Global Electrification

Electricity is essential. This book examines how multinational enterprises and international finance influenced the course of electrification around the world. Multinational enterprises played a crucial role in the spread of electric light and power from the 1870s through the first three decades of the twentieth century. But their role did not persist, as over time they exited through "domestication" (buy-outs, confiscations, or other withdrawals), so that by 1978 multinational enterprises in this sector had all but disappeared, replaced by electric utility providers with national business structures. Yet, in recent years, there has been a vigorous revival. This book, a unique cooperative effort by the three authors and a group of experts from many countries, offers a fresh analysis of the history of multinational enterprise, taking an integrative approach, not simply comparing national electrification experiences, but supplying a truly global account.

William J. Hausman is Chancellor Professor of Economics at the College of William & Mary. He was president of the Business History Conference, 2006–2007. Hausman has written extensively on the history of the U.S. electric utility industry.

Peter Hertner has just retired as Professor of Economic and Social History at the Historical Institute, Martin-Luther-University of Halle-Wittenberg. He returns to the European University Institute, Florence, Italy. Hertner is an expert on the history of German foreign investments, particularly in the electrical industry and banking.

Mira Wilkins is Professor of Economics at Florida International University. She is a former president of the Business History Conference and in 2004 was given the Lifetime Achievement Award by that organization. Her expertise and publications are on the history of multinational enterprise and the history of foreign investments.

Cambridge Studies in the Emergence of Global Enterprise

Editors

Louis Galambos, *The Johns Hopkins University*

Geoffrey Jones, *Harvard Business School*

Other books in the series:

National Cultures and International Competition: The Experience of Schering AG, 1851–1950, by Christopher Kobrak, ESCP-EAP, European School of Management

Knowledge and Competitive Advantage: The Coevolution of Firms, Technology, and National Institutions, by Johann Peter Murmann, Australian Graduate School of Management

The World's Newest Profession: Management Consulting in the Twentieth Century, by Christopher D. McKenna, Said Business School, University of Oxford

Global Brands: The Evolution of Multinationals in Alcoholic Beverages, by Teresa da Silva Lopes, Queen Mary, University of London

Banking on Global Markets: Deutsche Bank and the United States, 1870 to the Present, by Christopher Kobrak, ESCP-EAP, European School of Management

British Business in the Formative Years of European Integration, 1945–1973, by Neil Rollings, University of Glasgow

Global Electrification

Multinational Enterprise and International Finance in the History of Light and Power, 1878–2007

WILLIAM J. HAUSMAN

Chancellor Professor of Economics, College of William & Mary, Williamsburg, Virginia, United States

PETER HERTNER

Professor of Economic and Social History, Historical Institute, Martin-Luther-University of Halle-Wittenberg, Germany

MIRA WILKINS

Professor of Economics, Florida International University, Miami, Florida, United States

CAMBRIDGE
UNIVERSITY PRESS

CAMBRIDGE UNIVERSITY PRESS
Cambridge, New York, Melbourne, Madrid, Cape Town, Singapore, São Paulo, Delhi

Cambridge University Press
32 Avenue of the Americas, New York, NY 10013-2473, USA

www.cambridge.org
Information on this title: www.cambridge.org/9780521880350

First published 2008

Printed in the United States of America

A catalog record for this publication is available from the British Library.

Library of Congress Cataloging in Publication Data

Hausman, William J.
Global electrification : multinational enterprise and international finance in the history of light and power, 1878–2007 / William J. Hausman, Peter Hertner, and Mira Wilkins.
p. cm. – (Cambridge studies in global enterprises)
Includes bibliographical references and index.
ISBN 978-0-521-88035-0 (hbk. : alk. paper)
1. Electric utilities – History. 2. Electrification – Economic aspects – History.
3. Power resources – History. I. Hertner, Peter. II. Wilkins, Mira.
III. Title. IV. Series.

HD9685.A2H35 2008
333.793′2 – dc22

2007048053

ISBN 978-0-521-88035-0 hardback

Contents

Tables and Illustrations

TABLES

FIGURES

MAPS

Series Editors' Preface

The availability of electricity is largely taken for granted in industrialized countries, and yet as the authors of this path-breaking study emphasize, the dissemination of electric power over the last century was a massive endeavor. The distribution of electricity was, the authors show, a global project. We see the enormous importance of global firms, in a wide variety of corporate forms, in electrification before 1914 and after; yet at the same time, a countervailing force mounted, that is, the reduction of the role of these global firms, as governments assumed the responsibility for providing electricity; and then the reemergence in the contemporary era of global businesses as major forces in the world industry. In this and other regards, the spread of electric utilities tells us much about the larger patterns of evolution of the world economy through the vast changes that have occurred as countries industrialized and then moved into the information age. The authors have done research in historical archives located all over the world and in dozens of languages. They have demonstrated a mastery of many different historical literatures. The book points to a new style of "global business history" where the linkages between national experiences are mapped out to become a central explanatory theme, and where national experiences are compared and contrasted rigorously. In short, the authors have created the ultimate work of reference on the electrification of our world.

Geoffrey Jones
Harvard Business School

Louis Galambos
The Johns Hopkins University

Preface

This book is a cooperative effort by three authors – William J. Hausman, Peter Hertner, and Mira Wilkins – and Dominique Barjot, Jonathan Coopersmith, Kenneth E. Jackson, Pierre Lanthier, H. V. Nelles, John L. Neufeld, Harm Schröter, and Luciano Segreto. It attempts to understand how electric light and power facilities were established and how multinational enterprise and international finance have influenced the course of electrification around the globe. The three authors took the initiative in developing the project. Although electrification is basic to our daily lives, we were convinced that the international business and financial dimensions of its history had been underestimated. The authors assembled a superb group of experts, who have contributed much time and good advice. We were prompted by several considerations:

1. Although there was a huge literature on the spread of global electrification and on the manufacturing companies (the industrial firms), no one had dealt systematically with the history of multinational enterprise and finance in driving forward the lighting up of the world and in providing electric power. Thus, there was a gap to be filled. We wanted to write about the supply of electric light and power, about the utilities.
2. New emphasis on markets – liberalization, privatization, and restructuring from the late 1970s and particularly the 1980s onward – brought with it a resurgence of multinational-enterprise involvements in public utilities and a new globalization. We wanted to study the past in the context of the present because there were obviously historical precedents for today's activities.
3. For one of us (Wilkins), the only nonspecialist on electrification, there was an additional challenge. Wilkins had long been interested in the history of multinational enterprise and in its relationships to international finance. She had been considering forms and conduits

in international transactions – that is, the actors involved in undertaking foreign investments. The history of electric utilities and their global spread would be a splendid testing ground. All the other participants in this project had written extensively on various cross-border as well as domestic aspects of electric public utilities. Wilkins was in the enviable position of being surrounded by knowledgeable individuals.

4. For all the other participants, this project gave new perspectives. Each was a specialist on particular countries and regions and on particular international connections. Each knew very well a part of the story. What our project offered was a global view. Our group asked, What is distinctive about individual countries and regions and cross-border transactions? What are the legitimate generalizations? What are the common features? How do we think in international rather than conventional national terms? To what extent was information about, and the installation of, electric light and power facilities actually diffused through multinational enterprise and international finance? We looked at change through time. There was nothing static in our approach. And even though we were asking questions relevant to the present, we all understood that history must be approached from evidence, that looking back from the present can distort.

While members of our group come from economics and history departments, we shared the strong belief that good theory must be based on evidence. This is a study based on what happened, as best we can reconstruct it.

The project had its genesis in the early 1990s. Activities on it accelerated after Hausman, Hertner, and Wilkins received approval in May 1999 for a session at the International Economic History Congress (IEHC) in Buenos Aires. At the Business History Conference meetings in Palo Alto, California, in March 2000, Hausman, Hertner, and Wilkins mapped out the plans. Four formal sessions followed: The group had a "pre-IEHC" meeting in Wittenberg, Germany, in May 2001, hosted by Hertner; met in Buenos Aires in June–July 2002 at the IEHC; gathered in Paris in May 2003 as guests of Électricité de France (EDF), with arrangements by Barjot and Hertner; and convened in Lowell, Massachusetts, in June 2003 at a panel organized by Hausman at the Business History Conference. The three authors and Nelles attended all four of these group meetings (and also subsets of them); others attended one, two, or three of the sessions. We have all been in e-mail contact with each other.

It became apparent in our research on global electrification patterns that we would have to pay close attention to technological change and that we would also have to look carefully at the critical roles of governmental bodies, as the roles of the latter evolved over the years. We would have to explore the economic and political as well as the business and banking history literature. Multinational enterprise and international finance had to be put into a broad context. We realized that we were making a contribution to modern international economic history. We decided to confine our principal research to the first round of private investors' international participation, from 1878 to 1978. The last chapter brings the story up to date and explains how relevant the topic is in the early twenty-first century. We found that the story of multinational enterprise and international finance was not peripheral but was basic to an understanding of the spread of electrification around the world. Our topic was, in fact, extremely important.

Our initial chapter sets the stage for our findings. It examines the significance of electricity in the modern world, provides some quantitative measures of its spread and extent, and makes the point that a sizable number of households in the less-developed world today still do not have access to electricity. It offers a brief technological survey of electric lighting, power, and traction, emphasizing the importance of large networks and the role of hydroelectricity. The chapter offers evidence on the extraordinary capital intensity of the industry, explores the economic implications of this capital intensity, and demonstrates how crucial this is to our study of multinational enterprise and finance. The chapter also contains a succinct commentary on the role of governments (municipal, state, provincial, and national) in facilitating, regulating, and owning light and power companies. We argue that a governmental role is inherent because of certain fundamental characteristics of the electric utilities sector. Finally, in this framework chapter, we provide our definition of foreign ownership and control and present a basic, newly developed table containing estimates of the percentage of a country's capacity, output, or assets owned or controlled by foreign firms, by country, for benchmark years. This table lies at the heart of our study, revealing how significant foreign ownership and control was to the early history of global electrification.

Chapter 2 treats multinational enterprise and international finance. It is designed to establish a foundation for analysis. It introduces the reader to existing thinking about multinational enterprise and juxtaposes earlier research with the forms and practices we uncovered in our empirical work on the history of global electrification. Because of the capital intensity of electric utilities (as shown in Chapter 1), finance was fundamental. Accordingly, we have sought to understand the interrelationships between multinational enterprise and international finance, the networks and clusters of firms, and the ever-present minority interests. We have found particularly useful the new writings on corporate governance and have tried to integrate others' insights with our own discoveries. For many years, but no longer, theories and descriptions of multinational enterprise were dominated by considerations of manufacturing firms; our story is about a service: the supply of electric light and power. To include the latter is perfectly consistent with the newer research on multinational enterprise. Our surprise finding was, however, that although multinational enterprises were ubiquitous in the history of the spread of global electrification, it is inappropriate, for the first century of the industry's existence, 1878–1978, to write on "electric public utility multinational enterprises." With rare exceptions, operating electric public utilities in these years did not extend internationally. Instead, a variety of forms of multinational enterprise participated in the diffusion of global electrification. This chapter maps the economic actors participating in the process of providing light and power around the world. We explain the differences between foreign portfolio and direct investment. Although the material is often abstract, it should offer a guide to the understanding of the complicated story that follows in the subsequent chapters. Hopefully, this chapter (as well as the documentation of the abstractions in what follows) will contribute not only to our knowledge of how the spread of electrification occurred, but also to the literature on the history of multinational enterprise.

The next three chapters take the concepts put forth in the first two and show chronologically, in considerable detail, the dramatic changes as they transpired over time. Chapter 3 deals with the first movers, the new forms of outward and inward investments that emerged as central power plants proliferated. It documents the spread of the facilities and the extent and characteristics of foreign ownership and control, along with the role of financial intermediaries. By 1914, when Chapter 3 ends, residents of every city around the world had some kind of access to (familiarity with) electricity – whether on a tram, a street corner, possibly at work, or, less likely, at home. This chapter reveals the beginnings of the rise of complex interactions between European and North American capital and entrepreneurship – as inhabitants the world over slowly became aware of the diffusion of electrification. The great creditor nation is the United Kingdom, and its businesses' role in the spread of electrification is weighed vis- à-vis those of many other key actors: American, Belgian, Canadian, French, German, and Swiss, for example. Electrification was piecemeal on all continents and often the result of multinational enterprise expansion. Our interest is in the process of global diffusion, so what happened in colonies and dominions as well as independent nations is included.

Chapter 4 moves the story through time from 1914, when Germans were major players and Russian electrification was dominated by foreign capital, to 1929, when after war, nationalization, restructuring, and renewal there emerged a different configuration of foreign ownership and control and of international finance, assisting in the development of electrification. Continuities and discontinuities are evident. World War I, however, had a dramatic impact by focusing new attention on electrification needs, in stimulating new government interventions, and in transforming the already important activities of Belgian and Swiss holding companies. The collapse of the Austro-Hungarian, German, Ottoman, and Russian empires and the forming of new nations affected the electrification mosaic. After World War I, U.S. companies (and U.S. finance) took on a newly heightened role. In the 1920s, no sector attracted greater outward foreign direct investments from the United States than that of utilities. This chapter covers system building as well as the spread of enclave type and power-hungry industrial investments. Foreign direct investment – accompanied by international finance – facilitated the vast extension in the global accessibility of electric light and power. Yet, coincidentally, there was a layering process with the emergence of domestic control in certain countries (thus, for example, nationalization in Russia closed that country to foreign direct investors in electric utilities). The forms of and role of multinational enterprise became extremely complicated, with overlapping international business groups crisscrossing national frontiers.

Chapter 5 turns to the period between 1929 and 1945, when the temporary momentum of multinational enterprise in global electrification was undermined by the worldwide depression, foreign exchange controls, inconvertible currencies, and then World War II. The global electrification of the 1920s with the widespread participation of multinational enterprise carried over to 1930, with ambitious plans for a unified Europe, united with an electric grid developed by multinational enterprise initiatives. Alas, the dream was shattered. The years surveyed in this chapter saw unprecedented risks, uncertainties, and conflicts facing international private-sector investors. Although the demand for electric light and power rose, these foreign investors became less able to fulfill the requirements. Some multinational enterprises retired from existing international commitments. On the other hand, there were also some new, purely financial investments (with particularly large ones in the United States), but not foreign direct investments. For multinational enterprises, which during the 1930s encountered blocked remittances and enlarged governmental interventions (from rate regulations to renegotiated contracts to new legislation), there was little incentive or capability to meet rising expectations. Everywhere, the public and governments recognized that electricity was part of the basic infrastructure. National grids emerged with all the attendant costs. More often than in prior years, there were new government-run activities. And then World War II turned attention to national wartime requirements. The large multinational enterprises persisted and responded in various ways, but there was a nearly complete absence of new entries into international business.

Chapters 6 and 7 pull the previously presented material together, providing conclusions. Chapter 6 is in two parts. It starts with the years 1945 to 1978, when private-sector multinational enterprises were still present – and in some cases even enhanced – yet the handwriting was on the wall, and what we have called the "domestication process" (domestic rather than foreign direct investment) picked up speed. The second half of the chapter puts the entire history in perspective, summarizing the domestication process from 1878 to 1978. The rationale for these two sections within Chapter 6 lies in the fact that while there was some new private-sector international investment after World War II, the scenario was increasingly one of an expanded governmental role in the provision of electric power – and if it was not governmental everywhere, there were national (rather than private-sector international) activities in this sector. Our findings are that early in the process of electrification, international private-sector involvements were – or if not initially, soon became – fundamental. Over the years, in a highly uneven manner, there was greater domestication. In some countries, there was more inward international involvement in 1929–1930 than in the decades before World War I. By 1945, however, when Chapter 5 ends, this first wave of multinational-enterprise participation had already begun to show clear signs of dissipating. With the new postwar multilateral financing sources, with the newly enlarged national governmental roles, foreign private-sector activities in electric light and power were dwarfed. On an overall basis, they were increasingly reduced in absolute as well as relative terms. Multinational enterprises continued in this sector; there was private finance, but it had become a shadow of times past. And, at an ever more rapid pace after World War II, in country after country, multinational enterprises in this sector exited. As decolonization brought forth new nations, the latter did not desire foreign private control over the provision of light and power. To be sure, after 1945 there were some few instances of surges of new multinational enterprise-type investments, as in the case of American & Foreign Power Co. in Cuba, which later encountered expropriation with the advent of Fidel Castro. Thus, Chapter 6 contains, along with its summary of the entire domestication process, the story of 1945 to 1978, since by then the trend toward domestication was well under way. For reasons that we subject to analysis over the decades throughout the world, what was once "foreign-owned and -controlled" became domestic, often – but far from always – government-owned. Part of this process of domestication involved nationalization, and part was caused by "creeping" expropriation, where foreign firms found operations untenable. Throughout, private foreign finance persisted, but in the post–World War II years it, too, was muffled. By 1978–1979, when Brascan moved from Canadian to Brazilian ownership, the last of the long-standing, once-large array of foreign-owned and -controlled firms became domestic. The private sector *in terms of foreign ownership and control* was for all practical purposes out of the picture. What was once a truly internationalized private sector became domestic, with only a few remnants of the past remaining. Authors wrote of the "old" foreign investments in public utilities.

Yet, as soon as the notion of "old investments of another era" was well accepted, privatization, restructuring, and reliance on the market began to become the "talk of the town," which was especially true by the 1980s and during the 1990s. By the 1990s, there was a dramatic resurgence of international direct investments in the electric utilities sector. New multinational-enterprise investments in electric utilities in that decade and in the early twenty-first century multiplied in both developed and less developed countries. Clusters, networks, alliances, and business groups reemerged. The writers of this history had a certain sense of *déjà vu*. At the same time – by the end of the 1990s and in the early twenty-first century – some of the new international investors were encountering difficulties. We think our story could have predicted some of the problems. A short Chapter 7 reviews some of the new multinational-enterprise involvements of the last decades and considers some of the lessons that emerge from the historical experiences. This is followed by a short conclusion.

To understand the lessons learned, we will discuss populist sentiments as well as conflicts between private goals and public needs and the clash between openness and state intervention. We deal with the special difficulties business enterprises face in investing in electric utilities in a world of fluctuating currencies. Our overall goal is a new narrative and analysis. The outcome is a unique and previously untold story that is fundamental to the economic history of the modern world.

Acknowledgments

This is not an edited volume of essays. Instead, it is an integrated study, the result of the close interactions between and among the participants. William Hausman wrote Chapters 1 and 7; Mira Wilkins wrote Chapters 2 through 6; and throughout, Peter Hertner made vital contributions. Note that the first page of each chapter cites in a footnote the main authors and other contributors to the chapter. The phrase "Significant advice from ... " acknowledges special contributions to the chapter.

In addition to the bountiful and splendid assistance of our core group (listed at the beginning of the preface and in the roster that follows), authors Hausman, Hertner, and Wilkins want to thank individuals from around the world – from North and South America, Europe, Asia, Oceania, and Africa – for the rich contributions that they so generously provided: Robert Aliber, Franco Amatori, Francesca Antolin, Christopher Armstrong, Anna Maria Aubanell-Jubany, Ann Booth, Lisa Bud-Frierman, Bernard Carlson, Alfred Chandler, Andrea Colli, Theresa Collins, John Dunning, Abdel Aziz Ezzel Arab, Maryna Fraser, Patrick Fridenson, Pankaj Gemawat, Andrew Godley, Leo Goodstadt, Peter Gray, Leslie Hannah, Jean-François Hennart, Dina Khalifa Hussein, Paul Israel, Charlotte Jackson, Geoffrey Jones, Stuart Jones, Joost Jonker, Takeo Kikkawa, Makoto Kishida, Christopher Kobrak, Stephen Kobrin, Ginette Kurgan-Van Hentenryk, Pamela Laird, Norma Lanciotti, Daniel Lecuona, Donald Lessard, Reinhold Liehr, Kenneth Lipartito, Robert Lipsey, Andrea Lluch, David Merrett, Rory Miller, Yumiko Morii, Ulf Olsson, Nikos Pantelakis, Ioanna Pepelasis Minoglou, Anders Perlinge, Francesca Pino, Francesca Polese, Samir Saul, Dieter Schott, Jonathan Schrag, Keetie Sluyterman, Richard Sylla, Robert Tignor, Gabriel Tortella, Teresa Tortella, G. P. J. Verbong, Kazuo Wada, and Bernard Yeung. Hausman would like to thank Alan Zoellner, government documents librarian at William & Mary, and Debbie Green, Sarah Stafford, Beth Freeborn, Will Armstrong, and Michael Blum for their gracious technical assistance. This book would not have been possible without the help of all these talented men and women.

Authors and Contributors

William J. Hausman
Chancellor Professor of Economics
College of William & Mary
Williamsburg, Virginia
United States

Peter Hertner
Professor of Economic and Social History
Historical Institute
Martin-Luther-University of Halle-Wittenberg
Germany

Mira Wilkins
Professor of Economics
Florida International University
Miami, Florida
United States

Dominique Barjot
Professor of Economic History
University of Paris-Sorbonne
Paris
France

Jonathan Coopersmith
Associate Professor of History
Texas A&M University
College Station, Texas
United States

Kenneth E. Jackson
Associate Professor and Director
Centre for Development Studies
University of Auckland
Auckland
New Zealand

Pierre Lanthier
Professor
Department of Human Sciences/CIEQ
University of Quebec at Trois-Rivières
Quebec
Canada

H. V. Nelles
L. R. Wilson Professor of Canadian History
McMaster University
Hamilton
Ontario
Canada

John L. Neufeld
Professor of Economics
University of North Carolina
Greensboro, North Carolina
United States

Harm Schröter
Professor of History
University of Bergen
Bergen
Norway

Luciano Segreto
Professor of Economic History and the History
of International Economic Relations
University of Florence
Florence
Italy

PART I

CONCEPTS

1

The Invention and Spread of Electric Utilities, with a Measure of the Extent of Foreign Ownership

Electricity is essential, but it was not always so. The vast benefits, as well as dependency, electricity has brought to the contemporary world are never more dramatically demonstrated than when a blackout occurs. In economically developed countries, even brief blackouts cause severe inconvenience, and extended blackouts can impose huge economic costs and even lead to breakdowns in civil order. In less developed countries, blackouts tend to be chronic, inhibiting economic growth and social progress.[1] Two massive blackouts, each affecting over 50 million people, occurred in August and September of 2003, one engulfing the midwestern and northeastern United States and part of eastern Canada, the other affecting most of Italy – the largest blackout in Europe since World War II.[2] These blackouts demonstrated both the importance of electricity and the imperfection of the industry that delivers it. As the final report of the task force investigating the U.S.-Canada failure noted, "Modern society has come to depend on reliable electricity as an essential resource for national security; health and welfare; communications; finance; transportation; food and water supply; heating, cooling, and lighting; computers and electronics; commercial enterprise; and even entertainment and leisure – in short, nearly all aspects of modern life."[3] Nitin Desai, Secretary General of the United Nations' World Summit on Sustainable Development (Johannesburg, 2002) emphasized the importance of electricity both for today and for the future: "Electricity has profoundly transformed the industrialized world and led from the era of smoke chimneys into the era of knowledge-based services shaping the 21st century .... Universal access to affordable energy services including electricity is a prerequisite for achieving the goals and objectives of sustainable development .... Electricity permeates every aspect of

---

Authors: William J. Hausman, John L. Neufeld, and Mira Wilkins. Significant advice from H. V. Nelles, Peter Hertner, Harm Schröter, Jonathan Coopersmith, and Pierre Lanthier.

economy and society."[4] Some observers anticipated the tremendous potential for electricity to transform the world – not just illuminate streets and homes – during the earliest days of the industry. An article in the *New York Times* of January 17, 1881, noted a full year and a half before Thomas Edison's pioneering Pearl Street station commenced operation: "That the remarkable tendency shown by inventive genius during the past ten years toward the application of electricity to the needs of modern life continues is a fact which is receiving fresh illustrations almost daily ... Never before were so many men of genius at work in shops and laboratories trying to harness the new force in the service of man, and never was capital more eager to meet the inventor half-way and push his schemes through the channels of business enterprise. Electric companies for lighting houses and thoroughfares, for supplying motors, and for innumerable other purposes are springing up with a rapidity that is marvelous."[5] This book describes the role of multinational enterprise and international finance in making global electrification possible.

Where does the world stand now in terms of global electrification? The use of electricity and the extent of electrification can be measured in different ways. Total production of electricity varies widely among countries. In terms of total national production, the United States dominates, with net electricity generation in 2003 of almost 3.9 trillion kilowatt hours (kWh), over twice the amount generated by the second largest producer, China, which produced 1.8 trillion kWh. Only one other country, Japan, produced more that a trillion kWh in 2003.[6] Two better measures of the relative importance of electricity across countries are per capita consumption (presented in Figure 1.1 for a selection of countries for 2001) and household access to electricity (presented in Figure 1.2 for 1984, the latest date for which comprehensive figures are available).[7] These measures highlight the vast discrepancies that remain between developed countries and less developed ones. The global electrification process, while highly successful in many countries, remains incomplete. Around two billion people, roughly one-third of the world's population, still do not have access to centrally generated electricity.[8]

Before we trace the role of multinational enterprise and international finance in global electrification, we offer a perspective on the underlying characteristics of the electric light and power sector. The chapter begins with the inventions and new technologies that made electricity possible. The capital intensity of this sector emerges, with its profound economic significance. The growth of the industry was accompanied by interventions by national and subnational governments, and we briefly discuss their roles. The growth in electricity usage is shown by aggregate production statistics, which closely paralleled consumption. At the end of the chapter, we present a table that is at the core of our study, showing by country changes over time in foreign ownership and control of electric

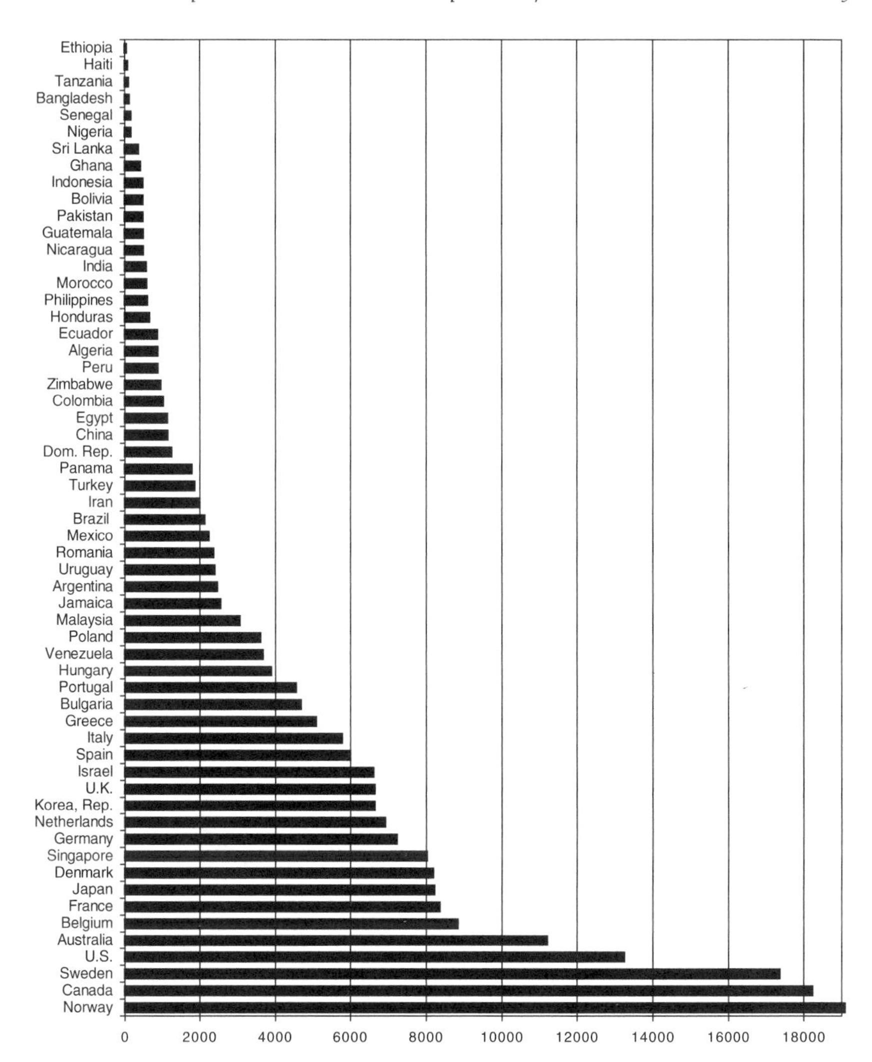

FIGURE 1.1. Per Capita Consumption of Electricity, Selected Countries, 2001 (kWh)
Source: United Nations Department of Economic and Social Affairs, Statistics Division, *Energy Statistics Yearbook* (2001) (New York: United Nations, 2004), Table 35, 478–94.

utilities. This table shows the importance of foreign-owned and -controlled firms (multinational enterprise) to the early diffusion of electricity. The table also reveals how in the course of time the role of multinational-enterprise activities were reduced (a process we call "domestication") until they were virtually gone by the mid-1970s. We consider the resurgence of foreign ownership of electric utilities over the past twenty years in Chapter 7.

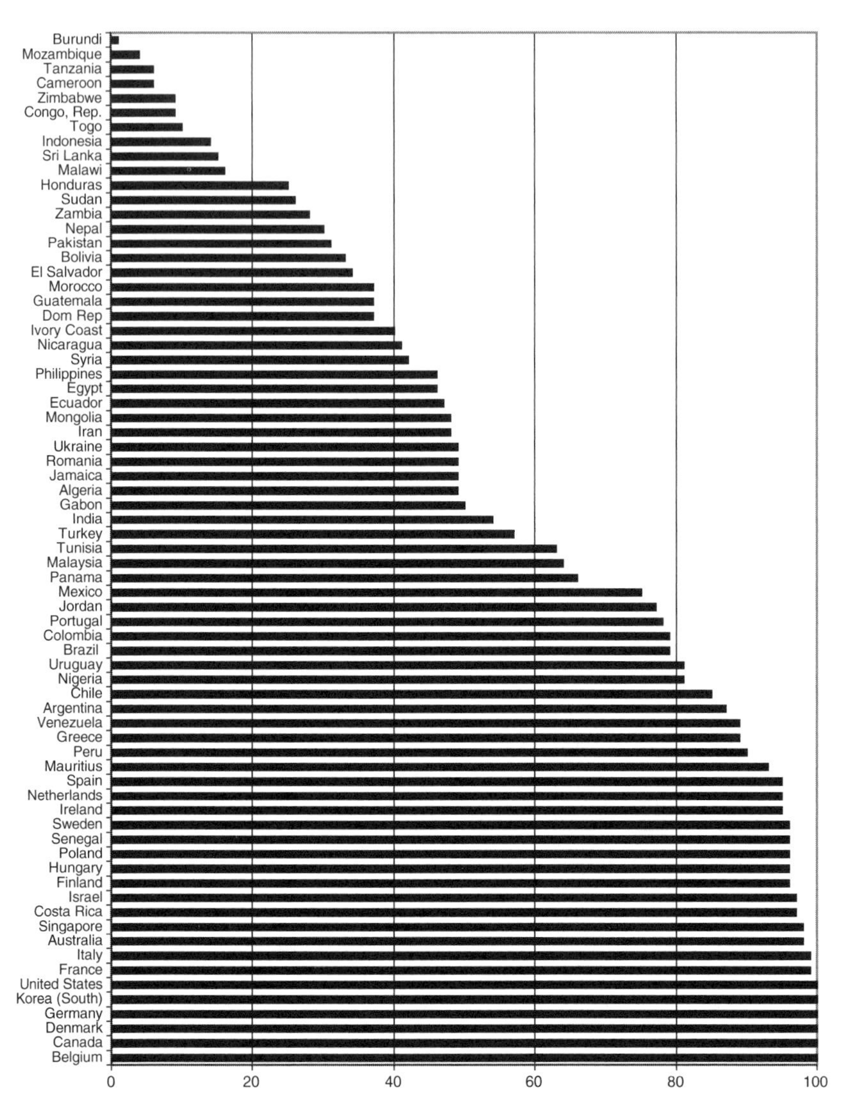

FIGURE 1.2. Percent of Households with Electricity, Selected Countries, 1984
Source: World Development Report 1994 (Oxford: Oxford University Press for the World Bank, 1994), 224–25.

THE PRECURSORS OF ELECTRIC LIGHT

The availability of a fully satisfactory form of artificial light is a relatively recent historical development: Until the middle of the nineteenth century, essentially all artificial light was obtained from some form of open flame. Ancient humans obtained light from fires and torches. The first great lighting innovation probably was the oil lamp, initially made from hollowed-out stones some 20,000 or so years ago.[9] The basic structure of the oil lamp, with its reservoir and wick, has remained essentially unchanged over the millennia, although many substances have been used as fuel, including both vegetable and animal oils. From the sixteenth through the nineteenth century, whale oil was a highly desirable fuel for lamp use. This was eventually supplanted by mineral oil, or kerosene, originally developed in the late 1840s and early 1850s by the Canadian Abraham Gesner and the Scotsman James Young. Kerosene became the dominant lamp fuel after the American Edwin Drake's successful oil discovery in 1859 led to an enormous expansion in the availability of the crude oil from which it was made.[10]

A variant of the oil lamp was the candle, whose origins are uncertain, but which is known to have been used by the ancient Romans. The first candles were made of either tallow (animal fat) or the superior, and hence more expensive, beeswax.[11] At the close of the eighteenth century, the use of spermaceti, obtained from the head of sperm whales, permitted an improved candle.[12] Candles remained a relatively expensive source of light until paraffin, a by-product of petroleum, became available.[13] All of these sources of light had one thing in common: They were stand-alone; none of them required a delivery network; none was provided by a "public utility," a term generally referring to a company or organization, either private or government-owned, that provides services to the general public over a network.[14] Electricity also could be and was provided by "isolated plants," essentially generators that were owned by the individuals or firms that used the power they produced.

The first public utilities devoted to illumination were gas lighting companies, which came to supply the main source of artificial light in urban areas for much of the nineteenth century, even into the twentieth century. The first gas lighting public utility was the Chartered Gas Light and Coke Co., which was granted a twenty-one-year charter by Great Britain's Prince Regent in 1812 to supply London and the surrounding boroughs.[15] By 1823, three different companies were supplying gas in the London area. Illuminating gas was manufactured by heating a fuel (usually coal, but also wood or oil) in the absence of air. The resultant gas could then be distributed in pipes to burners that initially produced open flames, like oil lamps or candles. Gas lights were convenient because they required substantially less attention and maintenance than the other forms of artificial light, and they became widely used for both interior and exterior (especially street) illumination. Although a number of refinements were made in the burners (or jets) over the course of the nineteenth century, the most dramatic innovation in gas lighting actually occurred after the development of the electric light. The gas mantle developed by the Austrian physicist Carl Auer von Welsbach in 1887 placed a solid substance in the flame that was then heated to incandescence, thus improving both the quality and the efficiency of gas lights. The Welsbach mantle gave gas lighting a powerful competitive weapon against the electric light and resulted in forestalling, and even in some cases temporarily reversing, the ultimate replacement of gas lighting by electric lighting.[16]

ELECTRICAL TECHNOLOGY AND THE BIRTH OF ELECTRIC UTILITIES

The path leading to the creation of the electric utility began in earnest at the start of the nineteenth century. The steps included discovery of the scientific principles of electricity, the invention of sources of power (the battery and dynamo), the creation of devices that effectively used electricity (lights and motors), devising a means of transmitting and distributing the electricity (especially over long distances), and finding a means of financing the whole operation.

The production of electricity with potential commercial applications did not occur until the invention of the battery by the Italian physicist Alessandro Volta in 1800. A battery (which Volta termed a "pile") produces a direct (or continuous) current of low voltage by chemical means. High levels of current (and/or voltage) could be obtained by connecting a number of batteries together. Soon after Volta's invention, the English scientists William Nicholson and Anthony Carlisle discovered electrolysis, the use of electricity to separate compounds into their elemental components by separating water into hydrogen and oxygen. By 1809, their compatriot Sir Humphry Davy had used more-powerful currents to isolate additional elements. This led ultimately to the discovery of electrochemical processes with significant commercial value, including electroplating and the smelting and refining of certain ores.

The significant technical breakthroughs that resulted in the creation of the electric utility industry came first in the field of electric lighting. Early electric lights were classified as either "arc" or "incandescent."[17] Sir Humphry Davy was a pioneer in both types of lighting. He demonstrated incandescent electric lighting in 1801 by using batteries to heat platinum strips. There is some evidence that Davy exhibited arc lighting the following year, and by 1808 he was able to provide a well-documented and impressive display of arc lights powered by two thousand battery cells to the Royal Institution in London. Davy's arc light essentially consisted of a continuous spark between two carbon electrodes, and all subsequent arc lights were based on the principles Davy discovered.[18] Incandescence requires that a material be heated, but it is difficult to maintain the stability of a substance at high temperatures because of its tendency to melt, vaporize, or oxidize. Most of the improvements in both incandescent and arc lighting involved methods of prolonging the life of the heated material. This initially proved easier to do when the heating was associated with a spark; thus, arc lights gained a slight lead over incandescent lights in becoming commercialized. Some of the earliest electric central stations, dating from the late 1870s, provided arc street lights in major world cities such as Philadelphia, San Francisco, New York, London, and Paris, as well as other cities.[19]

Electric power had a separate but related history. The electric motor's impact was destined to be profound, and the provision of electricity to motors, which were used to power machinery, played a major role in the industry. The first electric motor probably was produced in 1821 by the English scientist Michael Faraday, who had worked as a laboratory assistant to Davy, after learning of the discovery the previous year by Hans Christian Ørsted that a wire conducting electricity produced a magnetic field surrounding it. Faraday also discovered induction, the ability of a moving magnetic field to create an electric current. In 1831, he developed the first electric generator, a copper disk rotating between the poles of a magnet.

Electric lighting and power remained curiosities until powerful and efficient generators significantly reduced the cost of producing electricity. Stimulated by the potential for commercial success, improvements in the technologies of lighting, power, and generation continued to be made after the middle of the nineteenth century. Beginning in the mid-1850s, electric arc lights powered by steam-driven generators were used at construction sites in France and by the 1860s in lighthouses in both France and England. Generators slowly began to replace batteries in other applications of electricity, and the use of generator-powered arc lighting spread to other areas, including military signaling.[20] None of the electricity produced for these uses came from central-station utilities; all of these uses were satisfied with isolated plants.

A major factor hindering the first generators was the lack of strength of the permanent magnets they employed. Although designs incorporating electromagnets to help increase the strength of the magnetic field were tried as early as the mid-1840s, the major advance occurred with the discovery and publication of the principle of self-excitation virtually simultaneously by Charles Wheatstone, the brothers C. and S. A. Varley, and Werner Siemens in 1866–1867.[21] The iron core of an electromagnet retains some slight magnetism even when the current is off. This residual magnetism is enough to generate a small amount of current in a rotating armature, and when the armature is appropriately wired the current will increase substantially. Originally, the term "dynamo-generator" was used to distinguish this from the "magneto-generator," which used permanent magnets. Ultimately, the former term was shortened to "dynamo," which came to be applied generally to all electric generators.

One important technical aspect of producing electricity that later was to create controversy was whether direct or alternating current would be used. Although batteries always produce direct current, generators can be designed to produce either direct or alternating current. Both direct- and alternating-current generators were developed almost simultaneously.[22]

The first commercially successful dynamo was produced in 1871 by Zénobe-Théophile Gramme, who was born in Belgium but did much of his work in France. It was significantly more efficient than any generator produced previously. Although until the late 1870s it continued to be used primarily by the electrochemical industries, it made the more widespread use of electric lighting inevitable, and by 1879 Gramme had sold over one thousand dynamos. Gramme's dynamo, furthermore, could also function as a motor, a phenomenon demonstrated at the Vienna Universal Exhibition of 1873. In the Philadelphia Centennial Exhibition of 1876, Gramme dynamos powered arc lights, electroplating demonstrations, and other dynamos run as motors.[23]

By the middle of the 1870s, the commercial prospects for electric lighting seemed clear, but the conditions required for an industry of centrally generated electricity required an additional technical advance: how to power multiple lights from a single generator. An inherent problem of an arc light is that the electrodes are consumed as the light burns, which increases the gap between the electrodes until the arc can no longer span it. Some means had to be devised to prevent this. Several "regulators" had been developed initially that adjusted the gap, but putting multiple lamps on the same circuit made these regulators inoperative.[24] This problem was addressed in a novel way by the invention in 1876 of a new type of arc light by the Russian military and telegraph engineer Paul Jablochkoff (Pavel Yablochkov), who worked mostly in Paris.[25] Jablochkoff's "candle" eliminated the need for a regulator by placing the electrodes in parallel with a solid material used as a spacer. The lamps were cheap but short-lived and could not be relit once they were turned off. Jablochkoff was able to install several lamps in series in a single circuit, and he was able to make lamps of varying brightness, although all were too bright for residential use. The connection of arc lights in series became the standard industry practice.[26] Jablochkoff's system, which used alternating current, was installed in numerous locations in Paris both by his Société Générale d'Électricité and by others, and was also used, in 1878 and 1879, in various locations in London.[27] Ultimately, however, Jablochkoff's system was superseded by those using lamps with superior regulating mechanisms, including the successful systems of R. E. B. Crompton in England and both Charles F. Brush and William Wallace-Moses Farmer in the United States.[28] A number of commercial enterprises in various countries began providing arc lighting both to municipal governments for street lighting and to private users, including large stores and factories, in 1879 and 1880. These systems, the first central stations, generally consisted of a number of arc lights connected in series to a generator, controlled by a common switch, which was suitable for street lights and for lights in public places. Residential lighting continued to be provided by gas, oil lamps, or candles.[29]

The problem of the excessive brightness of arc lights was well known, and many inventors tried to tackle this problem, sometimes called "subdividing the light," by developing a fundamentally different form of electric light. If electricity was allowed to flow through an appropriate conductor, the conductor could become hot enough to incandesce. Such an approach to producing light held the promise of permitting a lower-intensity light than that produced by an arc light. A major technical impediment was that the conductor thus heated had a tendency either to melt or to burn up, thereby breaking the circuit. A method had to be found either to increase the life of the incandescing conductor or to automatically replace conductors consumed in the current.

Considerable progress in the development of incandescent lamps had been made in the 1840s and 1850s. Heinrich Goebel, a German who had emigrated to the United States, used incandescent lamps to illuminate a display window in his New York City watch shop in 1854. The Russian Alexander de Lodyguine used two hundred incandescent lamps in 1856 to light up the harbor of St. Petersburg. While Goebel tried to keep his conductor in a vacuum, Lodyguine used a nitrogen-filled bulb.[30] These two methods – vacuum and nitrogen – were pursued by a number of inventors as a means of avoiding oxidation of the conductor. The Englishman Joseph Swan also worked on the incandescent light during this time and determined that carbon was the best conductor. Thirty years later, he returned to his work on the incandescent light and became one of its commercially successful pioneers.[31]

Although numerous inventors had appreciated the problem of protecting the incandescing conductor from the destructive effects of oxygen, they were unable to produce either a complete enough vacuum or a container of inert gas sufficiently devoid of oxygen to enable an incandescent light to have a reasonably long life. This changed in 1865 with the invention of the mercury drop pump by the German chemist Hermann Sprengel. With subsequent improvements, these pumps dramatically improved the ability to produce a vacuum. Swan used a Sprengel pump to demonstrate a workable incandescent light before the Royal Institution in February 1879. Eight months later, Thomas Edison also demonstrated a workable incandescent lamp with a carbon conductor produced with the aid of a Sprengel pump.[32]

While Edison probably should not be remembered as the inventor of the incandescent electric light (for which Swan has an equal claim), he deserves to be remembered as the inventor of the modern electric utility – that is, a system for the production and delivery of electricity.[33] Edison was not a solitary inventor, but rather the head of a multiperson inventing enterprise, and many of the ideas that came from that enterprise may have originated with others.[34] Edison was a successful promoter and had the backing of established financiers willing and able to bring his ideas to market.

Edison approached the problem of the incandescent light as a piece of a larger plan to develop a new utility to replace the gas-lighting utility – one that would provide lighting in residences, commercial establishments, workshops, and factories. This required an electrical infrastructure very different from that used by arc-lighting utilities and one closer to that of the gas-lighting industry. Unlike in the case of arc lights, incandescent lights needed to be individually controlled, and the control had to be in the hands of the customers, not the utility. This meant that incandescent lights had to be connected in parallel rather than in series, and this had implications for the equipment that would be required.

Edison became convinced that a high-resistance filament would be required for his new system. Arc lights, and the incandescent lights designed by previous inventors, had low resistance, which was appropriate for devices connected in series. Without high resistance, parallel connection would have resulted in the need for high current, requiring thick distribution wires with unacceptably high costs.[35] Unlike others, Edison designed his incandescent light within a framework of a wholly new system, whose costs he believed had to be as low as that of gas. Actual costs turned out to be much higher than his initial calculations anticipated, but his reasoning proved to be sound.[36] Edison opened his first central stations in London and New York in 1882.[37]

BEYOND EDISON: THE ADVANTAGES AND EARLY DEVELOPMENT OF LARGE NETWORKS

The most significant competitor to the electric utility Edison envisioned was the isolated plant, where users produced electricity with their own generator, rather than purchasing electricity from a central-station utility.[38] This became a common practice for factories and large commercial establishments that, at least in the early days, were able to employ the same basic equipment as that used by a utility.[39] Isolated plants were cheaper to build because they avoided the costs of constructing a transmission and distribution system over a large geographic area, something a central station required. But the network that a larger transmission and distribution system entailed – particularly one connecting many consumers and many generating stations – provided a utility with several economic advantages that eventually became decisive. These included the ability to take advantage of scale economies, the freedom to separate the decisions of generator location from the location of electricity use, the reduced cost of improved reliability through the use of backup generators, the reduced cost of supplying electricity to users whose consumption is not steady throughout the day and not perfectly correlated, and the ability to make more efficient use of hydroelectricity, made possible by long-distance transmission.

Scale economies in generation eventually made the optimum size of generators far exceed that required by almost any single user. The use of such equipment was justified only within the context of a network, where the combined demand of many users allowed the adoption of generators of the optimum scale. By separating the location decisions of electricity production and consumption, less expensive real estate could be used for siting a utility generating plant. Sites suitable for hydroelectric generation are inflexibly provided by nature and also often are not suited for locating industrial plants, nor are they necessarily near population centers. But a network with long-distance transmission lines allows a hydroelectric plant to be sited some distance from the users of its electricity. In addition, a given level of reliability could be attained more cheaply by utilities with networks than by isolated plants. The American-born head of Sofina, Dannie Heineman, made a similar point at the First World Power Conference in 1924 regarding larger- versus smaller-scale units: "Every circumstance which may increase the number of kW. installed or which may diminish the annual utilization of these kW., will augment the cost of production. Subdividing the production among a large number of small central stations, when a few big central stations would suffice, is pernicious because ... smaller generation units not only greatly increase capital expenditure, but are far less efficient ... [and require] the installation of a much greater number of reserve (stand-by) units, which, while necessitating an increase of invested capital, diminishes the utilization of the installed machinery."[40]

Most importantly, a network also has an advantage if the consumption patterns of customers peak at different times. It is very expensive to store electrical energy. Without storage, the amount of generating capacity required to supply any electricity use is determined by the maximum power requirements of that use, even if that maximum is used for only a brief period, a phenomenon known as the "peak-load problem."[41] At all other times, the system will be operating well below capacity. If different customers on a network have their maximum power requirements at different times, the unused capacity of one customer can meet the increased demand of another customer. Thus, the total generating capacity required to meet everyone's needs on a large network will never be as much – and may be much less – than the total generating capacity required if each customer had his own isolated plant or was part of a small network.

The ability of a network to allow flexibility in siting a hydroelectric plant has already been mentioned, but networks also facilitated the exploitation of hydroelectricity in other ways. The generation of electricity from most hydroelectric sites is uneven and often unpredictable because it depends on the availability of falling water, which itself often depends on rainfall. By combining steam with hydroelectric generation, shortfalls in hydroelectric generation could be made up with steam generation, making the total supply of electricity to users more valuable than if users obtained electricity from a single hydroelectric site.[42]

A given amount of power can be transmitted either with low voltage and high current or with high voltage and correspondingly lower current. As a practical matter, the transmission of large amounts of power over long distances must be done at high voltage because the conductors (wires) required for low voltage would be unfeasibly large. At the same time, very high voltage is not practical for use in many electric devices because it poses extreme safety risks for ordinary electricity users. A large network therefore needs a way to change voltages: generation at a relatively low voltage suitable for generator design, much higher voltages for transmission, and reduced voltages again for final use. It soon became apparent that it was much easier in a system using alternating current than in a system like Edison's, which used direct current, primarily because the relatively simple transformer initially worked only with alternating current.[43]

Alternating current and transformers were in use before Edison designed his direct-current system, yet no one initially recognized that they offered a solution to the problem of enlarging the geographic scope of an electricity network. An important advance was made by the Frenchman Lucien Gaulard and his English business partner John Gibbs. Gaulard and Gibbs demonstrated in 1883 a transformer in which the voltage could be varied according to the needs of the load. This permitted lamps with different voltages to be used on the system. Gaulard and Gibbs also realized that their transformers could be used in a system to convert the high voltage necessary for long-distance transmission to the lower voltage needed for end use.[44] The Gaulard and Gibbs system, however, suffered from several problems, including inadequate voltage regulation. Improvements were forthcoming, including those made by the Hungarian engineering firm Ganz & Co., which displayed its system at the Hungarian National Exhibition in Budapest in May 1885.[45] The system was refined further by the firm of George Westinghouse in the United States. Westinghouse, using the technical expertise of William Stanley and patents developed by Nikola Tesla, was the pioneer in commercializing the alternating-current system.[46] Other pioneers in alternating-current systems included Sebastian Ziani de Ferranti, chief designer of the London Electric Supply Corporation's Deptford power station, and the Thomson-Houston Co. in the United States.[47]

The use of direct current, even for transmission, did not immediately disappear. The development of alternating-current motors lagged that of direct-current motors, and direct-current motors retained a significant advantage where applications required speed control and high starting torque, such as in elevators and short-haul transit.[48] Alternating current's share of generation increased through the use of rotary converters and motor-generators, devices that could convert electricity transmitted as alternating current to direct current for final use.[49] These devices enabled a utility to build and maintain a large alternating-current network and provide direct current for those uses for which it was best suited. Sometimes whole urban areas were supplied with direct current in this way, maintaining the service that had originally been supplied by direct-current generating stations.[50] An example from 1895 of the configuration of an alternating-current system, with both alternating- and direct-current end uses, including traction, is illustrated in Figure 1.3. This style of network would be common by the end of the nineteenth century.

ELECTRIC TRACTION

Tramways, which used rails to reduce friction and horses, mules, and other draft animals to provide motive power, predated electricity. Steam railways provided some intra-urban transit; but for purposes of short-distance transportation, the electric motor had important advantages over the steam engine. Compared with steam engines (or draft animals), electric motors could be made very powerful for their size. In addition, electric motors were much better suited to the erratic pace of urban transit than were steam engines, because they were easier to start and stop and their performance at varying speeds was superior. Electric motors were also cleaner and quieter than steam engines or draft animals. A major problem with the mobile electric motor, however, was that a method of providing electricity to it had to be devised, and this took many years to develop.[51] Attempts were made to do this with on-board batteries by a number of companies in the United States, France, and Britain, but these efforts generally were not successful.[52] The critical problem was devising a means to provide electricity to moving vehicles from stationary generating plants in a way that was economical and that prevented even brief interruptions. Achieving this goal was the most serious technical issue for electric public transportation.[53]

The first time an electric motor was used for traction was at the Berlin Industrial Exhibition in 1879, where Siemens & Halske installed a small, narrow-gage electric train that carried visitors in a circle around the exhibition grounds: "The train was originally designed for use in a mine tunnel and a complete [electric] railway was installed later by Siemens in 1882 in a coal mine in Saxony."[54] In 1881, Siemens & Halske constructed the first electric tramway using externally generated current (and the first to collect fares), a 2.5 km experimental line running between Groß-Lichterfelde and the Royal Cadet College south of Berlin. Two running rails on the ground provided current, which was dangerous, resulting in occasional shocks to unwary horses and pedestrians and highlighting the severe limitations of this technology.[55]

Siemens's French subsidiary, Siemens Frères, demonstrated a tram that used safer, overhead lines at the International Electricity Exhibition held in

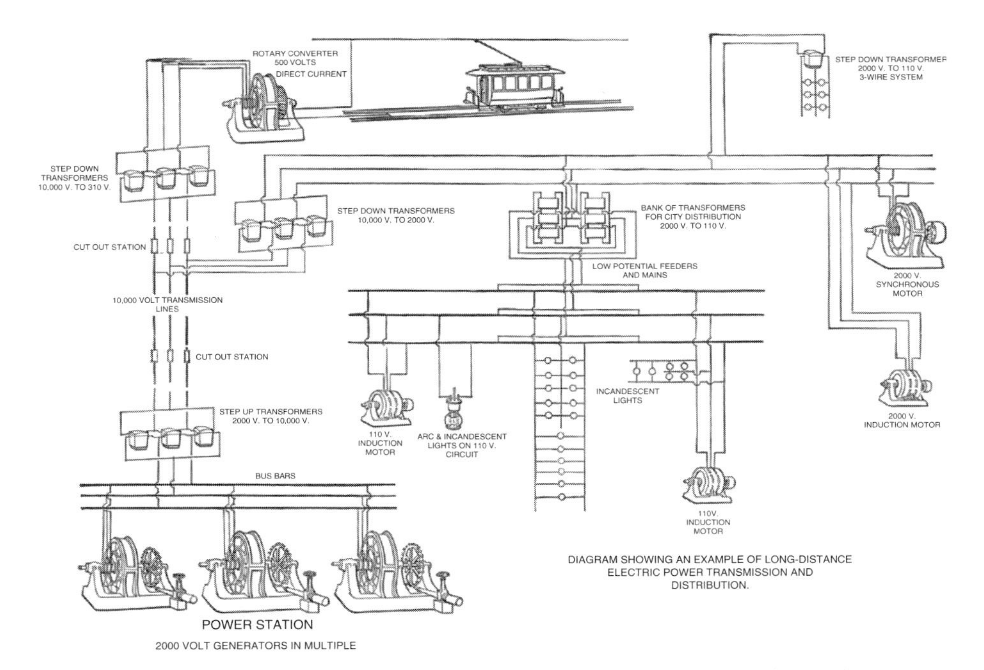

FIGURE 1.3. Diagram Showing an Example of Long-Distance Electric Power Transmission and Distribution, 1895
Source: S. Danna Greene, "Distibution of the Electrical Energy from Niagara Falls," *Cassier's Magazine*, 8 (1895), 358.

Paris in 1881.[56] Three years later, a similar system, comprised of a conductor surrounded by a split overhead pipe, was used on the tramway between Frankfurt and Offenbach constructed by Siemens for the Weinmann Bank.[57] Despite these early efforts, the widespread adoption of electric trams in Europe did not occur until after trams had become well established in the United States, already a leader in the adoption of new technology in public transportation.[58] But taking the lead from American innovators, by the late 1890s the electric streetcar had "completely transformed European urban transportation."[59]

Thomas Edison also experimented with electric railways. In 1881, he was given a contract by Henry Villard, president of the Northern Pacific Railroad, to construct a 2.5-mile electric railway at Menlo Park, New Jersey, which he proceeded to do. If the railway proved to be successful, Villard was to pay for installation of fifty miles of electric road in the wheat region of the northwest. The bankruptcy of the Northern Pacific in 1883 caused Villard to withdraw from the presidency of the railroad and return to Germany in January 1884 (where he stayed four years before returning to the United States), and Edison's attention was directed elsewhere.[60]

The first commercially successful, large-scale urban electric tramway in the world was built by the firm of Frank J. Sprague in Richmond, Virginia, in 1887–1888. Sprague accepted a contract that called for the construction of a system of forty cars, twelve miles of track, and a 375-horsepower power plant. Once the task was undertaken, it became clear that Sprague had underestimated the challenge, and the project ultimately cost him nearly twice what he was paid. Nevertheless, the system was very successful. Sprague solved numerous engineering problems during construction, and the Richmond system became a prototype for urban electric tramways.[61] The electrification of urban tramways was quite rapid after this. In 1890, of the 5,783 miles of tramways in existence in the United States, only 16 percent were electrified; but by 1902, of the 16,652 miles in existence, 97.5 percent were electrified. The corresponding 1902 figures were 59 percent for Great Britain and 91 percent for Germany.[62]

Another area where electricity became a part of intra-urban transit was in subways. Once transit became motorized, the desirability of removing it from street traffic became apparent, particularly in areas of high density. This could be done either by elevating the vehicles above the level of the streets or by putting them underground. When steam engines were the motive power, elevated railways became common in many large cities. The combustion products of steam engines generally made them unsuited for underground use, although London did use steam engines underground beginning in the 1860s.[63] Virtually all other urban subway systems were electrified from the beginning.

The earliest inter-urban lines, initially extensions and connections of existing suburban lines, were established shortly after the development of trams.[64] The electrification of main-line railroads in Europe and the United States followed, gaining momentum after the turn of the twentieth century.[65]

THE PATTERN OF DEVELOPMENT OF THE ELECTRIC UTILITY INDUSTRY

Once all of the components of the technology had been developed, the process of electrifying homes, shops, factories, tram lines, and farms could begin. While the story in each country had unique aspects, the process of electrification followed certain patterns. Globally, urban areas became electrified before rural ones. There was a strong preexisting demand for light, power, and transportation. Over time, new devices to connect to the system were invented or adapted, including products such as electric irons, fans, water heaters, ranges, vacuum cleaners, shavers, toasters, hot plates, and refrigerators.[66] Every city and town in the world wanted electric service. By the turn of the century, or shortly thereafter, with the exception of the least developed areas of the world, nearly every city and most of the larger towns had electric service of some type, at least in central areas.[67] Factories and plantations where processing occurred were quick to adopt electricity and occasionally began supplying surrounding areas, especially when they were geographically isolated.[68] Electric motors were quickly adopted for industrial uses. With the development of the steam turbine and improved transmission technology, an increasing number of systems extended their networks to suburban and surrounding areas, and smaller towns were integrated into networks.[69]

Hydroelectricity's role came early in the process of electrification and played an important role in stimulating developments in transmission.[70] The costs of hydroelectric production were almost entirely capital costs; because there was no fuel to acquire and burn, there was very little additional (marginal) cost to putting those facilities to use. The initial capital cost of a hydroelectric plant, of course, could be very large. By 1895, the crucial year that alternating current was selected for the hydroelectric project at Niagara Falls, there was a growing number of "long-distance" alternating-current systems in operation, the vast majority of which were hydroelectric. The longest and highest voltage system in the world was the largely experimental line from Lauffen (where a relatively small, 150 kW hydroelectric generator provided electricity to a cement plant) to Frankfurt, Germany, at 175 km (109 mi) and a quite remarkable 40,000 volts.[71] There were, in 1895, six other transmission lines ranging from seven to eighteen miles in length and carrying current of 6,000 to 11,500 volts in California, Connecticut, Mexico, and Italy, and twenty-four smaller lines in the United States, Mexico, Canada, and Europe.[72]

The size and scale of potential networks increased dramatically after the turn of the century with technical developments in transmission. By 1914, there were fifty-five transmission lines of 70,000 to 150,000 volts in the world, ranging in length from 19 to 245 miles. Of the highest-voltage lines, fifteen of the top twenty were in the United States. The eleven highest-voltage transmission lines, and twenty-one of the top twenty-five lines, were operated as part of hydroelectric power systems, confirming its role in the development of transmission systems. Information on the longest, highest-voltage lines outside the United States is presented in Table 1.1. While these lines could be found all over the world, none of them crossed national boundaries in 1914.

The increases in generation and transmission capabilities enabled the size of electric utilities to rise dramatically after 1900. As electricity in the household came to be viewed no longer as a luxury but as an essential commodity, it became imperative in developed countries to extend service to rural areas, often under the stimulus of governments at various levels. This process began effectively in the 1920s and continued at varying paces throughout the century.[73]

THE CAPITAL INTENSITY OF THE CENTRAL-STATION ELECTRIC UTILITY AND ITS IMPLICATIONS

The equipment needed to generate, transmit, and distribute electricity had distinctive economic characteristics. It was expensive and relatively complicated (hence the need for skilled labor to manufacture and maintain it), and it quickly became obsolete. There was a continuous need for replacement, upgrading, and new investment. The most salient feature of the electric utility industry was its extraordinarily high capital intensity.[74] The relative capital intensity of the central-station electric power industry in the United States, for example, is illustrated in Figure 1.4. With the exception of steam railways during that industry's formative years, no other public utility or manufacturing industry came close to approaching the capital intensity of the electric power industry from its inception in the late nineteenth century up to World War I. After the war, as output expanded dramatically and new uses that vastly improved the load factor were found, the capital/output ratio tended to converge toward that of other industries, but it still remained quite high.[75] This pattern was repeated, at varying paces, throughout the developed world in the twentieth century.

High capital intensity influenced the industry's development in several ways. In every country, a huge capital investment had to be made before an electric utility could even begin operation. Expensive equipment had to be bought and installed, and interest costs had to be paid before any revenue was received. Initial investment and rapid subsequent expansions simply could not be financed out of retained earnings; outside sources of funds were essential. Capital was not easy to obtain because starting a utility was perceived to be a very risky proposition in the early days. The initial and constantly increasing need for capital led to both traditional financing

Table 1.1. *The 25 Highest-Voltage Transmission Systems Outside the United States, 1914*

Company Name	Voltage (000s)	Type	Distance (miles)	Plant Location, Terminus
Inawashiro Hydroelectric Power Co.	115	hydro	144	Lake Inawashiro, Tokyo, Japan
Hydro-Electric Power Commission of Ontario	110	hydro	135	Niagara Falls, Toronto, Canada
Lauchhammer AG	110	steam	35	Lauchhammer Mines, Riesa, Germany
Mexican Northern Power Co.	110	hydro	47	Boquila, Parral, Mexico
Ebro Irrigation & Power Co.	110	hydro	105	Serge River, Barcelona, Spain
Chile Exploration Co.	110	steam	86	Tocopila, Chuquicamata, Chile
Shawinigan Water & Power Co.	100	hydro	87	Shawinigan Falls, Montreal, Canada
Tata Hydroelectric Co.	100	hydro	43	Khopoli, Bombay, India
Pfalzwerke, AG	100	steam	65	Hamburg, Ludwigshafen, Germany
Società Italiana di Elettrochimica	88	hydro	124	Pescara River, Naples, Italy
Rio de Janeiro Tramway, Light & Power Co.	88	hydro	51	Lages River, Rio de Janiero, Brazil
São Paulo Electric Co.	88	hydro	56	Soracabo, São Paulo, Brazil
Tasmania Hydroelectric & Metal Co.	88	hydro	64	River Ouse, Hobart, Tasmania
Mexican Light & Power Co.	85	hydro	169	Necaxa, Mexico City, Mexico
Toronto Power Co.	85	hydro	80	Niagara Falls, Toronto, Canada
Victoria Falls & Transvaal Power Co.	84	steam	30	Vereenigung, Johannesburg, South Africa

Company Name	Voltage (000s)	Type	Distance (miles)	Plant Location, Terminus
Energía Eléctrica de Cataluña	80	hydro	107	Pyrenees Mountains, Barcelona, Spain
Katsuragawa Denryoku Kabushiki Kaisha	77	hydro	48	Komahashi, Tokyo, Japan
City of Milan	72	hydro	93	Grossoto, Milan, Italy
Società Generale Elettrica dell' Adamello	72	hydro	72	Cedegolo, Milan, Italy
Hidroeléctrica Española Molina	70	hydro	158	Molina, Madrid, Spain
Compañía Hidroélectricae Irrigadora del Chapala	70	hydro	71	Santiago River, Guadalajara, etc., Mexico
Società Elettricità Rivieradi Ponente	70	hydro	155	S. Dalmazzo, Novi, etc., Italy
Swedish State Railways	70	hydro	73	Porjus, Kiruna, Sweden
City of Winnipeg	66–72	hydro	77	Point Dubois, Winnipeg, Canada

Source: U.S. Department of Commerce, Bureau of the Census, *Central Electric Light and Power Stations and Street and Electric Railways, 1912* (Washington, DC: USGPO, 1915), opposite p. 132.

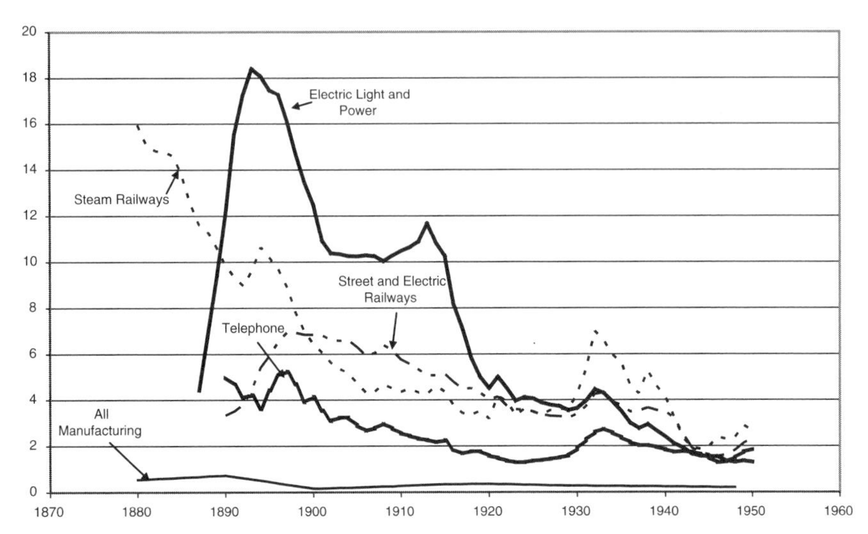

FIGURE 1.4. Capital/Output Ratio for U.S. Utilities, Transportation, and Manufacturing, 1880–1950
Source: Melville J. Ulmer, *Capital in Transportation, Communications, and Public Utilities* (Princeton: Princeton University Press, 1960), 256–57, 320, 374–75, 405–6, 472–73, 476, 482, 486; Daniel Creamer, Sergei P. Dobrovolsky, and Israel Borenstein, *Capital in Manufacturing and Mining* (Princeton: Princeton University Press, 1960), 265–67.

methods (issuance of equity and debt) and to the design of imaginative ways of attracting new investment, primarily through the use of leverage via holding companies and by drawing funds from abroad.[76]

The large amount of capital and the near impossibility of employing that capital in any other use once it was in place had other major implications for the industry. The revenues required to cover operating costs were a small portion of the total revenue required to also service the huge capital costs. If revenue only covered operating costs, a utility could remain in operation but would be unable to maintain or expand its capital. The difference between the level of prices that would permit a utility to operate in the short run versus the level that would enable it to operate in the long run was large; it created a situation that could contribute to uncertainty in consumers' minds over what level of prices was proper or fair. Competition was problematic because it could force prices to a level that covered only short-run operating costs, thus discouraging future investment and making potential competitors reluctant to compete with an existing firm. These economic factors eventually resulted in utilities becoming monopolies in their service area, with the market power to earn supernormal profits. The growth in scale economies in generation and the inherent scale returns in network expansion led to fewer utilities serving larger areas, each increasing its apparent monopoly power and creating suspicions about the prices being charged. The utilities were not unfettered, however. Distribution systems had to use land that the utility did not own, typically the rights-of-way of public streets, and this generally required the assent of government, often in the form of a franchise, which required some political accommodation between the utility and community it served.

Because electricity cannot easily be stored, nor can it be traded among users once it is generated, it becomes possible for a utility to engage in price discrimination, charging different prices to different consumers or groups of consumers, a practice that could well lead to higher profits. This situation could pit groups of consumers against one another, and the tension thus produced could be played out in the political arena. As electricity became more ubiquitous and more essential to modern life, the requirement that utilities have government approval at least for their distribution systems made them dependent on politicians, made their behavior an object of political concern, and also created opportunities for corruption. These problems were compounded when the utilities were owned and operated by foreigners.

GOVERNMENTS AND THE ELECTRIC UTILITY INDUSTRY

The state in its various forms – including municipal, provincial, and national governments – has participated extensively, as both regulator and owner, in the electric utility industry. In summarizing a series of papers given at the Third World Power Conference in 1936, William H. England noted, "Electric and gas utilities in the various countries have developed in a variety of ways. In some countries foreign capital has played a major part, in other nations public ownership and operation has dominated these industries, in other lands private control has been entirely or almost entirely responsible for their growth and development, while in still other lands private companies, municipal plants, State or Province ventures, and mixed public and private schemes have each contributed in building and operating these industries."[77]

The precise nature of government participation has varied tremendously in different countries and over time, and its desirability often was the cause of bitter political battles.[78] As cities became electrified, utilities virtually everywhere had to obtain municipal franchises, which invited some measure of public oversight or control. Many municipalities already had experience with water and gas utilities, so some basic rules, regulations, and procedures previously existed. One feature of the utility franchise that was common in many countries was that municipalities retained the right to purchase or take over the utility after the expiration of the franchise, which could be granted for as little as a decade or as long as half a century.[79]

As electric utilities grew in size and as long-distance transmission became increasingly important, government involvement and concern tended to move to higher levels.[80] The First World War placed a great demand on resources and awakened governments to the necessity of strategic planning.

They came to realize that electric utility networks were strategically important and that large regional, even national, systems would be desirable. The governments of many countries studied the possibilities of rationalizing transmission and distribution systems and creating national grids, either through direct public control or by encouraging private electric utilities to adapt their own systems.[81] These plans foreshadowed the nationalization of electric utilities that occurred in many European countries in the post–World War II era, a process that also took place in many former colonial dependencies (principally in Africa and Asia), in Central and South America, and, of course, in the centrally planned economies.

In countries where foreign companies participated in electrification, the relationship between electric utilities and governments (at the national or subnational level) could be even more complicated than it was where the conflicts were simply between domestic consumers, domestic private capital, and the various levels of governments. Foreign investors were crucial, of course, and they were encouraged and welcomed at first, but once the electricity supply was established and deemed essential, complications ensued: Relationships between the company and its consumers, suppliers, and competitors and with labor were subjected to close scrutiny and frequent intervention by the state. Foreign-owned companies often were subjected to severe criticism; after all, the provider of this critical service was a monopolist, and in most cases the owner was far away. When domestic economic times became difficult, particularly when exchange rates deteriorated, foreign-owned electric utilities, with their large amount of fixed and unmovable capital, became targets for extreme government intervention. In many cases, the government took actions that led to the redirection, withdrawal, or confiscation of foreign capital, through either purchase or expropriation – a process called by us "domestication" of the electric utility sector.

TRENDS IN ELECTRICITY PRODUCTION AND THE IMPLICATION FOR CAPITAL INVESTMENT

Today, there is a massive amount of data, much of it quite detailed, on the electric utility industry worldwide.[82] Most countries (or subnational political units), however, did not collect data on capacity, investment, and costs, much less patterns of consumption, in any comparable, systematic way until well into the twentieth century. Only scattered data are available for the early years of the industry's history. The only data that are consistent for a large number of countries across a long time period are for total electricity production.[83] Because all electricity produced must be consumed instantaneously, the only differences between production and consumption in various countries are line losses.[84] Furthermore, because international trade in electricity was relatively minor (as will be shown below), national production and consumption figures should be roughly comparable.

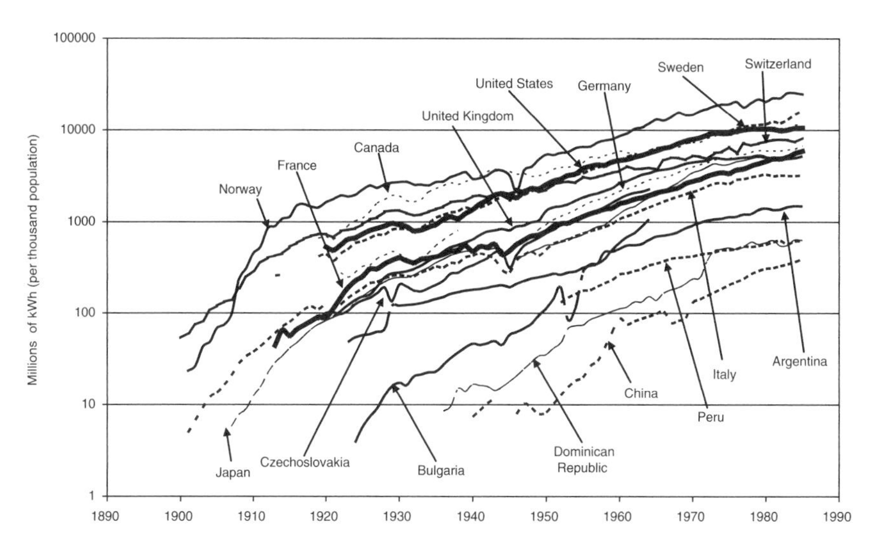

FIGURE 1.5. Per Capita Output of Electricity, Selected Countries, 1900–1985
Source: Bouda Etemad and Jean Luciani, *World Energy Production 1800–1985* (Genève: Librarie Droz, 1991), 91–165.

A major influence affecting the total output of electricity, of course, was population. Figure 1.5 presents information on the growth of per capita production of electricity for sixteen countries for which we have long-term data. Fortunately, these countries include some whose economies developed early as well as others whose economies developed later or remained less developed.[85] The vertical axis in this chart is logarithmic in scale, so a straight line represents a constant rate of growth of output (the steeper the slope of the line, the higher the rate of growth). The pattern of growth in per capita production across these countries is quite clear: There was very rapid early development followed by slower but steady growth. The figure also shows that there were significant differences between countries in the level of per capita electricity production and that these differences tended to persist over time. Many of the differences were related to the level of economic development. China, for example, had roughly the same amount of per capita production in 1950 as Japan did in 1910 or Italy did in 1900.

Growth in electricity production requires the expansion of capacity, which must be funded through domestic private capital, public capital, or foreign capital. Table 1.2 presents estimated growth rates for fifteen countries (those with the longest data series are listed first).[86] Overall growth rates in per capita production (essentially equivalent to growth rates in consumption) for countries with the longest series of data (1900–1902 to 1985) were roughly 5–7 percent per annum. If capacity grew at the same rate as output, the implications for capital investment are clear. With overall growth at 5 percent per annum, capacity would have to double

Table 1.2. *Per Capita Electricity Production Growth Rates, Selected Countries, 1900–1985*

Country	Years	Growth Rate (% per annum)†	Early Period	Early Period Growth Rate	Later Period	Later Period Growth Rate
Switzerland	1900–85	4.9	1900–19	14.6	1920–85	3.7
Italy	1900–85	6.6	1900–18	18.6	1919–67	5.1
Norway	1901–85	6.2	1901–17	29.0	1918–85	4.5
United States	1902–85	5.4	1902–29	9.1	1930–85	5.2
Japan	1907–85	7.5	1907–29	10.5	1950–85	7.4
Sweden	1913–85	5.6	1913–19	9.2	1920–85	5.6
Germany	1913–85	5.5	1913–29	8.4	1930–85	5.6
France	1913–85	6.0	1913–29	13.8	1950–85	5.6
Canada	1919–85	3.9	1919–29	11.9	1930–85	3.4
United Kingdom	1921–85	6.4	1921–29	13.2	1930–85	5.7
Hungary	1923–73	6.6				
Bulgaria	1924–73	12.2				
Dominican Rep.	1929–85	9.2				
China	1940–85	10.42				
Peru	1950–85	4.72				

† Growth rates are based on regressions of time on the log of per capita electricity production.

Source: See Figure 1.5

roughly every fourteen years. With a 6 percent growth rate, capacity would have to double every twelve years, while with a 7 percent growth rate it would have to double roughly every ten years. Most countries exhibited much higher growth rates for earlier periods than they did for later periods.[87] This highlights just how important financing was for the early periods of the industry's history in nearly all countries. With a growth rate of 18 percent per annum, as Italy had from 1900 to 1918, capacity would have had to double a little less than every four years. That represents a substantial amount of new capital that had to be raised.

CHARACTERISTICS OF A MATURING INDUSTRY: A SNAPSHOT AT 1933

By the second quarter of the twentieth century, the electric utility industry was beginning to mature. Electrification had spread to a greater proportion of the world's households, new electrical devices were being adopted, and rural areas were becoming integrated into networks in an increasing number of countries.[88] Factories in the industrialized world became almost completely electrified. Electric drive enabled greater flexibility in the organization of the factory floor, thus enhancing productivity.[89] The decade of the 1920s also witnessed grand plans for ever larger and more complex regional and national networks – Superpower and Giant Power in the United States and the national grid in Britain, for example.[90]

The publication in 1936 of the first statistical yearbook of the World Power Conference, containing data for 1933 and 1934, provides an opportunity to compare some aspects of the structure of the industry in various countries of the world.[91] Figure 1.6 presents a cross-country comparison of the percentage of the population that lived in areas supplied with electricity, a measure of the potential availability of electric service.[92] It is clear that the smaller, more densely populated Western European countries had done the best job of providing the opportunity for electric service to their residents. This is not surprising given their size, level of development, and access to capital. Several larger, highly developed countries, such as Germany and the United States, had progressed tremendously but still had a substantial portion of their populations residing in areas where electric service was not available. In other countries, some (but not all) of which had relatively high income, a substantial amount of work remained to be done as of 1933.

By 1933, the uses of electricity were quite varied, including traction; public street lighting; private lighting in homes, shops, and offices; metallurgical processes; and powering motors in factories. While the relative importance of each of these uses varied considerably across countries, electricity provided for industrial uses and by industrial establishments was exceedingly important.[93] Table 1.3 contains information on both the consumption of centrally generated electricity by industry and the

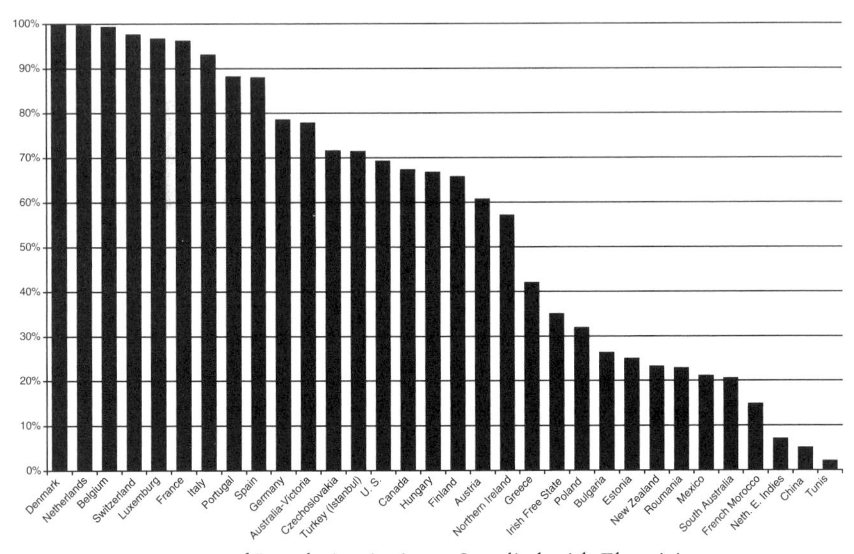

FIGURE 1.6. Percent of Population in Areas Supplied with Electricity, 1933
Source: Frederick Brown, ed., *Statistical Year-Book, 1933 & 1934* (London: World Power Conference, 1936), 102.

Table 1.3. *Industrial Electricity, Selected Countries, 1933*

	Industrial Consumption as Percent of Total Consumption, Central-Station Utilities	**Percent of Total Capacity (kW) Provided by Industrial Undertakings**	**Percent of Industrial Establishment Electricity Sold Outside Establishment**
Austria	23	22	64
Belgium	72	n.a.	n.a.
Czechoslovakia	n.a.	60	15
Denmark	n.a.	19	0
Estonia	67	49	0
Finland	92	n.a.	n.a.
France	65	32	39
Germany	66	43[‡]	n.a.
Greece	45	55	0
Hungary	62	12	0
Ireland	30	4	0
Italy	75	n.a.	n.a.
Latvia	57	22	n.a.
Luxembourg	n.a.	100	7
Netherlands	53	14	14

	Industrial Consumption as Percent of Total Consumption, Central-Station Utilities	Percent of Total Capacity (kW) Provided by Industrial Undertakings	Percent of Industrial Establishment Electricity Sold Outside Establishment
Norway	16[†]	58	2
Poland	n.a.	40	2
Portugal	55	23	0
Romania	n.a.	43	4
Spain	69	n.a.	n.a.
Sweden	79	n.a.	n.a.
Switzerland	39	25	6
U.S.S.R.	n.a.	30[±]	n.a.
Canada	73	21	0
United States	50	23	4
Mexico	55	17	3
Morocco	33	n.a.	n.a.
Tunisia	44	27	0
South Africa	70	n.a.	n.a.
China	77	37[§]	n.a.
Japan	n.a.	10	0
India	n.a.	6	n.a.
Neth. East Indies	31	15	4
South Australia	62	n.a.	n.a.
Aus. (Victoria)	35	n.a.	n.a.
New Zealand	25	n.a.	n.a.

Source: Unless otherwise noted, from Brown, *Statistical Year-Book*, 1936, pp. 103, 108–9.

‡ The figure is the proportion of output from C. Krecke and G. Seebauer, "Organization and Regulation of the German Electricity and Gas Supply," *Transactions, Third World Power Conference*, vol. 5 (Washington, DC: USGPO, 1938), 131.

† The figures are for 1935 from Brown, *Statistical Year-Book, 1938*, pp. 129, 134–5.

± The figure is for the year 1935 from U.S.S.R. Committee for International Scientific and Technical Conferences, "National and Regional Planning and Their Relation to the Conservation of the Natural Resources of the U.S.S.R.," *Transactions, Third World Power Conference*, vol. 6 (Washington: USGPO, 1938), 526.

§ The figure is for 1932 from C. Yun, "A Statistical Investigation of Electric Power Plants in China, 1932," *Transactions of the World Power Conference, Sectional Meeting, Scandinavia*, vol. 2 (Stockholm: Svenska Nationalkommittén för Världkraftkonferenser, 1934), 530.

production of electricity by industrial establishment. The first column of figures, which refers only to electricity produced by central stations, contains the proportion of total electricity consumed by industry. These figures range from around 25 percent (Austria and New Zealand) to over 90 percent (Finland), but most of them are quite large. The second column of figures shows the proportion of a country's total electricity-generating capacity from isolated plants installed by industry, a figure that varied considerably and that also could be quite high, as in Norway. The third column of figures provides information on the proportion of electricity produced by isolated industrial plants that was sold outside the establishment itself. With the exceptions of Austria and France, virtually all power produced by industry in isolated plants was used by the firm that produced it. Most industrial establishments eventually abandoned their isolated plants and connected to central-station networks.

Information contained in the statistical yearbook also makes it possible to determine the extent to which electric energy was traded internationally in 1933.[94] Only a handful of countries imported or exported more than a small fraction of the electricity produced.[95] Capital flowed across borders a lot more freely than did electricity. There were a few exceptions. Switzerland and Austria exported 26 percent and 13 percent, respectively, of the electricity produced there (and imported virtually none). The country with the most balanced trade in electricity was Denmark, which imported an amount equal to 9 percent of its production and exported 6 percent of its actual production. Canada exported 6 percent of its production and imported virtually none, while the United States imported the equivalent of 1 percent of its production.[96] Germany, France, Italy, Czechoslovakia, and Mexico all reported importing 4 percent or less of the amount produced domestically. The low level of international trade in electricity is remarkable.[97]

THE EXTENT OF FOREIGN OWNERSHIP AND CONTROL OF ELECTRIC UTILITIES

This book is about multinational enterprise and global electrification. We have sought to collect information to measure the participation of multinational firms in some meaningful way. We chose to focus on four benchmark time periods and then to assemble data for as many countries as possible for those years. The years selected were (1) 1913–1914, the eve of World War I, by which time cities had electricity, long-distance transmission had become established, and regional networks had begun to take shape; (2) 1928–1932, to account for the disruptions caused by the First World War and the development of larger networks after the war, some of which were beginning to become national in scope; (3) 1947–1950, to capture the changes wrought by the Great Depression, the Second World War, and the immediate postwar nationalizations; and (4) 1970–1972, near the end of our story, when the domestication of electric utilities was practically complete.

We thought carefully about what we meant by "foreign ownership and control," and ultimately we settled on the following definition: If a firm (directly or indirectly) had an equity interest and a significant degree of

Table 1.4. *Foreign Ownership of Electric Utilities, Four Periods: Percent of a Country's Capacity, Output, or Assets of Electric Utilities Owned and Controlled by Foreign Firms, 1913–1914, 1928–1932, 1947–1950, and 1970–1972**

	1913–1914	1928–1932	1947–1950	1970–1972
Europe				
Albania	x	100[1]	100	0
Austria	60–90[2]	20[3]	0[4]	0
Belgium	10[5]	10[6]	0	0
Bulgaria	95[7]	75[8]	0	0
Czechoslovakia	0[9]	0[10]	0[11]	0
Denmark	0	0	0	0
Finland	22[12]	9[13]	0	0
France	ca.15–25[14]	ca.10–15[15]	0[16]	0
Germany	ca.10[17]	<10[18]	0	0
Gibraltar	0[19]	0[20]	0	0
Great Britain (U.K.)	1–2[21]	5–10[22]	0[23]	0
Greece	ca.50[24]	ca.80–85[25]	ca.85[26]	0[27]
Hungary	<20[28]	<20[29]	0	0
Ireland	0[30]	0[31]	0	0
Italy	30[32]	0[33]	0	0[34]
Latvia	95[35]	50[36]	0	0
Luxembourg	0[37]	?[38]	0[39]	0[40]
Malta	ca.10–20[41]	0[42]	0	0
Netherlands	0[43]	0	0	0
Norway	ca.5[44]	ca.2[45]	0	0
Poland	<45[46]	74[47]	0	0
Portugal	?[48]	ca.30[49]		?[50]
Romania	95[51]	50[52]	0	0
Russia/U.S.S.R.	90[53]	0[54]	0	0
Spain	29/33[55]	27[56]	0[57]	0
Sweden	0[58]	0	0	0
Switzerland	10[59]	0[60]	0	0
Yugoslavia	95[61]	40–50/85[62]	0	0
Australasia				
Australia	15[63]	4[64]	0	0
New Zealand	18[65]	0	0	0
Africa				
Algeria	100[66]	100	0[67]	0[68]
Egypt	90+[69]	90+[70]	90+[71]	0
Ethiopia	x	100[72]	80–100	0
Kenya	100[73]	100[74]	100[75]	0[76]
Libya	100[77]	100	80–100	0

(continued)

Table 1.4 *(continued)*

	1913–1914	1928–1932	1947–1950	1970–1972
Morocco	100[78]	100	100	0[79]
Mozambique	x	x	x	95+[80]
Nigeria	0[81]	ca.10[82]	ca.10[83]	ca.10[84]
South Africa	ca.78[85]	65[86]	0[87]	0
Sudan	x	100[88]		0
Uganda	x	100[89]	0[90]	0
Asia				
Burma (Myanmar)	100[91]	40[92]	0	
China	<10[93]	51/62/65[94]	0	0
Hong Kong	ca. 17[95]	0[96]	0	58[97]
India	ca.80[98]	31[99]	0[100]	0
Indonesia (Dutch E. Ind.)	100[101]	100[102]	0[103]	0
Japan	0	0[104]	0	0
Korea (Chosen)	100[105]	ca.100[106]	0[107]	0[108]
Malaysia (Fed. Malay States)	0[109]	46[110]	ca.46[111]	ca.13–20[112]
Manchuria (Manchukuo)	83[113]	75[114]	0	0
Philippines	ca.100[115]	97[116]	ca.70[117]	0[118]
Singapore (Str. Settlements)	100[119]	0[120]	0	0
Sri Lanka (Ceylon)	100[121]	0[122]	0	0
Taiwan (Formosa)	100[123]	100[124]	0[125]	0
Thailand	ca.50[126]	ca.50[127]	0[128]	0[129]
South America				
Argentina	ca.85–95[130]	90+[131]	ca.70–80[132]	9[133]
Bolivia	ca.75[134]	ca.75[135]	ca.75[136]	ca.50–75[137]
Brazil	ca.67–82[138]	67/80[139]	67/82[140]	ca.34[141]
Chile	ca.95[142]	88[143]	80[144]	0[145]
Colombia	0[146]	ca.10[147]	ca.5[148]	0[149]
Ecuador	18[150]	ca.87[151]	ca.87[152]	ca.50–87[153]
Paraguay	100[154]	100[155]	0[156]	0
Peru	ca.85[157]	ca.85[158]	ca.85[159]	0
Uruguay	ca.15[160]	ca.15[161]	0[162]	0
Venezuela	ca.15[163]	ca.15[164]	ca.15[165]	<10[166]
Central America				
Costa Rica	ca.85[167]	ca.72[168]	ca.60[169]	0[170]

	1913–1914	1928–1932	1947–1950	1970–1972
El Salvador	0[171]	43[172]	0[173]	0
Guatemala	ca.95[174]	ca.95[175]	ca.95[176]	0[177]
Honduras	0[178]	ca.36[179]		0[180]
Nicaragua	0[181]	ca.80[182]	0[183]	0
Panama	77[184]	ca.100[185]	ca.100[186]	0[187]
Caribbean				
Barbados	100[188]	100[189]	100[190]	100[191]
Cuba	ca.90[192]	ca.96[193]	ca.96[194]	0[195]
Dominican Republic		100[196]	100[197]	0
Guyana (British Guiana)	ca.100[198]	87[199]	ca.87[200]	0[201]
Haiti		100[202]		0[203]
Jamaica	100[204]	100[205]	ca.100[206]	0[207]
[Smaller Islands]	0[208]			51–59[209]
Trinidad and Tobago	100[210]	100[211]	0[212]	0
North America				
Canada	ca.13[213]	34[214]	24[215]	5[216]
Mexico	ca.90[217]	ca.90[218]	60[219]	0
United States	<1[220]	ca.0[221]	0[222]	0[223]
Middle East				
Israel (Palestine)	x	100[224]	0[225]	0
Turkey	80[226]	20[227]	0[228]	0[229]

* In this table, we are trying to ascertain, as best possible, the share of a country's electricity provided by foreign firms. For countries that did not exist in certain years – because they were part of empires, for example – we have given percentages that relate as closely as possible to their boundaries when they first became nations. We have attempted to measure the percentage of centrally generated electric power (that is, of public utilities) that was foreign owned and/or foreign controlled. We exclude industrial and other isolated plants except where it can be shown that they provided a substantial portion of their output to a network. The notes to the table are in Appendix B.

An "x" indicates that electrification was negligible. If not otherwise indicated in a previous note, a "0" or "100" that is not footnoted represents general knowledge. When there is no entry in a box, we are too uncertain to even make a guess.

influence on the management of an enterprise in another country (that is, a country other than the investor's home country), the firm in that host country was deemed to be foreign-owned and -controlled. Some cross-border equity interest was necessary for foreign ownership and control and the phrase "significant degree" meant the potential for a firm to alter a key aspect of the business or affect a major decision of the business. For a firm to be "foreign-owned and –controlled," it had to be owned and controlled by nonresident investors. We then sought information on the presence of foreign ownership and control from documents, secondary sources, and the opinions of experts.

The results of our endeavors are contained in Table 1.4, where we present our best estimates for as many countries as possible, for the benchmark years, of the percentage of the electric utility industry (measured as either capacity, output, or assets) that was foreign-owned and -controlled. For example, for a country whose electric utility industry was entirely foreign-owned and -controlled (such as Korea's in 1915), this percentage is 100; if there was no foreign ownership at all (such as Japan in 1929), the percentage is 0. If a country had negligible electrification in a benchmark year, this is indicated by an "x." The entries in the table often required a substantial amount of judgment, and each carries an implicit standard error, sometimes large. Source notes on each entry in the table are included in Appendix B. The following chapters fundamentally are an extensive elaboration and explanation of Table 1.4.

2

Multinational Enterprise and International Finance

When electrification became a viable proposition in the late nineteenth century, communications on a global scale were easy. People traveled. Steamships and cables linked distant continents, making for "rapid" contacts – not with the speed of today's internet world, but faster than ever in history. Railroads and telegraph lines stretched into interiors of independent as well as colonized countries. Ideas, knowledge, and technology could (and did) circulate through individuals, companies, and imperial administrators. Capital was more mobile than ever. The modern multinational enterprise, with coordination and control within the firm, came of age. So, too, did international banking acquire new dimensions. Stock markets in the more advanced nations in Europe handled a greater quantity of securities, domestic and international, than ever before, facilitating financial transactions throughout the world. The New York Stock Exchange, while still fundamentally a domestic market, had begun listing some foreign issues, even though it remained subordinate to London and in international activities to the bourses on the European continent. This was the very time – the late nineteenth and early twentieth century – that the introduction and spread of electrification had begun, varying in pattern and swiftness from one country to the next.

Because the beginnings of the diffusion of light and power facilities worldwide coincided exactly with the beginning of the age of globalization and at the identical time when the modern multinational enterprise emerged, the latter could and did assist in the international spread of electrification. Over the years, the world economy changed markedly, due to World War I and subsequent events, and so did the operations of multinational enterprises. The United States, which was a debtor nation before

Authors: Mira Wilkins, H.V. Nelles, and William J. Hausman. Significant advice from Peter Hertner, Ginette Kurgan-Van Hentenryk, Pierre Lanthier, Robert Lipsey, Kenneth Jackson, and Luciano Segreto.

World War I, became a creditor nation, and in the process world capital markets were transformed. During the interwar years and then World War II, new forms of multinational enterprise became predominant as older forms lost significance. Financial intermediation was affected in the short term by wars and business cycles and in the long term by economic growth. From the electricity supply sector's very beginnings, but especially from the 1930s onward, public policies with respect to financial systems – and more specifically electric utilities – had a formidable impact on the ways business was done and on the ownership and control of the businesses that furnished electric light and power. After World War II, there was a dramatic shift in the sources of capital and the operations of enterprise, with governments playing an ever larger role.

This chapter seeks to abstract the diverse forms that multinational enterprises took as they contributed to the global diffusion of electric light and power. We agree with Thomas Hughes that the management of networked electric power systems cries out for attention, and we see the management and financing as going hand-in-hand.[1] Multinational enterprise can take various forms, and the ones we delineate herein should help to guide the reader through the chronological narrative that unfolds in Chapters 3 through 6. In the present chapter, we begin by establishing a framework and vocabulary. Then we focus on the different actors and forms, including a section on the impact of railroads (a sector with immense influence on the actors and forms previously presented). Next, we summarize the actors and forms of business organization that multinational enterprises adopted. We offer some general comments on the significant political dimensions of our story line, 1878–1978. Finally, we conclude with a short Chapter 7 on how circumstances have gone full circle in recent years.

THE FRAMEWORK

Before we proceed, an understanding of the multinational enterprise is required. First and foremost, it is a business or, as economists use the term, a "firm"– a producer of goods and/or services. Second, it operates across borders. It has a home, where it is headquartered, and it operates abroad in one or many host countries. The home is typically a single country, although it need not be. Most multinational enterprises operate in more than one host country – some, today, in as many as 150 (or even more) host countries. Independent nations as well as colonies are included by us under the rubric "hosts to foreign investment," including those investments from the mother country.[2] In sum, the multinational enterprise is a business that is an organized (administered) unit; it produces goods and/or services; and it has a home office and business operations outside the home country headquarters.

Multinational enterprises make foreign direct investments, which occur when the investor intends to have some influence or control over the foreign activity in which the company is investing. Multinational enterprises have strategic goals in their investment patterns. Their investments tend to be long-run, and they are not volatile. The management of the multinational enterprise expects a return not only from the capital invested, but from the business "package," including technology and its application. Multinational enterprises are able to concentrate knowledge.[3] Their investments abroad are far more than financial flows. They involve managed resources, managed within the cluster of firms that comprise the multinational enterprise.

Nonetheless, because light and power facilities were capital intensive (as shown in Figure 1.4 in Chapter 1), fundamental to their development was the mobilization of financial resources, which could be domestic and/or international; if domestic resources were inadequate, money could be raised abroad. In the late-nineteenth- and early-twentieth-century world economy, at the beginning of our story, financial capital for the introduction of electrification could be assembled by multinational enterprises and financial institutions outside the location of the operations, collected where savings were available, and directed to where they could be productively used – at home and abroad. With the demand for electricity and the presence of business organizations to meet that demand, the new electricity supply industry was able to obtain the available capital, although not always easily. It was not uncommon for host nation nationals to participate with foreign multinationals in ventures within their countries. This was the case in such host countries as Germany and England, but also in China and Egypt. Ours is the story of how capital was collected – internationally and domestically – through time for the purpose of global electrification. We concentrate our focus on the role of multinational enterprises in that process.[4]

Electric utilities that had, or could create, known and trusted reputations, were able to float bonds domestically and internationally and obtain funds without foreign ownership and control. For others that required large amounts of capital, they needed aid in creating business organizations perceived to be trustworthy.[5] Through different forms of multinational enterprise, the reduction of economic (and political) risk occurred, so as to facilitate the intermediation of capital internationally (and in the process to attract local capital as well).

As with all long-term international investments, there are two fundamental ways of transferring capital for global electrification. The first (sometimes called "foreign portfolio investment") relates to international finance, where lenders or securities' owners take no direct interest in management (unless things go wrong) and the corporate recipient of the funding makes the fundamental decisions on the operations of the business. The second (foreign direct investment), identified with multinational enterprise, involves ownership and control, as defined in Chapter 1.[6] Academic research on these two types of investment has often been separate, with the first set of researchers primarily concerned with governmental *and* corporate finance (along with banking), frequently with a more general interest in financial systems and securities markets. For some writers, the term "foreign portfolio investments" includes government as well as private-sector securities; with this definition, students of foreign portfolio investments have considered not only corporate but also – indeed, in large part – governmental debt (and credits).[7] The second group of researchers has studied multinational enterprises, focusing mainly on individual firms as they invest abroad.[8] The literature on multinational enterprise (once principally on manufacturing) now includes banks, other financial intermediaries, and service providers as well as a range of other businesses as they make foreign direct investments – that is, as they extend as a firm over borders. In keeping with this body of works, we use the words "business" and "firm" to embrace enterprises in all sectors. The provision of light and power is that of a service, so the enlarged literature is especially germane and provides insights for our study. There have been attempts to provide historical statistics on foreign direct investment, by sector, which we have used with great caution.[9]

Although our emphasis is on the activities of multinational enterprises, we found it imperative to consider foreign portfolio as well as foreign direct investments, because we have found that the two were not mutually exclusive. Moreover, throughout we have discovered a considerable number of "cross-investments" (inward and outward foreign investments), especially among the more advanced countries, accompanied by the highly uneven foreign direct/foreign portfolio investment ratios.[10] In exploring the associations between multinational enterprise and international finance, we often encountered ambiguities. As Geoffrey Jones has put it, "[There is] a grey world between direct and portfolio investment"; we can add that probably in no sector is this more evident than in the provision of light and power services.[11] The reason lay in the heavy capital requirements in this sector. We are compelled to look at both direct and portfolio investments and their relationships.

Enriching our study on multinational enterprise and foreign finance has been a relatively new literature on corporate governance, a large part of which has emerged as a direct offshoot from the field of corporate finance. While much of the published literature is still surprisingly narrow in that it does not cover multinational enterprises, the questions dealt with do illuminate our understanding of the latter within the electricity supply sector. This is especially true when authors on corporate governance confront the complexities of pyramided business groups.[12]

Scholars considering corporate governance have argued that "different countries' economies are organized in very different ways, and corporate governance – decisions about how capital is allocated, both across and within firms – is entrusted to very different sorts of people and constrained by very different institutions."[13] By contrast, we have been wary of references to national style, preferring instead to focus on how the national decision making by firms is transformed in an international setting.[14] Yet there were clear national differences in both home and host countries over time. These variations in home and host country experiences (juxtaposed by us into an international context) will emerge as our story unfolds; we accept (and endorse) the view that there were varieties in the evolution of capitalist systems.[15] But there were also differences within countries, so, even more important, our focus is on how what emerged inside particular countries crossed over borders to provide the basis for the worldwide growth of light and power facilities.[16]

Although typically national in their discussions, the studies of corporate governance cast light from the standpoint of home countries on the history of the international networks associated with electric utilities. They highlight the profound concerns of financial actors (shareholders and bondholders) as they made investments or provided the underwriting of and placement of such investments. The writings on corporate governance, integrated by us into the literature on multinational enterprise, seem to add clarity to that "grey" area between foreign direct and portfolio investments. A 2002 statement by the president of the Federal Reserve Bank of New York captures the connection. He associated financial stability with sound leadership at a firm level: "Sound leadership … begins with good corporate governance: capable and experienced directors and management, a coherent strategy and business plan, and clear lines of responsibility and accountability."[17] And, of course, that was what multinational enterprises hoped to accomplish.

When, historically, financial intermediaries – whether they were American, Canadian, British, Swiss, Belgian, or German – looked to international investments in public utilities (as well as in other sectors), they wanted to be assured of good governance. Most of the time, they did not want to run the business, which was the prerogative of management. It is here that the issues of control become important. Two corporate structures may be identical, but the intended control over management, over administering the business, may be highly diverse. We will see this murkiness as we monitor multinational enterprise and foreign financing of public utilities.

Early and many recent studies of multinational enterprise see the firm as starting business at home and then moving abroad and, in the course of doing so, extending the firm's core competencies. In this generally accepted pattern, the management of the firm learned from its experiences at home and developed international activities based on its accumulated knowledge. This can be labeled the "classic form" of multinational enterprise.[18] It was present in the late nineteenth and early twentieth centuries (as well as more recently). Before World War I, however, literally thousands of companies were set up in the United Kingdom and to a lesser extent within Western Europe (France and The Netherlands in particular) to undertake business over borders.[19] These companies had a head office at home, but they did not have operations in the home (domestic) market. They assembled talent at home and abroad to pursue their business in a foreign country (or region). In a 1988 article in the *Economic History Review*, Mira Wilkins called these "free standing companies," a form of multinational enterprise that did not fit the standard, classic model.[20]

The authors of the present volume wondered: To what extent were electric utilities started as free standing companies? Were there other variants to the classic model? In the writings on free standing companies, scholars had grappled with issues on the line between foreign portfolio and direct investments, with what constituted control, clusters of companies, business groups, and informal networks.[21] Jean-François Hennart expanded the thinking on free standing companies in an attempt to formulate a theory of minority equity stakes.[22] We found that such minority interests were ubiquitous in international investments in the electric utilities sector. Thus, while the literature on the classic multinational enterprise has informed our inquiry, we have not been fettered to it. We found the research on free standing companies particularly stimulating. Indeed, remarkably many of the insights from the studies on free standing companies coincided with the separate (and entirely independent) work on corporate governance, both paying heed to clusters and business groups.

To be sure, multinational enterprises technically comprise clusters of affiliates (although we will not use the expression in this manner). A loosely structured multinational enterprise is sometimes referred to as a "business group" (and at times, we adopt that formulation). Close associations of otherwise independent firms have also been designated as clusters, business groups, or networks. Often authors (including those writing this volume) want to differentiate between what is "internalized" – that is, owned and controlled within a multinational firm – and what is "outsourced" to a cluster of firms that may constitute a business group – what happens within a firm and across firms.[23]

Writers on multinational enterprise consider manufacturing, banking, and trading companies as multinationals.[24] When we tried to define a "public utility multinational," we discovered that we could not do so, at least during the first century of electrification (1878–1978). Multinational enterprises were deeply involved in this sector, but with very few exceptions public utility *operating* companies did not expand over borders. The closest resemblance to a multinational public utility enterprise was the public utility *holding company* that owned public utility operating (and holding) companies at home and abroad; many of these had core competencies that were extended internationally, yet this was only one way – albeit an important way – by which global electrification spread through multinational enterprise. The categories (forms of multinational enterprise), outlined in this chapter are culled from historical evidence. Rather than limiting ourselves to the classic multinational enterprise, or to the sometimes uneasy division between foreign direct and foreign portfolio investments, our sources have pushed us to probe the wide variety of conduits for foreign investments.[25] We hope the originality of our approach set out in this chapter will not only steer our reader through what follows in subsequent chapters, but also contribute to the theoretical (as well as the descriptive) literature on the history of multinational enterprise.

We identified a number of separate businesses and financial intermediaries that marshaled capital and in the process accelerated the spread of electrification around the world. The story is complicated, not only because of the many participants and how they interacted with one another, but also by the confusion that occurs when the same company has two or more names (one each in German, French, Italian, and English, for instance). Short names and abbreviations of companies were differently used by different authors.[26] For the sanity of our readers (and of the authors!), this volume contains an appendix that identifies companies with two or more names along with alternative short names and abbreviations. We do not want our reader to get lost in the forest of company names and the jungle of business groups. In addition, it was not unusual for large multinational enterprises to have so-called "paper companies" – set up to protect assets, to minimize tax burdens, and for a variety of other reasons. We will – as our text progresses – encounter such corporate "shells." They add complexity – and grief – in the targeted task of understanding. We hope our readers will bear with us as we make our way through the labyrinths and that this chapter will provide guidance for what follows.

In writing this chapter, we found a muddiness in our group's thinking about such terms as "types," "forms," "styles," "structures," "modes," and "patterns." For clarification, we arbitrarily use the term "type" to make the broad differentiation between foreign portfolio and direct investments; and we use the word "form" to designate the different business organizations that we outline in this chapter. "Structure," "style," "mode," and "pattern" are employed rather more freely to cover the behavior of firms: the way business was done in the electric public utilities sector. On occasion, the words "form," "structure," "style," and "mode" will be used as synonyms; the term "pattern" is more general, including nationality prominence and geographical spread. "Strategy," about which we found little confusion, relates to broad long-term policies of firms. "Conduits" are the channels through which capital, technology, and knowledge are moved over borders.

In this chapter, we offer a framework for identifying and classifying the conduits for foreign investments into electric utilities and how these conduits altered over time. In subsequent chapters, we will implicitly insert our ideas into the actual chronological story, as tools for understanding. We argue that not only were there technological applications, adaptations, diffusion, and reverse diffusion, but there was a learning process in international business as such and that it was this dynamic learning process that assisted the expansion of electrification on a global scale. Without the managerial and financing structures, electrification would not have spread internationally as rapidly as it did. As we cover the companies that supplied the management that accompanied the foreign investment, sometimes this meant cutting through corporate veils, collapsing the legal architecture. There was nothing static about the processes that we are considering: Major changes occurred in the international investments from the late nineteenth century onward, reflecting the growth and transformations in the businesses participating, the new entries, and also the economic, technological, political, social, and general business environments. Ours is a discussion not only on the nature of firms and the organizational forms that they take, but also on the growth of firms, their changes through time, their retreats as well as expansions, and on what motivated the enterprises.

As we study the investments of a multinational enterprise type – that is, those that carried ownership and control (management) across borders – we have always recognized the need to carefully define what we mean by, and what the businesses that used the term meant by, "control." The very notion of control was too often elusive. Among our group, we found that defining "ownership and control" resulted in ambiguous conclusions. In Chapter 1, Table 1.4, we did our best to cut the Gordian knot and accept an operative definition of the phrase "ownership and control." In this chapter and those to come, we adopt the same definition, but we take a more nuanced approach.

As we try to set forth the basis for systematic analysis, we have many times found rough edges and intersections. Our taxonomy is compromised by our identification of categories that are not mutually exclusive. Networks, alliances, webs, and minority interests comprising intricate interconnections were the norm, not the exception. Business groups overlapped. The reader is forewarned that what we will be presenting is on chains, imbrications, and associated clusters of firms.

What then were the forms of enterprise used to provide electric light and power over borders? Our tale is far from trivial. Private-sector international capital was fundamental to the introduction and, for many decades, to the spread of electrification on a global scale. How, from an organizational standpoint, did that capital cross borders? How were management and capital linked?

MANUFACTURERS' SATELLITES AND EXTENDED MANUFACTURERS' SATELLITES

Although ours is a story about the supply of electric light and power, about the provision of a service, we must start with the manufacturers. Electrical manufacturing companies made foreign direct investments that initially involved the installation of isolated plants and then the participation in the establishment of public utilities.[27] Electrical facilities set up abroad by manufacturers, we have labeled "manufacturers' satellites."

Here the pattern fits a scenario familiar to students of multinational enterprise. In the late nineteenth century, when our narrative begins, numerous U.S. and European manufacturers with new technologies and trademarked or branded goods not only sold these goods domestically but exported and marketed them abroad. These manufacturers did outside their domestic market what they did at home. They invested in marketing organizations. They also invested in manufacturing plants in foreign countries, when required, in order to fill the foreign demand. This was true, for example, of the American company Singer, which organized an international sewing machine distribution network and then built factories in major markets abroad.[28] British manufacturers, such as the then large thread company J. & P. Coats, followed an identical pattern.[29] Similarly, the principal U.S. and German electrical manufacturers invested in marketing and manufacturing outside their home country. Today, this has been the pattern for such companies as Toyota, which invested initially in marketing and then in manufacturing abroad. In each case, the manufacturer developed competence at home and transferred technologies abroad.

In addition, and most important for our purposes, the very same electrical manufacturers that exported, developed foreign marketing organizations, and then manufactured abroad also aided in establishing and participating in setting up electric light and power facilities at home and abroad. When they did so, they were doing what all manufacturing firms do when they create a complementary basis for distribution. But whereas a sales network designed to market sewing machines or thread – or, for that matter, soap, harvesters, elevators, automobiles, or electrical products – linked the manufacturer directly (although perhaps through a vertical wholesale and retailing chain) with the end consumer, the founding of an electric utility was different.

The manufacturer of electrical goods had a dual relationship with the electricity supplier: First, the supplier was the final customer for power equipment, and second, there were consumers who required access to electric power in order to use the products made by the electrical manufacturer (the more homes, factories, and communities with access to electric power, the greater the sales by the manufacturer of electrical goods). Thus, from the start, electrical manufacturers had a strong incentive to support the emergence of light and power facilities.[30] They did this at home, and they did it abroad.[31] While electrotechnical manufacturers were central to this manufacturing story, there were also manufacturers of boilers, insulated cables, and other equipment that perceived the development of electric utilities as key in their sales and would also participate in investments to encourage the installation of light and power facilities.

Sometimes the manufacturer acted as a "contractor," which might or might not have an investment in the foreign public utility.[32] When, as was frequently the case, an electrical (or other) manufacturer took part in the inauguration of or expansion of electric generation abroad and did make an investment, we have called this form of multinational enterprise activity "manufacturers' satellites." As we follow the chronology on the spread of electrification worldwide, we will observe numerous cases where equipment (particularly electrotechnical equipment) manufacturers, desiring to raise exports, took the initiative and responsibility for the setting up, first, of isolated stations and then on a broader basis electric utilities. They provided the engineering talents and the technological know-how.

Often, when a manufacturer got involved in sponsoring a utility, it would obtain only a partial interest in the newly established or acquired electricity supply unit. Because electric utilities were capital intensive, manufacturers looked for outside funding for them. Over time, the partial interest of the manufacturer might be reduced or, indeed, not maintained. New investors might be brought in. And these might or might not have an arm's length (totally independent) relationship to the manufacturer. For the manufacturer, ownership was not always needed to ensure the continuation of orders of machinery from the utility. (A utility designed to use a specific type of equipment would frequently buy from the same source when the equipment wore out or needed to be updated or new equipment was required for expansion.) Another reason why electrical manufacturers wanted electrification was that once a utility was in operation, consumers would buy electrical lights and appliances irrespective of the ownership of the utility. Indeed, the opposite side of the coin now took effect: The utility wanted to encourage the purchase of electrical goods so that consumption of electricity and revenues would grow.[33]

Sometimes, in a hierarchical fashion, an electrical manufacturer would establish or acquire an interest in a foreign manufacturing affiliate, which would, in turn, invest in utilities. We have called this form the "extended manufacturers' satellite." This was a typical "chain." An example of an extended manufacturers' satellite was when General Electric held an interest in the French manufacturer Thomson-Houston, which, in turn, had interests in electric utilities in France and abroad. Note that the international choices here involved a manufacturer's exporting machinery with no investment in its customer (a utility) or alternatively investing in the utility (or possibly in an extended manufacturers' satellite arrangement) in order to enhance goods exports (or to build the business of its manufacturing affiliate abroad).

There is a large literature on manufacturing multinationals that concentrates on the trade-offs between exports and foreign direct investment in producing abroad. There is also a literature on manufacturing multinationals and their investments in supply-related manufacturing – that is, investments for purposes of gaining inputs into the production process and importing these inputs back to the home country.[34] For the history of foreign direct investments in electric utilities such discussions of trade are generally (but not always) irrelevant. Historically, power lines seldom crossed national frontiers. Interestingly, however, when this did occur there did appear to have been cross-border investments.[35]

For the electrical manufacturer that invested abroad, there was, however, an important trade and investment story that related to the manufacturer's choices. While there was no neat association between the size of direct investments by a manufacturer in an electric utility and the former's sales to that utility, clearly contacts by the manufacturer with a public utility (formal or otherwise) added to the volume of that manufacturer's sales. Accordingly, minority interests or other sorts of relationships between the equipment manufacturer and the public utility often were evident.

In thinking about the manufacturers' choices on investments in electric power supplies and the forms used, it is crucial to keep in mind the capital intensity and "lumpiness" of investments in public utilities. And then there was the matter of returns on investments. Often, an equipment manufacturer's profits would come from equipment orders. The manufacturer counted less on the return on its investment in the electric utility and more on its *equipment sales*. Yet, the public utility had to be viable in order to maintain those sales/exports.

Characteristic of international investment in the electric utilities sector has been that while revenues are in the currency of the country where these ventures are located, substantial costs may be incurred in a foreign currency – especially in the case of developing countries. This does not matter if currencies are stable and readily convertible. In periods of currency fluctuations and blocked currencies, this could (and would) create major risks. It meant that the manufacturer assumed considerable risk in remaining involved in a public utility foreign investment whenever there was no special advantage in doing so – that is, if through contractual "deals," through "friends," or through small minority stakes, the manufacturer could continue to get assurance of equipment orders and if it was possible to find alternative investors. In addition, as noted, equipment orders tended to be cumulative. Once a light and power facility was established, its corporate owner (or, alternatively, its management) often continued to buy from familiar suppliers. If the manufacturer had been involved in the engineering and the construction design of the public utility, this might ensure a continuation of orders with no requirement for investment by the manufacturer in the foreign public utility (which was especially true with so-called "dedicated technology," distinctive to the particular activity). Remember, too, sales of end products of the electrical manufacturer *to the public* were – once the electric power plant was established – not dependent on the ownership of the utility.[36]

BANKS AND OTHER FINANCIAL INTERMEDIARIES

When many manufacturing companies went into international business in the late nineteenth century, reinvested earnings were, for the most part, adequate to finance their expansion in marketing, assembling, processing, and manufacturing abroad. By contrast, because the electricity supply systems were so capital intensive, from the start banks and other financial intermediaries were always involved. Thus, they become the second set of important actors in the establishment of electric utilities abroad. There were sizable capital costs before a utility was able to produce an output (or revenues) to offset the costs. Manufacturers did not want to tie up capital for this purpose; the needs of electric utilities surpassed their available reinvested earnings.

The financing of electric utilities over borders meant not only (1) raising the initial capital (and the ongoing recapitalization with growth), but subsequently, (2) the usual commercial accommodation for deposits and short-term borrowing associated with any form of commercial undertaking, and (3) the continuous return flow of funds from operating income to provide the return on investment. And then there were the added investments to assist the introduction of new, changing technology, the replacement of worn-out machinery, and new extensions as the business grew, whether through mergers and acquisitions or through internal expansion. Sometimes, these financial arrangements were intimately tied with equity investments (multinational enterprise activities), and sometimes they were exogenous to the operating firm. Whether internalized or separate, the roles of banks, a variety of other financial intermediaries (including insurance companies, securities companies, investment trusts, and investment companies), and individual promoters and brokers (separately or jointly) were critical. The role could be internalized, by which we mean that the banks or other financial intermediaries had representatives on the board of directors of the parent of the electric light and power company and played an active role in the latter. When technology changed from the late 1870s to the 1890s, there was a jump in the amount of capital required as new systems emerged. As a consequence, the activities of financial institutions became even more widespread in this sector.

At times, financial intermediaries saw opportunities and took the initiative; at other times, they were followers, brought in by manufacturers or other parties. Sometimes it is uncertain whether the manufacturer or the bank (or another financial intermediary) took the lead in establishing new enterprises abroad. Clearly, providers of capital desired to be assured of sound direction at the firm level. Sometimes the financial intermediaries participated in introducing management; sometimes their associated companies or the company in the host country took the lead. Arrangements were different in different situations. As H. V. Nelles has written, enterprise and finance are two parallel supporting institutional systems. Both operated at home and abroad. The identifiable processes of multinational enterprise investment in electric utility companies involved at the start the scouting and negotiation of the franchise, the securing of the contract, engineering, company promotion, underwriting, construction, operations and management, and primary and secondary distribution of securities. Sometimes these functions were performed within a single firm, but sometimes they were not internalized – that is, they were performed outside the firm that was the initiator and operator of the public utility.[37] If the latter, there were frequently very personal networks of social relationships that facilitated the raising of capital.

Sometimes, however, the international financial relationships were entirely separated from multinational enterprises, and established nationally owned and controlled utilities were able to locate underwriters and to float bonds in international markets; in many cases, financial institutions within these host countries aided in the process. As we study the role of financial intermediaries in the spread of electric utilities worldwide, we will make the distinctions.

Banks and other financial intermediaries had an interest in seeing to it that not only were good financial returns forthcoming, but that there was a solid productive activity to ensure that return in the future. Many financial institutions, especially those heavily involved in electric utilities, employed specialized talent, skilled individuals (engineers, for example) to evaluate investments. To the extent that the financial intermediaries became directly involved in the operations to make sure that the returns were forthcoming, they became direct investors, furnishing contacts and information, so as to lead the operation of the electric utility to success.

In this regard, it is useful to consider the dissimilarities between bank financing and capital market financing.[38] The former often tended to be short-term financing. As for the later, financial intermediaries (investment banks, merchant banks, universal banks, affiliates of commercial banks, or brokers) were involved in arranging access to capital markets, underwriting corporate bonds, and providing for the distribution of equity. They might do this without an extension of operations over borders. Many, however, had close relationships with other firms over borders. Once the utility was beyond the start-up phase and in operation, it had new requirements for financing that posed different problems, although often the same actors were involved. Other financial intermediaries – such as insurance companies, investment trusts, and investment companies – also assisted in the financing of utilities abroad.

Banks (of all sorts), other financial intermediaries, and promoters aided in accelerating the spread of electric utilities worldwide. Some of these players were highly entrepreneurial. However, in different settings (defined by space and time) the mix of such financial actors varied widely, and even the very term "bank" had distinct meanings in different national contexts.[39] "Merchant banks" in the United Kingdom, such as J. S. Morgan & Co. (and its 1910 successor, Morgan Grenfell), the Barings, and the Rothschilds, were not called "banks," although the phrase "banking houses" was used. The line between a stockbroker and a merchant bank in the United Kingdom often was tenuous.[40]

In the United States, Drexel, Morgan and its 1895 successor, J. P. Morgan & Co., were "private banks," which took deposits as well as carrying out investment banking functions. As in the United Kingdom, so in the United States, stockbrokers became investment bankers.[41] National City Bank, New York, was a "national" bank, regulated under federal law (yet before the passage of the Glass Steagall Act of 1933, it had a subsidiary that handled underwriting and securities' sales). Deutsche Bank has often been called a "universal bank." Laws that were distinctive to individual countries defined the spheres of "banks." As Daniel Verdier writes, "Universal banking is commonly believed to have existed before 1913 in Belgium, Germany, Austria, Italy, whereas specialized banking was mostly encountered in France and the Anglo-Saxon countries."[42] Verdier recognized that this generalization was overly broad. Within countries, regulatory regimes changed over time, as did banking functions. Functions performed in one country by a bank might be performed in another country by a differently designated financial intermediary. What was permissible in one era might be different from what could be done in the next. Banking reforms in the United States and Belgium in the early 1930s and in Italy in 1936 would radically alter what "banks" could do. After 1933 (and all through the subsequent period on which this book concentrates), in the United States there was a separation of investment and commercial banking. In recent years in the United States, this "wall" has crumbled. In Germany, there was never such a wall.

There were sharp country-specific differences in rules and traditions on bank branches. In the United States, branching was very limited; in Canada there were a few big banks and a substantial number of branches.[43] In the United Kingdom, in the nineteenth and much of the twentieth century, domestic commercial banks did not invest abroad, but there were important overseas banks that had branch networks that supplied financial accommodations to British enterprises (including those in electric utilities) that operated globally. Before the Federal Reserve Act of December 1913, national banks in the United States could not branch abroad; there were no similar constraints on the Bank of Montreal or on Deutsche Bank, which set up branches and subsidiaries in foreign countries. On the other hand, after 1914 National City Bank could and did branch abroad, providing financial services to U.S.-owned public utilities located in foreign markets. (Note that while it could not branch across state lines, it was permitted to set up branches in foreign countries.) The term "syndicate" had different meanings in various contexts. "Promoters" could be bankers, but they need not be.

Peter Hertner and H. V. Nelles have described the entrepreneurial character of certain Canadian investors in foreign public utilities. The "Canadian entrepreneurs understood the revolutionary effect hydroelectricity had upon the cost structure of electric utilities. By greatly increasing the scale of production and lowering operating costs, electric utilities could serve a much larger market, at lower prices, and still make healthy profits. Indeed, properly managed, a utility needed only a small fraction of its income to cover operating expenses. The rest could go toward extensions, upgrades, rate reductions, debt service, and ultimately dividends on common stock. Of course, the capital costs of the new hydroelectric installations, long-distance transmission, and extended distribution facilities increased dramatically. The Canadian entrepreneurs did not see that as a problem, but rather as an opportunity, for *they were first and foremost financiers, investment bankers, bond salesmen, and company promoters*. The more debt the better, as it meant higher commissions and more good 'stuff' (as they colloquially referred to the stocks and bonds they created) to spread around. The new economics of production meant that these companies could readily serve the mountains of debt piled upon them and still perform adequately for the shareholders" (our emphasis).[44] Entrepreneurial behavior in the financial sector in connection with public utilities was not uncommon.

Electrical equipment manufacturers (like many other manufacturers) had special domestic relationships with banks (and other financial intermediaries) that usually extended into the electric utilities sector, domestically and internationally. While there were some "banks" (for example, Bonbright & Co. in the United States) and some brokerage houses (Foster & Braithwaite in England, for instance) that specialized in electric utilities at home and abroad, and while there were certain "investment companies" that limited themselves to public utility investments, many, probably most, of the financial intermediaries that participated in stimulating the spread of electrification worldwide did not confine themselves to electric utility finance. This was true of insurance companies, which had an important role in financing certain public utilities, and also of many investment trusts and investment companies.

In 1899, Canadian regulators removed certain restrictions on the kinds of securities life insurance companies could hold; as Christopher Armstrong and H. V. Nelles have written, this "suddenly freed up millions of dollars of Canadian savings for placement in the relatively secure utilities sector" – at home and abroad.[45] So, too, the vast British insurance companies' resources could be, and were, used for investments in public utilities – at home and abroad. British insurance companies became part of the cluster of participants in international investments. Indeed, as we explore the forms and behavior of multinational enterprise taking part in the spread of utilities, we can identify financial intermediaries active in a variety of roles. At the same time as these financial intermediaries might take on a multinational enterprise form, they might also participate directly or indirectly in expediting purely financial transactions. Financial institutions ranked as key actors in facilitating the process of spreading electricity around the world.

So, too, the very presence of stock markets was significant in mobilizing funds and encouraging the global development of electric utilities. Securities markets were part of the financial system, and their use came to be crucial in the international financing of public utilities, both in relationship to multinational enterprises and also vis-à-vis the domestic and international financial transactions of what were domestically managed utilities. In a review, Richard Sylla commented on Ranald Michie's findings that "the value of securities in 1913 was three to four times greater than worldwide deposits, which makes one wonder why banks and banking have received such disproportionate attention from financial historians."[46] The point made by Sylla (and Michie) is well taken. Key stock markets were available to aid in the assembly of capital for public utilities around the world. Yet, here, too, change was very evident. The role of financial intermediaries and stock markets altered through time. London was by far the most important international securities market in 1913–1914, while in the 1920s the U.S. stock markets took on new significance. An individual public utility might be traded on a number of stock exchanges. The insights of Joost Jonker on the financial systems of Britain, France, and Germany are very germane to our story. In the first two countries, Jonker sees securities markets as playing a vital, central role, while the German stock exchanges "firmly chained to banking interests[,] ... keen to protect the internalized markets, remained rather listless considering the huge economy surrounding them and would remain so until the 1980s."[47] Canadians had very thin stock markets, but they effectively used London and then New York, as well as Brussels and Paris, in public utilities finance. The New York stock market was essential for public utilities finance in the 1920s. For stock markets to operate, there had to be actors to arrange the underwriting and the listings – and stockbrokers to facilitate transactions. In sum, financial intermediaries – banks, insurance companies, securities companies, investment trusts, investment companies, individual promoters, and brokers – were business organizations that played a variety of roles in the spread of electric utilities.

THE ENCLAVE FORM

From the 1880s onward, whenever a multinational enterprise set up a company town associated with plantations, mining, or oil drilling, these had some kind of electric power facilities. At the same time as electrification was taking hold and the world economy was being integrated by railroad networks, new resources were being utilized on a global scale. As businesses developed these resources and brought them into international trade, a company would typically install power plants to meet the requirements of the new, frequently remote, economic activity. Such light and power facilities introduced the initial electrification in diverse areas around the globe, from Europe to Latin America, Africa, the Middle East, Asia, and North America. We have called this international structure, an "enclave form" establishment.

Before the First World War, companies such as United Fruit (in countries washed by the Caribbean Sea), the Guggenheim's Chile Exploration Co. (at Chuquicamata in Chile), and Río Tinto (in Spain) were multinational enterprises in this category – and there were numerous others. In the 1920s, company towns multiplied around the globe, many with modern amenities, including electric power.[48] In terms of power generated, with some important exceptions, these activities both within and outside of empires probably added up to relatively small amounts of kilowatt hours, at least as compared with urban electrification. Yet some facilities were quite large, and in consideration of the *geographical* spread of electricity, spurred by international enterprise outside then-existing urban areas, all of them brought standards from the most advanced countries to far-off locales around the world. In time, with varying degrees of rapidity, these areas would become urban. Even before World War I, and certainly by the 1920s, as mining and oil communities were urbanized, the power plants would be spun off and run not by the multinational enterprise, but by a local (national) power company – not foreign-owned. Or alternatively, they might be spun off and continue to be foreign-owned. Sometimes, the power facilities that related to a particular enclave form of activities were placed in separately incorporated operating companies, and sometimes they were not. If substantial additional financing was required, the separate company was very likely. If not, the electricity supply system could be financed through the plantation, mining, or oil-drilling enterprise. In certain locales, where there were many mining companies, a single foreign-owned power company might come to serve the community or region.

In addition, there was a comparable political (as distinct from economic) enclave in the extension of electrification: As European administrators of empire went abroad, they came to expect to have electrified homes and offices. Here, the provision of electricity seldom extended beyond the European expatriates, and the linkages appear to have been less than with the company towns. Nonetheless, this, too, was a form of spatial diffusion of the supply of electric power on a global basis.[49]

LARGE POWER CONSUMERS

As electrification came of age, innovations in many industrial sectors created new industries requiring substantial power – for example, aluminum production as well as some electrochemical processes. Paper and pulp making came to be very energy intensive. Large power consumers were not a subset of the enclave form. This form was distinctive. Enterprises in these specific industries took the initiative and invested at home and over borders to obtain the required power; and at the same time, potential developers of power resources in what were remote areas sought out large industrial power users. These power consumers represented a further set of business actors that participated in building up power sources outside a particular home country. Whereas with the enclave form, the power facility was located where the agricultural endeavor, the mine, or the oil well had been or was being established, the large power consumers sought locations where there were potentials for cheap power. The development here combined firms with huge power requirements with a previously undeveloped source of power. After such facilities were built, they often served more than just the founding enterprises; they would become public utilities. This occurred from the late nineteenth century onward. Before (and after) World War I, Canada and Norway – with possibilities of hydroelectric power – were particularly attractive to companies with heavy power requirements. Switzerland, which was becoming rich in financial resources, also was appealing (but more often than in Canada or Norway, Swiss activities could draw on domestic finance). In the post–World War II years, in almost an encore, foreign aluminum companies in West Africa provided the stimulant for the exact same development of power resources. But while the aluminum companies were participants in the arrangements, the financing of this power generation was seldom provided by the aluminum producers.

HOLDING COMPANIES

One very important set of initiators in spreading electricity around the world were holding companies.[50] A holding company was a pyramided corporate structure that came to be an umbrella designation for highly diverse underlying behavior. Some holding companies were rather flat and extended. Others were highly layered, with one layer above another and control concentrated at the pinnacle. Many combined these corporate architectures. In a holding company structure, in a hierarchical manner, affiliates at home and abroad might themselves serve as holding companies, owning securities in separately incorporated entities within the home, host, and third countries. Most multinational enterprises had (and have) a holding company edifice, at least in a technical sense: The parent holds stock in companies that operate abroad, and control is concentrated in the parent company. Usually, however, these multinational enterprises have not been described as holding companies, because the entire enterprise integrated the business operations.[51]

In the summer of 2001, the U.S. Department of Commerce noted that in the "last two decades" U.S. multinational enterprises had been funneling an increasing share of direct investments abroad through holding companies, many of which were organized "primarily to coordinate management and administration of activities – such as marketing, distribution, and financing – worldwide or in a particular geographical region."[52] The use of holding companies with this intent is far from confined to recent decades.

In the electric utilities sector, from the mid-1890s both home-country *and* third-country holding companies emerged in Europe with efficiency rationales.[53] These engaged in international business: They organized and managed new public utilities projects; they assembled engineering talent; they arranged for equipping the utilities; they found management; and they set up and combined existing operating companies in single, more efficient utilities. They also financed or arranged the financing of the utilities. Third-country holding companies were frequently organized in Switzerland and Belgium. They did what is described in German as *Unternehmergeschäft* – that is, they served as entrepreneurial enterprises, and they behaved as multinational enterprises.[54]

To what extent did the ownership interests (by manufacturers and banks, for example) in these holding companies carry control? Definitions of "control" are slippery. Obviously, one purpose of information that came from ownership for a manufacturer was to be in an advantageous position to sell equipment to the power stations. The manufacturer, *through* the holding company, wanted to influence this facet of the holding and control the utility's management.[55] It certainly did not want to control the running of the operating company's business, except in a manner related to equipment supply. So, too, did banks involved in the holding companies have separate agendas.

Sometimes, the very same holding company did not exercise ownership and control over some of its holdings; it was simply an owner of securities, with special expertise in the public utilities sector that informed its financial portfolios. The mix of the active and passive investments by holding companies often changed through time. The legal structure was frequently complicated by the varieties of interests. There were holding companies that might be owned by other holding companies that were solely financial in nature. There were cross-holdings within a holding company group. Ginette Kurgan-Van Hentenryk has suggested that the Belgian group Empain, up to the 1950s, might be analyzed as a Japanese *zaibatsu*, with each having a "pyramid-like structure, with a family at the top, supported by a holding company and by various joint stock companies."[56]

As in Europe, U.S. holding companies emerged in the 1890s[57] in various industries – soon, particularly, in electric utilities. In 1913, *Electrical World* commented (in the U.S. domestic context) that the weakness of holding companies "lies in the temptation to use ... [their] undeniable operating advantages as a cloak to cover the issuance of more securities than the properties should be required to support." Historian Richard Hirsh added: "While recognizing the existence of opportunities for exploiting the holding company structure, [U.S.] industry insiders preferred to focus on the risk-reducing advantages offered by the new financing scheme, which engendered investment bankers' support for the new holding company structure." In the U.S. public utilities sector, domestic experience with holding companies would subsequently be replicated in the international context.[58] As in Europe, many of the leading U.S. electric utility holding companies, as Thomas Hughes has insisted, were to be "found rooted more deeply in technology and management history than in finance." Key holding companies were led by engineers and technically trained managers. At the same time, these men were able to raise money, so technology and management history were not divorced from finance.[59] The German word *Unternehmergeschäft* was applicable to their activities.

So, too, holding companies took shape with Canadian-headquartered firms to do business in public utilities outside the Dominion. Canadian holding companies for international business were a later phenomenon than those in Europe and the United States and had markedly different relationships with financial intermediaries (banks, brokers, securities companies, and investment companies). Yet, they, too, served the same functions, organizing the business abroad in public utilities and raising money for these capital-intensive projects. They also engaged engineering talent and were part of "management" history.

In the United States, the holding company came of age in the public utilities sector, both domestically and internationally, in the late 1920s. Companies were stacked on top of other companies, and at each level there was a gathering of new financial resources. Control at the pinnacle could be achieved with only a small amount of equity, and this control was often concentrated in the hands of a single individual or by a small group of individuals. In North America, as in Europe, the holding companies that took part in international investments ranged from entrepreneurial enterprises that organized and managed operations abroad to those with purely financial holdings (and some that mixed both sorts of holdings). A few combined holding and operating company activities in the pinnacle organization.

Electric utility holding companies that did international business can be seen as structures for rationalizing the management of large, integrated operations (integrated by knowledge and talents) of geographically dispersed companies, but they rarely physically integrated properties across borders. But on occasion – for example, over Swiss borders or over the U.S.-Canadian border (as noted above) – holding/operating companies might integrate a power system.[60] This was not, however, the typical pattern. The largest public utilities holding companies in international business would integrate the *operations* of what had been separate companies *within* particular foreign cities or regions inside a foreign country, but not across national borders.

Sometimes (in the pre–World War II literature), holding companies were seen as identical with "trusts." Some holding companies were equated with investment companies. And certain holding companies came to be known as "power finance" companies, or simply finance companies. When U.S. legislation in 1935 tore apart public utility holding companies, there were long discussions of definitions, and policy exceptions were made in the international business arena.[61] What is very apparent is that holding companies differed from one another, and the same ones differed over time. Pyramids and diagrams did not look alike. Were the differences based on "national" business systems? This does *not* seem to be the case. Within individual countries, various sorts of holding companies coexisted. Also, the term was often differently used in different contexts. As we studied holding companies in the electric utility sector, we found distinctions between direct and portfolio investments to be frequently muddy, and this complexity had nothing to do with national business systems. In some cases, the holding company seemed to be making direct investments – that is, planning its investments with more than purely financial aspirations and having a representative on the board of the recipient company – but when the coin was turned over and the perspective of the recipient company was considered, these same investments seemed to be portfolio rather than direct ones – for in these particular cases, there was no running or intention to run the host country enterprise; the entrepreneurial activity was in the host country. Is it conceptually possible for the home country enterprise to be making a foreign direct investment, while within the host country the same investment would be legitimately considered as a portfolio one? The idea is a bit iconoclastic, but it clearly should be entertained.[62]

OPERATING COMPANIES: HOLDING/OPERATING COMPANIES, "FREE STANDING COMPANIES," AND OTHERS

Operating companies would typically be established for a particular public utility, at home or abroad. If a holding company, with existing know-how and experience, set up or acquired the operating company abroad, this operating company could be seen as fitting neatly into a model of a classic multinational enterprise, emerging from existing competencies held by the parent. The standard theoretical treatments that have seen multinational enterprises evolving and going abroad, transferring their core competencies to the foreign affiliates, conforms perfectly to this pattern. Some operations were "greenfield" – that is, set up anew. Often, there were takeovers (acquisitions) of existing companies. That pattern, too, would square with the classic multinational enterprise.

Sometimes, however, foreign-owned operating companies would be (or appear to be) "free standing." In the introduction to this chapter, we introduced the reader to the term "free standing company," which was identified as a special form of multinational enterprise that did not arise from the core competencies of an existing firm, but was set up afresh to do business abroad. A number of the enclave form of companies – in agriculture, mining, and oil, where the electric power plant was built by the agricultural, mining, or oil firm – began as free standing companies. More important for our purposes, many operating electric utilities were initially free standing companies. The latter were organized to channel advanced country funds into a project abroad. Because of uncertainties and risk, money did not automatically go to businesses, including public utility projects. Investors wanted a company formed in a familiar setting and controlled by reliable individuals to intermediate their investments.

This was the genesis of many free standing companies. Because they were established anew and at origin had no operations at home, in order to conduct business abroad these companies drew on the talents of outsiders. There were clusters of individuals and other firms that surrounded the free standing companies, serving on the boards of directors and owning stock in the company. Included, for example, were promoters, prominent individuals with standing, solicitors (lawyers), accountants, engineers, men identified with construction firms, and those with trading companies. A manufacturer that wanted to sell to the new electric utility might have a place on the board of a free standing company. So, too, investment trust companies and other financial intermediaries that saw the free standing company as a good investment might be involved. Sometimes, these categories were not mutually exclusive: Promoters could be lawyers or engineers; prominent individuals with standing could be identified with investment trust companies; and engineers and men tied in with construction companies were sometimes one and the same. With the free standing companies in electric utilities (as well as in the general case), there were always clusters of individuals and companies with different competencies and contributions that joined together to undertake a set project. That these free standing companies had well-known, responsible boards of directors made them easier than an unfamiliar venture to float and to raise money at home or in the appropriate capital market(s). Home country investors (the providers of capital) did not have to worry about foreign exchange. When they invested in the free standing company stock or debentures, they were making a "domestic" investment. It was the company that made the foreign direct investments (and presumably exercised control over the business abroad). In time, successful free standing companies came to internalize many of the required talents and to look more like classic multinational enterprises. Also, in time many such free standing companies or groups of companies would be drawn into the investment orbit of larger holding companies. Before that happened, free standing companies were an important form in the public utilities sector. There were in Great Britain, France, Canada and some other source-of-capital countries many free standing companies set up to operate public utilities abroad. There were U.S.

free standing companies, but they tended to be less in evidence. Often, free standing companies were sequential. A free standing company would be formed to acquire assets. New financing might be needed and a new corporate structure superimposed (a newly named free standing company created); a merger or mergers might occur, and again a new corporate entity would emerge. There were "sister" companies that might later be combined. Operating companies were frequently formed to take over a prior activity or company or to merge two earlier companies. In the public utilities sector around the world, many foreign-owned operating companies began as (or became) free standing companies.

When this was the case, we asked, Who took the initiative? Because these companies were organized anew, the initiative had to come from somewhere. The clusters of participants became ever more significant. As the operating companies – with the goal of running an electrical facility abroad – were set up in capital-rich countries (or in countries such as Canada with a favorable legal system and the ability to tap British and other capital markets), the initiative was specific to the particular operation. A new company would be constituted to represent a particular activity. (What is key here is that the parent – the company itself – was *not* an operating utility in the home country.) Home country registration might remain the same over a period of time, but ownership could change as new actors came to participate. Thus, a project set up by Britishers, registered in the United Kingdom, might be taken over by German capital, with no alteration in the U.K. registration. The activity itself might be in South Africa or Chile.

Free standing companies often were part of a loosely defined business group – so the same people were frequently involved in a number of such companies. There were overlapping clusters of companies. Many times, as indicated earlier, the companies were sequential, often associated with mergers, and with each new incorporation raising additional capital. With free standing companies, this sequential pattern was common in many sectors, but there was far more of it in public utilities. Because scale economies came to be important, there was a tendency to want to suppress competition in a particular market. Operating companies often merged rather than competed. Accordingly, the business was then rationalized. Part of the sequential corporate structure was directly associated with that push toward consolidation. The aim was an organizational form that served that purpose and became a means of obtaining new funding for the public utilities project.

OPERATING COMPANIES: CONCESSIONS AND FRANCHISES

The clusters of participants that surrounded a free standing operating company interacted with host country actors. Sometimes, the promoter was an individual from the host country who was seeking financing abroad. Around the world, municipalities (and sometimes other governmental bodies) offered concessions to domestic or foreign firms. Utility typically required a concession from a public authority. Sometimes, the initiative came from the municipality (or the province or other regional governmental unit) and sometimes from the concession seeker, domestic or foreign. Often, municipalities gave the initial concessions to a country national, who discovered that he needed to go abroad for additional funding. This individual was on the spot, often well-connected. Sometimes he believed he could develop the concession on his own and discovered that he did not have adequate funds or access to technology; sometimes from the start, he planned to peddle the concession. Concessions that went to local people within a host country might thus end up in foreign hands. The foreign involvement might be purely financial. At times, a large power consumer might be attracted to the opportunity. Very often, the free standing company form would be used.

Sometimes, it is difficult to determine the initiator of a free standing operating company, whether it be domestic or foreign, for it was the complex interactions between the outsiders, local individuals, and the governmental unit that resulted in the power generation project being undertaken. In addition, concessions were often linked with (developed on the basis of) prior ones in gas, tramways, or water. Sometimes, they came to include telephones. Gas preceded electricity, and existing gas companies that supplied municipal lighting long before electricity was available would often be transformed into gas and electric companies; international gas ventures, in turn, were metamorphosed into international gas and electric companies. Frequently, in the early days, electric companies competed with gas companies and offered alternatives to them. Local authorities that owned gas suppliers often made it difficult for electric power companies to enter markets, fearing the competition. With the gas companies, there would be in the early period competition and then the co-opting of the new technologies.

It was very common for concessions for power facilities to be associated with tramways, as indicated in Chapter 1. The first trams were not electrified, but later ones were, and there came to be an intimate connection between the electrification of tramways (city transport) and electric light and power, based on technological considerations. Light and power facilities were also associated with other forms of urban transportation, from elevated (and flat) electric railways to subways (the "underground" in Europe). These public services required concessions and therefore political relationships.

Sometimes, gas, power, light, telephone, tramway, and, on occasion, water and ice concessions were intermixed, all part of a "modern" urban infrastructure. If waterpower was to be used for hydroelectric plants, there were usually legal issues regarding industrial and commercial water rights.[63] Also included in infrastructure were ports and harbors, and often it was the same actors involved in construction of these facilities as in the electric utilities. And these, too, required governmental authorizations and government contracts. Thus, from the earliest days, there was an admixture of government, domestic, and foreign participation in different proportions in individual countries in different parts of the world. Moreover, in the provision of electric power, there were sometimes separate contracts for generation and for transmission and distribution. although usually, they were joined. Many of the foreign-owned operating companies, based on concessions (or hopes for concessions), were set up initially (or very near the start) as free standing companies.

THE MANY BUSINESS ACTORS: CLUSTERS, NETWORKS, AND BUSINESS GROUPS

As concessions were granted, initiators of the process of global electrification, home and host country participants, continued to interact. Some of the foreign actors involved were representatives of independent firms, and some might be officers or employees of the multinational enterprise that ran the operating company. The line was not always clear for multinational enterprises that outsourced – that is, in many cases they engaged independent firms: financial intermediaries, lawyers, or engineers. Some free standing electric utilities had men from manufacturing companies on their board, men who expected export orders from the operating firm. Because of the capital needs of electric utilities, companies often planned to go to stock markets for their financial requirements, and thus one could find on the board important bankers, officers of other financial intermediaries (including securities companies, investment trusts, and insurance companies), and/or well-known promoters, who gave confidence to the investors and helped with the procedures. The relationship between foreign-owned operating companies and investment trusts is of particular interest. For a public utility overseas, a free standing company would be floated in London. Investment trusts would guarantee that all or a large portion of the equity would be picked up. On occasion, investment trusts also acquired debentures of these companies. To assure its securities' standing, a representative of the involved investment trust(s) would serve on the board of the company. And then there was the relationship of the free standing company with banks. Bank branches, for example, frequently attended to the operating companies' basic needs. Insurance companies also were part of the financing cluster.

It was not only manufacturers and financial intermediaries that played important roles in the clusters involved with public utility companies abroad. Other key individuals (and their firms) included the lawyers (or in the British case, solicitors). As a foreign investor negotiated with governmental entities, it became essential for the multinational enterprise to be able to arrange an appropriate concession contract. Lawyers figured in the public utility story in matters of patents, developing sound corporate structures (limiting liability, tax considerations, meeting legal requirements, etc.), and maintaining property rights, and they were often major negotiators with regulators. In some cases, especially from the 1930s onward, they handled trade union negotiations. In general, it does not seem that lawyers took the initiative in the spread of light and power facilities – although in Edison's international expansion, there is strong evidence that the lawyer G. P. Lowrey was a principal participant, and there were other cases where men with a legal background headed public utilities holding and operating companies. Law firms came to specialize in, or employed specialists for, electrical public utilities matters, and multinational enterprises required legal assistance when they went into business internationally.[64]

Among the major players in the networks surrounding the globalization of electricity were engineers and engineering firms. Sometimes, the involvement of engineers did not mean multinational enterprise participation. In Japan, for example – where there were sizable foreign direct investments by multinational enterprises in the electrical *manufacturing* sector – with the public utilities, Western engineers were hired, Western equipment was purchased, and Western finance was utilized, but neither the engineers nor the financial institutions made or facilitated multinational enterprise–type investments in any of the Japanese public utilities.[65] On the other hand, engineers and engineering firms were obligatory for multinational enterprise activities. Engineers could take the initiative (that is, promote new projects) or, alternatively, be engaged to evaluate a potential project. Even before a contract was negotiated – sometimes even before an operating company was set up – engineers were brought in by foreign direct investors (and sometimes by a lender) to determine the feasibility of a particular proposal. Sometimes, the engineers (and their firms) were independent, playing an advisory role. And sometimes, an engineer might have board membership in a number of different operating companies. Engineers (or their firms) were employed by (or became closely associated with) groups of actors involved in the setting up and running of the utilities in a foreign locale. The engineering function could be completely endogenous – that is, the multinational enterprise would have a full engineering staff and not use outsiders. There were holding companies engaged in international business that were run by engineers. In Britain, the term "engineering firm" had a different meaning from that used in the United States and Canada. (In Britain, an engineering company included manufacturers, while in the other two countries it referred only to professional engineering services.)[66] The legitimate confusion blurs further when both types of engineering firms were part of the clusters taking part in utilities abroad.

New and expanding public utilities required the efforts of construction companies. At times, engineering and construction firms were one and the same (since engineering was required in construction), and sometimes the firms were separate. In addition, a multinational enterprise sometimes internalized the construction functions, while in other cases independent outside companies were called on to undertake construction activities. Some construction companies became important multinational enterprises and initiated the process of developing public utilities, assuming ownership and control.[67]

And then there were the accountants: men and their firms that rarely initiated new public utility investments abroad. However, they did serve to verify records and to assure a wary public of the worth of certain ventures. Many of the free standing operating companies established in England to do business abroad had a close relationship with accounting firms, which helped facilitate international finance by vouching for the recipient of the funding.

Finally, trading companies took on vital roles in the formation of companies in the public utilities sector. Trading company personnel typically had unique knowledge of opportunities in particular regions. They often filled equipment needs of companies abroad that imported machinery. Some were borderline merchant bankers, handling securities. Some served as managing agencies. On a number of occasions, trading houses participated in, or even initiated, particular light and power projects.

The presence on a company's board of manufacturers, important bankers, officers of other financial intermediaries, well-known promoters, lawyers/solicitors, engineers, construction companies, accounting firms, and trading company representatives – in various configurations – attested to the safety of a traded security, from the underwriting of the initial issue onward, but it also served as a way of protecting the interests of the particular board member and his firm. Various clusters of involvement and network relationships were ubiquitous in projects in the electric utilities sector.

ENLARGING OUR THINKING ON MULTINATIONAL ENTERPRISE FORMS

The study of operating companies abroad in the electric utility sector has expanded and clarified key aspects of the original free standing company model, which in turn helps us to understand the forms of doing business abroad in this sector. First, research on free standing companies has brought out the fact that many *apparent* free standing companies were not "free standing" at all, but rather were part of established business groups or even affiliates of particular multinational enterprises. One could not rely solely on directories to count (or identify) free standing companies. With electric utilities, as we looked at the various participants, it was often possible to identify business groups and sometimes overlapping business groups. Sometimes, the business group was associated with families; other times, it was not. When there was a clearly defined business group, it often seemed inappropriate to call the operating companies free standing. In the chapters that follow, we have tried to identify the groups, or groupings, and, when present, the overlapping clusters.

Second, discussions of free standing companies had understood that a particular free standing company set up in England might in fact be German. There had been questions as to whether, for example, a free standing company registered in Canada was really Canadian. What had not been adequately grasped was that registration in a particular locale did not need to be identified with that country's capital markets. Thus, some Germans used British registration but ran their business abroad. Registration might, however, be identified with management: An operating company's registration in Canada gave the U.K. and other third-country investors security. These companies, *unlike* the German ones that used a U.K. registration, were Canadian-run, even though the actual capital supplied to the affiliates abroad came from places other than Canada and other than the nation that was host to the investment. The major financial contribution to the Canadian-registered firm might be from England or from continental Europe. U.K. and Canadian registrations gave confidence not only to the U.K. investor but to other investors as well. The notion of using a locale of registration to reduce uncertainty extended far beyond free standing companies. Holding companies that carried on operations abroad were registered in countries that provided assumed assurances and special benefits – true, for example, of Switzerland and Belgium. In short, ownership need not be in the country of registration, whereever the registration was.[68]

Third, there was another similarity between free standing companies and the holding company form. The clusters of participants involved in free standing companies often resembled (in their functions) those in the holding companies. Thus, on the board of the largest U.S. international holding company in the 1920s, for example, there were key bankers, a law firm representative, and the chairman of a leading electrical manufacturing company (General Electric).[69]

Fourth, while the literature emphasized that the free standing company form of multinational enterprise was an advantage in reducing risk and uncertainties, this is vividly illustrated in the electric utility sector.[70] The registration of operating companies in Canada and the United Kingdom, for instance, created a sense of security, of trust; it lowered transaction costs; and it created efficiencies in the financing process. The registration of holding companies in Switzerland and Belgium (at least before the outbreak of World War I) achieved the same purposes.[71] The free standing company form, with its cluster of participants, each with its special interests and competencies, furnished a mutuality of benefits. In a sense, the free standing company was a counterpart of the holding company structure, which involved the same grouping of participants, albeit often internalized within the holding company. The weakness of the free standing company was its absence of an internalized technical staff, which many holding companies provided.[72]

Fifth, the clusters of firms that were assembled and put into place with the successions of free standing companies frequently had the same kind of effect as, for example, the holding companies in Switzerland and Belgium. The companies set up and managed under these holding companies' initiatives were not free standing by any stretch of the imagination, yet the Swiss headquarters gave access to third-country capital markets that would not otherwise have been accessible. The Belgian holding companies achieved the same goal. The companies set up by American & Foreign Power and those purchased by that enterprise, once brought under the holding company, were no longer free standing. So, too, over time, many free standing companies were metamorphosed and rationalized into a holding company structure and no longer were free standing.

Sixth, looking at the boards of directors of the operating companies provides a good first step in considering the actors involved. Beyond that, one has to delve deeper and look within the particular groupings to understand the dynamics involved in the multinational enterprises' role in establishing electric utilities in foreign locations. Often there are ambiguities in what constituted ownership and control that even careful readings of corporate histories do not effectively resolve.

RAILROADS

Before we complete this discussion of forms, there is one more private-sector actor, whose role was indirect, yet crucial, especially at the beginning of our narrative. The relationships between railroads and the spread of light and power companies were several. Many of the banks and financial intermediaries that took part in financing electric utilities gained their initial experience in international transactions in railroad finance. Some had subsidiaries or sister companies engaged in railroad finance. Prior to the development of electric power, railroads had been the most capital-intensive sector in history (see Figure 1.4, for the American example). There was a somewhat similar gray area between foreign direct and foreign portfolio investments in the railroad sector, as we found in electric utilities.[73] Swiss holding companies were established in the 1870s for the control and financing of railroad companies.[74] In Belgium, railroad finance set the precedent for electric power developments.

Some of the engineers and construction companies that were key in electric utilities had a background of experience in railroad endeavors. Often, once electrification was possible, the process would follow the railroad lines to the places where the lines extended. To the extent that there was foreign ownership in the railroad sector, it might prompt foreign ownership in related activities. The linkage effects could be foreign or domestic. They could be internalized by the railroad company itself, or be set up separately by foreign investors, or be entirely domestic.[75]

Train terminals were among the first places to be electrified. Railroads required signals, which required electricity. The requirements of running a railroad motivated the initiation by foreign-owned railroads of their own power facilities. Railroads made possible the development of global resources. The enclave form of electrification would not have occurred were it not for the existence of steam-powered railroads. In addition, railroads and urbanization were closely associated, as destinations on the railroad lines were, or became, urban. Typically, railroads (especially foreign-owned ones) had connections with port cities, which became electrified. While most electric tramways replaced horse-driven tramways, some had their genesis in steam railroad construction and finance.[76]

Often railroads required concessions, and the experience with negotiating them, including rights of way, had carryovers into the electric utility sector. Railroads offered critical infrastructure for modernization, as did light and power facilities. Associated with this was the regulatory story, which Hirsh has told in the U.S. context, but which had broader implications. Railroads were the first target for U.S. regulation; electric utility regulation had the same antecedents in the United States.[77] This was true elsewhere as well: Typically, railroads often became government-owned before electric utilities, setting a precedent.

There came to be many forms of competition for railroads during the twentieth century: among them, cars, trucks, buses, and airplanes. Tramways, one of the earliest uses of electrification, met competition from alternative forms of transportation. With electric lights and motors, however, there were no other satisfactory options. True, the way electric light and power was generated changed over time – for instance, different fuels were used. But, electric lights and power did not follow the path of railroads and become a declining industry. During the twentieth century and continuing to today, worldwide, new end products have been developed that use electricity, so the supply of electricity has become more rather than less essential.

CONSIDERING THE ACTORS AND THE FORMS: A SUMMARY

In terms of home and host countries, did one form of conduit in the introduction of global electrification by multinational enterprise exceed all others? The manufacturers' satellites (and extended manufacturers' satellites) were key forms where there were strong electrotechnical equipment manufacturers, particularly in the United States, Germany, and Switzerland. As for host countries, the manufacturers' satellites (and extended manufacturers' satellites) that inaugurated the process of setting up utilities on a large scale were global in their reach. Yet early on, manufacturing companies became aware that integration into the light and power supply business was not a good use of capital, nor was it a sensible use of organizational talents, either domestically or internationally. Manufacturers retained minority interests at first, but often later not even that was necessary.[78] Manufacturers wanted to remain in an advantageous position to sell equipment to the power stations. They did not want to control the day-to-day running of the business (except in a manner related to equipment supply). Clearly, in the expansion phase all the major electrotechnical manufacturing multinationals had associations with the companies that built and then operated and refurbished electric utilities, at home and abroad. Domestic patterns were replicated internationally. Over time, manufacturers' satellites tended to morph into operating companies (sometimes foreign-owned and controlled, sometimes domestically owned and controlled).

By 1913, Britain's output of electrical goods was little more than a third of Germany's, and its electrical goods exports were not competitive. Britain's electricity supply industry was, in fact, markedly inferior to that in the United States and Germany, and it had no "competitive advantage" in electric utilities.[79] Nonetheless, British manufacturers, boiler makers, cable producers, and electrical manufacturers hoped to export. A substantial number of foreign-owned, free standing operating companies in electric utilities were headquartered in the United Kingdom. The British advantages were a creditor nation status, a vigorous stock exchange, a strong construction sector, an established engineering community, and formidable long-term trading and banking expertise in international markets. Likewise, Canada did not have any strength in electrotechnical manufacture (or in any manufacturing activity, to speak of, related to supplying a generation plant or distribution network), but Canadian entrepreneurs were key in the spread of electric utilities into Latin America – and for a time, in the exceptional European case, into Spain. Here again, the Canadian advantages lay in experience with home electric utilities, access to British capital markets, and the ability to tap U.S. engineering talent. A strong domestic electrotechnical manufacturing industry was not an imperative for large-scale international investments in public utilities.

Banks, insurance companies, other financial intermediaries, and investment bankers/stockbrokers/promoters played different roles in different countries and periods. They cooperated and competed for business with one another. They were critical in networks and alliances. Overall, there tended to be more capital market financing than bank financing, because of the capital-intensive nature of this industry. Even though the roles of individual financial intermediaries were different and even though they changed over time, they were important in all the principal home countries, because electric utilities required so much capital. Some of the largest European banks became depositories of vast amounts of expertise in relation to the electric utility sector. Likewise, in the United Kingdom, Canada, and the United States certain banks and other financial intermediaries accrued specialized expertise in public utilities finance. Within host countries, banks (and other financial intermediaries) in various continental European countries played very different roles from those financial institutions headquartered in the United Kingdom, Canada, and the United States (based on the separate home country national banking histories). In every country, change occurred through time.

As the decades passed, the enclave form of foreign-owned companies came to be found principally in the less-developed world. Within Europe and the United States, by the end of the 1930s the enclave form had disappeared. Globally, however, it remained, and new such facilities emerged. Large power consumers continued to stimulate added facilities, and facilities set up to meet such needs persisted, often, however, transformed into separate operating companies. Holding companies (broadly defined) in their various forms originated, in their application to electrification, in the 1890s, came of age in Europe in 1900–1914, and reached their heyday in the 1920s. They survived, albeit with some restructuring, until the underlying ventures were no longer part of a multinational enterprise. Some survived well beyond that as investment companies. Holding companies are critical to the story of the international diffusion of electric utilities by multinational enterprises. By the 1930s, while remaining important, the process of *Unternehmergeschäft* (entrepreneurial holding companies, as explained earlier) went into partial retreat in Europe, and there were no longer newly inaugurated "investor-owned" public utilities. This was not true of American holding companies – for example, American & Foreign Power, which, despite adversity, continued in an entrepreneurial role well into the 1960s, but it, too, was a creature of the 1920s and not of a later era. Throughout, it could be said to be following the *Unternehmergeschäft* model. The holding companies in all their configurations were able to mobilize vast amounts of capital required by public utilities worldwide. They were able to effectively use securities markets to assemble money for productive purposes. Many also did much more: They deployed knowledge, including engineering expertise and managerial talents, on a global scale, although the extent to which they carried on such functions varied by parent and affiliate and over the course of time.

Foreign-owned operating companies in public utilities developed their own managerial staffs within the multinational enterprise. Everywhere, governments pushed for lower rates. Companies found that governments (whether local, state, provincial, or national) increasingly influenced their business in a material manner. The passage of time within host countries brought major changes in operating companies: name changes, mergers, new owners (foreign or domestic), and restructuring. Operating companies became part of enterprise groups, often holding companies. In some cases, they became affiliates of holding companies within an individual host country.[80] Over time, the notion of the free standing company became increasingly out of place. Yet the *clusters* surrounding the free standing companies – the manufacturers, financial intermediaries, lawyers, accountants, engineers, people identified with construction firms, and so forth – continued to be participants, with some directly involved in the individual holding and/or operating company, frequently internalized within larger multinational enterprises.

Everywhere, foreign as well as domestic operating companies faced political constraints. Often the foreign-owned operating companies had a monopoly, usually for a city and its suburbs or a larger region within a country. A rare exception was American & Foreign Power Company, which supplied electricity to all of Cuba from the late 1920s. Usually, when national grids took shape in developed countries, the ownership was not foreign. Over the years (as indicated in Chapter 1, Table 1.4, and as will be spelled out in detail in Chapter 6), foreign investors lost out, and domestication of the operating company occurred. In many cases, the newly expanded role of state, provincial, and national governments made the difference.

THE POLITICAL DIMENSION

This brings us to the important political dimension. There are two separable "political" aspects. The first is specific to public utilities, and in Chapter 1 we included a brief overview of the role of governments at all levels – including subnational (municipal, state, and provincial) and national governments – in facilitating, regulating, and owning light and power companies. As a Nova Scotia (Canada) politician put it in 1914: "If the legislature [with its granting of a franchise] allowed businessmen to monopolize heat and light of a city," the businessmen in turn "owed" something to the community; "the citizens had a special right to be protected." By definition, the granting of a franchise (or a concession) engaged the government. Yet the political dimension went beyond the matter of "concessions" and "franchises."[81] National, regional, and municipal politics had profound impacts on domestic companies and domestic finance and on multinational enterprises and international finance. We in no way desire to underestimate this impact. Indeed, as Christopher Armstrong and H. V. Nelles have put it, utilities furnished basic services; everywhere there arose the dilemma of how to cope with "powerful economic institutions" and render them accountable "to some judgment other than that of the owners."[82] Put slightly differently, foreign ownership and control of a sector whose output (light and power) over time became a necessity of life (for both households and industry) meant that political conflict would often characterize the relationship between the foreign-owned enterprise and the customer.[83] This was true in both developed and less-developed countries, although in less-developed countries there probably was less intense concern prior to World War II than there would be after the war, when tensions heightened.[84] In the more advanced countries, there was a true ambivalence about foreign investments in the light and power sectors, which surfaces in all the contemporary literature. Different countries dealt in different ways and at different paces with the specific problems at hand. But everywhere, this predicament arose: Electric light and power companies by the 1920s were clearly "natural monopolies" – that is, efficiencies came from large-scale operations, and it did not make sense to have competition. This led to concentration in the industry. It also created controversy over the proper methods of fixing rates. What was a "fair return"? And how were costs to be measured when determining that rate of return?[85] Could a government have effective control with the presence of foreign investors?

The second political dimension was more general (not specific to the public utilities sector). Often, however, the first and second political dimensions converged in the formulation of government policies. The century 1878–1978 was one during which nation states achieved great importance. Historians and political scientists have studied the clash of nations in two world wars; the experiences of empires; after World War I, the end of the German, Ottoman, Austro-Hungarian, and Russian empires; and after World War II, the end of the European powers' overseas empires, which was accompanied by the emergence of a multitude of new nations. Multinational enterprise and international finance were deeply impacted by these political events, which were exogenous to the public utilities sector. Everywhere, capital movements were evaluated by politicians and general commentators, who viewed their economic, political, social, cultural, ethical, and moral aspects. The political economy of national economic growth was different in different periods and countries. In the determination of national and subnational policies, the very term "foreign" often carried a pejorative connotation, for the word by its nature had a slightly (and at times far more than slightly) negative taint. Sometimes the antagonism toward the foreigner was general; at other times, it was related to specific foreigners. Our narrative will distinguish the rhetoric from the actual consequences of these sentiments. Needless to say, the roles of multinational enterprises and international finance were usually perceived differently from those of domestic business and finance.

This said, we must never forget that multinational enterprises were actors in their own right. They operated in sovereign states, subject to national and subnational rules, regulations, and attitudes, and the concerns over their activities were based in part on the reality that at times multinational enterprises had the means to circumvent national political considerations. Thus, historians point out that the initial use of Swiss and Belgian holding companies served as a way of joining German and French business in a "neutral" environment. In nationalistic Germany and France before 1914, there was a great suspicion about international bankers. Many in France yearned to correct the injustices that they saw as imposed by the Franco-Prussian War of 1870–1871. Cooperation between French and German finance could be interpreted as "treachery." Similarly, after World War I many politicians in Germany sought to regain the "dignity" lost in Germany's defeat and tried to mold international investment to achieve national goals.

All through the century, 1878–1978, in numerous countries there were debates on whether foreign capital in general (inward and/or outward) was desirable. Both foreign policy and national security concerns came into play. Sometimes, governments wanted to use – or, alternatively, thought rival governments were using – foreign investors for political and/or economic ends. Thus, in a parliamentary debate in France in 1912, the Minister of Foreign Affairs said of French business abroad, "We ask ordinarily that France be represented in the boards of directors that may be set up as a result of the operation [abroad], so that our commerce and industry are enabled to profit as much as possible from the use of the borrowed funds."[86] As another, earlier example, in 1903 the French government, which regarded the Baghdad railway as a means of German imperial spread, refused to allow a stock exchange listing to the railroad bonds that had been acquired by French banks.[87]

Many people took for granted that "politics and finance go hand in hand."[88] Writing in 1914, before the outbreak of war, C. K. Hobson held the widely accepted view that: "European States are at present day anxious to gain political and economic advantage for themselves and their subjects, and readily make use of their financial power."[89] In 1912, French Prime Minister Raymond Poincaré was explicit in this regard, insisting that his government would do all it could to link French military (and naval) power with its financial power, "which is so great an aid to France."[90] Much of the pre- and post-1914 "finance and politics" discussions related to lending to governments, but the subject was extended more broadly to assume political intent related to nongovernmental recipients and political considerations connected to all foreign investments.

During and after both World Wars, the political plans of the victors had profound impact on the nature and structure of multinational enterprise and international capital movements. The predecessor company to American & Foreign Power was pushed to go abroad in the first instance by the U.S. government, so as not to have German interests near the Panama Canal.[91] To the extent that foreign investment in electric utilities was linked with trade (manufacturers' exports), there was an important role of Europe (in particular, Germany and Britain), as well as the U.S. government, in encouraging export activities. Political goals were general, with foreign investments in the public utility sector swept up in the politics of both home and host nations.

Political considerations were linked with national economic development aspirations, from both a home and host nation standpoint. European governments wanted to support exports; and if foreign investment (outward or inward) accomplished that, it was to be favored. Thus, in the 1920s the British passed Trade Facilities Acts (1921, 1922, 1924, and 1926). The British Treasury would guarantee loans to projects, including a number of foreign nongovernmental electrical projects, on the condition that the loaned money be used to purchase British goods.[92] Within host nation states, views varied on where foreign multinational enterprises and foreign capital fit into national goals; there were general views, but many of the latter became specific to basic infrastructure, particularly light and power. If foreigners were in a "vital sector" and if they had not merely "monopoly power" but actual monopolies, there was a questioning of their legitimacy, as newly independent nations emerged and pushed forward their own economic development agendas; these sentiments were also present in already advanced countries. At the end of the 1920s, within Western Europe a large number of companies took steps – some approved and others not necessarily approved by governments – to protect themselves from "foreign" control by, for example, confining voting rights or board membership to nationals.[93]

"Political risk" was something that multinational enterprises and actors participating in international finance always had to consider. Again, while some of the risks were special to the public utilities sector, many were more general. Broadly speaking, the international relationships between states posed problems for foreign investors. More specifically, and from a different perspective, government policies to cope with balance-of-payment woes created political risk. New governments accompanied by policy changes along with the incapacity of a government to provide law and order frequently altered the overall conditions for all international investors, including those in public utilities. There was a long-standing, pervasive view (to quote from a book published in 1914) that "[g]overnments of weak and backward countries often fall an easy prey to the wiles of financiers...."[94] A wariness about the intentions of participants in international finance and multinational enterprise activities made for political perils far more widespread than those confined to the public utilities sector. Government corruption (and the inability of a political system to remedy it) posed further difficulties for foreign direct and portfolio investors. And then there were the issues that were more specific to this industry: Were "powerful" foreign investors in vital sectors permissible? If a host nation (or subnational governmental agency) answered that question with a "no," that meant a major political risk. For many foreign investors, "politics" created "hazards of which businessmen have to beware," and this was as true in the late nineteenth and early twentieth centuries as in the 1950s and beyond.[95] Thus, as our story moves through time, we will keep in mind the municipal, regional, national, and international political environment, even though economic considerations rather than political ones were usually foremost in the strategies of the private-sector actors in the international transactions related to electrification. Yet politics did intervene. Politics did matter. The state assumed various, mounting economic and political functions that affected all outgoing and incoming international investors. And, indeed, because – specifically in the public utilities sector – large sums of money were involved and concessions from governments and regulation by governments were critical; because these investments were basic infrastructure investments; and because investments in light and power were imbued with public interest considerations; the overall political environment became fundamental.

As time passed in the century 1878–1978, for various reasons (high among them the attitudes of host country governments – local, regional, and national), the role of multinational enterprises in all forms in the electric light and power sector decreased. Alternatives to private finance became available after World War II on a previously unprecedented scale. In Chapter 6, we will summarize the "domestication process" and how even though multinational enterprises in the public utilities sector persisted for a long time after 1945, the overall process of domestication was (and had been through the decades) a steady one. Over time, public utility regulation – or, alternatively, public ownership – had become more and more prevalent in developed and less-developed countries alike.

LIBERALIZATION, RESTRUCTURING, AND PRIVATIZATION

By the late 1970s, this process had gone so far forward that attitudes reversed and questions began to be asked – especially in the more advanced countries – about the extent of regulation and government ownership in general and specifically in public utilities. For the 1930s and post–World War II generation, there had been a distrust of the market. At one pole, there had been the assumption that the market could not work well without government help, and at the other pole there was the assumption that the market would never work and so government intervention was a given.[96] The long and short of it was the viewpoint – at both ends of the spectrum – that some or a great deal of government regulation and ownership was required. Indeed, many within that generation saw no costs in the extension of government, which they perceived as a counterbalance to greed in the private sector.

Gradually, however, it became increasingly apparent that the enlarged governmental involvements did have both direct and indirect costs. Regulations, it was suggested, were impeding entrepreneurial activities rather than correcting inequities. With government ownership, where were the incentives to reduce costs? From a range of different perspectives – as the world economy slowed down from the high growth rates of the 1950s and especially the 1960s – economists and political leaders began to ask whether expanding governmental activities were the problem rather than the solution.

Indeed, no sooner had private international investments in electric light and power been judged "old" investments and inappropriate in a modern age, the climate changed. After 1978, with the new emphasis on markets, once again – quite gradually and then rather dramatically – public utilities became attractive investments to foreign multinational enterprises. As is well known, in the Ronald Reagan and Margaret Thatcher era in the 1980s, new attention was focused on the problems of "bloated" government. The failure of command societies to achieve the growth rates of the West placed added attention on removing the heavy hand of the state.

Forgetting why electric light and power companies had been regulated and become government-owned in the first place, there came to be, in some instances (far from universally), substantial deregulation and privatization. At times, the removal of regulations and the privatization process were not very skillfully accomplished, and deregulation was frequently partial, creating a mixture of regulated and deregulated sectors. Many times, privatization was combined with a new regulatory regime. The consequences of the restructuring were not simply domestic. They opened up the possibility of new multinational enterprise investment. We had come full circle. By the late 1990s, overnight, this sector once more became international.[97] We are not saying that everything was the same, for it was not. Business enterprises were larger; and so was the size of the market. Financial instruments were more numerous, and so were the financial needs. The speed of transactions became unprecedented. The density of the transactions – the numbers of mergers and acquisitions – was greater. In the late 1990s, there emerged "public utility multinational enterprises" – that is, public utility operating companies that extended over borders (which had been rare in prior years). There were other variations in the forms of investments. What is fascinating, however, is that many of the earlier forms, as outlined above, reemerged. The clusters of participants involved in a single operating company abroad bore a striking similarity to the historical structures. And what is perhaps more germane is how quickly some problems began to arise – and how by the time the twenty-first century was less than a decade old, a number of the new international businesses in this sector had retreated from foreign investments. Some had failed. Others had been spun off. It is possible that the wheel was turning once again, although as we write in 2007, the signs were not altogether clear and, in some cases, failed ventures had been replaced with different international businesses. We will save for our last chapter that story as well as the lessons to be drawn from it.

PART II

CHANGES

3

Every City, 1880–1914

Even before it became clear that electric lighting would be economically feasible, there was an international electric lighting business. We begin this chapter by considering the pioneering manufacturers – Jablochkoff, Siemens, Edison, and Thomson-Houston – examining their business over borders, which involved the setting up of manufacturing facilities abroad, as well as the sale of isolated plants and the sponsorship of central power stations. We will explore the manufacturers' relationships with other key players. As the chapter evolves, the activities of the many added actors that contributed to the spread of electrification on a global basis will emerge. By 1914, due to these actors' efforts, the residents of every major city around the world had become aware of the existence of electric light and power.

In 1877, the Société Générale d'Électricité (SGEl) was formed in France with capital of 8,000,000 francs. It arranged to install the Jablochkoff arc-electric lighting system in Paris, Le Havre, and London. By November 1880, over 2,500 of its lights were shining in Europe, and plans were being made to introduce this system in New York City. SGEl organized a Russian subsidiary to spread electric lighting eastward. By 1881, Jablochkoff enterprises were described as active in Europe, Asia, and South America. Paul Jablochkoff's firms manufactured the lights as well as installing the electric lighting system.[1]

Meanwhile, the German manufacturer Siemens & Halske was providing competition. By 1880, lights at the British Museum had been put in place by its British affiliate, Siemens Brothers.[2] In 1847, the Siemens & Halske Telegraph Construction Company had been founded. That German firm had formed an affiliate in England in 1858, which would become in 1865 Siemens Brothers. By then, the German Siemens had a subsidiary in

Authors: Mira Wilkins, William J. Hausman, H. V. Nelles, Peter Hertner, and Pierre Lanthier.
Significant advice from Theresa Collins, Christopher Kobrak, Ginette Kurgan-Van Hentenryk, David Merrett, and Luciano Segreto.

St. Petersburg, and in 1878 it set up an ongoing subsidiary in Vienna.[3] In 1881, the British manufacturing affiliate Siemens Brothers inaugurated a hydropower station on the River Wey, in Godalming, Surrey, England, which municipality would later boast it was the first town in the world to have electric public street lighting, a boast that could be disputed. Be that as it may, Siemens Brothers installed the facility and operated the new power plant under a yearly contract with the Town Council. The streets were lit with both arc and incandescent lamps, and current was made more generally available to the townsfolk. But the project proved to be unprofitable; there was inadequate demand in the small town; and the hydropower plant discontinued operations in 1884, and gas lighting was restored to the streets.[4] Elsewhere, Siemens was active in demonstrating dynamos and arc lamps.[5]

Everywhere during the late 1870s and early 1880s, profound uncertainty prevailed as to whether electric lights – and the various proposed systems – would be able to compete effectively with gas. In the United States, Thomas Edison was making promises about his new electrical system. In August 1880, the *New York Times* (in an article on the progress of electric lights) was convinced that foreign inventors were surpassing American ones.[6] By then, Edison had begun to promote his system, domestically and internationally.

While the story of the global spread of light and power facilities did not begin with the Americans Edison (1847–1931) and J. Pierpont Morgan (1837–1913), these two men were critical to the subsequent far-reaching diffusion of incandescent electric lighting that occurred through a collection of companies and worldwide investments. Both of these entrepreneurs had an international perspective; both had taken part earlier in activities outside the United States; and both had vision and imagination. Edison's other inventions – the phonograph, microphone, and telephone – had been introduced abroad; and he was not satisfied to limit his electric lighting system to the United States.[7] Morgan, who supported Edison in all of his endeavors, had long had intimate transatlantic associations; his father, Junius Spencer Morgan, was the principal in J. S. Morgan & Co., a prominent American merchant bank in London.[8]

As early as October 1878, J. P. Morgan had been aware of the potential of Edison's electric light system and had noted that rumors about Edison's achievement had sent gas prices plummeting on the London Stock Exchange. (It wasn't only Edison's success; it was Jablochkoff's, Brush's, and others' as well.) By November 1878, J. P. Morgan was writing his brother-in-law, Walter Burns, that he had "secured one third [of the] whole thing [the Edison thing] with complete control and management. Our idea is to offer London [J. S. Morgan & Co.] joint account for Great Britain if satisfactory. ... Impossible overestimate result if such success attained."[9] Morgan feared that his father would find the project too speculative, but he was convinced "he will change his mind."[10]

From 1880 to 1883, a variety of Edison companies related to electric light and power, for business outside the United States, were organized; the J. P. Morgan papers make it evident that the banker was closely involved, as was Edison himself.[11] Edison and Morgan interests (Drexel, Morgan & Co., the banking house with which J. P. Morgan was then connected) were direct investors in these pioneering foreign companies, which among their many activities participated in installing isolated plants and inaugurating lighting systems around the world.[12] New York lawyer Grosvenor P. Lowrey, who had "fallen under the spell of Edison," saw to it that Edison's patents were secured in foreign markets.[13] The relationship between the banker and the inventor appears to have been one of mutual self-interest. Lowrey intermediated the contacts between Edison and the Morgan partners (partners other than J. P. Morgan were active in these international affairs). Abroad, markets were delineated. Patent rights (licenses to operate under Edison patents) were exchanged for equity interests, which was not atypical in early international businesses.

The first of these Edison companies was the Edison Electric Light Company of Europe Ltd. incorporated in New York on December 23, 1880. It controlled Edison's electric light patents in Europe, excluding the United Kingdom, which was covered by a separate agreement between Drexel, Morgan and Edison dated December 31, 1878.[14] In June 1881, two companies were incorporated in New York: the Edison Electric Light Company of Cuba and Porto Rico and the Edison Electric Light Company of Havana, the first to promote the Edison system of electric lighting on the two islands, the second specifically for Havana, Cuba. In 1882, there was formed the Edison Spanish and Colonial Electric Light Company, incorporated in New York to control Edison's electric light patents in Cuba, Puerto Rico, and other Spanish American colonies. Meanwhile, in the summer of 1881 Edison Electric Light Company of Europe paid for an exhibit of the Edison system at the Paris International Electrical Exhibition. Visitors were ecstatic.[15] And, in 1882, new Edison companies were organized in England (the Edison Electric Light Company Ltd. of London) and France (Compagnie Continentale Edison, Société Industrielle et Commerciale Edison, and Société Électrique Edison), while for Australasia, Ceylon, India, and South Africa, a company was registered in England (Edison's Indian and Colonial Electric Company, Ltd.) to promote the Edison system in those parts of the British empire. In 1883, Edison companies were constituted in Germany, Italy, Switzerland, and Argentina. There were separate Edison arrangements for Sweden and Norway, and others for Portugal, New Zealand, and New South Wales, Queensland, and Victoria in Australia, always with Drexel, Morgan & Co. involved.[16]

This multiplication of these new business ventures, which can be seen as part of a multinational enterprise group, spurred the diffusion of the Edison system. These firms arranged to show off the Edison system and to advertise incandescent lighting. Thus, from 1882 to 1884, the Edison Spanish and Colonial Electric Light Company operated an "exhibition" plant in Havana, Cuba.[17]

The Edison Electric Light Company, Ltd., of London, demonstrated the Edison system in London, where city streets, homes of the wealthy, and prosperous businesses had long been lit by low-priced gas, which was highly competitive with electricity. The Jablochkoff "candle" (arc light) had already made an impression. Edison's English representatives obtained approval to run electric lines beneath the Holborn Viaduct, and Edison Electric Light Company, Ltd. of London leased a property. On April 12, 1882, the *New York Times* ran a terse item stating that "Edison's system of electric lighting with the incandescent lamp was satisfactorily demonstrated on Holborn Viaduct London last evening." This trial – like the earlier exhibit in Paris in the summer of 1881 – gave further proof that the Edison system could work. The Holborn Viaduct installation served as a "testing ground for Edison's first permanent station," the Pearl Street central power station in New York City, which began service on September 4, 1882.[18]

The path-breaking Edison activity at the Holborn Viaduct station was short-lived. In 1882, the British Parliament passed the Electric Lighting Act, with new regulatory restrictions. The following year, the Edison Electric Light Company, Ltd., of London, was absorbed into the Edison & Swan United Electric Light Company. (Recall that Joseph Swan had invented his own incandescent lamp, and for a while he and Edison had been rivals.) The Edison Holborn Viaduct station became an asset (or more properly, a liability) of Edison & Swan. By November 1884, Edison & Swan's management was reporting to the company's stockholders that the central station was a money-losing proposition. By 1886, Edison & Swan had "abandoned" it.[19]

Meanwhile, the 1880 Edison Electric Light Company of Europe, Ltd. had given birth in France in 1882 to the three affiliates mentioned earlier. For example, Société Électrique Edison set up isolated plants to light large stores, railroad stations, and printing houses. The working capital for the three French enterprises was provided by Seligman Frères & Co., Drexel, Harjes & Cie. (Morgan's Paris house), Banque d'Escompte de Paris, Banque Centrale de Commerce et de l'Industrie (Paris), and Speyer Brothers (London). In 1886, the three French Edison companies were merged into Compagnie Continentale Edison (CCE).[20] CCE gave up manufacturing (which had been done by one of the Edison firms) and specialized in producing and distributing electricity in Paris. Subsequently, it had nothing more to do with the Americans.[21] Meanwhile, the Jablochkoff system (and the business organization formed to introduce it) proved unable to compete with Edison's system or his companies. Jablochkoff lost out, as one writer put it, a victim to its too rapid success. The minutes of the Edison Electric Light Company of Europe, Ltd., board of directors meeting, January 21,

1885, included a note that the fusion in Europe with the Jablochkoff Company was planned.[22]

In Germany, where Deutsche Edison Gesellschaft had started in 1883, it emerged as a new and strong manufacturer, the precursor to the important 1887 Allgemeine Elektrizitäts Gesellschaft (AEG). Whereas Siemens had German origins, Deutsche Edison Gesellschaft was the result of U.S. multinational enterprise expansion. While it was a manufacturer, over time it would become responsible for the inauguration of numerous electric utilities. From its beginnings, the firm had associations with the well-established Siemens & Halske, links of both competition and cooperation and for a considerable time of deference. Siemens and AEG (and its predecessor) had banking connections, sometimes separate, sometimes shared.[23] Not until 1889 could Emil Rathenau, head of AEG, declare his firm's "independence" from its Edison ancestry. When Thomas Edison had written to request AEG not to compete in Japan, Rathenau countered (February 19, 1889), "You have not taken into consideration the fact that we have during the last year entirely discharged all the duties toward your rightful successors in Europe. ... [A]nd since we have accomplished this we do not stand any longer, as you describe it, as one of the Edison companies, confined to a certain territory. ... The market for our product is the entire world."[24]

When later in 1889 the Edison General Electric Company was organized in the United States as a manufacturing company, the coin was turned over: Siemens & Halske and AEG, along with the Deutsche Bank, apparently owned $8.3 million of the $12 million capital of Edison General Electric. Cross investments (and complexities) in the international business story had begun to take shape. The new Edison General Electric, as well as being a manufacturer, also had interests in electric utilities – in some 375 central stations – and had done some 2,300 isolated plant installations in the United States.[25] Edison General Electric took stock in electric utilities in exchange for the sale of Edison equipment and for patent licenses. The Germans' ownership and control of Edison General Electric proved transitory; and when in 1892 Edison General Electric and Thomson-Houston merged to form General Electric, the German investment had already been withdrawn.[26] This did not mean, however, an end to international business by AEG, Siemens, or the Deutsche Bank, which, as we will see, expanded greatly in the years that followed. For the manufacturers, much of the international business investments would be in manufacturing abroad, although a substantial part of it was in stimulating the development of public utilities (as manufacturers' satellites or extended manufacturers' satellites).[27]

In the meantime, Henry Villard (the Deutsche Bank's U.S. representative, who had brought the Germans into Edison General Electric) formed the holding company North American Company in June 1890. This new company, capitalized at $50 million, was designed to participate in the electrification of railroads and the transmission of the electric energy required. It would build central power stations in Milwaukee, Cincinnati, St. Paul, and Minneapolis. The company had a broad charter, giving it authority to transact business not only in the United States, but also in Mexico, Central and South America, British North America, including Canada, and all of Europe. The plan was that it would acquire Edison General Electric's holdings in the operating utilities. At its start, the new company attracted Deutsche Bank backing, although when it was in trouble in the fall of 1890 (with the "contagion" from the Baring Crisis), the Deutsche Bank was not listed as one of its creditors – or at least was not on the reorganization committee. The North American Company survived the crisis of 1890 (althought there is no evidence that North American ever used its broad mandate to expand internationally).[28]

By this time, the initial group of Edison foreign companies had either been liquidated around the world or, more often, transformed. We have discussed what happened with the principal British, French, and German Edison enterprises. In Milan, Società Generale Italiana di Elettricità Sistema Edison (set up in 1883, renamed in 1895 Società Generale Italiana Edison di Elettricità, and sometimes called Società Edison or the Edison Company) had become Italy's foremost electric utility. Like the British, French, and German Edison companies, it quickly became detached from Edison ownership and control.[29]

The fate of each of the pioneer Edison companies was distinct: In 1886, Edison's Indian and Colonial Electric Company had been brought into the Australasian Electric Light Power and Storage Company; in Latin America, where Edison representatives and affiliated companies had sold isolated plants and where there were attempts to develop and promote Edison's lighting system, Thomas Edison felt that his efforts were thwarted; and in Japan, the Edison system was adopted, but there were never any Edison-owned and -controlled enterprises. Indeed, by the mid to late1880s – certainly by the time Edison General Electric was organized in 1889 – the outward foreign direct investments by Edison were history. The remaining companies had declared independence. Yet, the legacies of these companies afforded a very strong foundation for the next phases in the international diffusion of electrical public utilities.[30]

In sum, when in the late 1880s Edison retired from active involvement in the Edison electric light enterprises, he personally maintained some minority interests in certain of the foreign companies and their successors, but there was nothing equivalent to direct investments.[31] Drexel, Morgan, and then from 1895 J. P. Morgan & Co., sustained its commitment to support the U.S. domestic electrical manufacturing industry and to develop U.S. light and power facilities, and it was never fully out of international business in electric power, although the firm and its successor's involvements ebbed and flowed. When Edison General Electric was folded into General Electric in 1892, Morgan took the initiative. General Electric at its origin did have an extensive international business, which (the Morgan-Edison connection apart) came from Thomson-Houston.

Thomson-Houston was the second of the two principal U.S. manufacturers that in 1892 combined into General Electric. At the dawn of the age of electric lighting – before Edison's systems were accepted – in the summer of 1878, Elihu Thomson had been in Europe, touring France, Switzerland, and Germany and visiting the Paris Universal Exposition. When in Paris, Thomson saw the Avenue de l'Opéra lit up with Jablochkoff "candles."[32] In December 1878, back in the United States, Elihu Thomson and Edwin J. Houston demonstrated their own alternating-current system of arc lights.[33] The stories of Thomson and Houston in the years from 1878 onward need not concern us except to note that on the eve of the 1892 formation of General Electric, the Thomson-Houston Electric Company had already built an international business and had taken part in the origination of some 870 central stations in the United States.[34] Unlike Edison General Electric, which acquired stock in utilities in exchange for equipment sales and patent licenses, Thomson-Houston took utility bonds, which it arranged to have converted into a series of trust funds, which next resold the securities to Thomson-Houston stockholders. Then in 1890, Thomson-Houston organized the United Electric Securities Company to specialize in the resale of utilities securities and to issue its own debt instruments (bonds and debentures). Thomson-Houston did not need (or desire) to run the utilities; it wanted them financed and functioning. The utilities would provide a market for Thomson-Houston's manufactured output. In 1885, Thomson-Houston International Electric Company had been formed to sell electric lighting systems worldwide. Its approach was to cooperate with engineering firms in foreign markets.[35] In 1889, Thomson-Houston acquired the controlling interest in the United States in Brush Electric Company. Although Brush Electric had once been involved in international business (and the "Brush" name was well known in Europe), by the time of the Thomson-Houston acquisition, Brush Electric seems to have added nothing to the by then rather extensive foreign operations of Thomson-Houston.[36] By 1889, Thomson-Houston was actively engaged in trying to market its own systems worldwide and was making foreign direct investments in order to do so.[37] When in 1892 General Electric was created, it not only obtained practically all its foreign direct investments from Thomson-Houston, but also inherited chief executive Charles Coffin, who had shaped, and would continue to shape, a strategy of running a domestic and international business. The domestic and international practices of General Electric came from its Thomson-Houston roots, not from Edison General Electric.[38]

General Electric took over Thomson-Houston International, which it would soon rename International General Electric. It also acquired

Thomson-Houston's 1890 holding company for public utilities securities: United Electric Securities (which retained that name). So, too, the French Thomson-Houston and the British Thomson-Houston (both manufacturing companies) would become General Electric affiliates. In addition, General Electric inherited from Thomson-Houston an equity interest in Union Elektrizitäts Gesellschaft (UEG), a new German manufacturer. While General Electric took over some miscellaneous (minor) foreign holdings from Edison General Electric, it did not acquire any stake in Villard's 1890 creation, the North American Company.[39]

Although at the start of the provision of electric light and power the line between the manufacturer and the electrical generation enterprise was often indistinct (manufacturing companies needed to set up their customers), over time the two activities would become clearly differentiated. As the principal electrotechnical manufacturers continued to participate in the setting up of public utilities (and spinning off the electric utilities), they and the utilities would continue to require banking connections to support the very capital-intensive processes of building and expanding the utilities. In the 1893 Crisis, the newly formed General Electric faced near bankruptcy and made particular efforts to gain revenues from its investments in electric utilities. Accordingly, General Electric "transferred reams of utility securities" to the unincorporated Street Railways and Illuminating Properties pool, which was strictly a liquidating firm, with no intention of entering the utilities business. The liquidators, however, created expert management and engineering skills to provide value for the shares that were being divested. Other securities went to General Electric's subsidiary United Electric Securities, which once again developed new expertise to make these assets viable. In these transactions, most of the public utilities securities were domestic, not international, but the precedent of establishing the separation between manufacturer and utilities was established.[40]

BANKS AND OTHER FINANCIAL INTERMEDIARIES

The identical banks associated with the electrotechnical manufacturers stayed deeply engaged in the financing of electric power plants, domestically and internationally. Although, until Junius Morgan's death in 1890, J. S. Morgan & Co., London, was the lead bank in the House of Morgan, the American J. P. Morgan rather than his father at the British house took the initiative in all aspects of the new electrical industry. The international cooperation that the two Morgan firms (and the Paris affiliate) had had in the financing of railroads carried over and was important in providing the U.S. banker's background and knowledge. The House of Morgan's involvements in railroad finance put it in a position to transfer that experience into the electric utility context at home and abroad. General Electric was Morgan's first big industrial combination, with J. P. Morgan and his partner Charles H. Coster serving on its board. So, too, Lee, Higginson, Boston, which had been the bankers for Thomson-Houston and had a long history in railroad finance, became important in aiding electrification. Henry L. Higginson, the senior partner in Lee, Higginson, was on the consolidation committee that put together General Electric and then joined the Morgan partners on the first General Electric board of directors.[41] Likewise, Kuhn, Loeb and Speyer & Co. in New York were able to apply the expertise they gained from railroad finance to electric utilities. So, too, in European cities, banks (broadly defined to include the merchant banks in London) had experience in railroad finance. The bankers had learned to cooperate with one another, and syndicates had often been made up of banks of different nationalities. Promoters/stockbrokers had organized capital for railroads and other ventures, and their knowledge was portable into electric utilities.

Wilkins's *The History of Foreign Investment in the United States to 1914* provides information on the principal international banks taking part in transatlantic railroad finance at the end of the 1870s – that is, at the birth of the electrical age.[42] Many of these financial institutions, with their established networks, assisted light and power developments. Bankers in both Europe and the United States not only participated in transatlantic networks but broadened their scope to take part in far more extensive international business. In addition, many of the same European bankers were involved in Latin American developments, first in railroads, in some instances in tramways, and then in light and power.[43] There were disparities among the European and U.S. bankers that had been in railroads and then became key participants in electric utilities. (The one giant difference that does stand out was in the Dutch role, which was highly significant in railroads but in the background vis- à-vis electric utilities.)[44]

The creditor committee for Villard's North American Company in November 1890 provides a glimpse of the U.S. bankers involved in railroads (and now in electric utilities). The committee included William Rockefeller (National City Bank), William Salomon (Speyer & Co.), J. H. Schiff (Kuhn, Loeb), and C. H. Coster (Drexel, Morgan). No German bank had representation on the committee, nor were there any Britishers present, but Speyer & Co. had both London (Speyer Brothers) and German (Lazard Speyer-Ellissen) houses, while Kuhn, Loeb had close British ties (especially with Ernest Cassel) and German family associations (in particular with M. M. Warburg, Hamburg, but much broader ones as well). Both Speyer & Co. and Kuhn, Loeb had ongoing relationships with the Deutsche Bank. And, of course, there were the intimate associations between the Morgan firms in New York, London, and Paris, and the house of Morgan also took part in syndicates with the Deutsche Bank.[45]

When viewing the apportionment of shares in the Edison & Swan company in Great Britain in 1883 (a firm that would initially participate in both manufacturing and electric utilities), there were no surprises in the ongoing Morgan involvement. What did jump out was the presence of Charles Lanier and Edward Dean Adams. Adams was a partner in the American banking house Winslow, Lanier & Co., which in the 1880s was deeply engaged in railroad reorganizations. According to one source, Adams had been a major stockholder in Edison companies since 1884 and would briefly own shares in Edison General Electric Co.[46] In 1889, promoters of Niagara Falls electrification sought financing from a banking group that consisted of Morgan, Brown Brothers and Winslow, Lanier. Before Winslow, Lanier was ready to make a commitment, it dispatched Adams to examine the feasibility of the project. For the next three dozen years, Adams was a key participant in the Niagara Falls developments. Indeed, from 1893 until 1914 Adams wore at least two hats: He headed the important Niagara Falls enterprise, and he also served as the Deutsche Bank's U.S. representative, having replaced Villard in 1893. The Deutsche Bank made a small investment in the Niagara Falls project, an interest that appears to have been for information purposes. The Adams connection, however, was central to Deutsche Bank's international business strategies.[47]

William P. Bonbright & Co. (later just Bonbright & Co.) was a Wall Street firm that would figure importantly in public utilities finance, both domestic and foreign. This banking/brokerage firm began in Colorado Springs in 1898, near the Cripple Creek mining district, "the first [western mining district in the United States] to possess an electric power system." The mining developments had been recently opened by the railroad's expansion westward. The Bonbright firm purchased a seat on the New York Stock Exchange in 1902, by which time it had offices in New York and London as well as its main office in Colorado Springs. By 1913, it was advertising its "long experience with Lighting and Electric Power Securities and the exhaustive engineering and accounting examinations upon which our recommendations are based." In 1908, William P. Bonbright & Co. had declared, for example, of a property in Mexico, "We will buy or sell any securities of Guanajuato Power and Electric Co."[48]

By the end of 1880s, the railroad network in Western and Central Europe was virtually completed. And, in an uneven manner, many of the European banks that had participated in railroad finance in the United States and internationally started, in different configurations, the financing of electric railways, tramways, and light and power facilities – first in Europe and then farther afield. If the Deutsche Bank's interest in the Niagara Falls company was small, in the 1890s and early twentieth century that bank came to be a major global participant in electric utilities finance (generally along with AEG and/or Siemens). Other German banks were involved, too, such as the Dresdner Bank and the Berliner Handels-Gesellschaft.

German banks branched abroad, and affiliates offered services for German commerce and German businesses abroad. In 1873, the Deutsche Bank opened a branch in London, and in 1886 it established the Deutsche Übersee Bank (renamed in 1893 the Deutsche Überseeische Bank) and in 1889 the Deutsch-Asiatische Bank. The Deutsche Überseeische Bank would become deeply engaged in South America, and came to be of assistance to the German-owned electric utilities in that region, especially in Argentina. As the big German banks, which were closely aligned with the electrotechnical manufacturers, encouraged German exports of electrical and other products, it was consistent for them to provide long-term financing to electric utilities abroad to stimulate the trade.[49]

In France, the large banks would also assume a role in public utilities finance, but it was initially with caution.[50] As we will see later in this chapter, Swiss and Belgian banks, principally associated with holding companies, also became deeply committed. And then there were individual promoters and stockbrokers – for example, the Belgian promoter/stockbroker/investment banker Alfred Loewenstein, who in the first decade of the twentieth century was involved in Brazil and was having his initial encounters with Canadian groups active in international business in electric utilities. Loewenstein made his "fortune" on the Belgian stock market, placing Brazilian railway securities there.[51]

In Italy, the German style of banking, the universal bank, was introduced in 1894 with the founding of the Banca Commerciale Italiana (BCI) by a group of German, Austrian, and Swiss banks. In 1894, BCI opened a credit line for Società Generale Italiana di Elettricità Sistema Edison.[52] BCI helped funnel foreign capital into Italy's electrical industry. By 1901–1902, the German, Austrian, and Swiss banks that had established BCI held less than 9 percent of its capital, and the Banque de Paris et des Pays-Bas (Paribas) had acquired an interest in BCI. BCI became an important participant in electrification in Italy and beyond. For Libya, in 1913, it took part in the founding of Società Elettrica Coloniale Italiana.[53]

Typically, banks and promoters on the European continent cooperated in the electrification process, both within their own nations and beyond their borders. Networks in the financial groupings were the norm. Spain, like Italy, was a major recipient of the new funding and of foreign direct investment. German and French banks played a key role. In 1894, Deutsche Bank, along with AEG, acquired controlling interest in Compañía Barcelonesa de Electricidad (Barcelonesa).[54]

As for Britain, its merchant banks joined in some of the European continental networks. Speyer Brothers, London (with its U.S. and German connections), Wernher, Beit & Co. (a firm that took shape based on money made in South African gold and diamonds), along with the Rothschilds, Barings, Glyn Mills, Sperling, Hambro, and Schröders, were all by the early twentieth century drawn, to varying extents, to some participation in international business in electric utilities.[55] And then there were individuals – for example, R. M. Horne-Payne of the British Empire Trust, who knew Canada well, through his prior railroad and land company investments, and who acquired a set of existing utilities in British Columbia, combining them into British Columbia Electric Railway Co.[56] All these financial intermediaries would employ engineers with expertise in this new economic activity.

A number of the British promoters/merchant banking houses were part of the clusters associated with free standing companies (see Chapter 2). For example, Wernher, Beit & Co. purchased horse and mule tramways in South Africa, Portugal, Chile, and Mexico. These, in turn, became electric tramways: the Cape Electric Tramway, the Lisbon Electric Tramway, the Chilean Electric Tramway and Light Co., and the Mexico Electric Tramways Co.[57] Investment trusts (for example, British Empire Trust and Trustees' Executors' and Securities Insurance Corporation) also became linked with the transfer of British money into electric utilities overseas.[58] Robert Fleming's coterie of trust companies, in their diversified investments, started to invest in electric utilities outside the United Kingdom.

There were particular British stockbrokers who came to specialize in electric utilities. The historian of Foster & Braithwaite tells us that the firm's "most consistent interest was in companies formed either for electrical engineering, or for the distribution of electric power in towns, or for electrical traction." Those companies in "the distribution of electric power in towns" included City of London Electric Lighting (1891) and County of London and Brush Provincial Electric Lighting (1894). In addition, Foster & Braithwaite became involved in firms formed in England in 1899 and 1905 for public utilities in Melbourne and Adelaide, Australia. We will have more on these Australian undertakings later in this chapter; what is important here is the role of stockbrokers in both domestic and international utilities promotions. Foster & Braithwaite also became active in British Electric Traction Co. (BET) in 1896 (if not before), which, in turn, had business abroad in electric traction.

But most central to Foster & Braithwaite's activities in the electricity supply industry was its 1890 participation in the formation of the Electric and General Investment Corporation, London, which would preside over the birth of many of the late-nineteenth- and early-twentieth-century British ventures in electric utilities at home and abroad. Electric and General Investment undertook negotiations for power station sites and arranged public issues of shares. The firm's prospectus indicated that "the principal Electrical Manufacturing and Contracting Firms in this country, as well as abroad . . . had neither the time nor the facilities for . . . promoting and financing new electrical undertakings." Electric and General Investment was designed to do this. The prospectus continued, "The corporation will not itself manufacture any electrical appliances; neither will it employ any staff for carrying out any installation contracts, but it will restrict itself to the financial and commercial operations of assisting in the promotion and the development of electrical undertakings." Profits were to come from underwriting commissions; from the acquisition and realization of concessions; from fees for examining, reporting on, and assisting the promotion and development of electrical undertakings; and from interest and profits on electrical undertakings. Electric and General Investment (often referred to as an investment trust and sometimes called Electric and General Investment Trust) served at the pinnacle of an "investment group." Historian William Reader writes that the cluster of electrical companies assembled at a later period "might have been fused together under a holding company, instead of remaining a relatively loose-jointed mutual aid society."[59]

British promoters/merchant banks, investment trusts, and stockbrokers were among the many financial actors that assumed a role in the informal groups surrounding the numerous British free standing companies involved in electrification abroad. They hired the appropriate engineering talents, and British overseas banks extended globally to promote British trade.[60] Indeed, when the German banks set up branches abroad, it was to make German foreign trade "independent of financing by British banks." The electrical industry was in the midst of a global British-German competitive "war." In Argentina, for example, the London and River Plate Bank and the Commercial Bank of the River Plate were well established when the Germans sought to compete.[61] Unlike the German banks, which were closely associated with assisting the exports of the electrotechnical manufacturers, the British overseas banks were less involved in financing trade in electrical equipment and end products. Yet the British overseas banks were often linked, creating information channels, with the British free standing companies in utilities that would be set up around the world. The banks were sponsors of tramway, light and power companies, and general utilities all through Latin America.[62] Elsewhere, on the European continent and around the world, the British competed with the Germans, with the latter often far more skilled in electric utilities finance.

From the mid-1890s, Canadian promoters/entrepreneurs enlisted a variety of financial intermediaries – banks and separate securities companies – to augment business abroad in electric utilities. In Canada, where there were no strong electrotechnical manufacturers to take the initiative (as was the case in the United Kingdom), Canadian financial intermediaries engaged in arranging for the establishment of public utilities abroad; the latter brought in engineering firms for investigations, design, and construction. "Because of the laxity of its securities and corporation law as well as the latitude permitted to controlling shareholders in the event of difficulties," Canada was an excellent legal domicile for corporate activities in public utilities outside the Dominion.[63] Canadians organized new free standing companies. The principal financing came from Great Britain, where the

Canadians had well-established relationships, but the initiative, interestingly enough, was usually Canadian.

When an electric utility began operations and started to report favorable earnings (with corresponding advances in the stock price), the Canadian underwriting syndicate would then conduct a primary distribution – that is, an initial public offering (IPO) – selling all or part of its portfolio to individual investors, unit trusts (mutual funds), insurance companies, and banks, principally in Canada and the United Kingdom. These financial intermediaries were passive investors and held the securities "as investments." (Banks, in turn, would play a role in financing the investments of individual investors.) In the early twentieth century, Canadian businessmen developed an internationally recognized specialization in the finance and operation of utilities, particularly, but not exclusively, in Latin America. Indeed, in 1911, when there was a major Canadian investment in Barcelona Traction, Light and Power Company, Spain, it was in effect an extension of what the Canadians had been undertaking in Latin America.[64]

Canadians were the entrepreneurs in these many international ventures because they knew the utilities business from their experiences at home. Canada had excellent hydroelectric power facilities and had early on been involved in domestic electrification. Thus, Canadians could transfer their domestic knowledge to the setting up and running of utilities abroad. The Canadian financial communities in Montreal and Toronto became deeply engaged, and the leading commercial banks – notably the Bank of Montreal and the Bank of Commerce, Toronto – participated in developing public utilities abroad, along with such Canadian entrepreneurs as William Mackenzie (earlier involved in railroads), American-born William Van Horne (also taking part in railroads, particularly the Canadian Pacific), and James Ross (who made his money in construction, linked with the Canadian Pacific). By the end of the first decade of the twentieth century, a group of forty or fifty Canadian bankers, securities companies' executives, brokers, lawyers, builders, and other businessmen formed free standing companies abroad in electric utilities. These Canadians operated in overlapping circles of relationships.[65]

Among the principal Canadian securities companies were (1) the Montreal-headquartered Royal Securities, organized in 1903, and identified at origin with Max Aitken (later Lord Beaverbrook), and (2) the Toronto-headquartered Dominion Securities, formed in 1901 and run by E. R. Wood.[66] Key among the involved law firms was Blake, Lash, and Cassels. Canadian-born Edward Peacock, James Dunn, and Aitken would move to London, further enhancing the ties between the Canadians and British financial groups.[67] American engineer Fred Stark Pearson was brought into, or imposed himself on, a number of the major Canadian projects abroad.[68] By contrast, the Royal Securities group would engage an affiliated company, Montreal Engineering (created in 1907), to handle its engineering needs.

Between 1896 and 1911, Canadians set up operating companies in electric utilities, incorporated in Canada, to run electric utilities in the United Kingdom (established in Birmingham in 1896, but short-lived and sold to British interests in 1902), Brazil, British Guiana (Guyana), Cuba, Jamaica, Mexico, Puerto Rico, Spain, and Trinidad.[69] In 1912, when the fledgling Alabama Power Company could not find financing in the United States, a Canadian company was established, the Alabama Traction Light and Power Company, Ltd., which tapped British capital markets on behalf of the American power company.[70]

ENCLAVE ELECTRIFICATION

In the late nineteenth and early twentieth centuries, plantation, mining, and oil-producing companies extended out from Europe, the United States, and, very occasionally, from elsewhere to develop new resources around the world. Because the products were typically exported from the country where they were produced, there would be within a host country a complementary development of port facilities and electrification in the port city.

With agricultural investments – such as those of United Fruit in bananas – operations had minimal electrification, and the linkage effects tended to be far less than in mining and oil; but where foreigners invested in processing the output – as, for example, in the case of sugar mills – there would be substantial electrification. Quite early, Cuban sugar mills came to be electrified, and soon after independence from Spain, Cuba witnessed a sharp rise in the number of electric utilities. Expatriates working for W. R. Grace on the west coast of Latin America installed electric generators. In another part of the world, the French Durand group received a concession for the development of forest land and mining properties in Madagascar; what followed was a company to develop water and electricity in the French colony.[71]

The industrial activities that accompanied mining and oil projects had new electricity requirements. Whether we are talking about gold- and diamond-mining groups in South Africa or the start of large-scale copper mining in Chile, electrification came on the heels of the industrial activity. In South Africa, British, German, and American entrepreneurs pushed forward electrification along with the mining. General Electric had a paid company representative in the Transvaal from 1894 onward. Wilfried Feldenkirchen reports that in 1897 Siemens & Halske built a 10,000 volt three-phase power plant for industrial purposes at Brakpan, near Johannesburg. Wernher, Beit & Co., first active in South Africa, would subsequently push electrification in Latin America. The British-registered Victoria Falls & Transvaal Power Co., Ltd. in South Africa was, in reality, German. In Chile, electrolytic processing of copper required major electrification.[72] The first hydroelectric power plant in what is now Malaysia was built in 1900 by the Raub-Australian Mining Company.[73] Similarly, the new developments in the oil industry in Iran, Mexico, and the Dutch East Indies (Indonesia) carried with them electrification. For all these enclave type activities and the port developments that accompanied them, electrification was secondary to the firms' primary agricultural, mining, and oil business, yet it was of vital importance and had impacts far beyond the company town and the port.

In addition, with fewer kilowatt hours and fewer consequences, when colonial administrators went abroad in the early twentieth century, if they had electrification in the European capitals where they had lived, they did not care to give up that comfort in the colonies, so they installed generators in their homes for lighting. The stores where they shopped might have electric lights or ice makers. Normally, this electrification (with the isolated plants) did not diffuse electrification beyond the European communities. Applications were still very partial. Nonetheless, the installations started to offer a demonstration effect, so that with the spread of colonization in the late nineteenth and early twentieth centuries, electrification followed, to be sure, slowly and unevenly. D. K. Fieldhouse has written that by 1914 "the proportion of the world's land surface actually occupied by European, whether still under direct European control as colonies or as one-time colonies [or as Europe itself]," was 84.4 percent.[74]

LARGE POWER CONSUMERS

One significant form of multinational enterprise activity that disseminated electrification in the early twentieth century was that pushed by demands from large industrial consumers of power. In certain industries, such as aluminum and paper and pulp, electrification was integral to the processes of production. These companies sited their business where there was – or was the potential for – cheap electric power. The German electrical manufacturer Allgemeine Elektrizitäts Gesellschaft (AEG) was one of the founders in 1889 of Aluminium Industrie AG (AIAG), the large Swiss aluminum company.[75] AIAG not only developed power resources in Switzerland, but also expanded in 1898 to build power facilities in nearby Lend-Rauris, Austria.[76] Similarly, U.S. entrepreneur/promoter/banker John Edward Aldred joined with the Pittsburgh Reduction Company – to be renamed the Aluminum Company of America (Alcoa) in 1907 – in the large Canadian public utilities venture Shawinigan Water and Power Company, incorporated in 1898. Soon this company had extra power and over a long-distance transmission line supplied wholesale power to the locally owned Montreal electric utility. U.S.-owned paper and pulp mills were set up in Canada, and some of the investors became suppliers of electric power, along with their manufacturing investments.[77] Elsewhere, the British Aluminium Company purchased a partially developed waterpower facility in

Norway in 1906, completing the power plant and the reduction works in 1908. Foreign-owned electrochemical enterprises also went to Norway, making investments there to enlarge power facilities, by far the largest being the huge operations of Norsk Hydro.[78] Virtually all of these power-intensive projects were associated with hydroelectric power, but there is some evidence that in Russia and perhaps Central Europe there were foreign industrial establishments developed near coal mines, with the subsequent buildup of utilities to use the excess coal.[79]

In some cases, the start-up initiative for a new electrical facility was provided by the owner of the rights to develop the power resources. Historian David Massell tells the fascinating story about how the Canadian Thomas Willson got those rights for the Saguenay River. But having acquired the rights, he needed customers. Thus, he invented an electrochemical process to make fertilizers and tried to market it in the United States to the principal fertilizer producers. Yet, as Massell writes, "It is one thing to purchase an option on a chemical process in order to prove or disprove its commercial prospect, and quite another, as Willson knew all too well, to take up vast outland water powers without a concrete plan for their future use." Willson attracted the struggling U.S. firm Interstate Chemical Co. to his as-yet-untested new fertilizer process. Through personal contacts Interstate Chemical, in 1911, attracted American tobacco entrepreneur James B. Duke, who was immediately tempted by the possibility of controlling the North American, if not the global, fertilizer industry and, more important, of obtaining new power resources. Duke had "deep pockets," earlier investments in fertilizer companies, and experience in developing waterpower sites in North and South Carolina, and he was ready after the breakup of his American Tobacco Company in 1911, to embark on a major new endeavor. As Massell puts it, "[F]rom the summer of 1912, the centre of command [for the Saguenay River development] shifted southward to the regional capital of Charleston, South Carolina, before gravitating ultimately to the continent's financial power centre, New York. From the moment in September [1911] that Duke showed interest in Interstate's fertilizer scheme, there was no doubt among Interstate's directors [and also Willson] as to who was running the show. The 'boss' was now James B. Duke," and so there was a transfer of this development from Canadian to U.S. control.[80]

MANUFACTURERS AND THEIR SATELLITES

By the mid-1890s, the big electrotechnical manufacturers General Electric, Westinghouse (founded in 1886), Siemens, Allgemeine Elektrizitäts Gesellschaft, and the Swiss Brown, Boveri (founded in 1891), as well as other electrical equipment manufacturers were undertaking large-scale international business, principally the establishment of manufacturing facilities and sales offices abroad.[81] By the eve of World War I, General Electric (GE) had associated manufacturing plants in Canada, England, France, Germany, and Japan, with a range of investments from 97 percent in British Thomson-Houston to a small stake in AEG (apparently acquired when, in 1903–1905, AEG merged with Union Elektrizitäts Gesellschaft). It is not clear that GE had any interest at all in its affiliated Canadian manufacturing business. From Mexico, to South Africa, to Australia, GE had wholly owned sales outlets. As for Westinghouse, it had large manufacturing operations in the United Kingdom, as well as plants in France, Russia, and Canada. As these American companies set up manufacturing and distribution abroad, there were new interests (often indirect and usually minority interests) in electric utilities. So, too, AEG, Siemens, and Brown, Boveri developed international networks of manufacturing and sales affiliates with impact on the establishment of electric utilities.[82]

General Electric would, through its international business, take the initiative in stimulating the establishment of foreign public utilities, as did Westinghouse to a lesser extent. Their international business in manufacturing was very extensive, and their interests in public utilities were an outgrowth of that business. In the cases of the two German giants and the Swiss electrical manufacturer, the arrangements to develop utility companies outside Germany and Switzerland became even more far-reaching. To jump ahead in time, as a 1927 publication put it, "Electrical manufacturers in the United States and Europe adopted very early the principle of large-scale production and of co-operative action, ... They recognized ... the need [for] the formation of new power supply companies, which would open up new territory and so create a demand for the products of the electrical manufacturer,"[83] domestically *and* internationally. The big electrotechnical manufacturers continued to compete *and* collaborate, depending on the circumstances. They divided markets and joined in cartel relationships. Patent licensing became a way of dividing up territories; and as the manufacturers formed alliances, this affected the patterns of investments in electric utilities.[84]

The beginnings of the French electric utility industry, as Pierre Lanthier has shown, were international: Compagnie Continentale Edison was established in 1882, as we have seen, with French capital but American patents (80 percent of the profits were to go to Edison interests, after cash subscribers were reimbursed for their contribution – which never happened). The French Thomson-Houston (FTH), a manufacturing firm, was an outgrowth, readers will recall, from Thomson-Houston after its merger into General Electric. FTH, involved in French public utilities, was American in origin but used French capital and over time came to be French-controlled. Formed in 1893, it was initially owned 40 percent by GE and 60 percent by French interests; by 1902, the U.S. interests had been reduced to 6.5 percent. The FTH group would have important outward foreign holdings in electric utilities. Compagnie Générale de Traction was linked with Westinghouse in a joint subsidiary called the Société Industrielle d'Électricité. And then there was Empain, with a Belgian head office which combined Belgian and French interests.[85] Compagnie Générale d'Électricité, founded in 1898, was an electrical manufacturing firm with a central power station in Rouen; Patrick Fridenson describes it as French in origin, with some Swiss capital involved. Two of the first five key administrators of CGE were Swiss; one was from the electrical manufacturer Brown, Boveri, the second from a bank.[86] Except for Empain (more on Empain to follow), all of these developers of light and power facilities in France could be seen as evolving in a manufacturing context (a type of manufacturers' satellite or extended manufacturers' satellite). CGE would also make investments outside France, particularly in Spain's Energía Eléctrica de Cataluña in 1911.[87]

When in 1893 the French Thomson-Houston was created, it was allocated a territory by General Electric. In 1898, with GE's German affiliate Union Elektrizitäts Gesellschaft (UEG), it formed the Belgian-registered Compagnie d'Électricité Thomson-Houston de la Méditerranée, otherwise known as Thomson-Houston de la Méditerranée (THM).[88] THM obtained from GE "territory rights" over the Mediterranean countries Egypt, Greece, Italy, and Spain, and in these countries THM acquired interests in and contracts for tramways and central stations. THM purchased in 1898 a power plant in Athens, built almost a decade earlier by a Greek (purely domestic) company. With that Greek firm and the National Bank of Greece, THM founded Compagnie Hellénique d'Électricité (CHdE) in 1899.[89] In addition, THM made investments in utilities in Egypt, Spain, and Italy. Separately, in 1911, with the Société Centrale pour l'Industrie Électrique (SCIE), Paris, FTH participated in the capital of the Constantinople Consortium (see below) and the Société d'Électricité de Rosario in Argentina. In 1913, FTH was also making investments in Énergie Électrique de Bakou in the key oil district of Russia (now Azerbaijan).[90]

Meanwhile, the German electrical manufacturing firm Allgemeine Elektrizitäts Gesellschaft (AEG) was investing in electric utilities, at first in Germany. It had the brief U.S. stake (with Siemens and Deutsche Bank) in Edison General Electric, discussed above. By 1890, AEG had entered the Spanish public utilities business. With the Madrid Gas Company and the Pereire Brothers, AEG formed Compañía General Madrileña de Electricidad (Madrileña). Note the cluster: a manufacturer (AEG) with a gas company (Madrid Gas) and a banking group with railroad experience (Pereire Brothers). For AEG, this was a short-lived investment, and in 1894 it divested.[91] In the same year, AEG acquired a local company in Barcelona, Sociedad Española de Electricidad, and transferred it to the newly created Compañía Barcelonesa de Electricidad (Barcelonesa). AEG (with Deutsche Bank and some other banks) obtained controlling interest (70 percent of the capital). The French company Société Lyonnaise des Eaux et de l'Éclairage took a 25 percent interest, and Spanish bankers picked up the remainder.[92] In 1894–1895, AEG undertook to electrify lighting and urban transport in Genoa, Italy, acquiring existing companies and modernizing their networks. There came to be an intimate nexus between the German electrotechnical industry and the emergence of public utilities in both Spain and Italy.[93] The same was true both in Central and Eastern Europe and much farther afield. Even though French and German companies sometimes cooperated, often the more aggressive Germans pushed ahead.

In general, manufacturers' satellites constituted an unstable mode. Once a utility was up and running, it would usually be spun off and sold. It did not remain a manufacturer's satellite, although the period and the amount of the manufacturer's involvements varied. Luciano Segreto writes that by the 1890s "the expanding market for electricity... brought new kinds of complications to... the electrical equipment manufacturers. Direct involvement in the management of electric [supply] companies ... became excessively complicated, because the activity of producing and distributing energy required an elaborate bureaucratic structure which the great electrical equipment manufacturers were not able to develop without incurring burdensome costs."[94] Another reason for the spin-offs related to the manufacturers' desire not to tie up capital in the utilities. Government regulations may also have affected the longevity of the manufacturers' involvements.[95] Clearly, however, administering an electrical manufacturing business and providing light and power services were different. Typically, there were lower costs in running them separately than in integrating them within a single firm. Yet, from a start-up standpoint the impetus often came from the manufacturer (frequently joined by a bank or banks).

The manufacturers' satellite initiatives were most evident where the big electrotechnical companies had specialties in generating equipment. Thus, the U.S. manufacturers General Electric and Westinghouse and their extended activities, the German Allgemeine Elektrizitäts Gesellschaft and Siemens, and the Swiss Brown, Boveri & Co. (which had special core competence in hydroelectric power) stand out. French manufacturers were important in certain markets. So, too, the Swedish Allmänna Svenska Elektriska AB (ASEA) had some interests in power companies abroad. The British manufacturers were affiliates of American ones or, in the case of Siemens Brothers Ltd. and Siemens Brothers Dynamo Works Ltd., the Germans. The way British overseas stakes in utilities most often manifested themselves was not through satellites of the electrotechnical manufacturers. Philips of Holland and Ericsson of Sweden, both important electrical manufacturers, had specialties outside of generation equipment; they were not caught up to any extent in the networks of electric utility finance.

Domestically and internationally, a manufacturer never acted alone when it entered the power supply business; it brought in (or associated itself with) others in the founding of the utilities. When the manufacturer expanded into international business and joined with national partners abroad, this often became connected with the domestication of the light and power facility, by which we mean the shift from the international genesis (international direct involvement) to domestic ownership and control. Thus, the European manufacturers and the utilities with which Edison had been involved had for the most part become "domestic." With General Electric, Westinghouse, Siemens, AEG, Brown, Boveri, and ASEA and their foreign affiliates, the pattern with the utilities was in some cases complete or partial domestication (the foreign retention of minority interests, often through other intermediaries). In Italy, for instance, German capital (principally that of the electrotechnical manufacturers and German banks) accounted for roughly 40 percent of the capital invested in the electricity supply sector in 1900, but in large part because of growing domestic involvements, this was reduced to about 16.5 percent in 1913.[96]

The great German electrical companies in the 1890s were at the same time manufacturers, suppliers of energy, and financing institutions. As the prominent German economist Jacob Riesser (in 1911 a professor at the University of Berlin) wrote, "[T]here was scarcely a form of management or financing which was not utilised in the nineties by the [German] electrical industry. There were syndicates, subsidiary companies (*Tochtergesellschaften)*, and trust companies, the latter especially intended to relieve the banks of part of their enormous financial and other tasks connected with electrical undertakings, operating companies proper, and manufacturing companies, as well as financing institutions, increases and reductions of capital, silent participations, commandites, issues and sales in the open market, fusions, pooling of profits (*Gewinngemeinschaften*), buying of shares, separations and combinations, independent and syndicated enterprises at home and abroad. In short, a medley of undertakings . . . ." By 1912, however, matters had calmed down, and prominent companies and forms of doing business had taken shape in this hugely important German industry.[97]

HOLDING COMPANIES

In 1895–1896, the major German and Swiss electrical equipment manufacturers (including AEG, Siemens, and Brown, Boveri) made the decision to organize holding companies to finance and manage electric utilities. Their precedent lay in the trusts that had been formed in continental Europe to finance railway companies. (Riesser and others called these holding companies "trust companies".) Unlike the railroad trusts, which tended to be exclusively for finance, the new holding companies involved in electric utilities would participate in all facets of the setting up of the electric utilities, including the planning of the projects and the supervising of construction, alone or with outside partners. They made foreign direct investments and ran the businesses. The electrical equipment manufacturers wanted to participate so they could sell their equipment. Once the electric utility was in operation, the holding company would arrange to float the shares of the operating company on the market, bringing in additional investors. These holding companies did what is known in German as *Unternehmergeschäft*. The word is important. The electrotechnical producers became – in the context of the holding company – electrical entrepreneurs (*Unternehmer*), creating their own market or business (*Geschäft*). The holding companies acted as entrepreneurs; they were not simply financial architecture. They sponsored efficiencies in the process of establishing and operating the business abroad. There were economies of scale in the communication of knowledge and general expertise vis-à-vis electric utilities. Sometimes these holding companies were called "power finance companies." The holding companies' principals had the advantage of attracting others' capital without relinquishing control.[98]

The first such European holding companies for electric utilities were incorporated in 1895–1896 in Switzerland, a congenial nation for tax and other reasons. Swiss commercial law allowed far larger bond issues than German law. Switzerland was a neutral ground, where German and French finance could meet and interact. And Switzerland already had an established, sophisticated banking sector. In addition, Switzerland was a splendid setting for hydroelectric power, and there was substantial investment within Switzerland in such facilities and great experience in the field. Because Switzerland had excellent polytechnical schools, engineering talent was readily available.[99]

A second group of holding companies, their origins also in the mid-1890s, were registered in Belgium, a nation where company law made it possible for firms to obtain "executive control … with little capital outlay, the real capital being furnished by debentures and bonds." Like Switzerland in the late nineteenth and early twentieth centuries, Belgium could bring together French and German capital.[100] Some of the Belgian companies were doing *Unternehmergeschäft*; some were purely investment companies (the word *Bankgeschäft* has been used for them). Sometimes the *Unternehmergeschäft* form and the investment company form were combined (in Switzerland as well as in Belgium). By way of precedent, Belgium stands out as the home of the first investment trusts and the first universal banks. The latter had been deeply involved first in railroad and then in tramway finance, where the Belgians took on the greatest importance.[101] There was no single model that covers the history of Belgian holding companies.[102] In time, Belgium became very much a tax haven for French capital, but this does not seem to have been the pre–World War I motive (or at least not the major one) behind the earliest Belgian holding companies.[103] What was perhaps most remarkable was the Belgian international role in tramway companies, providing power for what had been horse- or mule-powered tramways. These investments were made, in the main, in association with holding companies and/or business groups. (As noted in Chapter 2, the terms "holding companies" and "business groups" sometimes blurred.) The Belgian-headquartered international tramway activities often anticipated and then overlapped with the more general Belgian involvements in electric light and power utilities. Around the world, the electrification of tramways was introduced by foreign entrepreneurship and international finance, with the Belgian role predominant but far from alone.[104]

While Switzerland and Belgium were conspicuous in the size and significance of the holding companies that participated in foreign investments in electric utilities, elsewhere on the European continent – especially in Germany and France – investors also formed such companies to provide a legal structure for business abroad in light and power facilities. The holding companies were sometimes a combination of holding and operating companies – that is, in some cases the firm at the pinnacle delegated the operations to separately established operating companies, and in others it acted directly to operate the business abroad. (The degree of delegation to an operating company varied: Sometimes there were contractual relationships that insisted on the purchase of equipment from a particular electrotechnical company; and at other times the delegation was nominal, with the holding company itself installing the management for the operations.)

Let's start with the pioneer Swiss holding companies and their networks of associations, through both their ownership and their holdings. In 1895, AEG established in Switzerland the Bank für Elektrische Unternehmungen (Elektrobank), Zurich, and Brown, Boveri founded the Motor für Angewandte Elektrizität (Motor), Zurich. The next year (1896), Siemens organized the Schweizerische Gesellschaft für Elektrische Industrie (Indelec), Basel.[105] The primary purpose of Elektrobank, Motor, and Indelec was to invest in and to run electric utilities abroad. These holding companies not only had representatives from the equipment manufacturer on their boards of directors, but also had significant connections with leading banks because the electric utilities had large financial needs. Indeed, a historian of the Deutsche Bank credits the latter with the formation of Elektrobank, which is not fully accurate.[106] The way the manufacturers and banks interacted was fundamental, with each acting in its own interest, yet the result was a mutuality of interest because the manufacturers wanted to increase exports and the banks wanted to finance exports and have the utilities provide financial returns to the banks and their clients.

As earlier indicated, the links between AEG and Deutsche Bank were long-standing and intimate. On the other hand, the Zurich holding company Elektrobank was associated not only with the Deutsche Bank but also with four other German banks – two large ones, Berliner Handelsgesellschaft and the Nationalbank für Deutschland, and two private ones,

Jacob Landau and Delbrück – as well as with key Swiss, French, and Italian banks: Credit Suisse, the Banque de Paris et des Pays-Bas (Paribas), and the Banca Commerciale Italiana.[107] The participant banks were not always "independent," for among the banks themselves there were interconnections.[108] While all historians agree that Elektrobank, set up in Switzerland, was a German "creation," apparently in order to reach French capital markets, in particular, Elektrobank's founders believed it was desirable to make it "look" Swiss. Its first president was from Credit Suisse.[109] In emphasizing the AEG and the more general German role, we should not shortchange the universal bank Credit Suisse, which had been since its origin in 1856 a major player in railroad finance. A Credit Suisse historian writes that "the years leading up to the First World War brought a hefty rise in underwriting activity and securities commission business. At the same time, the provision of funds for Switzerland's young electricity industry came to assume the same importance as support for railway construction 40 years earlier."[110] Credit Suisse was involved in railroad construction in Switzerland and abroad; likewise, it became a participant in public utilities finance at home and abroad.

At its origin, the second of the key 1895 Swiss holding companies, Brown, Boveri's Motor had more limited banking ties than Elektrobank, with its banking associations solely with Leu & Co., Zurich. Later, Union des Banques Suisses (otherwise known as Union Bank of Switzerland) came to be a shareholder in Motor.[111] As for Siemens's Indelec, Basel, the third of the three principal 1895–1896 Swiss holding companies, it originally had its own banking alliances, although there were overlaps with the other Swiss holding companies: For example, Leu & Co., Zurich, was involved with Indelec as well as with Motor. Historian Serge Paquier believes that from the start the Basler Handelsbank ran Indelec, while Peter Hertner argues that early on Indelec was closely supervised by both Siemens & Halske and the Basler Handelsbank, but over time, because Siemens was not willing to increase its share of Indelec capital, its influence slowly declined.[112] Once again, depending on whether one reads the electrotechnical or the banking literature, the lead player in the Swiss holding companies might be differently interpreted. We are convinced that the appropriate way to reconcile this divergence is that the manufacturer was crucial in the choice of the public utilities' power equipment needs, whereas the bank(s) handled the financing requirements. Control was partial, and there were the separate benefits.

By 1904–5, each of these three Swiss holding companies – Elektrobank, Motor, and Indelec – had acquired its own technical staff, fully *au courant* in the electricity supply business. Initially, AEG's Elektrobank and Siemens' Indelec directed their activities mainly to building up public utilities in Italy, Spain, and Germany, as well as in Switzerland, but by 1914 Elektrobank had direct investments in electric power companies in nine European countries, while Indelec was a direct investor in seven European countries.[113] Elektrobank was far more important than Indelec and had a far stronger set of banking connections. For example, in 1905–1906, Elektrobank arranged that the shares of the German-controlled Spanish public utility Compañia Barcelonesa de Electricidad be traded on the Barcelona, Berlin, Zurich, Basel, and Geneva stock exchanges.[114] In 1913–1914, Elektrobank's portfolio was divided in these proportions: Germany (53 percent); Italy (18.1 percent); Switzerland (8.6 percent); Spain and Portugal (4.6 percent); France (1.8 percent); and Russia, Eastern Europe, and countries outside of Europe (13.9 percent, of which 3.4 percent was in South America). That same year, Indelec's portfolio was divided differently: Italy (38.9 percent), Germany (38.6 percent), Russia (18.0 percent), France (1.4 percent), and other countries (3.1 percent). As for Motor, its initial activities had been at home in Switzerland, but it expanded to neighboring countries and beyond, so that by 1913 the distribution of its holdings was Switzerland (61.2 percent), Italy (25.9 percent), Germany (9.2 percent), France (3.2 percent), and Denmark (0.5 percent). The small interest by these three Swiss-headquartered holding companies in Latin America did not reflect the actual German or Swiss participations; different financial intermediaries (or holding company structures) handled these investments. Likewise, these lists do not adequately portray the German or Swiss interests in the Austro-Hungarian or in the Ottoman empires.[115]

The international activities of the Germans and the Swiss in electric utilities, while very important in Europe, were not confined to that continent. In 1897, AEG obtained concessions from the municipal governments in Buenos Aires, Argentina, and Santiago, Chile, to set up electric generation stations. To carry on these activities, in January 1898 AEG formed Deutsch-Überseeische Elektrizitäts Gesellschaft (DUEG), Berlin, known in Argentina as Compañía Alemana Transatlántica de Electricidad (CATE), with financing from a group of banks, including Deutsche Bank and Berliner Handelsgesellschaft. (DUEG and CATE were the same company; in some instances, DUEG/CATE operated directly, in others it served as a holding company.) A Siemens historian notes that shortly after the formation of DUEG, Siemens also became a participant in this company, which was not odd, for as we have often noted AEG and Siemens both cooperated and competed in their international business.[116] CATE expanded rapidly in Buenos Aires, buying other providers of electricity and increasing its capacity. Its first power station had a capacity of 5,130 kW; by 1907, when its new power station came into operation, CATE's total capacity was 78,300 kW. That year, when it was the sole public provider of electricity in Buenos Aires, it received a fifty-year concession from the municipal government to supply electric power (although the concession did not give it exclusive rights). By 1914, the capacity of its central power stations in Buenos Aires was 179.4 million kW. CATE was by then the single largest German direct investment overseas. It was also an investor in electric utilities in Chile and Uruguay. AEG/CATE's main interest in Chile followed a different path from that in Argentina. In 1898, the Chilean Electric Tramway & Light Co. Ltd., London, was founded by the Gesellschaft für Elektrische Unternehmungen (Gesfürel), Berlin, one of the holding companies associated with Union Elektrizitäts Gesellschaft (UEG) and then (after the merger between UEG and AEG was completed in 1905) with AEG. In 1905, Chilean Electric (retaining its British registration) became an affiliate of CATE. In a pyramided relationship, in 1914 AEG's Elektrobank acquired a large quantity of CATE shares. Deutsche Bank historians point out that the consortium that had floated DUEG/CATE was headed by that German bank; indeed, in 1919, when decisions were to be made on purchasers who could "run the company properly," it was not AEG (or Siemens) but the Deutsche Bank that set the strategy (see Chapter 4).[117] In 1913, the DUEG/CATE enterprises formed the largest public utility group in Latin America.[118]

In addition, in 1905, after the completion of its merger with UEG, AEG came to play a material role in Belgian business abroad.[119] In 1895, the German UEG (then a General Electric affiliate) had participated in the organization in Belgium of Société Générale Belge d'Entreprises Électriques (SGB). UEG's partner in this precursor of Electrobel was Société Générale des Chemins de Fer Économiques (one of the oldest Belgian tramway holding companies); also involved were key Belgian, French, and German banks.[120] SGB "carried out consultative engineering works and act[ed] as main contractors with the right to sub-contract for machinery and other equipment."[121] It took part in electric utilities in Belgium and abroad. As Herman Van der Wee and Martine Goossens have written, "[A]t the end of the [19th century] the quickly developing electricity industry and the financial sector were ... integrated into the foreign investment strategy of [Belgian] mixed banks."[122]

If AEG after its merger with UEG played a role in SGB, far more significant was AEG's participation in what became one of the world's premier public utility holding companies: Société Financière de Transports et d'Entreprises Industrielles (Sofina). Headquartered in Brussels, Sofina had been established in 1898 by UEG/Gesfürel, in cooperation with Belgian banks and the two large German banks Disconto Gesellschaft and Dresdner Bank. With the AEG-UEG merger, AEG came to control Sofina. AEG dispatched American-born engineer Dannie Heineman to Sofina in 1905. At that time, Sofina had only two other employees on the payroll![123] It was a "paper" company. Heineman would transform the organization: Sofina expanded its international investments in operating companies in the electricity supply and tramway business in Austria-Hungary, Belgium, Denmark, France, Italy, Portugal, Russia, Spain, and Turkey, and, in addition, it developed an important presence in Latin America, principally in Argentina. It also did business in the Far East. By 1913, it had interests in forty-four companies in thirteen countries.[124] In 1914, Sofina organized an English affiliate to take over the principal tramway and lighting companies in Calcutta, Madras, and Bombay (now Mumbai), India, a plan that was abandoned with the advent of World War I.[125] In short, by the start of World War I, AEG was participating in an extended business group that included Swiss, Belgian, and German holding companies, as well as British companies, in a far-flung international business in the electric utilities sector.

For a hint of the complexity of these developments, one has only to view the diagrams in Jacques Thobie's article "European Banks in the Middle East." In December 1911, the Constantinople Consortium was formed in Brussels; it comprised German, French, Belgian, and Swiss groups. Its aim was to seek business in energy and transport. The Constantinople Consortium, in turn, organized in June 1914 the Société des Tramways et de l'Électricité de Constantinople (STEC), registered in Belgium. In this company, the French contingent (35 percent interest) was apparently the largest; it had Société Centrale pour l'Industrie Électrique (SCIE) and French Thomson-Houston (FTH) taking part, along with a coterie of French banks. The German group (32.2 percent) was in second place; it was made up of Elektrische Licht und Kraftanlagen AG (ELK), a Siemens holding company, and Gesellschaft für Elektrische Unternehmungen (Gesfürel), as we have seen, associated with AEG; the Deutsche Bank; and a bevy of other German banks. The third-ranking group was Belgian (24.55 percent) and dominated by Sofina (which, as we have also seen, was in 1914 an AEG-controlled company); in addition, there were ten other Belgian firms included. Thobie concluded that the "formal structure masked the reality of German domination, based on the weight of German capital in SOFINA . . . ."[126]

Brown Boveri's holding company, Motor, had focused first on public utilities at home in Switzerland, where there was rapid electrification, but as noted above, by 1913 its financial holding company, Motor, had investments in power companies in five European countries. In 1913, Brown Boveri established, along with "Italian allies," a second holding company, Columbus AG für Elektrische Unternehmungen, to invest in public utilities in South America, beginning with the prosperous Argentina, where its interests at origin were in Compañía Italo-Argentina de Electricidad. Shareholders in Columbus in 1913 were Motor, a group of Swiss banks, and an Italian contingent, including Pirelli (a manufacturer of insulated cables), Franco Tosi (an electromechanical firm), and the London branch of Credito Italiano. (The Pirelli group was among the main shareholders in Credito Italiano.) The principal Swiss banks linked with Columbus were the private banking house Leu and Union des Banques Suisses (Union Bank of Switzerland), both of which were close to Motor and Brown Boveri.[127]

Meanwhile, in 1897–1898, the Société Franco-Suisse pour l'Industrie Électrique (Franco-Suisse) was founded, with headquarters in Geneva. (German-dominated holding companies in Switzerland tended to be in Zurich or Basel, while French ones gravitated toward Geneva.) Franco-Suisse was yet another of the Swiss holding companies organized to offer funding (and more) for the construction, introduction, and expansion of public utilities at home and abroad. In this case, the French manufacturer Société Schneider & Cie. obtained a minority interest (8 percent); Schneider intended to supply the newly financed utilities with equipment from its electrical works at Le Creusot and then, after 1901, those at Champagne-sur-Seine. Other participants were Swiss and French banks, including Credit Suisse, Zurich; the private Geneva banks Lombard, Odier and Pictet & Cie, and representatives from l'Union Financière de Genève and the Banque de Paris et des Pays-Bas (Paribas).[128] Hubert Bonin points out, however, that typically "[t]he French banks did not favor the creation of financial holding companies for industry, unlike the German, Belgian, or Swiss conglomerates, which served as spearheads for penetration of markets for capital goods in the new countries." In 1902, Franco-Suisse did, however, participate in the organization of Société Financière Italo-Suisse, Geneva (Italo-Suisse), which became heavily involved in the financing of Italian utilities. Franco-Suisse's activities notwithstanding, it remained a modest enterprise when compared with such Swiss holding companies as Elektrobank or Indelec – or Motor, for that matter.[129]

In the early twentieth century, the Swiss "*elektrizitäts-trusts*" (as they were often called) expanded greatly, principally within Europe, although, as noted, Elektrobank had interests in DUEG/CATE, and with the formation of Columbus in 1913 the holding companies showed new interest in South America. From 1898 to World War I and beyond, Swiss *elektrizitäts-trusts* had larger outward foreign investments (three years excepted) than the sum total of all other Swiss direct investments abroad.[130] Switzerland's central geographical position – bordering Germany, France, Italy, and Austria – made a difference, accenting and shaping its international role. Often the cross-border involvements seemed regional – that is, related to the strategic position of particular Swiss cities. The Swiss holding companies overlapped with and worked with (and at times separately from) the Belgian companies. We have noted AEG's Elektrobank in Switzerland and AEG's involvements in two Belgian holdings companies, SGB and its even more important role in Sofina. SGB and Sofina were not alone among the Belgian holding companies.[131]

A prominent player in the international financing of electric utilities was the Belgian Empain group, organized by the great Belgian industrialist Baron Edouard Empain (1852–1929). Empain had founded a bank in Brussels in 1880. His group's activities – which came to comprise a formidable number of holding and operating companies, intricately interwoven – started in the early 1880s in local railways in Belgium and France.

While remaining involved in railways, the group expanded its interests, first into horse-drawn tramways, then into their electrification, and subsequently into providing light and power. In 1892, Empain established a holding company, the Compagnie Belge des Chemins de Fer Réunis (Réunis); Réunis's initial interest in electricity was in 1894, when it took over a tramway company in Lille, France, from the Belgian Philippart group. Note that this mid-1890s date coincides closely with the origins of the other key electrical holding companies in Switzerland and Belgium. Twenty years later, Réunis had important investments in railways and tramways throughout Europe (in Belgium, France, Greece, Ireland, Italy, Luxembourg, Portugal, Russia, and Spain), as well as in Argentina, Belgian Congo, Chile, China, Egypt, and Turkey. In 1896, the Empain group had organized a Belgian holding company, Société Russe-Française de Chemin de Fer et Tramways (RF), which invested in France and Russia. Its main goal was to participate (in 1898) in the Paris Metro, from the start an electric subway. The Empain group would be, until the Metro's municipalization after World War II, the largest single shareholder in the Paris Metro (RF's equity ranged from 15 to 30 percent). The Paris Metro served to stimulate the formation of electricity producers and distributors as well as electrical manufacturers, in which Empain then became involved. Thus, the Empain group in 1900 took part in the creation of Société Parisienne pour l'Industrie des Chemins de Fer et des Tramways Électriques (commonly known as Parisienne Électrique). RF provided a significant part of its portfolio in exchange for shares in Parisienne Électrique. The next step for Empain was an investment in the construction in 1903 of a power station in Paris by the Société d'Électricité de Paris (SEP); Parisienne Électrique became the French holding company for that property. Finally, the Empain group moved into electrical manufacturing in 1904 in Belgium and France (through an acquisition). Ateliers de Constructions Électriques de Charleroi (ACEC) was organized that year to serve as a manufacturing subsidiary; Parisienne Électrique managed the French manufacturing plant in Jeumont until in 1906 the Empain group created an additional subsidiary: Ateliers de Construction Électriques du Nord et de l'Est (ACENE). Meanwhile, in 1904 Empain had merged RF and another of its Belgian holding companies to form Compagnie Générale de Railways et d'Électricité (known as Railways et Électricité), a giant Belgian holding that would invest in many subsidiaries in Belgium and, along with the other members of the Empain group – Réunis and Parisienne Électrique – make investments in Europe, Asia, Africa, and South America. Gradually, electricity had become the principal activity of the Empain group, with a span of dramatic international involvements. The overlapping holding and operating companies from Spain to Russia, from the Belgian Congo to Egypt, were formidable. In Egypt, Edouard Empain built a mansion for himself in Heliopolis, a suburb of Cairo. His Cairo Electric Railways and Heliopolis Oasis

Company got a concession in 1906 from the Egyptian government, built an electric tram line linking Cairo with Heliopolis, and developed a housing project in Heliopolis. The group would become a major investor in Egypt. The Empain group's closest ties were with France, and its largest foreign investments were there. In its international business, it hired French as well as Belgian managers and engineers and used French along with Belgian banking services. By 1913–1914, Empain was a global group, with a complex maze of overlapping holding and operating companies with interests in Argentina, Belgian Congo, Belgium, Brazil, Chile, China, Egypt, France, Germany, Greece, Ireland, Italy, the Netherlands, Portugal, Russia, Spain, and Turkey.[132]

The European holding companies we have been considering were frequently linked with one another in criss-crossing business groups.[133] By the time of World War I, the many holding companies in Europe usually tied in with manufacturers, always involving banks, had been established to finance, set up, and facilitate the development of tramways and electric utilities across borders in continental Europe and in Latin America, with occasional forays into Asia, North Africa, and sub-Saharan Africa. German, Swiss, and Belgian universal banks were deeply engaged in these developments, as were French investment banks ("*banques d'affaires*"). Many of the holding companies were engaged in *Unternehmergeschäft* (that is, they had construction and engineering expertise internal to the firm); others used outside construction and engineering expertise within a loosely constituted group (with the groups varying in their cohesion); and still others were purely financial holdings. Often, to repeat, there was a combination of functions within a holding company – that is, the holding company would have financial holdings, exercise portfolio management, and also have a direct investment in certain electrical activities where it provided or hired the managerial talents.

Meanwhile, across the Atlantic, the holding company form for *international* business was slower to evolve. Within the United States, from Thomson-Houston's United Electric Securities Company (1890) onward, there had been holding companies that helped finance domestic activities. Villard's North American Company (also 1890) had that goal.[134] In 1904, General Electric established Electrical Securities Corporation, and, more important, in 1905 it formed Electric Bond and Share Company "to become an investment specialist and engineering and service organization, providing expert services to operating companies." Electric Bond and Share was primarily designed to hold domestic investments, although in its original portfolio it did have interests in three French Thomson-Houston companies and in Chatham & District Light Railways (Chatham, England) and Lanarkshire Tramways Co. (London).[135] Other substantial U.S. holding companies were formed for domestic business.[136] One that undertook U.S.-Canadian business was the Niagara

Falls Power Company, which desired a second source of power on the Canadian side of the falls. It got consent of the Canadian and provincial governments to locate and to construct a power plant inside the Queen Victoria Niagara Falls Park. This subsidiary, Canadian Niagara Power Co., would supply power in New York State as well as in Ontario. The first power was delivered January 1, 1905. This was one of the few instances of a holding company's subsidiary undertaking cross-border power exports back to the parent.[137]

From Canada, outward foreign investments took the form in the main of loose relationships between different financial groupings (as described above) rather than a unified holding company edifice. While Canadians had holding companies that involved single-country relationships, as far as we can establish, the first (1913) of the dedicated Canadian holding companies with multicountry foreign investments appears to have been International Light & Power Co. Ltd., Toronto, which had interests in public utilities in Argentina, Mexico, and Venezuela. Its companies were managed by J. G. White & Co., a New York–based engineering consultant/construction firm/contractor about which we will have more to say.[138]

OPERATING COMPANIES: CLUSTERS, ENGINEERING, CONSTRUCTION, AND TRADING FIRMS

To operate a public utility in urban areas, a company typically would be established that would get a concession from a government body. In international business, operating companies could be spun off from the electrotechnical manufacturing companies' ventures.[139] Financial institutions, in their various configurations, set up operating companies. Within enclave communities, operating companies for public utilities were organized. Separate operating companies were formed by large power consumers. Holding companies also founded and acquired ongoing operating companies. Sometimes, as noted, holding companies were both holding and operating units. We have seen all these origins.

Now is the time to turn to a sample of the hundreds of foreign-owned operating companies, including those that were set up in a fashion other than the above-mentioned forms.[140] Often, in Great Britain operating companies would be registered there to do business abroad. Directories offer long lists of them. Many such companies were short-lived.[141] Table 3.1 provides an incomplete 1915 roster of British-organized or -controlled electric light and power companies with properties located outside of the United Kingdom, the United States, Canada, Latin America, and the Caribbean. The table reveals the worldwide reach of such companies. Ostensibly, like most companies that we have called "free standing" (see Chapter 2), all appear to be independent – but that was not the case.

Table 3.1. *Partial List of British-Organized or -Controlled Electric Light and Power Companies (Including Electric Tramway Companies) with Properties Located Outside the United Kingdom, United States, Canada, Latin America, and the Caribbean, 1915*

Name	Location of property	Approx. Capitalization (in U.S. dollars)
Adelaide Electric Supply Co. Ltd.	Australia	3,240,000
Auckland Electric Tramways Co. Ltd.	New Zealand	5,042,000
Bombay Electric Supplies & Tramways Co. Ltd.	India	9,878,000
Burmah Electric Tramways & Lighting Co. Ltd.	Burma (Myanmar)	1,000,000
Brisbane Electric Tramways Investment Co. Ltd.	Australia	7,125,000
Calcutta Electric Supply Corporation Ltd.	India	5,000,000
Calcutta Tramways Co. Ltd.	India	6,440,000
Cape Electric Tramways Ltd.	South Africa	4,479,000
Capetown Consolidated Tramways & Land Co. Ltd.	South Africa	3,750,000
Colombo Electric Tramway & Lighting Co. Ltd.	Ceylon (now Sri Lanka)	1,254,000
Delhi Electric Tramways & Lighting Co. Ltd.	India	858,000
East India Tramways Co. Ltd.	India	500,000
Electric Supply Co. of Victoria Ltd.	Australia	2,267,000
Electricity Supply Co. for Spain Ltd.	Spain	1,182,000
Hankow Light & Power Co. Ltd.	China	100,000
Hong Kong Tramway Co. Ltd.	China	1,295,000
Huelva Gas & Electricity Co. Ltd.	Spain	279,000
Hydro-Electric Power & Metallurgical Co. Ltd.	Tasmania (an Australian state)	3,337,000
Indian Electric Supply & Traction Co. Ltd.	India	715,000
Kalgoorlie Electric Power & Lighting Corporation Ltd.	Australia	1,300,000
Kalgoorlie Electric Tramways Ltd.	Australia	1,999,000
Lisbon Electric Tramways Ltd.	Portugal	7,780,000
Lobito Benguilla & Catembella Electric Light & Power Co., Ltd.	South Africa (*sic*)	908,000
Madras Electricity Supply Co. Ltd.	India	2,942,000
Madras Electric Tramways Ltd.	India	1,088,000

Name	Location of property	Approx. Capitalization (in U.S. dollars)
Malaga Electricity Co. Ltd.	Spain	500,000
Malta Tramways Ltd.	Malta	715,000
Melbourne Electric Supply Co. Ltd.	Australia	4,800,000
Melbourne Tramway & Omnibus Co. Ltd.	Australia	4,800,000
Nairobi Electric Light & Power Co. Ltd.	(British) East Africa (now Kenya)	250,000
North Melbourne Electric Tramways & Lighting Co. Ltd.	Australia	1,661,000
Rangoon Electric Tramway & Supply Co. Ltd.	India	3,600,000
Shanghai Electric Construction Co. Ltd. (tramway)	China	1,680,000
Singapore Electric Tramways Ltd.	Straits Settlements	1,863,000
South African Lighting Association	South Africa	575,000

Source: U.S. Federal Trade Commission, *Report on Cooperation in the American Export Trade* (Washington, DC, 1916), II, 543–44. The locations, except those in parentheses, are as given in this source. In one place we have put a *sic* after South Africa because of an error in the source: this should have been southern Africa or Portuguese East Africa (now Angola). We have confirmed in Garcke, 1914–1915, that Malta Tramways and East India Tramways were electrified and that South African Lighting provided both gas and electric power. We have made very minor corrections in the titles of companies. To the best of our knowledge, all the companies included were controlled by nonresident British owners; we have not included any company known to be controlled by Germans (or other nationalities) in the locale of doing business.

Frequently, operating companies were clustered in informal (or formal) groups. Thus, for example, the Melbourne Electric Supply Co. Ltd. and the Adelaide Electric Supply Co. Ltd., at origins and throughout their history, were associated with the same set of British firms. Joseph Bevan Braithwaite, MIEE (Member of the Institution of Electrical Engineers), was listed on the board of each company. The "head office" of each was at Finsbury Pavement House, London. When the two Australian companies were set up in 1908 and 1905, respectively, Braithwaite (1855–1934) had long been engaged with English electric utilities. In 1893, his application for membership in the U.K. professional society for electrical engineers, the Institution of Electrical Engineers read: "In 1882 I became chairman of the Great Western Electric Light & Power Co. and during the two or three years that I held that position I devoted much time to the development of early electric lighting stations at Bristol and Cardiff. ... [M]y firm [the stockbrokers Foster & Braithwaite] were largely instrumental in obtaining the capital for the City of London Electric Lighting Co. ... As a director of the Electric & General Investment Trust ... I have been able to render valuable financial assistance." The Melbourne Electric Supply Co. Ltd. (1908) was the successor to the 1899 English-registered Electric Lighting and Traction Company of Australia Ltd. (which had brought together several Melbourne-based utilities). The Adelaide Electric Supply Company Ltd. was formed afresh in England in 1905.[142]

The companies associated with British Electric Traction Co. (BET), the largest private tramway and motor bus company in the United Kingdom, were tied in with another overlapping cluster, approximating that of a multinational enterprise. BET was formed in 1895 (the issuing house was Electric & General Investment Trust). In 1899, when its affiliate Auckland Electric Tramways Co. Ltd. (New Zealand) was organized, BET already had developed operations in the United Kingdom and was well acquainted with this business. The Auckland company combined tramway services and electricity supply. It was separately set up (and floated) within the United Kingdom, with BET the largest single investor.

Consider the important Bombay Electric Supplies & Tramways Co. Ltd. (India). It came into being in 1905 in India and the United Kingdom (with a pattern of dual boards common among free standing companies); it was the successor to and broadened the functions of the earlier Bombay Tramway Co., which in 1901 had been purchased by the British firm Anglo-American Brush Electric Light Corporation. In a complex transaction, the 1905 Indian company was promoted by BET, which retained a smaller stake in it than it held in the just discussed Auckland venture. Electric & General Investment Trust was involved, purchasing "debenture stock" from BET and offering that Bombay Electric stock for sale in the United Kingdom. Raphael Schapiro found, in his scrutiny of BET records, that after these transactions in 1907 BET owned two-thirds of the ordinary stock and one-third of the preference shares of Bombay Electric; BET participated in managerial decisions and had two seats on the board of directors of Bombay Electric. The company was run from England and did business in British pounds. Anglo-American Brush Electric Light Corporation had come to concentrate on the manufacture of traction equipment and from the end of 1896 had worked closely with BET; by 1906, if not earlier, BET had obtained control of Anglo-American Brush Electric Light.[143]

In addition, BET had minority financial interests in a number of other operating companies – for example, the Buenos Ayres and Belgrano Tramway Company Ltd. and the Anglo-Argentine Tramways Co. – as well as tramway and light and power companies in Australia, Canada, and China, where it did not provide managerial expertise.[144] The latter were part of its financial portfolio, although its expertise in the field directed it to invest in these activities. And to add to the network (as we pointed out much earlier in this chapter), the stock brokerage firm Foster & Braithwaite was active in the parent, BET.

As noted, Table 3.1 does not include the numerous companies in Latin America.[145] It also omits the many free standing British gas companies that by 1915 had developed electrical as well as gas concessions. This was true of the large and important Imperial Continental Gas Association (ICGA), with a 1915 capitalization of $30,875,000 (denominated in pound sterling), and operating companies in Austria, Belgium, France, Germany, and The Netherlands[146] ICGA began with gas concessions and then combined gas and electricity. Since its origins in 1824, it had internalized engineering talents that could be spread over each public utility project.

What Table 3.1 does is push us to uncover the varieties in modes of operations of British-registered companies that operated abroad: with some in a cluster surrounding a key stockbroker/engineer; with others fitting more into the model of a classic multinational enterprise (as with the activities of tramway and motor bus company in the United Kingdom); and with some emerging from prior activities in gas.

Indeed, as we peruse the operating companies – British and others as well, if they seem to be free standing – it is often possible to find a cluster of related firms. All operating companies required engineering and construction talents. Such activities could be fully or partly "internalized" within the parent firm, as in the *Unternehmergeschäft* model. Other times, joined in with this expansion were separate outside (otherwise independent) engineering and/or construction companies – including, for example, the German firm Philipp Holzmann. When, as a case in point, Deutsch-Überseeische Elektrizitäts Gesellschaft (DUEG), Berlin, developed the Buenos Aires light and power facilities, it contracted with Philipp Holzmann to build the plants and distribution networks, using materials and equipment imported from Germany.[147] So, too, by 1913–1914 the French construction company Société Générale d'Entreprises (SGE), which specialized in erecting electricity supply facilities, did roughly half of its business outside France. SGE developed a far-flung international business, from Russia to Italy and farther afield. Its subsidiary Société Générale d'Entreprises dans l'Empire Ottoman had twelve branches with ten thousand employees in Turkey.[148] In 1911, SGE founded the Société Ottomane d'Électricité de Constantinople (SOEC).[149]

Sometimes, it was engineering/construction firms that took the lead in the establishment of free standing companies. In Great Britain, a group of builders and construction firms had long taken part in infrastructure investments on a global basis. Some took the initiative in the organization of free standing companies in electric utilities. This was the case of the important British firm S. Pearson & Son, about which we will have a great deal more to say when we consider developments in Mexico.

In the United States, an important avenue for involvements in operating utilities abroad lay in the entrepreneurial activities of construction/engineering enterprises. Stone & Webster and J. G. White & Co. are two key examples. Before undertaking overseas projects, both of these firms obtained experience with financing electric light and power companies domestically in the United States. Stone & Webster started as consulting engineers in 1889; the firm moved into construction; it became a participant in managing and supervising public utilities; it developed the ability to raise capital for utilities; it took on the roles of underwriter and investment banker, and it transmitted these talents to the international arena. By 1913, Stone & Webster had offices in twenty-five U.S. states and in Canada and the West Indies.[150] So, too, the New York–headquartered J. G. White & Co., which specialized in electric power construction engineering, came to combine this with the management of utilities and dealing in securities. In the United States, it was identified with the holding company Associated Gas & Electric.[151] In 1903, together with Speyer & Co. and Westinghouse Electric & Manufacturing Co., J. G. White & Co. obtained a concession to build street railway and lighting plants in Manila, The Philippines. That year, the White firm took part in constructing Dutch street railways, and by 1905 it was participating in electrical projects in England, Ireland, Mexico, and in various parts of South America.[152] In 1906, the Canadian company Royal Securities joined with White to develop a major power project in Puerto Rico.[153] By 1913, White was deeply involved in designing and constructing electric light and power plants as well as street railways; for this purpose, it had offices in London, and in Argentina, Brazil, and Chile.[154] When in 1913 International Light & Power Co. Ltd., Toronto, was established, as we have noted earlier, the White firm became manager of its operating companies in Argentina, Mexico, and Venezuela.[155]

Many of the Canadian promoters of free standing operating companies in Latin America used the New York–based F. S. Pearson firm for engineering services. Fred Stark Pearson (1861–1915) was often the key individual in electric utilities developed under Canadian registration in Latin America and then in Spain – for instance, when the Canadians formed Barcelona Traction, Light and Power in 1911.[156] Pearson was frequently described as the driving force in these projects.[157] As part of the bundle of firms taking part in the international spread of operating companies before World War I, it is necessary to include trading companies. These well-established firms were familiar with the areas in which they traded; they knew about handling and financing trade in equipment; they could provide information of a very specialized kind. Thus, in 1898, when the Brasilianische Elektrizitäts-Gesellschaft, Berlin, was organized, participants included (1) Theodor Wille (a German import-export house), (2) the Deutsche Bank, and (3) the Siemens holding company Elektrische Licht und Kraftanlagen, AG (ELK). Both the Deutsche Bank and ELK also served in other clusters in pursuing international business in utilities.[158] Additional trading companies involved in the networks surrounding operating companies in electricity supply ventures included, for example, the British trading company Anthony Gibbs & Co. In the early 1880s, Gibbs was reported to be the principal participant in the British free standing company Mexican Gas and Electric Company.[159]

This barely skims the surface. What is important is that in the establishment of operating companies there were different foreign initiators and a bevy of out-of-country participants. This becomes clearer when we consider foreign-owned operating companies in certain key countries where foreign owners played a dominant role.

OPERATING COMPANIES IN LATIN AMERICA (MEXICO IN PARTICULAR) AND EUROPE (RUSSIA IN PARTICULAR)

European- and North American–owned operating companies were active in Latin America. British free standing companies were particularly in evidence. Wherever there had been gas companies, electric companies followed. Electricity found its way to market, often through preexisting utility companies that provided other infrastructure services. Water, gas, tramway, and telephone companies served as conduits for electrical services in Latin America as well as elsewhere around the world. It was very evident in the case of tramways. Early, unelectrified tramway concessions became electrified. Often, the line between tramways and electric light and power companies was indistinct – sometimes concessions were for both; sometimes they were separate. A study of electric light and power by necessity deals with tramways.

In each country of the world, but particularly in Latin America, there were sequences in the electrification process from new entries to mergers and consolidations. Municipalities might give concessions for only part of a city, and they might give nonexclusive concessions. Firms of one nationality might be followed by those of another nationality. The complexities were not only in clusters of initiators and participants, but in the very sequencing of the investments. Within a single country, because typically the concession was for a single geographic area, "monopolies" were confined to that part of the city, that city, or that region. (Even if concessions were nonexclusive, existing companies tended to divide up areas of service.)

In Latin America, a large number of foreign companies participated in supplying electricity. Different industries and cities within these countries attracted different – or overlapping – investors. The networks, the pyramids of companies, the sequencing, and the interactions of individuals of various nationalities meant that the combinations and permutations at times seemed overwhelming.

Mexican electrification – which came to be dominated by foreign concerns – illustrates many of the tangled relationships of the various operating companies. Historians Reinhard Liehr and Georg Leidenberger found that the earliest electrification in Mexico began in 1879, as cotton mills and mining and refining activities acquired generators related to their industrial activities.[160] In Mexico City, the British-registered Mexican Gas and Electric Light Co. Ltd. set up between 1881 and 1888 the first system of electric street lamps. They were of the Brush type. However, not until February 1894 were the first lights actually shining.[161] The system was not satisfactory, and on December 15, 1896, the Mexico City municipal council signed a contract with the German firm Siemens & Halske to introduce a second public lighting system.[162] In 1897, the Germans formed the Mexican Electric Works Ltd., London, a free standing company, with one-quarter of the capital owned by Siemens & Halske and Indelec (its Swiss holding company) and three-quarters by the Dresdner Bank. It did well, offering strong competition to the Mexican Gas and Electric Light Co.[163]

The next step involved a Halifax (soon to become a Montreal) group of investors, with the American engineer F. S. Pearson. This group obtained key waterpower concessions in Mexico in 1902 and organized the Mexican Light and Power Co. Ltd., incorporated in Canada.[164] Quickly, under Pearson's initiative, Mexican Light and Power Co. was "metamorphosed from a marginal speculation into a property controlled by the leading men of Canadian finance." The new company had among its directors, E. S. Clouston, then general manager of the Bank of Montreal, and George Drummond, who became president of that bank in 1905. The "cluster" of men involved included the very wealthy James Ross, who was a participant in Canadian utilities as a contractor; a number of key Canadian railroad entrepreneurs; and E. R. Wood, the prominent stock broker associated with Dominion Securities.[165] In July 1903, the Mexican Light and Power Co. acquired from the Germans the Mexican Electric Works Ltd., which resulted in Canadian control of this prominent firm, which by this time led in providing electric power to Mexico City. In the transaction, the prior owners obtained the right to appoint two board members: Those selected were Arnold Ellert, London manager of the Dresdner Bank, and Alfred Berliner of Siemens & Halske.[166] Siemens & Halske continued to receive orders to supply generators to the Canadian-controlled company. In 1905, the Mexican Light and Power Co. established a new Canadian subsidiary, Mexican Electric Light Co., which in turn purchased the Mexican Gas and Electric Light Co., as well as another locally owned, but Sofina-financed, Mexican company, La Compañía Explotadora de las Hidro-Eléctricas de San Ildefonso.[167] Mexican Light and Power Co. would make further acquisitions in Mexico in 1907–1910, in the process integrating and modernizing the facilities.[168] Encouraged by the opportunities in Mexico, on May 6, 1906 the Bank of Montreal set up a branch in Mexico City.

Clouston declared Mexican investments were safer than in Canada.[169] The Bank of Montreal in 1905 had guaranteed a million-dollar underwriting for the Mexican Light and Power Co. and also made an $800,000 loan to the company.[170]

Meanwhile, in 1882 a Mexican group had established the Compañía Limitada de Ferrocarriles del Distrito (CLFD), which combined a number of tramway companies formed since the 1870s.[171] CLFD was acquired by the British merchant bankers Wernher, Beit & Co. in 1896 and subsequently began electrification of streetcar service in Mexico City (although the first line was not electrified until 1900).[172] In 1898, an English free standing company, Mexican Electric Tramways Ltd. had been organized, a company in which Wernher, Beit had a substantial interest.[173] It apparently acquired CLFD.[174] Armstrong and Nelles tell an extraordinary story of how in 1906 (the same year Alfred Beit died) Canadian interests (along with F. S. Pearson) took over Mexican Electric Tramways. The entire Montreal group already participating in the Mexican Light and Power Co. was not interested at this time, so Pearson assembled a separate (albeit overlapping) set of Canadian and European investors. Clouston of the Bank of Montreal remained involved. The Canadian-incorporated Mexico Tramways Company Ltd., headquartered in Toronto, acquired Mexican Electric Tramways. Participating in this new activity were the Belgian entrepreneur Alfred Loewenstein and the British trust company pioneer, now London-based, Robert Fleming.[175]

Armstrong and Nelles explain the relationships between the two sizable Canadian-incorporated companies, Mexican Light and Power Co. and Mexico Tramways Co. In 1909, Pearson, as a participant in both ventures, arranged a hostile takeover by Mexico Tramways Co. of the Mexican Light and Power Co. The two firms technically stayed separate, but they would subsequently be managed jointly.[176]

Canadians took on the management of these Mexican companies, in cooperation with Pearson, while at the same time they were able to tap British capital markets in an effective manner. Investors in England were assured by the Canadian registration and by the Canadian participants that these were "safe" investments. The Canadian domicile provided comfort and security to the "portfolio" investors, who were not only English but came from the European continent as well. The corporate structure offered a way of raising large amounts of capital required for the undertakings.

Before 1914, these were not the only foreign-owned and -run electric power companies in Mexico. There was, for example, the Guanajuato Power and Electric Co., set up by Americans in 1902 in a silver- and gold-mining area of Mexico. This was one of the earliest – or perhaps the earliest – ventures of William P. Bonbright in electric utilities. In 1903, Stone & Webster organized the El Paso Electric Co., which provided electric lighting, power, and traction in both El Paso and across the border in Ciudad

Juarez, Mexico. In other parts of Mexico, there was the Monterey Railway, Light & Power Co. Ltd., formed in Toronto in 1905, and there was also the U.S.-owned Compañía Hidroeléctrica de Chapala to service the Guadalajara region.[177] Compañía Hidro-Eléctrica del Rio de la Alameda SA was organized in 1909 by a French group to provide power for textile factories in Mexico City.[178] Some Canadians – including E. B. Greenshields, Edwin Hanson, and G. F. Greenwood from Montreal; the lawyer/promoter B. F. Pearson and the contractor S. M. Brookfield from Halifax; entrepreneur and manufacturer S. J. Moore from Toronto; and John D. Paterson from Woodstock, Ontario – established in 1909 the Mexican Northern Power Company to develop the Conchos River in the Mexican state of Chihuahua and to provide electricity to mining towns and cities in that state.[179]

In addition, there was the coincident and extremely important collection of ventures of Weetman D. Pearson (not to be confused with F. S. Pearson or B. F. Pearson).[180] Weetman Pearson's family firm was S. Pearson & Son, a London-headquartered construction company, with contracts all over the world. By the end of 1889, that firm was involved in dock, harbor, and railroad tunnel construction in Egypt, Nova Scotia, and the United States; in December of that year, it got its first Mexican contract, a contract for the Grand Canal. The president of Mexico, Porfirio Díaz, met with Weetman Pearson, and the contract was rapidly negotiated. This was the start of a deep involvement in Mexico for Pearson, as well as a close friendship with the Mexican president.[181] One project led to another. The perils of getting construction materials landed in the treacherous harbor in Vera Cruz led to a contract to improve the harbor. While that work was underway, in 1901, S. Pearson & Son obtained a contract for drainage and water supply at Vera Cruz.[182] Then, in 1906 Díaz asked Pearson to take over the locally owned tramway system in Vera Cruz and electrify it. Pearson received a concession from the municipality and organized the Vera Cruz Electric Light, Power and Traction Ltd.[183] According to his biographer, J. A. Spender, this was Weetman Pearson's first entry into construction related to electrification.

For advice, Pearson turned to Alexander Worswick, a Canadian, who was the engineer on the spot in Mexico City, acting for Mexican Electric Tramways. (Worswick had been the resident engineer on behalf of the Wernher, Beit group.) Pearson followed Worswick's advice and did not restrict his activities to traction, but acquired and reconstructed the existing, though rather primitive, electric light and power business in Vera Cruz. John Young of Chicago had earlier set up El Portezuelo Light and Power Company, incorporated in Illinois. Pearson formed the Anglo-Mexican Electric Company Ltd., a free standing company registered in England in 1906 that took over the El Portezuelo company. Pearson also obtained an interest in the Canadian-incorporated Puebla Tramway, Light & Power Co. Ltd. and sold shares in Anglo-Mexican Electric to this firm. S. Pearson & Son, Weetman Pearson, and Worswick retained debentures in Anglo-Mexican Electric.

Listed among the debenture holders in this British-registered firm in 1909 were two Germans: "Luebeck and Ellert." We are unable to identify Luebeck (he might have been associated with Siemens & Halske). Arnold Ellert was the London manager of the Dresdner Bank, and we have come across him in connection with the Mexican Light and Power Co. During 1909, Anglo-Mexican Electric acquired bonds and shares of Puebla Tramway Light and Power. The two were obviously closely associated, each owning shares in the other.[184]

This was just the beginning of Weetman Pearson's forays into electrification: Soon other light and power projects in Mexico attracted his attention.[185] In Nova Scotia in the 1880s, Pearson had become friends with the Halifax contractor S. M. Brookfield. Years later, the two worked together in Mexico: S. Pearson & Son got a construction contract with Mexican Northern Power Co. in 1909; we have noted earlier that Brookfield was one of the investors in this company.[186]

As Weetman Pearson became active in various Mexican electrification projects, he was also becoming a major player in the Mexican oil industry.[187] Worswick advised Pearson to buy the tramway system and the two competing electric light companies in Tampico, the center of the Mexican oil industry boom. It is not exactly clear when this purchase took place, but it appears to have been during the Porfirio Díaz administration, which came to a close May 25, 1911.[188] A new English company, the Tampico Electric Light, Power & Traction Co. Ltd. was incorporated in 1912. Pearson was involved in other Mexican projects as well, among them one at Orizaba, where Pearson had built a power station for a local jute mill in 1906.[189]

Weetman Pearson shared Porfirio Díaz's desire to modernize Mexico. After Porfirio Diaz's ouster in 1911, the Mexican revolution continued, with its succession of Mexican leaders, uncertainties, disruptions, and physical damage to properties. Pearson (made Lord Cowdray in 1910) remained as a large investor in Mexico, as did the Canadian groups involved in electrical light and power. But the confidence that the Bank of Montreal had expressed in 1906 had waned, and losses appeared on the financial statements of some of the companies participating in electric utilities in Mexico.[190] By 1914, there were five sizable Canadian-incorporated ventures in Mexico: Mexico Tramways Co., Mexican Light & Power Co., Mexican Northern Power Co., Puebla Tramway, Light & Power Co., and Monterey Railway, Light & Power Co., along with the other, principally British-incorporated, free standing companies – in the main, Lord Cowdray's companies. There were some U.S.-owned companies as well.

In 1913, the International Light & Power Co. Ltd. had been set up, the first of the Canadian holding companies. It acquired a small existing power plant in Merida, Yucatan, Mexico (Compañía de Electricidad de Merida became its operating company), with J. G. White & Co. as manager.[191] The vast expansion of electric utilities in Mexico – which had occurred during the era of Porfirio Díaz and came to a close in 1911 – took place to aid industry, to light up cities, and to electrify tramways. There was nothing approximating a "national" system. Separate companies served individual cities and regions, although there was some regional integration.

Miguel S. Wionczek writes that of the approximately two hundred concessions granted or confirmed by the Mexican central government between 1895 and 1910, the vast majority had gone to Mexicans, who rapidly sold them to foreign investors. Why? Because foreign investors had the know-how and ability to develop power facilities, as well as access to capital for this very capital-intensive industry.[192]

While the progress of foreign companies in Mexico was shaped by Porfirio Díaz's attempts to modernize the nation and the "age of electricity" came to Mexico "with remarkable speed," the foreign direct investment story mirrored parallel developments elsewhere in Latin America and worldwide, although the national actors and forms of multinational enterprises in each case represented a different set of configurations.[193]

In Europe, a large number of companies that were foreign-owned and -controlled participated in electrification. This was particularly true in Italy and Spain, but also in Central and Eastern Europe and in Greece. Russia provides an important example of the diffusion of electricity vis-à-vis multinational enterprise. As in Mexico, Russian electrification came rapidly and soon was dominated by foreign direct investors. Siemens & Halske had long done business in Russia, so it set up an electricity supply company: the Company for Electric Lighting, known as the 1886 Company. It was the first commercial electric utility in Russia, and it built a thermal plant in St. Petersburg. Note that this was a decade before Siemens & Halske's participation in Mexico, and, as in Mexico, this was a typical manufacturer's satellite.

Shares of the 1886 Company were quoted on the Berlin stock exchange and subsequently on the St. Petersburg stock exchange. The key German banks participating were the Deutsche Bank, the Bank für Handel und Industrie, and the Mitteldeutsche Credit Bank. The 1886 Company, the largest and most prominent of the foreign-owned Russian public utilities, came to hold ownership interests in electric light and power companies in Moscow, Nishni Novgorod, Riga, Baku, and Lódź. In the late 1890s, Société Générale, Brussels – through the Belgian holding company Société Générale Belge d'Entreprises Électriques (SGB) and in cooperation with some German banks – obtained concessions to supply electric power in St. Petersburg (in competition with the 1886 Company). For this purpose, it organized the operating company: the Company for Petersburg's Electric Lighting (CPEL). Société Générale, Brusssels, was also involved in the Belgian-registered Compagnie Centrale d'Électricité de Moscou, a firm that attracted French capital, through the intermediation of Société Générale pour Favoriser le Développement du Commerce et de l'Industrie en France and the Banque des Pays du Nord. In addition, Sofina acquired interests in various Russian utilities. For example, it was involved in the foundation (through the Société Centrale pour l'Industrie Électrique [SCIE], Paris) of the Société d'Électricité d'Odessa; it, too, participated in the Compagnie Centrale d'Électricité de Moscou. AEG was represented in Russia through its interests in SGB and Sofina. And then, as noted earlier, Empain had interests in Russian tramways and in light and power companies. To add to the complexity, in 1899 the syndicate Russiches Syndicate für Elektrische Unternehmungen was formed by Siemens, AEG, and UEG (soon to be acquired by AEG) to develop electrical undertakings in Russia. Siemens's and AEG's involvements –respectively, in Indelec and Elektrobank – in Switzerland meant it would not be long before the Swiss holding companies held a tranche in Russia. Both acquired securities of the 1886 Company. In 1914, the Basler Handelsbank (key in Indelec) had a representative on the board of the 1886 Company, as did the Credit Suisse (the principal Swiss bank in Elektrobank). The French Rothschilds, who were deeply involved in the development of the Russian oil industry, became participants in the Russiches Syndicate and its electrification activities in Baku. Earlier, we noted the investments of the manufacturer French Thomson-Houston in Énergie Électrique de Bakou. Sofina was likewise a participant in the electrification of the Baku region.

By the early 1910s, the 1886 Company and CPEL were no longer competing but rather cooperating in developing hydroelectric power in St. Petersburg. Another sizable investor in Russia beginning in the 1890s was the German manufacturing company Helios, which became the leader in Petersburger Gesellschaft für Electroanlagen (PGE). In 1913, when Helios went out of business, the ownership of its Russian affiliate was reorganized, and Belgian and French investors took over. PGE became the Société Saint-Petersbourgeoise de Transmission Électrique de la Force des Chutes d'Eau (SSPT). Meanwhile, Siemens-Schuckertwerke had set up the Kiev Electric Company. In November 1912, Elektrobank and Indelec participated in Imatra, a giant venture organized in Brussels, with Swiss, Belgian, and Russian capital (30 million francs) and with plans for a central hydroelectric power station in Finland that would distribute energy in Finland and in the St. Petersburg region. (The reader will remember that at this time the Grand Duchy of Finland was part of the Russian empire.) The Imatra waterfall on the Upper Vuoksi River in Finland was a scenic spot, comparable to Niagara Falls. Serge Paquier writes that the participation in the Imatra project (which never materialized) reflected a new spirit of cooperation between the Swiss and Belgian holding companies; in each case, the participating companies were partly controlled by the German groups.

This is barely an introduction. But we can conclude that a labyrinth of German electrotechnical companies and banks, Belgian holding companies and banks, Swiss holding companies, French banks, and at least one French manufacturer were engaged in seeking to develop and actually developing light and power facilities in Russia. Belgian tramway operations, including many by Empain, proliferated in Russia. Sometimes these were linked to (and sometimes not) the light and power activities. Whereas German interests dominated light and power facilities, in tramways the Belgian groups were supreme. By the eve of World War I, 90 percent of the light and power produced in Russia came from facilities of foreign companies.[194]

Each host country around the world had a distinct mix of foreign investors. And within each host country, various cities attracted different configurations of such investments. We could tell countless other stories about each country in Latin America. Whereas Mexico came to be dominated by Canadian and British firms in electric utilities (with some U.S. firms, especially enclave form companies), that pattern was *not* general for Latin America. Mexico was not the model. Prosperous Argentina, for example, which attracted giant foreign involvements, had a more continuous and far more substantial German presence. The Chilean story is yet another case, with some of the same players; as in Argentina, the German role in Chile was very large. Each Latin American country went through a different course of electrification and had a different mix of foreign involvements.

Similarly, Russia was not the model for Europe, where the pattern of foreign operating companies once again varied by nation. For example, Spain, which also attracted heavy foreign direct investments, represented a separate set of experiences, with many of the same players involved, but with an important Canadian firm not present in Russia. Greek electrification had major French involvements, far greater than in Russia. In Europe, as in Latin America, the forms used by inward foreign investors varied according to each host nation (and also often according to particular cities within the host nation). Within Europe, as in Latin America, the nationality "mix" (Belgian, British, Canadian, French, German, Swiss, and U.S., for the most part) of the foreign ownership and control of the operating companies took on unique characteristics, depending on the host locale, although there were clear, overlapping networks of participants in what were global involvements. Indeed, the tissue of multinational enterprises' relationships with the operating companies in public utilities was not confined to Latin America and Europe.

FINANCE

Thus far, we have concentrated our attention on the various actors involved in foreign direct investments in public utilities in the years before 1914. At the same time, a substantial amount of international investment did not carry ownership and control – that is, it was purely financial. Some of it dovetailed with the direct investments, for frequently direct investors in this capital-intensive sector sought outside financing for their projects. Lance Davis and Robert Gallman note that between 1906 and 1914 the capital flows from the United Kingdom into Canada (measured by calls on capital) that went to electric light and power companies included Vancouver Power, Calgary Power, Cascade Water Power, and a number of others, with the largest single light and power company recipient, Toronto Power, with sixteen calls that totaled $10 million. Of the light and power companies listed by Davis and Gallman, only one was a British direct investment (Vancouver Power being a subsidiary of British Columbia Electric Power).[195]

The Canadian-registered companies that operated in Latin America also drew on British portfolio investors: Bonds were floated in London and often sold elsewhere as well. A report issued by Dominion Securities Corporation, Toronto, found that bonds issued by these Canadian-registered corporations, 1909 through 1913, came to $120.5 million, of which only $7.2 million were taken up in Canada.[196] While typically Canadians went to British capital markets, this was not always the case. When the Toronto group set up a free standing company in Spain in 1911 – the Barcelona Traction, Light and Power Company Ltd. – the distribution of the bonds was divided one-third Belgium and France, one-third England, and one-third Canada.[197] We must beware of "double counting." When there was a direct investor running the show, as in this Spanish example, we should identify the corporate structure and consider the entire investment as owned and controlled by the direct investor. Swiss and Belgian holding company structures also contributed greatly to the abilities of operating firms to use international capital markets. As in the Canadian cases, the security of a "metropolitan" country head office provided the means for tapping capital markets beyond those within the headquarters' country.

The direct investments of British free standing companies achieved the same goal. Thus, the Lima Light, Power and Tramways Co. – formed in 1910 as a British free standing company and designed to acquire and merge a number of existing utilities in Lima, Peru – was able, because of this British corporate structure, to raise substantial funds through capital markets. The British banking house J. Henry Schröder & Co. sponsored an issue of £1.2 million debentures for Lima Light (known in Peru as Empresas Eléctricas Asociadas). The issue was offered by Schröder in London and by Schröder Gebrüder in Hamburg; the bonds were also made available in Belgium and Switzerland.[198]

Belgium, Canada, and Switzerland – key locales for holding companies and registered companies – did not have "deep" stock markets in these years. Domestic and foreign entrepreneurs, however, were able to take the operating companies directly (in the Canadian case) and through the holding company structures (in the Belgian and Swiss cases) to more robust securities markets. As indicated earlier, an important reason Credit Suisse provided the president for Elektrobank lay in the ability of the Swiss to tap French and English capital markets. The Belgians used mostly French capital, as well as mobilizing capital in many other countries where they had investments.[199] In short, the companies registered in these countries could draw on the capital surpluses in England, France, and Germany. Before 1914, the London stock market was a truly international market, while those on the continent were international to a lesser, but important, extent. The availability of securities markets for purely financial transactions aided both multinational enterprises and purely domestic firms. Multinational enterprises through the various business groups could retain control, while obtaining funds from numerous share and bond holders.

Aside from the very early years, there was minimal inward foreign direct investment in U.S. electric utilities; by contrast, the foreign financial participation in U.S. utilities was far from trivial. Cleona Lewis records that Cities Service, St. Lawrence Power (Massena, New York), American Water Works and Electric, Consolidated Gas & Electric Light & Power of Baltimore, Great Western Power, Middle West Utilities, and Mississippi River Power were among the U.S. utilities listed on one or more European stock exchanges in 1914.[200] The principal investor in Illinois Traction Company was the Canadian Sun Life Assurance Company. As noted earlier, the Canadian-incorporated Alabama Traction Light and Power Company Ltd. gave the critical financial assistance needed for Alabama Power Company. U.S. firms used international financial markets to obtain financing, but the firms' management was American.[201]

The Japanese sought foreign financing. There were no foreign direct investments in the Japanese electric utilities, although there was one project proposed that might have taken that form but that failed to materialize.[202] The Japanese did get some short-term foreign finance, but they were unable to obtain any long-term foreign financing before World War I. Japanese entrepreneurs did, however, move forward with building electric utilities, considerably faster than anywhere else in Asia. Domestic sources provided the basic financing and managerial control.[203]

THE STATUS OF MULTINATIONAL ELECTRICAL INVESTMENTS ON THE EVE OF WORLD WAR I

In the United States, there was inward foreign finance and major utilities (holding and operating companies) that were traded on securities markets abroad. On the other hand, in 1914, by our definition, within the United States there was virtually no inward foreign direct investments.[204] Within the vast American nation, the process of electrification had been accomplished in the major cities. In rural areas and mining camps, isolated plants filled some of the needs, but large numbers of Americans still had no access to electricity. As for outward foreign investments, the electrotechnical giants General Electric and Westinghouse were global, although their involvement in electric utilities abroad was limited and mainly in the form of extended manufacturers' satellites.[205] Yet, domestically they had set the basis for the public utilities that would later have lives of their own and vigorously expand. In 1905, General Electric had organized Electric Bond and Share; in time, it, and then its offspring, would assume a major role in international business.[206]

Aside from the extended manufacturers' satellites and some enclave form investments, U.S. business abroad in the electric utilities sector was principally in the areas to which U.S. investment generally "spilled over," that is, in Canada, Mexico, Central America, and the Caribbean islands.[207] In Canada, there were sizable U.S. outward foreign direct investments in electric utilities, while the U.S. foreign direct investment in electrification across America's southern borders existed but was far more limited. Outward foreign finance from the United States for utilities was available, but it was not yet consequential (at least in comparison with what was to come in later years and with what was taking place from Europe or even Canada). The large outward financial investment from the United States (which might possibly be classified as an outward foreign direct investment) in the early twentieth century in the London underground (subway) was an exception.[208]

By contrast, by 1914 Canadians were far deeper into internationalization in this sector than were U.S. companies. Not only was there large inward foreign direct investment from the United States (principally in Quebec and Ontario), but there were also inward British foreign direct investments (the largest being in British Columbia).[209] Moreover, over the years Canadians had become very knowledgeable in the electric utilities sector and through various interconnections were well established in Latin America, especially in Mexico and Brazil, where large Canadian free standing companies were very much in evidence. Indeed, by 1914 Canadian investments in Mexico and Brazil had for more than a decade overshadowed the earlier German involvements. (Important Canadian and British direct investments in light and power coexisted in both of these Latin American countries.) And then there was the newer significant activity in Spain.[210] Canadians skillfully intermediated British and continental European portfolio investments. Key Canadian groups depended heavily on the talents of the American engineer Fred Stark Pearson.

Throughout Western Europe, by 1914, there were both outward and inward investments of different sorts in electric light and power. That Britain was the world's leading creditor nation was not, however, reflected in its business abroad in electric utilities, although by 1913 British capital was reported to be interested in some eighty electrical concerns within Latin America.[211] British outward investments took several forms. Britain was the principal country for the registration of free standing companies. The reasons for these British stakes abroad lay in British joint-stock company law, the presence of the London stock market, stockbrokers with special know-how in electrical issues, and investment trusts that would buy these securities. Initiators of British free standing companies in electric utilities worldwide were construction companies (such as S. Pearson & Son), trading companies, engineers, stockbrokers, and the like. There were also important outward British direct investments associated with enclaves, such as those linked with Rio Tinto in Spain or Anglo-Persian in Iran. While there were inward foreign investments in electric utilities in the United Kingdom, by 1913–1914 they were not substantial.[212]

In 1914, German outward investments in electric utilities far exceeded those of the British. The forms were not the same, with many of the German direct investments associated with the strong electrotechnical sector – that is, with AEG and Siemens. The Germans used Swiss, Belgian, and German holding companies to pursue their direct investments. By 1914, Swiss and Belgian holding companies had developed extensive business abroad in public utilities. There were also German direct investments abroad through British free standing companies. The presence of "universal" banks in Germany, Switzerland, Belgium, and Italy was important in financing electrification on the entire European continent. Southern and Eastern European utilities were large recipients of inward direct investments.

While North America and Europe (including countries not mentioned above, such as France) were both homes and hosts to international investments that stimulated the spread of electrification, Latin America, Australia/New Zealand, Asia, and Africa had a far lower level of electrification; moreover, countries in these regions (Japan excepted) were hosts rather than homes to foreign investments. Of these four continents, Latin America attracted the most inward foreign investments in electric utilities, practically all of them direct investments going principally to Argentina, Brazil, and Mexico, although smaller economies in Latin America also were targets for foreign direct investments. In 1914, prosperous Argentina was particularly appealing for foreign investors. Estimates indicate that about one-half of all Argentine capital in 1913 was foreign-owned, probably the highest percentage of any major debtor nation at the time.[213] The investments in electric utilities (light and power companies and tramways) were part of these investments. German investments in this sector predominated in the electrification of Buenos Aires, but there were also British interests, as well as those of other nationalities – Swiss, Belgian, French, and U.S. firms – involved in Argentine electrification. The foreign investments were not only in Buenos Aires, but in Tucumán, Córdoba, Rosario, and other Argentine cities. Peter Hertner estimates that German investment in the Argentine electricity sector (including electrified tramways) amounted to 230 million marks (ca. $55 million) at the outbreak of World War I, a figure that was three to four times higher than the amount the Germans had invested in Italy or Spain, where they had substantial interests. Throughout Latin America, as we have already indicated, countries had different nationality combinations of inward investments in electric utilities; in many nations on this continent, electric utility investments in the early twentieth century had become an attractive sector for foreign investors.[214]

Certain cities in Australia and New Zealand, as we have seen, attracted British free standing companies to tramway, light, and power companies. It was the European, not the Asian, parts of the Ottoman Empire that were being introduced to electricity. As for the rest of Asia, overall inward foreign direct investments were not large, nor was electrification very extensive. Once again, what predominated were British free standing companies in the cities of Bombay, Calcutta, and Delhi (in India); Colombo (Ceylon); Hong Kong and Shanghai (the latter for tramway only); and in Singapore. There also were some enclave-type investments. In Chinese port cities, Belgian, British, French, German, and Japanese companies provided some electric power, especially for tramways, and Sofina had investments in Thailand.[215] The Japanese direct investments in Chinese electrification were in the main associated with the South Manchuria Railway from 1906 onward. In addition, Japanese direct investors had interests in electric utilities in the Japanese colonies of Korea and Taiwan.[216] For most of the African continent, there was no electrification, except in South Africa and in North Africa, where there were inward foreign direct investments and in coastal cities in the rest of Africa, where colonial administrators might have generators (isolated plants). There was a British free standing electric light and power company in Nairobi, British East Africa (Kenya).[217] There was some electrification embedded within enclaves; Belgian investors had barely started electrification in the Congo. In Latin America, Oceania, Asia, and Africa, often electrification was associated with mining or oil operations (and to a lesser extent agricultural ventures) – developed by companies from Britain, continental Europe, and the United States.

In short, by the eve of the First World War in 1914, foreign investors had spread electrification on a vast, global, but very uneven scale. Domestic and international investments had reached the point that some electrification was present in every large city in the world. This did not mean, by any stretch of the imagination, that every household in these cities had electricity. Indeed, in 1912 less than 25 percent of nonfarm dwellings *in the United States* had electrical service.[218] Thus, the world of 1914 was still very far from the contemporary one, where electricity is taken for granted as ubiquitous – at least *expected* to be ubiquitous. Nonetheless, by the summer of 1914 every large-city dweller around the world was familiar with electric lights at the very minimum and possibly also electric tramways. All parts of a city might not have access to electricity, but all large cities had at least the rudiments of electricity and often more. For instance, large European and North American cities had more, as did some Latin American urban areas. In Barcelona, Buenos Aires, Cairo, Constantinople (Istanbul), Mexico City, Moscow, and Petrograd (St. Petersburg), foreign-owned companies provided virtually all the electric lights and electric power. The process of global electrification was underway, spurred by multinational enterprise and the availability of international finance.

4

War, the First Nationalization, Restructuring, and Renewal, 1914–1929

"Civilization has broken down, and there is the most absolute derangement of a great part of our affairs," wrote Frank A. Vanderlip, President of National City Bank, on August 4, 1914. World War I had just begun. Great Britain, France, and Russia (the Entente) were on one side with Germany and Austria-Hungary (the Central Powers) on the other. The major stock markets had stopped functioning. International business and international finance were in total disarray.[1]

The war was a turning point in the evolution of global electrification. Even though the United States did not enter the war until April 1917, the country, its businesses, and its banks were immediately affected. From 1914 to the armistice in 1918 (and the German acknowledgment of defeat), many changes had profound consequences for globalization and for the role of multinational enterprises and international finance in the electrification sector. This introduction briefly lists the key changes, taking the story line to roughly 1923–1925, when, as the problems germane to the immediate postwar years seemed to be straightened out, ambitious plans could – and did – unfold.

1. During the war years, everywhere a new nationalism arose, and with it increased government intervention, including in the electricity supply industry. Government spending soared as the nations at war needed to finance their military forces. Taxes mounted and for the first time started to impact the organization and plans of modern business. War brought government-induced restrictions on trade and international capital movements. Britain suspended the gold standard, as did most other countries (whether the United States did

Authors: Mira Wilkins, William Hausman, Jonathan Coopersmith, Peter Hertner, Pierre Lanthier, and Luciano Segreto.

is controversial).[2] The precedent for later large governmental participation in economies was set.

2. The Russian Revolution occurred. Whereas before the war 90 percent of the Russian light and power supplies were foreign-owned and -controlled, that came to an abrupt end.
3. The German defeat devastated that nation. As we have seen in Chapter 3, German businessmen were deeply involved in multinational enterprises and the financing of global electrification.
4. The collapse of the Russian, German, Austro-Hungarian and Ottoman empires led to new political boundaries in the postwar years with substantial repercussions on multinational enterprises and international finance, particularly in the electric utility sector.
5. Great Britain was the great creditor nation before World War I, and British companies and British finance had assisted in the spread of electrification. That Britain could not remain on the gold standard during the war meant that it was no longer the pillar of international finance. Its strategic position in the world economy, already being challenged before the war by the United States and Germany, deteriorated relative to the United States. Germany, by contrast, came out of the war "a loser" in every way.
6. Although Canada joined its mother country in the wartime effort, the war years pushed it economically closer to the United States, setting the stage for the future.
7. The United States came of age in the war years, catapulting forward as the world's economically strongest nation. Because it was neutral from the summer of 1914 to the spring of 1917, its business leaders were able to move into markets once dominated by Europeans (principally the British and the Germans). Before the war, the United States had already ranked as the world's leading industrial nation, including a strong electrotechnical sector; but in finance, Britain had been supreme. Indeed, prior to 1914, the United States had been a debtor nation in world accounts. By 1918, it emerged as a key creditor nation.

To some extent, these seven topics overlap; they need to be explored to understand how the war and its immediate aftermath significantly shaped the global development of electric light and power. We will begin by covering these topics from 1914 to roughly 1923–1925. Then we will consider the vast spread of electrification from 1923 to 1929, through the formation of enclaves, the new large enterprises linked with power-intensive industries, the revived European plans that stretched beyond that continent, the role of Canadian enterprise, and, finally, in the penultimate section, the unprecedented experiences of U.S. companies and financial intermediaries in providing vast amounts of capital for global electrification.

The concluding section will give a brief overview. In the late 1920s, we will see the proliferation of holding companies as organizational devices for assembling both domestic and international capital, engineering skills, and managerial know-how. Some of these holding companies were by any definition multinational enterprises. Some had minority stakes where the investments were part of the firm's strategy, but there was no attempt to run the venture abroad. We reintroduce the iconoclastic thought presented in Chapter 2 that certain of the holding companies made foreign direct investments (followed strategies as multinational enterprises), but the companies in which they invested were not in any meaningful sense run from abroad.[3]

NATIONALISM, GOVERNMENT ENLARGEMENT, AND THE WARTIME ECONOMIES

The war and its immediate aftermath resulted in a formidable surge in government participation in the electrical business in many countries. National, state, provincial, and municipal governments woke up to the economic and military significance of electric energy as industrial demand to fill wartime needs soared. The war disrupted prewar flows of fuel, equipment, and people across borders, causing shortages and bottlenecks. In numerous countries, the growing imbalance between supply and demand stimulated inflation, raising costs for utilities and curbing the construction of new facilities. Obtaining adequate fuel and producing electric energy more efficiently became important priorities, not just at the local level, but increasingly at the regional and, in some countries, national levels. Nonetheless, many nations saw the construction of new electricity supply facilities. These wartime investments had payoffs for the years to come. For example, the great expansion in the energy-intensive aluminum industry, a private-sector activity, resulted in heavy calls for electricity. Likewise, demands for nitrates for explosives and fertilizers focused attention on electrochemical processes and the need for more electricity generation.

During the war, government engagements in the electricity supply sector occurred on several levels:

- Creating new institutions to understand and handle electric power shortages. Usually these governmental bodies were part of larger agencies for industrial mobilization (such as the British Ministry of Munitions, set up in 1915).
- Establishing the magnitude of the problems by surveying generation, transmission, and consumption patterns. These pioneer government-sponsored surveys of electrical use formed the initial comprehensive studies.

- Setting priorities of users to allocate limited amounts of electric energy. This was a significant expansion of state jurisdiction.
- Closing the power plants of factories and connecting them to central stations for more efficient use of fuel. Firms were often wary of giving up their assured role in return for the promise of utility-generated electricity (creating inherent conflicts between the state and private suppliers of electricity).
- Interconnecting previously separated electrical grids to raise overall efficiency or send surplus electricity to another area. This was a quick, low-cost way of increasing available electric energy.
- Promoting development of local or domestic fuel supplies instead of imported or distant fuels. In a number of countries, this meant the use of hydroelectric power; and because many of these sites were located far away from the consumption centers, it was necessary to install sizable transmission networks. Another approach was the construction of large thermal power stations generating inexpensive electricity through improved steam turbines with low-quality "color coals" as fuel and sent by high-voltage transmission lines to distant points of consumption.
- Providing tax incentives to electricity supply companies in some countries.

These new roles, all sizable enlargements in the prerogatives, interest, and knowledge of national governments, were directly spurred by the demands of the war. National security was a powerful reason to do what previously could not be done. The results were greater electrification during the war years and certainly afterward.

Obviously, the war's combatants were the most affected by the war. Frequent fuel shortages created serious problems. For instance, St. Petersburg lost access to British smokeless Cardiff coal, which its utility boilers had been designed for, forcing engineers to find substitute fuels for the city. Imports of coal to northern German ports also stopped, compelling the creation of new internal flows of coal from the Ruhr and Silesia to feed war industries. Wartime shortages of coal and oil raised their prices, accelerating development of hydro power in France, Italy, Japan, Norway, and Sweden, which stimulated greater government involvement in electrification in each country.[4]

The growing gap between supply and demand of electric power stoked the fires of inflation. Coupled with the uncertainty about whether postwar demand would continue at the same high level, utilities were understandably leery about adding expensive capacity that might soon become surplus. Governments gave direct assistance for expanding capacity that was considered essential. Thus, the British Ministry of Munitions provided

£3.15 million of the £23 million (almost 14 percent) in capital expenditures for power stations and transmission during the war.[5] In the United States, the army and navy paid for some improvements in the Pittsburgh and New York industrial areas, respectively, while the War Finance Corporation advanced $41 million to utilities. As in many sectors within the U.S. economy, the government's role was greatly enlarged.[6] In both the United States and Germany governments developed synthetic nitrates, which required energy-intensive processes.[7]

War fostered the formation of new state agencies to solve electricity crises, and these agencies had lives of their own. Unsurprisingly, the people involved tried to expand their horizons to shape postwar electrification as well. In Britain, the Ministry of Munitions created a Department of Electric Power Supply in June 1916. Major tasks were coordinating the role of electric power within the ministry, establishing priorities for supply, encouraging munitions factories to electrify for more efficient fuel use, and in other ways promoting the rational use of a limited resource.[8] The government proved to be reluctant to retreat from its involvements after the war.

Prior to the war, industrial leaders from Buffalo, New York, had financed the development of Ontario Power Co., which was acquired in 1917 by the newly formed Hydro-Electric Power Commission of Ontario (a body owned by a group of Ontario municipalities and designed to provide cheap power to the municipalities). The properties moved from foreign ownership to local government ownership and control. Because of the nature of the charter, the Canadian subsidiary of Niagara Falls Power Company, Canadian Niagara Power Company Ltd., situated nearby, remained U.S.-owned.[9] Other key foreign investments in electric power in Canada (the American ones in Shawinigan Water and Power and the British ones in the British Columbia Electric Railway) were sustained during the war, although regulation increased.[10] But James Duke, with his big plans for Saguenay's development in Canada, found his project stymied because, as historian David Massell concluded, "business and government failed to reach accord on the industrial use of Lake St. John within the time frame dictated by wartime power needs."[11] The "government" involved in this case was not the Canadian federal government, but that of the province of Quebec. For six years, Duke's project was dormant. Indeed, it was provincial governments in Ontario and Quebec that expanded state activities. In Canada, as in Europe and the United States, governments were playing a larger role.

The war, as engineers insisted, demonstrated the "necessity of organization and rational utilization" of all resources.[12] This lesson would not be forgotten, as engineers and government officials tried to make the nation, or a region within the nation, and not merely the city the basic unit for postwar development.[13] At the war's end, many governments, backed by electrical engineers and industrial leaders, were convinced that electrification was too important to be left to the private market (domestic or foreign) or to local governments. The need to look at electrification from a regional or national level, its importance as a vital economic resource, and its insatiable demand for funding would make electrification a continuing object of state interest long after the last shells were fired.[14]

In a number of cases, nationalism reflected itself in antiforeign measures. In 1920, in the immediate aftermath of the war, the United States set up for the first time a Federal Power Commission (FPC). The legislation (the Federal Water Power Act) had a clause restricting licenses to build facilities at federally controlled water sites to "citizens of the United States … or to any corporation organized under the laws of the United States or any State thereof." This act was part of a collection of postwar U.S. nationalistic measures, but unlike others that impacted inward foreign investment negatively, this one proved to be more symbolic than effective, for it allowed licenses to corporations organized under U.S. or state laws (and said nothing about the ownership or the board of directors of those corporations).[15] Yet this kind of legislation was indicative of comparable measures in other countries that appeared to reserve the development of waterpower resources to their nationals.

"Nationalism," moreover, did not require the exercise of *national* state authority; it might mean a domestication on a subnational basis. In Canada, provinces, particularly Ontario, took the initiative. In 1919, British Electric Traction Co. sold its affiliate Auckland Electric Tramways Co. Ltd. (New Zealand) to the City of Auckland.[16] In Australia in 1920, the State Electricity Commission of Victoria acquired two large power stations from the English-registered Melbourne Electric Supply Co. Ltd.; these then became public-sector activities.[17] Similar transfers from private sector/ foreign to the public sector/domestic occurred in other parts of the world.

On the whole, however, the commitments during the war years to enhanced governmental participation in general, and particularly in the electric utility sector, would in most countries begin to dissipate (but not by any means disappear) in the war's aftermath, especially after the sharp international 1921 downturn and as recovery took place. Yet the precedent remained, although for most of the rest of the 1920s, with some marked exceptions, there was a renewed openness to new private-sector activities on a global scale.

A crucial impact of the war was the rise in taxes, although there were certain tax incentives to the electricity supply industries. The expansion of government meant the need for greater tax revenues, which in turn often necessitated companies' restructuring of the conduits for international investments. This was particularly true in relation to British overseas investments. Thus, the Bombay Electric Supply and Tramways Company Ltd. was run from England and operated in British currency until 1916, "when management and currency operations shifted to India for tax reasons."[18] Whether tax was the only consideration, and whether *management* actually shifted for "tax reasons," is not entirely clear. During the First World War and subsequently, colonial India developed more independence in its policies, and the Colonial Government of India often wanted to set its agenda separate from that of the mother country. Moreover, while the Bombay company shifted to a local currency and seems to have become domesticated, other British electricity supply companies in India remained U.K.-registered. This was the case, for example, of the large Calcutta Electric Supply Corporation Ltd. On the other hand, elsewhere in the empire, in 1922 the new company Hong Kong Tramways Ltd., with registered offices in Hong Kong, would replace the formerly London-registered Hong Kong Tramway Ltd.[19] Taxes during the 1920s would have immense impact on the structure of British overseas investments.

THE RUSSIAN SHOCK

If in many countries during the war years nationalism and government activities took on new importance, nowhere was this more evident than in Russia, and here there would be only a very limited retreat in the postwar years from the commitment to government direction and ownership (a retreat that did not involve the provision of electricity). When the war began, takeovers of enemy German properties in Russia occurred early, first undertaken by city councils, then by tsarist officials, although they trailed by many months.[20] The councils acted from patriotic motives and to legitimate or accelerate previous plans for municipalization. The steps by tsarist officials were in keeping with the expanded government role, but ultimately that did not matter, for after the Russian Revolution all foreign properties were nationalized. The Russian Revolution marked the first case, worldwide, of comprehensive expropriation. Private-sector investments, domestic and foreign, in the electrical industry came to an abrupt halt. This was consequential because the substantial prewar development of electric utilities in Russia had been dominated by foreign, particularly German, capital. There was no opportunity for other foreign investors to replace the German role, because the revolution ended all foreign direct investment and foreign lending to the electric utility sector. From a foreign investment standpoint, electric light and power suppliers became domesticated.[21] The "first nationalization" in the title of this chapter refers to the dramatic happenings in a country where once foreign investors had owned and controlled the principal suppliers of electricity.

TAKEOVERS OF GERMAN ASSETS, RESPONSES, PROTECTIVE MEASURES, AND CHANGES

Although some German properties had been seized in Russia even before the revolution, in general it was unacceptable to belligerents to allow enemy ownership. Thus, national governments helped themselves to enemy assets located within their frontiers.[22] This was true in both England and the United States (after the U.S. entry as a combatant), although the German investments in electric utilities in both countries had been small, which was not the case elsewhere. Sometimes there was a cutting through "corporate veils" to attempt to figure out what was really enemy-owned. Subsequently, in many instances the victors would sell confiscated assets to nationals of their own country. The takeovers of enemy properties occurred at different speeds – on occasion not until after the war was over. Because German businesses had had major investments in electric utilities around the world, the disposition of these properties had significant postwar implications. At war's end, the Treaty of Versailles seemed to ratify the sequestration of German properties. Moreover, the treaty required heavy reparation payments by Germany. Defeat in the war profoundly influenced German business and finance in subsequent years.

Siemens historian Wilfried Feldenkirchen writes that the shares of that firm's British affiliate, Siemens Brothers & Co. Ltd., with its Woolwich factory, were acquired by British shareholders (after expropriation), while Siemens Brothers Dynamo Works Ltd., with its Stafford factory, was sold to the newly formed English Electric Co. Both of these were manufacturing interests, not those in electric utilities. All the extensive Russian interests of Siemens were confiscated after the revolution. In France, Italy, and Belgium, in particular, Siemens "suffered considerable losses." As Feldenkirchen put it, "[A]s a result of the First World War, Siemens had lost almost all its foreign manufacturing facilities ...."[23] Siemens also lost interests that it had in public utilities on the European continent, in Latin America, and in Africa. It was the same story with Allgemeine Elektrizitäts Gesellschaft (AEG), the international business of which was shattered. Yet in 1919, with the war barely over, Siemens resolved to set up new distribution companies and manufacturing facilities abroad. As early as 1921, through Siemens-Bauunion, its construction subsidiary, Siemens won a major contract to build a giant Shannon, Ireland, hydroelectric plant. Siemens made no investment in the utility, however, which came to be crucial in the electrification of Ireland.[24]

There had been sizable prewar German direct investments in Italy in electric utilities, controlling some 17 percent of the capital invested in this sector. Italy entered the war in May 1915, first as an enemy of Austria-Hungary and then, in August 1916, it declared war against Germany. The German investments in electric utilities did not survive into peacetime, for Italy took them over.[25] Other foreign (especially U.S.) investors would come to play a sizable role in assisting the development of Italy's electricity supply sector. Many of the German investments in Italy had been through Swiss holding companies. (Switzerland remained neutral throughout the war.) The Swiss holding companies' investments were not taken over and indeed would grow as some of the confiscated German assets migrated to Swiss ownership and control.[26]

At the start of the war, Germany had overrun Belgium, and the Belgians hated the Germans. Dannie Heineman, who represented German (AEG) interests in Société Financière de Transports et d'Entreprises Industrielles (Sofina), stayed in Brussels during the war, "careful to keep his distance from the German occupiers." At war's end, Heineman was forced to resign from his position in Sofina, but after a brief interlude the Belgians permitted him to return as the key administrator in the formerly German-controlled Belgian holding company. His activities in Belgian war relief boded well for him. The nationalistic Belgian banks had been responsible for insisting that Heineman step down from his presidency of Sofina; he "lost his mandates on the boards of the Belgian electrical companies." Then, Maurice Despret, president of the Banque de Bruxelles, which had become an important shareholder in Sofina, helped Heineman to reclaim his leadership. Despret, however, became president of Sofina; on his return, Heineman did not hold that title. Nonetheless, it was under Heineman's direction during the 1920s that Sofina would assume an even larger significance in the international financing and development of electric utilities.[27]

Spain was neutral throughout the war. Spanish tramways and electric utilities had long attracted foreign multinational enterprises, although at the start of World War I, as in Italy, German interests were less than they had been in prior years and, in the Spanish case, nearly all German investments were through Swiss or Belgian holding companies (principally Elektrobank or Sofina).[28] Because Germany was not an enemy of Spain, no attempts were made to take over the remaining German properties. When the German army moved into Belgium, however, Alfred Loewenstein, who had been active in the Canadian-registered Barcelona Traction, Light and Power Co. (BTLP), fled to England, where he remained for the duration of the war.[29] With BTLP's ambitious plans, its multinational financial structure, and the Canadian group's key London broker (Dunn, Fischer & Co.) in difficulty, BTLP went into bankruptcy on December 31, 1914.[30] The bankruptcy notwithstanding, BTLP, through its subsidiary Ebro Irrigation and Power Co., developed during the war years an integrated hydroelectric system and electrified the transportation system for Barcelona and the Catalan region.[31] Canadian born, but a British resident, Edward Peacock took over the reorganization of BTLP.[32] Ultimately, Spanish capital would substitute for some of the foreign debt, but as Peter Hertner and H. V. Nelles insist, foreign control was not replaced.[33] The Talarn dam (on the Noguera Pallaresa River, near Lleida, Catalonia), then the tallest in Europe, was begun in 1913 and completed in 1916.[34]

Fred Stark Pearson, the American principal engineer-promoter of the Barcelona project, did not live to see the dam in operation. Pearson, who was so important in the many Canadian entrepreneurial ventures in Brazil, Mexico, and Spain, died in 1915 with the sinking of the *Lusitania*. Nevertheless, his New York firm, Pearson Engineering, continued to take part in Canadian ventures abroad, including BTLP.[35] Loewenstein, from his London outpost, kept involved and soon took on a more instrumental role in BTLP, as well as in other Canadian ventures. In 1917, Morgan Grenfell, London, advised Morgan in New York: "We see no harm in ordinary Banking transactions with this gentlemen."[36] Loewenstein would figure as a "market operator" during the 1920s, deeply involved in electrification ventures.[37]

BTLP emerged from the war a strong company, and in 1920 it merged with Energía Eléctrica de Cataluña. (In 1913, BTLP had already acquired control of this one-time French direct investment.)[38] While BTLP maintained its Canadian-registered office, Belgian interests – those of the now truly Belgian Sofina as well as Loewenstein – would vie for its leadership.[39] By 1922, BTLP was able to obtain its peak efficiency. From that point on, it produced sufficient energy to support the industrialization of the Catalonian region of Spain.[40] From the war years to 1922–1923, the Germans were very much in the background and not directly involved.

Indeed, overall, German businessmen and bankers at war's end recognized that "any investment of German capital outside Germany must, for political reasons, be handled with utmost caution, inasmuch as the Allies would be quick to point out that, if Germany can find foreign exchange for foreign investment, she should also be able to do so to meet her reparations bill."[41] In July 1920, an AEG representative told Hugo Hirst of the General Electric Company Ltd., London (the British manufacturing firm that had no relationship with the U.S. General Electric) that "they [AEG] were not yet out for a world policy again, because they needed time to recover their credit and to develop hydroelectricity within Germany to balance the postwar German coal shortage."[42]

The British had not been competitive in the electrotechnical industry before the war and worried about German recovery. Within Britain, new attention was paid to manufacturing, and it was thought that perhaps Britain would be able to build on what foreign investors had established. Not only would British owners take over the German (Siemens) factories, but British interests (associated with Dudley Docker) also bought the American Westinghouse plant in the United Kingdom. English Electric was formed to acquire Siemens's Stafford factory in England, and Metropolitan Vickers became the new owner of the Westinghouse facility.[43] Although the British hoped to be able to take advantage of Germany's reduced role, it proved to be an idle aspiration.

In 1919–1920, Deutsche Bank decided it was imperative to sell Deutsch-Überseeische Elektrizitäts-Gesellschaft (DUEG), the German-controlled giant Argentine electric utility, known in Argentina as CATE (Compañía Alemana Transatlántica de Electricidad). This sale was not forced by the Allies, but rather occurred because of German capital shortages, the Mark's depreciation, and Deutsche Bank's anxieties related to German reparation obligations. Argentina – like Chile, Colombia, Mexico, Paraguay, Spain, and Venezuela – had stayed neutral during World War I.[44] In Central America and the Caribbean, after the United States entered the war, Costa Rica, Cuba, Guatemala, Haiti, Honduras, Nicaragua, and Panama all declared on the side of the Allies. In South America, only Brazil joined the Allies (in 1917). Although Bolivia, Ecuador, Peru, and Uruguay did not become combatants, they eventually severed diplomatic relations with the Central Powers.[45] Argentina, however, had the largest German investments in all of Latin America, and it was the most prosperous before the war of all the nations in that region. Three specific reasons motivated the Deutsche Bank's postwar decision to sell DUEG: (1) the Bank no longer had "the capital necessary to invest in the amounts and with flexibility required for the company to perform effectively"; (2) "the shares of DUEG were denominated in Marks, and the depreciation of the Mark meant that foreign shareholders, especially the Swiss [including the Swiss holding company Elektrobank], who were heavily invested in the company, were receiving no dividend and were holding a depreciating asset"; and while the wartime and postwar Swiss and German ties stayed close, other foreigners were now taking advantage of the depreciated Mark to buy shares in DUEG (the Germans believed that by early 1920 almost 50 percent of the shares were in foreign hands); and (3) there was a fear that the German shares might be seized for reparations. The Germans sought to locate a friendly buyer for these large assets. Deutsche Bank officials considered the Swiss, but they decided that the latter's capital markets were "overstrained and not of sufficient size"; moreover, the Swiss were under pressure from the Allies not "to rescue" the Germans. Finally, there was a better alternative.

In 1920, a Spanish banking consortium (including the influential private bank Banco Urquijo) made the purchase. A new parent company emerged, Compañía Hispano-Americana de Electricidad (CHADE), and overnight it became Spain's largest multinational enterprise.[46] It acquired DUEG's huge Argentine investments, some smaller ones in Chile, and an electric tramway operation in Uruguay.[47] The transaction was arranged and structured by none other than Heineman, at the time temporarily expelled from his Belgian role in Sofina. When CHADE was organized in 1920, the Spanish banks and Heineman promised the German electrical manufacturers that they "would be entitled to 50 per cent of all contracts for CHADE projects if their prices were competitive, and that Germans could reappear on the supervisory board in due course."[48] Soon Sofina and Heineman would be active in CHADE (as well as in BTLP).

Meanwhile, German interests in the Swiss holding companies were reduced. Before the war, Elektrobank and Indelec had been intermediaries for AEG and Siemens, respectively. After the armistice, with the depreciating Mark, these Swiss holding companies, which had large interests in Germany, went through crises. By 1920–1921, they, along with other Swiss firms, were in financial difficulty.[49] Elektrobank collapsed and had to be reorganized.[50] Indelec was particularly hard hit by the expropriations during the Russian Revolution. The Swiss holding companies with German origins tried to detach themselves from their former parents and in the process became dominated by Swiss banks. Whereas before the war Swiss leadership had been present, now Elektrobank and Indelec came under the direct management of large Swiss banks – Credit Suisse and Basler Handelsbank, respectively.[51] Serge Paquier writes that only after the defeat of the Central Powers in November 1918 did Elektrobank and Indelec become genuinely Swiss. At the same time, the holding companies retained their prewar linkages, even if informal and even if the German equity interests were in a minority.[52] A Credit Suisse representative was on the board of CHADE, the Spanish company that acquired the former German assets in Argentina.[53] As earlier noted, many of the German assets in Italy moved to Swiss holding companies.

Motor für Angewandte Elektrizität (Motor), Zurich, which was allied with the Swiss manufacturer Brown, Boveri, had its main investments in Switzerland and neighboring France, Germany, and Italy. During the war years, it recognized the need for connected systems within Switzerland and with the adjacent countries. In the immediate postwar turmoil, like Elektrobank and Indelec, Motor faced serious financial troubles and found its resources strained. Brown, Boveri's other holding company (jointly owned with Italian interests), Columbus AG für Elektrische Unternehmungen, had its principal interests in South America and did much better than Motor. During and after the war, Columbus had expanded in Argentina. Indeed, its Argentine affiliate Compañía Italo-Argentina de Electricidad (CIAE, or Italo-Argentina) – having completed a central power station in 1916 and electrified important districts in Buenos Aires – offered some competition to the giant Compañía Alemana Transatlántica de Electricidad (DUEG/CATE) and in the postwar era to CHADE. Columbus, owing to its profitable Argentine business, did not pass through the postwar trauma that Motor and most of the Swiss *elektrizitäts-trusts* faced. In November 1923, the two Brown, Boveri affiliates, Motor and Columbus, merged, forming Motor-Columbus.[54]

German interests in France ended with World War I. German shareholding in the French holding company Société Centrale pour l'Industrie Électrique (SCIE), for example, ceased, but the Swiss and Belgian bank-dominated holdings of Elektrobank and Sofina kept their stakes in France.[55] When the capital of SCIE was raised in 1920, the French banks Banque des Pays du Nord and Banque Impériale Ottomane became shareholders, as did a Spanish banking group associated with CHADE (including Banco Urquijo). SCIE had had interests in Turkish utilities before World War I and in 1921 made investments in CHADE. If the intertwinings of financial connections had been complex before World War I, they would become ever more tangled in the 1920s. Companies were frequently cross-investors – that is, a parent invested in a "daughter company" *and* vice versa. For example, Sofina maintained in the postwar years its prewar investment in SCIE; in 1923–1925, SCIE invested in Sofina. A labyrinth of business groups spanned political boundaries.[56]

Around the world – not only in the countries considered above, but in Chile, Eastern Europe, Finland, South Africa, Turkey, and throughout the countries in the Caribbean – the effects of the war on German interests were profound, with prewar German interests in electric utilities replaced by foreign capital intermediated by companies domiciled in the homelands of the victors, in countries that had been neutral, or in countries that had been occupied by Germany (namely Belgium). Alternatively, German interests were sometimes replaced by governments, principally local government-owned utilities. In the new configurations, however, the one-time principally German-dominated holding companies in Belgium (Sofina) and Switzerland (Elektrobank and Indelec) stayed on (the latter surviving the debilitating 1920–1921 crisis); the much lessened German influence was backstage.

NEW POLITICAL BOUNDARIES: THE END TO THE RUSSIAN, GERMAN, AUSTRO-HUNGARIAN, AND OTTOMAN EMPIRES

The war's end saw a redrawing of maps, with new countries carved out of the former Russian, German, Austro-Hungarian, and Ottoman empires. The newborn nations faced formidable problems in developing appropriate political and economic institutions and in dealing with the rampant inflation that followed the war. The countries were all capital short, and because electric utilities were capital-intensive, it was not surprising that foreign investments were sought. Indeed, when the new countries had been part of empires, foreign (particularly German) involvements in their light and power facilities already had a presence in varying amounts. Finland, for example, which achieved independence in 1917 from the former Russian empire, during the war sequestered the German investments in its territory. After the Peace of Brest-Litovsk (March 1918), unlike in the many nations that never returned enemy assets, the confiscated properties in Finland reverted to German ownership. Within Finland, however, there was an eagerness to municipalize utilities, and AEG, which had controlled the properties prior to the war, readily negotiated. AEG transferred three of its four major power facilities immediately after the war to Finnish municipalities (with appropriate compensation). The town council in Viipuri did not accept the terms of AEG's tender, so the fourth power station stayed in AEG's possession.[57] That AEG was not reluctant to sell its utilities to town councils was in line with the Germans' shortage of capital and linked with German concerns over reparation demands (the same factors motivating German strategies vis-à-vis the transformation of DUEG into CHADE).

New borders meant that Swiss companies found their "German" investments in Alsace were now under a new flag, becoming inward French investments.[58] Often German prewar investments in electric utilities in Eastern Europe had been undertaken through Belgian and Swiss holding companies; these were retained with their German influence sharply reduced. The Swiss Bank Corporation affiliates' investments in electric utilities in Austria-Hungary were now in Austria and in the Kingdom of the Serbs, Croats, and Slovenes (set up December 4, 1918), which became Yugoslavia in October 1929.[59] Certain prewar French investments in the new countries were maintained. Some prewar investments in Eastern European electric utilities of the Gesellschaft für Elektrische Unternehmungen (Gesfürel), a Berlin holding company, appear to have been sustained. Foreign entries into additional eastern European investments did not occur quickly at war's end, because the immediate priority in the new countries lay in creating the basis for sovereign states and foreign (as well as domestic) investors hesitated in undertaking large investments under conditions of great uncertainty. Yet the demand for electricity was there, and firms in Western Europe and the United States were poised to fill the need.

In general, the newly constituted states in Central and Eastern Europe in the immediate aftermath of the war excluded explicit German interests (those few of Gesfürel were exceptional). For example, in Poland, which emerged anew out of the Russian, German, and Austro-Hungarian empires, the prewar German involvements in that territory disappeared entirely, replaced in good part by state enterprises and other foreign interests. Likewise, in the new states in the Middle East the German presence practically vanished. For instance, the sizable prewar German interests in Turkey came to a close, while the French and Belgian ones persisted.

In the aftermath of the collapse of the Ottoman Empire, Greece and Turkey fought a war in 1921–1922. Greece had some small, inefficient providers of electricity, while, as noted in Chapter 3, approximately 50 percent of Greek electricity was furnished by Compagnie Hellénique d'Électricité (ChdE), an affiliate of the French Thomson-Houston (the manufacturer in which General Electric had a minority interest). To surmount the various difficulties that the electricity supply industry faced during World War I and its aftermath, the National Bank of Greece sought additional funding abroad. In 1923, the British government was involved in a Greek refugee loan, and it would become helpful in providing capital for electrification.[60] Indeed, in all these developing nations there was a search for outside money for electrification, but only after 1923–1925 was there much success in finding new funding.

THE BRITISH DILEMMA

During the war and for a few years afterward, as the British had taken over the Siemens properties in Great Britain, they also sought to help themselves to German assets farther afield. Because Britain had been the preeminent creditor nation before World War I and British registration of free standing companies had been a way of raising capital, some German prewar investors had used or maintained British registration as they became owners of the equity of certain free standing companies in electric utilities. For example, Germans had been the principals in the very profitable British-registered Victoria Falls & Transvaal Power Co. Ltd., which operated in South Africa. In the postwar years, these German interests passed to British ownership and control (with the control now linked with British South African mining interests). British registration had opened the way for this takeover.[61]

A similar situation applied in Chile, where the British S. Pearson & Son was successful in replacing large German interests. The prewar activities in electric utilities of the British construction company S. Pearson & Son had been confined to Mexico, where that firm had accumulated substantial expertise. Weetman Pearson (later, Lord Cowdray) had stayed involved in Mexico during the Mexican Revolution, difficulties notwithstanding, combining and further developing existing electric utilities there.[62] Cowdray hired the Canadian Alexander Worswick as his chief engineer. (We have encountered Worswick earlier, in Chapter 3, as encouraging Cowdray to expand his pre–World War I Mexican investments into electric light and power.) In 1920, Worswick reported to the British Pearson group that "there are exceptionally good opportunities for a powerful public utility company in Chile," where there was splendid hydroelectric capacity and where the Germans had been solidly entrenched before the war.[63]

The German-owned Chilean Electric Tramway and Light Company had been registered in the United Kingdom. As with Victoria Falls & Transvaal Power Co., registering a company in a "safe" location had been seen as a form of protection. World War I radically altered that picture. German properties in the United Kingdom and those with British registration that operated overseas were taken over by the British government, which encouraged British capital to replace the German businesses.

This was the case in Chile, even though the country was neutral during the war. Chile was well known to British foreign investors due to the sizable long-standing British mining investments there. The Central Mining and Investment Corporation (CMIC), a British–South African mining group with Chilean interests, turned to S. Pearson & Son, with its experience in electric utilities, to take charge of what the British government had confiscated from the German owners. There had been some earlier connections between CMIC and the British Pearson group. CMIC was formed in 1905 by the big South African mining houses. It has been described as "an ambitious reconstruction by Wernher, Beit"; our readers will recall from Chapter 3 that Wernher, Beit & Co. had participated in Mexican and Chilean tramways.[64] In 1919–1920, the British firms CMIC and S. Pearson & Son put in a successful bid of £1 million, on a 40–60 percent basis, to acquire the former German assets in Chile, once owned by the German-owned Chilean Electric. CHADE, the new Spanish company, tried to buy these Chilean properties from Lord Cowdray, who refused to sell after receiving "strong representations" from the British Foreign Office. CMIC, which had favored the sale to CHADE, sold its minority stake in Chilean Electric to S. Pearson & Son. And in 1920, Chilean Electric merged with Compañía Nacional de Fuerza, a Chilean-owned firm, forming Compañía Chilena de Electricidad (Chilena). The latter continued to expand. In early 1923, CHADE, which had inherited some Chilean assets from DUEG, sold them to Chilena.[65] Thus, British interests substituted for the substantial prewar German stakes in Chile. Chilena, the largest electric power company in Chile, was now controlled by the British Cowdray group.

S. Pearson & Son (the "Cowdray group") had close British government connections. During the war, the Bank of England had "forced" Lazard Frères, New York, to sell its interests in its British house Lazard Brothers & Co. to the Cowdray group. Sir Robert Kindersley – on behalf of that group – took charge of this prominent investment house.[66] Another key figure in Lazard Brothers was Robert Brand.[67] In December 1916, Brand had published a report on "Industry and Finance," which compared British and German banks and, in the praise of the latter, wrote: "There are no first-class financial institutions in London which act as organisers or reorganisers of companies, or which issue on their own responsibility industrial securities .... In a word, there are no financial institutions in London whose aim it is, as it is the aim of the German banks, to act as a kind of general staff to industry."[68] Others in England pointed out that "there was no bank in England of any size that would offer to finance a new proposition of any magnitude [something] of the nature of Victoria Falls [& Transvaal] Power Co., and say 'Here are a couple of million for you in order that this contract may be placed with a British manufacturer.' The Deutsche Bank and their friends did that operation in that way."[69]

The group surrounding Cowdray hoped to rectify this British deficiency and to fill in where the Germans had acted. The British government was sympathetic. In 1919–1922, Cowdray restructured his various businesses, "transforming his organization into a great Investment Trust controlling and directing numerous enterprises at home and abroad." In 1919, his firm set up Whitehall Trust Ltd. as a finance and issuing house; Kindersley was appointed chairman.[70] In addition, S. Pearson & Son had two holding companies for electrical securities: The first, Whitehall Securities Corporation Ltd., had been formed in 1907, but not until 1919 did it become the holding company for S. Pearson & Son's important interests in Mexican utilities. The second, Whitehall Electric Investments Ltd. (organized in 1922), became the holding company for Cowdray's electric utility interests. From a direct-investment standpoint these interests were confined to Mexico and the new Chilean business. S. Pearson & Son had controlling ownership of Whitehall Securities, which in turn controlled Whitehall Electric, which raised funds in Britain for the large projects in electric utilities of the Pearson group; in time, these would extend beyond Mexico and Chile.[71] Whitehall Trust served as trustee for the securities of a number of companies where there appears to have been no direct investment by the Pearson/Cowdray group. In 1921, Brand noted that Lazard Brothers had in the last two years opened branches in Belgium and Spain.[72] Why those nations? Recall our earlier commentary on Sofina, Loewenstein, and CHADE. Belgium and Spain (temporarily) were the new postwar centers of finance *and* management of electrical activities abroad, although obviously Lazard Brothers had broader plans beyond electrification.[73]

In December 1921, the British industrialist-entrepreneur Dudley Docker registered in the United Kingdom the private company Electric and Railway Finance Corporation (Elrafin). Its directors were Docker's son Bernard, Dannie Heineman (Sofina owned part of the capital of Elrafin), and Cowdray's brother, Sir Edward Pearson (representing Whitehall Securities; Whitehall Electric had not yet been formed). Elrafin, run by Docker, was an attempt to create a British industrial bank. Was this to be a bank of the sort Brand envisaged in 1916? What is most interesting about Elrafin are the networks of capital and how interdependent were the British groups. Elrafin and its cluster of firms came to be cross-linked with those on the continent and around the world.[74] Dudley Docker was keen on Britain having its own electrical manufacturing sector; he was deeply involved in Metropolitan Vickers, which as noted had acquired the British Westinghouse factory.

In 1921, in keeping with the view that British finance should support *British* exports, the British parliament passed the first of a series of Trade Facilities Acts. These authorized the British Treasury to guarantee both the principal and the interest on low-interest loans in exchange for the money's being used to purchase British goods. These loan guarantees were often associated with British overseas investments in electric utilities. Thus, for example, the Treasury guaranteed $5\frac{1}{2}$ percent second-mortgage £500,000 debentures for Calcutta Electric Supply Corporation Ltd., a British free standing company.[75]

To enhance the nation's weakened post–World War I global position, the British government retained wartime controls over capital movements for a number of years. The governor of the Bank of England had to be consulted on all foreign securities issues over £1 million, for fear that capital exports would restrict domestic credit and require a rise in the bank rate.[76] But the controls deliberately exempted security issues by British concerns to finance direct investments in other countries (especially those direct investments that would encourage British exports) and in addition left large institutional investors (with their political clout) free to acquire foreign securities issued abroad. Investors could also repurchase securities originally issued in London and held abroad by foreigners.[77] Thus, the capital controls were far from all-inclusive (and would be relaxed to meet conflicting priorities). Historian David Kynaston writes, "[O]ne is struck by the global ubiquity of the City's tentacles during the first half of the 1920s," in spite of the Bank of England's attempt to limit capital outflows so as "to prop up sterling and hasten the return to the gold standard."[78] This was the British dilemma. The British government wanted to restore London's position as the world's greatest financial center; to do so, it felt it needed to return to the gold standard. But returning to the gold standard required government policies antithetical to free international capital markets. Moreover, by 1924 New York City was coming of age as a locale for foreign lending, and this took "some of the strain off London." The British, however, were not very comfortable with the challenge from across the Atlantic.[79]

The British were not alone, of course, in seeking to go back to the gold standard and in retaining capital controls. As Charles Feinstein, Peter Temin, and Gianni Toniolo have written, the attempt to restore "the gold standard dominated the financial policies of Britain, France, Germany, Italy, Belgium, the Scandinavian countries, Czechoslovakia, and many other Central and Eastern European nations" in the period after the war. Yet, nowhere were the problems more fundamental to globalization than in the United Kingdom, for it had been the greatest creditor nation.[80] In addition, Britain wanted to export. Within Britain, there were calls for more attention to be paid to British industry, seen as being sacrificed to finance. Outward foreign investments in electric utilities were caught up in the vigorous debates.

THE ROLE OF CANADIANS

Long before World War I, as we saw in Chapter 3, Canadian groups had developed a specialty in both domestic and international public electric utility finance; these groups' prewar activities in Latin America and Spain had continued through the war and extended into the postwar era. Just as Cowdray's Mexican business had persisted after the downfall of Porfirio Díaz in 1911 and through the war years, so, too, the largest foreign electrical investments in Mexico, those of the Canadian-registered firms – Mexican Tramways Company, Mexican Light and Power Co. (controlled by Mexican Tramways), Monterey Railway, Light & Power Co., Mexican Northern Power Co. (reorganized as Northern Mexican Power and Development Co. in 1919), and the holding company International Light & Power Co. – remained in business, the great unrest within Mexico notwithstanding.[81] Christopher Armstrong and H. V. Nelles tell how the management of Mexican Tramways and Mexican Light coped with the antiforeign rhetoric within Mexico and other adversities.[82]

In Brazil, the Canadian-registered holding company Brazilian Traction, Light and Power Co. (formed in 1912) had been "a creature of the last bull market before the First World War."[83] It was established by the "Canadian" group, made up of the U.S. engineer F. S. Pearson, the Canadian stockbroker who lived in London James Dunn, the Belgian promoter Loewenstein, and the Canadian William Mackenzie. It combined the earlier acquisitions by the Canadians in São Paulo and Rio. Like this group's other, nearly simultaneous promotion, Barcelona Traction, Light and Power (1911), the Brazilian venture had relied on British and continental stock markets for funding.

During the First World War, this large Brazilian enterprise was able to expand, despite such obstacles as the withdrawal of London's participation in its financing. As an alternative, the group had turned to U.S. capital markets (and to the New York issue house W. A. Read & Co.), but the loan proved inadequate. By 1917, Brazilian Traction suspended its dividend, as stockholders "fumed at the realization that steadily rising revenues in Brazil were being used to retire debt and extend the plant," rather than pay out dividends. The depreciation of the Brazilian currency (milreis) meant that earnings in local currency "could not be exchanged for enough pounds to pay the thousands of shareholders in Europe and North America."[84] After U.S. entry into the war, when Brazil joined the Allies, its involvement as a belligerent put it into ever closer relations with the United Kingdom, Canada, and the United States.[85]

Once the war was over, in 1919 the Canadian leadership of Brazilian Traction turned again to London (to Peacock) for a refinancing loan.[86] In 1919, Peacock's City connections notwithstanding, the British were not prepared to authorize new capital outflows to meet Brazilian requirements. Thus, Brazilian Traction appealed to its U.S. friends to renew for another three years the loan earlier issued by W. A. Read & Co. (a firm that would become, in 1921, Dillon, Read & Co., as its senior partner Clarence Dillon put his name in the title).[87] This reliance on the United States was indicative of the new Canadian-U.S. relationships. As far as London (the City) was concerned, as Gaspard Farrer, a director of Barings, put it in 1922, they saw the business ventures of the late F. S. Pearson – Brazilian Traction, Mexican Light and Power, and Barcelona Traction, Light and Power – as "all in the same state of utter impecuniosity [*sic*]. ..." And Farrer added, Peacock "has brought them through in a wonderful way."[88] In the early 1920s, as Great Britain struggled to resume the gold standard, it was unable to accommodate all the calls for capital from abroad.

Indicative of the new Canadian-U.S. relationships are data on all foreign capital going *into* Canada. The Dominion of Canada was both an exporter and an importer of capital. Before the war, British investments in Canada far exceeded those from the United States ($1.86 billion vs. $417 million). In 1923, British investments were slightly larger than before the war, while

U.S. investments had soared past those of the British ($1.89 billion vs. $2.42 billion).[89] These general figures were reflected in British and U.S. investments in electrification. Thus, even though some inward investments into Canada's electricity supply industry were reduced as regional governmental bodies took over, that decline was more than compensated for by the further increase in U.S. direct and portfolio stakes in this sector (the pie grew as the percentage of government holdings rose).

THE COMING OF AGE OF THE UNITED STATES

Out of World War I came a dramatic role for the United States and American business. Its businesses would not only be deeply involved in outward foreign direct investments, but Americans became leading players in global finance. The New York Stock Exchange was transformed from an essentially domestic body to one newly engaged in major international transactions. In electric utilities, both U.S. foreign direct investments and U.S. finance took on immense importance in the 1920s. The wartime transformation of the United States from debtor to creditor nation set the stage.

In 1917, when the British firm Metropolitan Carriage, Wagon and Finance Co. Ltd. desired to buy the American Westinghouse's properties in Great Britain, the latter agreed to sell. Westinghouse's giant factory in Manchester had never been a financial success. Subsequently, the American Westinghouse also divested its French and Italian manufacturing businesses. These retreats were, however, unusual and only partial, for Westinghouse took part in international business, mainly through exports and a network of licensing agreements (and by the very end of the 1920s, it would renew its international investments). In the early 1920s, however, it was not prominent in the international electric utilities field. By contrast, the opposite was true of its rival General Electric, which steadily expanded its multinational business activities in sales, manufacturing, and public utilities.[90] GE's affiliate Electric Bond and Share Company substantially enlarged its electric utilities investments abroad, including replacing German interests in Latin America.

World War I made the U.S. government nervous over German investments near the Panama Canal. General Electric had organized Electric Bond and Share in 1905. GE's strategy had been to combine domestic (U.S.) operating utilities under a single umbrella in a unit large enough to raise money in American capital markets; it would supply management and technical expertise to the constituent companies, resulting in more efficient operations. The learning experiences developed in the United States could be employed in its foreign direct investments. Electric Bond and Share's pre–World War I foreign investments had been very limited. In 1917, encouraged by the U.S. State Department, Electric Bond and Share made its first significant foreign direct investments, deploying its talents, sharpened in the domestic market, and acquiring the electric systems in Panama City and Colon, Panama. Its next foreign direct investment was in 1920 in Guatemala, where it purchased from the Guatemalan government the formerly German-owned electric company that Guatemala had seized as enemy property during the war. Two years later, Electric Bond and Share took over an electric power company in Santiago, Cuba, which was rapidly followed by a larger acquisition of a Havana utility (apparently, once controlled by German capital). Panama, Guatemala, and Cuba had all declared war against Germany in 1917.[91]

In 1920, Electric Bond and Share (with GE's subsidiary International General Electric) started to build an electric railway and a hydroelectric plant for the state government of Santa Catarina in Brazil.[92] This was not a direct investment, which in the early 1920s were confined to Panama, Guatemala, and Cuba. Electric Bond and Share's investments should not be seen solely in political terms. While the U.S. government did prompt the company to invest abroad, the latter hoped that "remodeling" and expanding the utilities abroad would result in purchases of GE machinery and equipment. In the early 1920s, as indicated, Electric Bond and Share was a GE subsidiary. Electric Bond and Share also hoped that its foreign investments would bring good economic returns. Its endeavors were in keeping with a fresh surge of U.S. business abroad. In December 1923, Electric Bond and Share organized American & Foreign Power to pursue international business.[93]

The new position of the United States in the world economy was consequential: With Europeans preoccupied and before the United States entered the war, Americans had moved into markets once held by Europeans. The American International Corporation (AIC) was symbolic. In November 1915, Frank A. Vanderlip, president of National City Bank, organized AIC to seek global opportunities for American business and finance. Its board included individuals interested in international business. Three of the participants were especially concerned with developing foreign electric utilities. One was AIC's president, Charles Stone of Stone & Webster, specialists in electric utilities. In 1917, Stone wrote, "The development of a country is essentially an engineering task – the building of railroads, of ports, of municipal works, of public utilities." He saw America as taking on that job internationally. Also on the board of AIC were Charles A. Coffin, chairman of the board of General Electric, and Guy E. Tripp, chairman of the board of Westinghouse Electric.[94] Westinghouse, even though it was divesting its foreign manufacturing operations, still wanted to export from the United States. At home and internationally, America emerged from the war as a giant. Huge opportunities beckoned for electrification. Even in the United States in 1922, only 39 percent of American homes had electric light and power.[95] Abroad, U.S. companies would assume leadership in spreading electricity worldwide. It was a dawn of a new age.

ENCLAVES

During the 1920s, multinational enterprises established plantations, mines, and oil properties worldwide; as in times past, the developers, principally Americans and Europeans, introduced electric power. Thus, familiarity with electrification would greatly extend beyond the cities to remote locales around the globe. Rubber plantations to meet the new demands for tires were set up and expanded in the Dutch East Indies (Indonesia), French Indochina (Cambodia, Laos, and Vietnam), Malaya (essentially Malaysia), Brazil, and Liberia, which meant new company towns and electrification. Other foreign-owned plantations for bananas, sugar, jute, hemp, and so on necessitated some electrification. To an even greater extent, the developments in mining worldwide prompted the introduction or expansion of electricity. Gold mining and electrification went forward in tandem. Other mining activities, from copper to phosphates, from bauxite to tin, also attracted new capital and signified new energy requirements, especially electricity. Société Générale, Brussels, through its interests in its subsidiary Union Minière, embarked on major copper-mining activities in the Belgian Congo, and electricity was introduced in the mining camps. Copper-mining facilities were also begun in Northern Rhodesia (now Zambia). Some of the most substantial increases in energy-intensive projects were in Chile, connected with the large-scale copper mining by the U.S. companies Anaconda and Kennecott. By the end of the 1920s, the American-owned (by Anaconda) Chilean Exploration Company at Chuquicamata owned the largest hydroelectric plant in South America, while Braden Copper Co. (controlled by Kennecott Copper) had electrified all its production processes at its Chilean mine. Oil drilling and refining brought modern infrastructure to company towns in Iran, the Dutch East Indies, and Venezuela. Foreign multinational enterprises located the crude oil, developed the resource, *and* supplied electric power in the numerous, often remote, company towns, as they organized the production, refining, transport, and marketing of the oil.

Many of these "enclave form" developments did not involve central power stations, although some of them were sufficiently substantial to do so. Typically, power generation plants were built to fill company town needs, lights for households, offices, and retail establishments, and, more important, power for industrial purposes. During the 1920s, company towns multiplied around the world, both within empires and in independent countries. Normally, they were connected to a port by a railroad, which required switching and other electrical apparatus. Port cities needed electrification. While the railroad or the port city might have public provisions, the company towns were private-sector activities, and electrification within the towns was commonly introduced by the dominant company. Sometimes, an entire region was electrified as a result of these economic activities.[96] The process that had begun before World War I expanded enormously during, and particularly after, the war. Through the enlarged span of activities of Belgian, British, Dutch, French, U.S., and, to a lesser extent, Australian, Italian, and Portuguese businesses, the first introduction of electric lights and power occurred within enclaves in many parts of the world. The financing of these activities was done concomitantly with the development of the specific primary resource.

LARGE POWER CONSUMERS

Certain new manufacturing industries required immense amounts of power. U.S. capital, in particular, became more involved in Canadian electrical facilities, linked with newsprint, paper and pulp, and aluminum production, and, to some extent, electrochemical plants. At decade's end, American and German chemical companies had investments in electrochemical and power operations in Norway.

The U.S.-controlled International Paper (and its holding company, organized in November 1928, International Paper and Power Co.) as well as Aluminum Company of America (Alcoa) made sizable investments where there was cheap power, especially in Canada.[97] Securities of International Paper and Power (IPP) and its Canadian subsidiary Canadian Hydro-Electric Corp. Ltd. were traded and bought for their portfolios by companies such as the U.S.-headquartered Public Utility Holding Corporation.[98]

Alcoa invested in power sites in Norway and France, but its biggest foreign involvements were in Canada. Earlier, we wrote of James Duke's dreams for the Saguenay development in Canada, which had been put on hold during the war and in its immediate aftermath. In 1922, Duke finally reenergized this project when he lined up Canadian newsprint titan William Price to be a major power customer. Duke's plans and those of the expanding Canadian newsprint industry coincided. But Duke wanted additional consumers for his ambitious hydroelectrical undertaking. Between 1922 and 1924, on behalf of Alcoa, John E. Aldred – the American banker who specialized in light and power projects and who before the war was deeply involved in the Shawinigan Water and Power Company – sought to become a participant in Duke's Saguenay venture. In 1924, Price died, which freed Duke to explore this possibility. Aldred joined with Alcoa's chief executive officer Arthur Vining Davis and opened new discussions with Duke. Davis was enthusiastic and desired to be more than a power facility customer; he wanted Alcoa to be an investor, which he achieved in July 1925, when Duke and Davis signed a formal contract to merge.[99] The Canadian "political processes" offered no barrier to the formidable new plans. Then Duke became ill and early in October 1925, at age 68, he died. Davis gladly took up full leadership in the huge Saguenay project. In April 1926,

Alcoa, through its subsidiary Aluminum Company of Canada, purchased a controlling interest in the Isle Maligne dam (which had been left out of the 1925 agreement).[100] If completed as planned, Alcoa's substantial venture would raise Canada's hydroelectric capacity by 34 percent.[101] By 1926, the work was well underway and went forward briskly in the late 1920s. In 1928, Davis spun off Aluminum Company of Canada, placing it under the holding company Aluminium Ltd., registered in Canada and owned by the shareholders of the closely held Alcoa.[102] Aluminium Ltd. acquired nearly all Alcoa's foreign properties, the major exceptions being the Dutch Guiana (Suriname) bauxite holdings (which supplied the U.S. Alcoa) and the uncompleted "lower development" on the Saguenay (which subsequently would be developed and transferred to Aluminium Ltd. in 1938).[103] Because in 1928 Alcoa and Aluminium Ltd. had identical shareholders (and family members in management), for all practical purposes, initially at least, they functioned as part of one multinational enterprise.[104]

Union Carbide was a U.S. chemical company that needed power for its electrochemical process. It established the Sauda Falls Co. Ltd., a public utility in Norway. Union Carbide not only had direct investments in Sauda Falls Co., but also in Meraker Smelting in Norway.[105] Because Sauda Falls Co. Ltd. required substantial capital, in 1925 it had a $4 million dollar bond issue on the U.S. market.[106] Union Carbide did not have to depend on its own resources to develop this power source.

Also in Norway, the power-intensive nitrate plant of Norsk Hydro supplied French needs during World War I; the remaining prewar (minority) German interests exited from involvements in Norsk Hydro. In 1927, however, when Norsk Hydro wanted to convert from the arc to the Haber-Bosch process, German chemical manufacturers (now combined into I. G. Farben) returned; in exchange for knowhow and licensing arrangements, Farben acquired a 25 percent interest in Norsk Hydro, which shares were lodged in the German firm's Swiss affiliate I. G. Chemie.[107]

ELECTRIFICATION IN THE LATE 1920S

Revolutionary Russia was the only nation that had inaugurated across-the-board nationalizations. Elsewhere, by the mid-1920s it became apparent that government ownership was not the solution to postwar reconstruction, although government (usually municipal or provincial) ownership had spread in the war years and in their immediate aftermath and was, in many instances, not reversed. On a global basis, government (mainly local or regional) ownership was larger than before 1914.

Not until the mid-1920s were the numerous postwar uncertainties and difficulties seemingly resolved. Inflation had been tamed in Central Europe and Germany. Britain succeeded in returning to the gold standard in 1925 and by the mid-1920s other major nations also returned to the gold standard. Arrangements for government debt rescheduling and settlement had taken shape. Finally, the private-sector international investments that had begun to resume immediately at war's end, but were temporarily halted by the global crisis of 1921, once again jumped, and soon there was a crescendo of new involvements. Foreign investments in electric light and power not only occurred in enclaves and locales offering cheap power, but also multiplied in Europe, in the western hemisphere, and, to a lesser extent, in urban areas farther afield. The vast buildup of electric utilities and the newly rationalized electric utilities systems required immense amounts of capital, which meant calls on international capital markets along with the new activities of foreign direct investors. Foreign direct and foreign portfolio investments marched together (and sometimes separately). Municipal and state-owned companies looked for capital beyond their nation's borders, raising funds in bond markets.

As the decade progressed and German currency was stabilized, it was unclear whether the Germans would or could reclaim their prominent prewar role in global electrification. Capital remained scarce. Reparation payments continued to be due. While the electrotechnical *manufacturers* recovered remarkably and engaged in international business, this failed to herald a strong German return to the international financing of electric utilities, although toward the later part of the 1920s German directors began to reappear on the boards of electric utility holding companies.[108] By decade's end, principally through Gesfürel, AEG was reported to have interests in electric utilities in Hungary, Poland, Portugal, Switzerland, and Turkey.[109]

Germany, which had been a creditor nation before the war, had become a heavy borrower abroad. German corporate borrowings in the United States were second only to those of the Canadians.[110] Prominent among the German borrowers were the electrotechnical manufacturers Siemens and AEG and also key German public utilities, especially the Rhine-Westphalia Electric Power Company (RWE).[111] We will return to a discussion of these borrowings and the inward (into Germany) direct investments by American business when we discuss the expansion of U.S. investments in this sector.

In 1927, the British Electrical & Allied Manufacturers' Association issued the report *Combines and Trusts in the Electrical Industry: The Position in Europe in 1927*, which documented the complex interrelationships among electrical manufacturers, electricity supply companies, and the so-called power finance companies in Europe. While at times not fully accurate, the report did give a glimpse of the intricate network of continental European finance. In power finance, the report concluded, "The war and its aftermath destroyed much of the system so carefully prepared by Germany, and allowed Switzerland and Belgium to obtain a hold in many countries once considered a German preserve, such as Italy, Spain,

Poland and South America."[112] The report also stated that by 1927 there was some revival of German activity in electricity supply, but that it remained a shadow of what it once had been.

In Switzerland, the prewar companies Elektrobank, Indelec, and Motor-Columbus (after 1923), once the early 1920s crises were past, maintained their activities as important investors in electrical securities. Increasingly, however, both Elektrobank and Indelec became more bank financing companies rather than following the *Unternehmergeschäft* form. Indelec, its ties to Siemens loosened, turned from its prewar focus on Germany, Italy, and Russia to place more of its investments in Switzerland, so the distribution of its participations in 1929 were Switzerland (26.4 percent), Czechoslovakia (24.3 percent), Italy (22.0 percent), Germany (10.7 percent), France (4.7 percent), and other countries (0.1 percent).[113] Regrettably, we have not been able to locate comparable 1929 geographical information for Elektrobank's investments, but it seems clear that the firm was very much involved in Swiss electrification and retained many international investments, particularly in Europe. When after World War I Alsace became French and some of its German assets changed nationality, new business emerged within France, much of it in connection with Sofina, especially after 1929.[114] Elektrobank, its links with AEG weaker but persisting, seemed, however, to have also enabled German transactions that might not otherwise have been possible. Thus, Thomas Hughes explains that for the German utility Rhine-Westphalia Electric Power Company to expand *within* Germany by acquiring controlling interest in Elektrizitäts AG vorm. W. Lahmeyer & Co. and its subsidiaries, the German utility RWE "had to deal with Elektrobank ... in Zurich, Switzerland, a company that financed electrical undertakings and owned shares in Lahmeyer."[115]

Motor-Columbus kept a sizable in-house engineering staff during the 1920s and remained highly entrepreneurial, strongly supporting the Swiss manufacturer Brown Boveri and taking the initiative in many new electrical endeavors. Luciano Segreto argues that Motor-Columbus held to the strategy *Unternehmergeschäft* throughout the 1920s. In 1926, Motor-Columbus helped organize in Zurich the Südamerikanische Elektrizitäts-Gesellschaft (Südelkra) and in 1928 the Schweizerisch-Amerikanishe Elektrizitäts-Gesellschaft (SAEG). Later that year, it participated in the creation of Foreign Light & Power Co. Ltd., Montreal, which would assemble Swiss, Canadian, and U.S. capital for investments in shares of European and South American electric supply companies. In the last case, Motor-Columbus, as was becoming increasingly common, used a Canadian holding company for its international business. In Argentina Motor-Columbus's principal involvements were in Compañía Italo-Argentina de Electricidad, which expanded greatly, from an output of 79 million kWh in 1921 to 144 million kWh in 1929.[116] Foreign Light & Power came to control Siebenbürgische Elektrizitäts AG (Transylvanian Electricity Co.), the operating company for a Romanian public utility.[117] Motor-Columbus also had many investments in Italy, where Brown, Boveri was active in the development of the Italian hydroelectric power industry.[118] One estimate of the distribution of Motor-Columbus's "participations" in 1929 was Switzerland (46 percent), South America (38 percent), Italy (12 percent), Germany (2 percent), France (1 percent), and other (1 percent).[119]

Two prewar Geneva-headquartered Swiss holding companies also maintained the important international investments: Société Franco-Suisse pour l'Industrie Électrique (Franco-Suisse) and Société Financière Italo-Suisse (Italo-Suisse). Both Franco-Suisse and Italo-Suisse took part in the financing of the large Italian electricity supply firm Società Meridionale di Elettricità (SME or Meridionale). Franco-Suisse participated in the financing of both Swiss and French electric utilities.[120] There were many other Swiss holding companies.

All of the Swiss firms cooperated with non-Swiss enterprises (and, at times, with one another) in making international investments that spurred electrification worldwide. Thus, for example, in 1923 the Lima Light, Power and Tramways Company Ltd., a poorly managed, capital-short enterprise with electric tramways and electric power supply in Lima and Callao, Peru, raised money with a £1.5 million debenture offering in London by J. Henry Schröder & Co. As we saw in Chapter 3, Schröder had sponsored a £1.2 million issue for the same company in 1910. By now, however, the Peruvian company was under the control of Italian and Swiss interests.[121] The Italian associations appear to have been with Banca Commerciale Italiana (BCI) and Impresse Elettriche della America Latina (Latina Lux), while the Swiss ones were with Motor-Columbus. For Lima Power & Tramways, its preference shares were payable in Geneva, London, Milan, and Zurich, while interest on debentures was payable in Basel, Geneva, Lausanne, London, and Zurich.[122]

In Belgium, Sofina, under the capable direction of engineer Dannie Heineman, expanded and developed new links with a dispersed group of partners. In Brussels in 1924, Heineman founded a scientific laboratory to develop research in the electrical industry. By the mid-1920s, Sofina was reported "to control" utilities in Algeria, Argentina, Belgium, Brazil, France, Italy, Portugal, Spain, Thailand, and Turkey. Sofina controlled the Spanish-registered CHADE, and in 1924, boasting about its activities in Argentina, Heineman indicated that CHADE had two central stations with 200,000 kW capacity and was planning to replace them with a single, more efficient central station. That year, Motor-Columbus's affiliate Compañía Italo-Argentina de Electricidad had a smaller central station of 35,000 kW. Together, Heineman claimed that these two companies, with their three power stations, provided Buenos Aires's 2 million inhabitants with the same amount of power as was supplied (inefficiently) by 32 central power stations in London, England, with a population of almost 4.5 million.

FIGURE 4.1. Dannie Heineman (1872–1962)
Note: Heineman was an electrical engineer by training who led Sofina for fifty years (1905–1955). The date of the photograph is unknown.
Source: Photograph courtesy of AIP Emilio Segre Visual Archives.

A new large central power station was completed by CHADE in Buenos Aires at Puerto Nuevo in 1928.

Everywhere, Sofina sought to rationalize production by creating grids within countries. It worked to regroup, reorganize, and make more efficient the production and distribution of electricity. It declared a "war on waste." It set up new holding companies to raise money for electrification. Very active in France, Sofina developed new relationships with the French Thomson-Houston group and retained its connections with Société Centrale pour l'Industrie Électrique (SCIE), with Société Générale d'Entreprises (SGE), and with Louis Loucheur and Alexandre Giros, who joined the Sofina board of directors in 1925. SGE had interests in Turkey and North Africa, as well as in France. Sofina was involved in the 1927 enlargement of the capital of Société Financière pour le Développement de l'Électricité, Paris, and its successor, Société Financière Électrique, Paris (Finelec), which assembled funds for French electrification. The latter became involved in several French colonial ventures. And as the decade progressed, Heineman began to contemplate a European grid, crossing national frontiers. Despite (or perhaps because of) its global reach and its ambitious plans, Sofina lost money in 1926, 1927, and 1928.[123]

Thus, Sofina sought additional financing on an international scale. On October 19, 1928, a new company was established – Trust Financière de Transports et d'Entreprises Industrielles – and on January 22, 1929, Sofina completed the merger with that company, transferring all of its assets and liabilities as well as its name. What emerged was Société Financière de Transports et d'Entreprises Industrielles (Sofina), the so-called new Sofina. Investors in many countries subscribed for shares in the greatly enlarged capital of the new Sofina, making the enterprise extraordinarily international in both its ownership and its activities. Its shares were owned by American, Belgian, British, French, Italian, Spanish, and even some German firms. The headquarters and formal registration remained in Belgium, and Maurice Despret became president of the Conseil d'Administration. Heineman continued as "Administrateur-Délégué, Président du Comité Permanent." Indeed, the *New York Times* discussed the broad participation and concluded that Heineman and Oscar Oliven in Berlin "are today the two outstanding figures in the public utility industry outside of the United States. They together handled the details of the plan which resulted in the creation of the new company." Oliven had been friends with Heineman since they attended the Technical College of Hanover together in the 1890s. Over the decades, they would stay close, as Heineman became involved in Sofina and Oliven remained with Allgemeine Elektrizitäts Gesellschaft (AEG) and the German holding company Gesellschaft für Elektrische Unternehmungen (Gesfürel). Oliven's role in the new Sofina symbolized the renewed participation of AEG and Gesfürel in international business.[124] In 1929, one of the British representatives on the Sofina board was Reginald McKenna, chairman of Midland Bank; McKenna was a major actor in the British electrical manufacturing merger in 1929 (see below). Dudley Docker, although not on the Sofina board, was probably Heineman's principal British ally. After the Sofina reorganization, U.S. stock interests in Sofina were reported to be 18 percent: 8 percent held by the "Morgan-General Electric group," 6 percent by the "Kuhn Loeb (Westinghouse?) group," with the remaining 4 percent comprised of independent U.S. shareholders.[125] *Moody's Manual (Utilities) 1930* noted that the new company "controls important electrical enterprises in France, Spain, Portugal, Germany, Italy, Turkey, Belgium, Far East, Argentina and owns interest in many industrial concerns." *Moody's* provided a list of forty-two principal subsidiaries and participations by Sofina, a number of which were holding companies that in turn held additional public utility properties. The only explicit Asian involvement listed was in Tramways et Électricité de Bangkok, a Brussels-registered firm. In the convoluted structures of 1920s finance, Banque de Bruxelles was listed in *Moody's Manual (Utilities) 1930* as one of the "principal subsidiaries and participations" of Sofina.[126] Actually, the Banque de Bruxelles, with Despret as its representative, continued in the leadership of Sofina.

Whereas before the First World War equipment for Sofina's utilities had come mainly from Germany, in the 1920s its supplier network was more far-reaching. While its 1920s associations with the French Thomson-Houston group were friendly, FTH was far from its sole – or even principal – supplier. Dudley Docker lobbied Heineman to buy from British manufacturers.[127] Throughout the decade, Heineman traveled widely, making extensive international contacts in high places, but at the same time retaining his German friendships.[128] By 1927, the Berlin holding company Gesfürel had direct representation (Oliven) on the Sofina-controlled CHADE board, and CHADE, of course, had important Argentine operations. At decade's end, Oliven was placed on Sofina's board.[129]

In 1929, Sofina organized the Canadian holding company Canadian International Light and Power Investment Company (Caninlipo), Toronto, to hold the securities of its French affiliates and to raise money on their behalf.[130] Note the tangled web of enterprises, involving a Belgian holding company, a Spanish holding company, operations in Argentina, German holding company interests, Canadian holding companies, and French holding and operating companies, along with American, British, French, Italian, and German shareholdings in the parent Belgian holding company as well as in a number of the operating companies. Other groups (not mentioned) were also cross-owners of many of these securities, including those in CHADE. In addition, Gesfürel was reported to have by 1927 minority interests in Tramways et Électricité de Constantinople and the Compagnies Réunies Gaz et Électricité, Lisbon. Although the Germans had become involved once more, Belgian interests were "the deciding factor" in the chain of command. Complexities and networks notwithstanding, Sofina was a Belgian enterprise, with Dannie Heineman in charge.[131]

Sofina spawned imitators. Belgian entrepreneur Alfred Loewenstein saw that firm as his model. In the early 1920s, he made plans to set up a utilities holding company to take over the old "Pearson group" of companies (here the reference was to American engineer Fred Stark Pearson).[132] In 1922, Loewenstein, who had earlier been a small investor in these companies, acquired sizable share holdings in Barcelona Traction, Mexico Tramways Co. Ltd., and its affiliated Mexican Light and Power Co. Ltd., all Canadian-registered firms. Loewenstein transferred these investments to his newly created Belgian-based holding company Société Internationale d'Energie Hydro-Électrique (Sidro), registered January 31, 1923. In what was now becoming a typical pattern, there were "cross-holdings," as Sofina (and CHADE as well) acquired shares in Sidro. From the start, Sofina and Sidro were closely associated; they shared a common president, Despret, by this time also chairman of the Banque de Bruxelles. Heineman was involved with both companies. Heineman had been an admirer of Pearson and, when the latter was still alive, Heineman had contemplated the possibilities of association with that American engineer's collection of Canadian-registered firms; Sofina would achieve that through Sidro.[133] In 1924, Sidro purchased added securities of the Mexican Light and Power group (Mexlight) and soon obtained voting control.[134] By that time, however, Loewenstein was in financial difficulty and "effective control" of both Barcelona Traction (in which Sofina already had a large interest) and the Mexican utilities passed to Sofina.[135] Meanwhile, both Sofina and Sidro had been buying shares in the Canadian-registered Brazilian Traction, Light and Power Co.

By 1924, Sofina held sufficient stock in Sidro to control that company. However, Loewenstein acted as though he were in charge, much to Heineman's chagrin.[136] Between 1924 and 1928, but especially between 1926 and 1928, Heineman and Loewenstein clashed on numerous occasions. In December 1926, Heineman wrote to Edward Peacock, "We wish to do constructive work and to do it calmly, Sidro represents only 2 p.c. of our business and we have no time to spend in endless discussions of fantasy projects of a boxing banker" (a reference to Loewenstein's infatuation with the sport). Loewenstein died on the night of July 4–5, 1928, a dramatic death, as he fell from his private airplane. By then, there was no doubt that Sofina controlled Sidro and, in turn, controlled the three key Canadian-registered companies – Barcelona Traction, Mexlight, and Brazilian Traction – in which Sidro had invested. Nonetheless, the direction of these utilities continued to be delegated to the Canadians.[137]

The Empain group also persisted in the 1920s, with important Belgian holding companies in international business in electric utilities. During World War I, the group had lost to the Germans its significant operations in France and it also lost its Russian operations. After the war, like Sofina, it was able to resume its business in France. (Actually, its French investments over the years had been much larger than those of Sofina.) The group's founder and head, Baron Edouard Empain, died in 1929. By then, a new generation of management had emerged within the group, which continued to be well connected within the Belgian political community. For instance, Georges Theunis (1873–1944) of the Empain group served as Belgian prime minister from 1921 to 1926. During the 1920s, Empain's business grew, both domestically and internationally. Parisienne Électrique and Railways et Électricité in Belgium remained the two main holdings of the group. These were involved in a variety of investments abroad, with new ones in the Congo and Turkey. The group continued to be particularly important in Egypt, where its Cairo Electric Railways and Heliopolis Oasis Company held controlling interest in a large number of related companies, including the Société Egyptienne d'Électricité, formed in 1929, which built and operated the important Shubra power station in the northern quarter of Cairo.[138] Other Belgian groups also expanded internationally in a spectacular fashion in the 1920s, including Société Générale Belge d'Entreprises Électriques (SGB), the precursor of Electrobel.[139]

THE OLD AND THE NEW

Before World War I, British and French free standing companies had proliferated. Some fell by the wayside during the war years and immediately afterward, while others continued. During the 1920s, such French companies in electric utilities were present in Brazil, China, and North Africa.[140] In Britain in the 1920s, this form came to be used less frequently for electric light and power facilities, although some such companies persisted in Latin America, Asia, and Africa, and some new ones were formed, principally within the empire.[141] For tax and other reasons (particularly laws within host nations), incorporation in the host country was more often required. Of course, a company registered beyond the reach of the home country could be controlled from the United Kingdom, but overseas registration (contemporary economists believed, probably correctly) had the effect of weakening the associations.[142]

The figures in Table 4.1 demonstrate the move in Britain to overseas registration by 1929. The very knowledgeable Sir Robert Kindersley, who assembled this information, noted that "the total British loan and share capital in the Electric Lighting and Power group [of companies registered *and* operating abroad] is £43 million, contrasted with only £16 million in the case of British [*U.K.-registered*] companies operating abroad." He commented that this comparison on British investment in the "younger

Table 4.1. *The Nominal Amount of British Capital Invested Abroad in the Electric Light and Power Sector, Dividends and Interest Paid, Percentage Return on Share and Loan Capital, 1929 (in £000s)*

Share Capital	Dividends	%	Loan Capital	Interest	%	Total Share & Loan Capital
A. Electric Light and Power Companies Operating Abroad and Registered in the United Kingdom						
8,886	888	10.0	7,542	480	6.4	16,425
B. Electric Light and Power Companies Registered and Operating Abroad						
11,820	600	5.1	31,002	1,724	5.6	42,822

Source: Robert M. Kindersley, "British Foreign Investments in 1929," *The Economic Journal*, 41(Sept. 1931), 377–81, with percentages added.

industries [electric light and power] bear out the view that the British [-registered] company operating abroad is no longer so favourable a medium for the investment of capital." In addition, he found "the proportion of British controlled [investments] is tending to diminish."[143] Mira Wilkins did the percentage calculations provided in Table 4.1, and they are striking. British-registered companies (part A of the table) that were clearly, by Kindersley's definition, controlled from the United Kingdom had a superior return to British investors, both on share capital and loans, compared with those companies registered abroad (Part B of the table). Why, then, did this form not prevail? According to Kindersley, "[T]he high rate of income tax now payable by British registered companies compared with companies registered abroad" had left little scope for the further development of this method of investment.[144] How Kindersley defined "controlled" investments is not articulated (for companies registered abroad could be British-controlled), but his conclusions appear accurate. Registration abroad often did serve to undermine the British influence and result in lower returns to the British investors.

After Britain returned to the gold standard in 1925, its leaders hoped to restore the country's paramount global position. Capital controls were removed. At the same time, within the United Kingdom many economists (including John Maynard Keynes) argued that the outflow of capital overseas was at the expense of domestic investment and that *domestic* industry should be encouraged. Globalization had its hazards. As historian David Kynaston put it, Montagu Norman – at the Bank of England – "attempted to walk a tightrope – on the one hand, seeking to reassert London's standing as an international financial centre and not entirely give the game to New York; on the other, fearful of what an avalanche of foreign loans would do to Britain's chances of staying on the gold standard, given that a high Bank rate was ... political dynamite."[145] Many British policies, from the Trade Facilities Acts to those in the tax arena, were in line with the "Buy British" sentiments of the time and were framed to spur domestic investments in manufacturing at the expense of international investments. In 1926, as the British made plans for an electrical grid, new investments at home were greatly encouraged.[146]

Within Britain, the prewar networks of merchant bankers, investment trusts, investment companies, and insurance companies – that is, the major players in the City – were well aware that the pound had to share with the dollar its important role in the world economy. Transatlantic financial relationships had altered with the rise of the United States to new prominence and with the new economic, including monetary, weaknesses within Britain; nonetheless, transatlantic ties were no less intimate than before the war. The important British merchant bank Schröders had set up a subsidiary in New York City in 1923, while Lee, Higginson, Boston, which became particularly significant in international finance in the 1920s, had long had Higginson & Co. in London.[147] The Morgan houses in New York and London continued to be closely linked. British–American relationships were complemented by the drawing in of continental alliances – a resumption of the pre–World War I linkages. What was new in the late 1920s were the ever increasing complexities of the transatlantic financial networks and the wealth in the United States relative to Europe.[148]

In Britain in the late 1920s, the Robert Fleming group of companies and those of Robert Benson – traditionally investors in American securities – filled their investment trust portfolios with stock of Insull's electric utilities.[149] When in January 1929 J. P. Morgan issued shares of the United Corporation (a major U.S. electric utility holding company), Morgan Grenfell, London and Morgan & Cie., Paris, took an allotment of shares to market in England and on the continent. So, too, Electric Bond and Share attracted investments from abroad in its securities.[150] Thus, at the same time as the United States was sending capital around the world, there were inward portfolio investments into the United States, from the United Kingdom and elsewhere.

During the late 1920s, the British Pearson group's Whitehall Trust participated in numerous bond issues for electric light and power. For instance, the group was involved in the British-registered free standing company Perak River Hydro-Electric Power Co. Ltd., operating in Malaya (now Malaysia), which included in its "loan capital subscribed" in 1928–1929 outstanding 5 percent £1,250,000 Debenture Stock, issued at 99.10 percent, November 1926, principal and interest guaranteed by His Majesty's Treasury. (Just under half its entire loan capital was British government–guaranteed.) This 1926 issue was "redeemable at par over the years 1931 to 1941 by a cumulative sinking fund operating by annual drawings and/or by purchase at or under par." Whitehall Trust was listed as "Trustees." When the power plant was completed in 1930, Perak River Hydro-Electric Power Co. Ltd. was the largest single producer of electric power in Malaya.[151]

Interlocking directorates of British-headquartered free standing companies were the norm, as in times past. Clusters of individuals and firms were ubiquitous. An example lies in the group surrounding the Sudan Light and Power Company Ltd., registered in England, January 7, 1925, which announced plans to install a new light- and power-generating plant at Khartoum, as well as other infrastructure within the Sudan. Its lustrous board of directors was chaired by the Rt. Hon. Lord Meston, K.C.S.I (Knight Commander of the Star of India). Meston (1865–1943) had been Finance Secretary to the Government of India and was also chairman of the Calcutta Electric Supply Corporation Ltd., and he was on the board of many other free standing companies in electric utilities. From its establishment in 1919, Meston had been active in the Royal Institute of International Affairs, London. Also serving on the Sudan company board was

Percy John Pybus, C.B.E. Before World War I, Pybus (1880–1935) had worked at the Siemens plant in Stafford, England. When in 1919 the plant was acquired by English Electric Co., Pybus moved to the newly formed British manufacturing company, where he became managing director in March 1921 and chairman in 1926. English Electric at that time was one of the four principal electrical manufacturers in Britain. English Electric did not do well under Pybus's tenure, which ended in 1929 when he became the government's Minister of Transport. The nearly bankrupt English Electric was then sold to Edmundson's Electricity Corporation, owned by Americans (see below); it did not disappear as an entity, however. Pybus served as a director of Société Générale Hellénique and of Power and Traction Finance (and its Polish subsidiary), and in 1927 he joined the board of Phoenix Insurance Co. and then became its chairman from 1933 to 1935.[152]

English Electric participated in several domestic and foreign power projects. In Egypt, where the Belgian Empain and Sofina were involved, a British Foreign Office dispatch of 1929 reported on English Electric's joint managing director Vernon Watlington's "clumsy attempts at bribery" in an unsuccessful attempt to win an Egyptian railway electrification contract. That year, Pybus at English Electric, a representative of Metropolitan Vickers, and someone from the Belgian Sofina were engaged, or so it was reported to the Foreign Office, "in abominable mud-slinging and vituperation" in relation to an Egyptian electrification project.[153]

Also on the board of Sudan Light and Power was George May, Secretary of Prudential Assurance. His presence on that board was not unusual, for Prudential Assurance was involved with a number of loans to encourage British activities in supplying electricity overseas. When Prudential took part and May was not on a board, E. H. Lever of Prudential represented the insurance company.[154] Prudential Assurance became an important actor in the overlapping clusters, not only with free standing companies but also with the financing of otherwise independent companies registered abroad. Thus, in 1925 Prudential Assurance acquired foreign bonds issued by Toho Electric Company that were guaranteed by the British Treasury under the Trade Facilities Acts.[155] Then, in 1926 Prudential Assurance provided a £2 million loan, backed by the British Treasury, to the Athens affiliate of the Power and Traction Finance Co. Ltd., which the insurer followed in 1927 by participation in the financing of the Palestine Electric Corp.[156] When potential business involving the electrification of Belgrade, Yugoslavia, was presented to the British Pearson group in the spring of 1929, the group learned that Prudential Assurance, "if they [the Pearson group] desired," would come into the financial arrangements with the Whitehall Trust or Whitehall Electric Investments Ltd. "at every stage and would share any profits which might be made on the finance in proportion to the risks assumed."[157]

Other clusters existed. The Hong Kong Electric Company was registered in Hong Kong. In 1929, its accounts were in Hong Kong dollars. Its board was predominantly of British nationality, although it listed two men with Chinese names. We found that the same sort of clusters that surrounded U.K.-registered companies were present on that board, including representatives from the British trading companies Jardine, Matheson (B. D. F. Beith) and J. D.Hutchison & Co. (T. E. Pearce). These trading companies had British bases: They monitored the performance of the company that was registered overseas. Even though Hong Kong Electric Company had no British registration, it was closely associated with those companies that did have imperial home offices. Was Hong Kong Electric controlled by "nonresident" Hong Kong investors? The chairman of the company was C. G. S. Mackie, from Gibb, Livingston & Co., a "British" trading company long established in Hong Kong. The matter of British nonresident ownership and control, however, is controversial.[158]

Meanwhile, during the 1920s the British electrical manufacturing industry remained noncompetitive in world markets. British industry counted on division-of-market agreements to safeguard its domestic turf and on the series of British Trade Facilities Acts to assist limping exports. The acts (of 1921, 1922, 1924, and 1926) were used in the case of numerous loans, both to companies incorporated abroad and to those registered in the United Kingdom. These acts required the borrowing firm to use the money to purchase British goods. Other loans under these acts were made to, for example, the Toho Electric Power Co. (1925), the Sudan Light & Power Co. (1925), the General Hellenic Co. (1926), the Perak River Hydro-Electric Power Co. (1926), the Palestine Electric Corp. (1927), and the Hungarian Trans-Danubian Electrical Co.(1928).[159] As this chapter progresses, we will provide more details on the British role in international investments in electric light and power in the 1920s, including the use of holding companies, and we will show how U.S. capital took over a (perhaps *the*) leading company within the U.K. electricity supply industry and how internationally U.S. capital often came to replace that of the British.

Before we proceed, however, we need once more to cross the English Channel and consider French outward investments, which should not be underestimated. As in the case of all advanced countries in the 1920s, there were both inward and outward foreign investments. French stakes abroad appear, at least up to 1929, to have kept separate from the German, ones unlike the cooperative ventures of the prewar years. And when, at the end of the decade, there were attempts through Sofina to bring the Germans back in, French companies – and of course the French government – resisted.

During the late 1920s, electrical securities became a significant part of French bank holdings.[160] More of the French outward investments appear to have been directed to firms within the French empire.[161] The story of the electrification of Morocco through French direct investments has been well told by Samir Saul.[162] It was based on the needs of the mineral industry, specifically phosphates. La Société Marocaine de Distribution d'Eau, de Gaz et d' Électricité (SMD) provided electricity to Casablanca and Rabat after 1915. SMD was part of the Petsche group of companies: Société Lyonnaise des Eaux et de l'Eclairage.[163] There was a demand for a larger hydroelectric facility to cover all of Morocco, and so on January 30, 1924, Énergie Électrique du Maroc (EEM) was organized, domiciled in Paris. Saul lists the cluster of French founders in five categories: railroad companies (50 percent of the shares in the syndicate), banks (15 percent), builders (*constructeurs*) (15 percent), entrepreneurs (15 percent), and customers (5 percent). There were two railroad companies. The lead bank was Banque de Paris et des Pays-Bas (Paribas), which was also represented among the founders through its subsidiary Compagnie Générale du Maroc. The *constructeurs* included the manufacturers Schneider et Cie. and the French Thomson-Houston. Among the customers was SMD (Albert Petsche). The president of EEM was Gaston Griolet, chairman of Paribas.[164] The coterie of interested parties made the electrification process possible. This is but one example of French direct investments in electrification within the empire.[165]

HOLDING COMPANIES

By the late 1920s, holding companies in the electrical public utilities sector had become omnipresent, and the best way to raise money for international business. They varied substantially, with some designed to rationalize business operations and others serving as financial holdings. Many of the holding companies made direct investments and at the same time held investment securities in companies in which they did not participate in management. A substantial number of holding company structures were tangled by cross-holdings, so that deciphering chains of ownership involves making one's way through a maze that became more and more complex as time passed. Sofina, for example, not only participated directly in the rationalization of electric utilities, but it had interests in other holding companies in the typical late-1920s pyramids. We have discussed Sofina and its labyrinth of holding and sub–holding companies and its substantial 1928–1929 restructuring. Sofina was not mere financial architecture. Heineman was determined to apply the latest engineering knowledge and to increase efficiency. His goal was to disseminate within the Sofina organization the best methods, and to do this required financial resources.[166]

In Belgium, a consolidation within the electric utilities sector occurred during 1928–1930. There emerged (1) Tractionel (Société de Traction et d'Électricité, a holding company for tramways), formed in 1929, (2) Electrobel (Compagnie Générale d'Entreprises Électriques et Industrielles), set up in 1929 and dominated by the Banque de Bruxelles; also involved were the Banque de Paris et des Pays-Bas (Paribas); Société Générale, Brussels; Mutuelle Solvay; and Sofina, and (3) Electrorail (Compagnies Réunies d'Électricité et de Transport), one of the Empain group's holding companies, organized in 1930, an "outcome of the Empain group's desire to unify the management of its companies' financial services" after the 1929 death of the group's founder. All of these holding companies had sizable domestic (Belgian) investments in public utilities and in fact dominated the domestic market. Electrobel (the successor to Sofina's onetime rival Société Générale Belge d'Entreprises Électriques, but now associated with the Sofina) had a vast set of international direct and portfolio investments in light and power companies, as did the Empain group (including more than Electrorail), which as we have seen continued to be heavily involved in French direct investments.[167] During 1928–1930, historian Ginette Kurgan-Van Hentenryk writes of the rivalries within Belgium between Société Générale and Banque de Bruxelles. Ultimately, the latter would draw back from its involvements in electricity, obliged to give up its controlling interest in Sofina and accept with Société Générale an equal one-fifth share in Electrobel.[168] While the span of investments of these Belgian holding companies was "global," Europe was foremost in their investment strategies.

Belgian involvements in electrification had long been impressive; in the early days, its companies had led in tramway investments, but by the 1920s investments in electricity supply companies were far more extensive than those in tramways. In Belgium, the older companies and their successors remained, but there continued to be new enterprises as well. For example, in July 1928 the Compagnie Financière d'Exploitations Hydroelectriques Société Anonyme (Hydrofina) was formed in Belgium, to hold shares in and to raise money for a number of Romanian electricity supply companies. By 1929, the key shareholders in Hydrofina were Belgian (Société Générale de Belgique, Banque d'Anvers, and Electrobel), French (Banque de l'Union Parisienne, Demachy, and Compagnie d'Enterprises Électromécaniques), and Austrian (Österreichische Brown Boveri and Niederösterreichische Escompte-Gesellschaft). The technical direction was undertaken by Electrobel, which managed the building of a new hydroelectric facility and parceled out the equipment orders among Belgian, French, and "Austrian" suppliers (Österreichische Brown Boveri was, of course, a subsidiary of the Swiss Brown, Boveri.)[169]

And then there was the Compagnie Italo-Belge pour Enterprises d'Électricité et d'Utilité Publique (CIBEE) or, in one English rendition, Italian-Belgian Electric & Public Utility Co. (Italo-Belge), formed in 1928 by Count Giuseppe Volpi. We will encounter Volpi, who had long experience in the electrical industry, frequently in connection with other international holding companies. Italo-Belge has been described as a "construction and managing company," and it was said to have at its disposal engineers from Società Adriatica di Elettricità (SADE), a major power company that Volpi headed.

Italo-Belge, in turn, owned shares in another Belgian registered company, the Compagnie Européenne pour Entreprises d'Électricité et d'Utilité Publique, also known as European Electric & Public Utility Company (Europel), formed in 1929, which held minority interests in "many European companies." According to one source, Europel was organized by Volpi along with the Swiss Elektrobank; a second source has Europel created by Sofina as an investment trust destined to acquire interests in numerous German and Italian electrical companies (this source compared it with Caninlipo, which Sofina had organized in 1929 to combine various holdings in French public utilities). Both were probably true, for the networks were linked.[170]

In France, there was Société Centrale pour l'Industrie Électrique (SCIE), which during the late 1920s made new investments for the first time in Portuguese utilities. It seems to have assisted the linkages between French banks and Sofina. It joined Sofina in the organization of Caninlipo. At decade's end, SCIE was making further investments in electric utilities in French colonies. SCIE was a financial holding company engaged in portfolio management, opening of current accounts for its subsidiaries, and selling its subsidiaries' bonds and shares to expand the pool of investors.[171] Its prewar relations with the manufacturing company French Thomson-Houston were retained, but SCIE clearly had a separate life.

Sweden, too, had new holding companies. In the summer of 1929, the Stockholms Enskilda Bank (SEB) and the large Swedish electrical manufacturer Allmänna Svenska Elektriska (ASEA) organized a jointly owned power-holding company, Electro-Invest, to acquire concessions abroad, especially in Eastern Europe.[172]

In Britain, holding companies *qua* investment companies emerged. Often, it was difficult to distinguish British holding from investment companies. For example, the Power Securities Corp. Ltd., formed in 1922, as a "means of handling new issues of electrical securities," appeared to be an investment company, with no direct investments in any of the electricity supply companies that were part of its portfolio, although key to its formation was Balfour Beatty, a British consultancy and management firm, with engineering experience; controlling interest was held by George Balfour and three British manufacturers: Armstrong Whitworth, Babcock & Wilcox, and British Thomson-Houston. It became the largest electric-utility holding company in Great Britain, with most of its investments domestic.[173]

More important in relationship to British international business was the Power and Traction Finance Co. Ltd. (PTFC), also established in 1922 by a group that included English Electric.[174] In 1929, Prudential Assurance (which had been involved from the start) was described as the "financial member" of the Power and Traction Finance Co. Ltd. group.[175] PTFC tried to identify light and power opportunities and to facilitate the translation of the prospects into working projects. In 1923, the National Bank of Greece had approached PTFC for aid in financing Greek electrification. In 1926, with a group of Greek banks that were involved in the Syndicato Meleton kai Epichiriseon (sometimes translated as Syndicat des Études et des Enterprises), PTFC formed a Greek affiliate, General Hellenic Company (Société Générale Hellénique), which for the next thirty-one years would supply electricity to Athens and its environs.[176] For these Greek operations, in 1926, as previously indicated, Prudential Assurance provided a £2 million loan, guaranteed by the British Treasury under the Trade Facilities Acts. English Electric Co. and Babcock & Wilcox were among the British manufacturers that hoped to export to the new Greek subsidiary. Babcock & Wilcox was a large producer of boilers that were used in steam-generating plants.[177] What was in evidence in this Greek investment was once again the cluster of related companies, an investment company, manufacturers, and an insurer, coordinated through PFTC. In these negotiations, the British government and the guarantee by the British Treasury of the Prudential loan were critical to the transaction.

All of the Greek electrification needs were not, however, fulfilled by General Hellenic Co. There was no monopoly – at least for the country as a whole. Earlier in this chapter, we noted that in 1923 the largest supplier of electricity in Greece in 1923 had been Compagnie Hellénique d'Électricité (CHdE).[178] As the Greek State and the National Bank of Greece were negotiating with Power and Traction Finance Company, the ChdE made its own plans and submitted a separate proposal to the National Bank of Greece. After the PTFC (and General Hellenic Co.) received its concession, CHdE obtained a concession for many of the other more important cities of Greece – outside of Athens and Piraeus, which was reserved for the PTFC group. CHdE got most of its financing from an Austrian group, which, in turn, was very much involved in international business – both inward and outward investments.[179]

PFTC's Greek activities involved General Hellenic (it did not take part in ChdE, nor as far as we can establish in any of the Austrian group that was financing the latter). But PFTC's business was not confined to Greece; it made investments in Eastern Europe and was heavily engaged in Polish electrification, establishing in 1923 an affiliate Power and Traction Finance Company (Poland) Ltd., which acquired the assets of an earlier British free standing company, the Anglo-Polish Electrical Development Corp.[180] During the 1920s, ten companies in which foreign capital was involved were established in Poland to construct and operate electric power stations on the basis of concessions. PFTC became an investor in several of these companies. When at decade's end an opportunity emerged for a large-scale electrification project in Belgrade, Yugoslavia, PTFC served as the intermediary in developing the plans.[181] While PFTC seems to have been entrepreneurial in these electricity supply ventures, its own holdings of securities do not reflect this. As of March 1927, its name notwithstanding, PTFC had less than 20 percent (19.92 percent) of its overall investment portfolio in "electrical railways and public utilities," with the other 80 percent in diversified investments; moreover, we do not know how much of the 20 percent was within Great Britain and how much was abroad (at that time, 36 percent of its total portfolio was in investments within Great Britain).[182]

By 1929, General Hellenic had built a new power station to supply the Athens-Piraeus area, but substantial added funding was needed. Thus, in 1930 Whitehall Securities/Whitehall Electric was ready to fill its requirements with a large capital contribution in exchange for control of the company in Athens. Like the earlier loan from Prudential, the money Whitehall Electric raised for this project seem to have had a British-government guarantee.

Whitehall Securities/Whitehall Electric conducted the international activities of the British Pearson group. In the early part of the 1920s, it looked as though the group might become a major player in global electrification. Based on Lord Cowdray's investments, the group had experience in Mexico and Chile and seemed committed to additional entrepreneurial activities in the electricity supply sector. Yet during most of the 1920s, its direct involvements in electric utilities did not extend beyond those two Latin American countries.[183] Then, in 1928–1929, during the sweep of U.S. business expansion throughout Latin America (see below), Whitehall Electric sold these large public utilities interests in Mexico and Chile to American & Foreign Power Company. The sale included electric light and power systems in Vera Cruz, Tampico, Puebla, Córdoba, and Orizaba, Mexico; street railway properties in Tampico and Vera Cruz, Mexico; and the electric light and power and street railway systems in Santiago and Valparaiso, Chile, and nearby.[184] The Pearson group's profits on the transaction were reported to be £2.7 million.[185] The Pearson group had sold out in Chile not only because of the attractive price, but mainly because its dealings with the Chilean government had over the years steadily deteriorated, so much so that in 1927, with a breakdown in negotiations, its Chilean affiliate, Compañía Chilena, was actually worried about the possibilities of expropriation.[186] After Whitehall Securities/Whitehall Electric retreated from Mexico and Chile, it entertained the possibilities in 1929–1930 of other major electrical industry propositions in Europe, including the one in Athens.[187]

Another British holding (free standing) company with large interests in Latin America was Atlas Light and Power Co. Ltd., organized in 1926 with a capital of £6,282,235 (ca. $30.5 million); Atlas Light was the successor to a series of British free standing companies, and at origin it controlled five separate companies in Argentina and Uruguay. In the standard pattern of holding companies, it consolidated existing companies and to do this raised money in the United Kingdom.[188] As Atlas Light, its role in Argentina proved to be short-lived, and like Whitehall Securities/Whitehall Electric, it, too, sold out in 1929 to the expanding American & Foreign Power.[189]

In April 1928, British and Foreign Utilities Development Corporation (BFUD) registered to do business in the United Kingdom with the goal "to secure openings for the employment of capital throughout the world."[190] Its board chairman was Arthur C. D. Gairdner, whose other directorships included the British Overseas Bank and the Anglo-Polish Bank. A representative of Prudential Assurance was a director of BFUD, which, invested in Poland in the newly established Utilities Corporation (Poland) Ltd., formed in October 1928, which in turn controlled Elektrownia Okrege Warszawskiego, a Polish public utility.[191]

With the qualified exception of Power and Traction Finance, the clear exception of Whitehall Securities/Whitehall Electric, perhaps Atlas Light and Power, and possibly BFUD, the "holding company" form (as distinct from the investment company and the free standing company) does not appear to typify British overseas stakes in electrical public utilities in the 1920s, although there were clusters of companies that had certain pyramid relationships. Yet in Britain, there was little that approximated the use of Canadian and U.S. holding companies for international investments where the holding company – as an entrepreneurial actor developing, rationalizing, and financing public utility properties – took on immense significance during the 1920s.[192]

Prior to the 1920s, Canadian-headquartered (Canadian-registered) holding companies had not been the norm. The prewar exception was International Light & Power Co. Ltd., Toronto, organized in 1913, with its interests in public utilities in Argentina, Mexico, and Venezuela. The Canadian pattern had been to set up free standing companies, which became holding companies *within* Mexico and Brazil. The holding company structure as such had not been evident *in Canada* as a means of carrying forth investments across borders. The Canadian style for business abroad in utilities, as we have seen, had been one of loose groups and clusters – that is, concentric circles. Some of this remained, but in the 1920s overall there was a change in the Canadian approach.

Very important, in a pyramid fashion, were foreign (non-Canadian)-owned companies that held stock in and continued to finance Canadian-registered firms, which did business abroad, sometimes as direct investors and sometimes as simply financial intermediaries. Thus, in 1928 Whitehall Securities/Whitehall Electric organized Whitehall Canada Ltd., which had a portfolio of "quoted and unquoted investments," most of which were U.S.-dollar-denominated securities.[193] For Whitehall Securities/Whitehall Electric, the investments made through Whitehall Canada were not foreign direct investments, but were part of its overall investment strategy.

Similarly, as we have noted, in the 1920s, although the Canadian registration persisted, Brazilian Traction, Light and Power Co., Mexican Tramways Co. and its affiliate Mexican Light & Power Co., as well as Barcelona Traction, Light and Power passed to Sofina control, and these firms became part of the Sofina/Sidro multinational network of enterprises. At the same time, the stock-holding interests notwithstanding, Canadians managed them.[194] In 1926, promoter I. W. Killam (head of Royal Securities, Montreal) founded the International Power Company, which joined under one corporate umbrella a collection of foreign utilities in Latin America that had been loosely associated with (controlled by) Royal Securities. Royal Securities and its subsidiary Montreal Engineering had electric utility interests in Bolivia, El Salvador, Venezuela, and Newfoundland. Royal Securities had followed the *Unternehmergeschäft* form of behavior for its group of companies even before 1926, when International Power was formed to furnish a formal unity to these Latin American utilities and to raise added funding. Royal Securities held 51 percent of the shares in International Power, which in turn had controlling interests in the foreign operating companies. During the late 1920s, International Power, one of the major utility holding companies in Latin America, expanded its activities.[195]

Another Canadian holding company *qua* investment company was the Hydro-Electric Securities Corp., registered in Canada in 1926 with the goal of acquiring interests in electric utilities. It was to be a "super Sidro," (an undertaking of Belgian entrepreneur Loewenstein replicating his existing Sidro). At first, its principal assets were Loewenstein's own holdings in Sidro – Barcelona Light and Power Company Ltd. – and in Rio de Janeiro – Tramway, Light and Power Company Ltd., one of the affiliates of Brazilian Traction. Loewenstein used the new firm for speculative purposes, and its holdings expanded even after its founder's death in 1928. Hydro-Electric Securities held stock and bonds of Brazilian, Italian, Mexican, and Spanish, utilities, but as of 1929 roughly 90 percent of its capital was placed in the United States. This firm was organized under the Canadian tax designation "4-K," meaning that it paid minimal Canadian taxes. However, under Canadian law it was not allowed to derive income from Canada or to own properties in the Dominion. By 1929, its "Belgian" origins notwithstanding, most of the investors in the stocks and bonds issued by Hydro-Electric Securities were from the United States and Canada.[196] In 1929, Hydro-Electric Securities and Central States Electric of New York formed Electric Shareholdings Corporation and helped organize U.S. Electric Power Corporation.[197] In short, like many other companies, Hydro-Electric Securities participated in pyramiding, the financial architecture so common in the 1920s. In the end, it was an investment company rather than an entrepreneurial venture.

Because of the favorable tax status and registration rules, holding companies registered in Canada were, as we have noted, not necessarily controlled from Canada: Whitehall Canada was English-controlled; Sofina, when it brought the large Brazilian, Mexican, and Spanish (Barcelona) properties into its sphere of influence, retained the Canadian registration; and Caninlipo, with its French investments, was Sofina-controlled. Canada had long had good corporate legislation, and in the 1920s, with new taxes everywhere, Canadian registration became even more attractive. In 1928, U.S. investors acquired 72 percent of the shares of International Light & Power, Toronto, formed in 1913 as the first of the Canadian holding companies. In 1928, J. G. White (of the eponymous construction company) became president of that holding company, which maintained its role in Latin America. At the end of the 1920s, International Light & Power held "all the capital, stocks, and debentures of the companies owning electric lighting, gas plants, and distributors systems in the cities of Caracas (Venezuela) and Merida (Mexico)," as well as the entire share capital of the South Brazilian Railways Co. Ltd., which owned electric lighting and tramways systems in Curitiba, in Southern Brazil.[198]

In 1917, the construction company J. G. White & Co. had become a subsidiary of the British trading firm Alfred Booth; by then, the White firm was already considered to be a specialist in the management of public utilities in Latin America and in contracting work. Once within the Booth group, however, it did not flourish. As a result, in 1929 Booth sold it back to its founder.[199] Before that occurred, in 1928, Foreign Light & Power Ltd., Montreal (allied with J. G. White) had been set up by Motor-Columbus.[200]

Indeed, within Canada, coincident with and sometimes indistinguishable from, the holding companies were the investment companies that specialized in electric light and power securities. Other investment companies did not specialize, but held sizable portfolios of light and power securities. Many of these companies were modeled after U.S. holding companies (or other U.S. enterprises) or after British investment trusts.[201] Canadian investment companies were typically linked with an investment banking–stock broker group: (1) Wood, Gundy & Co. Ltd., Toronto; (2) Nesbitt, Thomson & Co. Ltd., Montreal; and/or (3) Arthur Meighen of Montreal.

For instance, Wood, Gundy in May 1928 organized London Canadian Investment Corp., with Sir Herbert S. Holt, head of Montreal Light & Power, as president. LCIC had three British directors on its eight-person board. It was purely an investment company. In February 1929, Wood, Gundy formed Consolidated Investment Corporation of Canada. Holt was a director, as was George H. Montgomery, a lawyer and chairman of the previously mentioned Hydro-Electric Securities.

A. J. Nesbitt of Nesbitt, Thomson had in 1925 set up the Power Corporation of Canada, designed to provide technical, managerial, and financial services to operating public utilities companies. Along with its role as a "utility holding company," which managed a range of utilities, it also had minority interests in numerous other Canadian and American utilities. Interestingly, in a 1928 bidding war Power Corporation of Canada acquired from English ownership the British Columbia Electric Railway Co., which in the course of the 1920s had itself become a utility holding company. This was a domestication of the largest U.K. direct investment in

Canada.[202] The prior year (1927), Nesbitt, Thomson (with A. Iselin & Co. of New York) organized the Foreign Power Securities Corporation (FPSC), which bought substantial interests in key light and power companies throughout France (and in a French company that had a small plant in Madagascar). In all, as of April 30, 1929, FPSC's operations served 2,539 communities, and the entire system had 601,709 connected customers.[203] In short, there was an extraordinary number of holding companies *qua* investment companies, often not independent of one another, but with substantial cross-pollination.

Just as in Britain, so in Canada insurance companies accumulated sizable financial resources. And just as in Britain, Canadian insurance companies took part in the financing of electric utilities at home and abroad. Sun Life Assurance Company of Canada in particular became heavily involved in U.S. public utilities investments, especially in the Insull group of companies. By May 1929, that Canadian life insurance company had almost 20 percent of its investment portfolio in electric power, light, and gas companies, mainly in the United States.[204]

U.S. BUSINESS AND FINANCE

So far, we have barely captured the vast, complicated international activities of European and Canadian firms in providing light and power in the late 1920s. The number of companies staggers the imagination. There were many countries, from Syria to Kenya and beyond, with foreign direct investments that we have not discussed and separate companies established for such purposes. Even were we to extend our coverage, it would seem less impressive than that of the spread of U.S. enterprise; U.S. involvements in electric utilities catapulted upward in the late 1920s, at home and abroad. In this decade, the United States became the world's first consumer society, and electrical goods that required the supply of electric power became commonplace. From irons to vacuum cleaners to radios, American households acquired appliances. While the figures vary, one set indicated that in 1922 a mere 39 percent of U.S. homes had electric light and power; by 1929, 68 percent were served with electricity. There was still a distance to go, especially in rural America, but the diffusion was dramatic.[205] Owing to the sizable rural areas in America and the country's huge geographical expanse, by 1929 certain other nations had a greater percentage of homes hooked up to electricity, but no nation had more capital invested in providing electric light and power. At the same time, as U.S. companies were providing for U.S. needs, U.S. companies and capital also went to foreign lands. No single sector attracted more outward foreign direct investment from the United States than public utilities.[206]

The U.S. private sector's international involvements were not only in direct investments; financing of foreign public utilities projects was similarly impressive. Often, as in the European and Canadian setting, there was the combination of outward U.S. foreign direct investment and finance. Sometimes, however, the foreign financing was separate from the foreign direct investment.[207] In the 1920s, the United States possessed what no other nation in the world had: a strong electrotechnical industry combined with a capital-rich economy. Its enterprises were investing in an efficient manner in establishing American electrical systems. The nation's important multinational enterprises developed resources around the globe and in enclaves they had instituted electrification. So, too, the country had technologically advanced industries that founded businesses abroad to obtain cheaper power. The United States had a vibrant stock market and a dynamic international banking community.

In manufacturing, the front-runner, General Electric, augmented its long-established strategy; as in the past, this included participation in international agreements accompanied by foreign direct investments. In the 1920s, GE and its subsidiary International General Electric set out to have a tranche in every major electrical manufacturing enterprise outside the United States. Its cartel arrangements in no way dampened these plans. Toward the end of the decade, Westinghouse's international investments were renewed, although when compared with GE its international stakes seemed modest.[208] In general, in the 1920s GE and Westinghouse had a separate set of international alliances, although the management of each firm was cognizant of what the other was doing. Just as with Siemens and AEG, albeit tempered by U.S. antitrust law, there was both competition and cooperation between the two leading enterprises (and with the German giants and with other electrical manufacturers around the globe).[209] Of the late 1920s, economist Frank Southard wrote, "Unquestionably first among European industries in which American corporations have a stake is the electrical industry."[210] GE also had sizable direct investments in Japanese electrical *manufacturing*.[211]

Toward the end of the decade, Gerard Swope of GE attempted to merge the four largest British lamp and heavy electrical equipment manufacturing companies: (1) British Thomson Houston, already controlled by GE; (2) Metropolitan Vickers, in which GE had "clandestinely acquired" a majority interest (and that had agreements with Westinghouse, stemming from the former's wartime absorption of the British Westinghouse enterprise); (3) English Electric, which had earlier taken over Siemens's British dynamo plant in Stafford and was by decade's end a weak company, soon to come under the control of the Chicago-based Utilities Power and Light Corporation; and (4) the independent General Electric Company Ltd., London. These merger plans did not materialize, although in their wake emerged in January 1929 the new Associated Electrical Industries which combined British Thomson Houston, Metropolitan Vickers, and a number of smaller British electric companies. GE had a large enough interest in AEI to exercise control. At origin, AEI was the premier British electrical firm, followed by the smaller General Electric Company Ltd. and English Electric.[212]

On the continent of Europe and around the globe, GE's influence was pervasive. It had long been involved in the giant French Thomson-Houston. In 1928–1929, it was instrumental in the merger of certain properties of FTH and the Société Alsacienne de Constructions Mécaniques into the Société Générale de Constructions Électriques et Mécaniques (known as Als-Thom and then Alsthom). This new company, the largest French electrical manufacturer, was 14 percent owned by GE and the rest owned by its two French founding entities.[213] In 1929, German businessmen were complaining of "*Überfremdung* – the unwelcome purchase ... of equity shares in German corporations." That fall, owing to a "cash-flow squeeze," Allgemeine Elektrizitäts Gesellschaft (AEG) sold one-quarter of its equity to GE. With resentment, Siemens's head of finance, Max Haller, cried out in frustration in a note of November 11, 1929, to Owen Young of GE, "The whole world belongs to the Americans."[214] He was right. Even though German manufacturers had sought to resume their worldwide role, their activities were dwarfed by the U.S. expansion. The interests of GE (and to a lesser extent Westinghouse) in manufacturing were global and far more important than those of either Siemens or AEG, much less Brown, Boveri (in which GE had a minority interest) or any other European electrotechnical manufacturing firm.[215]

Although GE and its affiliates' principal domestic and international interests were in manufacturing, GE directly and through its affiliates spurred the development of electric utilities. As in years past, manufacturers desired to encourage public utilities so as to enlarge their markets.[216] Long before World War I and clearly by the 1920s, electric utilities and their holding companies might be in clusters with the manufacturers, but the activities from a corporate standpoint were now distinct. This is very important, for as we document the role of U.S. direct investment in utilities, the big interests were not by the manufacturers. GE was ubiquitous, but it became increasingly remote from direct investments in foreign (and domestic) utilities. The latter were now separate. Indeed, in February 1925 GE completed the distribution to its shareholders of its interest in the important holding company Electric Bond and Share. The latter, however, continued as the parent company of American & Foreign Power, and the chairman of the GE board remained on the board of directors of American & Foreign Power long after the spin-off.[217] GE and Westinghouse did keep (or establish) minority interests in European public utilities and in U.S. holding companies designed for international business, interests that were primarily for information purposes and part of the manufacturers' general network of contacts.[218] When, for example, the U.S. holding company Intercontinents Power Company was formed in 1928 to obtain properties in Argentina, Brazil, and Chile, on its board were the president and the general manager of Westinghouse Electric International.[219] However, as we consider U.S. investments in foreign electric utilities, we must go far beyond the role of the manufacturers.

By the 1920s, the requirements of electric utilities had reached proportions that only the wealthiest countries could, and did, fill: U.S. finance was there to support the spread of public utilities worldwide. The London market – with its bond and share offerings in the electric utility sector – was small relative to its U.S. counterpart. Continental European stock markets, from Paris to Zurich, handled the securities of electric utilities, but each transacted less than London, and London transacted much less than the New York Stock Exchange and the Curb. Many electric utility securities in the 1920s were listed on two or more stock exchanges at home and abroad and were traded internationally. The incomplete Table 4.2, which covers only 1922 to 1925 (that is, the beginnings of the U.S. financing story) provides an idea of the start of what became a crescendo of bond and stock issues in the United States for public utilities abroad. American participants in foreign public utilities created and took part in a very tangled web of international corporate structures. Indeed, the very word "foreign" in the title of the table is indicative of the labyrinth. "Foreign" could mean an otherwise independent firm resident abroad, where there were no direct investment interests – as in the case of the Japanese public utilities or, by 1922, the Melbourne Electric Supply Co. Alternatively, it could signify financing for a company set up in the United States that, in turn, invested in utilities abroad, as, for example, the collection of holding companies participating in Italian finance or the holding company American & Foreign Power Company. For instance, the Havana company listed on the table was an operating company under the hierarchy of American & Foreign Power.

Bankers raised money for utilities around the world. The large New York banks were not allowed to underwrite securities, but that did not stop them: Chase, National City, and Guaranty Trust (controlled by J. P. Morgan & Co.) formed affiliates (Chase Securities, National City Co., Guaranty Co., respectively) to take part in underwriting and distributing securities of electric utilities at home and abroad.[220] This was especially true of National City Co. and Guaranty Co. J. P. Morgan & Co.'s participation in international public utility finance was not only through Guaranty Co., but its partners took on an especially critical role in financing the Japanese electric utilities industry. Japanese electric utilities relied heavily on U.S. bond markets and to a lesser extent on borrowing in London (dollar borrowings of Japanese electric utilities far exceeded their sterling-denominated debt).[221] Thomas Lamont, a key Morgan partner, facilitated the U.S. transactions. J. P. Morgan & Co. was the fiscal agent for the Japanese government in the late 1920s, so it had access to an immense amount of information on the Japanese economy. In 1927, Lamont visited Japan, where he was lavishly entertained at the highest levels of the

Table 4.2. *Some Securities of "Foreign" Electric Light and Power Companies Outstanding in the U.S. Market, 1925*

Country Company	Rate (%)	Date of Issue/ Maturity	Amount ($000s)	Offering or Lead (L) House	Notes
Australia					
Melbourne Electric Supply	7½	1922/1946	2,500	Lee, Higginson	£ issue; $2.5 million in U.S.
Austria					
Lower Austria Hydro-Electric Power	6½	1924/1946	3,000	F.J. Liseman (L)	Guaranteed by province
Tyrol Hydro Electric	7½	1925/1955	3,000	F.J. Liseman (L)	
Canada					
Montreal Tramways & Power	6	1924/1929	8,000		Partly sold in Canada
Duke Price Power	6	1924/1949	12,000		
Cuba					
Havana Electric Ry Light & Power	5	1922/1954	3,600	National City Co.	
France					
International Power Securities (Union d'Électricité)	6½	1924/1954	4,000	Aldred & Co.	Indirectly connected with GE
Germany					
Electric Power Corp.	6½	1925/1950	7,500	Harris, Forbes; Lee, Higginson; Brown Bros.	

(continued)

Table 4.2 (*continued*)

Country Company	Rate (%)	Date of Issue/ Maturity	Amount ($000s)	Offering or Lead (L) House	Notes
Italy					
Italian Power	6½	1923/1928	2,000		
Japan					
Gt. Consolidated Electric Power	7	1924/1944	15,000	Dillon, Read	
Gt. Consolidated Electric Power	6½	1925/1950	13,500	Dillon, Read (L)	
Toho Electric Power	7	1925/1955	15,000	Dillon, Read; Guaranty Co. NY; Harris, Forbes	
Ujigawa Electric Power	7	1925/1945	14,000	Guaranty Co. NY (L)	
Tokio Electric Light Co.	6	1925/1928	24,000	Guaranty Co. NY (L)	
Latin America					
American & Foreign Power		1923	40,000		Stock, sold partly in Europe, covering Guatemala, Cuba, Panama

Source: Robert W. Dunn, *American Foreign Investments* (New York: B.W. Huebsch and Viking, 1926), 36–43, supplemented by ibid., 11–12. The above table only covers borrowings specific to electric light and power; it does not include borrowings by manufacturers (Siemens, for example) or by enclave-type companies that installed electric power as part of their resource development. Even so, it is incomplete. Note that the name of Italian Power Company was changed to International Power Securities Corporation in November 1924; Dunn's book does not reflect that change.

government. While there, he advised on the merger between Tokio Electric Power and Tokio Electric Light and how the combination would make the financing process in the United States easier. In December 1927, Lamont received a cable from Yasuzaemon Matsunaga, the principal person on the Japanese side in this combination: "Merger done Matsunaga responding Your advise splendid Merry Christmas." The merger occurred in April 1928.[222] In that year, when its 1925 bond issue matured, Tokio Electric Light refunded it; and in the same year, a New York banking group, led by the Guaranty Co., floated $70 million 6 percent first mortgage gold bonds for the Tokio Electric Light, due in 1953. A lesser amount of that same issue was introduced in London by Lazard Brothers and Whitehall Trust Ltd.[223] Other Japanese companies borrowed in New York, including Great Consolidated Electric Power Co., Toho Electric Power Co., and Ujigawa Electric Power Co. Some of these also had smaller sterling issues.[224] By year-end 1930, Japanese corporate bonds held in the United States amounted to $143 million and were entirely the obligations of electric light and power companies. These large borrowings were all publicly offered between 1924 and 1929. By way of comparison, the level of the entire (*all sectors*) U.S. foreign direct investment in Japan at year-end 1930 was a mere $61 million.[225] There were no foreign direct investments by Americans or other nationalities in Japanese electric utilities. However, Japanese investors were making outward foreign direct investments in electric utilities in Korea and Manchuria.[226]

If the large New York commercial banks were involved in international electric utilities finance, so, too, were U.S. investment bankers: Prominent examples were Kuhn, Loeb; Dillon, Read; Lee, Higginson; W. A. Harriman & Co.; Brown Brothers (these last two combined into Brown Brothers Harriman in 1931); Harris, Forbes; Bonbright & Co.; and Aldred & Co. Display advertisements in the *New York Times* covered share and bond offerings, and on the "tombstones" (as the advertisements for the securities listings were called) appeared the subsidiaries of the commercial banks along side the investment banks. Foreign banks, often with agencies in New York, might join in the offerings. Typically, for a securities issue there would be a lead bank, with other banks participating.[227]

The principal foreign *corporate* borrowers in the United States in the 1920s were from Canada, Germany, Italy, and Japan.[228] A large part of the Italian borrowings appear to have been through public utility holding companies set up in the United States, which we will discuss shortly. On the other hand, Società Generale Italiana Edison di Elettricità (the Edison Company, Milan) – the dominant factor in the hydroelectrical industry in the Lombardy region of northern Italy – issued on October 10, 1929 American depository shares for the convenience of U.S. securities holders, shares that were traded on the New York Stock Exchange. The firm (like some of the other big Italian electric utilities) also issued dollar bonds.[229]

ADSs (American depository shares) and ADRs (American depository receipts), which became very popular in the United States toward the end of the 1980s, were first introduced in the late 1920s, as Americans came to hold sizable foreign portfolio investments. Investors paid for the stock in dollars. The shares or receipts traded on exchanges along with other dollar-denominated issues.[230]

German corporate borrowers included manufacturers as well as electric utilities; we do not know the proportion of German corporate borrowings that went to the electric utilities.[231] Among the German light and power companies that raised money in the United States in the late 1920s were the Electric Power Corp. (1925), Consolidated Hydro-Electric Works of Upper Württemberg (1926), Silesia Electric Corp. (1926), Berlin City Electric Co. (1926 and 1929), Brandenburg Electric Power Co. (1928), and East Prussia Power Co. (1928).[232] Beginning in 1925, National City Bank's subsidiary, National City Co., managed a series of sizable bond issues for the majority state-owned German public utility Rhine-Westphalia Electric Power Corporation.[233] National City Bank had close relationships with General Electric and American & Foreign Power Co. Networks of participants in these financial transactions were conversant with the ins and outs of the electric utilities sector, with German, Italian, and Japanese borrowings.

The largest of all foreign corporate borrowings in the United States in the 1920s were by Canadian firms. Far more than in previous years, Canadian companies drew on U.S. capital resources. Canadian brokers were comfortable trading on U.S. exchanges, and it is not at all surprising that Canada ranked first in the number of corporate issues. During the 1920s, there were important U.S.-dollar-denominated bond issues for Canadian power companies.[234] At the same time, U.S. direct investors in Canada supplemented their own reinvested earnings with added U.S. borrowings.[235] A large number of American electric utilities had Canadian investments, some of which were direct investments; typically, these U.S. utilities obtained outside financing – that is, they went to the public for such financing.[236]

When there were offerings of the foreign securities, U.S. and foreign public utilities, holding companies, investment companies, and individuals would fill their portfolios with the securities. Much criss-cross ownership occurred by (and of) holding company and operating company securities doing business outside the United States (that is, foreign firms invested in securities of electric utilities in the United States as these same companies were investing abroad). This cross-ownership story involving inward and outward investments was not merely a U.S. phenomenon; it was true of European and Canadian firms as well. Moreover, after 1924, as bonds of light and power companies came to be seen as reliable investment securities, insurance companies operating in the United States acquired foreign, particularly Canadian, corporate bonds for their portfolios.[237]

Bankers, who placed their firms' names on the "tombstones," were often active in structuring the financing of the foreign (or domestic) utility, as in Thomas Lamont's role in the large Japanese merger. At other times, bankers did far more. Thus, by the end of the 1920s Harriman & Co. was making ambitious plans for the electrification of Poland, plans that were clearly those of a direct investor.[238] In 1929, press reports indicated that Harriman had acquired a "large block of shares in Oberschlesischen Elektrizitäts und Gas AG, which accounted for more than 25 percent of Polish power production."[239]

As an intermediary for U.S. investments in Germany, there was Paul Warburg's American & Continental Corporation, designed to provide financial assistance to German borrowers. Many European banks took part in this holding company, and its general financial contribution to German business included electric utilities. The initiative was a combination of Americans and Germans.[240]

Longer and more deeply engaged in international business in the electric light and power sector was the Boston banker John E. Aldred. In the 1920s, he set up investment houses in New York, London, and Paris, and he became a participant in complex holding company structures that related to Italian and French financing of public utilities (see below). We have mentioned his involvements in the Shawinigan and Saguenay developments in Canada. In January 1927, the Shawinigan Water and Power Co. purchased all the common stock of Eastern Canada Power Company Ltd.; it also held interests in a number of other Canadian utilities.[241] William J. Hausman and John L. Neufeld described Aldred "as both a utility executive and a financier." He had a vast web of contacts, but no full-scale in-house engineering and managerial services unit.[242]

By contrast, the engineering firm *qua* underwriter and investment banker Stone & Webster continued to be engaged in ownership and contractual dealings with foreign public utilities during the 1920s. Thomas Hughes writes that "Stone & Webster, while performing most of the functions of a holding company," did not take the first step in that direction until 1925, when it participated in the formation and financing of the Engineers Public Service Corporation. While heavily involved in domestic utilities, Stone & Webster also participated (with Aldred) in holding companies that were engaged in financing Italian and French electric utilities. Separately, Stone & Webster, for example, had interests in utilities in Poland in Utilities Corporation (Poland) Ltd. (12 percent of the voting stock), in Italy in Società Idroelettrica Piemonte, Turin (18,702 shares), and in Jamaica in Jamaica Public Services Ltd. (a joint venture with the Canadian industrialist Russell Bell).[243]

In the United States, by the end of 1929, key utility holding companies dominated the domestic market; each was domestically controlled as were the subsidiary operating companies. All were traded on stock exchanges and attracted inward portfolio investors at the same time as the holding companies made outward foreign direct investments.[244] In September 1929, Harris, Forbes and the American Founders group (a U.S.-based investment company group) organized the Public Utility Holding Corporation, with plans for South American, French, and German investments. (Above, we noted that it picked up shares in International Paper and Power Co., which operated in Canada.) The Deutsche Bank und Disconto-Gesellschaft (from a 1929 merger of Deutsche Bank with Disconto-Gesellschaft), for example, made investments in this U.S.-based holding company.[245] The inward investments in U.S. utilities were part of the complicated cosmopolitan finance of the 1920s that combined inward and outward international investments and foreign portfolio and foreign direct investments.[246]

It was the outward foreign investments from the United States, however, that made the difference and truly mattered, and the holding companies took on great importance. Most of the large *domestic* holding companies had outward foreign investments – and not only in Canada.[247] In addition, some holding companies held foreign portfolio investments, but more significant were the sizable foreign direct investments, often replacing (substituting for) the overseas investments of other nationalities, particularly the British in Latin America. For the direct investors, the strategy for the most part became that of merger and acquisition, not "greenfield" (new) operations.[248] This was in keeping with the wave of mergers occurring in the United States in the late 1920s. It was also in line with the fact that many separate electric utility companies had been set up around the world, and U.S. utility holding companies perceived the need for rationalization of these often inefficient units. American engineers could do this, and their companies would profit in the process. Americans did what the Belgian-based Sofina was undertaking, so they were not exceptional in this regard.

Holding companies took different forms, as our text above and the U.S.-Italian financing story that follows illustrate. The latter had a subtext of U.S.-French financing. As in the case of the American & Continental Corporation, in German finance these U.S. holding companies were created with the cooperation of Italians and Frenchmen in order to finance their enterprises. Many of the key players in the internationalization of electric utilities participated. Right after the World War I armistice, a representative of American International Corporation (see above) traveled to Italy to study the opportunities in electrification, and in the immediate postwar period it developed a financing plan that came to naught.[249] In 1920, Count Giuseppe Volpi, the founder and head of a leading Italian power company, Società Adriatica di Elettricità (SADE), organized a financial holding company in Italy, with subscriptions from the principal Italian electric groups and with the aim of obtaining support from Wall Street. Volpi contacted General Electric and John E. Aldred; the latter formed companies in New York City and London to issue bonds to finance Italian electric companies. Once again, nothing came of these trial runs. Not until 1922–1923 was the first noteworthy agreement reached between representatives of Società Generale Italiana Edison di Elettricità (the Italian Edison Company), Credito Italiano (a large Italian bank and one of the main shareholders in the Edison enterprise), Stone & Webster, Aldred, and General Electric (the last three had been active in the formation of American International Corporation). The result was that in April 1923 the Italian Power Co. came into being and started business that October. Its stated purpose was to finance in the United States electric light and power companies operating in Italy. It would invest American capital, under the "supervision of a specialized group of American businessmen." Italian Power raised $2 million in the U.S. market for the Italian Edison Company.[250] The next step (in November 1924) was the renaming of Italian Power; it morphed into International Power Securities Corporation (IPSC), which would acquire securities of electric utilities in the United States and abroad; like its predecessor, it was involved in the financing (through credits and/or bonds) of the Italian Edison Company and other key Italian electrical enterprises. The name change, however, reflected the extension of its activities into French electric utilities finance. The prime mover continued to be Aldred, IPSC's president. Aldred was also on the board of the Italian Edison Company. Alcoa's head, Arthur Vining Davis, along with GE and Stone & Webster representatives served on the IPSC board, continuities from Italian Power. In 1926, Giangiacomo Ponti, a member of the Italian parliament and head of Società Idroelettrica Piemonte (Turin), one of the Italian firms for which IPSC raised money, applauded the significance of the marriage between "Italian electrical and American financial genius in the development of electricity and its application to industry in Italy." In addition, IPSC developed financing for French electric utilities through Union d'Électricité, a utility identified with the French entrepreneurs Albert Petsche and Ernest Mercier (French Thomson-Houston was also involved). Petsche joined the IPSC board (he had not been on the board of its predecessor). IPSC had shareholdings in Union d'Électricité and extended a $4 million long-term loan to that company. Aldred, with his investment house in Paris, built up strong French connections.

As IPSC expanded, an agreement was signed between the Italian and U.S. governments on Italian war debts. (Negotiations were led on the Italian side by Giuseppe Volpi, Italian Minister of Finance, 1925–1928.) This accord gave new and stronger guarantees of reliability to all the Italian economic actors coming to Wall Street in search of capital. Between 1925 and 1928, a number of projects were discussed within Italy and the United States on how to move greater amounts of capital from the United States to the burgeoning Italian electric power industry.[251]

This would not occur through IPSC. In *Moody's Manual (Utilities) 1928*, Carlo Orsi of Credito Italiano was listed as being on the board of IPSC, but in *Moody's Manual (Utilities) 1929* and subsequently, IPSC had no Italian directors. Petsche, however, remained on the IPSC board, indicative of that holding company's new focus on French finance. Indeed, it was suggested that IPSC's role in Italy might bring orders to French manufacturers. Throughout the 1920s, IPSC continued under Aldred's direction.[252]

Meanwhile, in January 1928 Italian Superpower Corporation was incorporated in Delaware to acquire a substantial interest (but in no case a majority) in the stock of a large number of the principal electric light and power companies in Italy. The latter provided their shares in return for preferred shares in Italian Superpower. All the major Italian electric utilities participated. Accordingly, the ownership of Italian Superpower was shared between Americans and Italians. The board had 23 members – 12 Italians and 11 Americans. There were representatives from such utilities as SADE (Volpi), Unione Esercizi Elettrici, and Società Idroelettrica Piemonte. First and foremost among the Italian banks involved was Banca Commerciale Italiana (BCI), but also taking part in the new venture were Credito Italiano, Banco di Roma, and Banca Nazionale di Credito. Also included on the board were Italian manufacturers, among them Pirelli (which made insulated cables). At origin, the vice chairman of Italian Superpower was Giuseppe Toeplitz, managing director of BCI. Toeplitz hoped through Italian Superpower to reduce the number of electric utility shares in the portfolio of BCI in order to introduce more liquidity in BCI's balance sheet. From the U.S. side, Italian Superpower was governed by individuals associated with Electric Bond and Share and American & Foreign Power Co. Its chairman and president was S.A. Mitchell, who was on the board of American & Foreign Power and was vice president of Bonbright & Co. The new company would furnish financing for the Italian electricity sector.

In June 1929, barely a year and a half after Italian Superpower had been organized, American Superpower Corporation (which had been formed by Bonbright & Co. in October 1923 as a public utility holding company) acquired 50 percent of the voting stock of Italian Superpower. American Superpower, which was categorized by the Securities and Exchange Commission under the rubric "Management Investment-Holding Companies," was huge, with assets totaling $225.5 million on December 31, 1929. By way of comparison, at that date the assets of International Power Securities (IPSC) were $43.7 million, while those of Italian Superpower were $38.9 million. The pyramiding did not stop. American Superpower, in turn, came to be one of the companies controlled by the Morgan-led public utility holding company United Corporation, organized late in 1929. As of December 31, 1929, United Corporation's assets were $332.5 million.[253]

Through these holding and sub-holding companies, U.S. finance and expertise became embedded in assisting the spread of electrification in Italy as well as in France. Did these holding companies make U.S. direct investments abroad? Were they entrepreneurial in nature? The answer is "yes" to both; but when we turn the coin over and ask, Through their ownership interests, did they "control" the Italian and French enterprises that they financed?, the answer becomes far more difficult. Clearly, the funds raised were significant and were provided with care and supervision. Both International Power Securities and Italian Superpower were administered by experienced men in the electric utilities sector. Yet to argue that these holding companies (and the U.S. participants involved) – rather than Giacinto Motta with the Edison company or Volpi with SADE – for example, ran the utilities would be wrong. It was Italian entrepreneurship that did that. Neither Motta nor Volpi "reported" to any American "boss"; and it is unlikely that the chief executives of the holding companies could have "fired" the Italians, who appear to have made the basic operating-company decisions. It is also improbable that Petsche's French businesses were U.S.-controlled. So perhaps we have a curious paradox, as suggested in Chapter 2, where direct investments could be made by a multinational enterprise (with overall strategic content) but without "control" of the companies in which it invested.

Among the new activities of the U.S. holding companies in the 1920s were the sizable foreign investments by Utilities Power and Light Corporation (UPLC). These were incontrovertibly U.S. direct investments abroad, and UPLC exercised control over the companies in which it invested. UPLC was a relatively small U.S. holding company, controlling less than 1 percent of the generating capacity in the United States, yet its investments in the United Kingdom have been described as the "most aggressive American initiative in electricity supply in Britain."[254] In 1925, Harley Clarke, head of the Chicago-based UPLC, dispatched his employee Massingberd Rogers to London to establish the Greater London and Counties Trust (GLCT). Rogers became the managing director, and on the board were Sir Philip Dawson, a prominent British consulting engineer and Conservative member of Parliament, along with William May of the London solicitors Slaughter and May. The initial capital came from America, and GLCT proceeded to acquire and to combine a number of small British electricity supply companies that could take advantage of British plans for a grid.

In a dramatic takeover in 1928, GLCT bought 95 percent of Edmundson's Electricity Corporation, a British enterprise that controlled directly or indirectly twenty-nine electricity supply companies. GLCT used the securities of these supply companies as collateral and borrowed from U.S. and British banks to finance that acquisition as well as others. By the end of 1929, virtually overnight, GLCT had control of fifty-four companies. As the purchases were occurring, Clarke's UPLC reorganized the group, rationalizing the operations and creating efficiencies in the process. When it first invested, UPLC had been secretive about its role, but after substantial equivocation in 1929 UPLC acknowledged publicly that it had obtained controlling interest in GLCT. By then, GLCT was either one of the largest (according to one source) or the largest (according to another source) distributor of power in the United Kingdom. U.S. business now had a major role in the U.K. light and power sector.[255]

Of all the U.S. holding companies that engaged in international business in light and power, by far the most substantial was Electric Bond and Share and its subsidiary American & Foreign Power Company. Electric Bond and Share, which had during the war and postwar years expanded in Cuba, Guatemala, and Panama, in December 1923 organized American & Foreign Power to acquire those foreign operations and to pursue further growth outside the United States. In February 1925, General Electric spun off its long-standing interest in Electric Bond and Share, severing GE's ownership, albeit retaining its "network" relationship with both Electric Bond and Share and American & Foreign Power.[256]

In the late 1920s, Electric Bond and Share had two principal subsidiaries with foreign investments. One was Electric Investors Inc. (formed in 1909) to trade, deal in, underwrite, and hold a diversified portfolio of securities (minority equity interests or bond holdings) in companies with operations (directly or indirectly) in Latin America, Canada, Europe, and Asia. By 1929, its holdings in public utilities included American & Foreign Power Co. (United States), Great Consolidated Electric Power Co. Ltd. (Japan), Toho Electric Power Co. Ltd. (Japan), Shawinigan Water and Power (Canada), British Columbia Power Corp. Ltd. (Canada), and Italian Superpower Corporation (United States). Electric Bond and Share did not exercise control over any of these companies (except for its American & Foreign Power subsidiary).[257]

American & Foreign Power was the more important of the two Electric Bond & Share subsidiaries, and in contrast with Electric Investors Inc., it did make direct investments; its activities were those of a multinational enterprise. The directors of American & Foreign Power in 1929–1930 reflected its cluster of contacts. Its chairman was S. Z. Mitchell, who had been president of Electric Bond and Share since its inception in 1905. On its board was Owen Young, chairman of the board of General Electric. Thus, even though after 1925 GE had no direct or indirect stock holdings in American & Foreign Power, GE sustained its association with that firm, and typically the utilities managed by American & Foreign Power purchased GE equipment.[258] The American & Foreign Power's board had several bankers: Charles E. Mitchell (National City Bank, New York), S. A. Mitchell (son of S. Z. Mitchell, a principal in Bonbright & Co., and chairman and president of Italian Superpower), Clarence Dillon (Dillon, Read & Co.), and A. A. Tilney (Bankers Trust Company). No Morgan representative adorned the board, but there were Morgan "connections." George H. Howard, president of Morgan's new United Corporation, the major public utility holding company established in

FIGURE 4.2. S. Z. Mitchell (1862–1944)
Note: Sidney Zollicoffer Mitchell led Electric Bond and Share from its formation in 1905 until his retirement in 1933. He was also Chairman of American & Foreign Power Company from its formation in 1923 until 1933.
Source: Photograph from Sidney Alexander Mitchell, *S. Z. Mitchell and the Electrical Industry* (New York: Farrar, Straus & Cudahy, 1960), Frontispiece.

1929, served as a director of American & Foreign Power, as he had in earlier years. (In 1927, he was identified as being with Simpson, Thacher & Bartlett, a Wall Street firm specializing in utility law that had been the firm of Morgan partner Dwight Morrow.) Also on the American & Foreign Power board was Sosthenes Behn, president of International Telephone & Telegraph (some of the American & Foreign Power concessions in Latin America involved telephones as well as light and power), who had close Morgan ties. Not only was United Corporation represented on the board, but so were two other U.S. holding companies: American Gas and Electric Company and United Electric Securities Company.[259]

From its origins in 1923, American & Foreign Power furnished managerial and technical expertise to the companies in which it invested. To use the German vocabulary, it followed an *Unternehmergeschäft* form. It made sizable direct investments in public utilities in Argentina, Brazil, Chile, Colombia, Costa Rica, Ecuador, Mexico, and Venezuela and China and India, as well as enlarging its investments in the countries where at its foundation it had inherited operations: Cuba, Guatemala, and Panama.[260] In 1926, it bought a Canadian free standing company located in Camaguey, Cuba, extending its vast operations on that island. By 1929, every small town in Cuba was electrified, virtually all of them by American & Foreign Power, and the latter's gross earnings from its Cuban subsidiaries were much greater than from its subsidiaries in any other country.[261]

During 1928, American & Foreign Power acquired the Mexican and Chilean electric power interests of the English-owned Pearson firm Whitehall Electric Investments Ltd. and in 1929 (1) the Argentine holdings of the English free standing company Atlas Light and Power Co. Ltd., (2) control of the Canadian free standing company Northern Mexican Power & Development Co., and (3) a 50 percent interest in the English free standing company Tata Hydro-Electric Agencies Ltd., Bombay.[262]

American & Foreign Power not only replaced prior English and Canadian enterprises, but the American giant also took over the properties of other U.S. investors. Thus, in 1928 American & Foreign Power acquired the majority of the outstanding bonds, preferred stock, and common stock of Mexican Utilities Company, a U.S. holding company that had earlier in the decade united hydroelectric properties in Mexico, including those in and adjacent to the states of Guanajuato (including the cities of León de los Aldama and Celaya) and San Luis Potosí.[263] American & Foreign Power's Mexican expansion that year swept up electric light and power companies in Mérida, Torreón, Aguascalientes, Saltillo, Durango, Zacatecas, and Mazatlán. By the end of 1928, its operating subsidiaries in Mexico supplied electric light and power (and/or other public utilities) to 89 communities; by the end of 1929, the number was 108 communities.[264]

By the end of 1929, American & Foreign Power supplied electric light and power services to 246 communities in Brazil. That year, its annual report recorded new concession contracts, new hydroelectric developments, high-voltage lines, and arrangements to interconnect with the power system of Brazilian Traction, Light and Power.[265] In Argentina, where it had acquired the properties of Atlas Light and Power as well as numerous other facilities, its 1929 annual report indicated that "to permit a proper and orderly development of power generation and transmission by zones, your Company has assisted the officers and directors of these properties to work out a complete corporate reorganization of such Argentine interests ...." The company's principal properties in Argentina were reorganized into five separate companies, which later came to be called the ANSEC group.[266]

One of the largest acquisitions of American & Foreign Power was its takeover of control of the Shanghai Power Company in 1929. This electric light and power company was in the International Settlement of Shanghai, and American & Foreign Power assumed control from the Municipal Council of the International Settlement. American & Foreign Power obtained a concession contract that was unlimited in duration (according to the firm's annual report); other sources indicate that its monopoly rights were for forty years, and the Municipal Council reserved the right to repurchase the plant at the end of the four decades. Local firms and residents were encouraged to invest in Shanghai Power, which was American & Foreign Power's global practice. At the same time as American & Foreign Power had control and provided the managerial expertise, shares in Shanghai Power were purchased by investors of British, Chinese, and Japanese nationalities. American & Foreign Power anticipated a vast expansion and modernization of the existing facilities.[267]

The enlargement of American & Foreign Power's span of influence, especially in 1928–1929, was awesome, as it built new facilities and took over existing ones. While often its expansion was favorably perceived, in other instances it was greatly feared. Thus, on January 10, 1929, the Calcutta Electric Supply Corporation Ltd., London, passed a resolution designed to bar hostile takeovers by foreign (not British) firms: No more than 20 percent of issued shares of any class could be controlled by foreigners, and all the directors of the company were required to be British subjects.[268] This was designed as protection against a possible move by American & Foreign Power. In 1929, its Asian expansion was not only to China but to India (with the aforementioned investment in the Tata company in Bombay).

By 1929, American & Foreign Power was the largest multinational enterprise in public utilities. It explained its own procedures: (1) to investigate and to acquire properties; (2) to rearrange the contractual relations with the governing authorities so as to open the way to development; (3) to reorganize the financial structures of the operating companies to permit improvements and plant additions at the lowest practicable cost; (4) to prepare plans for development and construction of new power plant capacity and modern transmission and distribution systems; (5) to apply the latest, most modern commercial development to the property, in the process selling new electrical merchandise in well-lighted, attractive stores; (6) to introduce new operating and accounting methods, so as to improve efficiency while upgrading service and lowering operating costs; and (7) to involve customers, employees, and the general public in the locale served by offering preferred stock. It summarized its goals as offering better, less costly, and more dependable service, while increasing profits to the company through larger volume and more hours of service.[269]

From the start, this had been no easy task. When, for example, American & Foreign Power took over Whitehall Electric Investments' holdings in Chile, the British Pearson group interests in that country had been in numerous disputes with Chilean governmental authorities. Indeed, when negotiations had broken down with the municipality of Santiago in 1927, Compañía Chilena had worried about expropriation.[270] Yet at the end of the 1920s, American & Foreign Power was confident that it could make a difference. By December 31, 1929, it provided light and power to some 755 communities in Latin America and Asia and was very much in a growth mode.[271]

CONCLUSIONS

During the late 1920s, there had been a formidable extension of electrification around the globe stimulated by the availability of domestic and international capital and private-sector economic activities. Webs of international interrelationships characterized the management and financing of the expansion. Direct investments were interwoven with portfolio ones. Holding companies with cross-ownership were ubiquitous. Canadian-registered and sometimes -directed firms rationalized prewar companies. Canadian firms remained as important players in mobilizing money needed to encourage the international spread of electrification. The Canadian role was more one of continuity than discontinuity, although there was the greater use of holding company structures and more sophistication in international finance, and, in certain cases, Canadians did abdicate to U.S. corporate expansion. The new involvements of Sofina in the Canadian story did not materially change the Canadians' role, for Sofina decentralized its activities.

After a searing interruption caused by World War I, by the late 1920s German electrotechnical equipment manufacturers had resumed exporting and were attempting to reestablish themselves worldwide, but there was little available German capital; throughout the decade, Germany was an importer of capital, having become a great debtor nation. Its public utilities (and its electrotechnical manufacturers) borrowed abroad. Attempts at revival notwithstanding, Germany's pre–World War I role as a pioneer in global electrification had disappeared, although there was not yet a full awareness of this. The structures that had been set up before the war – the once German-dominated Sofina, Elektrobank, and Indelec – assumed lives of their own, yet many of the prewar personal networks and relationships endured. Informal associations often replaced more formal ones, and toward the end of the decade Germans began to reappear on corporate boards of companies outside Germany.

Great Britain failed to prosper in the 1920s, and the British global role in electrification had, if anything, diminished over the postwar years. Great Britain not only had a relatively backward electrical manufacturing (and electric utilities) sector, but it had lost its premier position in finance. Securities issues were floated in London; free standing companies persisted, operating from Hungary to Malaya (Malaysia) to the Sudan; from a global perspective, however, British involvement (like that of Germany) had become far less significant than in the pre-1914 years. The United Kingdom was still a creditor nation, yet in Latin America and Canada and even in Asia, British direct investment was in retreat, challenged by the rise of U.S. businesses.

From the immediate aftermath of World War I onward, Belgian, Swiss, and French firms participated in the international spread of electrification, and there were some new outward Italian corporate involvements abroad. Among the Belgian firms, Sofina, in particular, took on more importance. The Japanese had foreign direct investments in electric utilities in Asia, mainly in Korea and Manchuria.

It was the monumental U.S. outward foreign investments in finance and in direct investments in electric utilities, however, that captured the spotlight during the 1920s. At year end 1929, the sector's most important U.S. corporate investor, American & Foreign Power's subsidiaries, had over 47,000 employees, virtually all stationed abroad.[272] American & Foreign Power's main involvements were in Latin America, where it dominated the supply of electric light and power. By 1929, it had made giant investments in China and smaller ones in India. At the end of the decade, outward U.S. foreign ownership and control in the electric utilities sector were far greater than before the First World War by every measure: (1) total value, (2) percentage of U.S. business abroad, and (3) percentage of global investment in the sector.

While U.S. foreign investments in electric utilities were global, the strategies and actors were different in different locations. The largest amount of the U.S. outward foreign direct investments was in the western hemisphere, from Canada to Argentina. This was supplemented with additional finance, often arranged by the direct investor. Within Europe, America's stakes in foreign electric utilities were widespread, but with the exception of the giant direct investment interests in the United Kingdom by Utilities Power and Light Corporation, they tended to be in various forms of partnership with key European players. Holding companies had direct investments, typically minority interests. Aside from certain enclave type investments, there was a marked absence of U.S. direct (or financial) investments in Africa. American & Foreign Power was the rare U.S. firm with direct investments in Asia in electric light and power. Likewise, Japan was alone in Asia in obtaining large amounts of U.S. finance.

Although by 1929 U.S. international investment in utilities was the largest, firms such as Sofina were more than minor players. Second only in size to Electric Bond and Share/American & Foreign Power, Sofina, from its Brussels head office, was involved globally in encouraging new electrification projects. Sofina was the center of a far-flung business group; its "ownership" as well as its operations were international; its major activities were in Europe. Its chief executives referred to its "partners" in international investments. By decade's end, Sofina had renewed its associations with the Berlin-based Gesfürel. In addition, the Belgian-based Empain group maintained its international business, as did other Belgian-French connections.

Over the course of the decade, the Canadian outward role in foreign investments had become more embedded in networks involving European investors. Canadians were still key international investors in Latin America, where Americans, British, and Swiss (albeit in a smaller role) – and to a lesser extent, Italian entrepreneurship (along with capital) – were very much in evidence in ownership of electric utilities. CHADE was technically Spain's largest multinational enterprise, with its giant stakes in Argentine electrification (actually, it is far better seen as part of the Sofina network). Indeed, for a very brief interval in the late 1920s, to many observers it seemed that the global economy of the pre-World War I era had been re-created and that this was reflected in the growth of electrification. To be sure, to some extent public-sector involvements were now infringing more than in earlier times on the rise in foreign direct investments in electric utilities; new public ownership and new regulations were unquestionably more in evidence than before World War I. There had been, of course, the dramatic Soviet takeover of foreign-owned properties during the Russian Revolution, prior to which time electrification in Russia had been overwhelmingly by foreign direct investors. From Australia to Finland, provinces and municipalities had replaced much of the pre–World War I foreign ownership with domestically run activities. In some countries – such as Germany, Italy, and Japan – there was clearly domestic management of public utilities, the large foreign financing notwithstanding. Understanding what were and what were not foreign direct investments in electric utilities (and how to consider ownership and control with pyramided holding companies) became increasingly difficult.

In the new nations carved out of the Austro-Hungarian, German, Russian, and Ottoman empires, the prewar German interests had to a large extent been replaced by both the renewal of and the new activities of Belgian, French, Swiss, Swedish, and, to a lesser extent, British investors. In Poland, there was sizable interest by American investors. Table 1.4, in Chapter 1, suggests that in many (but far from all) countries the foreign role was probably less as sovereign states wanted to set the rules of the game. But if the dominance, measured in these crude percentages, was smaller, the size of (the amount of, the quantity of) foreign private-sector involvements appears to have been far greater.

Overall, while there had been an immense increase in foreign financing without foreign direct investments, nonetheless in 1929–1930 multinational enterprises continued to be highly significant in the spread of electrification, in the construction of large-scale power stations, and in the rationalization of systems. Foreign direct investment was substantial in the numerous enclaves around the world and in less remote places, where power-hungry industries made investments. In Latin American urban areas, five giant companies, owned and run by foreign investors, towered over markets: American & Foreign Power (with operations in Argentina, Brazil, Chile, Colombia, Costa Rica, Cuba, Ecuador, Guatemala, Mexico, Panama, and Venezuela), Mexican Tramways/Mexican Light and Power Co. Ltd., Brazilian Traction, Light and Power Co., CHADE (with Argentine business), and International Power Company Ltd. (with operating companies in Bolivia, British Guiana (Guyana), El Salvador, Mexico, and Venezuela).

In some parts of the world in 1929, inward foreign direct investments were far more evident than they had been in 1914. This was the case from Canada, to China, to Great Britain, to Greece. In Canada, the big U.S. developments at Saguenay made the difference. In China, American & Foreign Power controlled Shanghai Power, the largest power company in the entire country. In Great Britain, Utilities Power and Light Corporation of Europe's subsidiary the Greater London and Counties Trust, with its acquisition of Edmundson's Electricity Corporation, had become a leader in that nation's electrification. In Greece, new British and French foreign investments had laid the groundwork for extensive electrification. In colonial Africa and Asia, there were new foreign direct investments in providing light and power, typically, but not always, by firms set up in the home of the imperial power.

Throughout Europe in 1929, there was a fear of an American invasion by multinational enterprises. In India, at least one company introduced "poison pill" defenses to prevent a U.S. corporate takeover. Concerns notwithstanding, worldwide the new financial structures established in the 1920s, combining multinational enterprises with finance, seemed destined to create the possibilities of worldwide electrification. Given the many interconnections, especially among holding companies, was international consolidation of "control" of a vast global system conceivable?

5

Basic Infrastructure, 1929–1945

On October 24, 1929, and in the weeks following, the stock market crashed in the United States. There were multiple problems in the workings of the international economy before the Wall Street crisis. Given America's pivotal role in the world economy, its aftermath meant cascading, albeit uneven, consequences around the globe.[1] Initially, however, it did not appear that the operations and growth of electric utilities would be seriously affected. People cut back on their electricity consumption very little. The expansion of electrification in the 1920s had created a global demand for more access to electric power and added supplies. There was a demonstration effect: As the average consumer became aware of the comforts that came with electricity and new efficiencies brought down its price, demand rose on a worldwide basis. To be sure, electric utilities would incur losses in revenues with the downturn, but contemporaries assumed that this would be merely temporary and that electric utility companies were fundamentally sound. Thus, when the prices of utility securities fell in 1930, along with those of other stocks and bonds, knowledgeable foreign investors saw this as an opportunity to buy American public utility securities on the cheap. The important Swiss holding company Bank für Elektrische Unternehmungen (Elektrobank), Zurich, for example, made its very first U.S. investments in 1930.[2] In that year and even in early 1931, respectively, J. P. Morgan & Co. had no problem arranging to float loans for Toho Electric Power Company and Taiwan Electric Power Company.[3] In 1930, the leading foreign businesses financed by publicly offered securities in the United States were those in electric light and power.[4] National City Bank – through National City Company – had a Rhine-Westphalia Electric Power Company (RWE) issue of $20 million in March 1930 and another, far smaller one, $7.5 million, in February 1931. RWE's impressive new plant at Herdecke on the Ruhr River, its construction long underway, began operations on

Authors: Mira Wilkins, Harm Schröter, and William J. Hausman.

January 28, 1930.[5] During 1930, Deutsche Bank und Disconto-Gesellschaft raised its investments in the American firm Public Utility Holding Corporation (formed in September 1929), as the latter acquired interests in Argentina, France, Germany, and Luxembourg.[6]

Indeed, in July 1930 the *New York Times* commented that the rapid growth of public utility holding companies in the United States – Insull, Electric Bond and Share, and United Corporation, as well as dozens of smaller ones – had "exhausted the possibilities of further expansion by consolidation in this country." The result was, in the newspaper's view, that leading U.S. utility executives and investment bankers were finding business abroad more attractive. Berlin City Electric Company (all of the stock of which was owned by the city of Berlin) had issued $15 million in sinking funds in April 1930. This was its third outstanding loan in the U.S. market (the other two were for $20 million in 1926 and $15 million in February 1929), all issued by Dillon, Read & Co.[7] This was pure finance, not foreign direct investment. Yet it was part of what seemed to be the on-going ability of foreign firms in electric utilities to get U.S. financing into 1930, U.S. economic problems notwithstanding. Berlin City Electric and the earlier mentioned RWE flotation were "government-guaranteed" loans.[8]

The *New York Times*, in its July 1930 story, noted that not only were American banking groups interested to an unprecedented extent in European utilities, but "the backward conditions of electric power and light . . . of most foreign countries leaves room for numerous investment opportunities which American bankers are eager to seize in collaboration with financial groups abroad." The paper identified Bonbright, Field Glore, Harris Forbes, as well as Chase Securities, Guaranty Co., E. Rollins & Sons, J. G. White & Co., G. L. Ohrstrom & Co., Aldred & Co., and National City Co., among the clusters of U.S. firms taking part in mid-1930 in the financing of electric utilities that operated abroad.[9] That July 1930, Bankers Trust, New York, was preparing plans for a new Superpower Corporation, which in cooperation with Deutsche Bank und Disconto-Gesellschaft, would acquire a number of German utilities.[10] The concentration so evident in the United States would be further extended.

Not only U.S. bankers and brokers saw opportunities outside the United States. There were numerous U.S. outward foreign direct investments. In 1930, for the first time, the Insull group, the Utilities Power and Light Corporation, and Iowa Southern Utilities invested in Canada. All (except perhaps Iowa Southern Utilities) had earlier made other outward foreign direct investments. By far the most important outward U.S. foreign direct investments in electric utilities in 1930 were those of American & Foreign Power Company, which obtained significant new properties in Argentina, Brazil, Chile, and Venezuela (while at home it borrowed heavily and paid no dividend on its common stock).[11]

As in 1928–1929, so in 1930, there were newly organized public utility holding companies in the United States and Canada, designed for international business. One was the European Electric Corp. (EElC), incorporated in Montreal, Canada, on February 3, 1930. EElC acquired substantial holdings in (1) Società Adriatica di Elettricità (SADE), the key Italian electricity supply company headed by Count Giuseppe Volpi; (2) Compagnie Italo-Belge pour Entreprises d' Électricité et d'Utilité Publique, a Belgian corporation (another unit in the Volpi group), (3) Compagnie Européenne pour Entreprises d'Électricité et d'Utilité Publique (Europel), and (4) Iberian Electric Ltd., a Spanish corporation. The reader will recall from Chapter 4 that Volpi had been involved in obtaining substantial sums in the U.S. market for Italian public utilities. He figures as an important individual in the overlapping networks of finance. By 1929–1930, he had his own cluster of companies. His new Canadian holding company (EElC) had minority interests in electric utilities in Austria, Germany, Greece, Italy, Poland, and Spain. Initially, EElC announced that it anticipated its income would be derived from investments, but it explained that it was "expected that as the activities of the company and its subsidiaries increased, income from the supervisory and engineering contracts and from commissions and fees incident to the financing and development will form an increasing part of the company's total revenue." Volpi was president of EElC. Directors included Marshall Field (investment banker and grandson of the namesake Chicago retailer), Giovanni Fummi (Morgan's representative in Italy), C. H. Minor (of International General Electric), and S. Z. Mitchell (chairman of the board of American & Foreign Power). EElC immediately had a debenture issue of $12.9 million, offered at par by Bonbright, Field Glore, and Banca Commerciale Italiana Trust Co. (New York). The last-named company was a subsidiary of the Italian bank BCI. Even though EElC was Canadian-registered, the interest on its debentures was to be paid in U.S. gold coin at the office or agency of the EElC in New York. Its Canadian registration notwithstanding, EElC was essentially an Italian-sponsored U.S. flotation. The individuals involved were those participating in the U.S. financing of the Italian electrical industry in the 1920s (see Chapter 4).[12] Volpi joined the board of directors of Société Financière de Transports et d'Entreprises Industrielles (Sofina) in 1930; in a reciprocal manner, Dannie Heineman of Sofina was elected to the board of Volpi's Italian utility Società Adriatica di Elettricità (SADE).[13]

Harold James has argued that the "depression" did not cross over the Atlantic from the United States to Europe until 1931; and if we consider electric utilities, this seems evident.[14] In 1930, for example, the Pearson group (Whitehall Securities/Whitehall Electric) in England had no qualms about making sizable new investments that would enable Greek electrification to expand and in the process give the Pearson group control over the Athens Piraeus Electricity Company Ltd. In addition, in December 1928 Fuerzas Motrices del Valle de Lecrin SA had been established in Spain to construct a large hydroelectric plant in the province of Almería. The contract for the work had been awarded to a Spanish company that was then unable to complete the project. Thus, in December 1930 the Pearson group obtained 91 percent of the share capital of this enterprise, with the goal of stepping into the breech.[15] The Pearson group also continued negotiations for other large projects – for example, in Belgrade, Yugoslavia.[16] Remember that the Pearsons had sold out to American & Foreign Power in Mexico and Chile and had both resources and experience to develop activities elsewhere.

In 1930, the British & International Utilities Ltd. (BIU), a corporation with plans to acquire stocks in utilities in the British Isles and the British Empire, was registered in England; control was shared by (1) Compagnie Italo-Belge pour Entreprises d'Électricité et d'Utilité Publique (Italo-Belge) – we have noted its participation a few months earlier in the formation of European Electric Corp. – and (2) Dawnay, Day & Co. Ltd., a new London issuing house. Volpi was chairman, and Lord Barnby of Lloyds Bank and the Earl of Westmoreland decorated the BIU board.[17] Earlier, a leading British engineer, Borlase Mathews, had obtained a franchise for a rural area in Lincolnshire that seemed to have great potential for bulk supply of electricity when the local grid lines had been constructed. When in 1931 Mathews found it difficult to raise money, he turned to the newly formed BIU, which took advantage of the opportunity. BIU (with its sister companies Italo-Belge and EElC) would in time extend its control to four other British power projects in Altrincham, Windermere, Thurso, and Campbell. These were relatively small investments, but they were indicative of the continuing international involvements and the continuing entrepreneurial role of Volpi.[18]

The French Durand group made new plans in 1930 for electrical developments in Constanta, a port city on the Black Sea in Romania.[19] Other firms explored more possibilities for electrical developments in Central and Eastern Europe. This was the case even as Harriman's grand plans for Poland – indicated in Chapter 4 – were being rejected by the Polish government. The new Swedish holding company Electro-Invest (formed in 1929) acquired concessions in Latvia, Poland, Romania, and Yugoslavia.[20] In Belgium in 1930, the reorganizations of the late 1920s took on new clarity: Société Générale de Belgique, Brussels, arranged a secret agreement between Sofina and Electrobel to "demarcate their respective zones of influence."[21] There were continuing attempts to rationalize the business in electric utilities, with Société Générale assuming an ever larger role. The rivalry between Banque de Bruxelles and Société Générale seemed to be resolved in the latter's favor. According to Réné Brion, from 1931 Sofina and Electrobel would be jointly managed through the association between Sofina and Société Générale.[22] After the elections in Egypt in January 1930, temporarily dormant negotiations between the Empain group and the Egyptian government on the Shubra power plant in Cairo were revived, and the Empain group would defeat its British/Belgian and British/German competitors in the Egyptian contest for contracts.[23]

During 1930, American bankers were reported to be increasingly active in the "Heineman-Oliven utility groups of Belgium and Germany, which, headed by Sofina and Gesfürel [Gesellschaft für Elektrische Unternehmungen], [had] electric power holdings throughout the world." Dannie Heineman (of Sofina) and his long-time friend Oscar Oliven (of AEG and the German holding company Gesfürel) were putting forward plans for the rationalization of electric utilities throughout Europe with a connecting grid.[24] Heineman and Oliven had dreams of a united Europe. Their plans, which seem to have taken shape in late 1929, were made public by Oliven in Berlin in June 1930 at the Second World Power Conference. In Cologne on November 28, 1930, and in Barcelona on December 2, 1930, Heineman (who described himself as an "engineer") gave a presentation titled "Outline of a New Europe," the text of which was published in 1931 in English as well as in French and German. Heineman and Oliven envisaged a Europe united by an electrical grid that crossed national borders. These two engineers, with their access to financial and managerial resources, would participate in creating a new Europe. There would be three North–South transmission lines and two East–West ones: The North–South lines would go: (1) Oslo–Hamburg–Berlin–Zurich–Genoa–Rome, (2) Calais–Paris–Lyon–Lisbon, and (3) Warsaw–Vienna–the Dalmatian coast across from Italy. The East–West lines, which intersected with the North–South lines,

MAP 5.1. The Project Heineman-Oliven
Source: Adapted by the authors from René Brion, "Le Rôle de la Sofina," in Monique Trédé-Boulmer, ed., *Le Financement de l'Industrie Électrique, 1880–1980* (Paris: PUF, 1994), 229.

would extend from (l) Katowice (Poland) to Berlin–Calais, connecting to Paris, and 2. Rostov (Russia) to Budapest–Vienna–Lyon, connecting to Lisbon.[25]

From Katowice to Lisbon, Sofina and/or AEG (directly or indirectly) had a tranche in the electricity supply companies.[26] The plans for a united European energy market were remarkable. Heineman's vision, in *Outline of a New Europe*, was even broader. He called for a "Europe, organized by statesmen, who with the co-operation of industrialists and business-men strive to attain economic ends by technical means," "a banking organization which, by careful utilisation of the gold reserves, assures the still precarious stability of many European currencies. . . . ," and a European customs union. European unity rested on "three pillars, the first *technical*, the second *administrative*, the third *financial*." Heineman said, "Federation is a necessity for Europe; it is bound to come."[27]

1931

Robert Kindersley, who published an article in *The Economic Journal* in September 1931 on British overseas investments in 1928 and 1929, never mentioned the 1929 U.S. stock market crash.[28] To be sure, there is always a time lag with publications in academic journals. September 1931 was when the United Kingdom finally abandoned its gold-backed pound. By then, the problems of the U.S. economy had engulfed Britain as well as the European continent. Remarkably, it was not until Kindersley's annual survey of British overseas investments for 1930, published in June 1932, that he acknowledged retrospectively that the close of 1929 "saw the beginning of a severe slump in the Stock and other markets, accompanied by the liquidation of international and other securities on a large scale."[29]

It was well over a year into the crisis before there came to be a worldwide awareness that the U.S. downturn was not an ordinary business cycle and that the entire international economy was at risk. The vision of Heineman and Oliven for a Europe united by electrical facilities across borders went unrealized. Technologically, it was entirely feasible, but it was an impossible dream, both economically (financial resources dried up) and politically (governments were turning increasingly to cope with purely domestic difficulties). Indeed, by the time Heineman's 1930 presentations were in print, in 1931, they were "dead on arrival."[30]

By the spring of 1931, it was unmistakable: There was a worldwide economic disaster. Capital flows from creditor nations (as measured by the balances on current account, gold, and foreign currency) plummeted from a high of $1,980 million in 1928 to a low of $510 million in 1930; "creditor" nations became net importers of capital by these measures.[31] There was by the spring of 1931 an awakening globally to how bad the situation was: Everywhere, banks were failing. The capital-intensive public utilities sector had relied heavily on renewals of financing from sources outside the operating firms. When the funding stopped, plans made could not be pursued.

As for Britain, Kindersley himself and his firm, Lazard Brothers, were in trouble by the summer of 1931. In July 1931, Kindersley, who was a director of the Bank of England, had gone to that bank with a plea for "rescue." Precipitating the problem was fraud at Lazard's Brussels office. Kindersley told the governor of the Bank of England that although help from S. Pearson & Son and Lazard's French parent house could be expected, it would be inadequate. (The reader will recall, Lazard Brothers was half owned by the former and half by Lazard Frères, Paris; Kindersley as chairman of the British Lazard house was acting on behalf of S. Pearson & Son.) The Bank of England stepped in and lent £3.5 million (ca. $17 million), not directly to Lazards but to S. Pearson & Son, which put the money at the disposal of its affiliate. And then, in May 1932, Lazards again had to be bailed out by the Bank of England (and the National Provincial Bank), this time to "the tune of" £2 million (ca. $6.8 million, after the devaluation of the pound).[32] According to Ioanna Pepelasis Minoglou, "in 1931 . . . with the intervention of the British government, the Whitehall Securities Corporation [an S. Pearson & Son affiliate] provided advances amounting to £2,000,000, thus enabling its [Athens electric power] subsidiary to bypass the foreign exchange shortage during the world financial crisis."[33] Was some of the £3.5 million loaned by the Bank of England to Pearson in 1931 devoted to that purpose? Probably. Our readers will recall from Chapter 4 that in 1926 Prudential Assurance had made a £2 million loan to the Athens company, guaranteed by the British Treasury.

Early in 1931, Dudley Docker reactivated his project proposal for Egyptian electrical developments, pressing the British Foreign Office for aid, in vain. In February, the British government's response was that such "super schemes for electric power development are so gigantic that we must walk delicately." At the end of March, Bernard Docker (Dudley's son) had arrived in Cairo, and London learned in May that Bernard had "'nobbled the principal potential customers of [electric] current' and was trying 'to absorb the existing concessionary companies.'" He was not successful in the big Aswan Dam project.[34]

The Italian electrical industry, which had depended on a steady stream of U.S. finance, faced major distress. By mid-1930 in Italy there was already a profound awareness that this was no ordinary downturn. In June 1930, Banca Commerciale Italiana had made plans to separate its banking from its industrial operations, which were to be transferred to its subsidiary Società Finanziaria Industriale Italiana (Sofindit). In 1931, the electrical sector had difficulty in meeting its obligations.[35] The Italian economy was in peril.

When the Berlin City Electric Co. was in difficulty in March 1931, depression conditions notwithstanding, Heineman of Sofina stepped in and arranged U.S. and other financing. Under the conditions of the loan, a new company – Berliner Kraft und Licht (Bewag) AG – was established in May 1931 to acquire from the city of Berlin the city owned plants and the leases of Berlin City Electric Co. Oliven became a vice chairman of the new venture.[36]

After the Creditanstalt crisis in May 1931, there was a run on German banks, and U.S. banks got nervous. The very banks with the broadest international banking contacts were those most involved in electric utility finance, domestically and internationally. The June 1931 Hoover Moratorium on reparations (affecting inter-Allied debt payments) was designed to deal with public (intergovernmental) debts, not private ones. Bankers insisted that there should be no moratorium on private obligations; and while there was none, that did not deter defaults. Borrowers stopped paying interest. Foreign bond prices depreciated sharply. This was true of corporate as well as government bonds. The problems that U.S. and U.K. lenders faced were not only in Europe; the crisis extended to Latin America, too, where countries put new restrictions on foreign remittances. On December 1, 1931, for example, interest on its debt was not paid by Intercontinents Power Co. That U.S. holding company – set up in the boom year 1928 to raise money for South American investments, which had had a $3 million debenture issue in 1930 – explained that it was defaulting on its interest payments because with the "sharp declines in exchange values of currencies" in Argentina and Brazil, "together with the necessity of providing locally for fixed capital expenditures from earnings... made it impossible for funds to be paid by [its] subsidiaries to Intercontinents Power. In Chile,... prohibitions on the transfer of money from that country have been in effect."[37]

In Asia, the 1931 Japanese invasion of Manchuria was the first step in aggression that would ultimately lead to World War II. The following year, the Japanese action in Shanghai in 1932 frightened lenders. There were no Japanese defaults, but from 1932 until the end of the decade no new money from abroad would be forthcoming. Japanese electric utilities, as we have seen, had been giant borrowers in the late 1920s.[38]

1932

In 1932 came the fall of the vast Insull empire. All through 1930 and 1931, with the shaky economy in the United States, the Insull investments in public utilities had seemed to the public to be a bulwark. The Insull collapse was caused in part by the group's inability to get additional domestic *or* international financing to refinance its debt.[39] By 1932, electric utilities everywhere were swept up in the worldwide financial maelstrom. The financial architecture (the pyramided structures and business groups) that had been so successful in drawing in money to new endeavors was vulnerable under the altered conditions. With Insull's defaults, nothing seemed safe any longer. In the United States, the holding company edifice became a target for government investigators and critics of the nation's "capitalist" institutions. Everywhere around the globe, economic problems escalated. Countries cried out for banking reform. Yet throughout, the basic demand for electrification persisted. Financial crises notwithstanding, customers still required electric power, for electricity was no longer a luxury – it had become a necessity.[40]

The Public Utility Holding Corporation (PUHC), formed in the United States in 1929 and expanding in 1930–1931, had acquired a one-third interest in the French utility Union Électrique Rurale, which in 1932 PUHC sold off to the French Durand group. In Germany, PUHC had obtained securities convertible into a one-half interest in the voting stock of the important utility Vereinigte Elektrizitätswerke Westfalen GmbH (Westphalia United Electric Corporation), Dortmund. In 1932, it seems to have traded that stock for the German bank holdings in PUHC. Thus, by 1933 PUHC had divested both of these French and German investments.[41]

Chicago-based promoter Harley Clarke, who had engaged in a substantial amount of pyramiding in the 1920s and in 1930, was involved with General Theaters Equipment Inc. and Fox Film; their defaults were linked with the financial excesses of the 1920s. Clarke's Utilities Power and Light Corporation (UPLC), at the height of its glory in 1930, was serving 488 communities in Britain through subsidiaries of Greater London and Counties Trust (GLCT)-Edmundson's and 587 more communities in the United States and Canada through other subsidiaries. By 1932, control of UPLC was held by the holding company Public Utilities Securities Corporation (Pusco). On top of Pusco was another holding company, which in turn was controlled by Clarke – and this hierarchical structure encountered grave financial woes. While the British would have liked to have had greater equity participation in GLCT, the American owners desired to keep control (this was a direct investment), and thus they sought out borrowings (*British* fixed-interest capital) to meet the group's financial requirements.[42] It was not atypical for multinational enterprises to assemble capital wherever it was available. Throughout the worst years of the early 1930s, UPLC's management kept the holding company alive and maintained control over its sizable British properties, as well as its Canadian acquisitions.[43]

AMERICAN & FOREIGN POWER CO., 1929–1932

In the contextof the worldwide economic crisis, it is useful to trace the experiences of one of the largest multinational enterprises in electric utilities, American & Foreign Power Co., which by year end 1929 operated in thirteen foreign countries, eleven in Latin America and two in Asia (China and India). In many ways, its experience mirrored the overall story. The company's annual report for 1929 (dated May 20, 1930) reflected some of the burgeoning economic distress, but there was no mention of the U.S. stock market crash. American & Foreign Power's expansion momentum seemed to be moving forward, with new acquisitions made after October 1929. In March 1930, American & Foreign Power was able to sell to a bankers' syndicate $50 million of gold debentures, 5 percent series due 2030; it also sold to its parent, Electric Bond and Share, $20 million of twenty-year 6 percent debenture bonds of Compañía Cubana de Electricidad, one of its many underlying operating companies. The proceeds from these two transactions were then used to pay the indebtedness of American & Foreign Power – as shown on its December 31, 1929, balance sheet – and also to provide extra working capital.[44] American & Foreign Power took advantage of its own well-established network relationships to obtain the outside financing. Its 1929 annual report discussed the depressed business conditions in Cuba, where American & Foreign Power had huge investments; but the company did not stop its on-going expansion there. The report also noted the worldwide drop in commodity prices, which "affected business conditions in many of the countries served during the last two months of 1929."[45]

American & Foreign Power's annual report of 1930 (dated June 12, 1931) revealed that the company's operating revenues had grown when compared with 1929 revenues, but so had its operating costs – and much faster. Foreign exchange problems in the markets of the affiliates of American & Foreign Power were escalating, causing earnings, when translated into U.S. dollars, to plummet. The most serious depreciations in currencies were in Argentina, Brazil, and China, where American & Foreign Power had major operations. Despite these difficulties, during 1930 the company had maintained its expansion, even more so than in 1929, carrying out planned construction for new, principally hydroelectric power plants and building and rebuilding distribution systems.[46] Its initial (1929) operations in India were enlarged with the acquisition of majority interest in United Eastern Agencies Ltd. of Bombay. A minority of the stock in United Eastern was owned by prominent Indians living in Bombay, some of whom also participated with American & Foreign Power in Tata Hydro-Electric Agencies Ltd.[47] United Eastern Agencies was the managing agent for the operating companies that supplied light and power to Poona, Broach, and Karachi.[48] During 1930, American & Foreign Power reorganized its subsidiaries in Argentina, rationalizing the corporate structure of its by now very large – and dispersed – operations.[49] In Brazil, Chile, Colombia, Cuba, Mexico, and Venezuela, American & Foreign Power bought new companies and properties.[50] And to finance its expansion, American & Foreign Power issued additional bonds.[51]

American & Foreign Power realized that if it was going to be successful in developing electric utilities, it would be wise to involve citizens of the host countries. Its 1930 annual report read: "In whatever country your Company may engage in business its fixed policy is to co-operate with the nationals of that country for the better development of the country, to foster its industries and to add to and improve the conveniences of the home. As a part of this policy the properties are operated to the fullest extent practicable by the nationals of the country." The annual report explained that "nationals" were trained to carry on the business activities in an efficient manner, following company policies. Of the total number of individuals that American & Foreign Power employed, about 85 percent were nationals of the countries where the operations took place; about 15 percent were nationals of other countries; and less than 1 percent were U.S. citizens.[52] Where possible, American & Foreign Power also encouraged the participation of local capital, without, however, sacrificing "control."

American & Foreign Power's annual report for 1931 (dated June 15, 1932) turned gloomy, reflecting the bleak outlook in the global economy.[53] Currency depreciations in the countries that the company and its affiliates operated were taking their toll. While revenues were up in local currencies, they were down 17 percent when translated into dollars. Some dividend payments on American & Foreign Power's stock (it had various classes of preferred and common stock) had been suspended in 1930 and 1931, and more were suspended in April 1932.[54] Its annual report for 1931 and 1932 (the latter dated September 15, 1933) surveyed the sorry conditions in Latin America, China, and India – the "derangement of foreign exchange."[55] By the end of 1932, about 64 percent of American & Foreign Power's affiliates' income was "subject to official regulations [within host countries] restricting conversion into United States currency."[56] The dismal financial situation notwithstanding, the company continued to invest in additions to properties, but on a much more constrained basis.[57]

1933–1939

England had gone off the gold standard in September 1931. While this meant its exports were more appropriately priced, worldwide demand had dropped. New barriers to trade proliferated. Britain turned inward, looking to the problems at home. The United States would abandon the gold standard in 1933. It had had larger foreign lending in the 1920s than any country, and by 1933 defaults were adding up. There were perils to being a creditor nation. Congressional (and then after 1934, the Securities and Exchange Commission) investigations of investment bankers paid special attention to the electric utilities sector; there were heightened concerns about the vulnerability in the financial architecture that had emerged in the 1920s.[58] Germany, as it sought to rebuild its fractured economy, turned inward to national needs, and often there were defaults on the borrowings – governmental *and* corporate. On June 9, 1933, the German (now Nazi) government passed legislation allowing the suspension of payments on contractual obligations.[59] The world economy was in shambles.

President Franklin D. Roosevelt had taken office in the United States in March 1933, following his promise to the American people of a New Deal. Roosevelt had long been an advocate of public power, and public versus private power had been a major issue in his presidential campaign. In May 1933, Roosevelt signed an act creating the Tennessee Valley Authority (TVA), a federal power and development project, which would become one of the largest power producers in the United States.[60] In 1935, the Rural Electrification Administration was started to provide subsidized government loans and to encourage cooperative utilities, aiming to bring electrification to rural America. The Roosevelt administration did not look kindly on the pyramiding by public utilities, and after extensive debate in 1935 the Public Utility Holding Company Act (PUHCA) was enacted, seeking to cope with the seeming abuses. The act gave primary jurisdiction over utility holding company finances and operations to the just established (in 1934) Securities and Exchange Commission (SEC). The act also contained the famous "death sentence," which limited (with a few exceptions, including – important for our purposes – foreign-owned subsidiaries) a utility holding company to ownership of a single integrated public utility system. For much of the rest of the decade, U.S. public utilities tried to get clarification of the extent of applicability of the PUHCA. In addition, the U.S. Congress passed legislation setting up a firewall between commercial and investment banking (the Glass Steagall Act of 1933) and took steps not conducive to corporations' expansion, at home or abroad.

Meanwhile, U.S. capital markets dried up. The British increased domestic investments at the expense of international ones. There was no money for international finance in general nor for public utilities in particular, which required immense outlays of capital. Companies in Canada, Germany, Italy, and Japan, which had been especially large borrowers for electric utilities, faced straitened circumstances. Canadian firms weathered the problems, managing to keep current on interest payments. It helped that much of the borrowing was associated with foreign direct investors. Of the German corporate dollar loans outstanding in 1935 (totaling $485 million), virtually all were in default as to interest.[61] We do not know what percentage of these corporate loans were for electric utilities, although German electric utilities (many of which were in the 1920s and 1930s completely or partly government-owned and where the loans may have been classified as government rather than corporate) had raised money on the U.S. market and now were unable to pay interest on those borrowings. The Bankers' Trust planned Superpower Corporation (referred to above as part of the momentum of 1930) never materialized, so there was no U.S.-based holding company structure playing a significant role as foreign direct investors in the German electric utilities sector. Individual Americans (and some holding companies) who did own German securities tried to extricate themselves from their German holdings, but the German government imposed stringent controls on capital outflows (the 1933 suspension of interest payments was extended), which meant for foreigners not only losses on interest but no means to withdraw their investments.[62]

Increasingly, German companies with business in utilities abroad had to justify them to the German government or, alternatively, had to develop various means to cloak those investments.[63] When the crisis came, German foreign stakes in utilities had been small, and by the end of the 1920s had been more for information purposes than otherwise. As we have noted, the considerable expansion abroad by Siemens and AEG in the late 1920s and into 1930 – in exporting, sales offices, technical service offices, and manufacturing – did *not* have its counterpart in investments in public utilities (and also, in general, did not involve big sums). Even so, in 1933 Reichbank president Hjalmar Schacht advised large German corporations to shelter their foreign assets from attachment. To the surprise of Siemens's finance chief, Max Haller, his counterpart at AEG had already taken such steps.[64] Particularly in Eastern Europe, the Germans had interests, mostly indirect ones, in electric utilities.

Gesellschaft für Elektrische Unternehmungen (Gesfürel), the Berlin holding company associated with AEG, divested some of its attempted post–World War I– revived activities; and probably for safety reasons (and to avoid German nationalistic controls), in 1935 it transferred its holdings in CHADE, for example, to a Swiss subsidiary. It seems to have kept its only substantial foreign direct investment in a Hungarian utility (as well as a minor stake in Sidro, which reflected its relationship with the Sofina/Sidro group). At some point in the 1930s, according to one source, Sofina acquired a majority interest in Gesfürel.[65] It is likely that Gesfürel got approval from the German government to continue its holdings in Hungary.[66]

The rise of Hitler had more personal impacts: Oliven (who was in charge of Gesfürel's international and domestic activities) and Heineman (of Sofina) were both Jewish. In 1933, Oliven fled to Zurich, where he died in 1939. (While in Zurich, he may well have had influence on Gesfürel's activities from a distance.) He was removed from the board of Berliner Kraft und Licht (Bewag), AG. Heineman was an American citizen, living in Belgium for many years, and until 1938 German anti-Semitism did not seriously affect him. However, he worked to avoid having Gesfürel completely absorbed into the more Nazified AEG. And naturally, German nationalism and the rise of Nazism repelled him and thwarted his international aspirations (and negatively affected the Sofina balance sheet). In 1937, Bewag was incorporated into the Hermann Göring Werke.[67]

In Yugoslavia, the Swiss holding company Elektrowerte, Basel maintained its interest in power facilities. For business in Bulgaria, there was the Swiss company AG für Elektrische und Industrielle Unternehmungen im Orient. It did not fare well, and in 1937 it cut down its capital by

90 percent.[68] At the same time, the Bank für Elektrische Unternehmungen (Elektrobank), Zurich slowly reduced its interest in German utilities that it had held over the years. One could almost describe these interests by the 1930s as "round-tripping." AEG appears to have continued its small interests in Elektrobank; but Elektrobank's interests in German utilities do not appear to have had any characteristics of Swiss direct investments.[69] Elektrobank's portfolio of securities was diversified within Europe and in the United States.[70] The dominant influence in that Swiss holding company appears to have been Credit Suisse. By 1938–1939, the geographic distribution of Elektrobank's assets was as follows: United States (24.5 percent), Switzerland (17.2 percent), Italy (14.6 percent), France (13.3 percent), Germany (7.5 percent), Spain and Portugal (6.6 percent), South America (6.1 percent), other countries (10.2 percent).[71] The "other countries" stakes seem to have included direct investments in Hungary.[72] The sizable investment of Elektrobank in the United States came to be associated with the sheltering of assets.[73] The U.S. stakes were all portfolio investments.

Historically, Elektrobank, Zurich, had been associated with AEG, while Schweizerische Gesellschaft für Elektrische Industrie (Indelec), Basel, had been tied in with Siemens. During the 1930s, Siemens – in sales and manufacturing – enlarged its international business, and Indelec provided short-term credits. Indelec's key bank connection continued to be with Basler Handelsbank, although Swiss Bank Corporation, Basel was also involved. As for long-term investments in electric utilities, by 1938–1939 Indelec had a far smaller portfolio of securities than Elektrobank. It seems to have kept a number of its long-standing interests in Italy, but it did not enlarge these stakes. As Siemens had expanded in Eastern Europe, Indelec had played a role in Poland and Czechoslovakia. The composition of its portfolio in 1938–1939 was: Italy (30.7 percent), Germany and Czechoslovakia (28.0 percent), Switzerland (21.0 percent), France (11.0 percent), Poland (6.5 percent) and Luxembourg (1.9 percent). (Germany and Czechoslovakia are put in one category, because after the Munich agreement in September 1938, the Germans had absorbed much of Czechoslovakia.) The French investments were with the Mercier and Durant groups; Sofina also was involved. Indelec's main French interests were in Alsace, which had been German before World War I.[74]

During the 1930s, Belgian holding companies maintained their role – as in earlier years, overlapping with Swiss companies. But the Belgian pattern was different. After the First World War, the Germans were not welcome to use Belgian intermediaries. And, while in 1930–1931, as noted above, there had been a close relationship between Heineman and Oliven, the Belgian story in the 1930s diverged from the German one. We will return with more details on the Belgian holding companies; but before we do so, we need to look more closely at what was happening to the other principal corporate borrowers in the electric utilities sector.

If Canadian utilities had been the top borrowers in the 1920s and German utilities probably in second place, Japanese electric utilities probably ranked third. In the 1930s, as Japan moved from a civilian to a military economy, Japanese-government subsidized electrification went forward. The Japanese utilities paid their debts throughout the decade without default. Yet no new money came from England or the United States.[75] The Japanese had never had inward direct investments in their electric utilities. As the Japanese took over Manchuria (and established Manchukuo), electrification went forth along the Japanese-owned South Manchuria Railway. During the 1930s, electrification in Taiwan and Korea, under Japanese direction, also went forward. The Japanese felt that electrification at home and in their colonial territories was essential; they had no technological or managerial constraints in proceeding; and they managed with government assistance to mobilize adequate funding.

Italy, as we have seen, had been the object of much foreign capital (direct and portfolio investments) over many decades. In Italy, as foreign (and domestic bank) investors failed to provide the added capital needed to continue the large-scale electrification projects embarked on in the 1920s, the state substituted. IRI (Istituto per la Ricostruzione Industriale) was formed in 1933 to take over the industrial securities of Banca Commerciale Italiana and Credito Italiano (actually of the holding companies set up by these two key Italian banks), planning to sell industrial securities to private parties and to loan, long-term, to Italian companies adversely affected by the economic crisis. In 1937, IRI's status became permanent, as it could not find buyers for the industrial securities. IRI came to play a major role in Italian electrification, filling in for the lack of portfolio and direct investments from outside Italy. Indeed, by the late 1930s – even after IRI returned to the Edison company the securities that it had acquired from it – some 27 percent of electric energy output in Italy remained under IRI control. The rest stayed in the private sector, dominated by Italian entrepreneurs. By the late 1930s, there was little that approximated foreign control of the major companies in the Italian electricity supply sector.[76] Indeed, in a 1936 study of U.S. direct investments abroad published in 1938, U.S. investments in Italian public utilities that were "previously carried as direct investments in the amount of $66 million" were reclassified by the U.S. Commerce Department as portfolio investments.[77]

The two sizable U.S. holding companies that we described in detail in Chapter 4 – International Power Securities Corporation (IPSC) and Italian Superpower Corporation – lasted through the 1930s, but they took on different attributes. The former (John Aldred's company) at year end 1929 was the larger of the two, with assets of $43.7 million; at year end 1937, it was the lesser one, with assets reduced to $28.8 million. As for Italian Superpower, it also was smaller at year end 1937 than in 1929 (1929 assets $38.9 million; 1937, $31.9 million). At the close of 1937, Italian Superpower still owned shares in a number of Italian utilities; the voting shares of Italian Superpower continued to be jointly Italian-U.S. owned, now 50 percent by IRI and 50 percent by Floyd Odlum's Atlas Corporation (see below).[78]

As for Aldred's company, International Power Securities, at the end of 1937 it had no Italian or French officers or directors. In addition, it had no subsidiaries. Over the years, it sold off assets. By the end of 1937, it no longer had any interests in French public utility finance. As of September 30, 1938, it owned 4,500 shares of the Italian Edison company (compared with the 60,000 shares in its portfolio as of September 30, 1929), and it had shares in several Canadian public utilities, but not sufficient interests to exercise control. Its principal holdings were its own bonds, issued in December 1925 and January and February 1927; these were direct obligations of IPSC, secured by mortgages on key Italian hydroelectric facilities.[79] There was no new money going from the United States (or the United Kingdom) to the Italian (or to the French) electric utilities industry.

The private-sector Italian outward direct investments in electric utilities in the United Kingdom were retained (we will say more about them shortly). These, as in the case of other outward Italian foreign direct investments (except those within the empire) were not through companies registered in Italy. By 1938, some of the Italian outward investments seemed clustered under Italo-Belge (or CIBEE), the Belgian holding company dominated by Volpi, which described itself as "engaged chiefly in the engineering and construction field for which work it has had at its disposal the engineering staff" of Volpi's Italian company SADE. In 1938, its subsidiary and affiliated companies were in Greece and Romania, while its British interests had been transferred to other sister companies, but it played a "supervisory role."[80] In addition, certain Italian outward investments seem to have been through Canadian intermediaries. Other outward Italian investments, those in Latin America (jointly with the Swiss holding company Motor-Columbus) continued during the 1930s. And then there were the relatively small outward Italian investments in electric utilities within the Italian empire (principally in North Africa).

The Swiss firm Motor-Columbus, Baden, which had been highly entrepreneurial in the 1920s, had a difficult 1930s. It had cut back its dividend in 1930–1931 and then stopped paying dividends. In 1935–1936, it divested its sizable interests in Società Meridionale di Elettricità (Meridionale or SEM) and some other Italian utilities. It concentrated more of its activities within Switzerland. In 1936, it went through a reorganization, partly owing to its own problems and partly because the Swiss franc was devalued that year. Nonetheless, Motor-Columbus continued in business. It maintained its connections with Brown Boveri and still ranked as a prominent Swiss holding company, keeping some investments in Italy and, through Foreign Light and Power (a Canadian holding company), in Romania. It had interests in Argentina and Ecuador, as well as in Lima,

Peru and Bogota, Colombia, where it owned directly or indirectly securities of companies that furnished power to South American cities. Some of its Latin American investments were through the holding company Schweizerisch-Americanische Elektrizitäts-Gesellschaft (SAEG), Zurich. Some were linked with Italian interests (Compañía Italo-Argentina de Electricidad, for example). In the 1930s Motor-Columbus reduced its interests in Germany. With exchange controls, it was difficult to get any current payments much less capital retrievals from either Germany or Italy. By 1938–1939, Motor-Columbus's investment portfolio was divided: Switzerland (45.0 percent), South America (41.2 percent), Italy (12.2 percent), Canada (0.7 percent), Germany (0.4 percent), and France (0.3 percent).[81]

Each European country had a distinct story of inward and outward investments in the electric utilities industry. The investment networks grew weaker in the 1930s as everywhere nationalism and autarchic polices prevailed. Yet as we have seen so far, the links, however tenuous they had become, had for the most part not disappeared. There was, however, a reallocation of resources within Europe. Swiss holding companies – including Elektrobank and Motor-Columbus but also Indelec and others – became relatively more important as "holding or investment" units rather than direct investors. In the interwar period, Belgium had resumed its central importance for electric utility supply finance. Problems in its economy in the 1930s and the major bank reform in the early 1930s did not interfere with the key place of Belgium in terms of electrical holding companies. History mattered, and the first-mover advantages were still sustained.

Most important, among the Belgian companies was Société Financière de Transports et d'Entreprises Industrielles (Sofina), Brussels, which, still under the direction of Dannie Heineman, completed a number of projects in the early 1930s in France.[82] It survived the 1930s, sustaining most activities notwithstanding the difficult economic conditions. When the Spanish Civil War started in 1936 and a Spanish Workers' Committee took over the operations of the Sofina-controlled Barcelona Traction, Light and Power, it stayed the course.[83] And despite the adversities Heineman reported in September 1940 that "only slight damage was done to [Barcelona] hydraulic works and transmission lines in the civil war" and "the output of electricity in Barcelona now is within 90 per cent of the 1935 figure."[84] What Heineman probably did not realize was that during the civil war Juan March, a wealthy Spaniard with close connections to General Francisco Franco, was beginning to buy on the market the greatly depreciated sterling bonds of Barcelona Traction, Light and Power – purchases that would later mount and ultimately have profound consequences for the enterprise's future.[85]

With the Spanish Civil War in progress in 1938, the owners of Compañía Hispano-Americana de Electricidad (CHADE) securities, now principally Belgian and Swiss (with Sofina in control) sought to protect these assets and, with shareholder approval, the assets of CHADE were transferred from

Spanish registration to a new Luxembourg company: Société d'Électricité (SODEC). Before that occurred, in Argentina in 1936 Compañia Argentina de Electricidad (CADE) became the holding company for Argentine assets of CHADE; CADE continued (through CHADE and then through the Luxembourg intermediary) to be controlled by Sofina.[86]

With problems in the French economy, in 1936 Sofina reduced its holdings in Société Financière Électrique, Paris (Finelec), its affiliate that had been so active in France; it retained its interests, however, in important French light and power companies.[87] The French government had started regulating electricity prices and by decree, under the government of Pierre Laval in 1935, it lowered electricity prices by 10 percent. That did not make for good operating conditions and could explain the reduction in Sofina interests. In 1938, Sofina sold its Turkish electric utilities to the Turkish government. In contrast, in October 1936 and subsequently, Sofina made sizable new investments in the United States, in Middle West Corporation (the reorganized Middle West Utilities Company, one of the key Insull companies). Through all of the 1930s, Sofina remained an international business.[88]

Heineman, by 1938, was deeply disturbed with the rise of nationalism worldwide. His address to Sofina shareholders that year was devoted to the "tendency amongst some governments to view with suspicion or even animosity the participation of foreigners in ... the management of ... public utility undertakings." He presented a plea for "international co-operation in privately managed public utility undertakings," by which he meant cooperation between foreign private capital and nationals within host countries. For host governments "to reject the co-operation of foreign talent is not rational; the goodwill of experience gained abroad is yeast to the technical progress of any country, however advanced it may be. ... There is nothing humiliating about opening the doors to foreign collaboration." Foreign involvement was not exploitation, but rather was to the advantage of all. The ever optimistic Heineman concluded his remarks with the comment, "... [I]n most countries in which Sofina has its undertakings the authorities show that friendly and loyal spirit which is the natural outcome of mutual confidence. And even where it has to cope with an attitude that can hardly be described as amicable, I trust the attitude the authorities have taken reflects no more than a transitory outlook." During the decade, for Sofina with its many affiliates, most of its foreign direct investments survived, battered by exchange controls, depreciating currencies in the host countries, ever increasing government regulation and interventions at the local, provincial, and national levels, and new taxation. All the while, Heineman maintained "hope" that what was happening to the world economy was "transitory."[89]

Other Belgian companies – difficulties aside – kept their foreign investments and even made some new ones. Second only to Sofina was its sister company Compagnie Générale d'Entreprises Électriques et Industrielles, Brussels (Electrobel). Beyond its sizable investments in Belgium and France,

Electrobel had smaller interests in Italy and Spain. It also had made and continued to hold in the 1930s important investments in Eastern Europe and the middle east, in Bulgaria, Egypt, Lithuania, Poland, Romania, and Syria. Electrobel was said to direct Société d'Enterprises Électrique en Poland (set up in Brussels in 1923). Unlike Sofina (which had the large Argentine holdings and through its affiliate, Sidro, large ones in Mexico and smaller ones in Brazil; see below), aside from some small holdings in Brazil, Electrobel had virtually no investments in Latin America.[90] And then there was Compagnie Financière d'Exploitations Hydroélectriques SA (Hydrofina), Antwerp, formed in 1928, which developed business in Romania (in tandem with the Swiss Motor-Columbus); it was said to be controlled by Electrobel.[91]

Société Internationale d'Énergie Hydro-Électrique, Brussels (Sidro), the one-time Loewenstein company, did not manage as well as Sofina or even Electrobel. Sidro stopped paying dividends in 1936. It was heavily invested in Barcelona Traction and during the civil war no returns were forthcoming from that company. Sidro also had holdings in Mexican Light & Power and in two highly regulated French utilities. Sofina/Sidro seems to have continued to have shares in Brazilian Traction (see below). In the late 1930s, Sidro increasingly took a back seat to Sofina. Sofina was the dominating element in Sidro, so what was "controlled" by Sidro could be called part of the Sofina/Sidro group or sometimes simply Sofina "controlled."

The Empain group – in particular, Electrorail (Compagnies Réunies d'Électricité et de Transport) – also retained most of its investments of the 1920s and earlier years. It had a number of long-standing tramway investments. Its Belgian-French characteristics remained pronounced. It continued to be important in France, the crises of the 1930s notwithstanding. Its significant stakes in Egypt were also maintained.[92]

Overall, foreign direct investors in the years 1933–1939 found doing business an unhappy experience. Yet only a very few important ones retreated in full from investments abroad. One that did was Utilities Power and Light Corporation (UPLC). Because Harley Clarke's Chicago based UPLC was in financial trouble, Clarke accepted a series of deals by which added *British* capital was brought into Greater London and Counties Trust (GLCT)-Edmundson's. Lazard Brothers, the British Lazards (now revived), came to play a material role in sustaining GLCT and encouraging Prudential Assurance to provide funds for the *ailing parent* UPLC. At every interest date, Clarke managed to keep UPLC out of receivership. But by 1935, it was obvious that the latter was ready to withdraw from its large British investments.

Meanwhile, another American entrepreneur stepped into the picture: Floyd Bostwick Odlum. Odlum was a lawyer, who had for many years been involved in Electric Bond and Share and in developing American & Foreign Power. He had been with Simpson, Thacher and Bartlett, the important law firm that handled complicated international negotiations for American &

Foreign Power. Odlum became a director of American & Foreign Power and, from 1928 to 1932, was its vice chairman.[93] With another director of American & Foreign Power, in July 1929 he formed in Delaware the Atlas Corporation, an investment company.[94] In the 1930s, Atlas acquired control of a wide variety of companies whose securities had hit rock bottom. In the early 1930s, Odlum had started to buy UPLC debentures. Then he gained control of the Public Utilities Securities Corporation (Pusco), which in turn controlled UPLC. This effectively gave Atlas control of UPLC, although Clarke stayed on as president. Next, Odlum arranged the divestment of the U.K. company GLCT. The proceeds of this sale (about $25 million) would allow UPLC to buy up its own outstanding bonds and leave it with some working capital. Thus, in 1936 Odlum sold back to British subjects the largest U.S. direct investment in the United Kingdom, and GLCT-Edmundson's became British-owned. The British were delighted at the repatriation. Edmundson's, the former sub–holding company, now became the parent, and the process of domestication was complete.[95]

This left only the Italian British & International Utilities Ltd. (BIU) involved as a multinational enterprise in providing electric power in Britain. Its was not a large investment, but in 1938 the British Ministry of Transport worried about strategic information on electricity supplies and munitions factories being passed on to the German General Staff through BIU's Italian management. Finally, on May 28, 1940, after the outbreak of World War II, the Ministry of Transport ordered (under wartime emergency powers) the U.K. government takeover of these properties.[96] Because these small rural utilities represented only a tiny percentage of British electricity output, for all practical purposes significant foreign ownership and control within the British public utility sector was over in 1936 with the UPLC divestment. Interestingly, as we mentioned earlier in this chapter, Odlum's Atlas Corp. by 1938 had acquired 50 percent of the shares in the American holding company Italian Superpower. While Italian Superpower did not have shares in BIU (remember that cross-holdings were commonplace), there were links. BIU was established by Volpi, and Volpi was on the board of Italian Superpower; Italian Superpower also owned shares in some of the sister companies of Italo-Belge (which was part of the Volpi group).[97]

Yet the retreat of UPLC from its sizable foreign direct investments in Great Britain was atypical. In September 1939, UPLC also disposed of all the Canadian investments of its subsidiary Central States Power & Light Company (the Canada Electric Co. Ltd., the Eastern Electric & Development Co. Ltd.; Moncton Electricity & Gas Ltd.; and Maritime Coal Railway & Power Co. Ltd.) These became the properties of Eastern Utilities Ltd., a Canadian enterprise.[98] There were some other pullbacks in foreign investments, which we have already mentioned – the 1938 sale by Sofina of its Turkish properties to that government, for example. Overall, however, the principal Swiss and Belgian holding companies, as well as the key North American holding companies, preserved their international business during the decade but added little. Under their auspices, the provision of electricity grew, although not as rapidly as many consumers (or potential consumers) would have liked.

1933–1939: LATIN AMERICA

In Latin America in the 1930s, the Roosevelt administration had inaugurated a "Good Neighbor" policy. The president of American & Foreign Power, Curtis E. Calder, wistfully reflected in 1941 on the "strange misunderstanding" of that policy in some nations, where "there seems to be a feeling that...[the United States] has gone soft and that we and our investments are fair prey for any leader who can trump some sort of excuse to abuse us, however flimsy."[99]

In Mexico, Compañía Electrica Mexicana, SA, one of American & Foreign Power's Mexican operating subsidiaries, "abandoned in 1937 a hydroelectric project which it had acquired for investigation and development in 1930." The Mexican subsidiary forfeited its concession, and American & Foreign Power wrote off about $1 million.[100] The Toronto management of Mexican Light and Power (Mexlight) was similarly hesitant to invest in Mexico.[101] Then, in 1938 there was the Mexican government expropriation of foreign-owned oil companies. Economist Miguel Wionczek wrote of a "cold war" between the state and the electric power industry from the mid-1930s on. It was quite possible, he claimed, that the electric power industry might have been nationalized in 1938 along with the oil enterprises. The threat was there.[102] The Mexican electric power industry was almost entirely under foreign ownership and control, with the key players the Sofina-dominated but Canadian-registered and managed Mexlight, American & Foreign Power, and the somewhat smaller Canadian-directed International Power Co. Ltd. (which supplied the industrial city of Monterrey). There was also a U.S. investment in the Compañía Hidroeléctrica de Chapala, which serviced the Guadalajara region; the Chapala company went bankrupt in 1940 and was purchased by the Mexican federal government from its U.S. owners. Further, in 1929 the U.S. holding company Standard Gas & Electric Co. had taken over a group of small public utilities on the west coast of Mexico; it seems to have kept them until 1940, when it had them no longer. All of the foreign multinational enterprises suffered under the rising tide of nationalism and anti-foreign sentiment that developed in Mexico during the 1930s and the greatly enlarged government regulatory role in this sector. Those foreign direct investors that remained cut back on new investments.[103]

In Brazil, foreign companies were similarly "under fire." The largest investments were by the long-standing Canadian-registered, Sofina-associated Brazilian Traction, Light and Power. It supplied the Rio and São Paulo areas, where much of the Brazilian population was concentrated. Duncan McDowall documents the company's history in the 1930s. Demand rose rapidly, but Brazilian Traction found it difficult to meet the demand. Canadian management was wary about making investments, "committing ourselves to unknown dangers in the future." In 1928, Miller Lash had become president of Brazilian Traction; he was a lawyer and was part of the Toronto business establishment. Although he traveled annually to Brazil, he did not speak Portuguese and he had no desire to live there. To be sure, the Canadians did have on the spot a resident executive vice president, English-born Herbert Couzens, as well as the experienced American Asa Billings, who had been hired away from the New York firm Pearson Engineering. McDowall writes nothing about any role of Sofina in the 1930s. Heineman – who figured in McDowall's rendition of the late-1920s disputes with Loewenstein of Sidro – is never mentioned in McDowall's history thereafter. Likewise, there is nothing on Brazilian Traction in the Sofina annual reports for 1929 or 1939. And yet, there is no indication that Sofina relinquished its existing interest, although in the 1930s, unlike its activities in Mexico, Sofina does not seem to have considered Brazilian Traction among its "principal interests." The "unknown dangers in the future" that the Canadians worried about were that financial returns on any large new investments would fail to be forthcoming, owing to the weakness of Brazil's currency and to the restrictive legislation enacted by Brazil's leadership (in this, the Getulio Vargas era), which "challenged the very existence of foreign utilities in Brazil." In 1934, a Water Code was promulgated that seemed to jeopardize foreign investment in hydroelectric supplies. In 1935, the vice president of Brazilian Traction Couzens reported that "Bank of Brazil is so much disorganized internally that they hardly know where they are." Regulation in Brazil was by states and municipalities until, in 1937, federal authorities began to regulate electric utility concessions. That year, the new Brazilian constitution prohibited any company with foreign shareholdings from obtaining new hydroelectrical concessions. While industry developed rapidly in Brazil in the 1930s, doing business there proved to be a constant frustration to foreign multinational enterprises, especially those in the public utilities sector.[104] American & Foreign Power had fifteen separate operating companies in Brazil, for the most part spread out along the very long coastline. By 1939, it was serving 309 different communities, with an estimated population of 5.4 million.[105] In the northeast, it supplied Natal and Pernambuco; in the south, it furnished power to Porto Alegre and Pelotas.[106] During the decade, the number of communities and population it serviced had risen. Both Brazilian Traction and American & Foreign Power's subsidiaries depended on imported equipment for their facilities, which was difficult to pay for with the depreciating currency and the blocked payments.

In Argentina, cities asserted themselves with a multiplicity of new rules and regulations, but there was no national regulation of electricity. Here the largest investments were still by CHADE (Compañía Hispano-Americana de Electricidad) and after 1936 by its subsidiary Compañía Argentina de

Electricidad (CADE). CADE's territory was Buenos Aires and its environs. In Chapter 4, we saw Heineman singing CHADE's praises.[107] Even though a May 1936 Sofina tribute to Heineman referred to CHADE's founding as destined to become "Le plus beau fleuron de la couronne de la Sofina [the most beautiful flower in the crown of Sofina]," the hyperbole seems to have reflected history rather than the reality of 1936. Over the years, there seems to have been a deficit of good management in Argentina. During the 1930s, Heineman had become preoccupied with European matters. Sofina's range was so wide that there seems to have been by necessity a decentralization of management; Heineman left the administration of Mexlight and Brazilian Traction to the Canadians, who had developed, for the most part, competent operating teams, but somehow the management and direction of CHADE/CADE seems to have fallen between the stools. Although CHADE added to its large Buenos Aires power station in 1931 and 1934, it seems that its power facilities became run down. Where was the old spirit of renewal and rationalization? It seems to have been absent. Mexlight and Brazilian Traction had developed their own managerial operating staff, based on their Canadian origins (with Americans and Britishers also participating), hiring and training Mexicans and Brazilians, if not at the highest level, certainly throughout the organization. These companies appear to have been competently run. That does not appear to have been the case with CHADE/CADE. Moreover, between 1932 and 1936 CHADE was in a major dispute with the Buenos Aires city council, which looked like it might culminate in expropriation.[108] The revised 1936 concession was said to be written in Brussels by Sofina officials and passed by the Buenos Aires city council after "secret contributions" were made to the Radical Party's 1937 election campaign. (The Radical party was "radical" only in name.)[109]

CHADE was not by itself among the foreign investors in electric utilities in Argentina. American & Foreign Power was new to Argentina in 1929. It arrived just as the depression hit. Its plants were all acquisitions, and they were widely dispersed around the country. Its capable management made an initial effort to rationalize the properties.[110] By 1939 in Argentina, American & Foreign Power served 182 separate communities, with an estimated population of 2.6 million.[111] Most appear to have been provided for by separate power plants. It supplied electricity for Córdoba, Jujuy, Mendoza, Salta, San Rafael, and Tucumán, as well as numerous other Argentine cities (see Map 5.2). In 1929, it sought to rationalize its business by setting up regional grids of companies that served the Andes and the north, south, east, and center of the nation. The properties that it acquired needed care, managerial attention, and new investments, but the U.S. depression made such pursuits nearly impossible. There was no readily available capital to pour into this activity.

Sofina had two other investments in Argentina, one of them in a Buenos Aires tramway company. The city of Buenos Aires took over the service of

Anglo-Argentine Tramways on February 16, 1939. (Lengthy litigation followed, not to be resolved until 1963.) Sofina's interests in the tramway company dated back before World War I. The other Sofina investment was also long-standing and continuing, in the Argentine port city of Rosario. There were additional foreign companies in Argentina, including CIAE (Compañía Italo-Argentina de Electricidad; also called Italo-Argentine Electric Co.), which served parts of Buenos Aires and several other cities.[112] CIAE and some sister companies were linked with the Swiss Motor-Columbus. The electric power they furnished was small relative to the giant CHADE/CADE (or for that matter American & Foreign Power). South American Utilities (the 1936 successor to Intercontinents Power; see above) owned properties in Argentina and in 1938 had more than 49,000 customers in 89 communities in that country.[113] There were additional foreign-owned companies, but overall Argentina was not well served. During the 1930s, sizable new investments were required, but they were not made. In most of the country outside of Buenos Aires, small, costly, inefficient plants existed. Electric cooperatives began to spring up to meet local requirements.[114]

It is frequently asked why Argentina, which had been so prosperous before World War I, fell behind. In looking at the electric power story, one wonders if the lack of a good electric power infrastructure was to a certain extent responsible. As the 1920s ended, it seems that CHADE had not attended properly to Buenos Aires or the rest of the country, and by the time American & Foreign Power was making investments the global economic crisis acted as a deterrent. Argentina did not have coal, there were not yet adequate discoveries of oil, and hydroelectric possibilities were not effectively employed. (The possibilities of hydroelectric power were in areas far away from population centers and would have required expensive transmission lines.) The nation did not manufacture the equipment needed and had to import. The political environment was not conducive to new investments.[115]

If problems for foreign investors in electric utilities abounded in Argentina, Brazil, and Mexico, in 1935 the Chilean government charged American & Foreign Power with having dealt on the black market for three years, seeking to avoid foreign exchange restrictions in order to remit profits. The issue was resolved in 1936, but the agreement required Chilean subsidiaries of American & Foreign Power to be placed under an eleven-person board of directors, seven of whom had to be of Chilean nationality. Profits were to be distributed one-third to the Chilean government, one-third to stockholders, and one-third to subsidize reduced rates.[116]

In those four countries – indeed, throughout Latin America in the 1930s – foreign-owned companies dominated the electric utility sector.[117] As there were new attempts to industrialize, everywhere there were concerns with low productivity, which economists believed could be traced in part to shortages of electric power. The response was in many cases more government intervention to attempt to rectify the problem.[118] The shortage of foreign exchange led to import substitution policies, restrictions on profit remittances, and the depreciation of currencies. To add to the woes of foreign companies, the governments in Argentina, Brazil, Chile, Mexico began mandating wage hikes for electric utility employees. At the same time, the governments would not authorize rate increases.[119]

THE U.S.-CANADIAN CONNECTION

In 1936, Herbert Marshall, Frank Southard, and Kenneth Taylor published a comprehensive book on Canadian-American industry, showing the formidable impact of U.S. direct investments on the Canadian economy. The book includes a section on light and power companies.[120] The authors concluded that in the mid-1930s, as a consequence of earlier investments, "the distinctly and definitely American owned companies in Canada [supplied] 34 percent of the electricity (in terms of kilowatt hours)."[121] Much of these activities were outside the Province of Ontario, where increasingly the provincial government was playing an important role.[122] In addition, there was a second group of companies in Canada in which U.S. financial interest "[was] pronounced but which [was] largely or entirely Canadian controlled."[123] In this second category, Marshall, Southard, and Taylor included Montreal Light, Heat and Power, where much of the financing had been done over the years in the United States, but which always seems to have been independent of U.S. control.[124] Marshall, Southard, and Taylor also included in this second category Shawinigan Water and Power, which was one of John Aldred's ventures. In 1933, only about 11 percent of the equity of this company was held in the United States, although Aldred was still chairman of the board. The suggestion was that this had moved from what was once (before World War I and in the 1920s) a U.S. direct investment to a Canadian-dominated one.[125]

The first group – that of the clear U.S. direct investors in Canadian electric utilities – was divided into two segments: the Canadian firms that were owned and controlled by the large U.S. public utilities holding companies and the power companies owned by American branch plants, paper mills, or mines, for example. There had been an expansion of U.S. interests in electric power in Canada in 1930 – and perhaps in 1931 as well. Offsetting this, in 1930 the Hydro-Electric Power Commission of Ontario (Ontario Hydro) acquired the Canadian properties of Public Utilities Consolidated Corporation (a Foshay company), one of the many U.S. public utilities holding companies that had expanded into Canada in the late 1920s and 1930.[126] Otherwise, the large investments present in the 1930s were carryovers from earlier years. A handful of U.S.-owned newsprint companies that supplied power went into receivership, but this did not seem to change U.S. "control." As they came out of receivership, they remained U.S.-owned and controlled.[127] International Paper and Power

Company with its vast network of power plants, principally in Quebec, retained its great importance.[128]

The U.S. reform of the public utilities sector – the Public Utility Holding Company Act of 1935 – did not immediately affect the holdings in Canada that for the most part seem to have continued. We did note earlier some exits in 1940 associated with the PUHCA reorganizations. Also earlier noted, PUHCA gave an exemption from the terms of the act to holding companies that had "all or substantially all of their operating companies outside the United States." Related, and more important vis-à-vis Canadian business, a U.S. subsidiary that derived no material part of its income from sources within the United States could be exempt from PUHCA rules.[129] Thus, U.S. holding companies with subsidiaries in Canada that obtained their income from producing and selling electricity in Canada qualified for exemptions.

During the 1930s, Canadian public authorities did, however, become concerned over the sizable role of U.S. companies and whether it was appropriate. Ontario Hydro (owned by the province of Ontario) was already by 1929–1930 supplying over three-quarters of the electric power generated in that province.[130] A number of U.S. electric utilities in Canada sold their power wholesale to Ontario Hydro.[131] The most important sales of power came from International Paper and Power Co.'s subsidiary Gatineau Power Co. During the 1930s, Ontario Hydro had the lowest residential and small-user rates in North America, and as a result other provinces began to follow the lead of Ontario Hydro, providing competition to private-sector companies and often replacing them – thus, in the long run serving to reduce foreign ownership and control.[132] Throughout the 1930s, however, while not increasing, U.S. direct investments in supplying electricity in Canada continued to be significant. By way of contrast, British direct investments in Canadian electric light and power seem in the 1930s to have been temporarily nonexistent (as indicated in Chapter 4, the last big British stake, that in the British Columbia Electric Railway Co., had been acquired in 1928 by the Canadian-controlled Power Corporation of Canada). But in 1938, the British firm Bowater purchased from International Paper and Power the latter's equity interest in International Power and Paper of Newfoundland (which the American giant had owned since 1927). Newfoundland was not yet part of Canada. Bowater acquired a large mill, the so-called Corner Brook company, which then became Bowater's Newfoundland Pulp and Paper Mills Ltd. It had a sizable power facility.[133]

THE MIDDLE EAST, ASIA, OCEANIA, AND AFRICA

During the 1930s, there were two aspects of foreign direct investments in electric utilities in the Middle East. The first had its genesis in the breakup of the Ottoman Empire and was in the mandated and independent territories. In Syria and Lebanon, there were the rudiments of electrification by

French/Belgian companies. In British territory, a free standing company had undertaken electrification in Palestine. In Turkey, the Turkish government had increasingly taken over the limited electrification, with the entire process culminating in 1938.[134]

A second aspect of electrification in the Middle East occurred as foreign companies explored for oil. Electrification was evident in Iran near the oil fields and the large refinery at Abadan. In Iraq, the first oil was exported in 1934. Oil was discovered in Kuwait and Saudi Arabia in 1938. As foreign companies looked for oil, electrification emerged in company towns.

In the 1930s, there was a larger foreign direct investment role in Asia (from Malaya to Thailand to India to China) than there had been in the 1920s. With the exception of Japan (where there was no foreign direct investment), the amount of electric power available was not substantial, measured by the size of Asian populations. Large rural areas throughout Asia were not electrified by either domestic or foreign investors. Everywhere, however, there was more access to electricity in 1939 than in 1929 because of the foreign investors' role, but the rise was small relative to the huge numbers of people. Thus, the British-owned free standing company Calcutta Electric Supply Corp. Ltd. in 1934 purchased the property and goodwill of the Bhatpara Power Co. and obtained the permission of the Bengal government to take over its license. The energy it sold increased from 230 million kWh in 1934 to 395 million kWh five years later. The area the company served had 1.5 million people, but by the end of 1939 merely 57,415 houses were connected with electrical wiring, a bare fraction of the houses in the area.[135] In short, there was a modest spread of electrification.

In China, by contrast, American & Foreign Power embarked on a major effort to modernize the Shanghai power system.[136] Before the Japanese moves into China in 1937, its subsidiary Shanghai Power Co. had contracted for equipment and machinery for a new 15,000 kW installation, to complement its existing capacity. Work started in March 1937, but with the Japanese aggression, it was halted in September 1937 and American & Foreign Power announced that "completion of the installation [would] be delayed until demand for service increase[d] sufficiently to require it."[137] In 1939, work resumed but was then quickly suspended once more, owing to "the Sino-Japanese conflict."[138]

By the 1930s in Australia and New Zealand, virtually all the electric power was supplied by municipalities or provinces and financed domestically, although in certain mining facilities British capital offered the funding to provide electricity in enclaves. There remained some other British direct investment in Australia – for example, in the Adelaide Electric Supply Co. Ltd.[139] Otherwise, there appears to have been no (or very minimal) foreign direct investment. The investments of earlier years, which we discussed in Chapter 4, had become domesticated.

Throughout Africa, electrification was associated with empire. It was limited to urban areas, to mining camps, and to other enclaves. North Africa (particularly Egypt and to a lesser extent Algeria and Morocco), the Sudan, Kenya, South Africa, and Nigeria and other parts of West Africa had rudimentary availability of electricity in urban areas. There was probably more in 1939 than in 1929, but not much more.

SUMMARY TABLE, 1937

Harm Schröter constructed Table 5.1, based mainly on data in annual reports and directories. In the present volume, we have encountered all of these firms. It is important to note that none was formed after 1931. The table excludes the large group of U.S. companies with direct investments in Canada.

The excellent overview that this table provides greatly oversimplifies the role of major actors in what had become very complex corporate structures with numerous cross-holdings. Moreover, as each of these major companies had taken over others, they often retained the earlier incorporations (registrations). Thus, the Canadian-registered Brazilian Traction, Light and Power had subsidiaries that operated in Brazil but were (for historical reasons) incorporated in Canada, Brazil, and Great Britain.[140] The table also omits the many free standing companies still in existence that electrified particular cities, as well as the enclaves that were electrified. And, as noted, it leaves out the significant U.S. interests in Canada that had been established by the major U.S. holding companies, as well as some miscellaneous U.S. holding company properties elsewhere abroad. In addition, it ignores the foreign industrial companies in Canada (and elsewhere) that provided electricity to the public along with fulfilling their own requirements.

The Belgian Empain group seems to be neglected in this table. There are no U.K.- or French-registered companies on the roster; this inappropriately suggests the absence of outward foreign direct investment from these nations. The U.K. free standing companies that still existed (some were actually holding companies) were not sizable. Yet there were groupings of British business abroad not reflected in the table. Thus, for example, the Pearson group (Whitehall Securities/Whitehall Electric) had in 1937 direct investments in Spain and Greece (as well as a number of other miscellaneous electricity supply holdings that were not direct investments). Data in the S. Pearson & Sons Papers suggest that the assets controlled by Whitehall Electric were sufficiently large that that firm should have been included in the roster below.[141] In addition, the British connections with Sofina, through Midland Bank chairman Reginald McKenna, Sir Edmund Wyldbore-Smith, and Dudley Docker that continued from 1920s are not shown in this table.[142] Likewise, there were French direct investments abroad not represented in the entries on this table.[143] Thus, the list given on

Table 5.1. *The Assets of Electric Utilities with Investments Abroad, 1937 (assets in millions of U.S. dollars)**

Company (Country/ City of Registration)	Assets	Notes
American & Foreign Power Co. (U.S.)	534.6	By far the largest electrical holding company (by assets) with direct investments in Latin America and Asia.
Brazilian Traction, Light & Power Co. (Canada/Toronto)	425.6	A holding and operating company in Brazil.
Sofina (Belgium)	398.6	Worldwide investments in holding and operating companies in Europe and Latin America.
Electrobel (Belgium)	217.8	Investments in holding companies with interests in Brazil, Bulgaria, Egypt, France, and Spain.
Barcelona Traction, Light & Power Co. (Canada/Toronto)	190.3	Controlled by Sofina; assets in Spain.†
Mexican Light & Power Co. (Canada/Toronto)	109.8	Part of the Sofina/Sidro group.
Sidro (Belgium)	91.4	Controlled by Sofina. Holdings in Mexican Light & Power, Barcelona Traction, and two French utilities.
Gesfürel (Germany)	62.9	Investments in a Hungarian utility (linked with Sofina/Sidro group and AEG).
Hydrofina (Belgium)	53.3	Controlled by Electrobel. Largest investment in Romania.
Motor-Columbus (Switzerland/Baden)	44.5	Controlled by Brown, Boveri. Direct and indirect investments in Argentina, Ecuador, Germany, Italy, Peru, and Romania.
CHADE (Spain)	38.4	Principal direct investments in Argentina (in CADE). Sofina had controlling interest.
Italian Superpower Corp. (U.S.)	31.9	Principal investments in Italy. Atlas Corp. (by 1938) owned 50 percent of the shares.
Electrobank (Switzerland/Zurich)	30.3	Mainly portfolio investments in Austria, Belgium, France, Germany, Poland, Portugal, Spain, United Kingdom, and United States.
International Power Securities Corp. (U.S.)	28.8	Held its own securities that had been sold for Italian finance. An Aldred company.
European Electric Corp. (Canada/Montreal)	27.9	Set up by Italian group, a Volpi company, associated with Italian Superpower.

Company (Country/ City of Registration)	Assets	Notes
Schweizerisch-Americanische Elektrizitäts-Gesellschaft (Switzerland/Zurich)	21.4	Affiliate of Motor-Columbus, with operations in four Latin American countries, including interests in Lima Light and Italo-Argentina.
International Power Co. (Canada/Montreal)	20.5	Holding company with interests in Bolivia, British Guiana (Guyana), El Salvador, Mexico, Puerto Rico, and Venezuela.
Elektrische Licht und Kraftanlagen AG (Germany)	19.4	Through a Swiss affiliate, held a portfolio that included securities of CHADE, Sidro, etc. Holding company associated with Siemens.
Société Financière Italo-Suisse (Switzerland/Geneva)	14.1	Involved in financing Italian utilities.
Société Générale pour l'Industrie Électrique (Switzerland/Geneva)	12.2	Took over Franco Suisse in 1932. Portfolio investments in France, Italy, and the United States.
Indelec (Switzerland/ Basel)	10.9	Investments in Czechoslovakia, France, Germany, Luxembourg, and Poland.

* Abroad is defined as outside the country of registration.

† In 1936, during the Spanish Civil War, a Spanish Workers' Committee took control of Barcelona Traction, Light and Power, but it continued to operate.

Source: Adapted from Harm Schröter, "Globalization and Reliability: The Fate of Foreign Direct Investment in Electric Power-Supply During the World Economic Crisis, 1929–1939," *Annales Historiques de l'Électricité*, 4 (Nov. 2006), 105–6.

Table 5.1 is far from complete, but it does indicate most of the major international investors in electric utilities in the late 1930s.

By 1939, Sofina, together with the electric utilities under its direction, was said to employ a staff of 40,000. American & Foreign Power in 1939 had a roughly comparable number: 35,260.[144] We do not have a total for employees of Sofina affiliates in 1929, but American & Foreign Power and its subsidiaries had over 47,000 employed that year.[145] Thus, over the course of the 1930s, American & Foreign Power had shed almost 12,000 employees. It is not clear whether the same was true of Sofina, but it seems likely. With fewer employees, American & Foreign Power was, however, producing and distributing more electricity – so there were gains in efficiency. Moreover, its assets far exceeded those of any other international electric utility company.

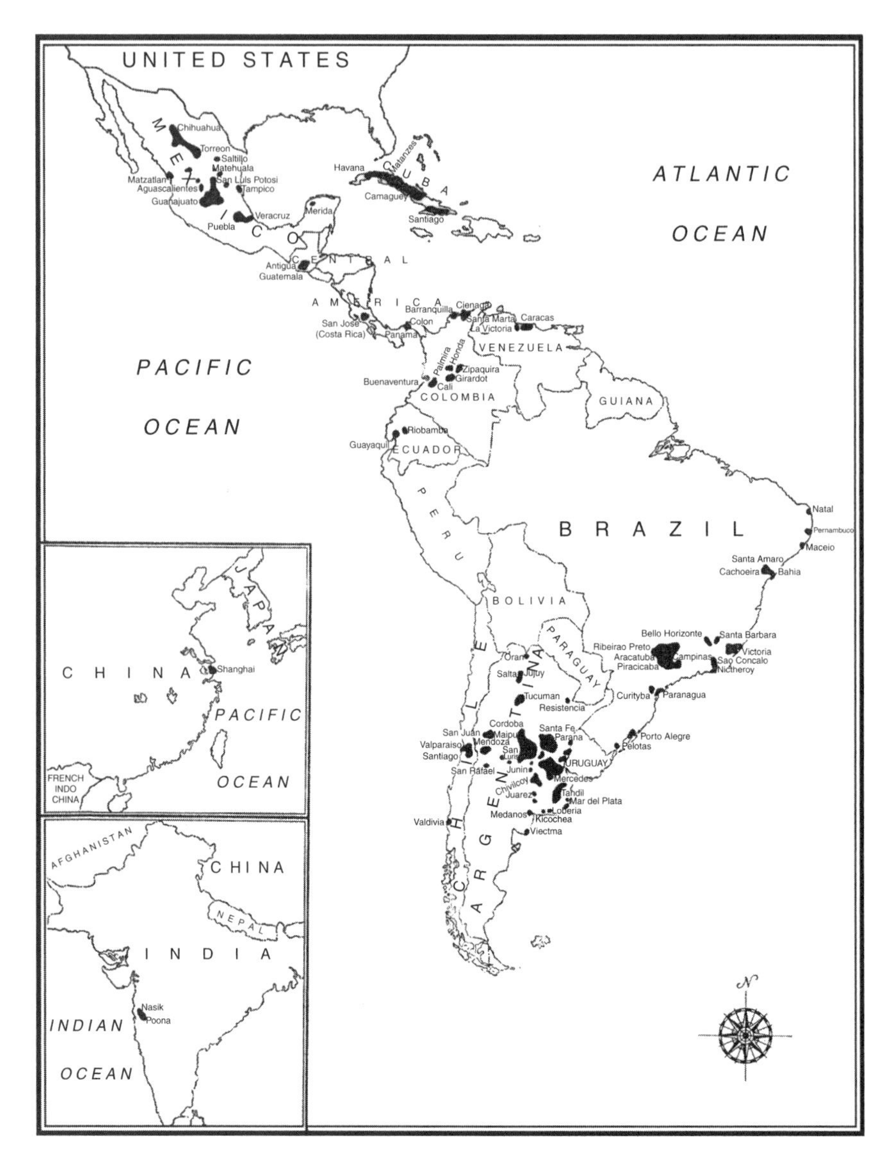

MAP 5.2. American & Foreign Power Operations, 1939
Source: American & Foreign Power Co., *Annual Report 1939*.

The map included herein covers the activity of just one holding company, although measured by assets in 1937 it was the largest one in the light and power sector. Within Latin America, where its operations were the greatest, American & Foreign Power provided light and power in Argentina, Brazil, Chile, Colombia, Costa Rica, Cuba, Ecuador, Guatemala, Mexico, Panama, and Venezuela. Were we to include the activities of Sofina, Mexican Light and Power Co. Ltd., Brazilian Traction, Light and Power Co. Ltd., as well as CHADE/CADE (in all three of which Sofina had an interest), along with those of Motor-Columbus and International Power Co. Ltd., the map of Latin America would reveal a far greater participation by foreign-owned companies in electrification.[146] At the end of the 1930s, American & Foreign Power Co., moreover, had no "operations" in Europe, Africa, or the Middle East, so this map does not capture the global span of foreign direct investments that we have discussed earlier and that are indicated on Table 5.1. American & Foreign Power did have a tranche in (or at least a relationship with) Sofina, however, which in turn had far-flung interests.[147] In short, toward the end of the 1930s there continued to be sizable foreign direct investments around the world, though it could be said that the links within and outside multinational enterprises (buffered by nationalist sentiments and activities) were weaker than in 1929–1930. Moreover, for businesses to prosper, it is not enough to simply survive; there needs to be new investments and ambitious new plans. These were constantly being thwarted. The Heineman-Oliven vision of a "European electrical grid," linked through a multinational enterprise structure, was on the eve of World War II a dim memory.

WORLD WAR II

World War II came as no surprise. Japanese aggression in Asia, Italian moves in Africa, the Spanish Civil War as a testing ground were all signs of the mounting world tensions. Then came the Anschluss, when in March 1938 the Germans incorporated Austria into the Reich. Later in that same year, the Munich Pact resulted in the German takeover of Czechoslovakia. And finally, less than twenty-one years after the 1918 Armistice, Europe was again – in September 1939 – at war. Little more than two years later, after the December 7th Japanese attack on Pearl Harbor, the United States became a combatant. The Second World War would be longer than the "Great War" had been. When World War I began, there was an international financial system dominated by the gold standard. Rates of exchange were for the most part stable. There was a general optimism about technological progress. The First World War abruptly shattered the complacency. By contrast, there was no global financial "system" at the advent of World War II. Autarchic conditions, fluctuating exchange rates, and restrictions on capital movements were the norm. Practically everywhere, there was little sanguinity about conditions within national economies.

Between the two wars, developed countries (the United States, Canada, Europe, and Japan) had become in large part electrified – principally with domestic capital, but in a number of nations with the assistance of foreign (direct and portfolio) investors that had stimulated the process – and at the margin if not more had had substantial impact. National grids had begun to connect distant points within advanced countries. Everywhere, national, regional, and local governments were playing a far larger role in the spread of electrification than had been the case in 1913, much less in 1918 or 1929. Even in the United States, rural electrification was occurring under government auspices. Having electricity had come to be accepted as living in the "modern" age. Electricity was part of the basic infrastructure. The New York World's Fair (which opened April 30, 1939) highlighted "the world of tomorrow" with its new uses of electricity – television, electric dishwashers, home air-conditioners, and other household appliances. The fair's exhibits provided an aura of the possibilities in an otherwise bleak world.[148]

If there was no international financial "system," there was on the eve of the World War II a highly complex maze of international investments in electric utilities, both direct and portfolio investments. There were inward and outward foreign investments that crisscrossed advanced countries in a highly unsystematic manner. Each advanced country had a different ratio of inward and outward investments and a different ratio of foreign direct investment to foreign portfolio investment. Even though capital flows had dried up in the 1930s, there persisted a lingering jungle of financial obligations that created unease among both debtors and creditors. In Latin America, foreign direct investors dominated the provision of electric power. Of the less-developed countries in the world, Latin America was far ahead in electrification. Foreign direct investors took part in electricity supply activities in Asia (excluding Japan, where they had never been present), Africa, and Oceania to a lesser extent. It is hard to overemphasize how complex the financial and multinational enterprise interrelationships had become.

Thomas Hughes ended his brilliant book *Networks of Power* (1930) by noting that by then in the more advanced nations, "the regional power systems, including those owned by private utilities, government agencies, and mixed private and government enterprises, had matured. After 1930 changes in these systems became less qualitative and more regular and predictable."[149] The regularity and predictability were technological, not political. The growth of electrification that occurred in the 1930s was slower than in earlier years, hampered by constraints on international capital flows and on the ability of multinational enterprises to set their own rates and to make remittances, on tax structures that left little profit for reinvestment, yet there was, nonetheless, an upward spiral in electrical generating capacity. And this was based on private- as well as public- sector companies – and in the private sector, on foreign as well as domestic companies. In 1939, worldwide, more homes had access to electricity than ever before in history.

The 1939 annual report of Sofina documented "the remarkable growth in the generation of electrical energy." American & Foreign Power supplied 755 communities outside the United States with electric light and power service as of December 31, 1929; as of December 31, 1939, the number had risen to 987 communities. In 1939, it served 1.3 million customers with electric light and power.[150] In the year 1929, generating- station output (including power purchased) for this single company was 2.1 billion kWh; the comparable figure for the year 1939 was 3.4 billion. Sofina's annual reports did not give a 1929 figure, but its 1939 annual report stated that "the companies in which we have our principal interests recorded ... a rise in their electricity output" in the last four years from 6.2 billion to 7.7 billion kWh and "an increase in the number of their customers" in the same period from 3.2 million to 3.7 million.[151] The seemingly unstoppable growth had continued through the 1930s.

In September 1939, with the start of the war in Europe, the private sector's international economic and organizational structures became increasingly fractured. Already in 1938, Heineman at Sofina was making plans just in case the Germans occupied Belgium. Sofina had sizable interests in gas and electric facilities in Portugal, and in August 1939 Heineman arranged for the transfer of Sofina's records to Lisbon – just in case. Even earlier, in March 1939, Sofina had set up the subsidiary American Intercontinental Trade and Services (Amitas) and opened an office in New York City. Well before the German invasion of Belgium, Sofina transferred a part of its administration, its entire shareholdings, and important members of its leadership to Lisbon and New York. While Sofina's main office remained in Belgium, its so-called permanent committee in Lisbon was provided complete control over Sofina's properties to avoid German seizure. Like many other companies from Europe, Sofina made plans to shelter its assets. Heineman himself did not leave Belgium until the Germans moved in, at which point he and his wife fled to France and then to Portugal and subsequently to New York.

After the Germans invaded Belgium in May 1940, the U.S. Treasury froze all Belgian assets in the United States to prevent German access to them. Aside from the new Amitas, Sofina had sizable investments in the United States in the Middle West Corporation. After the German occupation of Belgium, the Military Commander for Belgium and Northern France attempted to interfere with Sofina's continuing its links with North American enterprises, sought to stop the removal of any added capital from Belgium, and took steps to avoid the "sale of the German values to [the] USA." Most physical assets could not be moved, of course, but the title to them was mobile. For the most part, the Germans were too late, because Sofina had already transferred the securities that represented its major investments out of the control of the former Brussels head office.[152]

Heineman and his family flew from Lisbon to New York in July 1940. That summer, Sofina's top management crossed the Atlantic, too. Sofina was not alone among Belgian companies in this move to New York. Executives of the Empain group and Electrobel also arrived in New York

City with plans to conduct business from there. Sofina operated in New York under the name Amitas, which in turn was controlled by a company called Securitas, designed to hold Sofina assets in safety during the war years. Amitas got licenses to do business in the United States, required because of the blocked assets. In the summer of 1941, American control regulations of foreign funds were extended, and there were new concerns in the United States over German business influences in Latin America.[153]

By this time, Heineman and Sofina were well installed in New York City, where Sofina occupied three floors at 50 Broadway and had about 300 employees who had escaped from Europe. Out of the New York office, Amitas's engineering and technical staff selected and purchased electrical equipment, generating supplies, and fuel in the United States to export to Sofina's affiliates in Argentina, Brazil, and Mexico. In the United States, Sofina owned 4.96 percent of Middle West Corporation stock (just below the trigger of 5 percent, which would put it under the scrutiny of the Securities and Exchange Commission). Charles Wilmers (a director of Amitas) represented Sofina on the board of directors of Middle West Corporation. Sofina also invested in other U.S. utilities, among them Electric Power & Light Corporation and Standard Gas & Electric Company. And in that fall of 1941, Heineman was reported to be making "quiet acquisitions" of stock in two American utilities, which in turn owned a 93 percent stock interest in Panhandle Eastern Pipe Line, the operator of a natural gas pipeline from the Texas oil fields to Michigan.[154]

By this time, Sofina had become an object of U.S. government attention: Did it fall within the purview of the Public Utility Holding Company Act? And what of its "frozen" assets in the United States? Was it, in its trade with Argentina and Brazil, acting to support German enterprise? Was it violating the new "blacklist" and trading with "German-controlled companies"? When Sofina set itself up in the United States, there had been suspicion on the part of U.S. authorities that it was acting as a front for German interests. Of course, Sofina claimed that it was escaping German control and that its affiliates in Latin America were not German. When the freeze on Belgian assets was put into effect in May 1940, Sofina had applied for and received permission to use its assets in America. In October 1941, however, as more attention was being placed on "blacklisted" companies, the U.S. Treasury Department became wary, and the *New York Times* reported that Treasury had put a "ban on additional Sofina permits to use its funds." There were concerns that a rumored-to-be "German-controlled" Sofina was a worry for national security as it sought to buy interests in an oil pipeline company.[155]

Heineman got permission to use Sofina funds, and all during the war years the New York office continued to operate. Neither the freeze nor the SEC inquiries jeopardized the existence of Sofina's operations within the United States or elsewhere. Like a number of other European companies,

Sofina set up an affiliate in Panama, Services Inc., designed to handle transactions with Latin America.[156] Meanwhile, Brazilian Traction, in one of the infrequent expansions of generating capacity, had in the late 1930s ordered equipment and contracted with Siemens in Germany to build a new generating unit, so-called Lajes "A." When the war started in Europe, many parts for that generator were sitting in German warehouses, not having yet been exported to Brazil. Brazil did not enter the war as a belligerent until 1942, but Brazilian Traction had a Canadian registration and Canada had followed Great Britain and was after September 1939 a combatant. Duncan McDowall, the historian of Brazilian Traction, explains that Brazilian Traction officials in London skirted the "embargo placed upon all British companies trading with the enemy by arranging to ship the remaining components to Rio via Switzerland and the Italian port of Genoa." McDowall continued, "This desperate move might easily have brought severe diplomatic repercussions from the British or the German government. None the less, it worked, and the Lajes 'A' generating unit came 'on line' in 1940."[157] It is useful to put this in the context of Sofina's activities in New York in 1940–1941, as explained above.

The outbreak of war in September 1939 affected all of Europe, both combatants and noncombatants. Switzerland remained neutral during the war, but from the start it was caught up in war-related problems. The large Swiss banks, fearful that Switzerland might not avoid invasion in the Second World War, like Sofina and other Belgian entities, organized a New York presence. For the Swiss financial institutions, this was a novel approach to their American business. Swiss Bank Corporation, Basel, applied for a New York agency license in July 1939 (its agency actually began operations in October 1939). So, too – and because of its long-standing ties to Elektrobank probably more important in terms of foreign interests in the electric utilities sector – Credit Suisse, Zurich, organized a New York subsidiary, the Swiss American Company, in July 1939, and opened a New York agency early in 1940. Credit Suisse was not only key in Elektrobank, but it was Sofina's principal Swiss bank.[158] Not until June 1941 were Swiss assets in the United States frozen. Because those in public utilities, particularly the sizable ones made by Elektrobank, were of a portfolio nature, the freezing of Swiss assets had little consequence in relation to multinational enterprise behavior in the public utilities sector. The Swiss banks obtained licenses to operate under the freeze. No business operations in the United States were in any way impacted. That same June 1941, German assets in the United States were frozen – but by this time, German holdings in U.S. electric utilities were nonexistent or cloaked through Swiss intermediaries.[159] As indicated, U.S. government officials were wary that Sofina and the Swiss banks were a "cloak" for German business.[160] There was undoubtedly reason for concern, as evidenced by the Swiss role in getting Siemens parts through to the Sofina-associated Brazilian Traction.[161]

The war broke down international business relationships, making contacts over enemy lines difficult. Basically, it meant the fracture of international business. The British Pearson group – for example, Whitehall Electric/Whitehall Securities – had, as we have noted, acquired controlling interest in the Spanish company Fuerzas Motrices del Valle de Lecrin in December 1930. The Pearson group had completed the building of the plant in 1933. Electrification was provided. The physical facilities survived the Spanish Civil War, but on June 27, 1942, the company was sold "by agreement" to Spanish interests, at an estimated loss by the Pearson group of over £1 million.[162] Spain was neutral during the war, but Franco was widely viewed as pro-German. In Spain, the Istituto Nacional de Industria (INI) had been created on September 25, 1941, setting up a public-sector company to spur industrialization. It was inspired by the Italian Istituto per la Ricostruzione Industriale (IRI), which, as we have indicated, had its origins in 1933 and came to play a leading role in Italian electrification. INI also came to participate in the electrical field in a major manner, spawning Endesa in 1944.[163] Increasingly in Spain, public-sector companies emerged to provide electric power and other utilities as well.

On the European continent, the Germans developed electricity for war purposes. Within Europe, the occupation meant German control over electrical facilities, which the occupier expanded as needed for wartime production. Everywhere, there were shortages of fuel. Energy-intensive industries – aluminum and fertilizer production, for example – put new pressure on the expansion of electric energy resources. Swiss electricity output rose as the Swiss sought to maintain neutrality, surrounded by occupied or "Axis" nations. As for Italian electricity production, it mounted to fill military, industrial, and household demand. In fact, demand far exceeded the existing production capacity.

Japan's expansion in China and the Dutch East Indies (Indonesia) brought it fuel for electrical facilities. A subsidiary of Japan's long-established Oriental Development Company, with aid from the Japanese government, created within Korea a new nitrogenous fertilizer industry, with the fertilizer exported to Japan. This activity came to be responsible for almost the whole of the electric power industry in Korea. The modest prewar start of electric power in Korea now became comprehensive.[164] Japan itself by the time of World War II was almost completely electrified (90 per cent of Japanese homes were wired for electric lighting).[165]

In less developed countries, as trade slowed (interfered with by wartime conditions), there was new demand for import substitution to fill requirements, which necessitated new electrification associated with the new industrialization.[166] Throughout Latin America, where major expansion of electric generating capacity depended on imports of machinery (and often fuel), there were difficulties everywhere as high demand strained existing facilities.

And then there were the problems in Argentina. Not until March 27, 1945, with the war almost over, did Argentina finally declare war on Germany. Sofina's assets in Argentina were through Compañía Hispano-Americana de Electricidad, CHADE (along with the Luxembourg stand-in and a Panamanian holding company). When in May 1940 the Germans occupied Luxembourg, SODEC (which had stood in for CHADE since 1938) suspended its activities, and because the Spanish Civil War was over, CHADE's role was reinstated as the parent for CADE (CHADE's principal Argentine operating company). During the war years, Sofina used a Panamanian company, Sovalles, Inc., to protect CADE's assets.[167]

In the fall of 1942, Heineman made a trip to Argentina, where he stayed for several months, trying to negotiate rate increases for CADE. The war years were not sanguine ones for private enterprise in Argentina. After the 1943 military coup, the Argentine government – soon to be led by Juan Perón – adopted a policy that endorsed state intervention in economic activity. As in Spain and Italy, in Argentina the federal government became a major participant in electricity generation. During 1943–1945, roughly 38 percent of the book value of American & Foreign Power Co.'s assets in Argentina was expropriated.[168] CHADE/CADE's assets in Argentina survived the war years with no expropriations, but barely so. When in the postwar period there was an audit of CHADE/CADE's books, a group of Swiss shareholders insisted that 1940–1944 expenditures of 15 million gold pesetas by CHADE were unaccounted for by its board and that profits made in those years, aggregating 204 million gold pesetas, "could not be traced either in the period [1940–1944] balance sheets of Chade or Cade" – or of the Panamanian intermediary, Sovalles.[169] CADE appears to have been appallingly managed in the 1930s (see above); Heineman's visits had not coped with its problems. And as the Perón administration dawned, CADE came under intense scrutiny. Perón had little patience with private enterprise, which was reflected in his administration's relations with CADE.[170] Nonetheless, CADE maintained operations during the war years, despite fuel shortages and its continued inefficient management. Needless to say, few Argentines were satisfied with the service it provided.

From 1942 to 1945, in country after country, new government involvements in the electricity supply industry emerged, sometimes related to wartime requirements and sometimes more generally based on the ever-strengthening ideological view that the market could not handle the provision of a country's basic infrastructure. In 1943 Chile, for example, the Corporación de Fomento de la Producción adopted a program for national electrification. La Empresa Nacional de Electricidad, SA (Endesa or Endesa of Chile, as it was often called, to differentiate it from the Spanish Endesa) was established in 1944 as a branch of the Corporación de Fomento.[171]

During the war, American & Foreign Power was, as noted, the largest of the global electric holding companies – if defined by the assets it controlled.

The war's impact was profound. Right after Pearl Harbor, the Japanese took over its sizable Shanghai properties, and American & Foreign Power wrote off its assets in China.[172] The loss of revenues from its Chinese properties, however, was more than offset by higher revenues from its Latin American subsidiaries – this despite the nationalizations in Argentina.[173] The rise of nationalism in Latin America did not bode well, however, for the future of foreign-owned companies involved in electric utilities. Inflation indicated a need for higher electricity charges, but everywhere governments were intervening to stop or at least slow electric rate increases because no government wanted to face popular complaints about higher electricity prices. As electricity increasingly became a necessity, its cost became a politically sensitive issue. But most promising for the future, the "war-induced prosperity" in Latin America encouraged industrialization. Living standards rose, and thus demand for electric power mounted rapidly. American & Foreign Power discovered that in some Latin American countries its production capabilities were lacking, so despite shipping delays and equipment shortages it undertook $45 million worth of wartime construction in Latin America, an amount barely adequate to meet the expanded demand.[174] In the eyes of corporate leaders, the increasing demand seemed to present promising opportunities for the postwar future.

In World War II, even more than in World War I, governmental functions and responsibilities expanded everywhere. Even before the United States entered the war, the federal government was planning for peace. Among those countries that would ultimately be victors (and not only the United States), there was a broad examination of what had gone wrong in the past. Although this search for answers was true in many of the Allied countries, it was particularly evident in the United States. Why, asked government officials and the academic community, did World War II happen so close on the heels of World War I? How was a Third World War to be prevented? World War I and its aftermath were judged an economic disaster. How could planners escape a similar set of post–World War II experiences? What could be done to deal with the expected short postwar boom, which might well be followed by massive unemployment and a global depression?

In July 1944, meetings at Bretton Woods, New Hampshire provided the basis for setting up the International Monetary Fund and the World Bank, with one goal being to identify past mistakes and rectify them. There had been problems with the monetary system, and the 1920s were perceived as "a sad chronicle of attempts, often high-minded and frequently ingenious, but in the final analysis doomed to futility, to deal with the tangled legacy of the Great War."[175] Once things went wrong in the 1920s, the world economy fell apart during the 1930s. In 1944, the pervasive notion was that not only must the monetary system be repaired, but there must be provisions for funding world reconstruction and development. Recovery would not be automatic. Governments had to play a role in a manner that involved international cooperation. Already in the 1930s, in numerous countries, this enlarged governmental role was taken for granted. In the United States, for example, the Export Import Bank had been doing substantial financing of public utilities abroad in the 1930s. Now, on a bilateral and multilateral basis, it was expected that governments would provide for the needs, given the inadequacies of markets. Whether it was coping with fuel requirements or with electrification, the private sector could not be relied on. If the 1930s had seen added governmental interventions to regulate the process of global electrification, World War II seemed to ensure that that role would continue into years beyond. Private-sector financing of basic infrastructure around the world would not suffice. Moreover, when the war was over, the internationally networked private enterprise system that over the years had established electrification on a global basis was in disarray. International business faced new circumstances and new challenges.

There was another major change that occurred in the world economy as an outcome of World War II. After World War I, the United States had emerged as a world leader – bar none. Yet in 1919, the nation did not recognize its strength and the British loss of leadership was fresh. Germans had been in denial. They had hoped to resume their key role. After World War II, the superiority of the United States was evident for all to see. Moreover, Americans were set to take leadership. At the same time, other nations hoped to be players in the world economy, and Britain was particularly fearful lest the erosion of its traditional international role continue and accelerate. Already, Britain had been supplanted in Latin America. Would this happen elsewhere?[176] Of course it would. America came out of the Second World War as the strongest country in the world. Apart from Pearl Harbor, there had been no physical destruction. America was ready to help the rest of the world rebuild. Where would private-sector multinational enterprise in the electrical sector fit into the scheme of things? No one knew.

PART III

CONCLUSIONS

6

Summary of the Domestication Pattern to 1978

When World War II was over, the challenges were immense. Everywhere, there was damage that needed repair. Everywhere, exchange controls were in effect; currencies were inconvertible; trade restrictions were abundant. The problems facing the world community were formidable. Although around the world there remained many areas (especially rural ones) untouched by electrification, an awareness of electricity as essential now prevailed. Home and industrial uses of electricity already had expanded tremendously and were continuing to grow. People wanted far more than lightbulbs; they wanted an ever wider range of electrical goods, including washing machines, refrigerators, and eventually television sets. Usages of electricity soared. Industry required power sources. Air conditioning opened previously unimaginable opportunities. In the big projects of the new World Bank, providing electrical infrastructure came to be a top priority.[1] Dams would be built and resources harnessed. And the world would be a better, more prosperous one as a consequence.

This chapter is titled "Summary of the Domestication Pattern to 1978," for by the end of the Second World War domestication (the elimination of the participation of foreign multinational enterprises) was well under way. Nonetheless, multinational enterprises were still present in many countries. The process of exits of multinational enterprise accelerated in the years 1945–1978, with only rare entries of new participants in that period. However, the process was not smooth. In the 1950s, existing multinational enterprises (particularly American & Foreign Power) went through some episodes of great optimism and expansion, but then, especially after 1960, the retreats became inexorable.[2] Thus, the first section of this chapter documents the domestication pattern as it proceeded in the postwar decades, while the second section flashes back to summarize the entire story

Authors: Mira Wilkins and William J. Hausman.

and to explain why domestication occurred. By 1978, the process was virtually completed.

Out of the war's experience, a pervasive view held that the market mechanism was by itself incapable of providing for recovery, reconstruction, and economic development, a part of which included establishing or reestablishing a working electrical network with reliable electricity supplies and distribution. Governments would have to be involved in a critical manner. Of course, governments had from the earliest days been participants in electrification, from the initial concessions that municipalities granted, to the emergence of local, regional, and national regulation, to the setting up of national grids, and, in many cases, to ever more frequent government ownership. In the United States in the postwar years, there remained a mix of investor-owned, municipally-owned, and state government-owned utilities, along with the large federal government power projects such as TVA and the Bonneville Power Administration.[3]

In the interwar period in Germany, many electric utilities had state, mixed, or municipal ownership, which had at varying speeds substituted for private-sector involvements. Governments in Germany had guaranteed foreign loans to utilities in the 1920s and 1930. In West Germany in 1948, of the nine large electricity supply companies linked into the German power grid, four were 100 percent state-owned; another four were more than 50 percent state-owned; and only the Rhine Westphalia Electric Power Company (RWE) had state ownership of less than 30 percent.[4] The post–World War II recognition of more government participation in economic life was particularly echoed in the light and power sector.

The government (national and subnational) involvements had another implication: They put foreign direct investments at serious risk. That there would be a government role from regulation to ownership of this basic necessity was taken for granted in the first postwar decade. Increasingly, it would be a national government role. The role might rise or fall, but few doubted that it would be significant. The more governments were involved, the less opportunities for private-sector multinational enterprises. At war's end in 1945, around the world foreign ownership and control that existed in electric light and power were carryovers from past times. But, for example, U.S. direct investments abroad in utilities were smaller than they had been in 1940.[5] In Canada, where, unlike most developed countries, inward foreign direct investments were still sizable, there would soon come to be a sharp drop in U.S. ownership and control in that sector. (The foreign direct investments in this activity in Canada were virtually all from the United States.)

In Latin America, the 1943–1945 expropriations of American & Foreign Power properties in Argentina were harbingers of things to come. In 1946, Mexico Tramways was taken over by the Mexican government, and a few years later the Mexican state obtained majority control of Mexican Light and Power Ltd. (Mexlight).[6] Yet, even though in 1950 the interest of Sofina, the dominant stockholder, in Mexlight was reduced to 36.4 percent, a writer in 1956 would refer to this Mexican public utility as being "largely European owned."[7] The Mexican government's insistence on over 50 percent of the equity meant foreign ownership and, more important, control were being eroded (even while not eliminated).[8]

The prewar Swiss and Belgian corporate institutions so crucial in past times to the dissemination of electrification on a global scale were restructured. In 1947, the Credit Suisse–dominated Bank für Elektrische Unternehmungen (Elektrobank), Zurich, for example, changed its name to Elektro-Watt. It became a sister finance company to Credit Suisse.[9] There is no evidence that in its new role in the late 1940s, 1950s, and 1960s that it made foreign *direct* investment. Indeed, as we have indicated, already before World War II Elektrobank had lost much of its *Unternehmergeschäft* characteristics – that is, it no longer served as an entrepreneurial enterprise in the electric power supply field. It had once stood in for Allgemeine Elektrizitäts Gesellschaft (AEG); it now seemed independent of that manufacturer.[10] In 1945, the Swiss Bank Corporation had taken over the Basler Handelsbank.[11] The latter had been the key bank in Indelec, Siemens's one-time Swiss holding company. Swiss Bank Corporation (SBC) was a major player in the postwar financial world with a long history of involvements in financing electrical projects. But far more than in the past, in the postwar years it had many other priorities beyond participation in the electric power sector.[12] Motor-Columbus, which had been entrepreneurial on Brown, Boveri's behalf, continued on; however, by 1970 it had only thirty employees. It became basically an investment house, holding securities.[13]

And then there were the Belgian firms, most notably Sofina, which survived the war with its top management in exile in New York City. After the war, its head office in Brussels was restored. Gradually, the *foreign direct investment* role of Sofina and the other Belgian firms in electric utilities began to dissipate. Dannie Heineman would retire in 1955 (he died in 1962), and after him what remained of Sofina was a shadow of the multinational enterprise that he had created.[14] There had been the Belgian bank reforms in the 1930s and the seeming separation of the Belgian banks from the holding companies. Nonetheless, a book published in 1959 described Société Générale de Belgique as having worldwide interests, embracing "some eighty companies in a score of major industries. It was and is the major factor in the Belgian Congo."[15] While this book does not deal explicitly with its interests in electrification, Société Générale de Belgique remained a participant. What electrification existed in the Belgian Congo (now the Democratic Republic of the Congo) was an outcome of its presence there.

Heineman's successors at Sofina were not engineers. In 1964, two years after Heineman died, the *Wall Street Journal* reported that Société Générale de Belgique had made a $168-million offer to take control over Sofina. It declared that the proposed purchase of Sofina shares would combine the efforts of a group of companies in expanding the Belgian economy. "This collaboration ... could lead the two principal financial companies [Société Générale and Sofina] interested in these operations to unite their destinies." By 1964, Sofina was an investment house. But this did not happen immediately after the war, as we will see; it was a gradual process.[16] As for the vast Empain activities in electric power supply and electric traction, these, too, would be increasingly curtailed. The Empain group, which had long had ties with the French firm Schneider, in 1950 acquired a more than 25 percent interest in that manufacturer, a harbinger for even closer connections in the next three decades.[17] In the immediate postwar years, Empain – like Sofina – still retained important international business (involving foreign direct investments), as did some of the other Belgian holding companies.

Both the Swiss and Belgian firms had had sizable direct investment interests in the electric power sector in France prior to World War II. Accordingly, they were profoundly affected when the French electricity supply industry was nationalized after the war. On April 6, 1946, Électricité et Gaz de France (EGF) became responsible for two new public companies: Électricité de France (EDF) and Gaz de France (GDF), set up to operate the newly nationalized electricity and gas suppliers.[18] After the French nationalization, the Swiss holding companies Elektrobank (renamed Electro-Watt in 1947), Indelec, and Motor-Columbus, as well as Société Suisse d'Électricité et de Traction, Basel, and Société Générale pour l'Industrie Électrique, Geneva, put in claims for compensation associated with their "lost" interests in France.[19] Comparable claims were made by the key Belgian groups; Liane Ranieri documents the indemnification of the French companies in which Sofina was involved.[20]

The Cold War began in the immediate postwar period. In the interwar years, as our readers know, sizable foreign direct investments from the United States and Western Europe were made in Eastern and Central Europe. The war and then the communist move into Eastern Europe put a close to those investments. There was a complicated claims process, with little in the way of reimbursements. Thus, just as the First World War had put an end to foreign direct investments in the Soviet Union, in the aftermath of World War II the advent of communism in Eastern Europe meant the termination of the interwar multinational enterprise investments that we have discussed in Bulgaria, Hungary, Poland, Romania, and Yugoslavia. For all practical purposes, the role of multinational enterprises in Eastern Europe seemed by the start of the 1950s to be ancient history. So, too, in Asia, there was a similar discontinuity. For instance, the war had cut off American & Foreign Power from its big stake in Shanghai Power. Once the war was over, American & Foreign Power sought to reacquire its properties and reestablish its business, but the communist takeover in China thwarted those intentions.[21] Before the war, there had been smaller British and French direct investments in electricity supply companies in China, which also were expropriated by the new Chinese regime. In 1949–1950, the Chinese communists brought to a conclusion any hope for revival of private-sector activities (much less foreign private-sector activities) for more than three decades.

In many countries – and not necessarily communist-dominated ones – it was widely and strongly felt that foreign ownership of electric utilities, because they were such an essential sector in the economy, was not tenable. As in France, public ownership was the key alternative. In Austria, public ownership of electric power generation was established in 1947, blocking the possibilities of foreign direct investment.[22] In Italy, public-sector activities were greatly enlarged in the electric power sector, and foreign ownership and control seemed increasingly irrelevant. (Full nationalization of the electrical industry did not come until 1962, but by then there were merely the remnants of earlier foreign direct investments.)[23]

In Spain under Franco (as we saw in Chapter 5), the state had become committed to a larger role within its economy. At war's end, Sofina had two key affiliates in Spain: Barcelona Traction, Light and Power Ltd. (with its sister firm, Ebro Irrigation and Power Co.) and Compañía Hispano-Americana de Electricidad (CHADE), registered in Spain, but doing no business there. (All of its assets were in Argentina.) CHADE was the first to seem to be in jeopardy. Sofina and Credit Suisse (which was also significantly involved) had interests in CHADE and through it in Compañía Argentina de Electricidad (CADE). The foreign investors became increasingly nervous as policies during the Franco regime seemed nationalistic and hostile to investors from abroad. In 1947, ownership of CHADE was reported to be about 35 percent Swiss and 25 percent Belgian – that is, roughly 60 percent of the equity was held by Swiss and Belgian owners; merely 15 percent was Spanish, with the rest by other nationalities. The Swiss ownership was reported to be widely held, but with a large holding by Credit Suisse, which had sold CHADE shares within Switzerland (and appears to have acted on behalf of Swiss shareholders). Belgian ownership was more concentrated, mainly in the hands of Sofina, which was the reason why Sofina was thought of (correctly so) as the controlling influence.[24]

On July 17, 1947, the Spanish government issued a decree designed to extend state authority. Sofina and Credit Suisse worried that Franco was aiming to obtain possession of CHADE with its assets in Argentina. "To frustrate such designs on its capital CHADE decided to place itself beyond the jurisdiction of the Spanish Government." Its plan was to take advantage of a decree enacted several days earlier (July 14, 1947) by the Luxembourg government, "allowing all companies formerly domiciled there, but suspended during the German occupation, to be revived." To protect their assets, the owners of CHADE had used a Luxembourg intermediary,

Société d'Électricité (SODEC), from 1938 to 1940. Sofina and Credit Suisse informed the Spanish government quite bluntly that its July 17, 1947, decree was "unsuitable." Their protests got nowhere, and at a general meeting of CHADE shareholders held in Luxembourg on November 18, 1947, by 61 percent of the votes of the total share capital, the transfer of CHADE assets to SODEC was approved. Reports explained that SODEC had been resurrected to execute the functions CHADE could no longer exercise properly, given the Spanish decree of July 17. After this maneuver, CHADE was left as an empty shell, and its liquidation would follow. A Spanish court tried to prevent a meeting (scheduled for January 8, 1949) and convened in Spain to accomplish the liquidation. Not to be deterred, on January 26, 1949, at a CHADE meeting held in Luxembourg, liquidators of CHADE were appointed. The assets of the dissolved CHADE remained intact – in SODEC's possession. The shareholders of CHADE became shareholders of SODEC, which promised that holders of CHADE bonds would get the "same security as heretofore." The shareholders were told that the Argentine government had recognized the validity of the transfer of the CHADE assets to SODEC.[25] Thus, it seems that from 1947 SODEC, based in Luxembourg, was the parent of CADE – and SODEC remained dominated by Sofina and Credit Suisse. SODEC was fundamentally a paper company. Decisions relating to Argentina appear to have been made in Brussels, where Sofina had restored its international head office after the war.

Meanwhile, in Spain a close friend of Franco's, Juan March (pronounced Mark), had been buying up sterling-denominated bonds of the other important Sofina company in Spain: the Sofina-"controlled" Barcelona Traction, Light and Power. March had made those purchases when the securities had seemed very cheap, and between 1948 and 1952 he managed a hostile takeover of Barcelona Traction and its sister firm Ebro Irrigation and Power. At this time, Barcelona Traction and its subsidiaries supplied some 20 percent of all electric power in Spain. The way March accomplished his coup was Machiavellian. If Sofina "played games" with CHADE and SODEC, so did March use devious tactics. In an obscure Catalan courthouse (dominated by March interests), on February 12, 1948, Barcelona Traction was declared bankrupt. Before Sofina's management understood what was happening, March had gained control, and Barcelona Traction moved from foreign ownership and control to Spanish ownership and control. The properties were said to be worth $350 million. In the process of assuming control, March had pushed Barcelona Traction into bankruptcy. (With Spanish government restrictions on foreign exchange, it had not paid interest on the bonds that required payment in British pounds.)[26] Next, new shares were issued to the bond owners (mainly March interests), which now had the equity and control. There was a diplomatic rumpus, with futile complaints from the Canadian government (Barcelona Traction was registered in Canada), the Belgian government

(Sofina, which had had control, was Belgian-based), and from the U.S. government, which thought March's behavior was imbued with fraud.[27] Franco could not have cared less. March changed the name of the company to FECSA (Fuerzas Eléctricas de Cataluña).[28] Sofina's management was very angry and did not give up. On behalf of the Belgian shareholders, the Belgian government took the matter to the International Court of Justice at the Hague, which eventually ruled (15 to 1) in February 1970 that Belgium did not have standing before that court. Why not? Barcelona Traction was registered in Canada and the shares "allegedly" owned by Sofina/Sidro were held – in February 1948, at the time of the declared Spanish bankruptcy – in the name of an American partnership: Charles Gordon & Co. This, of course, was done during World War II to *protect* Sofina's assets.[29] All the corporate disguises had ultimately defeated their purpose, the protection of assets. In 1972, *Moody's Manual (Utilities)* listed Barcelona Traction for the last time; the stated reason it was dropped was "no public interest."[30] The phrase seemed to convey several meanings, but the bottom line was that international investors no longer could participate in this Spanish-owned utility. (Foreign direct investment, which had earlier come to an end, was now confirmed as out of the picture.)

The "domestication" process that took place in noncommunist Western Europe also occurred elsewhere. In 1947, the year of Indian independence, its new government pressed American & Foreign Power to give up control of its properties there. Reluctantly, the American enterprise did so. It had little choice. By 1951, American & Foreign Power had divested all of its direct investments in India.[31] In Egypt, a new public utilities law was passed in 1947 that mandated Egyptian state control over foreign-owned firms. No new concession was to last more than thirty years. Foreign-owned and -controlled companies remained, but the new legislation left a bleak future for foreign direct investors in this sector.[32] In South Africa in 1948, the state-owned Escom (Electricity Supply Commission), which had been formed in 1923, finally took over Victoria Falls and Transvaal Power Co., the last of the large foreign direct investment in public utilities.[33] In Algeria, electric utilities were nationalized in 1946, following the pattern in France.[34] In 1947 in Australia, the South Australian state government took control of the English free standing company Adelaide Electric Supply Co. Ltd., which seems to have been the only remaining nonresident British private-sector company in Australia. The others had been taken over by state governments in earlier years.[35] And so it went; around the globe, there were fewer and fewer possibilities of foreign ownership and control and far more public-sector involvements.

Latin America, where foreign direct investment had been formidable, followed the trend of domestication. In 1947, the municipal government of Cali, Colombia, expropriated the plant of American & Foreign Power.[36] This was just one of ten principal communities in Colombia served by

American & Foreign Power, but it was a foreboding of what was to come. More serious was what was happening in Argentina. In 1946, the municipal authorities in Rosario informed Sofina's affiliate there that it intended to take over that property when its concession expired in 1952. Sofina was also having problems getting appropriate treatment of its Buenos Aires tramway investment (see Chapter 5).[37] Otherwise, so far, there were no more expropriations in Argentina in the light and power sector beyond what had happened with the American & Foreign Power properties in 1943–1945, which was also discussed in the last chapter. (Argentina had, however, nationalized the big British investments in railroads and was trying to digest that acquisition.) In 1946, the largest foreign investor in Argentina in electric utilities was CHADE, which supplied light and power to Buenos Aires. At the same time as the dominant investors in CHADE were in conflict with the Spanish government and were rearranging the European corporate structures to their liking (see above), in Argentina Perón was threatening to nationalize CHADE's (and then SODEC's) giant assets, principally those of Compañía Argentina de Electricidad (CADE) – or, if not exactly nationalize, at least hold down electricity rates so as to make the company unprofitable. The Argentine government put restrictions on remittances. CADE's earlier conflicts in Argentina (see Chapter 5) suggested that there was a possibility that its concession would be revoked and its properties confiscated. Later, subsequent to Perón's leaving office in 1955, there would be allegations that CADE had bribed Peronist officials to keep under raps the accusations made by government investigators against this foreign-owned utility.[38] Not only Sofina's interests, including those of CADE, were under attack, so battered did American & Foreign Power's management in Argentina feel that in despair in 1950 the U.S. company (the second largest supplier of electricity in Argentina) offered to sell out to the Perón government. Negotiations proceeded, only to be suspended in 1952.[39] These negotiations were revived in September 1954, but they made little headway.[40] Both CADE's and American & Foreign Power's departures from Argentina were postponed until after Perón was out of power. With the change in government in 1955, American & Foreign Power's management was hopeful. The new Minister of Industry, who had jurisdiction over electric services in Argentine, assured officials of American & Foreign Power's so-called ANSEC group of companies that the longstanding quarrels over payments for the properties that had been expropriated in 1943–1945 (and for which American & Foreign Power had never been compensated) and the operating conditions of the properties still under ANSEC control would be studied "in an atmosphere of good will." Corporate euphoria was brief. As the 1955 annual report (dated April 27, 1956) of American & Foreign Power went to press, the company inserted the following passage: "[R]eports have been received that the Argentine Consultative Councils ... has advised the Government to expropriate the foreign electric companies. ... [T]he implications of this development are not yet clear."[41]

In Porto Alegre in southern Brazil, a subsidiary of American & Foreign Power owned and operated the street railway system. In May 1952, the municipal government refused to authorize higher fares. The subsidiary claimed it could not raise wages, and so the workers went on strike. Not surprisingly, the municipal government took over the operations of the properties. "Judicial protests" (the phrase is in American & Foreign Power's annual report) notwithstanding, the municipal government stood firm. The company suggested that it sell the property to the municipal government.[42] As in Colombia and Argentina (in the case of the tramway and Rosario companies), this was one small part of the business, but it suggested future troubles. In Brazil, American & Foreign Power served hundreds of communities around the country. Despite its difficulties in Brazil, American & Foreign Power tried to be positive in its outlook. Its 1952 annual report included these comments: "We are glad to report that the activity of the Brazilian Government and some of the State Governments in developing electric power projects has not been directed against the interests of private electric utility companies; nor does it appear to present any imminent threat to investments in privately-owned utility enterprises."[43]

Nonetheless, throughout Latin America in the late 1940s and the first half of the 1950s, American & Foreign Power was struggling to place its operations on a sound financial basis. In its view, its most serious problem was the control by governmental authorities over rates. American & Foreign Power found it was impossible to provide "adequate and dependable supplies of power while service rates fail by wide margins to provide a reasonable rate of return on existing investments."[44] In Chile and Mexico, as in Argentina and Porto Alegre, Brazil, faced with conflicts with governmental authorities, American & Foreign Power became more and more receptive to the idea of pulling out entirely and letting governments take over the provision of light and power.[45] If the "threat" in Brazil was not "imminent," as its management said, the threat of grave difficulties in the future resembled the sword of Damocles. Throughout most of Latin America, problems of a similar nature were emerging.

In short, around the world the trend toward more governmental involvement – or at least more national (domestic) involvement – in generating and distributing electric power was pronounced and carried with it major reservations about foreign direct investment. If state-owned companies could do the job, what was the need for foreign multinational enterprises? Within Latin America, in nearly every country, new public enterprises took form.[46] By 1953, the Chilean government's electrical company Endesa provided 48.3 percent of that country's electric generation capacity.[47] In addition, government-sponsored projects multiplied in Brazil, Colombia, Costa Rica, and Mexico.[48] Much of the new governmental activity in electrification, especially in Latin America, was supported by the World Bank, which in the early 1950s gave credits of $64 million to the Mexican Federal Electric Commission and Nacional Financiera; $13.5 million to the Corporación de Fomento in Chile; and $40 million to various federal and state agencies in Brazil.[49]

Even so, in the 1950s businessmen, bankers, and engineers still perceived (or hoped) that there might be a possible role for foreign direct investors. Between 1949 and 1951, for example, the World Bank also made substantial loans to existing foreign direct investors in Latin America – $26 million to Mexican Light and Power and $90 million to Brazilian Traction.[50] American & Foreign Power got $50 million in credits from the U.S. Export-Import Bank to equip its many Brazilian subsidiaries and $12 million for its Cuban expansion.[51] Despite adversities, the largest multinational enterprises in Latin America tried to frame plans for a prosperous future, where new capacity would fill the obviously growing demand for electrification. They believed that they were more efficient than government enterprises and could coexist with them. It was in Latin America where the greatest foreign direct investment remained in the aftermath of World War II and where in the early 1950s it appeared to somewhat wary, and ambivalent, corporate executives that there were new opportunities for private-sector expansion programs.

THE END TO OVERSEAS EMPIRES: NEW COUNTRIES AND THEIR NEW ASPIRATIONS

India led in the decolonization process. Overnight, in the postwar years, new countries emerged, with many dreams and plans. For these countries, private enterprise in the electric utility sector was not part of the agenda. It was perceived as integral to the colonial heritage. Where there had been foreign ownership of public utilities, practically everywhere these became properties of new government companies. In Egypt, for example, "anti-colonial" rhetoric was the order of the day. The 1947 legislation referred to above was followed by additional Egyptian supervision of the private utilities. Still, there were aims by private (foreign) enterprises to take part in this sector – but not for long. When in the 1950s Egyptians began to renew plans for the Aswan Dam project (which had been on the drawing board in the interwar period and even earlier), a European group came forward that included the German construction and engineering firm Hoctief, backed, we are told, by the German manufacturers Siemens and AEG. The prime mover in this group was said to be English Electric, always eager to sell its equipment and whose activities in relationship to public utilities we have earlier documented. Historian Robert Tignor explains that the Egyptian government had turned to European private enterprise, preferring a "mix of European business interests to the overpowering influence of a business group from a single national state [which would use its imperialistic clout]." But the consortium was not prepared to go it alone. English Electric insisted that the British government provide the project with full financial guaranties, "in the event of an Egyptian default;" and then English Electric decided it also wanted World Bank involvement. The financing did not come through. In the 1950s, no private group would proceed without it. The contract was not signed.[52] This unrealized investment, which Tignor has documented, was not atypical. Private construction companies were often involved in electrification projects; but private enterprise did not provide the financing. The Aswan Dam would be a public sector endeavor.[53] After the failed British, French, and Israeli invasion of Egypt in 1956–1957, a nationalization of British and French firms occurred.[54] It is not clear whether any nonresident foreign-owned electric utilities were swept up in this Egyptianization, although the Suez Canal Company had provided enclave-form electrical services and there does seem to have been some French investment in electric utilities (in Lebon & Co., for example).[55]

More important, a few years later, in a display of outrage over the presumed Belgian role in the murder of Patrice Lumumba (in the newly independent Belgian Congo), in a wave of "anti-colonial fervor" in 1961, Colonel Gamal Abdel Nasser nationalized Empain's important properties, Cairo Electric Railways and Heliopolis Oasis Company and its subsidiaries. The Empain companies were among Egypt's firms with the largest capital. Other Belgian-owned utilities, which like Empain's ventures had been subject to earlier criticisms, were now nationalized as well.[56] The nationalizations ended foreign direct investments in electric utilities in Egypt.

1960S AND 1970S

As the 1950s turned into the 1960s and 1970s, the world economy had successfully revived from the world war. Major currencies became convertible. Foreign exchange controls began to be dismantled. Trade became more liberalized, and the European community emerged. However, the world was now divided between the West and the East. The Korean War had been fought, and the prolonged Vietnam War was over by 1975. By the end of the 1960s, the decolonization process was virtually complete, with new nations proliferating. The 1960s world growth rates had been spectacular, far greater than in the 1950s. By contrast, the 1970s were a disappointment, with high oil prices, inflation, and a general slowdown in the world economy. Accordingly, the optimism of the 1960s faltered. Throughout the 1960s and 1970s, electrification around the world spread, but for the most part it was without the aid of foreign direct investments.

In the 1960s and 1970s, there emerged in many developing nations what has been called "mass-expropriating political regimes and expropriation acts." The vulnerable foreign enterprises were the utilities, mines, oil producers, and enclave agriculture.[57] This was not the milieu for new foreign direct investments in public utilities. In Latin America, which, for the most part, had gone through the decolonization and nation formation process in the nineteenth century, there continued to be at an accelerated rate the nationalization of utilities, mines, oil producers, and agricultural properties – the "old" foreign investors. At the same time, in many Latin American countries there was a desire for new direct investments by multinationals in *manufacturing*, designed to contribute to industrialization and import substitution policies. A contrast was seen between the "old" exploitative direct investments and the new ones that carried technology and might assist economic development.

LATIN AMERICA IN THE 1950S, 1960S, AND 1970S

It is important to note that in the middle and late 1950s there were still significant functioning foreign-owned and -controlled electric utilities in Latin America. For a 1956 master's thesis at MIT, Charles F. Mallory documented the role of four holding companies in North America: the New York–headquartered American & Foreign Power Company, the Toronto-based Brazilian Traction, Light and Power Company Ltd., the Montreal-headquartered International Power Company Ltd., and the Toronto-domiciled, although "largely European owned," Mexican Light and Power Co. Ltd. These four companies together owned operating companies in fourteen Latin American nations and produced and distributed more than one-third of the electrical energy consumed in Latin America.[58] In addition, throughout Latin America there were foreign-owned (principally American) oil-producing properties, mining companies, and plantations involving company towns, all of which were electrified or becoming fully electrified. The ownership of the electricity production, transmission, and distribution was by the existing oil, mining, or agricultural enterprises.[59] The U.S. mining companies in Chile and Peru in particular were large producers and consumers of electricity. These included Anaconda and Kennecott in Chile and the Cerro de Pasco mine in Peru (along with its refinery at La Oroya).[60] Also, CADE in Argentina – and, to a lesser extent, the Swiss Motor-Columbus's Argentine affiliate CIADE – represented important European investments. In Peru, the foreign-owned and -controlled Lima Light dominated that market (an investment that combined British interests with those of Motor-Columbus and Brown Boveri). It is probably legitimate to estimate that in the mid-1950s, despite the wartime and postwar governmental activities, roughly two-thirds of the electric energy consumed in Latin America continued to be provided by foreign owners. (This may have been a lower share than in 1929–1930, but not by much.) Throughout Latin America, foreign companies still lorded over the provision of electric light and power. Just over two decades later, the story line would be entirely different. At the end of the 1970s, foreign-owned and -controlled electric utilities in Latin America were few and far between.

The phrase "creeping expropriation" came into the vocabulary of executives of multinational enterprises. Often it was not clear when an electric utility became "domesticated." Was it when the government no longer allowed the company to set prices? Probably not, for companies still thought they could negotiate rates. Yet rate control meant lower profits. Was it when remittances were blocked? Again, the assumption was that this would be temporary; but with depreciating currencies, blocked remittances diminished profits. Private enterprise cannot survive without profits. Was it when the government insisted on 51 percent (or more) ownership? Again, returns were lowered; sometimes, however, companies thought they could maintain control despite the lack of "controlling equity." Yet, all these conditions, short of formal nationalization, indicated creeping expropriation – that is, a decrease in foreign control and a reduction in profits. The trend had been in evidence since the 1930s, but in the 1960s and 1970s it took on more cogency.

Indeed, since the 1930s government-developed power facilities in Latin America had proliferated. Sometimes, government power was sold to the consumer through the existing foreign-owned power companies and coexistence seemed feasible.[61] In the postwar years, however, problems facing foreign electric utilities in Latin America mounted. Governments put pressure on the foreign companies to raise production and enlarge distribution to meet the ever expanding demand. Throughout Latin America, there were longings for economic growth, and energy – including, importantly, the provision of electricity – was fundamental to achieving that growth. By the mid-1950s, it had long been established that governments had a major role in regulating the electric power sector. And as the state role expanded throughout Latin America, it seemed inevitable that there should be more attention paid to electrification. Foreign companies with large investments were prepared to make even larger ones, but they obviously could not and would not do so unless they would receive adequate returns on their investments. Within Latin America, inflation and depreciating currencies led to the corporate desire to hike utility rates to obtain appropriate returns. Governments, on the other hand, wished to keep the price of this essential service low, for the public clamored for low electricity rates. This became a political issue. Because revenues of the utilities were in local currencies, when the value of the currencies fell what might seem to be good local profits were eaten up by the foreign exchange loss. Moreover, most Latin American utilities imported basic equipment from abroad. Depreciating currencies raised the price of imports, running up corporate costs. There came to be a fundamental clash between governmental (and public) expectations of excellent, extended service at low rates and corporate wishes for an environment that would allow expansion with good returns on investment. And in this context, electric utilities increasingly came "under fire."[62]

Despite these difficulties for foreign investors, from 1945 to 1954, according to one estimate, the overall growth in energy generation by the four big North American–registered holding companies in Latin America was about 8 percent per year,[63] and new hydroelectric plants were still being built. In the late 1950s, completely convinced of the promising future of Cuba and that there was no xenophobia there, American & Foreign Power embarked on a formidable expansion program. When Fidel Castro came to power in January 1959, it was a chastening experience. The giant operations of American & Foreign Power in Cuba were expropriated on August 7, 1960. American & Foreign Power was probably the largest single loser in the sweep of Castro's takeovers.[64] The naiveté of American & Foreign Power executives seems in retrospect to have been profound. They were in a state of denial. The actual taking of the properties had been foreshadowed by a mandatory rate decrease in August 1959. Executives at American & Foreign Power could not believe that this was happening. There was political-risk insurance available to them, but the company had not anticipated any political risk in Cuba, which was only 90 miles off the Florida coast. It had long been part of the spillover of American capital. The shock of Castro's expropriations had profound reverberations.[65]

Already in 1958, after a long period of frustration and off-and-on negotiations going back to 1950, American & Foreign Power had arranged to sell its remaining properties in Argentina to that nation's government. The agreement was signed on November 28, 1958 and approved by the Argentine National Congress on January 16, 1959, having effect as of November 28, 1958.[66] Earlier in 1958, CADE had sold out as well. The Argentine "purchase" of CADE's properties was especially nasty. CADE was accused of bribery and other misbehavior. In that year, the Argentine government passed a law putting Buenos Aires's electricity supply system under national (rather than municipal) control and placing CADE's assets in a newly created public company: Servico Público de la Electricidad del Gran Buenos Aires (SEGBA). The foreign investors in CADE received a minority interest in SEGBA by way of compensation, but in 1961 they were bought out entirely.[67] Compañía Italo-Argentina de Electricidad, CIADE, Motor-Columbus's affiliate, which had far smaller operations in Argentina than either CADE or American & Foreign Power, actually had its concession renewed in 1961 and apparently it survived until 1979, when it, too, was acquired by the Argentine government and folded into SEGBA.[68] In effect, in 1958 – with the end to CADE's and American & Foreign Power's interests in Argentina – it was the end of an era. Argentina was far from Cuba and so events in Argentina had not been seen as a precedent for the Cuban takeovers. At the time of the sale of its Argentine properties, American & Foreign Power valued its Argentine subsidiaries (on its books) as $117.4 million.[69] When Cuban Electric was confiscated, the "total stated value of the outstanding securities" was $280 million; American & Foreign Power owned $168 million of these securities, or about 60 percent of the total.[70] The Cuban investment of American & Foreign Power was greater than its Argentine investment, so with the Cuban expropriation without reimbursement the loss was far larger.[71]

During the 1960s, all the foreign-owned utilities remaining in Latin America faced higher taxes, governmental controls over rates, remittance restrictions, and everywhere a nationalist environment in which corporate profits seemed to be under fire. Often there were employees' demands for higher wages, which the foreign-owned utilities saw as raising their costs. The exit process was uneven, but from 1958 to 1979 it was steady. Sometimes there was expropriation and sometimes an agreement that carried with it compensation, which the companies felt was inadequate but preferable to remaining in operation in what had become hostile business climates, where profits were increasingly elusive.

In 1960 in Mexico, Nacional Financiera SA, a Mexican-government agency, purchased the properties of American & Foreign Power.[72] In the same year, Mexican Light and Power (Mexlight) – the Sofina affiliate – sold out to the Mexican government.[73] These two large foreign enterprises had accounted for 60 percent of the industry's capacity in Mexico in 1945. But by 1960, just before the takeovers occurred, with the expansion of the government-owned Comisión Federal de Electricidad (CFE), Mexico had control of some 40 percent of the industry's capacity and the two foreign companies' share had been reduced to about 33 percent.[74] In 1962, a subsidiary of Canadian International Power Co., Monterey Railway, Light and Power Co., sold its physical assets in Mexico to that country's government. (Canadian International Power was the successor company to International Power Co. It was registered in Canada in December 1956 and had acquired over 97 percent of the stock in International Power in January 1957.) Monterey Railway, Light and Power had been a subsidiary of the Montreal-headquartered International Power.[75] With this sale, all the key properties of the giant multinationals in Mexico were no longer in foreign hands.[76]

In 1961, a Colombian government enterprise bought the rest of American & Foreign Power's properties in Colombia. (The Cali properties had already been expropriated in 1947.) The purchase was approved in 1962, retroactive to 1961.[77] American & Foreign Power noted that "since government-owned utilities are the principal suppliers of electricity in Colombia, the acquisition of our Colombian subsidiary's properties is in line with the Government's policy of bringing the electric power industry under the administration of government agencies." Unlike in many other cases, American & Foreign Power was not required to invest the proceeds from the sale in Colombia.[78]

The process of private corporate withdrawals in the public utilities sector continued. During 1959, the electrical properties of the American & Foreign Power subsidiary serving the city of Porto Alegre in the State of Rio Grande do Sul in Brazil were expropriated by the state government.[79] In 1961, the State of Pernambuco, Brazil notified the American & Foreign Power subsidiary there that its concession-contract, due to expire on July 17, 1962, would not be renewed and that the state would take over the electrical service in the area served by the company.[80] A third Brazilian state, Espírito Santo, also expropriated American & Foreign Power's utility subsidiary.[81] And finally, in 1963 American & Foreign Power arranged to sell its remaining Brazilian electric utilities (in ten states) to the Brazilian government. But the government did not make the first payment, and it seemed likely that it would not pay up. In 1964, there was a revolution in Brazil, and Brazil's new president, Humberto Castelo Branco, wanted to reverse the bargain made by his predecessor. American & Foreign Power, however, was determined to get out. It had had enough. It insisted that Castelo Branco honor the original agreement. New negotiations resulted in the payment to American & Foreign Power of $135 million over 45 years, and American & Foreign Power agreed to reinvest in bonds of a Brazilian government–owned company.[82] In 1964, Brazilian Traction, Light and Power was also prepared to sell out after it experienced huge losses in 1963. Yet when João Goulart was overthrown by Castelo Branco, unlike American & Foreign Power, Brazilian Traction, Light and Power chose to stay the course. Under the new administration, it received permission to make rate changes that would reflect its costs – or so it thought. With American & Foreign Power's subsidiaries under Brazilian government control, Brazilian Traction – with far larger assets in Brazil than American & Foreign Power – was the only foreign-owned utility still in Brazil.[83]

Early in 1964, American & Foreign Power sold its holdings of stock in its Venezuelan subsidiary, Luz Eléctrica de Venezuela, to La Electricidad de Caracas, a privately owned Venezuelan utility. When the transaction occurred, La Electricidad already had an 18.5 per cent interest in the common stock of Luz Eléctrica and supplied practically all the energy requirements for its operations. Both companies were in Caracas, serving neighboring communities.[84] International Power (and then its successor, Canadian International Power) had had two electric utilities in Venezuela, one in Maracaibo and the other in Barquisimeto. Its Barquisimeto franchise, for 50 years, dated from 1913, but on its expiration in 1963 it does not seem to have been renewed. The Maracaibo franchise ran from 1926 to 1976 and seems to have moved to Venezuelan control at the very time of the oil nationalizations in 1976.[85]

There were more withdrawals from Latin America in 1965. In that year, American & Foreign Power arranged to sell its properties to the Chilean government and reinvest in Chile.[86] By the end of the 1960s, with very few exceptions, American & Foreign Power had, either through nationalization or through "voluntary" sales, gotten out of the public utilities business. Each retreat was different and the terms separately arranged. In 1968, the name of American & Foreign Power was changed to Ebasco Industries, and in 1969 Ebasco Industries was merged into Boise Cascade Corporation.

Thus, at the start of the 1970s, American & Foreign Power was out of the picture, CADE's large Argentine properties were government–owned, and in Mexico practically every foreign-owned utility was now under Mexican control. By 1971 in Chile, the large mines of Anaconda and Kennecott, with their important power facilities, were in Chilean government hands.[87] In Peru between 1968 and 1975, a wave of takeovers of foreign-owned properties occurred, amounting to twenty-eight expropriation acts involving forty-seven foreign companies. Lima Light was prominent among the expropriated companies, which had included other important, long-standing foreign investments in oil, mining, and agriculture.[88] Lima Light was nationalized by the Peruvian government in 1972. American & Foreign Power never had any investments in public utilities in Peru.

In the mid to late 1970s, the only truly sizable foreign-owned property in public utilities remaining in all of Latin America was in Brazil. (There were some smaller foreign-owned utilities in Bolivia and Ecuador, for example; and as noted CIADE in Argentina did not divest until 1979.) In 1969, the Canadian government had repealed "4-K" tax provisions. This category of the tax code had historically protected from Canadian taxation the non-Canadian income of Brazilian Traction (and the many other Canadian-registered enterprises). By 1969, Brazilian Light (Brazilian Traction, Light and Power had been renamed Brazilian Light and Power in 1966) was probably the most important company taking advantage of this tax benefit. In that year, Brazilian Light changed its name to Brascan Ltd. and restructured its Brazilian operations.[89] Brascan's board of directors at the start of the 1970s reflected (1) the retreat of Sofina as an actor, (2) the continued Canadian dominant role, and (3) the sustained, truly international characteristics of this venture. There were twenty-two board members, only one of them from Belgium. Canada had ten representatives (six of whom were from Toronto). Six board members had U.S. addresses, while Brazil, England, Germany, and Switzerland each had a single individual on the board.[90] The historian of the company documents the difficulties that Brascan had in doing business in Brazil during the 1970s. To finance its activities, the company had to turn to syndicated bank loans, arranged by international banks, and bond issues on the Eurobond market. By 1978, the interest rate on these foreign borrowings exceeded by about 4 per cent the 10 percent return permitted by the Brazilian government on the company's rate base. The outlook was not promising. On December 28, 1978, Brascan's president, John Moore, announced that the Brazilian government had given its final approval to its purchase of Brascan's Brazilian subsidiary.

The transaction occurred on January 12, 1979, when, for $380 million, Brascan sold all its shares in its Brazilian subsidiary to Centrais Eléctricais Brasileiras SA (Eletrobrás). The sale resolved the problems of mounting friction all during the 1970s between the Brazilian government and the foreign-owned utility and the inability of the private company to meet Brazil's swelling demand for energy.[91] This sale was essentially the culmination of the process of domestication. Brascan was the last giant foreign-owned utility – not only in Brazil, but anywhere in the world – at least the last in the long history of foreign ownership and control up to this point in time.

CANADA

In Chapter 5, we noted that in the early and mid-1930s, the "distinctly and definitely" American-owned companies in Canada supplied about 34 percent of the nation's electricity (in terms of kilowatt hours). We also indicated that during the late 1930s and World War II, that percentage had been reduced – with divestments and the expansion of provincially owned electrical companies. (Many foreign-owned companies in the public utilities sector were registered in Canada, but did business outside the country, to take advantage of the tax laws; these are not the companies that we are discussing here. And, as noted above, that long-standing advantage came to an end in 1969.)

The Province of Ontario had taken the lead in playing a governmental role in Canadian electrification. After World War II, the pattern of provincial provision of electricity grew in other provinces, too. In the process, there came to be an ever reduced role for U.S.-owned companies. British Columbia, Quebec, and Saskatchewan had set up provincial power companies between 1944 and 1949. The process of domestication was gradual. By the mid-1970s, merely 18 percent of Canada's power was being produced by private utilities.[92] And most of that 18 percent was by Canadian-owned and -controlled firms, although there did remain a tiny part of that share that was American-owned and -controlled – and an even smaller part that was British-owned. The American-owned Niagara Falls company still generated power in southern Ontario, grandfathered in for many years. Yet given the extensive electrification throughout Canada, the role of foreign direct investment in this sector had become unimportant. In a book published in 1970 titled *Silent Surrender: The Multinational Corporation in Canada*, Kari Levitt described American business as "recolonizing" Canada. Levitt claimed that Canada had become economically, politically, and culturally dependent on the United States. But in her account, the *only* sector that between 1926 and 1963 "had experienced a marked reduction in foreign control" was that of utilities. Regrettably, her data include telephones and other public utilities as well as light and power. Nonetheless, they mirrored the trend. In 1926, foreign control of *all* public utilities in Canada was 26 percent, while in 1963 it was only 4 percent. In 1979, the percentage would be still lower. In short, when the

Canadians worried in the 1960s and 1970s about U.S. domination, it was the U.S. role in *manufacturing* industries that triggered the apprehension. The foreign direct investment in electric power still existed, but no longer had major consequences.[93]

THE REST OF THE WORLD IN THE 1950S, 1960S, AND 1970S

By 1950, most of the ownership and control of Europe's electric utilities had become domestic. In Asia, this was also the case in Japan, where there had never been foreign ownership and control. In China, the communist takeover ended any former large investments. But what about the rest of the world, aside from Latin America and Canada, which we have already discussed in detail? Everywhere, in the 1950s, 1960s, and 1970s, there was a retreat from foreign ownership and control of electricity supplies. Part of this accompanied decolonization, for the new nations did not want any domination from abroad, and part came with the nationalizations of large oil, mining, and plantation properties. These had once been electrified by the dominant company, but after nationalization that was no longer the case. When there was new electrification, as on the west coast of Africa with the development of aluminum smelters, virtually all of the power supplied was separately financed, usually by the World Bank or other governmental bodies. Foreign investors – British as well as American – saw no future in private investments in Indian public utilities because former colonial powers were not appreciated in this newly independent nation. It is true that state-owned companies such as Électricité de France (EDF) developed certain international business in the 1950s, 1960s, and beyond, but these were governmental not private-sector activities. The ever optimistic 82-year-old Heineman of Sofina wrote in 1954:

> The fulfillment of the legitimate aspirations of nationalism in dependent territories has, I would say, produced a fundamental change in the political, social, and even economic environment, making undoubtedly for greater stability in the long run, but for the time being introducing new uncertainties into the international scene.[94]

By the end of the 1960s, the decolonization process was almost completed. Société Générale de Belgique had been expelled from the Congo. Change was everywhere in the offing. Foreign direct investors in electric utilities were not welcomed. Heineman was wrong, for greater stability did not follow – in most cases.

Internationally, U.S. foreign direct investment grew dramatically in the 1950s and 1960s, and by the 1970s large European multinational enterprises (most of them not state-owned) were competing once again with U.S. international business on a global scale. Contemporaries mistakenly thought that this multinational enterprise activity was "new." As the readers of this volume are aware, they did not know their history.[95] What was important about the U.S. multinational enterprise's activity was its heavy concentration in the manufacturing sector. And when studies were made of European multinational enterprise, once again it was manufacturing firms that were in the spotlight.

The "old" direct investments in mining, agricultural plantations, and public utilities seemed to have been eclipsed.[96] And then in the 1970s, there had been a dramatic shift from private-sector multinational enterprises to host country companies in the production of oil.[97] What happened in electric utilities was more extreme than what occurred in the oil industry, but it was part of the same pattern. When we write "more extreme," we point to the fact that in 1979 the seven major international oil companies still produced 23.9 percent of the crude oil outside of the United States and communist countries. On the other hand, in 1979 probably less than 1 percent of the world's electric power could be said to be supplied by foreign direct investors.[98] Indeed, by the end of the 1970s, in the electric utilities sector, most economists and other commentators assumed that these infrastructure activities in advanced countries would be by government companies or heavily regulated investor-owned companies. In developing countries, in the main, it was assumed that the provision of infrastructure would be by government entities, financed by the World Bank and other international agencies. And in communist countries, there was the belief that these services would best be provided by the state.

When in late 1978 Brascan announced that its subsidiaries in Brazil would become government-owned, it was, to repeat, the last of the giant foreign direct investments of times past. Financial intermediaries, banks, holding companies, investment trusts, investment companies, and so forth would maintain portfolio stakes in electric utilities, international bank lending to *governments* did continue, but the first round of private-sector foreign direct investments – investments that included ownership and control and carried with them management and technical services – was over. American & Foreign Power, once the largest (at least as measured by assets) and most entrepreneurial of the multinational enterprises in this sector, no longer existed, having been folded into Boise Cascade in 1969. Sofina survived as part of a Belgian financial group – as an investment company. And Brascan would become an investment unit of Peter and Edward Bronfman.[99]

THE SEQUENCING

It is worthwhile to summarize the course of domestication that occurred through the first round of multinational involvements in global electrification and culminated at the end of the 1970s. We have been selective and do not deal with every country in the world, but rather we attempt to put into a broad perspective the overall story line.

Table 6.1. *The "Domestication Process" of Electric Utilities in Selected Countries*

Period	Country	Comments
From the beginning	Japan	A brief attempt to establish before World War I the Anglo-Japanese Water Power Co. was futile. Otherwise, there is no evidence of any foreign direct investment in any Japanese light and power company. The newly organized Tokyo Electric Light Co. built the first power station in Japan in 1888, using the Edison system but with no foreign direct investment. There were substantial foreign long-term borrowings in the 1920s, but these were not accompanied by foreign direct investment.
Virtually from the beginning	United States	The Deutsche Bank, Siemens & Halske, and AEG had a brief investment in Edison General Electric in 1889–1891 and through EGE in utilities. There were minor foreign direct investments in the nation's electric utilities: In the mid-1890s, Canadian utility entrepreneurs were investing in power facilities for street railways in Minneapolis, Detroit, and Toledo, Ohio. There were other, more ambiguous foreign direct investments (for example, Table 1.4 gives >1 percent in 1913–1915). We have not included Middle West Corp. (the Sofina investment). Fundamentally, U.S. light and power facilities were domestic from origin.
1917	Russia/Soviet Union	Expropriation of the large foreign direct investments in electric utilities came with the Russian Revolution. While in some cases the formal process was not completed until 1923, for all practical purposes 1917 is the appropriate date for the domestication.
1923	Italy	There had been substantial foreign direct investment before the First World War, but it gradually dissipated. By the early 1920s, there was still a foreign presence, but nothing that approximated foreign ownership and control. There would be substantial portfolio investments in the 1920s. Nationalization did not come until 1962.

(continued)

Table 6.1 (*continued*)

Period	Country	Comments
1936	Great Britain	Utilities Power and Light Corporation (an American holding company) sold its significant direct investment in Great Britain to a British group. Some small direct investments in British electric utilities remained after 1936, but none was significant.
1938	Turkey	The Turkish government had completed the process of assuming control over French-owned public utilities. Sofina sold its Turkish utilities to the government in 1938.
1940s	Germany	After the end to the brief Edison impact, practically all electric power suppliers were German-owned and controlled; there was large outside financing (especially in the 1920s) and nominal "Swiss" control, but not foreign direct investment if one removes the corporate veil. The Bewag investment of Sofina in the early 1930s did not survive World War II. On Table 1.4 we have put 5 percent for Germany 1913–1915 and 1928–1932 and 0's for the post–World War II years. Brown, Boveri/Motor's German interests were not "nominally" Swiss, but were actual Swiss foreign direct investments, the former in manufacturing and, with the extended manufacturers' model, in power generation facilities.
1945–1948	Czechoslovakia Hungary Poland Romania Yugoslavia	Nationalizations – as communist regimes installed.
1946	France	The process of domestication was gradual, but when France in 1946 nationalized its electrical industry, there clearly was an end to all foreign direct investment involvements.

Period	Country	Comments
1947	Austria	Government ownership established throughout nation.
1947	Australia	There had been sizable British direct investments that diminished over time; and when in 1947 the South Australian state government took over the Adelaide Electric Supply Co. Ltd., this appears to have been the end of the sequence.
1948	South Africa	The state-owned Escom (Electricity Supply Commission), which had been formed in 1923, took over Victoria Falls and Transvaal Power Co., the last remaining large foreign direct investment in public utilities.
1949	China	The communist takeover in China ended American & Foreign Power's ownership of Shanghai Power, the biggest foreign investment in light and power in China.
1949	Spain	Barcelona Traction and Ebro Irrigation and Power came to be owned and controlled by a Spanish group (Jean March). Earlier, in 1942, Franco had created INI (Industrial National Agency), which, in turn, in 1944 set up Endesa and in 1946 Enher. Both Endesa (in thermoelectricity generation) and Enher (in hydroelectric generation) were state-owned companies.
1958	Argentina	American & Foreign Power arranged to sell all its properties to the Argentine government. CADE sold to the government that year as well. The largest once foreign-owned properties became government-owned.
1960	Cuba	Fidel Castro's expropriations included the huge American & Foreign Power's facilities.
1961	Egypt	While the 1947 public utilities law gave the Egyptian state control over foreign-owned public utilities, Belgian direct investments remained in this sector until 1961, when Nasser nationalized Empain's important properties. This marked the end of foreign direct investments in electric utilities.

(continued)

Table 6.1 (*continued*)

Period	Country	Comments
1962	Mexico	The government takeover was completed with its acquisition of Monterey Railway, Light and Power. Two years earlier, the Mexican government acquired practically all the key foreign-owned utilities (American & Foreign Power had sold its properties to Nacional Financiera SA, a government agency, and the important Mexican Light & Power had become fully government-owned.)
1965	Chile	American & Foreign Power arranged to sell its properties to the Chilean government. (The foreign-owned electricity suppliers associated with the mining industry did not become government-owned until 1971.)
1978–1979	Brazil	With the domestication of Brascan (the renamed Brazilian Light), the last big Brazilian utility property became domestically owned.

Source: Based on the text of this book.

Over time, foreign direct investors played a major role in stimulating electrification. They provided management, technology, knowledge, and experience, along with capital. They built generating plants, and they constructed transmission and distribution lines. They created networks of power. For small, inefficient plants, they substituted larger, more efficient ones. All of these efforts increased productivity. They led in technical rationalizations. In the end, direct investors contributed in an important fashion to electrification within the world economy.[100] By the time of the 1978 Brazilian decision to purchase the Brascan properties and the actual consummation of the deal in 1979, however, the first round of domestication was over. Foreign direct investors in electric utilities were few and far between.

A PERSPECTIVE

Are there any generalizations that can be made about the conclusion to the first round of globalization in electric light and power and the domestication that occurred from the late 1870s to the end of the 1970s, a process encompassing developed and less developed countries alike? Why, if these multinational enterprises contributed to making more electricity more available around the world, did their participation in this global activity virtually cease? Why did this sector become "domestic"? It seems clear that the reasons for the domestication were both economic and political, and the two were in many instances inseparable. Often, but not always, domestication was linked with nationalism and populism. Sometimes, it was yoked with socialist and communist movements. Other times, it was connected with national security. Frequently, it came to involve government (national and subnational) ownership.

Before we discuss what was behind the move toward domestication, we need to ask why there was internationalization in the first place. In many cases, international investment coincided with the start of electrification – for example, the Edison companies' spreading out internationally. In some instances, there was an aborted internationalization, domestication, and then a return to greater internationalization. Thus, in China, for example, the beginnings of electrification in Shanghai may have been foreign-inspired, by an early free standing company; alternatively, it may have been started by local capital. In any case, in 1893 the plant and the plans for electrification were taken over by the Shanghai Municipal Council. The latter tried to divest in 1899, but it found no buyers, domestic or foreign. Not until 1929, when American & Foreign Power invested in and took over the management of the Shanghai power facilities, did foreign direct investment in this sector in China become significant. So, too, many of the municipalities within Latin American countries had their own power plants, domestically established. Promoters who got early concessions were at times from the host country and recognized the need to attract outside investments and entrepreneurial talents. In advanced countries – for example, in Great Britain – the largest inward foreign direct investments in electric utilities did not occur at the birth of the electrification process, but rather in the late 1920s, with the U.S. ownership and control of Greater London and Counties Trust–Edmundson's. The patterns differed by country.

Multinational enterprises go where there are opportunities. They carry with them ownership and control – and far more. The foreign direct investors were able to assemble capital and direct it to productive purposes. Of greater importance, they introduced technology, management, and experience and raised productivity. They knew the logistics of organizing purchasing as well as planning distribution. They provided more reliable service, based on the knowledge that they could transfer from one operation to another. The initiative in developing foreign direct investments in this sector had come from various sources, which we spelled out in Chapter 2. It could come from the host country, which wanted the development to take place, or from a developed nation, whose companies' management saw good prospects abroad. Obtaining foreign finance (money that came without the ownership and control that accompanied multinational enterprises) was difficult for an aspirant company that was not well placed (in an international social network, if you like): investors hesitated to take the risks. Associated with a multinational enterprise, the projects could acquire the needed financial resources accompanied by managerial and engineering know-how. For the recipient country and the investor, foreign direct investments should have been a "win-win" proposition, with each party benefiting. The domestication process, however, shows that it was not so perceived. Why, then, did the domestication process occur?

The economic reasons lay squarely in the nature of the business. First, historically, the light and power company has been a natural monopoly. There were scale economies. A natural monopoly occurs in sectors where with decreasing average unit costs as production rises, given the demand, it makes sense to have a single producer. Competition meant smaller plants, higher unit costs, and inefficiencies. Typically, but not always (at least in the early concessions), a company that made a commitment to electrify a part of a city, the whole city, or a region, got a franchise that gave it a monopoly. And as is the case of any unregulated monopoly, the consumer faced higher prices and lower volume than under competition. This encouraged the introduction of government regulation or, alternatively, government ownership (in the case of government ownership, by definition, there is domestication). Second (and related), the investments are "lumpy." The start-up capital/output ratio is very high, but once the construction phase is over the marginal costs of operations (until a new round of investments is necessary) tend to be low. Yet the investor desires to recover the initial "sunk" costs and thus is wary of marginal cost pricing. The host state or community often disagrees and looks at marginal costs. Conflict is inevitable. Third, light and power supplies are a basic good, providing infrastructure needs. The companies furnish a "public service." Politically, it is difficult for a governing authority to let prices rise, and this becomes particularly untenable when it is a "foreign" company that is seen as "exploiting" the opportunity. This encouraged regulation and often government ownership. Fourth, if there are depreciating local currencies, returns on foreign investments are reduced. Foreign investors desire to raise prices to compensate for this, and unavoidable conflict once again looms. Often host countries perceived an "obsolescing bargain" (a phrase introduced by Raymond Vernon). Yes it was necessary to bring in foreign direct investors when the project started; the nation, municipality, or region needed capital (and perhaps more than capital). As investments were made and operations begun, the public and the governing authority saw the utility was in place and believed the bargaining advantage had shifted into the host country's hands. Why was a foreign investor necessary now that the power plant had been built?[101] This perception of the altered bargaining conditions often had counterproductive consequences. Foreign companies, which were no longer appreciated, became wary of making new and necessary capital investments lest returns be inadequate, owing to government interventions. With the generating plant came transmission and distribution systems, which needed further extensions, which in turn required more investments. Without new investments, facilities became run-down. Needs were not fulfilled, because as demand rose there was not enough capacity. Service deteriorated. Growing populations, with rising expectations, put additional demands on the foreign public utilities for extended services, often service to distant areas where the costs of building power lines might mean little in the way of profits. Governments called for more investment and more comprehensive electrical services, while at the same time expecting (even requiring) low rates. In many countries, foreign companies feared the "political" risks and found themselves in a business environment not conducive to big business activities, much less the activities of foreign companies. As a result, they hesitated to make the necessary extra investments. And in a chicken-and-egg fashion, this induced more hostility toward the foreign-owned utility. Sixth, and part of the same story line, consumers of electricity wanted a secure supply, without power interruptions. Because companies hesitated to make new investments, aging power plants and distribution facilities became unreliable. Companies found making repairs costly and postponed doing so. Service – once appreciated as the only electricity supply available – became inadequate and resentment mounted. As the role of governments expanded everywhere, more and more of them felt that there were political requirements that mandated the extension of and the steadiness of electrical services, and they objected to foreign companies making the decisions. Thus, in time foreign companies appeared to be no longer needed for capital, engineering, or management skills, which came to be perceived as available at home or through other channels. Or, alternatively, they were taken for granted – as being readily accessible. Seventh, domestication occurred in both developed and developing countries. While in industrial countries domestication frequently involved government companies' substituting for the private foreign investors, in less developed countries it nearly always did. Domestication in industrial countries took place when foreign firms no longer had an advantage, when capital, engineering, and management skills were present locally or through international financial channels. In less developed countries, governments believed that they could just as effectively (or even more effectively) operate the electric utility business as the alien companies. Particularly in the post–World War II years, international financial options (from sources such as the World Bank and other multilateral lending agencies) provided the possibilities of capital and engineering skills. In many less developed countries, the provision of management by private enterprise was seen as irrelevant, because it was presumed that government companies could manage resources as well as private foreign ones. Moreover, there was a widespread belief that utilities were not "management intensive" or "knowledge intensive" and anyone could run them. And, so, gradually, for some or all of these reasons, foreign ownership and control receded and domestic companies and governments came to supply light and power the world over.

As governments came to play a larger role in national economies, they watched their balance of payments. They put restrictions on the movements of money. Foreign investors in electric utilities needed "hard currency" for imports of generating equipment, supplies, and sometimes fuel. They also required hard currency to pay dividends to stockholders and interest on corporate debt. Many of the direct investors had borrowed from outsiders to add to the financing of their projects. But governments did not want their monetary and industrial policies to be determined by outside direct investors. With the notion of the obsolescing bargain in the forefront, the thought was that foreign direct investors, with their foreign exchange needs, could be easily dispensed with. It was better to have a domestic activity, with no need to pay dividends and interest to foreigners and one that could be encouraged to buy domestically.

Other reasons for the domestication were nationalistic and populist in nature. It was believed that outsiders should not be involved in vital sectors of the economy. Electricity and waterpower resources were too fundamental to be left to nonresident owners. "Foreigners" were perceived as suspect. They made "excessive" profits. They cheated. They corrupted public officials. They were "bad news." Because multinational enterprises were "sophisticated" and "experienced," it was often assumed that they had more opportunities to be deceitful – to get around national laws, to use transfer prices to the disadvantage of the host state, or to evade taxes. Hence, there was an inherent distrust between the host nations and the foreign companies. In certain countries, this distrust was fueled by labor unions, who felt that employees did not share enough of the "rents." Very often such feelings were visceral, not founded on realities and based on faulty assumptions. Such negative views toward multinational enterprises had their cycles, which surfaced periodically in both developed and less developed countries over the course of the twentieth century. In various configurations, they were present in advanced countries and in the many new nations that obtained sovereignty during the century. It did not matter whether the beliefs were true or untrue; they had a life of their own.

In some countries, foreign direct investors were seen not as private-sector actors but as representatives of colonial powers (or in certain renditions as representatives of U.S. government policies). Popular sentiment often saw them as imposing imperialist norms. In many countries, private investors had attracted (assembled) local capital, for multinational enterprises found capital where it was available and put it to productive uses. Yet the collection of local capital was often believed to be either exploitation (instead of adding capital, multinational enterprises were mopping up limited domestic resources), or coalition building with despised local elites. In less developed countries, individuals often became wealthy by working for or with foreign multinational enterprises, which benefited local businesses. To most economists, the mobilization of local capital for productive purposes and the enrichment of nationals within a host country were viewed as a favorable attribute of foreign direct investments – the ability to have positive linkage effects. For many "antibusiness" observers, the local alliances were perceived negatively, as local and foreign capitalists joined together to the disadvantage of the developing nation. This view was often fostered by sociologists and an articulate group of development economists, who described foreign direct investors – and particularly those in the "old" activities of utilities, oil, mining, and agriculture – as adding nothing and creating dependent development. Foreign direct investment in manufacturing, where there was new technology to be transferred, might be approved because it was necessary, but electric utilities were not seen in that light for they were viewed as one of the "old" industries. On the other side of the coin, multinational enterprises had other opportunities that appeared more promising. For one reason or another – or more often, a combination of reasons – by the end of the 1970s private foreign direct investment in electric utilities in advanced and in less developed countries seemed to be part of the past.

7

Coming Full Circle, 1978–2007, and a Global Perspective

After the long process of domestication, which included numerous nationalizations of electric utilities and during which foreign ownership had all but disappeared, the political landscape shifted rather dramatically in the late 1970s and early 1980s. In many countries, government-owned electric utilities now were being criticized for their poor performance, high costs, and unreliable supply, problems (especially in less developed and developing countries) deemed to have been caused by inadequate maintenance and expansion due to the inability or unwillingness of the state to invest needed capital.[1] By the end of the 1980s and throughout the 1990s, new government policies of liberalization, privatization, and utility restructuring were being implemented in many countries.[2] These policy changes, along with loosened restrictions on capital outflows and inflows, opened up the prospects for renewed foreign direct investments, and once again companies began investing in foreign electric utilities. As the International Energy Agency (IEA) – a unit of the Organization for Economic Cooperation and Development (OECD) – stated in one of its "Messages for Governments" in 1994, "Investment by international electric companies in other markets plays an important role in transferring technology and capability/knowledge, as well as improving technical and economic efficiency, capital availability, energy security, and the environment."[3] Such statements viewed foreign direct investment as desirable. Today, cross-national ownership patterns of electric utilities again have become quite common. The situation around the world, however, remains in a state of constant flux, with a substantial amount of reform and counter-reform, merger activity (especially in Europe) and divestiture, buying and selling of light and power firms, and international investment and disinvestment in the sector.

The initial structural reforms in the industry were stimulated in part by the oil crises of the 1970s, during which the relative price of raw energy as well as

---

Authors: William J. Hausman and Mira Wilkins. Significant advice from H.V. Nelles.

electricity increased dramatically, contributing to a widespread feeling of general economic malaise.[4] The adoption of reforms that forced firms to rely much more heavily on the market to guide decision making became part of the international agenda, endorsed enthusiastically by multilateral aid organizations such as the International Bank for Reconstruction and Development (World Bank) and the Asian Development Bank, and commended by the International Monetary Fund.[5] State enterprises and heavily regulated utilities now were deemed in many countries to be inefficient and an actual deterrent to economic growth.[6] Whereas most electric utilities from the very earliest days of the industry were vertically integrated, monopolist firms providing generation, transmission, and distribution services in a single package, many reformers believed that this structure had become obsolete and ineffective by the 1980s. Reformers argued especially that the generation function, because of changes in technology, had become naturally competitive and could be split off from the other two major functions, creating major gains in efficiency. As one World Bank document stated, "Since the 1950s, the power sector had been dominated by government-owned monopolies over the full range of sector activities from production to distribution. This was in accordance with the prevailing notion that large-scale technologies and their high fixed costs favored state financing, and that monopoly stewardship by the state enhanced consumer welfare. The sector was also considered critical to national security and a tool with which governments might pursue social equity objectives in their development efforts. These views prevented competition and discouraged foreign investment. From the 1980s, however, the promise of greater efficiency through market-based competition and technological advances encouraged the vertical unbundling of power generation and an increase in private investment."[7]

Eventually, policies implemented in many nations (with differing particulars and varying degrees of success) resulted in the "unbundling" of the industry – that is, the separation of each of the three major functions (as well as marketing and billing in some cases), with the possibility of different firms performing the functions in the different segments of the industry.[8]

One of the first pieces of national legislation passed in response to the energy crises of the 1970s was the Public Utility Regulatory Policies Act of 1978 (PURPA) in the United States. This act focused on the generation sector and sought to open up the transmission network to small power producers and co-generators (such as industrial establishments) by requiring integrated utilities to purchase power from these producers at their own, relatively high, marginal cost. This "opened the door to greatly expanded participation by nonutility generators in electricity markets, and it demonstrated that electricity from nonutility generators could successfully be integrated with a utility's own system supply."[9]

Chile was one of the first countries to substantially reorganize its electric utility sector, and it became a model to other South American countries.

In 1982, Chile's government, then under the military dictatorship of General Augusto Pinochet and with the advice of "free market" economists associated with the University of Chicago, enacted a law that allowed some choice of electricity providers for large consumers.[10] This was followed by reforms that introduced more extensive competition and used explicit market mechanisms to determine prices. The industry eventually was completely restructured. By 1996, Chilean companies were the only ones in Latin America to control electric utilities in other Latin American nations. Chilectra, Chilgener, Chilquinta International, Endesa (Chile), Enersis, and National Electric of Chile all owned generation or distribution assets in Argentina and/or Peru.[11]

In England and Wales, the large-scale privatization and unbundling of the electricity supply system was carried out under the Electricity Act 1989. Under the provisions of the act, generation and marketing were to be treated as competitive industries, while transmission and distribution – still viewed as natural monopolies – remained subject to regulation. A wholesale electricity pool, where electricity could be traded competitively, was created in 1990. As William W. Hogan has stated, "The initial reforms in England and Wales in 1990 were highly influential in subsequent developments in electricity restructuring around the world."[12] Power pools, often formed in conjunction with privatization, were established in other countries around the globe in the 1990s: Norway in 1991 (extended in 1996 to include Sweden); Finland and Denmark in 1996; Victoria, Australia in 1994 (merged with the New South Wales pool in 1997); and New Zealand in 1996. Competitive power exchanges began operating in Spain in 1998, and in regions within the United States (California, Pennsylvania-New Jersey-Maryland, New York, and New England) around the same time. The Amsterdam Power Exchange began operating in 1999.[13]

THE RESURGENCE OF FOREIGN OWNERSHIP AT THE END OF THE TWENTIETH CENTURY

As the privatization, liberalization, and restructuring movement gathered momentum in the 1990s and multilateral aid institutions became very supportive of power sector reform, the entry of foreign companies into this sector, as noted previously, was welcomed more frequently. Unlike in the earliest days of the industry, when foreign firms often inaugurated electric power service, this recent phase more closely resembles that of the late 1920s and very early 1930s, in that it has occurred largely through mergers and acquisitions. Given the ever-present need for expansion, many of these mergers and acquisitions were accompanied by new infrastructure investments, as was the case in the late 1920s and 1930. In addition, however, some of these firms entered the industry by creating brand new, independent power producers.[14] A wide variety of companies acquired or created electric utility assets in various regions of the world in the 1990s.[15] Companies invested individually or, in the case of "project management" in developing nations, in clusters with networks of both private and government participants.

Some of those involved in foreign electric utility investments at the end of the twentieth century were large multinational firms with familiar names. A major investor worldwide was ABB Energy Ventures, a subsidiary of ABB Ltd., created in 1988 by the merger of two long-standing electrical manufacturers: the Swedish ASEA and the Swiss Brown, Boveri et Cie. In 1989, ABB acquired the transmission and distribution assets of the Westinghouse Electric Corp., another of the venerable names among electrical equipment manufacturers. By 1999, ABB owned generating plants in Colombia, China, and the United Kingdom, transmission lines in Argentina, Brazil, France, Greece, Italy, Kenya, Saudi Arabia, and the United Kingdom and distribution systems in Georgia (the country) and Kazakhstan. ABB, however, subsequently divested its nuclear power and power generation businesses, choosing rather to focus on other business sectors.[16] General Electric Power Systems, a subsidiary of General Electric, made investments in hydroelectric projects in Australia, Brazil, Canada, Finland, Norway, and Sweden, but by 2006 did not appear to own and control any foreign electric utilities or generating assets. GE remains a major provider of power equipment and services to the industry, as does Siemens, which also in 2006 did not appear to own foreign electric utilities. Notably absent from any participation was AEG, which became in the 1980s a relatively minor subsidiary of the then DaimlerBenz.[17]

Among the more active investors in foreign electric utilities were operating utilities already in the industry, something that was rare in the first round of global electrification. Twenty-seven U.S. electric utilities or their subsidiaries had made direct investments in utilities around the world by the end of the century. These included many traditional utilities, such as Duke Energy, Entergy, and Central and South West. There were several U.S. firms that would come to specialize in ownership of foreign utility assets, including AES Corp. and Edison Mission Energy, a subsidiary of Edison International (formerly Southern California Edison). AES's very rapid rise and recent setbacks reflect many of the benefits and perils of foreign ownership of electric utilities. Founded in 1981, shortly after passage of the Public Utility Regulatory Policies Act (1978), the company began with the purchase and construction of domestic generating assets, but it moved aggressively into foreign countries in the 1990s. The *New York Times* described AES in 1998 as "the largest United States-based power plant developer."[18] In 2000, AES was operating in twenty-four countries and by 2002 had operations in thirty-two countries, sometimes under joint agreements, including those with such traditional U.S. utilities as the Southern Company and Public Service Enterprise Group (PSEG) in Brazil and sometimes with other foreign utilities, including Tractebel in Northern Ireland and Électricité de France (EDF) in Brazil. AES got into deep financial trouble shortly after the turn of the millennium and had to scale back substantially and restructure. Its Latin American (especially Brazilian) utilities were particularly problematic, but it also ran into serious difficulties in Georgia (where it owned the electricity system in Tbilisi, its capital), Kazakhstan (where it was forced to agree to barter arrangements for some cash-strapped large customers), Uganda (where "traditional spirits" are said to have blocked a $500 million dam project), and England (where in 2003 it walked away from its Drax power station in North Yorkshire, having purchased it for US$3 billion in 1999).[19]

A variety of other U.S. firms entered the foreign electricity market. These included the oil giant ExxonMobil (with generating assets in Italy and China[20] and plans to enter other countries), Bechtel (Chile and India), Foster Wheeler (China), Sithe Energies (Australia, Canada, China, Mexico, the Philippines, South Korea, and Thailand), Coastal Corp. (Dominican Republic), Tenneco (Ecuador), Goldman Sachs (Dominican Republic), and Enron (with generating assets in Brazil, Ecuador, Guatemala, India, Israel, Italy, Nigeria, Panama, the Philippines, Spain, and the United Kingdom and distributing systems in Brazil and Venezuela). Before its ignominious bankruptcy in late 2001, Enron had encountered major obstacles in its investment in the Dabhol power project in India. In May 2006, the international assets of the bankrupt Enron were sold to a consortium of hedge funds, with 60 percent British and 40 percent U.S. participation, for $2.1 billion.[21]

Two Canadian utilities had foreign utility investments at the end of the twentieth century. Hydro One (formerly part of the state-owned Ontario Hydro) owned a distribution utility in Peru, and TransAlta Corp. owned independent power producers in Australia, Mexico, and New Zealand.[22] Since then, a number of Canadian companies have acquired foreign utility assets. Fortis, Inc. controls the major utility in Belize, has holdings in the Cayman Islands, and owns four hydroelectric facilities in New York State.[23] By 2004, the venerable Canadian corporation Brascan, formerly Brazilian Traction, Light and Power and as of 2006 a subsidiary of Brookfield Asset Management, had returned to its roots and owned generating properties in Brazil, as well as in the United States.[24]

Several European and British electric utilities also actively entered foreign markets in the 1990s. EDF, a state-owned enterprise, was particularly active, with generating plants in China, Italy, Mexico, Portugal, and Spain, electricity distribution systems in Hungary, Lebanon, Morocco, South Africa, Sweden, Switzerland, and the United Kingdom, and both generating and distribution assets in Argentina, Austria, Brazil, and Ivory Coast. EDF remains very active in foreign electric utility markets. In spring 2006, EDF and AEM, Milan's municipal electricity utility, combined to purchase the Edison Company, Italy's second-largest electric utility.[25] As of March

2006, EDF also held a 25 percent stake in Atel, a firm created by a consolidation of the Swiss operating company, Atel, and the holding company Motor-Columbus (which thereby ended its long corporate existence).[26]

Britain's National Power (now International Power) and PowerGen (now owned by the German firm E.ON) had generation or independent power investments in Australia, China, the Czech Republic, Hungary, India, Indonesia, Kazakhstan, Malaysia, Pakistan, and Thailand.[27] For the first time ever, some major U.S. electric utilities became foreign-owned.[28] One large foreign investment was made and then withdrawn. Scottish Power purchased PacifiCorp in 1999 and then sold that company in early 2006 to MidAmerican Energy, a unit of Warren Buffet's Berkshire Hathaway.[29] Scottish Power in November 2006 agreed to be acquired by the Spanish utility Iberdrola, a transaction completed in April 2007.[30] A strong presence in the United States was created by National Grid Plc, which owns the high-voltage transmission system in England and Wales and which purchased the New England Electric System (comprised of four relatively small utilities in the Northeast) in 2000 and then in 2002 acquired the much larger Niagara Mohawk Power Corp., a New York utility. In early 2006, National Grid announced the planned acquisition of KeySpan, a major U.S. gas distributor that operates an electric utility on Long Island, New York. The transaction was completed in August 2007.[31]

E.ON has become a major player in the field of international electric utility investments. The company was created in 2000 with the merger of two German energy firms, Viag and Veba, and in 2006 it was the largest electric utility in Europe by market capitalization. It purchased the British PowerGen in 2002 and through that acquisition obtained the U.S. utility Louisville Gas and Electric (now E.ON-USA). In February 2006, E.ON, in the biggest takeover bid in the history of the electric utility industry, offered to purchase the Spanish firm Endesa, the fifth-largest European electric utility, for around $35 billion, which was later raised to $52 billion. The Spanish government threw numerous roadblocks in the way of the merger, some of which were ruled illegal by the European Union.[32] In early 2007, Italy's Enel (Ente Nazionale per l'Energia Elettrica), privatized in 1999 and the second-largest European electric utility by market capitalization, and Spain's Acciona teamed up and made a competing offer. In April 2007, E.ON yielded and dropped its bid, accepting Endesa's assets outside Spain and some of Enel's Spanish assets as consolation. Acciona's participation meant that Endesa remained in Spanish control, with significant Italian participation.[33]

Other European participants included British Gas Group International (the Philippines), Royal Dutch Shell (with generating assets in Brazil, Brunei, China, Colombia, Malaysia, Mexico, Oman, and the United Arab Emirates), the German Ruhrkohle AG, parent of RAG Coal International (generation assets in Colombia), the Finnish Fortum Oil and Gas Oy

(Estonia, Hungary, and Thailand), and the Belgian (now French-controlled) utility Tractebel (Canada, Chile, China, Hungary, India, Italy, Kazakhstan, Luxembourg, Peru, Portugal, Qatar, Singapore, Thailand, and the United Kingdom). Tractebel, which had been formed in 1986 with a merger of Tractionel (formerly Traction et Électricité) and Electrobel, merged with Société Générale de Belgique in 2003 to become Suez-Tractebel, a subsidiary of the French water and electric utility Suez.[34] In early 2006, the Italian electric utility Enel offered to purchase Suez, the third largest European electric utility. The French government, not wanting to lose a "national champion" to Italian control, intervened and arranged a merger (still pending in early 2007) between the state-owned Gaz de France and Suez.[35]

The Swedish power company Vattenfall, which traces its origins to 1909, expanded into other nations nearly a century later. It acquired several German electricity suppliers as well as utilities in Poland and Denmark.[36] Some European firms are on the cutting edge of technology, investing in solar and wind farm generators in various nations. EHN (Corporación Energia Hidroeléctrica de Navarra, S.A., acquired in 2005 by the Spanish firm Acciona) owns wind farms in Germany, France, and the United States (including one in New York State as a joint venture with AES).[37]

Finally, a number of Asian multinationals recently have become active in the electricity sector. An international subsidiary of Hongkong Electric Holdings Ltd., part of the Cheung Kong group, owns several distributing companies in Australia and a generating plant in Thailand.[38] CLP Holdings (formerly China Light & Power), another Hong Kong firm, jointly owns a coal-fired power plant in mainland China with EDF and has generating plants in Australia, India, and Thailand. J-Power, formerly the Japanese Electric Power Development Corporation, owns generating plants in China, the Philippines, Taiwan, and Thailand and in 2006 purchased a wind power facility in Spain and an independent power producer in Texas, its first investment in the United States.[39] Meiya Power Company (MPC) began in the early 1990s as a joint venture between the U.S. utility PSEG, the Asia Infrastructure Fund, and Hydro Quebec. The Canadian and U.S. firms have been replaced by a consortium of investors, with major participation by the BTU Power Company, part of a Middle Eastern group.[40] The firm has independent power plants in China, South Korea, and Taiwan.[41] Singapore Power owns a transmission and distribution network in Victoria, Australia and a power plant in Taiwan.[42] YTL, a Malaysian firm, owns and operates the transmission grid in South Australia and owns an independent power plant in Indonesia.[43] Japan's Tomen Corp. and Sumitomo own generating stations in Hungary and the United States (Oregon), respectively. Sumitomo also owns generating plants in Turkey and, in a consortium with Tokyo Electric Power and EDF, in Vietnam.[44] Tokyo Electric Power and Marubeni in late 2006 purchased the power assets in the Philippines of Mirant, a U.S. company.[45] South Korea's Korea Electric

Power Corp. owns generating assets in China, North Korea, and the Philippines. The activities of the Asian multinationals have been extensive.[46]

The number, magnitude, and complexity of these new investments across borders attest to the resurgence of the multinational firm in global electrification. If we could add a column for 2006 to Chapter 1's Table 1.4, there would be nontrivial entries for most of the nations listed in the table. We have not attempted to catalog every foreign direct investment of the past decade, partly because there are so many, but also because the landscape continues to change. While the resurgence is manifest, there are many lingering uncertainties about where the process is heading, and there have been retreats.

The privatization/restructuring/deregulation movement may have peaked very early in the new millennium.[47] The dramatic electricity crisis in California in the fall of 2000 – during which markets were manipulated by firms such as the now-infamous Enron, wholesale prices increased for a time by up to 500 percent, and several venerable electric utilities became insolvent or declared bankruptcy – shocked the world and "halted the momentum of electricity reform in many locales."[48] There is evidence that privatization efforts in Latin America and Europe have been losing support among the public. While the stabilization and liberalization policies of the 1980s, which curbed hyperinflation and attracted foreign capital, received strong support from public opinion in Latin America, "the decision to sell public firms, to deregulate utilities and to allow the entry of foreign capital proved divisive very soon. By the late 1990s almost half of the public thought of privatizations as not beneficial. By 2003 the proportion of respondents unsatisfied with them had roughly doubled to 75 percent."[49] Even in a mature nation like Britain, a recent poll indicated a growing skepticism about foreign ownership in general: 68 percent of respondents in one survey thought it was "too easy" for foreign companies to take over British businesses.[50] Attitudes such as these signal potential difficulties for foreign utility investors in Britain, Latin America, and elsewhere.

LESSONS

This book describes in detail the history of multinational enterprise and international finance in global electrification. In times past, foreign direct investment played a major role in the process of global electrification, supplying modernizing infrastructure more widely, sooner, and more efficiently than would otherwise have been the case. The enterprises that pioneered in foreign direct investment in this sector were the electrical manufacturers and banks, but eventually complex holding companies and clusters of firms specializing in the financing, construction, and operation of electric utilities emerged and came to dominate international investment in electric utilities. These firms frequently had international cross-equity ownership networks, had directors and officers in common, shared information, and often were configured and reconfigured to enhance the ability to raise capital. As time passed, electricity grew to become such a vital service and key driver in economic development that its effective provision came to be viewed as a necessity, and governments at all levels vigorously intervened in the industry, through price and other regulations or through direct ownership. Foreign capital often was welcomed at first; but as the industry matured, dissatisfaction tended to grow and focus on long-distant owners. As technology became increasingly standardized and local technical and managerial skills improved, governments gained confidence that the utility could be run without the foreign owners. As we have seen, these forces, among others, led to the almost complete disappearance of foreign ownership of electric utilities by the mid-1970s.

Is the scenario evident in round one of globalization – engagement and then withdrawal – likely to be repeated? We cannot say for sure. There have been major structural and technological changes in the industry. It may be that there is no longer an economic necessity for the (always politically vulnerable) natural monopoly, which may mean that foreign investors in this sector will find themselves to be less under attack. On the other hand, basic reactions to foreign investments over the years have fluctuated. There is no reason to assume that the friendliness to foreign investments in public utilities will continue. In fact, it is quite possible that this industry once again could become a scapegoat, thus putting the foreign owner particularly at risk.

What lessons, then, can we learn in the midst of a second round of global electrification? Fundamentally, there has been both continuity and change:

1. For most of the world, what used to be new, unusual, and exciting – access to electricity – now is a necessity. When the power goes off and daily patterns are disrupted, it gets noticed. In the contemporary world, there is a real and profound dependence on electricity, which affects people's attitudes toward the industry.
2. The electric utility industry has been and remains extraordinarily capital intensive, particularly in the transmission and distribution functions. Though a single generating plant can now be relatively small, many still comprise very large projects. The sheer amount of capital required by this industry has had implications for its history and will continue to in the future. Projected growth rates for developing countries today are similar to growth rates attained by many developed countries in the past, during the early phases of electrification.
3. In the past, any community that wanted to see electric service initiated and expanded would take capital from anywhere it was available. This included private foreign capital. Also, the state

(municipality, state, province, or nation) often participated because of its ability to raise capital and the strong desire on the part of citizens for access to electricity. Both private (foreign and domestic) and public financing are likely to remain important in the future. Much capital is needed.

4. Once a utility's capital was in place, it represented a very large sunk cost. An electric system could not be moved, but it could be sold or taken over. A system also could be allowed to deteriorate. The sunk nature of this massive investment meant that private owners were especially vulnerable to authorities changing the rules of the game after the investment had been made.[51] If this served to discourage further investment in order to maintain the system, then government policy might turn increasingly hostile. This remains as true today as it ever was. There is little reason to believe that liberalization, privatization, and deregulation (where it has occurred) are permanent states of affairs.
5. Today's technology that allows smaller, efficient generating plants still requires that they be connected to the transmission and distribution system. This creates a whole new set of problems related to access pricing that involve regulation.
6. Utilities today face many and various risks.[52] Internally, there are the normal project risks; at the national level, there are regulatory risks, political stability risks, and macroeconomic (inflation, interest rate, and business cycle) risks; and internationally, there are exchange rate risks, the risk of war, and now we might add the risk inherent in climate change and potential government responses to that. In those countries where the generating sector is unregulated or lightly regulated, the macroeconomic risks may have been enhanced (for example, when an economic downturn causes electricity prices to fall, thus hurting the generating sector).[53] There is always a risk that policy changes will tighten rules on capital mobility, which heightens the risk of retaliation by other countries. The United States, for example, in the aftermath of the September 11, 2001 terrorist attack, has been considering tightening the rules on who can own certain strategic assets in the country.[54] While recent legislation did not do so, in a substantial manner the threat remains and if, in the interest of national security there are new restrictions on foreign direct investment, those with interests in electric utilities could well be affected. It is almost certain that there will be similar rules adopted elsewhere. Exchange rate risks are especially important to electric utilities because of the magnitude of the sunk costs. A multinational enterprise, like a private domestic company, can operate in a regulated environment if the regulations are "fair and appropriate." Where the multinational enterprise differs from the domestic

company is that it must remit profits to a parent abroad. If what is "fair and appropriate" in one period turns out – based on currency depreciation (with no change in the operations of the enterprise) – to be unfair and inappropriate in a subsequent period, the multinational enterprise is stuck. This, of course, is possible even in the absence of strict regulation.

7. Many individuals believe that there have been two eras of globalization: one that began in the 1880s and ended either in 1914 or 1930, and a second that began in the post–World War II era and only came of age at the end of the twentieth and beginning of the twenty-first centuries. If the first age of globalization was reversed, so may be the second wave, and if a reversal were to occur, the electric light and power sector – because of the public's dependency on electricity – would be particularly at risk. Many economists believe that globalization is "good," and that means it is probably good for electric utilities as well. But globalization also tends to create a few big winners and many losers, at least in the short term. Much of the literature on economic history would confirm that the distribution of income worsens, sometimes substantially, during the industrialization/development process. The losers tend to make political demands, including the demand for cheap electricity (often cheaper than it costs to produce). This could create serious problems for the industry, leading to onerous regulations and perhaps the reappearance of extensive state ownership. In fact, in early January 2007 Hugo Chávez, President of Venezuela, announced plans to nationalize the country's electricity and telecommunications industries.[55]

CONCLUSION

Multinational enterprises and international finance were deeply involved in the electric light and power industry at its birth and for many decades thereafter. Businesses that participated in the spread of electric light and power systems were buffeted by winds of tumultuous economic, political, and social change as they served as important catalysts in the transformation of electricity from a luxury to a necessity. The process of global electrification was neither quick nor easy.

Manufacturers of electrical equipment, which were pioneer multinational enterprises, aided in the development of their customers, electric utilities, at home and abroad. German and American manufacturers were innovators from the late 1870s forward, but electrical manufacturers were not alone. Because electric utilities were capital intensive, banks and other financial intermediaries were needed to facilitate the process of setting them up. The banks and other financial intermediaries took part in two ways: first, as multinational enterprises themselves, and second, as underwriters and marketers of bonds for and, to a lesser extent, providers or arrangers of loans to existing utilities at home and abroad. The two roles were often blended in a complex manner. Canadians, Britishers, Germans, Americans, Italians, Swiss, and others participated.

As already urbanized areas were being electrified, frequently by multinational enterprises, company towns founded by other multinational enterprises (associated with plantations, mining, and oil production) were introducing modern infrastructure, including electrification. We called this the enclave form of doing business, and it greatly expanded the geographical span of electrification. So, too, international businesses in aluminum and electrochemicals (processes that required cheap energy) assisted the development of hydroelectric power. From the 1890s onward, holding companies, headquartered in Switzerland, Belgium, the United States, and Canada (and other countries), served as a mode of corporate governance and were linked with clusters of electric utilities, electric tramways, and related companies at home and abroad. Holding companies typically owned controlling interests in diverse operating companies. Other operating companies were free standing – that is, companies that had been formed for the purpose of operating abroad but with no parent carrying on that activity in the home country. These firms frequently were part of a loosely formed business group. The international clusters, with their networks, encompassed various knowledge workers, including lawyers, engineers, construction company executives, accountants, and their firms. Trading companies also played a role in identifying opportunities, investing in public utilities and providing supplies for the utilities abroad.

Thus, in the establishment of electric light and power around the world a wide variety of multinational enterprise actors served to get the task accomplished. Rather remarkably, absent for the most part were electric utility operating companies that extended over borders. Instead, the various other forms of multinational enterprise activities coalesced in providing light and power facilities internationally. Our text describes multinational enterprise in various nonconventional forms, moving capital, ownership and control, management, technology, processes, procedures, and know-how across borders. The story adds substantially to our understanding of the ways in which multinational enterprises, making their foreign direct investments, developed their strategies over time as they diffused electrification around the globe. Many countries had businesses that were investors abroad *and* recipients of foreign investments, with no uniformity in the mix.

Public utilities in some countries obtained foreign finance without inward foreign direct investment, as was the case in the main with the United States and Japan. In Italy, France, and Spain, as well as the

United Kingdom, inward foreign direct investment was crucial for many years. From Russia (before 1917) to Mexico (up to 1960), foreign multinational enterprises dominated the provision of electric power. Our narrative and analysis of the role of multinational enterprises in the spread of electrification has brought together many national accounts in a totally unique manner, casting new light on the actors in what was a highly internationalized process. Multinational enterprises mattered.

By 1930, among the many multinational enterprises, two major companies stood out as global leaders in electric utilities. One was American & Foreign Power Co., a U.S.-headquartered holding company with widespread interests in Latin America, new foreign direct investments in China and India, and a tranche (minority, portfolio investments) in activities within Europe. The second company, Sofina, was also structured as a holding company, headquartered in Brussels. Its hundreds of affiliated companies formed a business group, with numerous cross-investments and minority interests. Its activities were concentrated in Europe but stretched into Latin America and to a lesser extent elsewhere beyond the European continent. So extensive were its foreign direct investments by 1930 that Dannie Heineman, its chief executive, was making plans for a Europe united by electric power companies' transmission lines as well as other fundamentals. The plans were before their time, and, in the autarchic conditions of the 1930s, their failure was inevitable.

Electric utilities were the pride and joy of countries. They were basic infrastructure. Business and government interactions were inherent, from the initial concessions, to the creation and administration of regulatory structures, to government ownership. Over time, around the world, countries wanted their power plants to be run by nationals and owned domestically. Thus, gradually and globally, multinational enterprise in this sector disappeared. Foreign finance remained, but much of it after World War II was provided by bilateral and multilateral aid agencies rather than by private-sector lending. National enterprises replaced multinational ones, with the process virtually completed at the end of the first century of electrification, in 1978.

And then, with globalization, privatization, restructuring, and deregulation, and a new emphais on "markets," a new wave of multinational enterprise activities began in the electric utility sector, activities that have recently mounted. Unlike the first round, described in detail in this book, now it is the giant, well-funded public utilities that are making acquisitions and spreading over borders in an unprecedented manner. We have asked whether these new investors, by the very nature of this essential service, would experience the same (or similar) nationalist reactions as did prior generations. Our tale links one age of globalization to the next.

One thing history teaches is that we can never know the future. There will always be surprises. And so it will be with foreign direct investment in the second round of global electrification. We will not and cannot predict the extent or even whether the second round will continue to flourish or will wither, and at what pace. We can predict that there will be surprises, and we can only hope that the story told in this volume will help us better understand the past and better prepare for what the future may bring.

Appendix A: Abbreviations, Acronyms, Company Names, and Variations on Company Names

1886 Company: Company for Electric Lighting, St. Petersburg
ABB: ASEA Brown Boveri, sometimes ABB ASEA Brown Boveri, ABB Ltd., or ABB followed by any member of the group
ACEC: Ateliers de Constructions Électriques de Charleroi
ACENE: Ateliers de Constructions Électriques du Nord et de l'Est
ADB: Asian Development Bank
Adriatic Electric Company: Società Adriatica di Elettricità (SADE)
ADRs: American depository receipts
ADSs: American depository shares
AEG, Berlin: Allgemeine Elektrizitäts Gesellschaft, sometimes rendered Allgemeine Elektricitäts Gesellschaft
AEI: Associated Electrical Industries
AFPC: American & Foreign Power Co.
AIAG: Aluminium Industrie AG
AIC, New York: American International Corporation
Alabama Traction Light and Power Company, Ltd. (ATLPC)
Alcoa: Aluminum Company of America
Allgemeine Elektricitäts Gesellschaft: AEG
Allgemeine Elektrizitäts Gesellschaft: AEG
Allmänna Svenska Elektriska AB (ASEA)
Alsthom: Société Générale de Constructions Électriques et Mécaniques
Aluminum Company of America (Alcoa)
Aluminium Industrie AG (AIAG)
American & Foreign Power Co. (AFPC)
American depository receipts (ADRs)
American depository shares (ADSs)
American Intercontinental Trade and Services (Amitas)
American International Corporation (AIC)
Amitas: American Intercontinental Trade and Services
Anglo-Japanese Hydro-Electric Company, Ltd.: otherwise referred to as the Anglo-Japanese Water Power Company or the Anglo-Japanese Water Power Electric Company

Anglo-Japanese Water Power Company: Anglo-Japanese Hydro-Electric Company, Ltd.
Anglo-Japanese Water Power Electric Company: Anglo-Japanese Hydro-Electric Company, Ltd.
APEC, Athens: Athens Piraeus Electricity Company, Ltd.
ASEA: Allmänna Svenska Elektriska AB
ASEA Brown Boveri: ABB
Asian Development Bank (ADB)
Associated Electrical Industries (AEI)
Ateliers de Constructions Électriques de Charleroi (ACEC)
Ateliers de Constructions Électriques du Nord et de l'Est (ACENE)
Athens Piraeus Electricity Company, Ltd. (APEC)
ATLPC: Alabama Traction Light and Power Company, Ltd.
Badische: see Badische Anilin- und Soda-Fabrik AG
Badische Anilin- und Soda-Fabrik AG: known as Badische before 1926 and BASF after World War II
Banca Commerciale Italiana: BCI, also known as Commerciale and Comit
Banco Hipotecario Suizo-Argentina: Buenos Aires "branch" of Schweizerisch-Argentinische Hypothekenbank, Zurich
Bank für Elektrische Unternehmungen (Elektrobank), Zurich: otherwise known as Banque pour Entreprises Électriques (Électrobanque), name change in 1947 to Elektro-Watt and in 1974 to Electrowatt.
Bankverein Schweizerische: Schweizerischer Bankverein
Bankverein Suisse: Schweizerischer Bankverein
Banque Commerciale de Bâle: Commercial Bank of Basel or Basler Handelsbank
Banque de l'Union Parisienne (BUP)
Banque de Paris et des Pays-Bas (Paribas)
Banque Française et Italienne pour l'Amérique du Sud (BFI)
Banque pour Entreprises Électriques (Elektrobank), Zurich: Bank für Elektrische Unternehmungen
Barcelona Electric Co.: Barcelonesa
Barcelona Traction, Light and Power Co.: BTLP, sometimes shortened to Barcelona Traction
Barcelonesa, Barcelona: Compañía Barcelonesa de Electricidad, also known as the Barcelona Electric Co.
BASF: Badische Anilin- und Soda-Fabrik AG
Basler Bankverein: after merging with Zürcher Bankverein, became in 1897, Schweizerischer Bankverein; in English Swiss Bankverein, in French Bankverein Suisse
Basler Handelsbank: otherwise known as Banque Commerciale de Bâle or Commercial Bank of Basel, acquired by SBC in 1945.
BCI, Milan: Banca Commerciale Italiana
BEAM: British Electrical & Allied Manufacturers' Association
Belgian Gas: Compagnie Générale pour l'Eclairage et le Chauffage par le Gaz, Brussels
Berliner Elektricitäts-Werke AG: Bewag
Berliner Kraft und Licht (Bewag) AG: Bewag

BET: British Electric Traction Co.
Bewag: Berliner Kraft und Licht (Bewag) AG, once Berliner Elektricitäts-Werke AG, hence the initials Bewag
BCER: British Columbia Electric Railway Co.
BFI: Banque Française et Italienne pour l'Amérique du Sud
BFUD: British and Foreign Utilities Development Corporation
BIU: British & International Utilities, Ltd.
Brascan Ltd.: Brazilian Traction, Light and Power Co. Ltd.
Brazilian Light and Power: Brazilian Traction, Light and Power Co. Ltd.
Brazilian Traction: Brazilian Traction, Light and Power Co. Ltd.
Brazilian Traction, Light and Power Co. Ltd.: became Brazilian Light and Power in 1966 and Brascan Ltd. in 1969
British and Foreign Utilities Development Corporation (BFUD)
British & International Utilities, Ltd. (BIU)
British Columbia Electric Railway Co. (BCER)
British Electric Traction Co., London (BET)
British Pearson group: S. Pearson & Son, also known as Cowdray group, Pearson group, Whitehall Securities/Whitehall Electric
BTLP: Barcelona Traction, Light and Power Company, sometimes shortened to Barcelona Traction
BUP, Paris: Banque de l'Union Parisienne
CADE: Compañía Argentina de Electricidad (initially abbreviated as CAE)
CAE: Compañía Argentina de Electricidad (CADE)
California Electric Light Company (CELC)
Canadian International Light and Power Investment Company (Caninlipo)
Caninlipo: Canadian International Light and Power Investment Company
CATE: Compañía Alemana Transatlántica de Electricidad, otherwise known as Deutsch-Überseeische Elektrizitäts Gesellschaft (DUEG)
CCE: Compagnie Continentale Edison
CCEE: Paris: Compagnie Centrale d'Énergie Électrique (with central power station in Rouen)
CEAG: Continentale Elektrizitätsunion AG
CELC: California Electric Light Company
Centrais Eléctricas Brasileiras SA (Eletrobrás)
Central Mining and Investment Corporation (CMIC)
Centrales Électriques de l'Entre-Sambre et Meuse et de la Region de Malmédy (ESMA)
CFE: Comisión Federal de Electricidad or Federal Electric Commission, Mexico
CGE, Paris: Compagnie Générale d'Électricité
CHADE, Madrid: Compañía Hispano-Americana de Electricidad
CHdE: Compagnie Hellénique d'Électricité
Chilean Electric: Chilean Electric Tramway and Light Company
Chilean Electric Tramway and Light Company (Chilean Electric)
Chilena: Compañía Chilena de Electricidad
Cia: Compañía
CIADE: CIAE
CIAE, Buenos Aires: Compañía Italo-Argentina de Electricidad, also called Italo-Argentina, CIADE, or Italo-Argentine Electric Co.

CIBEE: Compagnie Italo-Belge pour Entreprises d'Électricité et d'Utilité Publique, also known as Italian-Belgian Electric & Public Utility Co. (Italo-Belge)
Cie.: Compagnie.
CLFD, Mexico City: Compañía Limitada de Ferrocarriles del Distrito
CMIC: Central Mining and Investment Corporation
CNEP, Paris: Comptoir National d'Escompte de Paris
Columbus: Columbus AG für Elektrische Unternehmungen
Columbus AG für Elektrische Unternehmungen (Columbus)
Comisión Federal de Electricidad or Federal Electric Commission, Mexico (CFE)
Comit: Banca Commerciale Italiana
Comitato per le Applicazioni dell'Eletricità Sistema Edison: became in Dec. 1883–Jan. 1884 Società Generale Italiana di Elettricità Sistema Edison; renamed in 1895 Società Generale Italiana Edison di Elettricità (Società Edison, Edison Company, Milan, or Italian Edison Company)
Commercial Bank of Basel: otherwise known as Basler Handelsbank or Banque Commerciale de Bâle
Commerciale: Banca Commerciale Italiana
Compagnie Centrale d'Énergie Électrique (CCEE)
Compagnie Continentale Edison (CCE)
Compagnie d'Électricité Thomson-Houston de la Méditerranée: also known as Thomson-Houston de la Méditerranée (THM)
Compagnie Européenne pour Entreprises d'Électricité et d'Utilité Publique: European Electric & Public Utility Company (Europel)
Compagnie Financière d'Exploitations Hydroélectriques SA (Hydrofina)
Compagnie Financière et Industrielle de Belgique (Finabel)
Compagnie Français pour L'Exploitation des Procédés Thomson-Houston: the formal name for French Thomson-Houston
Compagnie Générale d'Électricité (CGE)
Compagnie Générale d'Entreprises Électriques et Industrielles, Brussels (Electrobel)
Compagnie Générale de Railways et d'Électricité: Railways et Électricité
Compagnie Générale pour l'Eclairage et le Chauffage par le Gaz, Brussels (Belgian Gas)
Compagnie Hellénique d'Électricité (CHdE)
Compagnie Italo-Belge pour Entreprises d'Électricité et d'Utilité Publique (CIBEE): also known as Italian-Belgian Electric & Public Utility Co. (Italo-Belge)
Compagnies Réunies d'Électricité et de Transport (Electrorail)
Compañía Alemana Transatlántica de Electricidad (CATE): otherwise known as Deutsch-Überseeische Elektrizitäts Gesellschaft (DUEG)
Compañía Argentina de Electricidad (CADE)
Compañía Barcelonesa de Electricidad (Barcelonesa)
Compañía Chilena de Electricidad (Chilena)
Compañía Energía Electrica de Cataluña: otherwise known as L'Énergie Électrique de Catalogne, also Energía Eléctrica de Cataluña (EEdC)
Compañía General Madrileña de Electricidad: also known as Sociedad General Madrileña de Electricidad (Madrileña)
Compañía Hispano-Americana de Electricidad (CHADE)
Compañía Italo-Argentina de Electricidad (CIAE): also known as Italo-Argentine Electric Co.

Compañía Limitada de Ferrocarriles del Distrito (CLFD)
Compañía Sudamericana de Electricidad (SUDAM)
Company for Electric Lighting, St. Petersburg: 1886 Company
Company for Petersburg's Electric Lighting (CPEL)
Comptoir National d'Escompte de Paris (CNEP)
Continentale Elektrizitätsunion AG (CEAG)
Corporación de Fomento (Fomento)
Cowdray group: S. Pearson & Son (British Pearson group)
Cowdray (Lord): Weetman Pearson
CPEL, St Petersburg: Company for Petersburg's Electric Lighting
Credit Suisse: originally, Crédit Suisse; in Italian, Credito Svizzero; in German, Schweizerische Kreditanstalt (SKA)
Credito Svizzero: Credit Suisse
Deutsch-Überseeische Elektrizitäts Gesellschaft (DUEG): otherwise known as Compañía Alemana Transatlántica de Electricidad (CATE)
Deutsche Bank und Disconto-Gesellschaft: name of Deutsche Bank 1929–1937, adopted after Deutsche Bank merged with Disconto-Gesellschaft in 1929.
DUEG, Berlin: Deutsch-Überseeische Elektrizitäts Gesellschaft
Ebro: Ebro Irrigation and Power Co., known in Spanish as Riegos y Fuerza del Ebro
Ebro Irrigation and Power Co.: Ebro
EDF or EdF: Électricité de France
Edison & Swan, London: Edison & Swan United Electric Light Company
Edison & Swan United Electric Light Company: Edison & Swan, London
Edison Company, Milan: Società Generale Italiana Edison di Elettricità
Edison General Electric Co. (EGE)
Edmundson's: Edmundson's Electricity Corporation
Edmundson's Electricity Corporation: Edmundson's
EEC: European Economic Community
EEdC: Compañía Energía Electrica de Cataluña
EElC: European Electric Corp.
EGE: Edison General Electric Co.
EIA: Energy Information Administration (U.S.)
Electrabel, Brussels: not to be confused with Electrobel; Electrabel, formed in 1990, had predecessor companies dating back to 1905; the Suez group became majority owner of Electrabel in 2003 and completed its takeover in 2005
Electric and Railway Finance Corporation (Elrafin)
Electric Lighting and Traction Company of Australia (ELTC)
Électricité de France (EDF or EdF)
Électricité et Traction: Société d'Électricité et Traction
Electricity Supply Commission, South Africa (Escom or ESCOM)
Électrobanque: Elektrobank
Electrobel, Brussels: Compagnie Générale d'Entreprises Électriques et Industrielles, Brussels, the successor to Société Générale Belge d'Entreprises Électriques
Electrorail: Compagnies Réunies d'Électricité et de Transport
Electrowatt (or Elektro-Watt): Bank für Elektrische Unternehmungen (Elektrobank)
Elektrische Licht und Kraft, AG (ELK)

Elektrizitäts A.G. vorm. W. Lahmeyer & Co. (Lahmeyer).
Elektrobank, Zurich: Bank für Elektrische Unternehmungen
Eletrobrás: Centrais Eléctricas Brasileiras SA
ELIN, Vienna: ELIN Société Anonyme pour l'Industrie Électrique, also known as Elin Aktiengesellschaft für Elektrische Industrie
Elin Aktiengesellschaft für Elektrische Industrie: ELIN Société Anonyme pour l'Industrie Électrique (ELIN)
ELIN Société Anonyme pour l'Industrie Électrique: Elin Aktiengesellschaft für Elektrische Industrie (ELIN)
ELK: Elektrische Licht und Kraftanlagen, AG
Elrafin: Electric and Railway Finance Corporation
ELTC: Electric Lighting and Traction Company of Australia
Empresa Nacional de Electricidad SA (Endesa): different Spanish and Chilean companies bore the same name and abbreviation; the Chilean company was sometimes called Endesa de Chile.
Empresas Eléctricas Asociadas: Lima Light
Endesa: Empresa Nacional de Electricidad SA.
ENEL or **Enel**: Ente Nazionale per l'Energia Elettrica; in English, National Agency for Electric Power
Energía Eléctrica de Cataluña (EEdC)
Énergie Électrique de Catalogne: Energía Eléctrica de Cataluña (EEdC)
Energy Information Agency (EIA)
Ente Nazionale per l'Energia Elettrica (ENEL or Enel)
E.ON: created in 2000 as a merger of Veba and Viag, two leading German energy concerns
Escom or **ESCOM**: Electricity Supply Commission, South Africa
ESMA: Centrales Électriques de l'Entre-Sambre et Meuse et de la Region de Malmédy
European Economic Community (EEC)
European Electric & Public Utility Company, Brussels (Europel): also known as Compagnie Européenne pour Entreprises d'Électricité et d'Utilité Publique
European Electric Corp., Canada (EElC)
Europel: European Electric & Public Utility Company
FDI: foreign direct investment
FECSA: Fuerzas Eléctricas de Cataluña
Federal Electric Commission, Mexico, in Spanish Comisión Federal de Electricidad (CFE)
Federal Power Commission (FPC): U.S. regulatory agency
Finabel: Compagnie Financière et Industrielle de Belgique
Finelec: Société Financière pour le Développement de l'Électricité, and its successor Société Financière Électrique, Paris
Fomento: Corporación de Fomento
Foreign Direct Investment (FDI), which is what multinational enterprises make
Foreign Portfolio Investment (FPI), a passive, financial investment
Foreign Power Securities Corporation (FPSC)
FPC: Federal Power Commission (U.S.)
FPI: foreign portfolio investment

FPSC: Foreign Power Securities Corporation
Franco-Suisse: Société Franco-Suisse pour l'Industrie Électrique, sometimes called Franco-Suisse pour l'Industrie Électrique
Franco-Suisse pour l'Industrie Électrique: Franco-Suisse
French Thomson-Houston (FTH): its formal name was Compagnie Français pour L'Exploitation des Procédés Thomson-Houston, often referred to as Société Thomson-Houston
FTH: French Thomson-Houston
Fuerzas Eléctricas de Cataluña (FECSA): the successor to Barcelona Traction, Light and Power
GE: General Electric, or The General Electric Company
GEC, London: General Electric Company, Ltd.
General Electric (GE)
General Electric Company, Ltd. (GEC): this British company was not associated with the U.S. GE
General Hellenic Co.: Société Générale Hellénique (SGH)
Gesellschaft für Elektrische Unternehmungen (Gesfürel)
Gesfürel, Berlin: Gesellschaft für Elektrische Unternehmungen
GLCT: Greater London and Counties Trust
Greater London and Counties Trust (GLCT)
Hydrofina: Compagnie Financière d'Exploitations Hydroélectriques SA
ICGA: Imperial Continental Gas Association
IEA: International Energy Agency
IGE: International General Electric Co.
IMF: International Monetary Fund
Imperial Continental Gas Association (ICGA)
Impresse Elettriche della America Latina (Latina Lux)
Indelec, Basel: Schweizerische Gesellschaft für Elektrische Industrie, otherwise known as Société Suisse pour l'Industrie Électrique (SSIE); the French rendition is sometimes given as Société Suisse d'Industrie Électrique
Independent Power Producers (IPPs)
INI: Istituto Nacional de Industria, Spain
Institute for Industrial Reconstruction: in Italian, Istituto per la Ricostruzione Industriale (IRI)
International Bank for Reconstruction and Development: World Bank
International General Electric Co. (IGE)
International Monetary Fund (IMF)
International Paper and Power Co. (IPP)
International Power Co. (IPC)
International Power Securities Corporation (IPSC): its predecessor was Italian Power Co.
IPC: International Power Co.
IPO: Initial public offering
IPP: International Paper and Power Co.
IPPs: Independent Power Producers
IPSC: International Power Securities Corporation

IRI: Institute for Industrial Reconstruction (in Italian, Istituto per la Ricostruzione Industriale)
Istituto Nacional de Industria (INI), Spain
Istituto per la Ricostruzione Industriale (IRI)
Italian-Belgian Electric & Public Utility Co. (Italo-Belge)
Italian Edison Company: Società Generale Italiana Edison di Elettricità
Italian Power Company: International Power Securities Corporation
Italo-Argentina: CIAE
Italo-Argentine Electric Co.: CIAE
Italo-Belge: Italian-Belgian Electric & Public Utility Co., also known as Compagnie Italo-Belge pour Entreprises d'Électricité et d'Utilité Publique (CIBEE or Italo-Belge)
Italo-Suisse, Geneva: Société Financière Italo-Suisse
J. Henry Schröder & Co., London (Schröders)
kW: kilowatts
kWh: kilowatt hours
Lahmeyer: Elektrizitäts A. G. vorm. W. Lahmeyer & Co.
Latina Lux: Impresse Elettriche della America Latina
LCIC: London Canadian Investment Corp.
Lima Light: Lima Light, Power and Tramways Company, Ltd., known in Peru as Empresas Eléctricas Asociadas; English name changed to Lima Light & Power Co. in 1935
Lima Light, Power and Tramways Company, Ltd.: Lima Light
London Canadian Investment Corp. (LCIC)
Lyonnaise des Eaux et de l'Éclairage: Société Lyonnaise des Eaux et de l'Éclairage
Madrileña: Compañía General Madrileña de Electricidad
Meridionale: Società Meridionale di Elettricità (SME)
Mexican Light and Power Co. (Mexlight)
Mexican Northern Power Company: reorganized as Northern Mexican Power and Development Co. in 1919
Mexlight: Mexican Light and Power Co.
MNE: multinational enterprise
Motor, Zurich: Motor für Angewandte Elektrizität, also known as Motor, Société Anonyme pour les Applications de l'Électricité and Motor, Société Anonyme pour l'Électricité
Motor-Columbus, Baden: Motor-Columbus AG für Elektrische Unternehmungen
Motor-Columbus AG für Elektrische Unternehmungen (Motor-Columbus)
Motor für angewandte Elektrizität (Motor)
Motor, Société Anonyme pour l'Électricité: Motor
Motor, Société Anonyme pour les Applications de l'Électricité: Motor
National Agency for Electric Power: ENEL
North Bohemian Electric Power Works: Severočeské elektrárny
Northern Mexican Power and Development Co.: Mexican Northern Power Co.
OECD: Organization for Economic Cooperation and Development
OEG, Genoa: Officine Elettriche Genovesi
OFE: Omnium Français d'Électricité
Officine Elettriche Genovesi (OEG)

OHE: Omnium Hellénique d'Électricité
Omnium Français d'Électricité (OFE)
Omnium Hellénique d'Électricité (OHE)
Organization for Economic Cooperation and Development (OECD)
Paribas, Paris: Banque de Paris et des Pays-Bas
Parisienne Électrique: Société Parisienne pour l'Industrie des Chemins de Fer et Tramways Électriques
Pearson Engineering, New York (F.S. Pearson's company)
Pearson group, London: S. Pearson & Son, Whitehall Securities/Whitehall Electric/ Whitehall Trust, British Pearson group, Cowdray group
Pearson, Weetman (Lord Cowdray, from 1910)
Petersburger Gesellschaft für Electroanlagen (PGE)
PGE, St. Petersburg: Petersburger Gesellschaft für Electroanlagen
Power and Traction Finance Company (PTFC)
Power Securities Corporation (PSC)
PSC: Power Securities Corporation
PSEG: Public Service Enterprise Group
PTFC, London: Power and Traction Finance Company
Public Service Enterprise Group (PSEG)
Public Utilities Securities Corporation (Pusco)
Public Utility Holding Company Act of 1935 (PUHCA): U.S. regulatory law
Public Utility Holding Corporation (PUHC)
Public Utility Regulatory Policies Act of 1978 (PURPA): U.S. regulatory law
PUHC: Public Utility Holding Corporation
PUHCA: Public Utility Holding Company Act of 1935
PURPA: Public Utility Regulatory Policies Act of 1978
Pusco: Public Utilities Securities Corporation
Railways et Électricité: Compagnie Générale de Railways et d'Électricité
RF: Société Russe-Française de Chemin de Fer et Tramways
Rheinisch-Westfälisches Elektrizitätswerk (RWE)
Rhenish-Westphalian Electric Power Co. (RWE)
Rhine-Westphalia Electric Power Company (RWE)
Riegos y Fuerza del Ebro: in English, Ebro Irrigation and Power Co. (Ebro)
RWE: Rhine-Westphalia Electric Power Company, otherwise known as Rheinisch-Westfälisches Elektrizitätswerk, sometimes translated as Rhenish-Westphalian Electric Power Co.
S. Pearson & Son, London (SP&S): also referred to as Pearson group, London, British Pearson group, or Cowdray group; Whitehall Securities/Whitehall Electric were part of this group
SADE: Società Adriatica di Elettricità, also called the Adriatic Electric Company
SAEG: Schweizerisch-Americanische Elektrizitäts-Gesellschaft, otherwise known as Swiss-American Electric Co.
SBC: Swiss Bank Corporation; Schweizerischer Bankverein
SBG: Schweizerische Bankgesellschaft; Union Bank of Switzerland (UBS)
SBS: Société de Banque Suisse; Schweizerischer Bankverein
SBU: Siemens-Bauuion
SBV: Schweizerischer Bankverein

Schröders: J. Henry Schröder & Co., London
Schweizerisch-Americanische Elektrizitäts-Gesellschaft, Zurich (SAEG), also known as Swiss-American Electric Co.
Schweizerisch-Argentinische Hypothekenbank, Zurich, known in Argentina as Banco Hipotecario Suizo-Argentina
Schweizerische Bankgesellschaft (SBG): Union Bank of Switzerland
Schweizerische Eisenbahnbank: renamed in 1924 Schweizerische Elektrizitäts- und Verkehrsgesellschaft (Suiselectra)
Schweizerische Elektrizitäts- und Verkehrsgesellschaft (Suiselectra)
Schweizerische Gesellschaft für Anlagewerte (Socval)
Schweizerische Gesellschaft für Elektrische Industrie: Indelec
Schweizerische Kreditanstalt (SKA): Credit Suisse
Schweizerischer Bankverein (SBV): Swiss Bank Corporation (SBC), or Société de Banque Suisse (SBS), names adopted in 1917; before 1917 in English, Swiss Bankverein and in French Bankverein Suisse
SCIE: Société Centrale pour l'Industrie Électrique
SEC: Securities and Exchange Commission (U.S.)
Securities and Exchange Commission (SEC): a U.S. regulatory agency
SEE, Barcelona: Sociedad Española de Electricidad
SEGBA: Servico Público de la Electricidad del Gran Buenos Aires
SEP: Société d'Électricité de Paris
Servico Público de la Electricidad del Gran Buenos Aires (SEGBA)
Severočeské elektrárny: North Bohemian Electric Power Works
SFMT: Société des Forces Motrices de Truyère
SGB: Société Générale Belge d'Entreprises Électriques
SGCF: Société Générale des Chemins de Fer Économiques
SGE: Société Générale d'Entreprises
SGEA: Società Generale Elettrica dell' Adamello
SGEl: Société Générale d'Électricité
SGH: Société Générale Hellénique, also known as General Hellenic Company
Shawinigan Water and Power Co. (SWP)
SIDRO or **Sidro,** Brussels: Société Internationale d'Energie Hydro-Électrique
Siebenbürgische Elektrizitäts AG: Transylvanian Electricity Co.
Siemens-Bauunion (SBU)
SIP: Società Idroelettrica Piemonte
SMD: Société Marocaine de Distribution d'Eau, de Gaz et d'Électricité
SME: Società Meridionale di Elettricità, sometimes shortened as Meridionale
Sociedad Española de Electricidad (SEE)
Sociedad General Madrileña de Electricidad: Compañía General Madrileña de Electricidad (Madrileña)
Società Adriatica di Elettricità (SADE): also called the Adriatic Electric Company
Società di Banca Svizzera: Schweizerischer Bankverein
Società Edison: Società Generale Italiana Edison di Elettricità
Società Finanziaria Industriale Italiana (Sofindit).
Società Generale Elettrica dell' Adamello (SGEA)
Società Generale Italiana di Elettricità Sistema Edison: renamed in 1895 Società Generale Italiana Edison di Elettricità (Società Edison, Edison Company, Milan, or Italian Edison Company)

Società Generale Italiana Edison di Elettricità: Società Generale Italiana di Elettricità Sistema Edison
Società Idroelettrica Piemonte (SIP)
Società Meridionale di Elettricità: SME or Meridionale
Société Centrale pour l'Industrie Électrique (SCIE)
Société de Banque Suisse (SBS): Schweizerischer Bankverein
Société de Traction et d'Électricité, Brussels (Tractionel): sometimes called Traction et Électricité
Société d'Électricité, Luxembourg (SODEC)
Société d'Électricité de Paris (SEP)
Société d'Électricité et Traction, Brussels: became Traction et Électricité (Tractionel)
Société des Forces Motrices de Truyère (SFMT)
Société des Tramways et de l'Électricité de Constantinople (STEC)
Société Financière de Transports et d'Entreprises Industrielles (Sofina)
Société Financière Électrique, Paris, successor to Société Financière pour le Développement de l'Électricité, also called Finelec
Société Financière Italo-Suisse, Geneva (Italo-Suisse)
Société Financière pour Entreprises Électriques aux Etats-Unis, Geneva
Société Financière pour le Développement de l'Électricité (Finelec)
Société Franco-Suisse pour l'Industrie Électrique (Franco-Suisse)
Société Générale, Brussels: Société Générale de Belgique, Brussels
Société Générale, Paris: Société Générale pour Favoriser le Developpement du Commerce et de l'Industrie en France
Société Générale Belge d'Entreprises Électriques (SGB): Electrobel
Société Générale de Belgique (Société Générale, Brussels)
Société Générale de Constructions Électriques et Mécaniques: commonly called Alsthom
Société Générale d'Électricité (SGEl)
Société Générale d'Entreprises, Paris (SGE)
Société Générale des Chemins de Fer Économiques, Brussels (SGCF)
Société Générale Hellénique (SGH): General Hellenic Co.
Société Générale pour Favoriser le Developpement du Commerce et de l'Industrie en France (Société Générale, Paris)
Société Internationale d'Energie Hydro- Électrique (SIDRO)
Société Lyonnaise des Eaux et de l'Éclairage (Société Lyonnaise)
Société Marocaine de Distribution d'Eau, de Gaz et d'Électricité (SMD)
Société Ottomane d'Électricité de Constantinople (SOEC)
Société Parisienne pour l'Industrie des Chemins de Fer et Tramways Électriques: sometimes called Parisienne Électrique; name change after 1945 to Société Parisienne pour l'Industrie Électriques (SPIE)
Société Parisienne pour l'industrie Électriques (SPIE)
Société Russe-Française de Chemin de Fer et Tramways (RF)
Société Saint- Petersbourgeoise de Transmission Électrique de la Force des Chutes d'eau (SSPT).
Société Suisse d'Électricité et de Traction, Basel
Société Suisse d'Industrie Électrique: Indelec

Société Suisse pour l'Industrie Électrique: Indelec
Société Thomson-Houston (STH): French Thomson-Houston (FTH)
Socval: Schweizerische Gesellschaft für Anlagewerte
SODEC: Société d'Électricité, Luxembourg
SOE: State-owned enterprise
SOEC: Société Ottomane d'Électricité de Constantinople
Sofina or **SOFINA**, Brussels: Société Financière de Transports et d'Entreprises Industrielles
Sofindit: Società Finanziaria Industriale Italiana
SP&S, London: S. Pearson & Son
SPIE: Société Parisienne pour l'industrie Électriques
SSIE, Basel: Société Suisse pour l'Industrie Électrique, otherwise known as Schweizerische Gesellschaft für Elektrische Industrie (Indelec)
SSPT, St. Petersburg: Société Saint-Petersbourgeoise de Transmission Électrique des la Force de Chutes d'Eau
State-owned enterprise (SOE)
STEC: Société des Tramways et de l'Électricité de Constantinople
Steiermark Electric Power Co.: Steiermärkishe Elektrizitäts-Gesellschaft.
Steiermärkishe Elektrizitäts-Gesellschaft: Steiermark Electric Power Co.
STH, Paris: Société Thomson-Houston
SUDAM: Compañía Sudamericana de Electricidad
Südamerikanische Elektrizitäts-Gesellschaft, Zurich (Südelkra)
Südelkra: Südamerikanische Elektrizitäts-Gesellschaft, Zurich
Suez Group: a broad collection of energy (and other) companies that emerged out of the old canal company after the expropriation of the canal in 1956.
Suiselectra: Schweizerische Elektrizitäts- und Verkehrsgesellschaft, new name in 1924 for Schweizerische Eisenbahnbank
Swiss-American Electric Co.: Schweizerisch-Americanische Elektrizitäts-Gesellschaft, Zurich (SAEG).
Swiss Bank Corporation (SBC): Schweizerische Bankverein
Swiss Bankverein: Schweizerische Bankverein
SWP: Shawinigan Water and Power Co.
Syndicat des Études et des Enterprises: in Greek, Syndicato Meleton kai Epichiriseon
Syndicato Meleton kai Epichiriseon: Syndicato Meleton kai Epichiriseon, sometimes translated as Syndicat des Études et des Enterprises
Tennessee Valley Authority (TVA): U.S. government-owned electric utility
THM: Thomson-Houston de la Méditerranée, or Compagnie d'Électricité Thomson-Houston de la Méditerranée
Thomson-Houston de la Méditerranée (THM): see also Compagnie d'Électricité Thomson-Houston de la Méditerranée
Traction et Électricité (Tractionel): Société d'Électricité et Traction
Tractionel: Société de Traction et d'Électricité
Transylvanian Electricity Co.: Siebenbürgische Elektrizitäts AG
TVA: Tennessee Valley Authority
UBS: Union Bank of Switzerland; the UBS designation was adopted in 1998 when Union Bank of Switzerland (UBS) merged with Swiss Bank Corporation (SBC).

UdE: Union d'Électricité
UEG: Union Elektrizitäts Gesellschaft, sometimes rendered as Union Elektricitäts Gesellschaft
UITE, Genoa: Unione Italiana Tramways Electtrici
UNES: Unione Esercizi Elettrici
Union Bank of Switzerland (UBS): otherwise known as Union des Banques Suisses, Unione di Banche Svizzere, Schweizerische Bankgesellschaft, formed in 1912
Union d'Électricité (UdE)
Union des Banques Suisses: Union Bank of Switzerland
Union Elektricitäts Gesellschaft: Union Elektrizitäts Gesellschaft
Union Elektrizitäts Gesellschaft (UEG): also rendered as Union Elektricitäts Gesellschaft
Union Financière: Union Financière de Genève
Union Financière de Genève: Union Financière
Unione di Banche Svizzere: Union Bank of Switzerland
Unione Esercizi Elettrici (UNES)
Unione Italiana Tramways Electtrici (UITE)
UPLC, Chicago: Utilities Power and Light Corporation
Utilities Power and Light Corporation (UPLC)
Vereinigte Elektrizitätswerke Westfalen GmbH, Dortmund: Westphalia United Electric Corporation
VFP: Victoria Falls Power Co. Ltd.
VFTP: Victoria Falls & Transvaal Power Co., Ltd.
Victoria Falls & Transvaal Power Co., Ltd. (VFTP)
Victoria Falls Power Co., Ltd. (VFP)
Westphalia United Electric Corporation: Vereinigte Elektrizitätswerke Westfalen GmbH, Dortmund
Whitehall Securities/Whitehall Electric/Whitehall Trust: Pearson group, London
WIR: World Investment Report
World Bank: International Bank for Reconstruction and Development
World Investment Report (WIR)

Appendix B: Notes to Table 1.4 Foreign Ownership of Electric Utilities, Four Periods

1. All figures for Albania were provided by Luciano Segreto.
2. Mira Wilkins and Harm Schröter educated guess.
3. Schröter educated guess.
4. For electric power generation, complete public ownership was established in 1947. Peter Eigner, "The Ownership of Austria's Big Business, 1895–1995," in Margarita Dritsas and Terry Gourvish, eds., *European Enterprise* (Athens: Trochalia Publications, 1997), 57.
5. Schröter educated guess.
6. Schröter educated guess.
7. This estimate is based on data for 1909 from Ivan T. Berend and György Ránki, *Economic Development in East-Central Europe in the 19th and 20th Centuries* (New York: Columbia University Press, 1974), 143.
8. The figure is based on the proportion of foreign direct investment in electric utilities for 1936 from R. Nötel, "International Credit and Finance," in M. C. Kaser and E. A. Radice, eds., *The Economic History of Eastern Europe, 1919–1975* (Oxford: Clarendon Press, 1985), II, 282.
9. We can find no evidence that any of the electric utilities in the part of the Austro-Hungarian Empire that became Czechoslovakia were foreign-owned. For a history of electric utilities in Prague, see http://muzeum.pre.cz/eng/hist/uvod.php, accessed Jan. 9, 2006.
10. By 1928–1932, Indelec had made investments in at least one Czech electric utility (in Podmokly), but we are uncertain about control. See notes to Chapter 4 herein. By 1934, 67 percent of Czechoslovakia's electric utilities were government owned. J. Tichý and F. Kneidl, "Power Resources, Their Importance and Utilization in Czechoslovakia," *Transactions, Third World Power Conference* (Washington, DC: USGPO, 1938), vol. 2, 144.
11. Nationalization occurred in 1945–1946 (http://www.muzeum.pre.cz/eng/hist/uvod.php accessed Oct. 2, 2007).
12. Timo Myllyntaus, *Electrifying Finland* (London: Macmillan, 1991), 44–45, 56–57.
13. Ibid. The figure assumes approximately equal growth rates among Finnish urban electric utilities.

14. Peter Hertner and Pierre Lanthier educated guess.
15. Hertner and Lanthier educated guess.
16. A state monopoly was created in 1946. David Levi-Faur, "On the 'Net Impact' of Europeanization. The EU's Telecoms and Electricity Regimes between the Global and the National," European Integration Online Papers, 6:7 (2002), 12 (http://eiop.or.at/eiop/texte/2002-007.htm, accessed July 28, 2006).
17. Hertner and Schröter educated guess.
18. Hertner and Schröter educated guess. By 1933, 83 percent of Germany's central-station electricity was produced by government-owned utilities. W. Leisse and G. Balzer, "Germany's Sources of Power, Their Development and Utilization," *Transactions, Third World Power Conference*, vol. 2, 202.
19. There was a municipal electric system. Emile Garcke, comp., *Manual of Electrical Undertakings* (London: Electrical Press, 1914–1915), 1473 (hereafter cited as Garcke, with appropriate year).
20. Garcke, 1928–1929, 1586.
21. The figure is an estimate provided by Leslie Hannah.
22. The figures are estimates provided by Hannah. The first figure represents capacity and the higher figure output.
23. A state monopoly was created in 1947. Levi-Faur, "On the 'Net Impact.'"
24. This figure is based on information provided for 1918 by N. Pantelakis in e-mail correspondence. The Compagnie Hellénique d'Électricité was foreign-owned. Pantelakis's book *From Private Initiative to State Monopoly (1889–1956)* is in Greek.
25. The figure is based on e-mail correspondence from N. Pantelakis. Prior to 1930, Greek investors held a majority of the shares of the General Hellenic Company, although control may actually have resided with British investors. After 1930, the British group S. Pearson and Sons, through its Whitehall Securities subsidiary, clearly had control. Compagnie Hellénique d'Électricité remained foreign-dominated.
26. The figure is based on e-mail correspondence from N. Pantelakis. The Athens electric utility remained under British control and produced approximately 85 percent of Greek electricity.
27. A state monopoly was created in 1950, and all electric companies were bought by the state company between 1956 and 1968. E-mail correspondence from N. Pantelakis.
28. By 1918, the Budapest electric utility, by far the largest in the country, was government owned. This was also the case in many municipalities. L. de Berebély, "National and Regional Planning and Their Relation to the Conservation of National Resources; Regional Integration of Electric-Utility Facilities," *Transactions, Third World Power Conference*, vol. 6, 410. According to Ránki, by the end of the 1920s "a few electrical trusts," presumably foreign, may have controlled several electric stations. György Ránki, "Electric Energy in Hungary," in Fabienne Cardot, ed., *Un Siècle d'Électricité dans le Monde, 1880–1980* (Paris: Presses Universitaires de France, 1987), 157. See Liane Ranieri, *Dannie Heineman* (Brussels: Éditions Racine, 2005), 62, 70, 72, on Sofina in Hungary 1907ff.
29. This is an estimate. In addition, British capital helped fund the state-owned Hungarian Transdanubian Electric Co. in 1928–1930. De Berebély, "National and Regional," 419.

30. Capital was entirely Irish or English, and the public sector was very large. Garcke, 1914–1915, 121–1074. Three privately owned companies were registered or had offices in London: Larne, Portarlington, and the only large one, Cork Electric Tramways and Lighting Co.
31. The Irish Electricity Supply Board was created in 1927 (http://www.esb.ie/main/about_esb/history_foundation.jsp, accessed July 28, 2006).
32. Luciano Segreto, "Imprenditori e Finanzieri," in Giorgio Mori, ed., *Storia dell' Industria Elettrica in Italia* (Rome-Bari: Laterza, 1992), 321–22, 332. The figure is for percent of total capital invested in 1913. Segreto believes most of this capital was foreign direct investment.
33. This figure, and the one for 1947–1950, was provided by Luciano Segreto. While there still was foreign participation, by the late 1920s there were no foreign-controlled electric utilities.
34. Italy's state electricity company, Enel, was formed in December 1962. Michael Polo and Carlo Scarpa, "The Italian Electricity Sector Between Privatization and Fear of Competition," in Mario Baldassarri, Alfredo Macchiati, and Diego Piacentino, eds., *The Privatization of Public Utilities: The Case of Italy* (London: Macmillan, 1997), 143.
35. Schröter educated guess.
36. Schröter educated guess. By 1935, over 98 percent of electricity in Latvia was generated by government, including municipal, plants. Alfred Bilmanis, "Production of Electricity in Latvia," *Transactions, Third World Power Conference*, vol. 2, 290.
37. Early electricity was supplied to Luxembourg City by the iron company Gallais-Metz, which merged with ARBED, SA in 1911. In 2006 ARBED was part of the giant steel company Arcelor Mittal (http://www.rail.lu/arbedhisto.html; http://www.cegedel.lu, accessed Nov. 21, 2006).
38. The Public Utility Holding Corp. of America had a 35 percent interest, which the company asserted was noncontrolling, in Cie. Grand Ducale d'Électricité du Luxembourg (CEGEDEL), which had been formed in 1928. *Moody's Manual (Utilities) 1930*, 2416–17. Also see *New York Times*, July 20, 1930.
39. The company was renamed Luxemburger Electrizitäts AG during the German occupation, by which time there appears to have been no foreign ownership (http://www.cegedel.lu, accessed Nov. 21, 2006).
40. The state became the principal shareholder in CEGEDEL in 1970 (http://www.cegedel.lu, accessed Nov. 21, 2006).
41. This is a crude estimate. Malta (Valletta) Lighting and Power was owned by the government. Malta Tramways, which generated its own electricity and may have supplied some to outside customers, was British-owned (by Macartney, M'Elroy & Co. Ltd.). Garcke, 1914–1915, 1481.
42. Garcke, 1928–1929, 1597–98 still lists Malta Tramways, but the company went bankrupt in 1929, and the trams were replaced by buses.
43. By 1910, virtually all power stations were government-owned enterprises. While there may have been some foreign investment in coal mines that provided some local power or in some border power stations, it is not likely that any of these operations were foreign-controlled. Information provided by G. P. J. Verbong via e-mail correspondence.

44. Schröter educated guess. If power generated by industrial firms were included, the figure would be close to 80 percent. By 1918, 80 percent of electricity supply undertakings were municipally owned. Robert Millward, *Private and Public Enterprise in Europe* (Cambridge: Cambridge University Press, 2005), 78.
45. Schröter educated guess. If power generated by industrial firms were included, the figure would be approximately 60 percent. By 1934, 88 percent of electricity supply undertakings were government, including municipally, owned. Norwegian National Committee of World Power Conference, "Power Resources, Development, and Utilization," *Transactions, Third World Power Conference*, vol. 2, 307.
46. This figure is based on the proportion of foreign-owned capital stock in electric, gas, and water companies. The figure for 1927 was 44.6 percent and subsequently increased. Zbigniew Landau and Jerzy Tomaszweski, "Foreign Policy and International Business in Poland: 1918–39," in Alice Teichova, Maurice Lévy-Leboyer, and Helga Nussbaum, eds., *Multinational Enterprise in Historical Perspective* (Cambridge: Cambridge University Press, 1986), 276.
47. The figure is for 1930. Landau and Tomaszewski, "Foreign Policy," 276. By 1934, 19 percent of electricity was generated in government-owned firms. Polish National Committee, "Statistical Tables of the Power Sources and Their Utilization in Poland," *Transactions, Third World Power Conference*, vol. 2, 332.
48. Pierre Lanthier indicates that in Portugal ownership and control are very difficult to assess. There were substantial foreign investments (by both Sofina and SCIE) by 1914, but also much participation by municipalities. The foreign investments persisted until nationalization, but control is uncertain.
49. Data provided by Francesca Antolin via e-mail correspondence, based on annual reports of Hidroeléctrica Ibérica.
50. The electric utility industry was nationalized in 1975–1976. Levi-Faur, "On the 'Net Impact.' "
51. Schröter educated guess, confirmed for 1910 in Berend and Ránki, *Economic Development*, 107.
52. Schröter educated guess. By 1934, 48 percent of electricity was generated by government-owned firms. Dorin Pavel and Eugen Bodea, "Power Resources of Roumania, Their Development and Utilization," *Transactions, Third World Power Conference*, vol. 2, 359–60.
53. Timo Myllyntaus, "Electrical Imperialism," paper presented at Business History Conference, Glasgow, 1997.
54. After the Russian Revolution, the properties of foreign utilities were taken over; foreigners participated in the electrification activities of the first five-year plan, but there was no foreign direct investment in the operation of Russian public utilities.
55. The first figure is for percent of total production in 1917 and was provided by Francesca Antolin, based on statistics found in *Anuario Estadístico de España*. The slightly higher figure is based on a separate calculation for installed capacity for major utilities and all hydroelectric facilities for the same period. In terms of capital investment in tramways, the figure would be 75 percent foreign-owned; however, not all tramway companies generated electricity, so this figure undoubtedly overstates the importance of electricity production by foreign-owned tramways. Philip S. Smith, *Electrical Goods in Spain*,

Department of Commerce, Bureau of Foreign and Domestic Commerce, Special Agent Series, 197 (Washington, DC: USGPO, 1920), 21–22, 54–56, 58–86, 131.

56. This figure was provided by Francesca Antolin, based on *Anuario Estadístico de España*.
57. In 1949, Juan March, with the help of the Spanish government, forced the last remaining foreign-owned electric utility in Spain – Barcelona Traction, Light and Power Co. Ltd. – into bankruptcy and seized control of the firm. *New York Times*, Dec. 19, 1948; Sept. 21, 1949; June 9, 1951.
58. There is no evidence of foreign ownership in Sweden. There was strong central control, with the State Power Board having been created in 1909. Arne Kaijser, "From Local Networks to National Systems," Fabienne Cardot, ed., *Un Siècle d'Électricité dans le Monde, 1880–1980* (Paris: Presses Universitaires de France, 1987), 15.
59. Schröter educated guess.
60. Schröter educated guess.
61. Schröter educated guess.
62. The lower figures are based on percent of FDI for 1938 from Nötel, "International Credit and Finance," 281. The higher figure is from Ránki, "Electric Energy in Hungary," 159.
63. Educated guess provided by David Merrett, based on Commonwealth Statistician, *Production Bulletin* (1906–1916 issues). The three foreign-owned firms were Melbourne Electric Supply Co., Adelaide Electric Supply Co., and Kalgoorlie Power Corp.
64. Information provided by Kenneth Jackson.
65. Based on installed capacity from Garcke, 1914–1915, 1417–61. The only foreign-owned firm was the Auckland Electric Tramways Co. Ltd., which was part of British Electric Traction Co. The municipality took over the tram company in 1919. Garcke, 1928–1929, 1469.
66. With the exception of some small operations, electric utilities prior to nationalization were all French- owned. Mohamed Messen, "Réseau Électrique Algérien: Naisance et Croissance," in Monique Trédé, ed., *Électricité et l'Électrification dans le Monde* (Paris: PUF, 1992), 261–74.
67. When electric utilities were nationalized in 1946–1947, shortly after they had been in France, authorities created Électricité et Gaz d'Algérie (EGA) (http://www.winne.com/algeria3/to12frinter.html, accessed Dec. 19, 2005).
68. The state-owned Société Nationale de l'Électricité et du Gaz (Sonelgaz) was created in 1969 to replace EGA (http://www.sonelgaz.dz/Francais/FRANCAIS/presentation/historique.htm, accessed Dec. 19, 2005).
69. Wilkins educated guess, based on Robert L. Tignor, *State, Private Enterprise, and Economic Change in Egypt, 1918–1952* (Princeton: Princeton University Press, 1984), 19, 182–83. Most electric utilities and tramways were British or Belgian-owned.
70. Calculations from Garcke, 1928–1929, 1423–61, put the figure at 95 percent.
71. Robert L. Tignor, *Egyptian Textiles and British Capital 1930–1956* (Cairo: American University in Cairo Press, 1989), 100, writes: "The campaign against public utilities culminated in the passage of a stringent public utilities law in

1947." Electric utilities were nationalized during the following period, the last of which were those of Empain, which were nationalized in 1961. See Chapter 6 herein.

72. All figures were provided by Segreto.
73. The Nairobi Electric Power and Lighting Co. Ltd. was registered in 1906. Garcke, 1914–1915, 1351.
74. The East African Power and Lighting Co. Ltd., formed by the merger of companies serving Nairobi and Mombasa, was registered in Nairobi, with both Nairobi and London Boards of Directors. Garcke, 1928–1929, 1433–34. Over the course of the following decade, this company became the monopoly supplier of electricity to Uganda and Tanganyika as well. Robert L. Tignor, *Capitalism and Nationalism at the End of the Empire* (Princeton: Princeton University Press, 1998), 304.
75. The properties of East African Power and Lighting in Uganda were nationalized in 1947–1948, but those in Kenya survived an attempt at nationalization. Tignor, *Capitalism*, 305. An ad for the company can be found in the *New York Times*, Jan. 20, 1964.
76. The government had a controlling interest in the East African Power and Lighting Co. by 1971. Nicola Swainson, "State and Economy in Post-Colonial Kenya, 1963–1978," *Canadian Journal of African Studies*, 12 (1978), 373.
77. All figures for Libya were provided by Segreto.
78. The first French-controlled company was established in 1913. Prior to nationalization, all electric utilities were French-owned, although the Moroccan government provided substantial assistance. Agnès d'Angio, "L'Électrification du Maroc Vue à Travers l'Action de la Société Schneider et Cie (1907–1954)," in Dominique Barjot, Daniel Lefeuvre, Arnaud Berthonnet, and Sophie Coeuré, eds., *L'Électrification Outre-mer de la Fin du XIXe Siècle aux Premières Décolonisations* (Paris : Publications de la Société Française d'Histoire d'Outre-mer, 2002), 317–29, and Samir Saul, "L'Électrification du Maroc à l'Époque du Protectorat," in ibid., 491–512.
79. Electricity was nationalized, and the Office Nationale de l'Électricité was created in 1963.
80. The large Cahora Bassa hydroelectric plant was constructed in the 1960s by a foreign consortium led by Harry Oppenheimer's Anglo American Trust. Upon completion, it was controlled by Portuguese interests. It was transferred to the government of Mozambique in 2005. In 1999, only 5 percent of Mozambique's households had access to electricity (http://www.eskom.co.za/live/content.php?Item_ID=892 and http://www.mbendi.co.za/indy/powr/af/mz/p0005.htm, accessed Feb. 2, 2005).
81. The first electric power station in Nigeria was constructed by the Lagos Public Works Department in 1896. Marcel N. Azodo Manafa, *Electricity Development in Nigeria (1896–1972)* (Yaba, Nigeria: Raheem Publishers, 1979), 14.
82. In 1923, Nigerian Power and Tin Fields Ltd., a British company, obtained the rights to supply power to companies operating in northern Nigeria and constructed a hydroelectric facility. In 1929, the company was reorganized and the name changed to Nigerian Electricity Supply Corporation Ltd. (NESCO). Most of the electricity produced was used in mining operations, but some bulk power was sold to small utilities in Jos and in towns such as Vom and Buruku,

which is the basis of the estimate in the table. Manafa, *Electricity*, 24–28. U.S. Department of Commerce, Bureau of Foreign and Domestic Commerce, Trade Information Bulletin, 423, *Central Light and Power Plants in Africa* (July 1926), 2. *Stock Exchange Official Intelligence* (1929), 1195. Nigerian towns were served by small, government-owned utilities that were not consolidated into a separate branch of government until 1946. Tignor, *Capitalism*, 199.

83. NESCO remained in private hands. Manafa, *Electricity*, 27–31.
84. The centralized National Electric Power Authority was created in 1972, although NESCO continued to exist. Its distribution system was not connected with the national grid. Manafa, *Electricity*, 31 (http://www.nopa.net/Power_and_Steel/messages/21.shtml, accessed Dec. 14, 2005).
85. The figure is based on installed capacity, with estimates for some small companies and excluding DeBeers and Randfontein mining operations. Garcke, 1914–1915, 1339–58.
86. Wilkins educated guess and Richard W. Hull, *American Enterprises in South Africa* (New York: New York University Press, 1990), 139.
87. In 1948, the Electricity Supply Commission of South Africa (ESCOM) took over Victoria Falls and Transvaal Power Co., the last remaining large foreign direct investment in public utilities. G. Boileau, "La Production Électricité en Afrique du Sud (1880–1922)," in Dominique Barjot, et al., *L'Électrification Outre-Mer* (Paris: EDF, 2002), 476.
88. Garcke, 1928–1929, 1455–56. The Sudan Light and Power Co. Ltd. was formed in 1925. It was registered in London but had a representative of the government of Sudan on its board. Tignor notes that while the company's capital was raised privately, the assets of the company were considered the property of the Sudanese government. Robert Tignor, "The Sudanese Private Sector: An Historical Overview," *Journal of Modern African Studies*, 25 (June 1987), 191.
89. Electricity was provided by the East African Power and Lighting Co. Tignor, *Capitalism*, 304.
90. Nationalization occurred in 1947–1948. Tignor, *Capitalism*, 304–5.
91. Garcke, 1914–1915, 1464–65, 1482–84.
92. Rangoon Electric Tramway and Supply Co., now registered and controlled in Rangoon (now Yangon). Utilities serving Mandalay remained British-owned. Garcke, 1928–1929, 1574–75, 1604–5.
93. The largest electric utility in China served the international settlement in Shanghai. It had been purchased from foreign investors in 1893 by the municipal council. There was a foreign-owned firm in Shanghai and a French-Belgian tramway operating in Tientsin. The approximate percentage given here is based on the relative size of these firms in 1932. C. Yun, "A Statistical Investigation of Electric Power Plants in China 1932," *Transactions of the World Power Conference, Sectional Meeting, Scandinavia*, 1933, vol. 2, 532. Also see R. A. Lundquist, *Electrical Goods in China, Japan, and Vladivostok*, U.S. Department of Commerce, Bureau of Foreign and Domestic Commerce, Special Agent Series, 172, (Washington, DC: USGPO, 1918), 62.
94. Figures are capacity, output, and investment, respectively. Capacity and output are from Electric Utility Regulation Board, "Electric Power Development in China," *Transactions, Third World Power Conference*,. vol. 2, 108, and investment is from Yun, "A Statistical Investigation," vol. 2, 536. Yun's paper

contains a list of power systems and industrial plants with annual output exceeding 10 million kWh. Many of these, including the three largest (Shanghai Power Co., South Manchuria Electric Supply Co., and Compagnie Française de Tramways et d'Éclairage Électrique) were foreign-owned.

95. This figure is based on an estimate of capacity. Hongkong Tramways Ltd. was British-controlled. Hongkong Electric Co. and China Light & Power (which served Kowloon) were registered in Hong Kong and appeared to be controlled by directors resident in Hong Kong. The capacity figures for Hongkong Tramways and Hongkong Electric are from Garcke, 1914–1915, 1474. The China Light & Power figure is based on a 1919 figure for capacity from Nigel Cameron, *Power: The Story of China Light* (Hong Kong: Oxford University Press, 1982), 268. On Hongkong Electric, see Austin Coates, *A Mountain of Light: The Story of Hongkong Electric Company* (London: Heinemann, 1977). We included only Hongkong Tramways as British-controlled.
96. By 1922, Hongkong Tramways had ceased producing its own power and was purchasing power from Hongkong Electric. Coates, *A Mountain of Light*, 59–60. Hongkong Electric was owned and controlled by Hong Kong residents.
97. In 1964, China Light & Power formed a joint venture with the American oil company Standard Oil Co. (New Jersey), resulting in the creation of a generating company, Peninsula Electric Power Co. Ltd., that was to generate power that China Light & Power distributed. The company was 60 percent owned by an affiliate of the U.S. oil company. The figure in the table is based on generating capacity in 1976–1977. Cameron, *Power*, 200–11; Coates, *A Mountain of Light*, 199.
98. Figures are from Garcke, 1914–1915, 1462–87. For several firms, capacity was estimated using assets or population of area served.
99. Garcke, 1928–1929, 1567–616. This figure considers the very large Tata Sons Ltd. enterprises (39 percent of total installed capacity in India) to be domestically owned and controlled even though American & Foreign Power Co. held substantial investments in the enterprise.
100. State electricity boards were created in 1948. James H. Williams and Navroz K. Dubash, "Asian Electricity Reform in Historical Perspective," *Pacific Affairs*, 77 (Fall 2004), 419.
101. Schröter educated guess.
102. Schröter educated guess.
103. PLN was nationalized in 1950. Williams and Dubash, "Asian Electricity."
104. Wilkins, general knowledge. Although Japanese electric utilities issued a substantial amount of debt in foreign nations, none of the Japanese electric utilities was foreign-owned.
105. All central stations were Japanese-owned. The lighting plant and tramway in Seoul were originally American owned, but by 1909 were controlled by a Japanese syndicate. R. A. Lundquist, *Electrical Goods in China, Japan, and Vladivostok*, U.S. Department of Commerce, Bureau of Foreign and Domestic Commerce, Special Agent Series, 172 (Washington, DC: USGPO, 1918), 170, 175.
106. Samuel Pao-San Ho, "Colonialism and Development: Korea, Taiwan, and Kwantung," in Ramon H. Myers and Mark R. Peattie, eds., *The Japanese Colonial Empire, 1895–1945* (Princeton: Princeton University Press, 1984), 374.

107. With the Japanese defeat in World War II, foreign ownership effectively ceased. In 1948, the year in which the U.S. military government handed over control of the country to an elected government, South Korea received 75 percent of its electric power from what became Communist North Korea. "Korea Power Threat Held to Be Political," *New York Times*, April 19, 1948. Also see Yang Jonghoe, "Colonial Legacy and Modern Economic Growth in Korea: A Critical Examination of Their Relationships," *Development and Society*, 33 (June 2004), 1–24.
108. Williams and Dubash, "Asian Electricity," 419. Electric utilities in South Korea were nationalized in 1961.
109. There were government, including municipal, plants in Georgetown, Kuala Lumpur, and Kampar. Garcke, 1914–1915, 1473, 1477; Muzaffar Tate, *Power Builds the Nation: The National Electricity Board of the States of Malaya and Its Predecessors*, I (Kuala Lumpur: National Electricity Board, 1989), 284. The first generating plants in Malaya were installed by foreign-owned tin-mining companies, but they were limited to industrial power. Robert F. Kinloch, "The Growth of Electric Power Production in Malaya," *Annals of the Association of American Geographers*, 56 (June 1966), 220–35, at 221.
110. The Perak River Hydro-Electric Power Co. Ltd., registered in 1926, was British-controlled. Garcke, 1928–1929, 1585, 1592, 1602–3. According to Kinloch, over 90 percent of the total power produced in the FMS was consumed by tin-mining operations. If mining operations were included in total utility production, the total foreign-controlled capacity would have been approximately 85 percent.
111. This is an estimate based on the 1928–1932 figure. The war substantially reduced operating capacity, but recovery began shortly thereafter. Muzaffar Tate, *Power Builds the Nation: The National Electricity Board of the States of Malaya and Its Predecessors*, 2 (Kuala Lumpur: Tenaga Nasional Berhad, 1991), 2–41.
112. This is an estimate based on increased capacity of government-owned plants between 1949 and 1970. The Central Electricity Board was created in 1949, but it was not until 1976 that the last privately owned (and foreign-controlled) firm, Perak River Hydro-Electric Power Co. – whose chairman was Hugh Balfour at the time – was purchased by the government. Tate, *Power Builds the Nation*, vol. 2, 268–69, 453–55.
113. T. Tsukuda, "Electric Power Projects for Future Supply in Manchukuo," *Transactions, Third World Power Conference*, vol. 5, 213.
114. By 1935, the percentages were 46 percent foreign, 54 percent joint Japanese-Manchukuo ownership (with less than 1 percent pure domestic ownership). Tsukuda, "Electric Power."
115. Charles M. Swift of Detroit, Michigan, received a 50-year franchise from the Municipal Board of Manila in 1903 and established the Manila Electric Railroad and Light Co. (Meralco; now Manila Electric Co.), which acquired all existing franchises in Manila. Gabriel Y. Itchon, Perla A. Segovia, and Arturo P. Alcaraz, *A Short Story of the National Power Corporation* (Quezon City, Philippines: National Power Corporation, 1986), 1–3.
116. There were two small domestic utilities; otherwise, all utilities were owned by the Associated Gas & Electric Corp. of the United States. *McGraw Central*

Station Directory (New York: McGraw-Hill Catalog and Directory Co., 1929), 677 (hereafter cited as *McGraw* with appropriate date).

117. The figures are for capacity in 1947. The National Power Corporation (NAPOCOR) had been created in 1936 in a law that reserved all future hydroelectric developments for the government-owned company. NAPOCOR was about to complete its first hydroelectric facility when World War II broke out. By 1956, the capacity of Meralco and NAPOCOR were about equal. Itchon, Segovia, and Alcaraz, *A Short Story*, 14. Also see http://www.napocor.gov.ph/historical_background.htm (accessed Jan. 16, 2006). In 1940, U.S. direct investment in public utilities in the Philippines comprised nearly 40 percent of total U.S. direct investment and was the largest single component of the total. By 1950, this proportion had fallen to 32 percent but remained the largest single component. A. V. H. Hartendorp, *History of Industry and Trade of the Philippines* (Manila: American Chamber of Commerce of the Philippines, 1958), 730.
118. A syndicate of Filipino investors led by Eugenio Lopez purchased Meralco (Manila Electric Co.) from its American parent in 1962. Itchon, Segovia, and Alcaraz, *A Short Story*, 22. Also see http://www.benpres-holdings.com/h-heritage.shtml (accessed Jan. 16, 2006). In 1978, the generating assets of Meralco were purchased by the National Power Corp. (http://www.napocor.gov.ph/historical_background.htm, accessed Jan. 16, 2006).
119. A municipal firm distributed electricity produced by the British-owned tramway company. Garcke, 1914–1915, 1462–87.
120. Garcke, 1928–1929, 1597, 1610–11. Singapore Traction Co. Ltd. remained British-owned but did not produce electricity. With the exception of one small plant, electrical plants were government owned. Frederick Brown, "Power Resources, Development and Utilization," *Transactions, Third World Power Conference*, vol. 2, 239.
121. Garcke, 1914–1915, 1469–70.
122. Garcke, 1928–1929, 1581–82, 1591. The utilities in Colombo and Kandy were taken over by the municipalities.
123. Most, if not all, of electrical development was financed with Japanese money. The Taiwan Electric Power Co., organized in 1919 through the consolidation of several smaller companies, was Japanese- owned, including 37 percent ownership by the Japanese government. The company also had issued debt in the United States, Canada, and Scandinavia. *New York Times*, Jan. 26, 1931. Mark R. Peattie, "Introduction," in Ramon H. Myers and Mark R. Peattie, eds., *The Japanese Colonial Empire, 1895–1945* (Princeton: Princeton University Press, 1984), 34.
124. Ho, "Colonialism," 357, 374.
125. Taipower was nationalized in 1945. Williams and Dubash, "Asian Electricity."
126. There was one municipal and one foreign-owned (at one time Danish) private plant of roughly equal size in Bangkok (http://ostc.thaiembdc.org/energy/egat.html, accessed Oct. 3, 2005).
127. http://ostc.thaiembdc.org/energy/egat.html, accessed Oct. 3, 2005.
128. Virtually all electricity was provided by municipal and regional authorities (http://ostc.thaiembdc.org/energy/egat.html, accessed Oct. 3, 2005).
129. Regional state enterprises were consolidated into the Electricity Generating Authority of Thailand in 1969.

130. There was substantial foreign ownership of electric light and tramway companies prior to World War I. The German Transatlantic Electricity Co. (Compañía Alemana Transatlántica de Electricidad, formed in 1898), the Italo-Argentine Electricity Co. (Compañía Italo-Argentina de Electricidad, which commenced operation in 1916), the Anglo-Argentine Electricity Co. (Cía. Anglo-Argentina de Electricidad, formed in 1911), and the English company Cía. Electricidad de la Provincia de Buenos Aires (1911) operated in and around Buenos Aires and in Mendoza. The Compañía Electricidad of Rosario was Belgian. The River Plate Electricity Company of La Plata was English. The Cordoba Light and Power Co. was American. Domestic companies existed in Corrientes, Bolívar, and Río Gallegos. Frederic M. Halsey, *Investments in Latin America and the British West Indies*, U.S. Department of Commerce, Bureau of Foreign and Domestic Commerce, Special Agent Series, 169 (Washington, DC: USGPO, 1918), 68–70, 483–97.
131. José A. Gómez-Ibáñez, "The Future of Private Infrastructure: Lessons from the Nationalization of Electric Utilities in Latin America, 1943–1979," Discussion Paper, Taubman Center for State and Local Government, John F. Kennedy School of Government, Harvard University (Jan. 1999), 8.
132. The figure was 92 percent at the outbreak of World War II. By 1943, 38 percent of American & Foreign Power Company's assets had been expropriated or seized, leading to this estimate. Simon G. Hanson, *Economic Development in Latin America* (Washington, DC: Inter-American Affairs Press, 1951), 306–7. *The Foreign Power System* (New York: American & Foreign Power Co., 1953), 10.
133. All major foreign utilities with the exception of the Swiss Compañía Italo-Argentina de Electricidad (CIADE) had been nationalized by 1960. CIADE was nationalized in 1979. Gómez-Ibáñez, "The Future of Private Infrastructure," 4, 9.
134. This is an estimate based on the 1928–1932 proportion. The Bolivian & General Enterprise Co. (Ltd.), serving La Paz, was owned almost wholly by the French firm Creusot & Schneider. Trams and lighting plants were operated by domestic firms in Cochabamba and Sucre, Bolivia. A German-owned firm served the tin-mining district in Oruro. Halsey, *Investments in Latin America*, 110–11. José A. Gómez-Ibáñez, *Regulating Infrastructure: Monopoly, Contracts, and Discretion* (Cambridge, MA: Harvard University Press, 2003), 129.
135. The figure excludes mining operations in Catari, Punutuma, and Uncia, which represented approximately 60 percent of the total capacity installed in Bolivia in 1929. Bolivian Power Company was now Canadian-owned, as was Oruro Light & Power Company. *McGraw*, *1929*, 766.
136. This estimate is based on the 1928–1932 figure. There was little change in the structure of the Bolivian electric power sector between these dates. Gómez-Ibáñez, *Regulating Infrastructure*, 129–30.
137. This is an estimate. Bolivia established a state-owned electric utility in the 1950s to promote rural electrification. Bolivian Light and Power remained foreign-owned. It was never nationalized. Gómez-Ibáñez, *Regulating Infrastructure*, 130–31.
138. The figure is an estimate based on the 1928–1932 figure. The Canadian-owned Brazilian Traction, Light and Power Ltd. was the largest and most prominent utility company in Brazil. In addition, there were British-owned lighting and tramway companies in Ceará, Santos, Recife, and Belém. There

was a French-controlled electric utility in Curitiba and municipally owned or local utilities in Bahia, Bello Horizonte, Nictheroy, and Rio Grande do Sul. Halsey, *Investments in Latin America*, 164–73.

139. Generation was approximately 67 percent; installed capacity probably was nearer 80 percent. Gómez-Ibáñez, "The Future of Private Infrastructure," 8.
140. The first figure is for capacity, the second is for output. Hanson, *Economic Development in Latin America*, 302–3; Werner Baer and Curt McDonald, "A Return to the Past? Brazil's Privatization of Public Utilities: The Case of the Electric Power Sector," *Quarterly Review of Economics and Finance*, 38 (Fall 1998), 509.
141. The figure is for 1965. Baer and McDonald, "A Return." By 1979, nationalization was complete, and the figure was 0. Gómez-Ibáñez, "The Future of Private Infrastructure," 9.
142. This is an estimate based on Ricardo Simpson, "Organization of Private Gas and Electric Utilities," *Transactions, Third World Power Conference*, vol. 5, 57–64. The figure is for public utilities and excludes industrial enterprises. See also Linda Jones, Charles Jones, and Robert Greenhill, "Public Utility Companies," in D. C. M. Platt, ed., *Business Imperialism* (Oxford: Oxford University Press, 1977), 77–118. The Compañía Alemana Transatlántica (controlled by Deutsch-Überseeische Elektrizitäts Gesellschaft, Berlin) owned an electric utility in Valparaíso, tramways in Valparaíso and Viña del Mar, and a large stake in the Santiago Electric Light & Tramway Co. Halsey, *Investments in Latin America*, 243. Also see Philip S. Smith, *Electrical Goods in Bolivia and Chile*, U.S. Department of Commerce, Bureau of Foreign and Domestic Commerce, Special Agent Series, 167 (Washington, DC: USGPO, 1918), 38.
143. The figure is for 1935. Simpson, "Organization."
144. Estimate based on Simpson, "Organization," and Hanson, *Economic Development*.
145. Rolf J. Lüders, "Early, Massive, Broad, and Successful Privatizations: The Case of Chile," in Melissa H. Birch and Jerry Haar, eds., *The Impact of Privatization in the Americas* (Miami: North-South Center Press, 2000), 13–49.
146. Gómez-Ibáñez, "The Future of Private Infrastructure," 12, asserts that there were no foreign investments in electric utilities in Colombia until 1927.
147. American & Foreign Power owned the utilities in Cali and Santa Marta. Utilities in Medellín and Bogotá were municipally owned. *McGraw, 1929*, 776–77. Also see Gómez-Ibáñez, "The Future of Private Infrastructure," 12.
148. The Cali property was nationalized in 1945, the remaining properties in 1961. Gómez-Ibáñez, "The Future of Private Infrastructure," 9.
149. Gómez-Ibáñez, "The Future of Private Infrastructure," 9, See also Joseph W. Mullen, *Energy in Latin America* (Santiago, Chile: United Nations, CEPAL, 1978), 65.
150. The Quito Electric Lighting & Power Co. was controlled by the British company Ecuadorian Corp. Other lighting plants appeared to be municipally or domestically owned. Halsey, *Investments in Latin America*, 290. The figure in the table is based on capacity as given in U.S. Bureau of Foreign and Domestic Commerce, Special Agent Series, 154, *Electrical Goods in Ecuador and Peru* (Washington, DC: USGPO, 1917), 11.

151. *McGraw, 1929*, 778–79. Quito, Guayaquil, and Riobamba were served by U.S.-owned companies.
152. This estimate is based on the 1928–1932 figure. American & Foreign Power retained its interests in Guayaquil and Riobamba. American & Foreign Power Co., *Annual Report 1952*.
153. This is an estimate. The Basic Electrification Law of May 1961 created the Ecuadorian Electrification Institute (INECEL), which gave the state exclusive responsibility for electric power development, and eventually all electric power was generated by government-owned utilities. While the foreign-owned utilities of Guayquil and Riobamba (by this time owned by Boise Cascade) were never nationalized, they became exclusively distributing utilities. Ecuadoran Foundation for Energy and Environment, *Economics of Greenhouse Gas Limitations*, Country Study Series, Ecuador, published by the Centre on Energy and Environment, Technical University of Denmark (Roskilde, Denmark: Risø National Laboratory, 1999), 47; Gómez-Ibáñez, *Regulating Infrastructure*, 115, 124.
154. Asunción Tramway, Light and Power Co. Ltd. was British-owned. Garcke, 1914–1915, 146. According to Halsey, *Investments in Latin America*, 312, the company entered receivership in October 1914.
155. The firm was then controlled by a Swiss-Argentine company, Compañía Americana de Luz y Tracción (http://www.ande.gov.py/Historia/historiadelaelectricidad-py.htm, accessed July 28, 2006).
156. Nationalization occurred in 1948.
157. This is an estimate based on the 1928–1932 figure. The largest electrical establishment in the country was a hydroelectric power plant constructed by the Cerro de Pasco Copper Corp. The power was used exclusively for industrial purposes. The electrical plant is described as being "owned by an American company." U.S. Bureau of Foreign and Domestic Commerce, Special Agent Series, 154, *Electrical Goods in Ecuador and Peru* (Washington, DC: USGPO, 1917), 25–26.
158. *McGraw, 1929*, 779. Lima Light, Power & Tramways Co. (Empresas Eléctricas Asociadas) was foreign-owned. The Cerro de Pasco plant comprised ca. 20 percent of total electrical capacity in the country. For an excellent history of Lima's tramways, see http://www.tramz.com/pe/li/li00.html (accessed April 24, 2006).
159. Lima's tramways were taken over by the government in 1934. *Moody's Manual (Utilities) 1937*, 770. Empresa Pública de Electricidad del Perú (ELECTROPERU) was created in 1972 as a holding company to unify the government's activities in the electricity sector. The state became an owner or majority shareholder for all previously held private concessions. Alfred H. Saulniers, *Public Enterprises in Peru* (Boulder, CO: Westview Press, 1988), 27.
160. The estimate is based on the 1928–1932 figure. The electric light plant of Montevideo and other cities and towns was owned by the government. There were two electric tramways in Montevideo, the British-owned United Electric Tramways and the other controlled by Compañía Alemana Transatlántica. Halsey, *Investments in Latin America*, 361–63. For a brief history of the state-owned electric utility, which dated to 1912, see http://www.ute.com.uy/empresa/informacion/historia.htm (accessed Jan. 26, 2006).

161. The Montevideo tramway was owned by the British Atlas Electric and General Trust Ltd. *Moody's Manual of Banks, 1930*, 2590. No other electric utility was foreign-owned. *McGraw, 1929*, 780. The estimate is based on the capacity of the tramway.
162. The Montevideo tramway company was sold to the state in 1947 (http://members.tripod.com/~lfu1/index-13.html, accessed Jan. 27, 2006).
163. The figure is an estimate based on the 1928–1932 figure. The Canadian International Light & Power Co. controlled the Venezuela Electric Light Co. United Electric Tramways Co. of Caracas (Ltd.) appears to be British-owned. Halsey, *Investments in Latin America*, 383, 529, 536.
164. There were several U.S. and Canadian-controlled utilities according to *Moody's Manual (Utilities) 1930*, 1502; see also Gregory Marchildon, "The Limitations of the Free-Standing Utility," in Mira Wilkins and Harm Schröter, *The Free-Standing Company in the World Economy 1830–1996* (Oxford: Oxford University Press, 1998), 398. Gómez-Ibáñez says that most electric utilities were owned by domestic investors. The figure here is based on *McGraw, 1929*, 780–82. There was a Canadian utility in Maracaibo, while the Venezuela Electric Light Co., which served part of Caracas, was still listed as British, although it was controlled by American & Foreign Power by this time.
165. This estimate is based on the 1928–1932 figure. There was little change in the structure of the electric utility sector between these dates.
166. The American & Foreign Power subsidiary serving part of Caracas was sold in 1964; the Canadian-owned Venezuelan Power Company, serving Maracaibo and Barquisimeto, was nationalized in 1976. Gómez-Ibáñez, *Regulating Infrastructure*, 125.
167. Costa Rica Electric Light and Traction Co. was British-owned. Garcke, 1914–1915, 338. It is likely that some municipal firms existed at the time.
168. Garcke, 1928–1929, 319. The utilities in San José and surrounding area were purchased by American & Foreign Power in 1928. *Moody's Manual (Utilities) 1929*, 1437. A number of municipal firms also existed. *McGraw, 1929*, 737–38.
169. Based on 1954 output, 40 percent of which was from government-owned plants. *New York Times*, Jan. 5, 1955.
170. Arrangements were made in 1969 for government purchase of the remaining foreign utility. *Moody's Manual (Utilities) 1968*.
171. There was little electrification and Halsey, *Investments in Latin America*, 447, identifies no foreign-owned electric utilities.
172. The San Salvador Electric Co. was Canadian-controlled. *McGraw, 1929*, 753–54.
173. Nationalization occurred in 1945 (http://www.cel.gob.sv/insti_historia.htm, accessed Jan. 25, 2006).
174. This is an estimate. Empresa Eléctrica de Guatemala was German-owned. Under the urging of the United States, the company was confiscated by the Guatemalan government during World War I. Thomas F. O'Brien, *The Century of U.S. Capitalism in Latin America* (Albuquerque: University of New Mexico Press, 1999), 42–43.
175. The figure excludes several coffee and sugar company generators. American & Foreign Power controlled Empresa Guatemalteca de Electricidad, the largest utility in Guatemala. *McGraw, 1929*, 739.

176. This estimate is based on American & Foreign Power's continued ownership (http://www.eegsa.com/historia.php, accessed Feb. 1, 2006).
177. In 1972, the concession of the company (now controlled by Boise Cascade) expired, and within several years the government negotiated the purchase of the company (http://www.eegsa.com/historia.php, accessed Feb. 1, 2006).
178. There were no tramways, and while several towns were electrified, Halsey, *Investments in Latin America*, 424–25, identifies no foreign-owned electric utilities.
179. Approximately 81 percent of the total installed generating capacity in Honduras was controlled by two companies, Cuyamel Fruit Co. and New York and Honduras Rosario Mining Co., but the electric power was used predominantly for industrial purposes. A U.S. firm controlled the electric utility in San Pedro, Sula. *McGraw, 1929*, 740. Public Utilities Honduras Corp. purchased Planta Eléctrica of San Pedro in 1930. *Moody's Manual (Utilities)* 1930, 1809.
180. The state-owned La Empresa Nacional de Energie Eléctrica (ENEE) was created in 1957 (http://www.enee.hn/quienes.htm, accessed Feb. 1, 2006).
181. There were several electric lighting systems, but there appears to be no foreign ownership. Halsey, *Investments in Latin America*, 435.
182. The Managua utility was controlled by Public Utilities Consolidated Corp., a U.S. firm. *McGraw, 1929*, 752.
183. The state purchased Managua's utility from Central American Power in 1948. The industry was nationalized in 1979 (http://www.iie.org/programs/energy/downloads/Proceedings/PresentationsResources/CentralAmericanPerspectives/CAPerspectiveCalderaNicaragua.ppt, accessed Feb. 6, 2006).
184. The utility in Colón appeared to be domestic; that in Panama City was controlled by Panama-American Corp., a subsidiary of Electric Bond & Share of New York. The figure is based on installed capacity in these two cities. *McGraw, 1913*, 572. Halsey, *Investments in Latin America*, 440.
185. All utilities except for the canal were controlled by American & Foreign Power. *McGraw, 1929*, 752–53; *Moody's Manual (Utilities)* 1930, 1502.
186. *Moody's Manual (Utilities)* 1950.
187. Nationalization occurred in 1968 or shortly thereafter.
188. Garcke, 1914–1915, 1360, indicates British ownership.
189. Barbados Electric Light Corp. Ltd. remained British-owned. Garcke, 1914–1915, 1360.
190. http://www.blpc.com.bb/aboutus/history/history2.cfm (accessed July 28, 2006).
191. In the mid-1960s, control of the power company passed into Canadian hands. By 1998, when the company was reorganized, 63 percent of shares were held domestically, while the remaining 37 percent were owned by Canadian International Power Co. Ltd., whose parent company was Leucadia National Corporation, a U.S. firm (http://www.blpc.com.bb/aboutus/history/history5.cfm, accessed July 28, 2006).
192. Between 1890 and 1910, numerous utilities were organized by British (Havana), Canadian (Havana and Camagüey), German (Cárdenas), and American (Cienfuegos) investors. Jorge R. Piñón, "Cuba's Energy Challenge," Institute for Cuban and Cuban-American Studies, Occasional Paper (March 2004), 13. In 1913, utilities in Santiago and Sagua La Grande appeared to be

domestic, that in Camagüey Canadian- controlled, and in Havana American-controlled. *McGraw, 1913*, 571.

193. After excluding the 16 percent of total capacity devoted to United Fruit and various sugar operations, the American and Foreign Power Company controlled virtually all of the rest of installed capacity in Cuba. *McGraw, 1929*, 784–90.
194. *McGraw, 1929*, 784–90.
195. Nationalization occurred in 1960.
196. The utilities were controlled by Central Public Service (Islands Gas & Electric), a U.S. firm. *McGraw, 1929*, 791.
197. The government-owned Corporación Dominicana de Electricidad purchased the U.S.-controlled firm in 1955 (http://www.monografias.com/trabajos6/redoz/redoz.shtml, accessed Feb. 16, 2006).
198. The Canadian-owned Demerara Electric Company was formed in 1899. See Marchildon, "The Limitations," 394. There may have been some enclave type electrification outside Georgetown through the whole period of the table.
199. Garcke, 1928–1929, 1289, and *McGraw, 1929*, 771. The figure is an estimate based on population. New Amsterdam was served by a municipal firm.
200. This is an estimate based on earlier figures.
201. Demerara Electric was taken over by the state in the 1960s and the company renamed the Guyana Electricity Company Carl Greenidge, "The State and Public Enterprise in Guyana," in *Studies in Caribbean Public Enterprise, Vol. I: An Overview of Public Enterprise in the Commonwealth Caribbean* (Georgetown, Guyana: Institute of Development Studies, 1983), 196. Also see the current Guyana Power and Light Inc. web site at http://goliath.ecnext.com/coms2/product-compint-0000467281-page.html (accessed July 28, 2006).
202. The utilities in Cape Haïtienne and Port-au-Prince were owned by Central Public Service (Islands Gas & Electric), a U.S. company. *McGraw, 1929*, 790, and William J. Hausman and John L. Neufeld, "U.S. Foreign Direct Investment in Electric Utilities in the 1920s," in Mira Wilkins and Harm Schröter, eds., *The Free-Standing Company in the World Economy, 1830–1996* (Oxford: Oxford University Press, 1998), 369.
203. Électricité d'Haïti, a public enterprise, was formed in 1971. As of 1986, only 45 percent of Port-au-Prince and 3 percent of rural customers had electric service (http://www.photius.com/countries/haiti/economy/haiti_economy_energy.html, accessed Aug. 26, 2005).
204. West India Electric Company, successor to the Jamaica Light and Power Company, was financed and controlled with Canadian capital (B. F. Pearson group) (http://www.jpsco.com/site.nsf/web/history.htm, accessed Aug. 25, 2005).
205. Jamaica Public Service Ltd., successor to West India Electric Co., was Canadian-controlled. United Fruit operated a plant in Port Antonio. *McGraw, 1929*, 783.
206. This estimate is based on the 1928–1932 figure.
207. By 1974, the government had acquired all outstanding foreign-owned shares in the island's only electric company, Jamaica Public Service. Richard L. Bernal and Winsome J. Leslie, "The Experience of Privatization in the Caribbean," in Melissa H. Birch and Jerry Haar, eds., *The Impact of Privatization in the Americas* (Miami: North-South Center Press, 2000), 118.

208. Smaller islands – such as Antigua, British Virgin Islands, Grenada, Montserrat, St. Kitts and Nevis, and St. Lucia – had no electric utilities. Halsey, *Investments in Latin America*, 449–79.
209. In 1977, the electric companies in Dominica, Grenada, Montserrat, St. Lucia, and St. Vincent were owned jointly by the British Commonwealth Development Corporation and the island governments. Patrick Emmanuel, "Public Enterprises in the West Indian Associated States," in *Studies in Caribbean Public Enterprise, Vol. I: An Overview of Public Enterprise in the Commonwealth Caribbean* (Georgetown, Guyana: Institute of Development Studies, 1983), 49.
210. The B. F. Pearson group purchased the lighting and tramway operations in Trinidad in 1901, creating the Trinidad Electric Company (http://www.biographi.ca/EN/ShowBio.asp?BioId=41766 and http://www.ttec.co.tt/about/history/default.htm, accessed Aug. 25, 2005).
211. http://www.ttec.co.tt/about/history/default.htm (accessed Aug. 25, 2005).
212. The franchise of the Trinidad Electric Company was allowed to expire in 1933, and the Trinidad and Tobago Electricity Commission, a public enterprise, was created in 1945.
213. There were four large foreign-owned utilities (British Columbia Electric Railway, Canadian Niagara Power, Ontario Power, and Shawinigan Water and Power). This percentage is based on the total capacity in kilowatts of these firms (Garcke, 1914–1915) divided by an estimate of total industry capacity in 1913–1915. The estimate of total capacity is 90 percent of total capacity in 1917 (to account for growth in total capacity between 1913–1915 and 1917). Leo G. Denis, *Electric Generation and Distribution in Canada* (Ottawa: Commission of Conservation, 1918), 4 .
214. The figure is the share of electricity output in 1935 from U.S.-owned firms. Herbert Marshall, Frank Southard, and Kenneth Taylor, *Canadian-American Industry: A Study in International Investment* (New Haven: Yale University Press, 1936), 141. In 1928, the domestic Power Corp. of Canada acquired the British-owned British Columbia Electric Railway Co.
215. This 1948 figure is from A. E. Safarian, *Foreign Ownership of Canadian Industry*, 2nd ed. (Toronto: University of Toronto Press, 1973), 14. It represents "non-resident control of utilities." Safarian's figures include all utilities (except railroads) and thus are not confined to electric utilities.
216. Based on Nelles's educated guess using an extrapolation of Safarian's "foreign ownership" figure of 11 percent for 1962. Safarian, *Foreign Ownership*, 14.
217. An estimate of the proportion of installed capacity for 1913 of 91 percent was calculated from *The McGraw Electrical Directory* (New York: McGraw Publishing, 1913), 564–71. An estimate of the proportion of foreign capital invested in 1910–11 is from http://www.sme.org.mx/sme_oficial/historia/Empresas percent20Generacion.htm, accessed April 24, 2006.
218. This is an estimate based on capacity from *McGraw*, 1929, 740–52. Because some firms were difficult to categorize as domestic or foreign, the percentage could range from around 85 percent to 95 percent.
219. The figure for generating capacity in 1945 is from Miguel Wionczek, "Electric Power," in Raymond Vernon, ed., *Public Policy and Private Enterprise in Mexico* (Cambridge, MA: Harvard University Press, 1964), 75–6. Government-owned

firms controlled 5 percent of capacity and small, locally owned firms controlled 35 percent. According to Wionczek, by 1960, on the eve of nationalization, foreign-owned firms controlled 33 percent of capacity, government firms 40 percent, and others 27 percent. The Centro de Investigaciones Económicas y Políticas de Acción Comunitaria has the following percentages for capacity in 1960: government, 54 percent; foreign, 37 percent; other 9 percent. See http://www.sme.org.mx/sme_oficial/historia/Empresas percent20Generacion.htm (accessed April 24, 2006).

220. There were substantial portfolio investments in U.S. public utilities but only a small number of direct investments, and control of these investments could be ambiguous. Canadian investors controlled several electric tramways, and the Alabama Power Company probably was controlled from 1912 to 1924 by British investors through a Canadian-registered company. Mira Wilkins, *History of Foreign Investment in the United States to 1914* (Cambridge, MA: Harvard University Press, 1989), 165, 551–55; United States Federal Trade Commission, *Control of Power Companies*, United States Senate, 69th Congress, 2nd sess., Document 213 (Washington, DC: USGPO, 1927), 36–37, 144–49.
221. There remained substantial (and important) portfolio investments in U.S. public utilities, but no major U.S. public utility operating or holding company was "owned and controlled" from abroad. Mira Wilkins, *History of Foreign Investment in the United States, 1914 to 1945* (Cambridge, MA: Harvard University Press, 2004).
222. Mira Wilkins, "History of Foreign Investment in the United States, 1945 to the Present," book-length manuscript in process.
223. Wilkins, "History of Foreign Investment in the United States, 1945 to the Present."
224. The Palestine Electric Corp. was financed with British capital, although the concession had been granted to Pinhas Rutenberg, a Ukranian resident in British Mandate for Palestine. Garcke, 1928–1929, 1601.
225. Nationalization occurred in 1953. Yossi Borochov, "Israel's Electricity Market," *Policy Studies*, 38, (Israel: Institute for Advanced & Strategic Studies, 1999) (http://www.iasps.org/policystudies/ps38.htm, accessed Feb. 14, 2006).
226. Schröter educated guess.
227. Schröter educated guess.
228. The Turkish Electric Authority, a public enterprise, was founded in 1970 (http://www.bsrec.bg/turkey/turkey_existing.html, accessed Aug. 26, 2005).
229. Most of the utilities were public with some privately owned distribution companies (http://www.photius.com/countries/turkey/economy/turkey_economy_energy.html, accessed Aug. 26, 2005).

Notes

1 THE INVENTION AND SPREAD OF ELECTRIC UTILITIES, WITH A MEASURE OF THE EXTENT OF FOREIGN OWNERSHIP

1. Chronic reliability problems also can occur in highly developed countries when there are disasters or extreme weather conditions. On the persistent problems with electric power in New Orleans nearly a year after 2005's devastating Hurricane Katrina, see *New York Times*, July 22, 2006.
2. Estimates of the cost of the blackout in the United States ranged from $4 billion to $10 billion. In Canada, there was a net loss of nearly 19 million work hours and gross domestic product was depressed by nearly 1 percent in the month of the blackout. U.S.-Canada Power System Outage Task Force, *Final Report on the August 14, 2003 Blackout in the United States and Canada*, April 2004, 1 (https://reports.energy.gov/BlackoutFinal-Web.pdf, accessed March 22, 2006). The Italian blackout was caused by a single tree falling over a Swiss interconnection line, which highlights remaining instability in transmission systems. Jacques de Jong, *The "Regional Approach" in Establishing the Internal EU Electricity Market*, Clingendael International Energy Program Report, Jan. 2005, 41–44 (http://www.clingendael.nl/publications/2004/20041200_ciep_paper_dejong.pdf, accessed March 22, 2006).
3. U.S.-Canada Power System Outage Task Force, *Final Report*, 5. Many historians have noted the profound social and economic consequences of electricity. Two of the more eloquent descriptions of the impact of electricity can be found in David E. Nye, *Electrifying America: Social Meanings of a New Technology* (Cambridge, MA: MIT Press, 1990) and Vaclav Smil, *Creating the Twentieth Century: Technical Innovations of 1867–1914 and Their Lasting Impact* (Oxford: Oxford University Press, 2005), Ch. 2.
4. "Foreword," *Electricity for All* (Paris: Électricité de France, 2002), 2–3. The view that electricity "is a crucial input to the development process" was reiterated in United Nations, Department of Economic and Social Affairs, Division for Sustainable Development, *Multi-Dimensional Issues in International Electric Power Grid Connections* (New York: United Nations, 2005), 6.
5. "The Uses of Electricity," *New York Times*, Jan. 17, 1881.

6. Energy Information Administration, *International Energy Annual 2003* (updated June 24, 2005) (http://www.eia.doe.gov/pub/international/iealf/table63.xls, accessed Dec. 20, 2005).
7. Although the levels of electrification have increased in the past two decades, the relative positions of the countries probably have not changed much.
8. The e7, an organization of electric utilities comprised of nine large private and public companies from G8 countries, has pledged to find imaginative, cooperative ways to increase access by the poor to electricity. They emphasize that a major impediment to progress is lack of sufficient capital. As Paul Loeffelman, Director of Environmental Policy of the American Electric Power Company, stressed, "We have to challenge countries to establish financial frameworks that will raise the capital for projects to be undertaken." United Nations' Johannesburg Summit, 2002 (http://www.johannesburgsummit.org/html/whats_new/otherstories_e7.html, accessed March 23, 2006).
9. G. W. Stoer, *History of Light and Lighting: Oil Lamps, Gaslight, Carbon-Arc Lamps, Incandescent Lamps, Discharge Lamps, Electricity Generation* (Eindhoven, The Netherlands: Philips Lighting B.V., 1986), 4.
10. For a history of early illumination, see Harold F. Williamson and Arnold R. Daum, *The American Petroleum Industry: The Age of Illumination, 1859–1899* (Evanston: Northwestern University Press, 1959), Ch. 1–5.
11. Brian Bowers, *Lengthening the Day: A History of Lighting Technology* (Oxford: Oxford University Press, 1998), 15.
12. Ibid., 16, 20.
13. Roger Fouquet and Peter J. G. Pearson have examined the type and price of illumination in Great Britain from 1300 to 2000. They found that the cost of candlelight declined gradually over the course of the eighteenth century. Each innovation in illumination in the nineteenth century – gaslight, kerosene light, and electric light – began at a higher price than the forms of illumination with which it competed or was destined to replace, but then its price declined dramatically. In 2000, the price of a lumen-hour was .001 what it had been in 1850 and .0001 of what it had been in 1300. Roger Fouquet and Peter J. G. Pearson, "Seven Centuries of Energy Services: The Price and Use of Light in the United Kingdom (1300–2000)," *Energy Journal*, 27:1 (2006), 139–77.
14. Jules Dupuit was one of the first economists to analyze what we would now call public utilities. See "On the Measurement of the Utility of Public Works," trans. R. H. Barback, orig. pub. 1844, in Alan T. Peacock, et al., *International Economic Papers*, 2 (London: Macmillan, 1952).
15. Bowers, *Lengthening the Day*, 44–45. The first gas company in the United States was the Baltimore Gas-Light Company, formed in 1816. Williamson and Daum, *The American Petroleum Industry*, 39.
16. Stoer, *History of Light and Lighting*, 11–12.
17. Arc lights are especially intense and suitable only for outdoor use or use in large spaces. Incandescence refers to the property of materials that cause them to give off visible radiation when sufficiently heated. Until very recently, all artificial lighting was based on incandescence.
18. Department of Commerce and Labor, Bureau of the Census, *Central Electric Light and Power Stations, 1902* (Washington, DC: USGPO, 1905), 86.

19. Harold C. Passer, *The Electrical Manufacturers, 1875–1900* (Cambridge, MA: Harvard University Press, 1953), 14–21.
20. W. James King, *The Development of Electrical Technology in the 19th Century: 3. The Early Arc Light and Generator*, Contributions from the Museum of History and Technology, U.S. National Museum, Bulletin 228 (Washington, DC: Smithsonian Institution, 1962), 352–62.
21. Ibid., 378; R.H. Parsons, *The Early Days of the Power Station Industry* (Cambridge: Printed for Babcock and Wilcox Ltd. at Cambridge University Press, 1939), 1.
22. Faraday's 1831 generator produced direct current. The next year, Hippolyte Pixii, a scientific instrument maker working in Paris, demonstrated a more efficient generator that produced alternating current. King, *Development*, 345, 349.
23. King, *Development*, 385; K. G. Beauchamp, *Exhibiting Electricity* (Stevenage, England: Institution of Electrical Engineers, 1997), 127, 134.
24. King, *Development*, 392.
25. After his success, Jablochkoff was enticed by the Russian military to open a factory in St. Petersburg (around 1878). The business failed in 1887, but Jablochkoff had already returned to Paris in 1880. Jonathan Coopersmith, *The Electrification of Russia, 1880–1926* (Ithaca, NY: Cornell University Press, 1992), 33.
26. A drawback to this arrangement was that an interruption in the flow of current through any device would shut down the entire circuit, so some means had to be found to solve this problem. King, *Development*, 396; Thomas P. Hughes, *Networks of Power: Electrification in Western Society, 1880–1930* (Baltimore: Johns Hopkins University Press, 1983), 86–87.
27. King, *Development*, 404; see also Chapter 3 herein. The cost of lighting by the Jablochkoff system was estimated to be three to four times that of gas for equivalent illuminating power in 1879. *Scientific American*, March 15, 1879, 164. On the London installation (encompassing Billingsgate Market, the Thames Embankment, and Holborn Viaduct), see *Scientific American*, Jan. 25, 1879, 51.
28. Brian Bowers, *A History of Electric Light and Power*, History of Technology Series, 3 (Stevenage, Herts., England: Peregrinus in association with the Science Museum, 1982), 103.
29. Ibid., 128.
30. Stoer, *History of Light and Lighting*, 21.
31. Bowers, *A History of Electric Light*, 64–65; Hughes, *Networks of Power*, 21–22.
32. The literature on the development of Edison's electric light is massive. A detailed account can be found in Robert Freidel and Paul Israel, with Bernard S. Finn, *Edison's Electric Light: Biography of an Invention* (New Brunswick, NJ: Rutgers University Press, 1987). The Thomas A. Edison Papers at Rutgers University contain over five million pages of documents, many of which are available in various print and electronic forms. See http://edison.rutgers.edu/, accessed March 27, 2006.
33. Edison was a brilliant publicist as well as prolific inventor. A lengthy and very favorable article on his new system of lighting was published in the New York

Herald on December 21, 1879. The author, Edwin M. Fox, was a freelance correspondent for the *Herald* who had known Edison for a decade and who was one of the small number of original stockholders in the Edison Electric Light Co. Payson Jones, *A Power History of the Consolidated Edison System, 1878–1900* (New York: Consolidated Edison Co. of New York, 1940), 29. For a discussion of Swan versus Edison, see George Wise, "Swan's Way: A Study in Style," *IEEE Spectrum*, 19:4 (1982), 66–70.

34. On the culture of Edison's laboratory, see Andre Millard, *Edison and the Business of Invention* (Baltimore: Johns Hopkins University Press, 1990), Ch. 2.
35. Walter G. Vincenti, "The Technical Shaping of Technology: Real-World Constraints and Technical Logic in Edison's Electrical Lighting System," *Social Studies of Science*, 25:3 (1995): 553–74.
36. Israel, *Edison's Electric Light*, 66–67. In the process of inventing the incandescent lighting system, Edison and his competitors filed numerous patents in many countries, although Edison believed that "continued innovation [was] the best means of defeating competition." Paul Israel, *Edison: A Life of Invention* (New York: John Wiley, 1998), 209. Over the years, Edison (at times reluctantly) both sued and was sued for patent infringement. Rather than fight a patent suit against Joseph Swan in Britain, he merged his company with Swan's (see Ch. 3). His Canadian patent for the incandescent light was canceled in 1889, on the grounds that he had not produced electric lights within two years after the patent was granted. He lost an important case at the U.S. Patent Office in 1881, but eventually sued successfully in District Court, a decision that was appealed. The U.S. Circuit Court of Appeals ruled in favor of Edison in 1892, and the Supreme Court in 1895 agreed that a rival incandescent light patent was invalid, while noting that Edison's patent had expired because of a decision the previous year that found that the patents dated from the time of application rather than the time of award. By this time, Edison's interest in electric lighting had long since waned, and he had moved on to entirely new endeavors. General Electric and Westinghouse carried on the battle, but in 1896 they agreed to share patents, which ended most of the remaining litigation. For short summaries of the role of patents to Edison, see Israel, *Edison: A Life*, 109–10, 218, 317–20, and W. Bernard Carlson, *Innovation as a Social Process: Elihu Thomson and the Rise of General Electric, 1870–1900* (New York: Cambridge University Press, 1991), 280–83. For details on some of the specific cases, see *New York Times*, Feb. 6, 1881; May 3, 1885; July 19, 1888; July 11, 1889; July 15, 1891; Feb. 21, 1892; Oct. 5, 1892; Dec. 16, 1892; March 6, 1895; Nov. 12, 1895; March 3, 1896; April 5, 1912.
37. The Holborn Viaduct station in London, which was meant to be temporary, first operated on January 12, 1882, and closed in 1884 (see Chapter 3 herein). New York's Pearl Street station commenced operation on September 4, 1882. The station initially supplied electricity from a single "Jumbo" Edison dynamo, connected directly to a Porter-Allen engine, with steam furnished by Babcock & Wilcox boilers. Jones, *Power History*, 9, 156. For a full, illustrated description of the station, see *Scientific American*, Aug. 26, 1882, 127. Later in September, the first Edison hydroelectric station commenced operation in Appleton, Wisconsin. Smil, *Creating the Twentieth Century*, 55.

38. Edison also produced isolated plants. Until 1887, Edison isolated plants in operation accounted for more lights than did Edison central stations. Passer, *The Electrical Manufacturers*, 118.
39. U.S. Department of Commerce and Labor, *Central Electric Light and Power Stations*, 1902, 3.
40. D. Heineman, "Electricity in the Region of London," *The Transactions of the First World Power Conference*, vol. 4 (London: Percy Lund, Humphries and Co., 1924), 1289. Heineman was highly critical of the system of small plants in London versus the larger operations found in many European and American cities. He especially complimented the systems in Paris, Chicago, and Buenos Aires (1291–98).
41. For a discussion of load curves and the peak load problem, see Joel D. Justin and William G. Mervine, *Power Supply Economics* (New York: John Wiley & Sons, 1934), Ch. 2, 4.
42. The authors of a paper on Germany given at the Third World Power Conference (1936) noted that almost all of Germany was by that time connected either directly or indirectly with the grid and that the "cooperation of steam and hydro plants permits the transportation of base loads from the increasingly larger central plants while the local stations cover the peak loads." R. T. Beall, "Significant Trends in the Development and Utilization of Power Resources," *Transactions, Third World Power Conference*, vol. 9 (Washington, DC: USGPO, 1938), 249.
43. Another method of conversion used batteries, which were charged in series at high voltage and then reconnected to the load in parallel, thus resulting in a lower voltage. Bowers, *A History of Electric Light*, 133–43; Hughes, *Networks of Power*, 85.
44. Hughes, *Networks of Power*, 86–91.
45. By 1892, Ganz & Co. (Ganz Electric Co. Ltd.) had installed alternating-current systems in Tivoli, Rome, Venice, and Leghorn (Livorno), Italy; Innsbruck, Austria; Marienbad and Karlsbad (Karlovy Vary), now Czech Republic; and Valréas and Dieu-le-Fit, France. The firm also was a pioneer in railway electrification in Europe. Killingworth Hedges, *Continental Electric Light Central Stations* (London: E. & F. N. Spon, 1892), v; Thomas Barcsay, "Banking in Hungarian Economic Development, 1867–1919, *Business and Economic History*, 20 (1991), 222. The firm exists today as Ganz Transelektro Electric Co. Ltd.
46. Hughes, *Networks of Power*, 98–105. Samuel Insull, who was Edison's secretary during the developmental phase of his system, praised William Stanley as being well ahead of his colleagues (including Edison) when it came to conceptualizing the large electric utility system. "At the time that Mr. Edison was engaged in installing his early central-station plants we had very little idea, and scientists and engineers the world over had very little idea, of systems of distribution that would even cover the ordinary limits of the metropolitan centers of population. If we could install a system that would prove a financial success over an area of a mile square, we had about reached the limit; and when inventors and engineers like Mr. Stanley had the vision to see the necessity of massing the production, of longer distances of transmission and distribution, we used to throw cold water on

their work." Samuel Insull, "Developments in Electric Utility Operating," in William Keily, ed., *Public Utilities in Modern Life: Selected Speeches (1914–1923) by Samuel Insull* (Chicago: Privately printed, 1924), 109.

47. J.F. Wilson, *Ferranti and the British Electrical Industry, 1864–1930* (Manchester, England: Manchester University Press, 1988), Ch. 2. By 1892, Ferranti also had installed a system in Barcelona, as well as systems for several French municipalities, including those in Paris, Nancy, Le Havre, Melun, Troyes, Dijon, Lens, and St. Céré. Hedges, *Continental Electric Light Central Stations,* 60. On Thomson-Houston, see Carlson, *Innovation as a Social Process*, 215, 259–68.
48. In the United States, alternating-current generating capacity was 50 percent of the total by 1898 and 98 percent by 1922. William J. Hausman and John L. Neufeld, "Battle of the Systems Revisited: The Role of Copper," *IEEE Technology and Society Magazine*, 11 (Fall 1992), 18–25. In some places, direct current persisted for quite a long time. In 1909, 67 percent of German central stations had direct current, and it was not until 1913 that alternating-current stations outnumbered direct-current stations. In 1908, 68 percent of central stations in Russia had direct current. Jonathan Coopersmith, "When Worlds Collide: Government and Electrification, 1892–1939," *Business and Economic History On-Line*, 1 (2003), 9 (http://www.thebhc.org/publications/BEHonline/2003/Coopersmith.pdf, accessed March 29, 2006). For the processes by which three German cities selected alternating current, direct current, or mixed systems, see Edmund N. Todd, "A Tale of Three Cities: Electrification and the Structure of Choice in the Ruhr, 1886–1900," *Social Studies of Science*, 17 (1987), 387–412.
49. Paul A. David and Julie Ann Bunn, "The Economics of Gateway Technologies and Network Evolution: Lessons from Electricity Supply History," *Information Economics and Policy*, 3 (1988), 165–202; Paul David, "The Hero and the Herd in Technological History: Reflections on Thomas Edison and the Battle of the Systems," in Patrice Higonnet, David S. Landes, and Henry Rosovsky, eds., *Favorites of Fortune: Technology, Growth, and Economic Development Since the Industrial Revolution* (Cambridge, MA: Harvard University Press, 1991), 72–119.
50. Direct current had its advocates and continued to be used well into the twentieth century. J.S. Highfield and W.E. Highfield, "High Voltage Direct Current Generation and Distribution of Electrical Energy," *Transactions of the First World Power Conference*, vol. 3 (London: Percy Lund, Humphries and Co., 1924), 1225–63. Since 1954, direct current also has been used commercially for long-distance, very high voltage transmission or transmission under water. Roberto Rudervall, J.P. Charpentier, and Raghuveer Sharma, "High Voltage Direct Current (HVDC) Transmission Systems," World Bank, Technology Review Paper, n.d.
51. Thomas Commerford Martin, an expert special agent of the U.S. Bureau of the Census, wrote as follows in a chapter on the history and development of electric traction: "It is an interesting problem to explain why the value of electricity as a motive power was so slowly recognized. The earliest efforts to apply the electric motor to locomotion purposes antedated the beginning of cable and

synchronized with the earliest attempts to utilize steampower, but it was not until fifty years after both of these methods of traction had been put into use that the electric street car or the electric locomotive could be pronounced a definite success." *Street and Electric Railways, 1902*, 160.

52. Hughes, *Networks of Power*, 181; Passer, *The Electrical Manufacturers*, 223–24. The Electrical Power and Supply Storage Co. of Millwall, England, demonstrated a tram powered by batteries ("accumulators") on March 10, 1883, but nothing came of this. Clement E. Stretton, *A Few Remarks on Electric Lighting* (London: Simpkin, Marshall & Co., 1883), appendix.
53. Passer, *The Electrical Manufacturers*, 217.
54. Beauchamp, *Exhibiting Electricity*, 138.
55. John P. McKay, *Tramways and Trolleys: The Rise of Urban Mass Transit in Europe* (Princeton, NJ: Princeton University Press, 1976), 38; Sigfrid von Weiher and Herbert Goetzeler, *The Siemens Company – Its Historical Role in the Progress of Electrical Engineering, 1847–1980*, 2nd ed. (Berlin and Munich: Siemens AG, 1984), 39–41; Wilfried Feldenkirchen, *Werner von Siemens: Inventor and International Entrepreneur* (Columbus: Ohio State University Press, 1994), 110–15.
56. The Paris Exhibition, which was conceived by the French Minister for Posts and Telegraphs, A. Cochery, was comprised of 1,781 exhibits from sixteen countries. In addition to the experimental transportation exhibit, every lighting system in existence was on display. A. Heerding, *The History of N. V. Philips' Gloeilampenfabrieken*, vol. 1, trans. Derek S. Jordan (Cambridge: Cambridge University Press, 1985), 86–104.
57. Siemens & Halske did not seriously enter the electric tramway industry until 1889, by which time the technology had been developed more fully. Feldenkirchen, *Werner von Siemens*, 114.
58. McKay, *Tramways*, 39–40.
59. Ibid., 40.
60. *Street and Electric Railways, 1902*, 161–62.
61. Passer, *The Electrical Manufacturers*, 243–48. William D. Middleton, *Metropolitan Railways: Rapid Transit in America* (Bloomington: Indiana University Press, 2003). Sprague's very successful company was merged into the newly formed Edison General Electric Co. in 1889. For Sprague's interpretation of the development of the electric railway, see Frank J. Sprague, "Electric Railway Not Creation of One Man," *New York Times*, Sept. 23, 1926. The "one man" was Edison, whom Sprague thought received too much credit in this particular field.
62. *Street and Electric Railways, 1902*, 6, 149–53.
63. Michael Ball and David Sunderland, *An Economic History of London, 1800–1914* (London: Routledge, 2001), 245) (http://www.tfl.gov.uk/tube/company/history/early-years.asp, accessed Sept. 15, 2006).
64. For a description of a 60 km (37 mi.) line from Milan to the area around Lake Como in Italy, constructed by Ganz & Co., see *Scientific American*, June 29, 1901, 408.
65. George W. Hilton and John F. Due, *The Electric Interurban Railways in America* (Stanford, CA: Stanford University Press, 1960), Ch. 1; see also Pierre

Lanthier, "Les Constructions Électriques en France: le Case de Six Groupes Industriels Internationaux de 1880 à 1940," Ph.D. diss., 3 vol. (Paris: University of Paris X (Nanterre), 1988).

66. Many electric utilities introduced appliance sales rooms to offer products to customers of the utilities during the teens and twenties.
67. In the United States, for example, in 1902, 80 percent of urban areas with a population of 2,500 or more had service; however, only 20 percent of towns with a population of less than 2,500 had service. By 1920, just under half of nonfarm households had electric service. J. F. Fogarty, "Organization of Private Electric and Gas Utilities," *Transactions, Third World Power Conference*, vol. 5 (Washington, DC: USGPO, 1938), 265; and U.S. Department of Commerce, Bureau of the Census, *Historical Statistics of the United States, Colonial Times to 1970*, part 2 (Washington, DC: USGPO, 1975), 827.
68. In Italy, for example, in 1898 there were 2,264 electric generating plants, all but 392 of which belonged to manufacturing establishments. The plants supplying the public, however, tended to be larger, and they comprised about 65 percent of the aggregate total kilowatt capacity. Tito Gonzales, Waldemar Mungioli, and Giorgio Valerio, "Organization of Private Electric and Gas Utilities," *Transactions, Third World Power Conference*, vol. 5 (Washington, DC: USGPO, 1938), 187–88.
69. Westinghouse installed the first steam turbine, which replaced a reciprocating engine, in its own plant in Wilmerding, PA, in 1898. The first use of a steam turbine in an electric central station occurred in 1901. Between 1901 and 1935, steam turbine capacity increased from 1,500 kW to over 200,000 kW. Robert Healy, "Organization of Private Electric and Gas Utilities," *Transactions, Third World Power Conference*, vol. 5 (Washington, DC: USGPO, 1938), 287.
70. In Sweden, for example, the first major transmission of electricity from a hydroelectric site was in 1893, from Lake Hellsjön to the Grängesberg ore fields, using a 9,500 volt line. In 1897, 95 percent of hydropower was produced by industrial establishments, and only 5 percent came from electric power stations. By contrast, in 1923 83 percent of hydropower was generated by central electric power stations. F. V. Hansen, "The Power Resources of Sweden," *Transactions of the First World Power Conference*, vol. 1 (London: Percy Lund, Humphries and Co., 1924), 1322–23.
71. Oskar von Miller and C. E. L. Brown – who later was one of the founders of Brown, Boveri – are credited with much of the technical expertise for the project. Hughes, *Networks of Power*, 133–35. See also ZEAG, *Moderne Energie für eine Neue Zeit. Die Drehstromübertragung Lauffen a.N. – Frankfurt a.M. 1891* (Heilbronn: ZEAG, 1991).
72. S. Dana Greene, "Distribution of the Electrical Energy from Niagara Falls," *Cassier's Magazine*, 8 (1895), 352.
73. The speed with which electrification spread should not be exaggerated; on the progress made in thirty-two countries around the world by 1933, see Figure 1.6. The point that electrification spread relatively slowly is also made by Paul David, "The Dynamo and the Computer: An Historical Perspective on the Modern Productivity Paradox," *American Economic Review*, 80 (May 1990), 355–61.

74. As Hunter and Bryant note, "In the evolution of central-station finances, three factors were largely controlling: the heavy investment in fixed capital, the wide variations, daily and seasonal, in demand for energy, and the peculiar necessity for simultaneous production and consumption of this commodity." Louis C. Hunter and Lynwood Bryant, *A History of Industrial Power in the United States, 1780–1930*, vol. 3, *The Transmission of Power* (Cambridge, MA: MIT Press, 1991), 275.
75. The load factor is the ratio of the average rate of production to the maximum rate for a brief period of time (e.g., fifteen minutes). The higher the load factor, the more economically the plant is operating.
76. See Sidney A. Mitchell, *S. Z. Mitchell and the Electrical Industry* (New York: Farrar, Straus & Cudahy, 1960), 79–80, for a discussion of how holding companies were expected to work.
77. William H. England, "Organization of Private Electric and Gas Utilities," *Transactions, Third World Power Conference*, vol. 9 (Washington, DC: USGPO, 1938), 329.
78. On the battle in the United States, see William J. Hausman and John L. Neufeld, "Public Versus Private Electric Utilities in the United States: A Century of Debate over Comparative Economic Efficiency," *Annals of Public and Cooperative Economics*, 65:4 (1994), 599–622.
79. On these provisions in some countries, see Dr. E. Haidegger, "Organization, Financing, and Operation of Publicly Owned Electric and Gas Utilities," *Transactions, Third World Power Conference*, vol. 6 (Washington, DC: USGPO, 1938), 117, 120; and L.T. Fournier and J. Butler Walsh, "Public Regulation of Private Electric and Gas Utilities," *Transactions, Third World Power Conference*, vol. 9 (Washington, DC: USGPO, 1938), 344–45.
80. A whole section of the Third World Power Conference was devoted to government-owned electric and gas utilities. *Transactions, Third World Power Conference*, vol. 6 (Washington, DC: USGPO, 1938), 3–305.
81. Georg Klingenberg, a German electrical engineer and eventually a director of Allgemeine Elektrizitäts Gesellschaft (AEG), first proposed in 1916 that the German state create a national network in a paper titled "The Superpower Supply in Cooperation with the State." "Klingenberg's investigations resulted in the conclusion that electricity supply on a large scale could not be attained with the existing system of individual plants, that only the State has sufficient power to overcome the legal difficulties, and that therefore the State was bound to intervene." The operators of municipal stations reportedly objected to the plan. In the 1920s, however, the plan became a model for rationalizing the German electrical network. Prof. Dr. W. Petersen and Prof. R. Tröger, "National and Regional Planning of German Electricity Supply," *Transactions, Third World Power Conference*, vol. 6 (Washington, DC: USGPO, 1938), 338–39. In the United States, Samuel Insull, in commenting on a proposal during World War I by the Fuel Administrator in Washington to "look for opportunities to establish temporary linking up at this time of all the great power-producing companies of a given territory," noted: "People are beginning to learn, as a matter of governmental necessity, that true economy can be reached by massing the production and distribution of energy. That is one of the lessons this war is going

to teach the country with relation to our business." Insull, of course, in the postwar period constructed one of the largest privately owned electric utility systems in the world. Samuel Insull, "The Electrical Industry and the War," in William Keily, ed., *Public Utilities in Modern Life: Selected Speeches (1914–1923) by Samuel Insull* (Chicago: Privately printed, 1924), 150–51.

82. See, for example, United Nations Department of Economic and Social Affairs, Statistics Division, *Energy Balances and Electricity Profiles, 2000*, (New York: United Nations, 2004), and United Nations Department of Economic and Social Affairs, Statistics Division, *Energy Statistics Yearbook, 2001*, (New York: United Nations, 2004).

83. Kilowatts (kW) and kilowatt-hours (kWh), respectively, are the two most common measures of the capacity of an electrical system and the amount of energy produced by that system. Several sources have sought to gather, synthesize, and present data on electric utilities across nations and over time. The three volumes of historical statistics compiled and edited by Brian Mitchell contain annual statistics of output (kilowatt-hours produced) for many nations. B. R. Mitchell, ed., *International Historical Statistics: Africa, Asia & Oceana, 1750–1993*, 3rd. ed. (New York: Stockton Press, 1998), Table D24, 490–503; B. R. Mitchell, ed., *International Historical Statistics: The Americas, 1750–1993*, 4th. ed. (New York: Stockton Press, 1998), Table D22, 404–12; B. R. Mitchell, ed., *International Historical Statistics: Europe, 1750–1993*, 4th ed. (New York: Stockton Press, 1998), Table D27, 562–67. Bouda Etemad and Jean Luciani, *World Energy Production 1800–1985* (Geneva: Librarie Droz, 1991), present annual electricity output in kilowatt-hours for numerous countries from 1900 (or when data begin) to 1985. They rely heavily on the statistics in the Mitchell volumes, but they add the important figures on hydroelectric output. The sources for the data in the Mitchell and the Etemad and Luciani volumes are principally international statistical yearbooks, supplemented with national statistical yearbooks and specialist publications, especially for the early years. Very useful data were collected for select countries by the Union Internationale des Producteurs et Distributeurs d'Énergie Électrique, Paris, which compiled returns from questionnaires. These have been published in Frederick Brown, ed., *Statistical Year-Book of the World Power Conference*, No. 1, 1933 and 1934 (London: World Power Conference, 1936), and subsequent volumes.

84. These varied from country to country and could be fairly substantial, depending on circumstances such as the length of transmission lines and the level of development. Line losses in 1933 as a proportion of production for countries contained in the *Statistical Year-Book* ranged from 9 to 10 percent in The Netherlands, Finland, and Czechoslovakia to 20 to 25 percent in Canada, New Zealand, France, Argentina, Ireland, and China. Brown, *Statistical Year-Book*, 103. In 1990, line losses were less than 10 percent in most high-income countries and up to 40 to 50 percent in some low-income countries. *World Development Report 1994* (Oxford: Oxford University Press for the World Bank, 1994), 224–25.

85. The data actually are millions of kilowatt-hours per thousand persons, which we call per capita production. Production figures are from Etemad and Luciani,

World Energy Production, 91–165. Population figures are from Mitchell, *International Historical Statistics: Africa, Asia & Oceana,* Table A5, 47–65; Mitchell, *International Historical Statistics: The Americas,* Table A5, 60–64; Mitchell, *International Historical Statistics: Europe,* Table A5, 81–90.

86. The growth rates were estimated using ordinary least-squares regressions.
87. This is not unexpected. It is easier to achieve higher rates of growth from a small base, which would be the case early in the process of electrification.
88. On the invention and adoption of various electrical devices, see Smil, *Creating the Twentieth Century*, 91–94; and Nye, *Electrifying America*, Ch. 6. For a discussion of electricial devices being used in many North and South American countries in 1927, see U.S. Department of Commerce, Bureau of Foreign and Domestic Commerce, *Central Light and Power Plants in the Western Hemisphere, with Notes on the Market for Electrical Goods*, Trade Information Bulletin No. 469, April 1927. A series of these bulletins published in the 1920s and 1930s discussed electrical appliances in various countries of the world.
89. See, for example, Sam H. Schurr, Calvin C. Burwell, Warren D. Devine, Jr., and Sidney Sonenblum, *Electricity in the American Economy: Agent of Technical Progress* (New York: Greenwood Press, 1990). Robert Whaples has shown that electrification of the factory floor in the United States was a significant factor in the reduction of the manufacturing work day in the early twentieth century. Robert Whaples, "Winning the Eight-Hour Day, 1909–1919," *Journal of Economic History*, 50 (June 1990), 393–406. In a study of factory electrification in the 1920s and 1930s, Ristuccia and Solomou found that electricity diffusion in the manufacturing sectors of the United States, U.K., and Japan resulted in significant positive effects on the growth rate of labor productivity. The authors conclude that their paper "confirms that electricity diffusion can persuasively explain the generalized growth in labour productivity in manufacturing in the industrialized world in the 1920s and 1930s." Christiano Andrea Ristuccia and Solomos Solomou, "Electricity Diffusion and Trend Acceleration in Inter-War Manufacturing Productivity," Feb. 2002, University of Cambridge Working Paper No. 0202, available at SSRN (http://ssrn.com/abstract=303799, accessed March 28, 2006). On the importance of the induction motor, see Smil, *Creating the Twentieth Century*, 79–83.
90. On the U.S. proposals, which never were implemented, see Leonard DeGraaf, "Corporate Liberalism and Electric System Planning in the 1920s," *Business History Review*, 64 (Spring 1990), 1–31. On the creation of the British grid, see Leslie Hannah, *Electricity Before Nationalisation* (Baltimore: Johns Hopkins University Press, 1979).
91. Brown, *Statistical Year-Book*, 1936
92. Note that this is not the same as the proportion of the population actually using electricity, because those in areas where electricity was available might not have been using it. Another source has Switzerland with the highest proportion (99 percent) of electrified homes in 1935. Some of the states in the northeastern United States and California had coverage that was slightly less than this (90–96 percent), while countries such as France, Norway, Sweden, Belgium, Germany, and the United States overall had middling percentages (60–70 percent). Italy and Great Britain were just over 50 percent. Floyd L. Carlisle,

"National Power and Resources Policy," *Transactions, Third World Power Conference*, vol. 9 (Washington, DC: USGPO, 1938), 174.

93. For countries included in the statistical yearbook of the World Power Conference, electricity for traction purposes ranged from negligible to around one-third of usage. Public lighting and indoor usage ranged from under 10 percent to around 75 percent. The use of electricity in agriculture was notable for its complete absence in most countries. Brown, *Statistical Year-Book*, 103–04.
94. Brown, *Statistical Year-Book*, 102.
95. Lewis L. Lorwin, economic advisor to the International Labor Office, Geneva, commented, "While it is true that for the time being power is not to any large extent, or in many places, an export product, it has immense significance in the field of international finance and investment, in its capacity for bringing about industrial and trade expansion, in the competitive power which it gives to newly industrialized countries, and in the dislocations of their industrial economy which such competition is producing in the older countries." "Discussion," *Transactions, Third World Power Conference*, vol. 9 (Washington, DC: USGPO, 1938), 226.
96. There are some discrepancies in the data. The amount reported as imported into the United States was only 64 percent of the amount reported as exported by Canada.
97. This remains the case today. In 2001, total world exports of electricity were only 3 percent of production. Exports were 7.4 percent of production in Europe, where the European Union in 2002 established a 10 percent interconnection target. The largest European exporter by volume was France (13 percent of production), and the largest importer by volume was Italy (17 percent of production). Moderately large net exporters, by percent of production, included Sweden, Ukraine, Russia, Poland, Czech Republic, and Lithuania. Moderately large net importers, by percent of production, included Belgium, Finland, Belarus, The Netherlands, Spain, and Hungary. Countries that were roughly balanced included Austria, Portugal, and Germany. United Nations, *Energy Statistics Yearbook, 2001*, 478–94.

2 MULTINATIONAL ENTERPRISE AND INTERNATIONAL FINANCE

1. Thomas Hughes, "From Firm to Networked Systems," *Business History Review*, 79 (Autumn 2005), 587–593, and his *Networks of Power: Electrification in Western Society, 1880–1930* (Baltimore: Johns Hopkins University Press, 1983).
2. Colonies were often hosts (and only rarely homes) to multinational enterprise. It is necessary to specify that we include them, for at times in the literature they are excluded. We define the term "foreign" with a broad brush. A British (or a German) nonresident investment in colonial India or a French (or a German) nonresident investment in colonial Algeria will be considered by us to be "foreign." By nonresident, we mean that there is a home office abroad.
3. Our definition is conventional. For a similar definition, see Mira Wilkins, "What Is International Business?" in Peter J. Buckley, ed., *What Is International*

Business? (London: Palgrave, 2005), 133. In our definition, we have been influenced by Oliver Williamson, who wrote, "[R]ather than characterize the firm as a production function, transaction cost economics maintains that the firm is (for many purposes at least) more usefully regarded as a governance structure." Oliver E. Williamson, *Economic Institutions of Capitalism* (New York: Free Press, 1985), 13. Alfred Chandler used the term "governance structure" in the same manner as Williamson in Alfred D. Chandler, Jr., "A Framework for Analyzing the Modern Multinational Enterprise and Its Competitive Advantage," *Business and Economic History,* 2nd ser., 16 (1987), 3–17, and subsequently in Alfred D. Chandler, Jr., *Scale and Scope* (Cambridge, MA: Harvard University Press, 1990), 14. When the authors of the present book write of the multinational enterprise as an administered (managed) unit, we are talking about a "governance structure" as the phrase was used by Williamson and Chandler.

4. We used the phrase "multinational enterprise and financial institutions" with great discomfort, falsely implying a necessary separation. Financial institutions could be multinational enterprises, extending themselves as firms over borders. See discussion below.
5. We are saying the same thing here about electric utilities as others have said more generally in a purely domestic context: "The financial market has been, is, and was willing and able to supply monies to established firms with good credit history and the potential for growth." Taking risks with new firms was more difficult. See Sue Bowen, "Corporate Finance," in Joel Mokyr, ed., *Oxford Encyclopedia of Economic History,* 5 vol. (Oxford: Oxford University Press, 2003), II, 5.
6. See Mira Wilkins, *The History of Foreign Investment in the United States, 1914–1945* (Cambridge, MA: Harvard University Press, 2004), 616–17, 626–27, for a concise discussion of the formidable problems of definitions of foreign portfolio and foreign direct investments and on statistical measures over time. (This book is henceforth cited as Wilkins, *History ... 1914–1945*.) See also the discussion in Mira Wilkins, "Conduits for Long-Term Foreign Investment in the Gold Standard Era," in Marc Flandreau, Carl-Ludwig Holtfrerich, and Harold James, *International Financial History in the Twentieth Century: System and Anarchy* (Cambridge: Cambridge University Press, 2003), 51–76.
7. Definitions of "foreign portfolio investment" vary widely. A recent example of the separation in thinking about foreign portfolio and foreign direct investment is Daniel Verdier, *Moving Money: Banking and Finance in the Industrial World* (Cambridge: Cambridge University Press, 2002). Examples of the definitional problems are: Sometimes foreign portfolio investment is defined as comprising everything in a country's international position that is not foreign direct investment (this is the usage, for example, in U.S. Congressional Budget Office, "Why Does U.S. Investment Abroad Earn Higher Returns than Foreign Investment in the United States?" Economic and Budget Issue Brief, Nov. 30, 2005, a study that sought to deal with both foreign portfolio and foreign direct investments). Sometimes, foreign portfolio investments include short-term foreign trade financing. Some definitions of "portfolio investment" are narrow, involving only equity holdings that are not direct investments and excluding debt. Discussions of international finance include debt, whether it be bank loans

or bonds. All foreign debt is not classified as portfolio investment. Today, the U.S. Bureau of Economic Analysis includes some foreign debt as foreign direct investment: if a foreign direct investment is established (by 10 percent or more of equity share in a foreign affiliate), then the net international debt financing of the foreign affiliate is included as foreign direct investment. In recent International Monetary Fund and Federal Reserve publications, there are discussions of foreign investments in "stock, bonds, and banking," with no differentiation at all between what is foreign direct investment and foreign portfolio investment; also there is a confusion in this literature between trade in foreign assets and investment.

8. There are some students of foreign direct investment who look at the macroeconomic picture, paying little attention to the individual players.
9. The writings on multinational enterprise are vast. For a start, see Geoffrey Jones, *Multinationals and Global Capitalism* (Oxford: Oxford University Press, 2005); Alan M. Rugman and Thomas L. Brewer, eds., *The Oxford Handbook of International Business* (Oxford: Oxford University Press, 2001); and John H. Dunning, *Theories and Paradigms of International Business Activities: The Selected Essays of John H. Dunning,* vol. 1 (Cheltenham, England: Edward Elgar, 2002). John H. Dunning's important *Multinational Enterprises and the Global Economy* (Wokingham, England: Addison-Wesley, 1993) is being revised and is scheduled for publication in late 2008, by Edward Elgar. Although Giorgio Barba Navaretti and Anthony J. Venable, *Multinational Firms in the World Economy* (Princeton, NJ: Princeton University Press, 2004), 11, recognizes that almost 60 percent of world foreign direct investment stock is in services, the book reflects the lingering *theoretical* bias toward manufacturing. In this regard, see also Richard E. Caves, *Multinational Enterprise and Economic Analysis*, 3rd ed. (Cambridge: Cambridge University Press, 2007), 5n; James R. Markusen, "International Trade Theory and International Business," in Alan M. Rugman and Thomas L. Brewer, eds., *Oxford Handbook of International Business*, 87; and many of the articles published in recent years in the *Journal of International Economics*. Yet Markusen's knowledge capital model can be more broadly applied, and as Peter Gray pointed out (conversation with Mira Wilkins, April 18, 2006), trade theorists now recognize that multinational enterprises in services export intangibles, including know-how and accumulated experience. For a broad coverage of the history of multinational enterprise, see Mira Wilkins, *The Emergence of Multinational Enterprise: American Business Abroad from the Colonial Era to 1914* (Cambridge: MA: Harvard University Press, 1970); Mira Wilkins, *The Maturing of Multinational Enterprise: American Business Abroad from 1914 to 1970* (Cambridge, MA: Harvard University Press, 1974); Mira Wilkins, *The History of Foreign Investment in the United States to 1914* (Cambridge, MA: Harvard University Press, 1989) (henceforth cited as Wilkins, *History ... to 1914*); and Wilkins, *History ... 1914–1945*. Geoffrey Jones has made a substantial contribution to bringing service sector multinationals into prominence. See his edited book, *Banks as Multinationals* (London: Routledge, 1990), his *British Multinational Banking 1830–1990* (Oxford: Oxford University Press, 1993), and his *Merchants to Multinationals* (Oxford: Oxford University Press, 2000). Aside from the authors cited above, works by Raymond Vernon,

Jean-François Hennart, Mark Casson, Peter Buckley, Robert Lipsey, Kenneth Froot and Jeremy Stein, and Benjamin Gomes-Casseres have been among the many influential studies on multinational enterprise that have enriched our analysis. Today, for statistical purposes, an equity stake of at least 10 percent defines a foreign direct investment (this is the International Monetary Fund criterion); historically, as statistical measures were introduced, different thresholds were used (some countries still retain different statistical criteria); indeed, as recently as 1997, for example, the United Kingdom defined a foreign direct investment as a firm's having an equity stake of 20 percent or more in the affiliate. See *World Investment Report 2006*, 293–98. For many years, a number of countries used a 25 percent cutoff. While we know and have always kept in mind the available statistical data, we have not set a percentage-of-equity statistical measure in defining foreign "ownership and control," trying instead to understand the behavior of multinational enterprise.

10. This is important. In one of our preliminary papers, it was suggested (in keeping with some of the established literature) that Canada was remarkable in having both inward and outward investments; we have found that this was true of all advanced nations – whether we are discussing the United Kingdom, the United States, or France, for example. There were, however, varying foreign direct/foreign portfolio investment ratios, as well as varying inward and outward investment ratios, but in all advanced nations we found both foreign direct and foreign portfolio cross-investments to be historically commonplace. See Mira Wilkins, "Dutch Multinational Enterprises in the United States: A Historical Summary," *Business History Review*, 79 (Summer 2005), 263–67, for this insight in an entirely different context. The electricity supply industry was not atypical.
11. Geoffrey Jones, *The Evolution of International Business* (London: Routledge, 1996), 33 (on the "grey world"). The gray areas are also particularly in evidence in foreign investments in railroads, as we note below.
12. For the genesis of some of the corporate governance literature in finance, see, for example, Oliver Hart, "Corporate Governance: Some Theory and Implications," *Economic Journal*, 105 (1995), 678–98; Andrei Schleifer and Robert W. Vishny, "A Survey of Corporate Governance," *Journal of Finance*, 52:2 (1997), 737–83. The relationship between corporate governance and the corporate finance literature is apparent in the entry on "Corporate Finance" in Mokyr's *Oxford Encyclopedia of Economic History* (2000), II, 5–8, where practically all of Sue Bowen's bibliography is on corporate governance; the encyclopedia does not have a separate entry for corporate governance. For an introduction to the corporate governance literature, see Randall K. Morck, ed., *A History of Corporate Governance Around the World: Family Business Groups to Professional Managers* (Chicago: University of Chicago Press, 2005), beginning with Randall K. Morck and Lloyd Steier, "The Global History of Corporate Governance – An Introduction," in ibid., 1–64. An earlier version of the latter (cited below) appeared as NBER Working Paper 11062, Jan. 2005. See also Mary A. O'Sullivan, *Contests for Corporate Control: Corporate Governance and Economic Performance in the United States and Germany* (Oxford: Oxford University Press, 2000), and Randall Morck, Daniel Wolfenzon, and Bernard

Yeung, "Corporate Governance, Economic Entrenchment and Growth," *Journal of Economic Literature*, 43 (Sept. 2005), 657–722. Whereas Williamson and Chandler used the phrase "governance structure" to refer to the management of firms and were not concerned with corporate finance or the ownership of the firm (see Chap. 2, note 3 above), this literature considers the relationships between the ownership of the firm and its governance. Its focus is on differences between nations: shareholder capitalism, family capitalism, bank capitalism, and state capitalism. The business groups we will be discussing are far more intricate than those presented in this literature, because ours crisscross borders.

13. Morck and Steier, "Global History of Corporate Governance," NBER Working Paper 11062, 1.
14. In one of the preliminary papers prepared in connection with this project, there were important explorations of German versus Canadian style. See Peter Hertner and H. V. Nelles, "Contrasting Styles of Foreign Investment: A Comparison of the Entrepreneurship, Technology, and Finance of German and Canadian Enterprises in Barcelona Electrification," *Revue Économique*, 58:1 (Jan. 2007), 191–214.
15. Peter A. Hall and David Soskice, eds., *Varieties of Capitalism* (Oxford: Oxford University Press, 2001), articulates this view.
16. One reader of our manuscript asked why, in a book on global business, we were "wary of references" to national style, to national comparisons. What is basic and original about our approach is not merely the comparisons of one home (or host) country to another, but the consideration of commonalties and differences in the forms of business that cross borders.
17. William J. McDonough, "Issues of Corporate Governance," *Federal Reserve Bank of New York, Current Issues in Economics and Finance* 8 (Sept.–Oct. 2002), 1–6; on the New York Federal Reserve's attention to corporate governance in the aftermath of the Enron collapse, see the entire issue of *Economic Policy Review* (a publication of the Federal Reserve Bank of New York), 9 (April 2003), 1–139.
18. Wilkins at first used the term "American model" to refer to such firms, because the initial research had been done on U.S. companies and this pattern was very apparent in U.S. business abroad. Mira Wilkins, "The Free-Standing Company Revisited," in Mira Wilkins and Harm Schröter, eds., *The Free-Standing Company in the World Economy* (Oxford: Oxford University Press, 1998), 5–6. Subsequently, she added – and adopted the designation – "classic form" of multinational enterprises: Wilkins, "Conduits for Long-Term Foreign Investment," 53, 64–65, 70–72. She did not use the word "classic" as associated with classical or neoclassical economic theory, but rather as serving as a standard model, accepted within the literature.
19. There were some such firms headquartered in the United States and Canada as well.
20. On the concept, see Mira Wilkins, "The Free-Standing Company, 1870–1914: An Important Type of British Foreign Direct Investment," *Economic History Review*, 2nd series, 41 (May 1988), 259–82; Wilkins and Schröter, eds., *Free-Standing Company*, passim; and Wilkins, "Conduits for Long-Term Foreign Investment," 51–76.

21. For example, Wilkins, "Free-Standing Company, 1870–1914," 261 (on the foreign portfolio investment/foreign direct investment categories); Mark Casson. "An Economic Theory of the Free-Standing Company," in Wilkins and Schröter, eds., *Free-Standing Company*, 102–06 (on control issues); and Wilkins and Schröter, eds., *Free-Standing Company*, passim (on clusters).
22. Jean-François Hennart, "Transaction-Cost Theory and the Free-Standing Firm," in Wilkins and Schröter, eds., *Free-Standing Company*, 65–74 (for insights on minority equity involvements).
23. Wilkins has in the past used the term "business group" to deal with the links between firms that often participated in the clusters surrounding free standing companies. Randall Morck has equated business groups with the complex holding company structures. (See Randall Morck, "How to Eliminate Pyramidal Business Groups: The Double Taxation of Inter-Corporate Dividends and Other Incisive Uses of Tax Policy," NBER Working Paper 10944, Dec. 2004.) Bernard Yeung has suggested three categories of business groups, those that are vertical (the holding company structure), those that are horizontal (same activities), and those that represent the kind of loose cluster, as in Wilkins's usage (Wilkins's discussion with Bernard Yeung, April 21, 2006). What the authors of the present volume are trying to capture are the sometimes uneasy distinctions between what happens within a business firm (a multinational enterprise) and across firms. Activities across firms can be with related (albeit "independent" entities) or with unrelated companies. See Mira Wilkins, "Defining a Firm: History and Theory," and Peter Hertner, "German Multinational Enterprise Before 1914: Some Case Studies," in Peter Hertner and Geoffrey Jones, eds., *Multinationals: History and Theory* (Aldershot, England: Gower, 1986), 80–95, 113–15.
24. See, for example, Jones, *Multinationals and Global Capitalism.*
25. In Chap. 2, note 9 above, we give only a small part of the huge literature on multinational enterprise that has influenced our analysis. We draw widely on the literature that has been developed by economists, historians, business school professors, political scientists, historians (in general), sociologists, and economic geographers. We have been most influenced by the economists, economic and business historians, and business school professors. Among the highly useful works by political scientists are those by Stephen Kobrin and Witold J. Heinsz (both are business school professors). Frequently, historians (and political scientists) have seen multinational enterprises solely in political terms, perceiving business–government relationships as central to the story line. Sometimes these studies are part of a broad political economy framework. Sociologists have focused on "political power" or "power relationships." A specific branch of the large political economy literature deals with "dependent development" and studies the politics of alliances, those between governments, local capital, and multinationals; it concentrates exclusively on multinationals in less-developed regions of the world. Robert Vitalis, *When Capitalists Collide: Business Conflict and the End of Empire in Egypt* (Berkeley: University of California Press, 1995), xii, for example, takes this approach as a point of departure and argues that "the politics of investment in Egypt was ultimately less a struggle between foreign and local capital than a conflict among local investors for access to resources and control over the rents...."

26. There are also other confusions in names that arise from translations: Thus, for example, the Anglo-Japanese Hydro-Electric Company, Ltd., when translated from the Japanese literature, is sometimes presented as the Anglo-Japanese Water Power Company or the Anglo-Japanese Water Power Electric Company. These are the same company.
27. See Chapter 1 on isolated plants.
28. Wilkins, *Emergence of Multinational Enterprise*, 37–45.
29. Wilkins, *History ... to 1914*. The international activities of J. & P. Coats are being documented by Dong-Woon Kim and others. See, for example, Dong-Woon Kim, "J. & P. Coats in Tsarist Russia, 1889–1917," *Business History Review,* 69 (Winter 1995), 465–93; idem., "J. & P. Coats as a Multinational Before 1914," *Business and Economic History,* 26:2 (1997); and idem., "The British Multinational Enterprise in the United States Before 1914: The Case of J. & P. Coats," *Business History Review,* 72 (Winter 1998): 523–51.
30. One is impressed with the historical analogies to the telecommunications industry. Producers of telephones needed a telephone network.
31. The earliest electrical manufacturers frequently aided their customers in setting up isolated plants; but when there was a move to establishing a central power station, there was typically a separate company established.
32. See Killingworth Hedges, *Continental Electric Light Central Stations* (London: E.F.N. Spon, 1892), v–vii; Wilfried Feldenkirchen, *Siemens* (Munich: Piper, 2000), 84, describes the "contractor business" as one where "the electrical company acts simultaneously as a manufacturer of electrical equipment, as an electricity supply utility and as a financing company." He dates this process, which he calls an important marketing strategy, to the 1880s. He adds a note: "Today [2000,] the contractor business is organized in the form of BOO (Build-Operate-Own)/BOT (Build-Operate-Transfer) models. . . . " Ibid., 401n54.
33. On this, see Thomas F. O'Brien, "The Revolutionary Mission," *American Historical Review,* 98:3 (June 1993), 774; and for the makers of boilers, insulated cables, and other such producer goods, this second reason for the initial investment in the utility was inapplicable. The Sofina *Annual Report, 1939*, 13, read: "Until recent years the producers and distributors of electricity have left it to the manufacturers of electrical plant and appliances to promote a more widespread knowledge of the various uses of electricity. Latterly they have departed from this policy. . . . [T]hey have seconded the efforts of those who sell and install this apparatus, and have set out to explain to their subscribers the advantages of their various and graduated scales of charges. The active part thus taken by the [electricity] distributing undertakings in promoting the use of electric energy has tended to maintain and increase the demand."
34. In recent literature, foreign direct investment in the first case is called "horizontal foreign direct investment"; in the second case, it is called "vertical foreign direct investment." See, for example, articles in the *Journal of International Economics*. The literature also discusses export platforms, where the export is to a third country, not back to the home nation.
35. See Chapter 1, herein, on this. One estimate, made by the Dresdner Bank for 1928, indicated that only 1 percent of the world's total production of current was transmitted across political frontiers. This export of current was mainly

accounted for by Switzerland, which was reported that year to export roughly 25 percent of its production to neighboring countries, and by Canada, which transmitted to the United States about 10 percent of its electricity output. *New York Times*, July 20, 1930. The high Swiss power exports that persisted all during the interwar years appear to be exceptional. Another estimate of Swiss power exports, 1930–1943, put them at 20–24 percent of output (with minor annual fluctuations). Independent Commission of Experts Switzerland – Second World War, *Switzerland, National Socialism and the Second World War: Final Report* (Zurich: Pendo Verlag, 2002), 221 (http://www.uek.ch/en/index.htm, accessed online March 12, 2006). Ibid., 220, describes Swiss hydroelectric power plants on the border rivers, the Rhine and the Rhône, and notes that "the bi-national hydroelectric power stations on the Rhine were subject partly to German and partly to Swiss law; their output was generally divided on a 50–50 basis, and their joint management usually functioned smoothly, even during the war [World War II]." Manufacturers' satellites were involved.

36. Here there was a major difference between electric power and telephones. For many decades, the provision of telephones to the final user (the consumer) was directly associated with the provider of the telephone service; telephone companies actually owned manufacturers (American Telephone & Telegraph, for example, owned Western Electric, which was a manufacturer). Electric light and power was different, probably because of the wide range of electrical goods that came to be available. One exception we have found to this was related to the sale of meters. In some cases (in Latin America, for example), German manufacturers that had ownership in public utilities insisted that the public pay for meters furnished by the public utility (imported from the German manufacturer by that electric utility). In other parts of the world, this was not a consideration. And in recent years – with deregulation, privatization, and especially the introduction of cell phones – the manufacturers of phones and the providers of telecommunication services are now rarely identical.
37. H. V. Nelles, in a preliminary paper for this project.
38. Takeo Hoshi and Anil Kashyap, *Corporate Financing and Governance in Japan* (Cambridge, MA: MIT Press, 2001), is very useful on this topic.
39. Charles W. Calomiris, *U.S. Bank Deregulation in Historical Perspective* (Cambridge: Cambridge University Press, 2000), 236–38, comparing "banks" and banking systems.
40. See Stephanie Diaper, "The Sperling Combine and the Shipbuilding Industry," in J. J. van Helten and Y. Cassis, *Capitalism in a Mature Economy* (Aldershot, England: Edward Elgar, 1990), 75; and Ranald C. Michie, *The London Stock Exchange: A History* (Oxford: Oxford University Press, 1999), 139.
41. See Vincent P. Carosso, *Investment Banking in America* (Cambridge, MA: Harvard University Press, 1970), on investment banks.
42. Daniel Verdier, "Explaining Cross-National Variations in Universal Banking in Nineteenth-Century Europe, North America, and Australasia," in Douglas J. Forsyth and Daniel Verdier, eds., *The Origins of National Financial Systems: Alexander Gerschenkron Reconsidered* (London: Routledge, 2003), 23.
43. For example, domestically: In 1913, Britain had 104 banks, which controlled 8,156 branches; in the United States, there were 24,524 banks, which had

merely 548 branches; and Canada had 24 banks, with 2,962 branches. Ranald Michie, "Banks and Securities Markets 1870–1914," in Forsyth and Verdier, *The Origins*, 47.

44. Hertner and Nelles, "Contrasting Styles of Foreign Investment," 201.
45. Christopher Armstrong and H. V. Nelles, *Monopoly's Moment: The Organization and Regulation of Canadian Utilities, 1830–1930* (Philadelphia: Temple University Press, 1986), 120. (We added "at home and abroad," for there came to be large Canadian insurance company investments in the U.S. public utility sector.)
46. Richard Sylla, Review for EH-Net, March 25, 2005, of Forsyth and Verdier, eds., *Origins of National Financial Systems*. Ranald Michie's contribution is Chapter 2.
47. Joost Jonker, "Competing in Tandem: Securities Markets and Commercial Banking Patterns in Europe During the Nineteenth Century," in Forsyth and Verdier, eds., *Origins of National Financial Systems*, 84.
48. Wilkins, *Emergence of Multinational Enterprise* and Wilkins, *Maturing of Multinational Enterprise*, document numerous such American companies.
49. Dominque Barjot, et al., eds., *L'ÉlectrificationOoutre-mer de la Fin du XIXe Siècle aux Première Décolonisations* (Paris: EDF, [n.d. 2002?]).
50. Our discussion of holding companies has been particularly influenced by conversations with and the works by Jean-François Hennart, Peter Hertner, Luciano Segreto, and Thomas Hughes. A large literature exists on the history of holding companies. On those in Europe, the standard sources are Robert Liefmann, *Beteiligungs- und Finanzierungsgesellschaften: Eine Studie über den modernen Kapitalismus und das Effektenwesen* (Jena, Germany: G. Fischer, 1913), and *Cartels, Concerns, and Trusts* (London: Methuen, 1932), which edition was originally published in German as *Kartelle, Konzerne und Trusts*. On U.S. holding companies, see James C. Bonbright and Gardiner C. Means, *The Holding Company: Its Public Significance and Its Regulation* (New York: McGraw-Hill, 1932), and William J. Hausman, "The Historical Antecedents of Restructuring: Mergers and Concentration in the U.S. Electric Utility Industry, 1879–1935" (unpublished paper prepared for the American Public Power Association, March 4, 1997). For insightful treatments of holding companies and their relationships with investment trusts and investment companies, see Theodore Grayson, *Investment Trusts* (New York: John Wiley, 1928), and Hugh Bullock, *The Story of Investment Companies* (New York: Columbia University Press, 1959). On holding companies, see also Richard F. Hirsh, *Power Loss: The Origins of Deregulation and Restructuring in the American Electric Utility System* (Cambridge, MA: MIT Press, 1999), and Hughes, *Networks of Power*. Morck, "How to Eliminate Pyramidal Business Groups," 38–42, deals with national (not multinational) enterprises, but his materials on holding companies are exceptionally valuable; see also Morck and Steier, "Global History of Corporate Governance," which like Morck's prior work takes the view that there were sharp differences by country in holding company structures. Morck sees the pyramided holding company as a means of concentrating control.
51. In 1936, after the 1935 Public Utility Holding Company Act had been passed in the United States and there was a governmental attempt to alter the structure of

holding companies in public utilities, Max Horn (from the Belgian holding company Sofina) at the Third World Power Conference came to the defense of holding companies and the coordination of business activities made possible by them. He contrasted the holding company with "investment trusts," arguing there was not the same "permanent relation" between the investment trust and the companies in which it is interested as between the holding company and the operating companies. Whereas the holding company had responsibility for the operating company, by contrast the investment trust, he argued, felt less responsibility for the operating companies' activities. He believed that a fundamental advantage of the holding company was its ability to supply technical advice in construction, in research, in obtaining the advantages of large-scale purchases, and in providing financing. Max Horn, "Comments," *Transactions, Third World Power Conference*, vol. 5 (Washington, DC: USGPO, 1936), 340–41. Plummer made the same distinction in 1938: "The term 'holding company,' as understood in England, means a company whose chief function is to hold the shares or stock of other companies, *with the intention of controlling* their operations or policy. It is this intention to exercise control which distinguishes the holding company from the investment or trust company." Alfred Plummer, *International Combines in Modern Industry* (1938; reprint ed., Freeport, NY: Books for Libraries, 1971), 33 (emphasis in original). Although the term "multinational enterprise" was not used, clearly Horn and Plummer's descriptions would fit neatly contemporary descriptions of multinational enterprise.

52. *Survey of Current Business*, July 2001, 23. In 1982, foreign affiliates of U.S. companies classified as holding companies had represented 9 percent of the U.S. direct investment position abroad. By 2004, holding companies comprised 35 percent of the American business-abroad position (in 2005, the percentage fell to 30 percent for very specific tax reasons). Ibid., July 2006, 24. Holding company affiliates meant that for the U.S. Bureau of Economic Analysis "the industry patterns and the country patterns of the position estimates differ from those of the estimates of the *operations* of foreign affiliates" (our emphasis). Ibid. When we read this, we had a sense of *déjà vu*; it echoed some of our frustrations in writing the present volume. Note that in this formulation the entire multinational enterprise is not thought of as a holding company, only the foreign affiliates that were in a different industrial classification and in turn had other holdings.
53. By "third-country" holding company, we mean a holding company owned in part by a foreign parent that in turn owns securities in affiliates that operate in another country(ies) abroad.
54. On *Unternehmergeschäft*, see Peter Hertner, "Financial Strategies and Adaptation to Foreign Markets: The German Electro-Technical Industry and Its Multinational Activities, 1890s to 1939," in Alice Teichova, Maurice Lévy-Leboyer, and Helga Nussbaum, eds., *Multinational Enterprise in Historical Perspective* (Cambridge: Cambridge University Press, 1986), 150.
55. Newly created affiliates of certain holding companies were sometimes forced by statute to buy their electrotechnical supplies from the manufacturer(s) that participated in the foundation of the holding company and of the operating

enterprise. Hertner, "Financial Strategies and Adaptation to Foreign Markets," 150.

56. Ginette Kurgan-Van Hentenryk, "Structure and Strategy of Belgian Business Groups (1920–1990)," in Takeo Shiba and Masahiro Shimotani, *Beyond the Firm: Business Groups in International and Historical Perspective* (London: Oxford University Press, 1997), 90. Wilkins wondered about this analogy in the international context: In the main, the *zaibatsu* structures brought in foreign investments; Empain spread it outward. Yet, when Wilkins tried out the idea on a Japanese audience (November 2005), they found it reasonable. On the *zaibatsu* form, see Hoshi and Kashyap, *Corporate Financing*, 8–10. Holding company groupings often had variations in the degree of looseness in the relationships between corporations involved.
57. For a broad U.S. context, an interesting discussion of holding companies is that in relation to Standard Oil. Originally, the Standard Oil group was organized as a "trust" (at the pinnacle was the trust, which was not incorporated anywhere); after an 1892 Ohio court decision, the group was reorganized so that some companies were holding companies, some were holding and operating companies, and others were purely operating companies. In 1899, Standard Oil of New Jersey was at the pinnacle, an operating and holding company, which ran a large integrated multinational industrial enterprise. Ralph W. Hidy and Muriel Hidy, *Pioneering in Big Business* (New York: Harper & Brothers, 1955), 3–4, 40, 219–32, 305–38.
58. Hirsh, *Power Loss*, 36 (both quotations); Hausman, "Historical Antecedents," 32, and passim; see also William J. Hausman and John L. Neufeld, "U.S. Foreign Direct Investment in Electrical Utilities in the 1920s," in Wilkins and Schröter, eds., *Free-Standing Company*, 361–90, for the replication of domestic experience.
59. Hughes, *Networks of Power*, 393.
60. In the late 1920s, Switzerland exported roughly 25 percent of its power production to neighboring countries, and the holding companies reflected these network connections. A U.S. company on the American side of Niagara Falls had a subsidiary across the border.
61. Numerous U.S. government hearings in the 1930s explored the terminology and the characteristics of holding companies, trusts, and investment companies. There was often confusion between (and long discussions about) investment companies, investment trusts, and holding companies. We have mentioned such distinctions in a note above. More recently, Serge Paquier in his "Swiss Holding Companies from the Mid-Nineteenth Century to the Early 1930s," *Financial History Review* 8 (Oct. 2001), 163–82, argued that there were two main types of holding companies: investment trusts and finance companies. The former "always acquired minority stakes in other concerns," and the aim of the management of the investment trust "was never to take over, or control, the companies whose shares were bought." The second, the finance companies, were "characterised by their controlling interests in firms that all operated in the same industry;" and they spread risk through geographical diversification. While Paquier's two types of holding companies (one without and one with controlling interests) correspond with the distinctions that others have made

between investment trusts *and* holding companies, the correspondence in added respects is uneasy (the first spreading risk by industry diversification, the second by geographical diversification); there were investment trusts that concentrated on investments in electric utilities and holding companies that confined themselves to a single country (foreign or domestic).

62. Normally, a company makes a foreign direct investment and the object of that direct investment is considered to be a "direct investment." What we are suggesting here is the possibility that a company may make a foreign direct investment (investing as part of an overall strategy, planning to have influence, its holding more than a purely financial one), yet the targeted firm is not influenced or controlled in a major manner by the company undertaking the investment. The targeted firm makes its own fundamental decisions quite independently of the investing company(ies). This situation prevailed particularly when minority interests were involved.
63. Pamela Laird pointed this out to Mira Wilkins in June 2003.
64. Hughes, *Networks of Power*, 30, goes so far as to suggest that Lowrey "was one of those who persuaded Edison to turn to electric lighting."
65. Hoshimi Uchida, "The Transfer of Electrical Technologies from the United States and Europe to Japan, 1869–1914," in David J. Jeremy, ed., *International Technology Transfer: Europe, Japan and the USA, 1700–1914* (Aldershot, England: Elgar, 1991), 224–26, on the engineers.
66. On U.K. definitions, see Derek F. Channon, *The Strategy and Structure of British Enterprise* (Boston: Harvard Business School, 1973), Ch. 5.
67. The best material on the history of international construction firms is in Marc Linder, *Projecting Capitalism: A History of the Internationalization of the Construction Industry* (Westport, CT: Greenwood Press, 1994).
68. In Wilkins, "Free-Standing Company," 263, she recognized that the British free standing company could be used to attract foreign as well as British investments. She did not recognize, however, how common this was. After World War I, when British tax laws changed, registration might be outside the United Kingdom with no change in ownership and control, even though registration overseas tended to loosen the potential for control.
69. See specifically American & Foreign Power Co., *Annual Report 1927*, for the board that year. The pattern was the same for the rest of the 1920s.
70. For the general proposition, see Wilkins, "Conduits for Long-Term Foreign Investment," 51–76.
71. See Peter Hertner, "Les Sociétés Financières Suisses et le Développement de l'Industrie Électrique Jusqu'a la Première Guerre Mondiale," in Fabienne Cardot, ed., *1880–1980, Un Siècle d'Électricité dans le Monde* (Paris: PUF, 1987), 341–55, esp. 342. There were also other advantages of Canadian, Swiss, and Belgian registration, based on those nations' corporate law.
72. See discussion of "lean governance" in Wilkins, "Free-Standing Company, 1870–1914," 279, and Wilkins and Schröter, eds., *Free-Standing Company*, 6, 67, 349–52, 355–56. The phrase "lean governance" was used to indicate the small (weak) head office of some free standing companies.
73. On the gray area related to railroads, see the dilemma faced by Michael J. Twomey, "Patterns of Foreign Investment in Latin America in the Twentieth

Century," in John H. Coatsworth and Alan M. Taylor, eds., *Latin America and the World Economy Since 1800* (Cambridge, MA: Harvard University Press, 1998), 171.

74. Jules Düblin, *Die Finanzierungs- und Kapitalanlage-Gesellschaften der Schweizerishchen Grossbanken* (Basel: Philographischer Verlag, 1937), 38–61.
75. Japanese direct investments in Chinese electric light and power that were intimately associated with the Japanese direct investments in the South Manchuria Railway were made from 1906 onward. In 1926, the South Manchuria Electric Company was organized, and it took over the electric power plants formerly owned by the South Manchuria Railway. C. F. Remer, *Foreign Investments in China* (New York: Macmillan, 1933), 427–30, 490.
76. Chapter 1, herein, explains the advantage of electric tramways over steam railroads in urban areas.
77. Hirsh, *Power Loss*, 12–31.
78. Sometimes the minority interests were above the 10 percent threshold that most modern scholars use to define foreign direct investment, and sometimes they were below. It did not really matter. The minority interests were principally for information purposes and to influence the purchasing decisions of the utilities.
79. Linda Jones, Charles Jones, and Robert Greenhill, "Public Utility Companies," in D. C. M. Platt, *Business Imperialism 1840–1930; an Inquiry Based on British Experience in Latin America* (Oxford: Oxford University Press, 1977), 81; Hughes, *Networks of Power*, 227, 232.
80. For example, the Canadian-registered Mexican Light and Power and Brazilian Traction, Light, and Power by the 1930s and well into the post–World War II years were both ranked among the top foreign-owned "holding companies" in public utilities in Latin America – indeed, worldwide – (as ranked by assets), while all their operations and operating companies were still confined within a single country.
81. The quotation is from Armstrong and Nelles, *Monopoly's Moment*, 321. There is a modern literature that seeks to understand the development of U.S. and Canadian (and by extension, global) electrification in a broadly defined political economy framework with the focus on the regulatory structures. See Mark Rose, *Cities of Light and Heat* (University Park: Pennsylvania State University Press, 1995), and Hirsh, *Power Loss*. In a certain sense, Armstrong and Nelles, *Monopoly's Moment*, falls into that category.
82. Armstrong and Nelles, *Monopoly's Moment*, 322.
83. This point is made in Chapter 1, but it seems important to reiterate.
84. On the other hand, we do not want to neglect the tensions of the earlier years. Miguel S. Wionczek, "Electric Power," in Raymond Vernon, ed., *Public Policy and Private Enterprise in Mexico* (Cambridge, MA: Harvard University Press, 1964), 28, writes of Mexico, 1906–1910, and the bitter negotiations between the municipalities and the companies, as the former complained about deficient services and high rates; so, too, there was the intense hostility in Mexico in the late 1930s. Ibid., 60. The more closely we look at the data, the earlier the clashes seem to emerge in Chile and Argentina, for example.
85. See George Soule, *Prosperity Decade* (New York: Holt, Rinehart and Winston, 1964), 183, for the U.S. problems in the 1920s, but these problems extended far

beyond the United States; there is an immense literature on public utility regulation and methods of rate determination.

86. Herbert Feis, *Europe: The World's Banker 1870–1914* (1930; reprinted New York: W.W. Norton, 1965), 131.
87. Ibid., 139. And as Sofina head Dannie Heineman recalled decades later, "In England, the storm of public protest against British financial participation in the Baghdad railway project frightened off the private group that had been organized in the City and led to a cabinet decision forbidding the investment." Dannie N. Heineman, "The Changing International Environment," address to the general meeting of shareholders of Société Financière de Transports et d'Entreprises Industrielles (Sofina), April 22, 1954 (published in booklet form), 10–11. For more details, see Jacques Thobie, "European Banks in the Middle East," in Rondo Cameron and V.I. Bovykin, eds., *International Banking* (Oxford: Oxford University Press, 1991), 434.
88. C.K. Hobson, *The Export of Capital* (London: Constable & Co., 1914), xxii.
89. Ibid.
90. Quoted in Feis, *Europe: World Banker*, 123.
91. Wilkins, *Maturing of Multinational Enterprise*, 16.
92. See Chapter 4, herein, on loans for Greek, Hungarian, and Yugoslavian (this last was planned but not made) as well as Japanese electrical ventures, based on British Treasury guarantees.
93. Frank Southard, *American Industry in Europe* (Boston: Houghton Mifflin, 1931), 181. Included in Southard's long list of companies was the Swiss, Motor–Columbus. See ibid., 176.
94. Hobson, *Export of Capital*, xxi.
95. The quotation is from Heineman, "Changing International Environment," 12, where the head of Sofina compared and contrasted conditions of doing business in 1953 with those of his early experiences in the company, 1895–1905, "then and now."
96. F.A. Hayek, *The Road to Serfdom* (1944; Reprinted Chicago: University of Chicago Press, 1994) was the rare exception in bemoaning this trend (and not sharing the assumption).
97. Donald R. Lessard, "Risk and the Dynamics of Globalization," in Julian M. Birkinshaw, et al., *The Future of the Multinational Company* (London: John Wiley, 2003), 76–85.

3 EVERY CITY, 1880–1914

1. On the technological contributions of Jablochkoff (1847–1894), see Chapter 1, herein. On SGEl, see chronology in d'Arnaud Berthonnet, *Guide du Chercheur en Histoire de L' Électricité* (Paris: Editions La Mandragore, n.d.), 21; *New York Times*, Dec. 30, 1878 (trial of electrical lights, Jablochkoff electric lighting system, Holborn Viaduct), Feb. 16, 1879 (Jablochkoff electric lighting system at Thames Embankment and Holborn Viaduct), Aug. 8, 1880 (capital of SGEl; SGEl have maintained light on the Thames Embankment for 18 months; plans for Russian company), Nov. 10, 1880 (2,500 lights); Serge Paquier, *Histoire de l'Électricité en Suisse* (Geneva: Éditions Passé Présent, 1998), I, 52–53; Jonathan

Coopersmith, *The Electrification of Russia, 1880–1926* (Ithaca: Cornell University Press, 1992), passim; http://archives.iee.org/about/Arclamps/jabloch.htm, accessed Oct. 2, 2007; and Allen M. Perry, "Tentative History of the Evolution of the Electrical Industry," 4 vol. typescript (Birmingham, AL: Alabama Power, c. 1936), I, 99 (1881 activities).

2. *New York Times*, Aug. 8, 1880.
3. An earlier attempt to establish a subsidiary in Vienna had failed. Wilfried Feldenkirchen, *Siemens* (Munich: Piper, 2000), 20, 35–36; Peter Hertner, "Financial Strategies and Adaptation to Foreign Markets: The German Electro-Technical Industry and Its Multinational Activities, 1890s to 1939," in Alice Teichova, Maurice Lévy-Leboyer, and Helga Nussbaum, eds., *Multinational Enterprise in Historical Perspective* (Cambridge: Cambridge University Press, 1986), 146–47. See also Sigfrid von Weiher, *Die Englischen Siemens-Werke und das Siemens- Überseegeschäft in der Zweiten Hälfte des 19. Jahrhunderts* (Berlin: Duncker & Humblot, 1990).
4. Godalming's web page (http://www.godalming-tc.gov.uk/, accessed Oct. 2, 2007); R.H. Parsons, *The Early Days of the Power Station Industry* (Cambridge: Printed for Babcock and Wilcox at the Cambridge University Press, 1939), 12; others claim that California Electric Light Company (CELC), founded in 1879 in San Francisco, was the first "central-station electrical utility." W. Bernard Carlson, *Innovation as a Social Process: Elihu Thomson and the Rise of General Electric, 1870–1900* (Cambridge: Cambridge University Press, 1991), 133–34; William J. Hausman, "The Historical Antecedents of Restructuring: Mergers and Concentration in the U.S. Electric Utility Industry, 1879–1935" (unpublished paper prepared for the American Public Power Association, March 4, 1997), 11. The CELC venture did not involve international business, but that is not at the heart of the dispute, which may lie in the terms "incandescent lamps," "entire town," and "street lights." David S. Landes, *The Unbound Prometheus: Technological Change and Industrial Development in Western Europe from 1750 to the Present* (Cambridge: Cambridge University Press, 1969), 285, writes that "the first public power station *in Europe* was established at Godalming in England by Siemens Brothers in 1881" (our emphasis).
5. For example, the Russian entrepreneur Vladimir N. Chikolev's company, Elektrotekhnik, had received permission in 1880 to light Nevskii Prospekt, the main boulevard in St. Petersburg. By 1883, out of money, he sold out to the Russian subsidiary of Siemens & Halske, which finished the project late that year. Coopersmith, *Electrification of Russia*, 48.
6. *New York Times*, Aug. 8, 1880.
7. Mira Wilkins, *The Emergence of Multinational Enterprise: American Business Abroad from the Colonial Era to 1914* (Cambridge, MA: Harvard University Press, 1970), 52.
8. Vincent P. Carosso, *The Morgans* (Cambridge, MA: Harvard University Press, 1987), and Ron Chernow, *The House of Morgan* (New York: Atlantic Monthly Press, 1990).
9. Theresa Collins found and directed our attention to two key letters: J.P. Morgan, New York, to Walter Burns, Oct. 30, 1878, and J.P. Morgan to Walter Burns, Nov. 19, 1878. They were found in a box labeled "Pierpont

Morgan (1837–1913)," binder stamped J. S. M. & Co., No. 12. Letterbook No. 12, pp. 457–59, 478, J. Pierpont Morgan Library (JPML).

10. Morgan to Burns, Oct. 30, 1878. This letter is also quoted in Jean Strouse, *Morgan* (New York: Random House, 1999), 182.
11. Data in the JPML, as researched by Collins, Stouse, and others. Wilkins used the Edison archives (EA) in the preparation of her *Emergence of Multinational Enterprise*. (The Edison papers that Wilkins used have subsequently been included in the Thomas A. Edison Papers (TAEP), some of which are accessible online; we have cited EA to indicate material taken from Wilkins's notes as distinct from the material that we have used from TAEP.) Note that some of the "foreign" companies were registered abroad, and some were registered in the United States to do business abroad.
12. They did this although many had other specific functions, i.e., their purpose was to undertake exhibitions and to hold patents.
13. On Lowrey, see Matthew Josephson, *Edison* (New York: McGraw-Hill, 1959), passim; the quote is on p. 185; Josephson, who used the Edison papers, notes how early Lowrey was involved; see also Strouse, *Morgan*, 182.
14. Strouse, *Morgan*, 183; Thomas P. Hughes, *Networks of Power: Electrification in Western Society, 1880–1930* (Baltimore: Johns Hopkins University Press, 1983), 49–50.
15. Paul Israel, *Edison: A Life of Invention* (New York: John Wiley, 1998), 214–15; for the excitement over this exhibit, see Luciano Segreto, "Ciento Veinte Años de Electricidad: Dos Mundos Diferentes y Parecidos," in Gonzalo Anes, ed., *Un Siglo de Luz: Historia Empresarial de Iberdrola* (Madrid: Iberdrola, 2005), 17.
16. A list of some of these Edison companies is included on the TAEP website (http://edison.rutgers.edu/list.htm#Lightfor, accessed Dec. 30, 2006). See also Wilkins, *Emergence of Multinational Enterprise*, 53–54, 57. The TAEP website notes that not included were many additional companies set up in foreign countries during the early 1880s. Thus, for example, a historian of Korea tells of Edison's seeking to obtain in the 1880s a concession for exclusive rights for electric light systems. Peter Duus, "Economic Dimensions of Meiji Imperialism: The Case of Korea, 1895–1910," in Ramon H. Myers and Mark R. Peattie, eds. *The Japanese Colonial Empire, 1895–1945* (Princeton: Princeton University Press, 1984), 139. Edison companies established central power stations from Rotterdam to St. Petersburg. Israel, *Edison*, 215–16. See also G.P. Lowrey to Drexel, Morgan & Co., March 25, 1880, JPML (p. 11 of Collins notes) on the foreign companies.
17. TAEP website (http://edison.rutgers.edu/index.htm, accessed Dec. 30, 2006).
18. *New York Times*, Dec. 30, 1878, reprinting an article from the *London News*, Dec. 16, 1878; see also *New York Times*, Jan. 16, 1879. Smithsonian website (http://americanhistory.si.edu/lighting/scripts/s19c.htm, accessed Sept. 26, 2007); *New York Times*, April 12, 1882; on the British Edison company, Wilkins, *Emergence of Multinational Enterprise*, 52–53, and data from EA and from JPML. See also Hughes, *Networks of Power*, 54–65. The British Edison company's memorandum of association was dated Feb. 8, 1882 and its articles of association were March 15, 1882; JPML (p. 8 of Collins notes on Drexel,

Morgan & Co. Syndicates); the display that the *New York Times* reported was on April 11, 1882.

19. Hughes, *Networks of Power*, 55–57 (Holborn Viaduct), 58–66 (details on the new legislation), 21–22 (Swan), 62 (Edison & Swan). Hughes attributes the abandonment, and the subsequent "backwardness," of British electrification, not to technology, but to the requirements imposed under the British political system. Ibid., 65–66. For an interesting discussion of the weak development of British domestic electrification (in the context of whether British capital went abroad rather than investing at home), see Michael Edelstein, *Overseas Investment in the Age of High Imperialism: The United Kingdom, 1850–1914* (New York: Columbia University Press, 1982), 64. His culprits are different from those of Hughes, as he seeks to explain why the anarchy of local regulation and the absence of appropriate British legislation were not challenged.
20. Wilkins, *Emergence of Multinational Enterprise*, 54, 57, with corrections by Pierre Lanthier.
21. Pierre Lanthier, "Les Constructions Électriques en France: Le Case de Six Groupes Industriels Internationaux de 1880 à 1940," Ph.D. diss., 3 vol. (Paris: University of Paris X (Nanterre), 1988).
22. Paquier, *Histoire de l'Électricité en Suisse,* 54–55. Minutes of Meeting, Edison Electric Light Company of Europe Ltd., Board of Directors, Jan. 21, 1885, EA. The failure of the Jablochkoff system was undoubtedly also the result of a noncompetitive technology.
23. Georg Siemens, *History of the House of Siemens*, 2 vol. (Freiburg/Munich: Karl Alber, 1957), I, 90–100, is excellent on the reaction of Werner von Siemens and his firm, "who were regarded as the supreme authority in all matters concerning electricity," to the involvements of Emil Rathenau (and Edison interests) in the German industry. Siemens & Halske actually contributed to the initial capital of AEG, and the latter's first chairman of the board was Georg Siemens, who was the key figure in the Deutsche Bank and was the cousin of Werner von Siemens, founder of Siemens & Halske. Family ties notwithstanding, the AEG–Deutsche Bank links were equally important. AEG was Deutsche Bank's first successful industrial flotation. Lothar Gall, "The Deutsche Bank from Its Founding to the Great War, 1870–1914," in Lothar Gall, et al., *The Deutsche Bank, 1870–1995* (London: Weidenfeld & Nicholson, 1995), 34.
24. Emil Rathenau to Thomas Edison, Feb. 19, 1889, EA. He added very bluntly and emphatically, "[A]nd we cannot restrict ourselves in the sale of the same [our product] any more than do Siemens and Halske and the other manufacturers of incandescent lamps." When Tokyo Electric Light Co. had ordered its first direct-current system in 1886, it had done so from the Edison Co. in the United States. Tokyo Electric changed to alternating current in 1894 and imported generators from AEG. Hoshimi Uchida, "The Transfer of Electrical Technologies from the United States and Europe to Japan, 1869–1914," in David J. Jeremy, ed., *International Technology Transfer. Europe, Japan and the USA, 1700–1914* (Aldershot, England: Elgar, 1991), 231. This related to trade, not to investments, but it shows the independence of AEG. Peter Hertner found in AEG archives, Berlin, documents on the relations between Siemens and AEG that indicated that

it was not until 1894 that Siemens "granted AEG complete independence." Data provided by Peter Hertner, June 2006.

25. Mira Wilkins, *The History of Foreign Investment in the United States to 1914* (Cambridge, MA: Harvard University Press, 1989), 434, and Christopher Kobrak, *Banking on Global Markets: Deutsche Bank and the United States, 1870 to the Present* (Cambridge: Cambridge University Press, forthcoming). Sidney Alexander Mitchell, *S. Z. Mitchell and the Electrical Industry* (New York: Farrer, Straus & Cudahy, 1960), 52 (on number of central power stations and isolated plants of Edison General Electric on the eve of the 1892 formation of General Electric). Hausman interprets the figures as the number of central stations and isolated stations set up by Edison General Electric; Theresa Collins suggests Edison General Electric and its predecessor companies would probably be even more accurate. There is no question that Edison General Electric, which was a manufacturing firm, had interests in electric utilities. See also Forrest McDonald, *Insull* (Chicago: University of Chicago Press, 1962), 42–43. As Carlson, *Innovation*, 289, points out, Edison General Electric accepted substantial amounts of utilities stock as payment for equipment; the predecessor companies seem to have followed the same path. In January 1890, Villard was reporting to Deutsche Bank that Edison General Electric was making investments in New York Illuminating Company and Boston Illuminating Company–insisting that such investments would encourage the sale of Edison equipment. The Deutsche Bank was extremely nervous about the amount of capital needs of Edison General Electric and that its receivables were to related companies. Kobrak, *Banking on Global Markets*. McDonald argues that Villard initially envisaged Edison General Electric as a holding company that would manufacture and sell only to its own central-station companies. McDonald, *Insull*, 42–43.
26. Wilkins, *The History ...to 1914*, 434–35.
27. As a reminder to the reader, this is the terminology we used in Chapter 2.
28. The North American Company is of interest to us as one of the ways the Germans participated in American business. It would become an important public utility holding company. At origin, it was a "Henry Villard" company, the successor to the Oregon & Transcontinental Company, which he had organized for railroad finance on June 28, 1881. *New York Times*, June 16, 17, 1890; Oct. 7, 1891; Dec. 16, 1891; Hausman, "Historical Antecedents," 17; North American Company, *North American Company* (Privately printed, 1926?), 15; Dietrich Buss, *Henry Villard: A Study of Transatlantic Investment and Interests, 1870–1895* (New York: Arno Press, 1978), 216 (on the charter); ibid., 217 (on initial Deutsche Bank backing); ibid., 217, 247 (on the withdrawal). Kobrak found in the Deutsche Bank archives, Frankfurt (September balances, HADB, A-0671) information on the latter's shareholdings in the North American Company, as of September 1890. In 1890, the Deutsche Bank was very unhappy with Villard's constant calls on the bank for more funding. A note below provides more on the Deutsche Bank–Villard relationship as it related to electrification in the United States.
29. Data on the TAEP website indicates that the Società Generale Italiana di Elettricità Sistema Edison was organized in December 1883, preceded by the Comitato per le Applicazioni dell'Elettricità Sistema Edison in Italia, which

built a central station in Milan in early 1883. According to *Moody's Manual (Utilities) 1930*, 1673, Società Generale Italiana di Elettricità Sistema Edison was incorporated Jan. 6, 1884. See also Denis Mack Smith, *Italy: A Modern History* (Ann Arbor: University of Michigan Press, 1959), 246, and Luciano Segreto, *Giacinto Motta* (Laterza, Italy: Roma-Bari, 2004).

30. See partial list of the companies on the TAEP website (http://edison.rutgers.edu/index.htm, accested Oct. 20, 2007).). The website provides links to the documents, which makes it possible to trace the course of many of the individual companies. Paul Israel makes the legitimate point that all the Edison foreign companies were set up individually. "Neither Edison nor his business associates seem to have considered [for example] bringing the European enterprises together into a single multinational business, although Drexel Morgan's interest in Edison's foreign patents and their international banking connections might have logically led to such an enterprise." Israel, *Edison*, 216. As indicated, each of the European companies became detached from its originators; so, too, did the companies around the world. In part, the loosely knit origins might have been responsible.
31. Wilkins, *Emergence of Multinational Enterprise*, 57.
32. Carlson, *Innovation*, 48, 87–91.
33. Ibid., 66, 101.
34. Mitchell, *S. Z Mitchell*, 52, and Hausman, "Historical Antecedents," 23.
35. Carlson, *Innovation*, 211–15, 224. United States Congress, Senate, *Report on Electric Power Industry: Control of Power Companies* (Sen. Doc. 213), 69th Cong., 2nd sess. (1927), 70, and William J. Hausman and John L. Neufeld, "U.S. Foreign Direct Investment in Electrical Utilities in the 1920s," in Wilkins and Schröter, eds., *The Free-Standing Company in the World Economy* (Oxford: Oxford University Press, 1998), 365, 371, on United Electric Securities Co., as one of the oldest holding companies. It should be noted that its origins in 1890 were at the identical time as the North American Co.
36. Brush had been an early contender in the electric light field, moving from arc lamps to incandescent lamps. Josephson, *Edison*, 341 (on Brush's competition with Edison); in 1885, Brush Electric in the United States began producing incandescent lamps and developing lighting plants. Even earlier, in 1880, Brush Electric had made a licensing agreement with Anglo-American Brush Electric Light Corporation, Ltd., in England. Wilkins, *Emergence of Multinational Enterprise*, 58. The latter became a manufacturing company and sold "concessions" to other British "Brush companies." In the early 1880s, there had been excitement as an array of Brush securities had been offered on the London Stock Exchange, in what was known as the Brush boom, followed by a collapse. David Kynaston, *The City of London* (London: Chatto & Windus, 1995), II, 148; Hughes, *Networks of Power*, 57, 61–62; and Arnold White, London, to Thomas Edison, July 20, 1882, EA; I.C.R. Byatt, *The British Electrical Industry, 1875–1914* (Oxford: Oxford University Press, 1979), 18–19. The Brush companies floated in England were both domestic and foreign. Included, for example, were the International Electric Company, Ltd. and the English-Austrian Brush Electric Company, Ltd., Vienna (set up Sept. 22, 1882). The latter two companies were associated with the building of

the first central power station in Bucarest (later in Romania). Paul Cartianu and Calin Mihaileanu, "Les Débuts de l'Utilisation de l' Électricité dans le Territoire de la Roumanie," in Fabienne Cardot, ed., *1880–1980, Un Siècle d' Électricité dans le Monde* (Paris: PUF, 1987), 167–68. Irving Stone, *The Global Export of Capital from Great Britain, 1865–1914* (Houndmills, England: Macmillan, 1999), 42–381, provides tabulations of British "Capital Calls" (1865–1914) in the electric light and power sector (he has no company names or numbers of companies). He found a surge in capital calls in this sector in 1882, including calls for capital for companies operating in Austria-Hungary, Chile, India, and South Africa. This obviously reflected the "Brush boom." This is part of a passing *British* business-abroad story rather than the American one, although the initial impetus came from the U.S. Brush company (we will return later in this chapter very briefly to the fate of the Brush companies). Apparently, the U.S. Brush company in its licensing never acquired an equity interest in Anglo-American Brush or in any of the other individually floated Brush companies within Great Britain or overseas. See Carlson, *Innovation*, 216, and *New York Times*, Oct. 17, 18, 1889, and Jan. 21, 1890, on Thomson-Houston's takeover of Brush Electric in the United States. The Brush and the Edison international business stories had something in common: Both spawned foreign business that bore the "brand" identification of the parent. But whereas Edison initially acquired stock in exchange for patent licensing, Brush apparently did not. And, as indicated, Edison did not maintain control.

37. Everett Frazar to Edison, Jan. 16, 1889, EA, writes of the "unexpected active competition of the Thomson-Houston Company, who are also represented in Japan and China." Frazar & Co. was a U.S. trading company that was Edison's representative in Japan. In 1887, it had sold the Japanese their first electric light plant, an Edison plant, installed in the Imperial Palace. William W. Lockwood, *The Economic Development of Japan, Growth and Structural Change 1868–1938* (Princeton: Princeton University Press, 1954), 329–30.
38. Wilkins, *Emergence of Multinational Enterprise*, 58, and Carlson, *Innovation*, 224.
39. Hausman and Neufeld, "U.S. Foreign Direct Investment in Electrical Utilities in the 1920s," 371 (on the absorption of United Electric Securities); Carlson, *Innovation*, 224 (on the French and British Thomson-Houston). The French Thomson-Houston was not formed until 1893 (that is, after the establishment of General Electric), even though Thomson-Houston was doing business in France much earlier. The full name for the French Thomson-Houston company was Compagnie Français pour L'Exploitation des Procédés Thomson-Houston; the name explains why the Thomson-Houston designation was retained after GE came into existence. The British Thomson-Houston was also organized after GE was established: Thomson-Houston had worked with the British engineering firm Laing, Wharton & Down, which in 1894 became the British Thomson-Houston. On the Thomson-Houston connection with Union Elektrizitäts Gesellschaft (UEG), once again, formed after General Electric's creation, see Liane Ranieri, *Dannie Heineman: Un Destin Singulier, 1872–1962* (Brussels: Éditions Racine, 2005), 40; UEG was a company of the German entrepreneur Ludwig Loewe.

40. Mitchell, *S. Z. Mitchell*, 67–68, and U.S. Senate, *Report on Electric Power Industry*, 71–73. Manufacturers would continue to build central power stations, sometimes under contract and sometimes as owners; but if the latter, there would rapidly be established separate companies and new financial arrangements.
41. On Morgan's and Higginson's roles in the formation of General Electric and the GE board membership, see Carosso, *Morgans*, 390–91; Vincent Carosso, *Investment Banking in America* (Cambridge, MA: Harvard University Press, 1970), 43 (identifies Lee, Higginson as banker for Thomson-Houston Electric). For Lee, Higginson's role in railroad finance, see ibid., 34. In 1906, Lee, Higginson would open a London office; Carosso writes that prior to that, its access to European capital "appears to have been through its connections with Speyer & Co." Carosso, *Investment Banking in America*, 91, 95n77.
42. Wilkins, *History ...to 1914*, 204–7.
43. On international banking relationships in these years, Rondo Cameron and V. I. Bovykin, eds., *International Banking* (Oxford: Oxford University Press, 1991); European Association for Business History, *Handbook on the History of European Banks* (Aldershot, England: Edward Elgar, 1994), henceforth cited as *Handbook on the History of European Banks*; Paul H. Emden, *Money Powers of Europe in the Nineteenth and Twentieth Centuries* (London: Sampson Low, Marston & Co., [1937]); Gall, et al., *Deutsche Bank, 1870–1995*; Kobrak, *Banking on Global Markets.* We have also relied on bank histories and gone into some European bank archives.
44. There seem to have been a number of reasons for this that came down to the absence in The Netherlands of any comparative advantage in electric utilities. The key Dutch participant in the electrical manufacturing industry, Philips, did not make turbines and other heavy electrical equipment. Also, perhaps the strength of Dutch banking in the age of railroads was greater than in the subsequent age of electric utilities.
45. *New York Times*, Nov. 14, 1890 (on the creditor committee); see also Buss, *Henry Villard*, 217.
46. Syndicate information, JPML, Collins notes, p. 10; Wilkins, *History ... to 1914*, 221. Interestingly, Winslow, Lanier, & Co. was one of the earliest customers of Edison's Pearl Street Station, which opened in 1882. Mitchell, *S. Z. Mitchell*, 37. The Pearl Street station began operations on September 4, 1882; by the end of that month, it had 59 customers, with Winslow, Lanier among them. The office of J. P. Morgan at Drexel, Morgan (23 Wall Street, New York) was lit when the current went on at the Pearl Street station. Ibid., 35. Jill Jonnes, *Empires of Light: Edison, Tesla, Westinghouse and the Race to Electrify the World* (New York: Random House, 2003), 282, 309 (on Adams and the Edison companies). On Winslow, Lanier's history and importance as an investment bank, see Carosso, *Investment Banking*, 12–13, 37, 91.
47. At the age of 81, in 1927, Adams would write a two-volume history of Niagara Power Company: Edward Dean Adams, *Niagara Power. History of Niagara Falls Power Company,* 2 vol. (Niagara Falls, NY: Niagara Falls Power Co., 1927); Wilkins, *History ...to 1914*, 221, 548, and Kobrak, *Banking on Global Markets* (on Adams). During the 1880s, Deutsche Bank had taken part in

financing the Northern Pacific Railroad; Villard, who had channeled Deutsche Bank money into that railroad, became the bank's representative in the United States in 1886 and had been (as noted earlier) instrumental in bringing Siemens and AEG as well as the Deutsche Bank into Edison General Electric, 1889–1891. In 1890, the British manufacturing affiliate of Siemens, Siemens Brothers, London, presented a proposal to supply the Niagara Falls project that was not accepted (Wilkins, *History ... to 1914*, 434–36, 549). While Deutsche Bank had become discontented with Villard from 1890, it had continued to use the man as its representative, and Villard brought Deutsche Bank investments into U.S. public utilities (portfolio, not direct investments) in 1891–1892. Indeed, when Deutsche Bank and the German banking house Jacob S. H. Stern were in 1892 considering supporting Cincinnati Edison Electric as part of a syndicate, the Deutsche Bank wrote Villard (Nov. 11, 1892) that it "would not have invested 'such considerable amounts' in a business so unfamiliar to them had it not been for Villard's confidence in the project." (Kobrak, *Banking on Global Markets*). In the crisis of 1893, Deutsche Bank and the banking house Jacob S. H. Stern were "disagreeably astonished" with Villard: They had made a loan to the North American Company, "solely to satisfy Villard" and now "refused to put any more in." They had relied on Villard "for protection of our interest," and Villard had let them down. (Based on Stern to Villard, June 23, 1893, Box 99, Folder 742, Villard Collection, Baker Library, Harvard Business School; we are indebted to Kobrak for this document.) In 1893, as Villard's Northern Pacific went into receivership, Deutsche Bank reached its last straw. Adams served on the reorganization committee for the Northern Pacific, and in 1893 the Deutsche Bank appointed Adams as its U.S. representative, finally replacing Villard. Kobrak documents the tumultuous Deutsche Bank–Villard relationship in Kobrak, *Banking on Global Markets*. Kobrak has used the very large collection of Villard–Deutsche Bank *and* Adams–Deutsche Bank correspondence in the German Deutsche Bank archives. For more on Adams, see also Manfred Pohl, ed., *Arthur von Gwinner. Lebenserinnerungen,* 2nd ed. (Frankfurt am Main: Friz Knapp Verlag, 1992), 62–64, and Karl Helfferich, *Georg von Siemens: Ein Lebensbild aus Deutschlands Grosser Zeit*, 2nd ed., II (Berlin: Julius Springer, 1923), 260–72.

48. *New York Times*, Aug. 8, 1898 (Cripple Creek), Dec. 6, 1902 (seat on Stock Exchange), Jan. 20, 1913 (advertisement on experience). On Cripple Creek mining promotions in London, see Wilkins, *History ... to 1914*, 242. Guanajuato Power and Electric Co. was to develop electric light and power in the Guanajuato district in Mexico. In 1910, Frederick Gerhard of William P. Bonbright & Co. was appointed assistant secretary of the Guanajuato Power and Electric Co. *New York Times*, July 1, 1908 and May 2, 1910. Bonbright was probably associated with this electric utility from its origins in 1902. The "Mexican" company was headquartered in Colorado Springs, CO. *Moody's 1914*, 375. On Guanajuato, Mexico, "the city that silver built," where in 1903 Porfírio Díaz inaugurated a new Opera House, see *New York Times*, Sept. 24, 2006.

49. On German banks abroad, see Hermann Wallich and Paul Wallich, *Zwei Generationen im Deutschen Bankwesen 1833–1914* (Frankfurt am Main: Fritz

Knapp, 1978), 274–338; Gall, et al., *Deutsche Bank,* esp. 16, 18, 58–59; Peter Hertner, "German Banks Abroad Before 1914," in Geoffrey Jones, ed., *Banks as Multinationals* (London: Routledge, 1990), 99–119; J. Riesser, *The German Great Banks and Their Concentration* (1911; reprinted New York: Arno Press, 1977), esp. 420–545. Hertner, "German Banks," 99, notes the growing share of world trade in manufactured products by German enterprises. See also Henri Hauser, *Germany's Commercial Grip on the World: Her Business Methods Explained* (New York: Charles Scribner's Sons, 1918), wherein he quotes (p. 64) Deutsche Bank's Georg von Siemens as having said (in 1907) "Every bank created abroad ...is the pioneer of national industry." The Banco Alemán Transatlántico opened as a branch of the Deutsche Übersee Bank, in Buenos Aires on Aug. 5, 1887. It continued to trade as the Banco Alemán Transatlántico after the name change of its parent in 1893; it would be helpful in the development of Compañía Alemana Transatlántica de Electricidad (CATE).

50. Albert Broder, in "Banking and the Electrotechnical Industry in Western Europe," in Rondo Cameron and V. I. Bovykin, eds., *International Banking* (Oxford: Oxford University Press, 1991), 468–84, emphasizes the initial caution of French banks. See also Lanthier, "Les Constructions Électriques en France."

51. In the first decade of the twentieth century, Loewenstein was a partner in the Belgian investment house Stallaerts & Loewenstein (Christopher Armstrong and H. V. Nelles, *Southern Exposure: Canadian Promoters in Latin America and the Caribbean, 1896–1930* [Toronto: University of Toronto Press, 1988], 305n13, 80, 149). David Kynaston, *The City of London* (London: Chatto & Windus, 1999), III, 145 (on Loewenstein's "fortune"). On the pre-1914 activities of Loewenstein in Brazilian electrification, see Duncan McDowall, *The Light: Brazilian Traction, Light and Power Company Limited, 1899–1945* (Toronto: University of Toronto Press, 1988), 106, 140–41, 156, 161, 183, 189–91.

52. Gianni Toniolo, *One Hundred Years, 1894–1994: A Short History of the Banca Commerciale Italiana* (Milan: Banca Commerciale Italiana, 1994), 34 (relation to the Italian Edison company). For the early years of the Italian Edison company, see Antonio Confalonieri, *Banca e Industria in Italia 1894–1906,* III (Milano: Banca Commerciale Italiana, 1976), 217–29. The initial shareholders in BCI in 1894 were the major German banks (including Deutsche Bank, the Berliner Handelsgesellschaft, the Disconto Gesellschaft, the Bank für Handels und Industrie, and the Dresdner Bank); the private German banking house S. Bleichröder, Berlin; as well as the Austrian and Swiss banks (the latter comprised one each from Zurich, Basel, and Geneva: Credit Suisse, Basler Bankverein, and Union Financière, respectively). Toniolo, *One Hundred Years*, 28.

53. Toniolo, *One Hundred Years,* 34, 36–37 (where it is noted that BCI took part in the financing the formation of thirteen firms in the electrical sector in the years before World War I); *Handbook on the History of European Banks*, 602; Luciano Segreto, "Electifier un Rêve," in Dominique Barjot, et al., eds., *L'Électrification Outre-mer de la Fin du XIXe Siècle aux Premières Décolonisations* (Paris: EDF [2002]), 237–38; Peter Hertner, "Il Capitale

Tedesco nell'Industria Elettrica Italiana Fino alla Prima Guerra Mondiale," in Bruno Bezza, ed., *Energia e Sviluppo: L'Industria Elettrica Italiana e la Società Edison* (Torino: Einaudi, 1986), 211–56; and Peter Hertner, "Il Capitale Tedesco in Italia dall'Unità alla Prima Guerra Mondiale," in *Blanche Miste e Sviluppo Economico Italiano* (Bologna: II Mulino, 1984), 209–25. On the Libyan company in 1913, see Atto Constitutivo delle Società Elettrica Coloniale Italia, in Sofindit (SOF), Box 33, BCI collection, Archivio Storico di Banca Intesa, for the BCI, Banco di Roma, and the electricity supply companies' involvements in the newly constituted Libyan enterprise.

54. An important source for foreign investments in electric utilities in Spain is Teresa Tortella, *A Guide to Sources of Information on Foreign Investment in Spain, 1780–1914* (Amsterdam: International Institute of Social History, 2000) (http://www.ica.org/en/node/30421, accessed Sept. 26, 2007); see also Peter Hertner, and H. V. Nelles, "Contrasting Styles of Foreign Investment: A Comparison of the Entrepreneurship, Technology, and Finance of German and Canadian Enterprises in Barcelona Electrification," *Revue Économique*, 58:1 (Jan. 2007), 191–214, and Anna M. Aubanell-Jubany, "La Industria Eléctrica y la Electrificación de la Industria en Madrid entre 1890 y 1935," Ph.D. thesis, European University Institute, Florence, 2001.
55. On this, we have found particularly useful Armstrong and Nelles, *Southern Exposure*, 6, and passim. So, too, the general banking literature has been invaluable.
56. Patricia Roy, "The British Columbia Electric Railway Company, 1897–1928: A British Company in British Columbia," Ph.D. thesis, University of British Columbia, 1970, and her "Direct Management from Abroad: The Formative Years of the British Columbia Electric Railway," *Business History Review*, 47 (Spring 1973), 239–59. See also Armstrong and Nelles, *Southern Exposure*, 151; Horne-Payne was also a director of Sperling & Co. (ibid., 151). On BCER and British direction, especially, the role of Horne-Payne, R. H. Sperling, and Sperling & Co., see Christopher Armstrong and H. V. Nelles, *Monopoly's Moment: The Organization and Regulation of Canadian Utilities, 1830–1930* (Philadelphia: Temple University Press, 1986), 97–100, 132–34, 207–8, 348–49, 369.
57. Nelles, *Southern Exposure*, 95. Wernher, Beit & Co. was founded by Alfred Beit and Julius Wernher. Both men were German-born and had made their money in South African diamonds, before founding the London house in the 1890s. They became involved in South African gold mining. Then they invested in electric traction. Beit died in 1906, Wernher in 1912. After Beit's death, the firm Wernher, Beit & Co. came to an end. Kynaston, *City of London*, II, 82–83, 123, 134. Dates of the men's death are from Emden, *Money Powers*, 420, 428. See also Maryna Fraser, "International Archives in South Africa," *Business and Economic History*, 2nd ser., 16 (1987), 168, on Wernher, Beit's tramway interests in Chile, Mexico, Portugal, and South Africa.
58. See text on British Empire Trust. On Trustees' Executors' and Securities Insurance Corporation, see Wilkins, *History ... to 1914*, 492–93; it participated in the Cataract Construction Company, which was involved in Niagara Falls power developments.

59. For Foster & Braithwaite's important role in electrification at home and abroad, see W. J. Reader, *A House in the City: A Study of the City and of the Stock Exchange Based on the Records of Foster & Braithwaite 1825–1975* (London: B. T. Batsford, 1979), 100–5, and Kynaston, *City of London*, II, 463. On Electric and General Investment, see also Raphael Schapiro, "Public Ownership and Private Investment: The Case of British Electric Traction," in his "Why Public Ownership? Urban Utilities in London, 1870–1914"(D.Phil. thesis, Nuffield College, Oxford University, June 2003), 209, 224.
60. See Chapter 2 on free standing companies. The best work on British overseas banking is Geoffrey Jones, *British Multinational Banking 1830–1990* (Oxford: Oxford University Press, 1993). Also useful are the earlier, A. S. J. Baster, *The International Banks* (London: P. S. King & Son, 1935), and A. S. J. Baster, *The Imperial Banks* (London: P. S. King & Son, 1929).
61. Gall, et al., *Deutsche Bank*, 58.
62. Baster, *International Banks*, 153. Baster notes the late-nineteenth-century, early-twentieth-century competition from German banks and from others on the continent. Ibid., 154–56.
63. Armstrong and Nelles, *Southern Exposure*, 48.
64. Ibid., ix. This book and H. V. Nelles himself (and his background papers) have been our principal source on the Canadian role in utilities in Latin America. On Spain, see Hertner and Nelles, "Contrasting Styles of Foreign Investment."
65. Armstrong and Nelles, *Southern Exposure*, passim, and Gregory P. Marchildon, "The Montreal Engineering Company and International Power: Overcoming the Limitations of the Free-Standing Utility," in Wilkins and Schröter, eds., *Free-Standing Company*, 391–418.
66. Gregory P. Marchildon, *Profits and Politics. Beaverbrook and the Gilded Age of Canadian Finance* (Toronto: University of Toronto Press, 1996). The date of formation of Dominion Securities is from the Royal Bank of Canada website (http://www.rbc.com/history/quicktofrontier/ds.html, accessed Sept. 26, 2007). Dominion Securities Corporation was set up by the Central Canada Loan & Savings Company, which had opened its doors in 1884. Armstrong and Nelles, *Southern Exposure*, passim. By 1902, Dominion Securities Corporation had a London office. The representative was Canadian-born Edward Peacock. See notes to Chapter 4, herein.
67. Armstrong and Nelles, *Southern Exposure*, 10 (on the law firms), 148–68 (on James Dunn, who made London his permanent home in 1907). See also Graham Taylor and Peter A. Baskerville, *A Concise History of Business in Canada* (Toronto: Oxford University Press, 1994), 257 (on Max Aitken, who settled in Great Britain in 1910).
68. Henry M. Whitney, the U.S. entrepreneur who took the initiative in transforming Boston streetcars from horse to electric power, had gone to Nova Scotia in the mid-1890s to obtain coal for his New England power plants. "As an afterthought," Whitney and his chief engineer Fred Stark Pearson became involved in a small Halifax streetcar promotion, turning it into a profitable business, which impressed the Canadians, not only in Halifax, but in Montreal and Toronto as well. Pearson, who had been the principal engineer

on the Metropolitan Street Railway in New York as well as the West End Street Railway in Boston, would bring the receptive Canadians into a wide range of electric traction, as well as light and power promotions. Armstrong and Nelles, *Monopoly's Moment*, 90. One writer argued that Pearson knew how "to enlist the support of the venture capitalists of the time." Gil Cooke, "An Extreme Power Engineer: The Accomplishments of Fred Stark Pearson, Part One," *IEEE Power and Energy Magazine*, 1 (Nov/Dec. 2003), 60–65. For the life and times of Pearson, see McDowall, *Light*, passim, and Armstrong and Nelles, *Southern Exposure*, passim.

69. Marchildon, "The Montreal Engineering Company," 393–94.
70. Wilkins, *History ... to 1914*, 554.
71. Wilkins, *Emergence of Multinational Enterprise* (on the American companies abroad); Catherine Vuillermot, *Pierre-Marie Durand et l'Énergie Industrielle* (Paris: CNRS, 2001), 45, 64 (on Madagascar).
72. Both Victoria Falls & Transvaal Power Co. and Chile Exploration Company are listed on Table 1.1 herein as owning among the highest-voltage transmission systems outside the United States. Victoria Falls & Transvaal Power Co.'s inclusion reflected the gold-mining requirements in the Transvaal, while Chile Exploration had heavy use of electrolytic processes in treating the copper ores. Interview by Mira Wilkins with P. M. Markert, General Electric, Johannesburg, South Africa, Aug. 3, 1965 (on GE history); Wilfried Feldenkirchen, *Siemens: From Workshop to Global Player* (Munich: Piper, 2000), 401 (on Siemens). Céline Boileau, "La Production Électrique Destinée à las Minière en Afrique du Sud (1880–1922)" in Barjot, et al., eds., *L'Électrification Outre-mer*, 474, writes that the first concession for electrification in South Africa was given to Siemens & Halske in 1894. United States Federal Trade Commission, *Report on Co-operation in American Export Trade,* 2 vol. (Washington, DC: USGPO, 1916), II, 544 (henceforth cited as *FTC Report*). Victoria Falls Power Co. Ltd. (VFP) was formed in 1906; it was renamed Victoria Falls & Transvaal Power Co. Ltd. (VFTP) in 1909. VFP obtained a monopoly for the generation and distribution of power for the mineral industry. AEG was involved, as were the Dresdner Bank and the Deutsche Bank. VFP and then VFTP appear to have acquired the power plant built by Siemens & Halske in Brakpan, South Africa. Boileau, "La Production Électrique," 459, 462, 469, 474. For this period, the Guggenheims made a huge (for a single firm) investment, some $12 million in the Chile Exploration Company. Wilkins, *Emergence of Multinational Enterprise*, 181–82.
73. "Windows to Malaysia" website (http://www.windowstomalaysia.com.my/nation/14_3_1.htm, accessed Sept. 27, 2005). It was built on Sungai Sempam near Raub, Pahang, Malaysia.
74. D.K. Fieldhouse, *Economics and Empire 1830–1914* (Ithaca: Cornell University Press, 1973), 3.
75. Hertner, "Financial Strategies," 149; Donald Wallace, *Market Control in the Aluminum Industry* (Cambridge, MA: Harvard University Press, 1937), 6; Karl Erich Born, *Internationale Kartellierung einer Neuen Industrie: Die Aluminum-Association 1901–1915*, in *Zeitschrift für Unternehmensgeschichte*, Beiheft 84 (Stuttgart: Franz Steiner Verlag, 1994), 14–31.

76. Wallace, *Market Control*, 33–34, 40. The initial aluminum production there was in the same year, 1898.
77. Aluminum Company of America Brief, U.S. *v.* Aluminum Company of America, Eq. # 85–73 (Southern District of New York, 1940), 103 (on the 1899 contract between Pittsburgh Reduction and Shawinigan Water and Power Co., under which Alcoa's predecessor obtained power at Shawinigan Falls; these rights were assigned to the latter's Canadian affiliate, Northern Aluminum Co. Ltd. in 1903); Wilkins, *Emergence of Multinational Enterprise*, 138–39; William J. Hausman and John L. Neufeld, "U.S. Foreign Direct Investment in Electrical Utilities in the 1920s," in Wilkins and Schröter, eds., *Free-Standing Company*, 369, 378–79; Thomas Heinrich, "Product Diversification in the U.S. Pulp and Paper Industry: The Case of International Paper, 1898–1941," *Business History Review*, 75 (Autumn 2001), 483; see also Claude Bellevance, *Shawinigan Water and Power, 1898–1963* (Montreal: Boreal, 1994), 225–33 (on Aldred's role in the financing of SWP); Herbert Marshall, Frank A. Southard, and Kenneth W. Taylor, *Canadian-American Industry* (1936; reprinted New York: Russell & Russell, 1970), 44–46; and Armstrong and Nelles, *Monopoly's Moment*, 104–6.
78. Wallace, *Market Control*, 38. L. F. Haber, *The Chemical Industry 1900–1930* (Oxford: Oxford University Press, 1971), 87, 167–69. German, French, and Swedish interests were involved in Norsk Hydro. The German interests were linked with the chemical industry. On Badische Anilin- und Soda-Fabrik AG's participation, see Jeffrey Allan Johnson, "The Power of Synthesis (1900–1925)," in Werner Abelshauser, et al., *German Industry and Global Enterprise: BASF: The History of a Company* (Cambridge: Cambridge University Press, 2004), 144–45. The French interests were those of the Banque de Paris et des Pays-Bas (Paribas). On the large French loans to Norsk Hydro in 1910 and 1911 (with Paribas and Crédit Lyonnais as underwriters), see Samir Saul, "Banking Alliances and International Issues on the Paris Capital Market, 1890–1914," in Youssef Cassis and Eric Bussière, eds., *London and Paris as International Financial Centres in the Twentieth Century* (Oxford: Oxford University Press, 2005), 134. On the Stockholms Enskilda Bank involvement in Norsk Hydro, see Ulf Olsson, *Furthering a Fortune* (Stockholm: Ekerlids Förlag, 2001), 11. Badische effectively pulled out from its controlling interest in Norsk Hydro in 1911, but there were some remaining German minority interests.
79. This came up in the discussion at the Buenos Aires meetings, July 2003.
80. The story of how Duke was brought into the Saguenay River development is told for the first time by David Massell, *Amassing Power: J. B. Duke and the Saguenay River, 1897–1927* (Montreal: McGill-Queen's University Press, 2000), 48–61. The quoted passages are on pp. 52 and 60. For more on Duke's background and his experiences in 1912–1914 with the men who brought him into the Saguenay River project, see ibid., 62–98. After the dissolution of American Tobacco in 1911, Duke had become chairman of British American Tobacco Company (BAT), London, one of the major companies spun off from American Tobacco. Although Duke held the title of chairman of BAT until 1923 and initially, at least, played an active role, BAT appears to have been

managed in the main by the highly capable Hugo Cunliffe-Owen. Over the years, Duke's participation in BAT management seems to have captured less and less of his attention. Mira Wilkins, *The History of Foreign Investment in the United States, 1914–1945* (Cambridge, MA: Harvard University Press, 2004), 141–42.

81. In 1886, Westinghouse Electric Company was incorporated in the United States; in 1889, it started the wholly owned (London) Westinghouse Electric Company, which had Westinghouse world patent rights outside the Western Hemisphere. This subsidiary started as a trading, constructing, and installing company, with no initial manufacturing; at the turn of the century, its successor company would embark on manufacturing. Wilkins, *Emergence of Multinational Enterprise*, 59. The German companies included both Siemens & Halske and Schuckert & Co. In 1902, these companies merged their power engineering activities to form Siemens-Schuckert. Feldenkirchen, *Siemens*, 93.
82. For the international business of General Electric and Westinghouse in the late nineteenth and early twentieth centuries, see Wilkins, *Emergence of Multinational Enterprise*, 94–96, which has nothing on investments in foreign utilities, only on foreign manufacturing and sales. GE's small interest in AEG apparently dated from sometime between 1903 and 1905, when AEG was acquiring Union Elektrizitäts Gesellschaft (UEG), one of the companies in which GE (through its Thomson-Houston heritage) had an interest. Ibid., 94. Before World War I, Siemens had manufacturing plants in Austria-Hungary, France, Great Britain, Russia, and Spain, as well as a large number of sales and technical bureaus around the world. Peter Hertner, "L'Industrie Électrotechnique Allemande entre les Deux Guerres: À la Recherche d'une Position Internationale Perdue," *Relations Internationales*, 43 (Autumn 1985), 293. When AEG acquired UEG, it acquired an interest in a group of foreign manufacturing facilities – in Riga, Vienna, and Milan, for example. Ibid., 296.
83. British Electrical and Allied Manufacturers' Association, *Combines and Trusts in the Electrical Industry: The Position in Europe in 1927* (1927; reprinted New York: Arno Press, 1977), 27. This is henceforth cited as BEAM, *Combines*.
84. In 1903, GE and AEG were dividing markets; so, too, in 1905, GE and British Thomson-Houston agreed to selling rights in particular territories. Wilkins, *Emergence of Multinational Etnerprise*, 94–95. The GE-AEG division of markets came at the same time as AEG was taking over UEG.
85. Pierre Lanthier, "Multinationals and the French Electrical Industry, 1889–1940," in Teichova, Lévy-Leboyer, and Nussbaum, eds., *Historical Studies*, 143–45; Patrick Fridenson, "France," in Alfred D. Chandler, Jr., Franco Amatori, and Takashi Hikino, *Big Business and the Wealth of Nations* (Cambridge: Cambridge University Press, 1997), 210; Wilkins, *Emergence of Multinational Enterprise*, 54. Lanthier writes that during the years 1880 to 1914 the French "electrical industry," manufacturing and electricity supply, was characterized by inward foreign investments that were sizable but did not imply "domination." He argues that in this period there were three waves of inward foreign investments, the first during the 1880s in electric lighting, the second in the 1890s concentrating on the electrification of tramways and the

development of power stations, and the third, in manufacturing plants to take advantage of an expanding French market. Lanthier, "Multinationals," 143–47. See also Lanthier, "Les Constructions Électriques en France."

86. Fridenson, "France," 210. Albert Broder, *Alcatel Alsthom: Histoire de la Compagnie Générale d' Électricité* (Paris: Larousse, 1992), 41; the second Swiss representative was from the Banque Suisse et Française, which had been founded in 1894. For the German prewar interests in France, see Peter Hertner, "Technologie et Capitaux Allemands dans l'Industrie Électrotechnique Français avant la Première Guerre Mondiale: Un Premier Bilan," in Michèle Merger and Dominique Barjot, *Les Entreprises et Leur Réseaux: Hommes, Capitaux, Techniques et Pouvoirs, XIXe–XXe Siècles, Melanges en l'Honneur de François Caron* (Paris: PUP, 1998), 499–521.
87. Marco Doria and Peter Hertner, "Urban Growth and the Creation of Integrated Electricity Systems: The Cases Genoa and Barcelona, 1894–1914," in Andrea Giuntini, Peter Hertner, and Gregorio Núñez, eds., *Urban Growth on Two Continents in the 19th and 20th Centuries: Technology, Networks, Finance and Public Regulation* (Granada, Spain: Editorial Comares, 2004), 245–46 (on EEdC). See Chap. 3, note 114 below for more on this venture.
88. The first board of THM, as of 1898, had as president Victor Fris (a Belgian politician and president of a Belgian local railway), along with representatives of FTH, GE, UEG, Gesfürel, and SGB. For details on the board and the shareholdings in THM, Lanthier, "Les Constructions Électriques en France."
89. Nikos Pantelakis, *The Electrification of Greece: From Private Initiative to State Monopoly (1889–1956)* (Athens: Cultural Foundation of the National Bank of Greece, 1991), 40, 55–57, 71. This volume is in Greek; the relevant portions have been translated for us by its author. Ibid., 74–75, gives the board of the Compagnie Hellénique d' Électricité, representing the founding group. See also Lanthier, "Les Constructions Électriques en France." Less ambitious, and later, but indicative of the general move abroad of French companies, in 1911 Joseph Bligny, engineer and a key individual in Omnium Français d' Électricité (OFE), had gotten concessions to develop electricity and other public services in two Greek cities: Larissa and Corinth. In 1912, OFE led in establishment of Omnium Hellénique d' Électricité to develop those concessions. See Vuillermot, *Pierre-Marie Durand*, 99n74.
90. Lanthier, "Les Constructions Électriques en France."
91. AEG's initial investments in utilities in Germany were by its predecessor company; see Hughes, *Networks of Power*, 71–75. AEG may have had some interest in the North American Company, associated with Deutsche Bank's involvement. On its Spanish interests, Gabriel Tortella, *The Development of Modern Spain* (Cambridge, MA: Harvard University Press, 2000), 217–18. The Pereire brothers were French. In 1852, they founded Société Générale de Crédit Foncier (a mortgage bank) and Société Générale de Crédit Mobilier (planned as a "railway bank"). For the Pereire brothers' international activities, see Cameron and Bovykin, eds., *International Banking*, 8–10, 75, 85, 145, 531. Before they got into public utilities finance, they had been deeply involved in railroads. On the divestment, see Doria and Hertner, "Urban Growth," 241n92: AEG explained its sale of the Madrid company in that the capital of

this company was mainly in "foreign [French]" hands, and the price AEG got was too good to refuse. From 1894, the Madrileña company came to be dominated by French interests (the company had a dual board of directors, one in Madrid and one in Paris). In 1897, Madrileña bought 62.5 percent of the British free standing company Electricity Supply Company for Spain Ltd., which had been established in Madrid in 1889. Information from Anna Maria Aubanell-Jubany, e-mail, Sept. 1, 2005, based on her thesis, Anna M. Aubanell-Jubany, "La Industria Eléctrica y la Electrificación de la Industria en Madrid entre 1890 y 1935," Ph.D. thesis, European University Institute, Florence, 2001, pp. 14–21. Madrileña merged with the electricity business of Urquijo, a key Spanish banker, forming in 1912 the Unión Eléctrica Madrileña. The French did not do well as investors, and in July 1913 "the French presence disappeared." (Ibid., 116–17). Although there had been a long history of foreign direct investment, by the end of 1913 there was none in the largest electricity supplier in Madrid.

92. Doria and Hertner, "Urban Growth," 231. Société Lyonnaise des Eaux et de l'Éclairage was founded in France in 1880. Before 1914, most of its investments were still in France (Suez website: http://www.suez.com/en/groupe/history/group-1822-1946/1822–1946/, accessed Sept. 26, 2007). This Spanish investment by Société Lyonnaise des Eaux et de l'Éclairage appears to be the exception. In 1905–1906, Electrobank would take over the financing of Barcelonesa. See text and Chap. 3, note 114 below.
93. Javier Loscertales, *Deutsche Investitionen in Spanien 1870–1920* (Stuttgart: Franz Steiner Verlag, 2002), 148–252; Peter Hertner, "The German Electrotechnical Industry in the Italian Market Before the Second World War," in Geoffrey Jones and Harm Schröter, eds., *The Rise of Multinationals in Continental Europe* (Aldershot, England: Elgar, 1993), 157; and Doria and Hertner, "Urban Growth," 219–30. UEG had interests in tramways in Naples. Ranieri, *Dannie Heineman*, 43–45.
94. Luciano Segreto, "Financing the Electric Industry Worldwide: Strategy and Structure of the Swiss Electric Holding Companies, 1895–1945," *Business and Economic History,* 23 (Fall 1994), 163.
95. The French Thomson-Houston, for example, had hoped to invest in both manufacturing and tramways (1896–1902), but it got out of the tramway (power) investments because it was not receiving adequate returns, owing to the low rate structure imposed by municipalities. Lanthier. "Les Constructions Électriques en France." Earlier, we noted that General Electric had intended in 1893 to realize capital for its core business in a crisis time by spinning off electric utilities.
96. Estimates made by Hertner, "Il Capitale Tedesco nell'Industria Elettrica Italiana," 242, 256; see also Doria and Hertner, "Urban Growth," 219–30, 247–48. For another estimate on foreign direct investments in Italian electric utilities that includes foreign capital other than that from the Germans, see Luciano Segreto, "Imprenditori e Finanzieri," in *Storia dell' Industria Elettrica in Italia*, vol.1 (Rome-Bari: Laterza, 1992), 332. (Segreto estimates that foreign investors held 30 percent of the capital of Italian electric utilities in 1913.) Considerable German investment was not made directly, but through Swiss

holding companies. The 16.5 percent estimate of Hertner's does not include that "indirect" investment. Thus, the reduction of German interests and the "domestication" was not as extreme as the reduction from 40 percent to 16.5 percent suggests.

97. Riesser, *German Great Banks*, 124–25.
98. For the beginnings, see Segreto, "Financing the Electric Industry Worldwide," 164, and Peter Hertner, "German Multinational Enterprise Before 1914," in Peter Hertner and Geoffrey Jones, eds., *Multinationals: Theory and History* (Aldershot, England: Gower, 1986), 128. The form was in part anticipated in the United States by Thomson-Houston's United Electric Securities Company (in 1890) (see above).
99. On the numerous advantages of Switzerland for such companies, see Segreto, "Financing the Electric Industry Worldwide," 163; Paquier, *Histoire de l'Électricité en Suisse*, II, 960ff; and Peter Hertner, "Les Sociétés Financières Suisses et le Développement de l'Industrie Électrique Jusqu'a la Première Guerre Mondiale," in Fabienne Cardot, ed., *1880–1980: Un Siècle d' Électricité dans le Monde* (Paris: PUF, 1987), 341–55. The "neutrality" of Switzerland was important, for in both France and Germany capital was "commonly regarded as a servant of national purposes rather than an ordinary private possession to be disposed of in accordance with the private judgment and on the private risk of the owners," and there was the long-standing political enmity between France and Germany. Herbert Feis, *Europe: The World's Banker 1870–1914* (1930; reprinted New York: Norton, 1965), 466.
100. BEAM, *Combines*, 55 (the quote). Jacques Thobie, "European Banks in the Middle East," in Cameron and Bovykin, eds., *International Banking*, 434 (on the bringing together of French and German capital). In the Middle East, there were particular conflicts between German and French governmental aspirations and the desire for influence. On Belgian capital markets, see B. S. Chelpner, *Le Marche Financier Belge Depuis Cent Ans* (Brussels: Librairie Falk Fils, 1930), and Herman van der Wee and Martine Goossens, "Belgium," in Cameron and Bovykin, eds., *International Banking*, 113–29.
101. Theodore J. Grayson, *Investment Trusts* (New York: Wiley & Sons, 1928), 11 (on the origins of investment trusts).
102. Ginette Kurgan-Van Hentenryk, an expert on this subject, made the comment on no single model.
103. On the other hand, C. K. Hobson, *The Export of Capital* (London: Constable, 1914), 44–45, found that a considerable amount of "French business" passed through Brussels and London brokers owing to various French government controls. He cites works on the history of "fiscal treatment of foreign securities" in France. See also Feis, *Europe: The World's Banker*.
104. On Belgian holding companies in tramways, see Alberte Martinez López, "Belgian Investment in Tramways and Light Railways: An International Approach, 1892–1935," *Journal of Transport History*, 3rd ser., 24:1 (March 2003), 59–77; on tramways in Europe, Ranieri, *Dannie Heineman*, 42ff; John McKay, *Tramways and Trolleys: The Rise of Urban Mass Transport in Europe* (Princeton: Princeton University Press, 1976); see also contributions of Peter Hertner, Harm Schröter, and Jean-François Hennart in Wilkins and Schröter,

eds., *Free-Standing Company*, 154, 335, 337–38, and P.V. Ol', *Foreign Capital in Russia*, translated from Russian with an introduction by Geoffrey Jones and Grigori Gerenstain (1922; New York: Garland Publishing, 1983), 8, 140–44, 222–23 (for Russian tramway companies); Tortella, *Development of Modern Spain*, 218 (the Belgians in Spanish tramways); Van der Wee and Goossens, "Belgium," in Cameron and Bovykin, eds., *International Banking*, 124, 126–27; and G. Kurgan-Van Hentenryk, "Finance and Financiers in Belgium, 1880–1940," in Youssef Cassis, ed., *Finance and Financiers in European History 1880–1960* (Cambridge: Cambridge University Press, 1992), 317–36 (general context).

105. Segreto, "Financing the Electric Industry Worldwide," 163–64. Swiss companies typically had both German and French names. Thus, Elektrobank was also known as Banque pour Entreprises Électrique, while Indelec was also known as Société Suisse pour l'Industrie Électrique. On Indelec, see Peter Hertner, "Espansione Multinazionale e Finanziamento Internationale dell'Industria Elettrotecnica Tedesca Prima del 1914," in *Studi Storici* (1987), 819–60.

106. Gall, "Deutsche Bank... 1870–1914," 15. By contrast, Peter Hertner sees Elektrobank as completely AEG-dominated. At one time, AEG held 95 percent of the equity in Elektrobank. Hertner, "L'Industrie Électrotechnique Allemande," 297. Swiss bank historian Hans Bauer agrees: Elektrobank was set up by AEG as its "financing company." Hans Bauer, *Swiss Bank Corporation* (Basel: Swiss Bank Corp., 1972), 93.

107. Segreto, "Financing the Electric Industry Worldwide," 163–64, and Paquier, *Histoire de l'Électricité*, II, 967ff. In mid-1895, Basler Bankverein (after an 1897 merger with Zürcher Bankverein, it became Swiss Bankverein, the predecessor of Swiss Bank Corporation) decided to take a 1.5 million franc interest in Elektrobank: "It was of importance in this context to cultivate relations with Berlin and Vienna which 'might be chilled by a refusal,' and at the same time it was desired ... not to let the Basler Handelsbank steal a march." Bauer, *Swiss Bank Corporation,* 93. Basler Bankverein/Swiss Bankverein had interests in Austro-Hungarian railways. On Basler Handelsbank and Indelec, see below.

108. Thus, as noted earlier, there was a strong Deutsche Bank influence in Banca Commerciale Italiana. Gall, "Deutsche Bank... 1870–1914," 15. So, too, as noted above, German, Austrian, and Swiss banks participated in the founding of BCI. And, Paribas would become involved.

109. Albert Broder, "Banking and the Electrotechnical Industry in Western Europe," in Cameron and Bovykin, eds., *International Banking*, 479.

110. "Credit Suisse," *Handbook on the History of European Banks*, 1090. Within the *Handbook*, there are general comments and also individual bank sketches, provided by the individual bank (with no author given). Railroad "banks" and holding companies in Switzerland provided a precedent for the holding companies in the electric utilities sector. In 1879, the Schweizerische Eisenbahnbank was founded by Credit Suisse (it was liquidated in 1885, long before Credit Suisse got involved in electrification). Jules Düblin, "Die Finanzierungs- und Kapitalanlage-Gesellschaften der Schweizerischen Grossbanken," Ph.D. thesis, University of Basel, 1931 (Basel: Polygraphischer

Verlag, 1937), 38–41. Another historian of Credit Suisse writes that the bank "traditionally had two representatives on Elektrobank's board of directors, and assumed the management of the business operations right from the start." Joseph Jung, *From Schweizerische Kreditanstalt to Credit Suisse Group. The History of a Bank* (Zurich: NZZ Verlag, 2000), 64. In 1910 Credit Suisse founded the Schweizerisch-Argentinische Hypothekenbank, Zurich (known in Argentina as Banco Hipotecario Suizo-Argentina) which was involved primarily in electricity and that year (1910) set up a branch in Buenos Aires. Ibid.

111. On Motor, see Segreto, "Financing the Electric Industry Worldwide," 162–175, and Luciano Segreto, "Du 'Made in Germany' au 'Made in Switzerland'," in M. Trédé, ed., *Electricité et Électrification dans le Monde 1880–1980* (Paris: PUF, 1992), 347–67. For Leu & Co. 's involvement with electric utilities and Motor see *Handbook on the History of European Banks*, 1056; Union Bank of Switzerland (UBS) was formed in 1912; on its history see ibid., 1121–22. On the importance of the private bank, Leu & Co., Jung, *From Schweizerische Kreditanstalt to Credit Suisse Group*, 18–20, 69 (by 1913, measured by total assets, it was Switzerland's fourth largest bank, larger than UBS). When Motor was established, the Basel bank, Swiss Bankverein (actually its predecessor, Basler Bankverein) conducted negotiations with Brown Boveri & Co., but "in view of the 'inferior representation on the Board of Directors as against Brown, Boveri's 'overpredominance', the business was 'ultimately declined with thanks.'" Bauer, *Swiss Bank Corporation*, 108. Swiss Bankverein, Basel–by 1913 Switzerland's largest bank–had become fully involved in financing electrification in Switzerland and abroad; in 1910, Swiss Bankverein was represented on the board of Brown, Boveri (ibid., 174); thus, although Motor had limited banking connections, Brown, Boveri came to cooperate with Swiss Bankverein in other projects. And while Swiss Bankverein was not the lead bank in Elektrobank, Motor, or Indelec, that bank's activities in electrification came to be ubiquitous. It assisted other Swiss manufacturers as well as Brown, Boveri. It had its own network. It developed, for example, close ties with the electrical equipment manufacturer, Alioth of Basel. Alioth, in turn, was linked with the Sarasin family group of Basel that was fascinated with the newly developing electrical industry. The latter had many French connections, including those with Giros and Loucheur. Alfred Sarasin-Iselin became allied with Swiss Bankverein as Alioth grew internationally; and just before World War I, Brown, Boveri took over Alioth and its sales organization in Spain, Italy, Austria, Holland, the United States, and South America. Although as late as 1908, Swiss Bankverein looked with "disfavor" on French "power stations," it did come to participate in assisting the financing of French electric power. It was also involved in Austria, through an associated railroad bank. That railroad bank (holding company) increasingly steered its activities toward electrification. It is not surprising to learn that Swiss Bankverein was one of the banks financing the projects of the American engineer Fred Stark Pearson. On Swiss Bankverein pre–World War I engagements in electricity, see Bauer, *Swiss Bank Corporation*, 90, 93, 108, 162–63, 173–75, 249; Paquier, *Histoire de l'Électricité*, I, 268, II, 633–35, 642–46; on Alfred Sarasin-Iselin and A. Sarasin & Co., *Handbook on the History of European Banks*, 1060; and on Swiss Bankverein's financing of Pearson, McDowall, *Light*, 235.

112. Segreto, "Financing the Electric Industry Worldwide," 163–64; Paquier, *Histoire de l'Électricité*, II, 1001; see ibid., 1006, on the first administrative board of Indelec. For more on Indelec, see Hertner, "L'Industrie Électrotechnique Allemande," 297, who notes that whereas AEG was dominant in Elektrobank, Siemens had only a minority interest in Indelec. In 1913, measured by total assets, Basler Handelsbank was smaller than Leu & Co. and UBS, and much smaller than Swiss Bankverein and Credit Suisse. Jung, *From Schweizerische Kreditanstalt to Credit Suisse Group*, 69. When Indelec was formed, the plan was that Basler Bankverein (soon to be Swiss Bankverein) and Basler Handelsbank would both participate, sharing the Swiss half of the capital equally, but the two banks could not agree on the seats on the board of directors, and Basler Handelsbank proceeded alone. Bauer, *Swiss Bank Corporation*, 93. Prior to the formation of Indelec, Basler Handlelsbank had partnered with Siemens (in 1893) in the construction of a hydroelectric power station at Wynau, Switzerland. Serge Paquier, "Swiss Holding Companies from the Mid-Nineteenth Century to the Early 1930s," *Financial History Review*, 8 (Oct. 2001), 175.
113. Segreto, "Financing the Electric Industry Worldwide," 165. In each country, Elektrobank and Indelec shared ownership of the utilities with other investors. Hertner, "Les Sociétés Financières Suisses," 347, lists nine European countries in which Elektrobank participated, as of June 1914: Finland, France, Germany, Italy, Portugal, Romania, Russia, Spain, and Switzerland, as well as Turkey, straddling Europe and Asia. All three holdings companies – Elektrobank, Indelec, and Motor – had important investments in Italy. For their inward Italian investments, see Paquier, *Histoire de l'Électricité*, II, 688–89, and various works by Segreto, especially "Imprenditori e Financieri," 333–35, which documents the Italian electrical investments of Elekrobank, Indelec, and Motor in 1913. See also Hertner, "Il Capitale Tedesco nell'Industria Elettrica Italiana," 211–56, and Hertner, "Les Sociétés Financières Suisses," 341–55.
114. Doria and Hertner, "Urban Growth," 231, explain Elektrobank's role in Compañia Barcelonesa de Electricidad (Barcelonesa); AEG had invested in Barcelonesa in 1894, and the initial management had been sent from AEG, Berlin, to Barcelona. When in 1905–1907, Elektrobank took over the financing of Barcelonesa and arranged for its shares to be introduced on a number of European stock exchanges, the Swiss holding company became highly entrepreneurial in its financing of the Spanish utility and also became relatively more significant as a decision maker in the actual Barcelona operations. Ibid., 231–35. In 1907, Elektrobank dispatched Carl Zander to Barcelonesa as "administrador delegado tecnico." Doria and Hertner argue that AEG "clearly had the last word in all strategic decisions" made by Barcelonesa; the latter was required to use AEG as a general contractor for all construction work and to purchase its electrotechnical material from AEG, Berlin. When after the 1907 business crisis there was a search for new shareholders, the AEG group did not hesitate to bring in Elektrische Licht und Kraftanlagen AG (ELK), which was a Siemens holding company and which in 1909–1910 acquired 9.17 percent of the shares of Barcelonesa. Ibid., 237.

115. Segreto, "Financing the Electric Industry Worldwide," 166. See Paquier, *Histoire de l'Électricité*, II, 716–18, for Brown, Boveri's interests in the Austro-Hungarian empire, which included financing of electric utilities. Schweizerische Eisenbahnbank – the second by that name – formed in Basel in 1890 became closely associated with Swiss Bankverein in 1907, and both it and Swiss Bankverein were involved through Steiermärkishe Elektrizitäts-Gesellschaft (Steiermark Electric Power Co.) in electric utilities in the Austro-Hungarian empire. Bauer, *Swiss Bank Corporation*, 162–63, 249. Swiss Bankverein, with its two subsidiaries, the Eisenbahnbank and Schweizerische Gesellschaft für Anlagewerte (Socval), actually founded the Steiermark company in 1910. Ibid., 174.
116. Siemens, *History of the House of Siemens*, II, 147 (Siemens & Halske participation). George F.W. Young, "German Banks and German Direct Investment in Latin America, 1880–1920," in Carlos Marichal, ed., *Foreign Investment in Latin America: Impact on Economic Development, 1850–1930* (Milan: Università Bocconi, 1994), 63, says Siemens did not come in until 1906.
117. On DUEG/CATE, see Young, "German Banks and German Direct Investment in Latin America, 1880–1920," 60–64; Gall, "Deutsche Bank ... 1870–1914," 61; Gerald Feldman, "The Deutsche Bank ... 1914–1933," in Gall, et al., *Deutsche Bank*, 182–83; and Peter Hertner, "Foreign Direct Investment and the Political Economy of Municipal Government: Compañía Alemana Transatlántica de Electricidad (CATE) and the Electrification of Buenos Aires and Santiago de Chile, 1898–1920," unpublished paper presented at the Business History Conference, Toronto, June 2006. An excellent contemporary description of CATE's holdings in Argentina, Chile, and Uruguay is in Frederic M. Halsey, *Investments in Latin America and the British West Indies* (U.S. Department of Commerce, Bureau of Foreign and Domestic Commerce, Special Agents Series No. 169 [Washington, DC, 1918]), 68–69, 75, 243, 363–64, 494. In Argentina, CATE was involved in Buenos Aires and later in Mendoza; in Chile, its interests were in Santiago, Valparaiso, and Vina del Mar; in Uruguay, it provided electric tramway service in Montevideo. For a brief review of the expansion of CATE in Buenos Aires and its taking over of the existing French and British companies there, see Andrea Lluch and Laura Sánchez, *De Movimiento Popular a Empresa El Cooperativisismo Eléctrico en La Pampa* (Santa Rosa: Fondo Editorial Pampeano, [2001]), 12–13. For background on Gesellschaft für Elektrische Unternehmungen (Gesfürel), Ranieri, *Dannie Heineman*, passim. Gesfürel was founded in 1894 by Isidore Loewe as the financial branch of UEG. Ibid., 43. Both UEG and AEG appear to have been involved in Argentina and Chile before the merger of the two manufacturers. For Oscar Oliven's stay in Argentina on behalf of UEG (and Gesfürel), see ibid., 36. The 1913–1914 Elektrobank interest in CATE was the 3.4 percent interest in South America that Segreto reported (see above), with confirmation in Hertner, "Les Sociétés Financières Suisses," 347.
118. Halsey, *Investments in Latin America*, 21.
119. Different sources give different dates for the AEG takeover of UEG, for it was a process. Hertner, "Financial Strategies," 151, says it was in two stages in 1902 and 1904. The full takeover was completed in 1905.

120. On UEG in Belgium, Van der Wee and Goossens, "Belgium," 127; Ginette Kurgan-Van Hentenryk, "Le Patronat de l'Électricité en Belgique, 1895–1945," in Dominique Barjot, Henri Morsel, and Sophie Coeuré, *Stratégies, Gestion, Management: Les Compagnies Électriques et Leurs Patrons, 1895–1945* (Paris: EDF, 2001), 56, 61–62. Electrobel (Compagnie Générale d'Entreprises Électriques et Industrielles, Brussels) was founded in 1929. Ranieri, *Dannie Heineman*, 43, writes that SGB was started in 1895 by the Banque de Bruxelles with the help of the two German firms UEG and Gesfürel. Martinez López, "Belgian Investment in Tramways," 68–69, indicates that the Belgian participant, Société Générale des Chemins de Fer Économiques (SGCF), was itself an important holding company. According to Martinez López, SGCF was formed in 1889 (we believe this is a typographical error for 1880) by Banque de Bruxelles, Paribas, and the private banks of Brugmann and Cassel; in 1913, its tramway portfolio included forty different companies in ten countries. It was particularly active in Mediterranean Europe, but it had investments worldwide. Also on SGCF, see Kurgan-van Hentenryk, "Finance and Financiers in Belgium," 318. For its predecessor in Belgium, see Ranieri, *Dannie Heineman*, 42, and Martinez López, "Belgian Investment in Tramways," 68 (Table 5, note b).
121. BEAM, *Combines*, 105.
122. Van der Wee and Goossens, "Belgium," 122.
123. The best source on Heineman (and on Sofina) is Ranieri, *Dannie Heineman*. Ranieri, 49, says SGB was involved in the 1898 formation of Sofina. See ibid., 55, on the important UEG/Gesfüral role in the formation of Sofina. Heineman (1872–1962), born in North Carolina, had at age 8 gone with his mother to Germany, where he received an electrical engineering degree from the Technical College of Hanover in 1895 and joined UEG. From that base, he had field assignments supervising the electrification of streetcar systems, construction of power stations, and the establishment of electricity distribution systems. When he joined Sofina, he was 32 years old. See ibid., 15–51; see also *New York Times*, Feb. 2, 1962 (obituary for Heineman). For basic data on Sofina in 1913, see Martinez López, "Belgian Investment in Tramways," 68–69 (No. 8 on Table 5 and No. 5 on Table 6).
124. Hertner, "German Electrotechnical Industry," 158; Jean-François Hennart, "Transaction Cost Theory and the Free-Standing Firm," in Wilkins and Schröter, eds., *Free-Standing Company in the World Economy* (Oxford: Oxford University Press, 1998), 94n21; Luciano Segreto, "Financing the Electric Industry in Europe (1880–1945)," unpublished paper presented in 1993 in Paris at a "pre-Milan-conference" meeting, henceforth cited as Segreto, Milan Paper. See also Ranieri, *Dannie Heineman*, and Martinez López, "Belgian Investment in Tramways," 68–69. Ranieri, *Dannie Heineman*, 76, indicates that on the eve of World War I Heineman was on the board of eighteen companies on four continents. In Argentina, CATE had in its expansion consolidated Argentine tramways. On March 5, 1907 (the same year as CATE got its fifty-year municipal concession), Sofina set up Compagnie Générale de Tramways de Buenos Aires. This company, associated with CATE, with Belgian, English, French, and German interests (a total of 26 participants), would take the initiative and consolidate the Argentine tramway system. Ibid., 64–66.

125. R. P. T. Davenport-Hines, *Dudley Docker* (Cambridge: Cambridge University Press, 1984), 201.
126. Thobie gives all the names of the participants. Thobie, "European Banks in the Middle East," 431–34. Adding to the complexity (and to the "German domination"), as indicated later in this chapter, in Sofina's sphere of influence was Société Centrale pour l'Industrie Électrique (SCIE), the biggest "French" participant in Société des Tramways et de l'Électricité de Constantinople.
127. On Motor, see text and notes above, specifically, Segreto, "Financing the Electric Industry Worldwide," 165; Paquier, *Histoire de l'Électricité*, II, 677–92; and Pierre-Alain Wavre, "Swiss Investments in Italy from the XVIIIth to the XXth Century," *Journal of European Economic History,* 17 (Spring 1988): 94–97. At the end of 1911, Motor had taken part in the formation of Compañía Italo-Argentina de Electricidad (CIAE). BEAM, *Combines*, 89, reports that when CIAE was formed in Buenos Aires, the Zurich banking firm Leu & Co. participated; CIAE "became ... a preserve for the Brown-Boveri Company." On Columbus, see Luciano Segreto, "Capitali, Technologie e Imprenditori Svizzeri nell'Industria Elettrica Italiana: Il Caso della Motor (1895–1923)," in *Energia e Sviluppo. L'Industria Elettrica Italiana e la Società Edison* (Turin: Einaudi, 1986), 200. At origin, CIAE was a shareholder in Columbus, and Columbus seems to have taken over Motor's investment in CIAE, a case of cross-investments. The Italian manufacturers investing in Columbus expected to sell to the South American electric power companies. On CIAE, as seen from an Argentine perspective, see Maria Ines Barbero, "Grupos Empresarios, Intercambio Comercial e Inversiones Italianas en la Argentina," *Estudios Migratorios Latinoamericanos,* 5:(1990), 327–33. Also on Motor, CIAE, and Columbus, see Hertner, "Les Sociétés Financières Suisses," 353.
128. Claude Ph. Beaud, "Investments and Profits of the Multinational Schneider Group: 1894–1943," in Alice Teichova, Maurice Lévy-Leboyer, and Helga Nussbaum, eds., *Multinational Enterprise in Historical Perspective* (Cambridge: Cambridge University Press, 1986), 87; Segreto, Milan Paper. Earlier, Schneider had shown little interest in this industry, although Schneider had participated in a small electricity distributing company in Paris. Broder, "Banking and the Electrotechnical Industry in Western Europe," 473; see also Paquier, *Histoire de l'Électricité*, II, 1033ff. Paquier lists the founding group of bankers on p. 1041. For the involvement of Swiss Bankverein (and its predecessor) in Union Financière de Genève and in Franco-Suisse, see Bauer, *Swiss Bank Corporation*, 73, 90.
129. Hubert Bonin, "The Case of the French Banks," in Cameron and Bovykin, eds., *International Banking*, 82; he argues that closeness between German banks and industry was absent in the French case, and, moreover, the French had no advantage in electrical equipment industries. Ibid., 82–83. Paquier, *Histoire de l'Électricité*, II, 1057–58 (Franco-Suisse and Italo-Suisse). Included on the board of Italo-Suisse was Ernest Hentsch, of the private Geneva bank Hentsch & Cie. Hentsch was associated with Franco-Suisse and with l'Union Financière de Genève. Others on the board had connections with Paribas. Its particular investments in Italy were in the Società Meridionale di Elettricità

(Meridionale) and the Société Générale d'Illumination de Naples. Ibid., II, 1042, 1060, and passim has a great deal on the activities of Franco-Suisse in France, Italy, Norway, Spain, and Switzerland.

130. Ernst Himmel, *Industrielle Kapitalanlagen der Schweiz im Auslande* (Langensalza, Germany: Druck von Hermann Beyer & Söhne, 1922), Table 11 (p. 136) and Recapitulation (no page number).

131. It is impossible to document the numerous Belgian holding companies. We cover only the principal ones. Martinez López, "Belgian Investment in Tramways," 68–69 (Tables 5 and 6), lists of a number of key Belgian *tramway* holding companies in existence in 1913. One of the important ones that we have not mentioned was Compagnie Mutuelle des Tramways, formed in 1895 and with holdings in forty-nine separate companies as of 1913. Its key holdings were in Eastern, Western, and Mediterranean Europe. In 1911, Société Générale, Brussels, obtained a major interest in the company. For more on Compagnie Mutuelle des Tramways, which would become part of Traction et Électricité (Tractionel) and much later Tractebel, see Ranieri, *Dannie Heineman*, 80n2, and Kurgan-van Hentenryk, "Finance and Financiers in Belgium," 322. Société Générale, Brussels, was slow to enter into the electricity sector and had not begun to do so until 1905 (some ten years after Banque de Bruxelles' involvement in SGB – see above). Ibid.

132. Lanthier, "Les Constructions Électriques en France" is splendid on the Empain group. See also Van der Wee and Goossens, "Belgium," 126–27; Herman Van der Wee and Monique Verbreyt, *The Generale Bank 1822–1997* (Tielt, Belgium: Lannoo, 1997), 111; Segreto, Milan Paper; Barjot, Morsel, and Coeuré, *Stratégies, Gestion, Management*, 7, 15, 59–60, 180–81; Kurgan-Van Hentenryk, "Finance and Financiers in Belgium, 1880–1940," 318–19; and specifically on Compagnie Générale de Railways et d'Électricité, see Martinez López, "Belgian Investment in Tramways," 68–69. Robert L. Tignor, *State, Private Enterprise, and Economic Change in Egypt, 1918–1952* (Princeton: Princeton University Press, 1984), 28, 182–83 (on the Empain group in Egypt).

133. Take another case, that of Société Centrale pour l'Industrie Électrique (SCIE), Paris, organized in 1909; we mentioned that in 1914 it had participated in Société des Tramways et de l'Électricité de Constantinople, registered in Belgium. In 1910, once again in partnership with the Belgian holding company Sofina and now with an existing French tramway company, Compagnie Centrale de Chemins de Fer et Tramways (in which Sofina had an interest), SCIE created yet another holding company, Compagnie Centrale d'Énergie Électrique (CCEE), which in turn acquired the central power station in Rouen (previously owned by CGE). CCEE in 1911 got a concession to produce and distribute electricity in the suburbs of Algiers (the capital of the French colony Algeria); CCEE did this directly and did not establish any separate corporate entity (until 1935). By 1914, SCIE had a tranche in utilities in Russia and Argentina, as well as in Turkey, in its headquarters nation, France, and in Algeria. Its initial shareholders included two manufacturers that were part of the U.S. General Electric network, the French Thomson-Houston and AEG, along with the AEG-associated holding companies Sofina and Elektrobank, and three major French banks, Comptoir National d'Escompte de Paris (CNEP), Banque de l'Union

Parisienne (BUP), and Société Générale, Paris. Pierre Lanthier emphasizes the importance of the role of the bank, CNEP, in SCIE's early years. (Note that CNEP was one of the banks involved in the Constantinople company.) Was SCIE a French equivalent of Elektrobank? Was it active in doing *Unternehmergeschäft*? Lanthier's findings are negative. From the start, it was meant to have a purely financial role in collaboration with other (and more important) holding companies and with key banks. Thobie, "European Banks in the Middle East," 432 (on CNEP's participation in the Constantinople group); Lanthier, "Les Constructions Électriques en France"; and Bonin, "The Case of the French Banks," 82. On the strong AEG influence on SCIE, see Hertner, "Technologie," 519. Hertner writes that AEG did not participate directly in SCIE, but rather through Sofina (Brussels), Gesfürel (Berlin), and Elektrobank (Zurich).

134. See text above and Hausman, "Historical Antecedents," 28. As noted, United Electric Securities Co. was absorbed into General Electric when the latter was formed in 1892. It became a holding of Electric Bond & Share in 1905. Mitchell, *S. Z. Mitchell*, 63. The North American Company survived as an independent firm, becoming a key multistate U.S. holding company; it did not ever seem to have utilities abroad. See Hausman, "Historical Antecedents," 38, 56, for North American Company's importance in 1915 and in the 1920s.

135. Ibid., 29, and Mitchell, *S. Z. Mitchell*, 62–63. The Thomson-Houston companies were Ateliers Thomson-Houston, Compagnie Français pour L'Exploitation des Procédés Thomson-Houston and Compagnie d'Électricité Thomson-Houston de la Méditerranée. Compagnie Français pour L'Exploitation des Procédés Thomson-Houston was, as noted earlier, the formal name for the French Thomson-Houston; Ateliers Thomson-Houston was a partially owned subsidiary of the latter. At origin, Electric Bond and Share Company owned preferred shares in United Electric Securities Co.

136. Hausman, "Historical Antecedents," 32, 38–39.

137. Adams, *Niagara Power*. I, 228, 240, 306–37; II, 290–91. Another case was the Ontario Power Company of Niagara Falls, which was incorporated under Canadian laws, June 23, 1887, as the Canadian Power Co. (the name change was in 1889). In 1914, its "executive office" was Buffalo, New York, and it furnished power both to Canadians and across the border in the United States.

138. Irving Stone, *The Composition and Distribution of British Investment in Latin America, 1865 to 1913* (New York: Garland, 1987), 457; J. Fred Rippy, *British Investments in Latin America, 1822–1949* (Minneapolis: University of Minnesota Press, 1959), 244. Halsey, *Investments in Latin America*, 536. The companies were Compañía Luz y Fuerza de Parana (Argentina), Compañía de Electricidad de Merida (Mexico), and Venezuelan Electric Light Co.

139. In the early years, central power plants might be established by existing manufacturing companies and owned with no separate corporations formed. By the 1890s, however, as indicated earlier, this was generally no longer the case. Power plants were owned by corporations dedicated to providing power services.

140. We have no idea of the number of foreign-owned operating companies at any point in time, but we hazard a very rough guess that in 1914 the number would be in the range of 800 to 1,000.

141. Stone, *Global Export of Capital*, 42–381, has tabulations of British "Capital Calls" (1865–1914) in the electric light and power sector. He provides no company names (or numbers of companies). Earlier, we noted that he found a surge in capital calls in this sector in 1882, including calls for capital for companies operating in Austria-Hungary, Chile, India, and South Africa; earlier, we identified these calls as associated with the "Brush boom." Most of these could be interpreted (based on information outside of Stone's book) as British free standing companies. The vast majority of the companies did not have a sustained life. The best source on them is the *Manual of Electrical Undertakings* (London: Electrical Press; cited hereafter as Garcke, after its original compiler, Emile Garcke); we have used various issues. Also useful are London stock exchange manuals. Some companies disappeared because they never found (adequate) financing; others started up and failed after several years of existence; a number dropped out because they were superceded by or merged into successor companies, or they might have moved their registration overseas and no longer be listed as British-registered entities. Thus, the number of British-registered formations before 1914 does not correspond with the number of operating companies in 1914. Moreover, this was just one way operating companies could be set up.
142. We began with the Australian *Nash Directory 1913/14* listings with help from David Merrett, Melbourne, Australia. Then we turned the coin over and looked at the British side of the story. We have earlier referred to Reader, *A House in the City*, on Foster & Braithwaite's activities in electric utilities. Braithwaite's application to the IEE is from Kynaston, *City of London*, II, 463. Ranald Michie, *London Stock Exchange* (Oxford: Oxford University Press, 1999), 139, first put us on to these connections. See also Lance E. Davis and Robert E. Gallman, *Evolving Financial Markets and International Capital Flows: Britain, the Americas, and Australia 1865–1914* (Cambridge: Cambridge University Press, 2001), 542, for calls on the London stock market by Electric Lighting and Traction of Australia (between 1899 and 1901) and its successor Melbourne Electric Supply Company (1909). Ibid., 171, indicates that Electric Lighting and Traction Company of Australia (ELTC) was one of the companies promoted by Foster & Braithwaite. On ELTC, see *Nash Directory, 1907*, 174. There is in the Thomas Edison Papers evidence of a continuity between Edison Indian and Colonial Company, Australasian Electric Light, Power and Storage Company, and its successor "Brush Electrical Engineering Company of London." See Eaton & Lewis, "Mr. Edison's Patent Obligations to Edison Indian and Colonial Company: Mr. Eaton's Opinion, December 1, 1891." TAEP. The Brush group of companies was associated with Foster & Braithwaite, and one can guess that the Melbourne companies were in this sequence.
143. Schapiro, "Public Ownership and Private Investment," 222–25; Byatt, *British Electrical Industry*, 148.
144. Schapiro, "Public Ownership and Private Investment," 225. On Anglo-Argentine Tramways Co. Ltd., see Halsey, *Investments in Latin America*, 483–84. This was a tramway company in which the Belgian Sofina was very much involved. Ranieri, *Dannie Heineman*, 64–66.

145. William Hausman, based on material in Garcke, 1913–1914, has prepared a more complete list. Rippy, *British Investments in Latin America*, 242, estimated, based on the *Stock Exchange Year-Book* for 1913 and 1914, that British investors had interests in some 80 "electric utilities" enterprises in Latin America in 1913 (this number goes far beyond U.K.-registered, free standing companies). See also Stone, *Composition and Distribution of British Investment in Latin America*, 78, 80–81, 83, 86–88, and 456–59, and *FTC Report*, II, 543–45.
146. Geoffrey Jones, *The Evolution of International Business* (London: Routledge, 1996), 148, 155; the English firm Imperial Continental Gas Association, which in 1825 made its first foreign direct investment providing gas in Ghent in The Netherlands (in 1830, part of Belgium), added electric utilities within its municipal concessions. On its 1915 capital, see *FTC Report*, II, 543. Rippy, *British Investments in Latin America*, 241, has a list of "British gas companies in Latin America, 1913," which reveals how many of them had become associated with electric light and power companies.
147. Marc Linder, *Projecting Capitalism: A History of the Internationalization of the Construction Industry* (Westport, CT.: Greenwood Press, 1994), 87, and Dominique Barjot, *La Grande Entreprise Française de Travaux Publics (1883–1974)* (Paris: Economica, 2006), 121. Ol', *Foreign Capital in Russia*, 113, notes that operating under Russian statutes was the German firm "Fillipp Golzman & Co., Russian Overground and Underground Construction Company"; this is surely a mistranslation of Philipp Holzmann. The Philipp Holzmann firm was closely associated with the Deutsche Bank on a number of projects, including the Baghdad Railway. Emden, *Money Powers*, 231.
148. The French group Giros et Loucheur had been the founders of Société Générale d'Entreprises (SGE). On SGE's business in Belgium, the Ottoman Empire, and then Russia, Italy, and Spain and also on Giros et Loucheur's international expansion, see Dominique Barjot, "Le Rôle des Entrepreneurs de Travaux Publics: L'Exemple du Groupe Giros et Loucheur (1899–1946)," in Monique Trédé-Boulmer, ed., *Le Financement de l'Industrie Électrique 1880–1980* (Paris: PUF, 1994), 75, 77, and Barjot, *Grande Entreprise Française*, passim. Davenport-Hines, *Dudley Docker*, 204, describes the careers of Louis Loucheur and Alexandre Giros in railroad electrification and hydroelectric developments in France and overseas, as well as their 1908 formation of SGE, which became a "great force in French electro-technology and electrical services, but also established subsidiaries in the Ottoman Turkey (1909–1910), Morocco (1911), Russia (1912), and elsewhere." In the 1910 formation of Société Générale d'Entreprises dans l'Empire Ottoman, two other French construction companies participated: Grands Travaux de Marseille and Fougerolle Frères. Barjot, *Grande Entreprise Française*, 196. See also Linder, *Projecting Capitalism*, 86; Feis, *Europe: The World's Banker*, 321; Barjot, Morsel, and Coeuré, *Stratégies, Gestion, Management*, 182.
149. Catherine Vuillermot, "Le Groupe Durand: Une Multinationale Française de la Distribution de l'Électricite (dans la Premiére Moitié du XXe Siècle)?" in Hubert Bonin, et al., *Transnational Companies (19th –20th Centuries)* (Paris: PLAGE, [2002]), 367. For SGE's role in the electrification of Turkey, see

Barjot, *Grande Entreprise Française*, 220. Barjot does not mention SOEC but writes of "L'Ottomane d'Électricité," seemingly referring to Société d'Eclairage Électrique de Constantinople, the Giros et Loucheur/SGE company in Constantinople. He writes that the French did not get into tramways, leaving that to the Germans and "Elektrobank's company," Société des Tramways de Constantinople. Ibid.

150. Hausman and Neufeld, "U.S. Foreign Direct Investment," 375–76; Linder, *Projecting Capitalism*, 108; Hughes, *Networks of Power*, 386–91.
151. Hausman, "The Historical Antecedents," 38.
152. Cleona Lewis, *America's Stake in International Investments* (Washington, DC: Brookings Institution, 1938), 324.
153. Marchildon, "The Montreal Engineering Company," 396.
154. Linder, *Projecting Capitalism*, 108.
155. In the literature, there is some confusion about the nationality of J. G. White & Co., which began as an American firm. Armstrong and Nelles, *Southern Exposure*, 128, correctly identifies it as a "New York firm of utility engineers and promoters." In 1917, it would become a subsidiary of the British trading firm Alfred Booth. Within the Alfred Booth group, its activities were constrained and temporarily eclipsed; and as a result, in 1929 it was sold back to its founder. Geoffrey Jones, *Merchants to Multinationals: British Trading Companies in the Nineteenth and Twentieth Centuries* (Oxford: Oxford University Press, 2000), 104 (on the 1917–1929 period). Jones wrongly identified the White firm, before its acquisition by Booth, as British. He correctly described the White firm in 1917 as "specializing in the management of public utilities in Latin America." The British journal *Engineer* in 1916 made the same mistake, assuming that J. G. White & Co. was a London-headquartered firm; see Linder, *Projecting Capitalism*, 108n109. Interestingly, a look at the board of the Canadian-registered (in 1913) International Light & Power Co. Ltd. finds George M. Booth among the directors. See Halsey, *Investments in Latin America*, 536.
156. When Canadian interests replaced the German ones in Barcelona, F. S. Pearson was the principal figure in the activities. In 1911, the Canadian-registered Barcelona Traction, Light and Power Company (BTLP) took over the German Barcelonesa (Elektrobank sold its 25 percent of the shares in the Barcelona company to BTLP, while at the same time Elektrobank loaned money to BTLP, accepting the latter's shares as collateral). Why were the Germans ready to sell out to the Canadian-registered firm? Doria and Hertner speculate that the cause was "chronic 'capital famine,'" combined with a need for liquidity for new investments in other places. And, the Canadians offered a good price. Doria and Hertner, "Urban Growth," 240–41. Meanwhile, in 1911, another Barcelona company, Energía Eléctrica de Cataluña (EEdC) was founded by the French firm Compagnie Générale d'Électricité (CGE); Siemens's holding company Indelec acquired EEdC securities. CGE would build the steam power plant, and Indelec supplied the technological know-how for the hydroelectric part of EEdC's project. Ibid., 245. CGE subscribed 47 percent of the shares and Indelec 33 percent, while the rest went to the Catalan owner of the waterpower concession. By 1913, BTLP had gained controlling interest in EEdC. Pearson was responsible. (In the process of gaining controlling interest,

shareholders in the EEdC obtained shares in BTLP, so there remained connections.) The Barcelona firms became part of "F. S. Pearson group" of companies (this was exceptional; the other key ventures were in Latin America, especially Mexico and Brazil).

157. Because F. S. Pearson was so closely associated with the Canadian ventures abroad, he was often thought of as Canadian, which was not the case: He was an American engineer, and his firm was in New York.
158. ELK served as a Siemens holding company for many domestic, German electricity supply companies and also had an interest in the German/Argentine DUEG, as well as in the Constantinople company. On the Brazilian operating company see Young, "German Banks and German Direct Investment," 60; on Theodor Wille, see Mira Wilkins, "An Alternative Approach," in Steven C. Topik and Allen Wells, *The Second Conquest of Latin America* (Austin: University of Texas Press, 1998), 194; on ELK, see BEAM, *Combines*, 143.
159. Armstrong and Nelles, *Southern Exposure*, 88; Gibbs, while a trading house was also involved in merchant banking. Jones, *Merchants to Multinationals*, 42, 53, 227. In Asia, British trading company interests, namely, Gibb, Livingston & Co. and Jardine, Matheson, were closely associated with the formation and operation of the large lighting and power station of Hong Kong Electric Co., registered in Hong Kong. See Austin Coates, *A Mountain of Light* (Hong Kong: Heinemann, 1977), 200–1, for the board chairmen and directors.
160. Reinhard Liehr and Georg Leidenberger, "From Free-Standing Company to Public Enterprise: The Mexican Light and Power Company and the Mexican Tramways Company, 1902–1965," typescript prepared for International Economic History Congress, Buenos Aires, July 2002 ("Part 2: Mexico Tramways Company" was separately prepared by Georg Leidenberger), 3. This article formed the basis of Reinhard Liehr and Georg Leidenberger, "El Paso de una Free-Standing Company a una Empresa Pública: Mexican Light and Power y Mexico Tramways, 1902–1960," in Sandra Kuntz Ficker y Horst Pietschmann, eds., *México y La Economía Atlántica (Siglos XVIII–XX)* (Mexico: El Colegio de México, Centro de Estudios Históricos, 2006), 269–309. There are differences, so at times we will cite the typescript.
161. Liehr and Leidenberger, "From Free-Standing Company," 3; Liehr and Leidenberger, "El Paso de una Free-Standing Company," 272; Armstrong and Nelles, *Southern Exposure*, 88.
162. Liehr and Leidenberger, "From Free-Standing Company," 3; Liehr and Leidenberger, "El Paso de una Free-Standing Company," 273.
163. Armstrong and Nelles, *Southern Exposure,* 88; apparently, a Mexican subsidiary of the Mexican Electric Works Ltd. was also established: Compañía Mexicana de Electricidad, SA; Liehr and Leidenberger, "From Free-Standing Company," 5.
164. Armstrong and Nelles, *Southern Exposure*, 85–88; the waterpower concessions had been earlier granted to Dr. Arnold Vaquié, a French citizen, and the Société de Necaxa, a French free standing company set up for the sole purpose of holding the concession. Miguel S. Wionczek, in his otherwise excellent discussion of electric power in Mexico, mistakenly assumed that F. S. Pearson was "Canadian." Miguel S. Wionczek, "Electric Power," in Raymond Vernon,

ed., *Public Policy and Private Enterprise in Mexico* (Cambridge, MA: Harvard University Press, 1964), 23.

165. Armstrong and Nelles, *Southern Exposure*, 87–88. Merrill Denison, *Canada's First Bank: A History of the Bank of Montreal,* 2 vol. (New York: Dodd, Mead, 1966, 1967), II, 419–20; Drummond was vice president, 1887–1905, and president, 1905–1910; Clouston was general manager, 1890–1911, and coincidentally vice president of the bank, 1905–1912.
166. Armstrong and Nelles, *Southern Exposure*, 89.
167. Ibid., 88–89, 91; as our readers know, Sofina was Belgian-headquartered but German-dominated at this time.
168. Liehr and Leidenberger, "From Free-Standing Company," 7.
169. Denison, *Canada's First Bank*, II, 281.
170. Ibid.
171. Liehr and Leidenberger, "From Free-Standing Company," Part 2, 7–8.
172. Ibid., 8. We discussed Wernher, Beit earlier in this chapter.
173. Armstrong and Nelles, *Southern Exposure*, 95.
174. Liehr and Leidenberger, "From Free-Standing Company," Part 2, 9, say that Mexican Electric Tramways Ltd., while still controlled by Wernher, Beit, was reincorporated in Canada in 1901; Rippy, *British Investments in Latin America*, 248, gives an 1898 date for the British company.
175. Armstrong and Nelles, *Southern Exposure*, 97–98. Robert Fleming had been based in Dundee, Scotland, but by this time he had moved its headquarters to London.
176. Ibid., 98–104.
177. On Guanajuato Power and Electric Co., see *New York Times*, Feb. 21, 1903; July 1, 1908; May 2, 1910. Henry Hine, president of Guanajuato Power and Electric, was also a director of the Guanajuato Reduction and Mines Co. Ibid., April 11, 1906. See also *Moody's 1914*, 375 (for the date of incorporation under Colorado laws); the main offices of this company were in Colorado Springs, CO. By 1913, the company owned the entire capital stock of the Michoacan Power Co. "and guarantees the principal and interest on the latter company's bonds." It also owned practically all the common stock of the Central Mexico Light & Power Co., "which was organized to carry on the light and power business of the company ...." Hausman and Neufeld, "U.S. Foreign Direct Investment," 376 (El Paso). Marchildon, "The Montreal Engineering Company," 394 (on the Monterey company). On the Compañía Hidroeléctrica de Chapala, see Wionczek, "Electric Power," 31; Wionczek does not give a date of formation, but indicates that with the revolution, in 1912, it stopped its expansion program, although it did resume at a later point. The *New York Times*, Aug. 21, 1903, had an item that said, "[A]n American syndicate, it is said, proposes to construct a huge waterpower plant near the city of Guadalajara, Mexico, to generate electricity for lighting, traction, mining and other purposes." See Table 1.1 on the Chapala company's transmission system (the name is slightly different, but this is clearly the same company). At some point, the Chapala company seems to have come under the control of the Banco Nacional of Mexico City; in 1926, however, it was back under U.S. ownership, acquired

by Morrison-McCall interests. Hausman and Neufeld, "U.S. Foreign Direct Investment in Electrical Utilities," 382.

178. Liehr and Leidenberger, "From Free-Standing Company," 18.
179. Armstrong and Nelles, *Southern Exposure*, 253, 344n9; Marchildon, "The Montreal Engineering Company," 394, 397.
180. Note that there are three (unrelated and not to be confused) Pearsons in the pre–World War I Mexican story: (1) the American engineer, F. S. (Fred Stark) Pearson; (2) the Canadian lawyer B. F. Pearson; and (3) the Englishman Weetman D. Pearson (from 1910 Lord Cowdray), associated with the construction firm S. Pearson & Son.
181. J. A. Spender, *Weetman Pearson: First Viscount Cowdray, 1856–1927* (London: Cassell & Co., 1930), 16–17, 84–100. William Hausman found (misfiled) in Box B4, S. Pearson & Son Ltd. Papers, Science Museum Library, London (henceforth cited as Pearson papers), a personal note from Porfirio Díaz to Weetman Pearson, dated June 1911, that reflected their closeness.
182. Spender, *Weetman Pearson*, 107.
183. Ibid., 109, 205; see Stone, *The Composition*, 459, for the date.
184. Stone, *The Composition*, 456, and data in Box B4, Pearson papers (on Anglo-Mexican Electric Company). Reinhard Liehr and Mariano E. Torres Bautista, "British Free-Standing Companies in Mexico, 1884–1911," in Wilkins and Schröter, eds., *Free-Standing Company in the World Economy*, 265; Spender, *Weetman Pearson*, 206. On Worswick's connection with Wernher, Beit, see Armstrong and Nelles, *Southern Exposure*, 196. We have tried in vain to identify Luebeck; our linking him with Siemens & Halske is a "guess."
185. Spender, *Weetman Pearson*, 106.
186. Ibid., 18 (on Brookfield), 289 (on the contract).
187. Ibid., 49–171; Geoffrey Jones and Lisa Bud-Frierman, "Weetman Pearson and the Mexican Oil Industry (A)," Harvard Business School Case N9-804-085 (Nov. 3, 2003).
188. Spender, *Weetman Pearson*, 206.
189. *FTC Report*, II, 545; Stone, *The Composition*, 459. Linda Jones, Charles Jones, and Robert Greenhill, "Public Utility Companies," in D. C. M. Platt, *Business Imperialism 1840–1930: An Inquiry Based on British Experience in Latin America* (Oxford: Oxford University Press, 1977), 80.
190. Spender, *Weetman Pearson*, 206 (on Lord Cowdray's experience during the revolution), and ibid., 36 (on his becoming Lord Cowdray in 1910).
191. The Canadian companies are given in the text above. Note that the Puebla company was associated with the Cowdray group of companies. *FTC Report*, II, 544–45 (on the English companies) and data in Pearson Papers. On International Light & Power Co. Ltd., see Halsey, *Investments in Latin America*, 536.
192. Wionczek, "Electric Power," 25–26. Wionczek estimates that some $75 million of British, Canadian, and U.S. capital was invested in Mexican electric power generation and distribution between 1900 and 1910. Ibid., 22.
193. Ibid., 21 ("remarkable speed").
194. We have used a variety of sources on this, including Jonathan Coopersmith, *The Electrification of Russia, 1880–1926* (Ithaca, NY: Cornell University

Press, 1992), 45–87. Coopersmith notes that Imatra involved nine Belgian, German, and Russian banks, a number of electrotechnical manufacturers, and three Russian utilities. Ibid., 85. We have also found useful Timo Myllyntaus, "Electrical Imperialism or Multinational Cooperation? The Role of Big Business in Supplying Light and Power to St. Petersburg Before 1917," *Business and Economic History*, 26 (Winter 1997), 540–49 (according to Myllyntaus T & F Mottart of Brussels was the banking house most closely associated with SSPT); P.V. Ol', *Foreign Capital in Russia* (New York: Garland, 1983; first published in Russian in 1922), esp. 47–49, 110–14, 141–42, provides lots of detail; see also Paquier, *Histoire de l'Électricité*, II, 990–91; Hertner, "Les Sociétés Financières Suisses," 347; and Ranieri, *Dannie Heineman*, 75 (on Sofina in Russia).

195. Davis and Gallman, *Evolving Financial Markets*, 389. On Vancouver Power as a subsidiary of BCER, see Armstrong and Nelles, *Monopoly's Moment*, 99. On Davis and Gallman's list was Shawinigan Water and Power Company, a *U.S.* direct investment. Davis and Gallman give the U.K. flow of funds into public utilities, 1906–1914, to Canada as almost $48 million (this figure includes $13.7 million for Bell Telephone of Canada, raised in the United Kingdom; the rest appears to have been for light and power companies). While not specified, I think one has to assume these figures provided in Davis and Gallman are in Canadian dollars.

196. Quoted in Jacob Viner, *Canada's Balance of International Indebtedness 1900–1913* (Cambridge, MA: Harvard University Press, 1924), 89.

197. Armstrong and Nelles, *Southern Exposure*, 164. Alfred Loewenstein in Brussels and Arnold Spitzer in Paris picked up the European bonds for distribution among their clients. In London, Fleming and other houses took up the issue, which was oversubscribed. E. R. Wood, of Dominion Securities, handled the distribution in Canada. As noted earlier, for the Canadians the Barcelona promotion was an exceptional one in Europe; most of the Canadian promotions were for companies in Latin America and the Caribbean (as well as in Canada). The initial issue for BTLP proved inadequate, and it was followed up by a further bond issue in 1913, with the ratios: 71 percent to continental Europe, 19 percent for Great Britain, and 10 percent to Canada. Both these bond issues for BTLP, although for a Canadian-registered company (located in Spain), were denominated in pounds. Ibid.

198. Richard Roberts, *Schroders* (Houndmills, England: Macmillan, 1992), 139; the following year, 1911, Schröder floated a loan for the Peruvian government. See also Rory Miller, "The West Coast of South America," in Wilkins and Schröter, eds., *Free-Standing Company in the World Economy*, 222, 234.

199. On the other hand, French banks when faced with French stock market regulations often invested through Belgian intermediaries. This is discussed in detail in Feis, *Europe: The World's Banker*, passim. Broder, "Banking and the Electrotechnical Industry in Western Europe," 479 (on Belgian use of French capital).

200. Wilkins, *History ... to 1914*, 550–55, 909n186; Lewis, *America's Stake*, 72; on the sizable London share in new bond issues for Consolidated Gas & Electric, 1911–1913, see Paul D. Dickens, "The Transition Period in American

International Financing, 1897 to 1914" Ph.D. diss. George Washington University, 1933, 259, 263, 265–67; Cities Service, formed in 1910, was a particularly large recipient of capital from abroad. For these U.S. companies, see Hausman, "The Historical Antecedents," 38–39. In addition, the Rothschild representative in the United States, August Belmont, attracted money from abroad to the New York City subway system – the Interborough Rapid Transit (IRT). Wilkins, *History ... to 1914*, 552–53. Stone, *Global Export of Capital from Great Britain*, 42–381, contains information on British "Capital Calls" (1865–1914) in the electric light and power sector. Based on his data, Wilkins calculated (for the present book) that in nine of the fourteen years, between 1901 and 1914, the United States ranked first by a substantial amount among all the countries around the world in tapping British capital markets for electric light and power facilities. Wilkins believes that these particular British interests in the United States were all financial – that is, portfolio investments.

201. Wilkins, *History ... to 1914*, 554. There may be some question as to whether there was direct investment in the United States by Sun Life Assurance Company and by Alabama Traction Light and Power Company Ltd. Lewis, *America's Stake*, 102, 566, includes Alabama Traction Light and Power Company Ltd. (ATLPC) as a "foreign" Canadian-controlled enterprise and has it on a list of foreign companies in the United States. But American managers made the allocation decisions. As in many large U.S. businesses, there was a separation of ownership and control. There was no need for ATLPC to install management and no indication that it did so (ATLPC was formed for purely financial purposes). With Illinois Traction, the Canadians played a larger role, and in our view there is more ambiguity.

202. The one plan for a British free standing company to invest in Japan was the proposed Anglo-Japanese Hydro-Electric Company Ltd. The project took various forms, but apparently by 1909 the proposal was that half the capital would come from Japanese sources and half from British sources. See inventory online for Public Record Office (PRO), Foreign Office (FO) files, FO 262/1475 (Reel 4). The inventory has the following extract from the "Minutes of a Meeting of the Most Influential Men Held at the House of Marquis Katsura on 14 March 1909": "Marquis Inouye declared the meeting open and explained the reasons for it being called which may be summarised as follows: He was happy to say that owing to the friendly relations existing between Japan and England, and to the Political Alliance, and the daily drawing closer of the bonds uniting the two countries which, on the economic side, was leading to the formation or consideration of joint commercial undertakings whose fruitful results would, he believed, add to the permanence and value of the Political Alliance, the joint Anglo-Japanese Hydro-Electric undertaking assumed a considerable national importance, intensified owing to the fact that owing to the present commercial depression in Japan, a difficulty had arisen at an advanced stage of the negotiations, viz: the Japanese side found it difficult to raise their half of the capital. At this juncture, the British side had come forward with an offer to find four-fifths of the capital if necessary, but he was of the opinion that the Japanese side should make a great effort to provide all of their half, especially as the money market is now easing." This project never materialized. We are indebted

to Makuto Kishida (Nov. 20, 2005) for initially acquainting Mira Wilkins with this proposed venture. Kishida directed us to the research findings of Takeo Kikkawa, who concluded that ultimately the foreign direct investment did not materialize, not because of the reasons given in the PRO document, but because the British did not have confidence in the outlook for electric power in Japan. See Takeo Kikkawa, "The Plan for the Establishment of the Japan-Britain Electric Power Joint Enterprise after the Japanese-Russian War," in *Enerugi shi Kenkyu* [*Research for the History of Energy*], 12 (June 1983), 46–60 (in Japanese), a paper that details the course of the failed negotiations from their beginnings in 1906 to 1910; see also Takeo Kikkawa, *Nihon Denryokúgyo no Hatten to Matsunaga Yasuzaemon* [*The Development of Japanese Electric Power Industry and Yasuzaemon Matsunaga*] (Nagoya: Nagoya University Press, 1995), 39; our thanks to Yumiko Morii for the translations.

203. In Japan, there were foreign direct investments in electrical *manufacturing*, but not in the utilities. Uchida, "The Transfer of Electrical Technologies from the United States and Europe to Japan, 1869–1914," 224–26; Toshiaki Chokki, "'Japanese Business Management' in the Prewar Electrical Machinery Industry: Emergence of Foreign Tie-up Companies and the Modernization of Indigenous Enterprises," in Takeshi Yuzawa and Masaru Udagawa, *Foreign Business in Japan Before World War II* (Tokyo: University of Tokyo Press, 1990), 198. Not only were there the unrealized plans for the Anglo-Japanese Hydro-Electric Company Ltd., but Japanese public utilities sought (in vain) to borrow in the London bond market. See, for example, Muneo Nitta, *Tokyo Dento Kabushiki Kaisha Kaigyo Gojunenshi* [*Tokyo Electric Light Corporation, Company History of Fifty Years*] (Tokyo: Tokyo Dento Kabushiki Kaisha, 1936), 93. The Japanese *government* was an established borrower in London with a good record for maintaining interest payments. Michie, *London Stock Exchange*, 91. Lockwood, *Economic Development of Japan* , 322, writes that the Japanese borrowed heavily abroad during the first decade of the twentieth century; it (Japan) sold national and local bond issues in Western money markets, and secondarily semiofficial companies and electric utilities. We are convinced that Lockwood is mistaken on the matter of pre–World War I foreign borrowings by Japanese electric utilities, at least in relation to long-term borrowings – i.e. on the bond markets. After much effort in Japan, although we can establish attempts to borrow and we can identify short-term borrowing, we have been unable to verify any actual borrowing abroad in foreign bond (or stock) markets by Japanese electric utilities in this period. Stone, *The Global Export of Capital from Great Britain*, 142–151, in his table on "Japan (1865–1914)," indicates zero "capital called" for companies in electric light and power. As Davis and Gallman, *Evolving Financial Markets*, 26, indicate, "capital called" statistics have their serious limitations: "[T]he term 'call' was used to describe the announcements of the 'periodic installments that were to be paid by the subscribers of the new issue.'" If the Japanese were financing their electric light and power facilities in London, however, there ought to be some indication in the "capital called" data. There is evidence of *short-term* yen-denominated borrowings by Nagoya Electric Light (in 1907), Hakata Electric (in 1910), and Kinugawa Electric (in 1911).

The first of these borrowings was from an unidentified London syndicate. The other two were from two trading companies: Sale & Frazar and M. Samuel & Co. See Harumi Matsushimi, "The Historical Importance of the Flotation of the Foreign Loan of the Power Industry," [Denryoku Gaisai no Rekishiteki Igi] in *The Socio-Economic History* [*Shakai Kezigaku*], 16–6 (1961), 95. Yumiko Morii provided the translation. On Sale & Frazar history, see Lockwood, *Economic Development of Japan*, 329–30. Frazar & Co., the long-established U.S. trading house, traded under the name Sale & Frazar from 1902 to 1927. M. Samuel & Co. was a British trading company *qua* merchant bank. On the latter, see Jones, *Merchants to Multinationals,* 73. With foreign financing lacking and domestic finance substituted, the Japanese made important strides in electrification before World War I.

204. As indicated above, others believed there were some sizable foreign direct investments, so the term "by our definition" is key here. Aside from those investments earlier mentioned, we have identified some small foreign direct investments in power facilities, but the output of these plants was so limited relative to the total output of U.S. electric utilities that one could justify the statement that there was "virtually no" inward foreign direct investment.
205. On the outward investments of U.S. electrical manufacturers, see Wilkins, *Emergence of Multinational Enterprise*. On an explanation of extended manufacturers' satellites, see Chapter 2, herein.
206. See Hausman, "Historical Antecedents," 31–33. As noted above, in 1905 it already had interests in five foreign companies. This was nothing compared with what would follow.
207. On the spillover, see Wilkins, *Emergence of Multinational Enterprise.*
208. The story of the Morgan-Yerkes rivalry over investments in the London "tube" made for high drama. In the view of many individuals in Great Britain, "American capital was taking over." In 1901–1902, J. P. Morgan (New York) with J. S. Morgan (London) competed with Chicago traction giant Charles T. Yerkes, backed by Speyer & Co. (New York) and Edgar Speyer in London, to finance the London underground. Yerkes won out. Securities were issued, and in 1903 alone the Underground Electric Railways of London received some $17 million in U.S. financing – a huge sum for that period. Only about one-quarter of the original shares of the Underground Electric Railways of London were sold in Great Britain. Yerkes was said to have invested "millions" of his own money with no returns. As a consequence of this contest for leadership in the financing, the unending distrust by the Morgans of the Speyer house was fortified; J. P. Morgan called Speyer's rivalry on this occasion the "greatest rascality and conspiracy I ever heard of." The press in London and New York carried the story. On Yerkes's victory, see *New York Times*, Oct. 22, 1902; Chernow, *The House of Morgan*, 100; Lewis, *America's Stake*, 340 (Lewis considers the $17 million a portfolio investment); Byatt, *British Electrical Industry*, 7 (on original shares); A. Emil Davies, *Investments Abroad* (Chicago: A.W. Shaw Co., 1927), 49 (on Yerkes's absence of return on his investments); and Hughes, *Networks of Power*, 206, 221 (on Yerkes in Chicago). The hostility of the House of Morgan to that of Speyer is evident in every study of Morgan. See, for example, Chernow, *The House of Morgan*, 74.

The "rascality" quotation is from Kynaston, *City of London*, II, 352. John H. Dunning, *American Investment in British Manufacturing Industry*, rev. ed. (New York: Routledge, 1998), 13, says British Thomson-Houston (GE's British manufacturing affiliate) supplied a major part of the electrical equipment for the London Underground Railway (and also for "more than fifty tramways systems" in the United Kingdom). Thus, even though Morgan lost out in the financing, a GE affiliate got the orders. Was Yerkes a direct investor? There is a possible argument for that view. We do not know how long the investment lasted.

209. For example, the U.S. interests in the Shawingan Water & Power Co. in Quebec, the Canadian Niagara Power Company and Ontario Power Company in Ontario, and British interests in the British Columbia Electric Railway, in British Columbia.

210. We have discussed above the Canadian (and English) interests in Mexico. For material on the Canadians in Brazil, see Armstrong and Nelles, *Southern Exposure*; McDowall, *Light*; Halsey, *Investments in Latin America*, 164–67. On the British free standing companies in Brazil, there was, for example, the Southern Brazil Electric Co., registered in 1913. Charles Franklin Mallory, "Financial Problems of the North American Owned Electrical Utilities in Latin America," MA Thesis, MIT, 1956, 86, and *FTC Report*, II, 544. Other British foreign direct investments in light and power in Brazil by the eve of World War I included those made by the British-registered Ceara Tramways, Light & Power Co. Ltd., Minas Gerais Electric Light & Tramway Co. Ltd., Manaos Tramway & Light Co. Ltd., and Pernambuco Tramways & Power Co. Ltd. Ibid., II, 544–45; Brazilian Traction, Light and Power Co. was formed in 1912. Halsey, *Investments in Latin America*, 168–69, 171, and Allen Morrison, "The Tramways of Manaus, Amazonas state Brazil," [n.d.] (http://www.tramz.com/br/mn/mn.html, accessed March 13, 2006).

211. Jones and Greenhill, "Public Utility Companies," 81, and Rippy, *British Investments in Latin America*, 242. These firms in the main appear to be foreign direct investments. Considerable information on British (and other foreign) investments in tramways in a number of Latin American countries is available on the website of Allen Morrison (http://www.tramz.com/index.html, accessed Sept. 26, 2007).

212. It is not clear whether Yerkes's earlier investment in the London underground (see above in this chapter) still remained in 1913–1914. Other inward investments consisted of extended foreign manufacturers' satellites and also investments that passed through the United Kingdom – that is, were in companies that in turn invested abroad. Leslie Hannah, *Electricity Before Nationalisation* (Baltimore: Johns Hopkins University Press, 1979), 71, refers to George Balfour as commercial manager of an unnamed American electric utility operating in Britain in 1902. We think this would go into the category of "extended foreign manufacturers' satellite" and was associated with the large Westinghouse manufacturing operation in the United Kingdom. The Westinghouse affiliate Traction and Power Securities Co. was financing the Mersey Railway electrification at this time, for which power facilities had been created. See John Dummelow, "Metropolitan-Vickers Electrical Co. Ltd.,

1899–1949" (http://homepage.ntlworld.com/jim.lawton1/index.htm, accessed Oct. 25, 2005).

213. John M. Coatsworth and Alan M. Taylor, eds., *Latin America and the World Economy Since 1800* (Cambridge, MA: Harvard University Press, 1998), 141, 189.

214. Halsey, *Investments in Latin America* (for overview of foreign investments in public utilities in 1914). Halsey omits French firms, but there was a French contribution associated with French industrial investments – isolated plants. There were also some Italian investments, often associated with Swiss interests. Rippy, *British Investments in Latin America*, 242; the *Stock Exchange Yearbook*; and Garcke, 1914–1915 (on British investments in Latin American utilities). Peter Hertner is doing major work on German investments in Argentina: See his "German Foreign Investment in Electrical Industry and in Electrified Urban Transport in Italy, Spain, and Argentina until the end of the 1920s: Some Preliminary Considerations," unpublished paper, [2005]. We used the pre–World War I exchange rate of 4.198 Marks to the dollar for the conversion.

215. The best description of the electrical industry in China at the eve of World War I is in Garcke, 1914–1915, 98–100. These pages discuss the French central station in the French concessions in Shanghai and Tientsin (now Tianjin) (that of the Compagnie Française de Tramways et d'Éclairage Électrique in Shanghai) and the German stations at Tsingtau (now Qingdao) and Tsinanfu. On the Compagnie Française de Tramways et d'Éclairage Électrique de Shanghai, see Damien Heurtebise, "L'Electrification Outre-mer à Travers les Fonds du Centre des Archives Diplomatique des Nantes," in Barjot, et al., eds., *L'Électrification Outre-mer*, 45, and ibid., 46 (for the electrification of the French concession in Tientsin, 1910–1925). According to Garcke, 1914–1915, 98–99, Chinese-owned power stations tended to be equipped with British, French, or German machinery, often installed by trading companies of the respective nationality. In British Hong Kong, Hong Kong Tramway Co. Ltd. was registered in London. The large lighting and power station of Hong Kong Electric Co., which was registered in Hong Kong, was equipped with English machinery; as noted earlier, British trading company interests, namely, Gibb, Livingston & Co. and Jardine Matheson, were closely associated with this venture. China Light and Power with a concession in Kowloon was likewise registered in Hong Kong. On Sofina's interest (as of 1912) in Bangkok tramways, see Ranieri, *Dannie Heineman*, 75.

216. The Japanese interests in China in electricity supply before 1914 were exclusively in Manchuria. C.F. Remer, *Foreign Investments in China* (New York: Macmillan, 1933), 427–30, 490; the South Manchuria Electric Company (which would be organized in 1926) would take over the electric power plants built earlier and once owned by the South Manchuria Railway. The process was started by the railroad company; Japanese ownership would continue, including both the railroad and the electricity supply company. The requirements of running a railroad motivated the initiation by this railroad of its own power facilities.

217. See Table 3.1.

218. The 1912 percentage was calculated by the authors from data in United States, Bureau of the Census, *Historical Statistics of the United States, Colonial Times to 1957* (Washington, DC: USGPO, 1960), 15, 510. If the less than 25 percent seems low, note that this includes *all nonfarm* households, encompassing those in small towns and rural areas; we have not been able to locate figures on the electrification of large-city urban households in the United States pre–World War I, nor have we found comparable figures for other countries. Figure 1.5, Chapter 1, herein, suggests, however, that on the eve of World War I Canada, Norway, and Switzerland (owing to their early development of hydroelectric power and relatively small populations) had higher per capita electricity output than the United States.

4 WAR, THE FIRST NATIONALIZATION, RESTRUCTURING, AND RENEWAL, 1914–1929

1. The quote is from Mira Wilkins, *The History of Foreign Investment in the United States, 1914–1945* (Cambridge, MA: Harvard University Press, 2004), 4.
2. On the controversy, see ibid., 678n52.
3. We introduce this notion in relation to some holding companies. We will not document this notion in other contexts here, although it seems to us to be applicable in a number of settings.
4. Jonathan Coopersmith, "When Worlds Collide: Government and Electrification, 1892–1939," *Business and Economic History, On-Line*, 1 (2003), 12–13; Jonathan Coopersmith, *The Electrification of Russia, 1880–1926* (Ithaca: Cornell University Press, 1992), 103–4; Gerald D. Feldman, *Army Industry and Labor in Germany, 1914–1918* (Princeton: Princeton University Press, 1966) 254–55; "English Summary," in *Storia dell' Industria Elettrica in Italia*, vol. 2 (Rome-Bari: Laterza, 1993), 949–53. W. Borgquist, "Regional Integration of Electric-Utility Facilities," *Transactions, Third World Power Conference*, vol. 7 (Washington, DC: USGPO 1936), 679; Gunnar Nerheim, "The Development and Diffusion of European Water Turbines, 1870–1920," in Kristine Bruland, ed., *Technology Transfer and Scandinavian Industrialisation* (New York: Berg, 1991), 355. M. Banal, "L'Électricité Pendant la Première Guerre Mondiale," in *Histoire Générale de l'Électricité en France*, vol. I (Paris: Fayard, 1991), 901–6, and G. Mori, "Le Guerre Parallele. L'Industria Elettrica in Italia nel Periodo della Grande Guerra (1914–1919), in *Il Capitalismo Industriale in Italia* (Rome: Editori Riuniti, 1977), 166–68.
5. Leslie Hannah, *Electricity Before Nationalisation: A Study of the Development of the Electricity Supply Industry in Britain to 1948* (Baltimore: Johns Hopkins University Press, 1979), 53; Kakujiro Yamasaki and Gotaro Ogawa, *The Effect of the World War upon the Commerce and Industry of Japan* (New Haven: Yale University Press, 1929), 336.
6. Charles Keller, *Power Situation During the War* (Washington, DC, 1921), 17–18, 46. Federal government spending rose from 1.5 percent of the U.S. GNP in 1916 (before U.S. entry) to 24.2 percent of U.S. GNP in 1918 (the last year of the war); on textbook treatment of U.S. government involvement in general, see, for one example among many, Gary M. Walton and Hugh Rockoff, *History of*

the American Economy, 10th ed. (n.p.: South-Western/Thomson Learning, 2005), 418, 421–24.

7. Williams Haynes, *American Chemical Industry*, 6 vol. (New York: Van Nostrand, 1945–1953), II, 90–111, and Thomas P. Hughes, *Networks of Power* (Baltimore: Johns Hopkins University Press, 1983), 287 (on the U.S. government nitrate program). The German government provided financial security for the construction and operation of two large lignite plants for fixing nitrogen from the air. Ibid., 287–89.
8. Hannah, *Electricity Before Nationalisation*, 53–57.
9. See H. V. Nelles, *The Politics of Development* (Toronto: Macmillan, 1974), 227; Edward Dean Adams, *Niagara Power. History of Niagara Falls Power Company*, 2 vol. (Niagara Falls, NY: Niagara Falls Power Co., 1927), II, 81.
10. Christopher Armstrong and H. V. Nelles, *Monopoly's Moment: The Organization and Regulation of Canadian Utilities, 1830–1930* (Philadelphia: Temple University Press, 1986), 207–10, 254–60 (on BCER's experience with regulation).
11. David Massell, *Amassing Power: J. B. Duke and the Saguenay River, 1897–1927* (Montreal: McGill-Queen's University Press, 2000), 147.
12. L. de Verebely, "National and Regional Planning and Their Relation to the Conservation of Natural Resources: Regional Integration of Electric-Utility Facilities," *Transactions, Third World Power Conference*, vol. 6 (Washington, DC: USGPO, 1936), 409.
13. Keller, *Power Situation During the War*, 46, 102–280.
14. As one example, "In 1920 Lenin defined communism as 'Soviet power plus the electrification of the whole country.'" "Energy Survey," *Economist* (June 18, 1994), 6.
15. Wilkins, *History ... 1914–1945*, 109; see also 41 U.S. Stat. 1065 for the relevant section of the act.
16. Raphael Schapiro, "Public Ownership and Private Investment: The Case of British Electric Traction," in his "Why Public Ownership? Urban Utilities in London, 1870–1914," D.Phil. thesis, Nuffield College, Oxford University, June 2003, 223.
17. Alex Hunter, *The Economics of Australian Industry* (Melbourne: Melbourne University Press, 1963), 131.
18. Schapiro, "Public Ownership and Private Investment," 225. The actual reincorporation with Indian registration appears to have taken place in 1920, based on Garcke, 1928–1929, 1572.
19. Garcke, 1928–1929, 1576, 1588. The only difference in the names of the Hong Kong companies was the 1922 addition of an "s" at the end of "Tramway." The Hong Kong registration appears to have been for tax reasons.
20. Coopersmith, *Electrification of Russia*, 104–6.
21. Later, as is well known, the Russian government called on foreign engineering talent to help build up the industry, but no foreign investments were involved, other than credits on equipment exports, which were not long-term foreign investments. Even earlier, with the New Economic Policy in Russia, there was some foreign investment allowed, but not in the electricity supply sector. The large German activities in the Russian electrical industry in the interwar period,

documented by Feldenkirchen, did not involve any long-term foreign direct investments. See Wilfried Feldenkirchen, "Siemens in Eastern Europe: From the End of World War I to the End of World War II," in Christopher Kobrak and Per H. Hansen, eds., *European Business, Dictatorship, and Political Risk, 1920–1945* (New York: Berghahn Books, 2004), 126–35. See Coopersmith, *Electrification of Russia*, 227, on the absence of foreign investment in contrast with the prewar years.

22. This happened on both sides of the war. See Mira Wilkins, *The Maturing of Multinational Enterprise: American Business Abroad from 1914 to 1970* (Cambridge, MA: Harvard University Press, 1974), 23–24, 40–42, on the takeovers of U.S. properties in Germany, which were far smaller in size than German properties in the United States. Wilkins, *The History ... 1914–1945*, Ch. 1, on the takeover of enemy assets in the United States.
23. Wilfried Feldenkirchen, *Siemens: From Workshop to Global Player* (Munich: Piper, 2000), 110, 202; apparently, what English Electric acquired from Siemens within England was no bargain. The large Stafford factory had been unprofitable and underused. I. C. R. Byatt, *The British Electrical Industry, 1875–1914* (Oxford: Clarendon Press, 1979), 194; Feldenkirchen, "Siemens in Eastern Europe," 126; Georg Siemens, *History of the House of Siemens*, 2 vol. (Freiburg/Munich: Karl Alber, 1957), II, 24–26.
24. Feldenkirchen, "Siemens in Eastern Europe," 126, 132. Construction of the plant apparently did not start until 1925. For the progress, see Sigfrid von Weiher and Herbert Goetzeler, *The Siemens Company: Its Historical Role in the Progess of Electrical Engineering, 1847–1980* (Berlin and Munich: Siemens AG, 1977), 95. On the Shannon plant, see Harm Schröter, "The German Question, the Unification of Europe, and European Market Strategies of Germany's Chemical and Electrical Industries, 1900–1992," in *Business History Review*, 67 (Autumn 1993), 382–83. Naturally, Siemens exported its own equipment under the contractual arrangement.
25. See Chapter 3 for Hertner's 16.5 percent estimate. On the "Italianized" foreign capital, see Luciano Segreto, "Financing the Electric Industry in Europe (1880–1945)," Unpublished paper presented in 1993 in Paris at a "pre-Milan-conference" meeting (cited as Segreto, Milan paper). For details on foreign capital in Italy before the first World War, Luciano Segreto, "Imprenditori e Finanzieri," in *Storia dell' Industria Elettrica in Italia*, vol. 1 (Rome-Bari: Laterza, 1992), 332. Hertner's 16.5 percent estimate was that made *directly* from Germany and not those made indirectly through Swiss holding companies. For the Italianization process during the war, see Luciano Segreto "Gli Assetti Proprietari," in *Storia dell' Industria Elettrica in Italia*, vol. 3 (Rome-Bari: Laterza, 1993), 94–110, and his *Giacinto Motta* (Rome-Bari: Laterza, 2005), 104–8.
26. German investments through Swiss holdings were not taken over. There was no attempt here to cut through the corporate veils. Italian banks, electric, and/or industrial firms set up special holding companies for the confiscated German assets. These companies then were merged with Swiss holding companies, such as Elektrobank and Indelec, to permit the latter to have the controlling interest in the Italian holding company. Alternatively, in neutral Switzerland German

and Italian electrical and financial groups met (discreetly) to develop strategies to mitigate the German losses during the war. Segreto, "Gli Assetti Proprietari," 94–110, and his *Giacinto Motta*, 104–8 See also Pierre-Alain Wavre, "Swiss Investments in Italy from the XVIIIth to the XXth Century," *Journal of European Economic History*, 17 (Spring 1988), 96. Swiss holding companies, however, with postwar Italian interests, including Elektrobank, Indelec, Motor, and Italo-Suisse, would be negatively impacted when in 1921 the Italian lire was devalued. Luciano Segreto, "Du 'Made in Germany' au 'Made In Switzerland," in M. Trédé, ed., *Électricité et Électrification dans le Monde 1880–1980* (Paris: PUF, 1992), 350.

27. Hans-Peter Schwarz, *Konrad Adenauer*, vol. 1 (Providence, RI: Berghahn Books, 1995), 120 (the quote). Réné Brion, "Le Rôle de la Sofina," in Monique Trédé-Boulmer, ed., *Le Financement de l'Industrie Électrique 1880–1980* (Paris: PUF, 1994), 217–20; Ginette Kurgan-Van Hentenryk's data cited in Herman Van der Wee and Monique Verbreyt, *The Generale Bank 1822–1997* (Tielt, Belgium: Lannoo, 1997), 162; and Ginette Kurgan-Van Hentenryk to Mira Wilkins, July 1, 2002. See also Liane Ranieri, *Dannie Heineman: Un Destin Singulier, 1872–1962* (Brussels: Éditions Racine, 2005), 79–130 (on Heineman and Sofina during World War I and its immediate aftermath; Ranieri is good on Heineman and Belgian relief, ibid., 89ff). American-born Heineman retained his U.S. citizenship. He was an exceptional individual. In February 1919, he published a plan for an International Clearing House and developed his first ideas about international cooperation to deal with stabilization of exchange rates, war debts, and the development of electrical networks. Brion, "Le Rôle de la Sofina," 221. He became a very visible figure. See, for example, his discussion of the inefficiencies in the provision of electric power in London. D. Heineman, "Electricity in the Region of London," in *Transactions of the First World Power Conference*, vol. 4 (London: Percy Lund Humphries & Co., 1924), 1285–1305. On his title, see Sofina, *Annual Reports*.

28. See Chapter 3 herein. Gabriel Tortella, *The Development of Modern Spain* (Cambridge, MA: Harvard University Press, 2000), 218; Teresa Tortella, *A Guide to Sources of Information on Foreign Investment in Spain, 1780–1914* (Amsterdam: International Institute of Social History, 2000) (http://www.iisg.nl/publications/guide-spain.pdf, accessed Sept. 26, 2007). Specifically on the Barcelona companies, Christopher Armstrong and H. V. Nelles, *Southern Exposure: Canadian Promoters in Latin America and the Caribbean, 1896–1930* (Toronto: University of Toronto Press, 1988), 163–67; Marco Doria and Peter Hertner, "Urban Growth and the Creation of Integrated Electricity Systems: The Cases Genoa and Barcelona, 1894–1914," in Andrea Giuntini, Peter Hertner, and Gregorio Núñez, eds., *Urban Growth on Two Continents in the* 19th *and* 20th *Centuries: Technology, Networks, Finance and Public Regulation* (Granada: Editorial Comares, 2004), 241; and Peter Hertner and H. V. Nelles, "Contrasting Styles of Foreign Investment: A Comparison of the Entrepreneurship, Technology, and Finance of German and Canadian Enterprises in Barcelona Electrification," *Revue Economique*, 58 (Jan. 2007), 191–214. Elektrobank and Indelec both had investments in Spain. In 1905, Sofina had created in Spain the Tramways de Barcelone and in 1906 Tramways

et Électricité de Bilbao. When Sofina sold its interests in 1913 in the Tramways de Barcelone to Barcelona Traction, Light and Power Co., it got stock as collateral for the tramway company's debt to Sofina; after the December 1914 bankruptcy of BTLP, Sofina obtained an interest in BTLP. Ranieri, *Dannie Heineman*, 74, 122.

29. Armstrong and Nelles, *Southern Exposure*, 257. Loewenstein had no known German ties.
30. Armstrong and Nelles, *Southern Exposure*, 167; Doria and Hertner, "Urban Growth," 243; and Hertner and Nelles, "Contrasting Styles," which is wonderful on the troubles with the financing.
31. Doria and Hertner, "Urban Growth," 242–43, explain that Ebro, founded in Canada at the same time as BTLP (1911) and then registered in Spain, was the main producing company, while BTLP served as the principal holding company for the electricity and transport firms that it acquired in Catalonia. According to Tortella, *Guide to Sources of Information on Foreign Investment in Spain*, item 410: Riegos y Fuerza del Ebro, Ebro was at origin a wholly owned subsidiary of BTLP.
32. Peacock, who became president of Barcelona Traction in 1915, resided in London; he was the London representative of the Toronto-headquartered Dominion Securities from 1902 to 1915. Peacock developed a close, informal relationship with Barings and was considered by them to be a specialist on electric utility enterprises in Brazil, Mexico, and Spain (that is, the Canadian activities). He would serve as a director of the Bank of England from 1921 until 1924, when he became a partner in the Barings merchant bank. (In 1924, Barings had a director on the Bank of England board; not until that man died did Peacock again, in 1929, become a Bank of England board member.) For background on Peacock, see Carroll Quigley, *The Anglo-American Establishment: From Rhodes to Cliveden* (New York: Books in Focus, 1981), 87 (which has a number of mistakes, but is good on context); Wilkins, *History ... 1914–1945*, 489, 848n250; and Duncan McDowall, *The Light: Brazilian Traction, Light and Power Company Limited, 1899–1945* (Toronto: University of Toronto Press, 1988), 212.
33. Hertner and Nelles, "Contrasting Styles," 16.
34. Armstrong and Nelles, *Southern Exposure*, 232.
35. Ibid., 232, 238, 240, 280 (on Asa Billings and Pearson Engineering). After the bankruptcy of Barcelona Traction in December 1914, it was already clear, even before the sinking of the *Lusitania*, that F. S. Pearson "would have to be dislodged" from the management; thus, Peacock had in 1915 become president of Barcelona Traction. McDowall, *The Light*, 212.
36. David Kynaston, *The City of London* (London: Chatto & Windus, 1999), III, 145.
37. The quoted passage was Edward Peacock's assessment in 1926. See Wilkins, *History ... 1914–1945*, 198.
38. Armstrong and Nelles, *Southern Exposure*, 232, and Albert Broder, *Alcatel Alsthom: Histoire de la Compagnie Générale d'Électricité* (Paris: Larousse, 1992), 88. On Energía Eléctrica de Cataluña, see Chapter 3 herein.
39. Armstrong and Nelles, *Southern Exposure*, 258–59.

40. Hertner and Nelles, "Contrasting Styles," 16; its sister company Ebro became the most important hydroelectric producer in Spain. Doria and Hertner, "Urban Growth," 242.
41. Lothar Gall, et al., *The Deutsche Bank, 1870–1995* (London: Weidenfeld & Nicholson, 1995), 182.
42. R. P. T. Davenport-Hines, *Dudley Docker* (Cambridge: Cambridge University Press, 1984), 200. Was this in part disingenuous? In August 1920, Walther Rathenau of AEG told General Electric (U.S.) men that he intended to take advantage of the depreciated Mark to reconquer export markets. Stephen A. Schuker, *American "Reparations" to Germany, 1919–33* (Princeton: Princeton Studies in International Finance, No. 61, Department of Economics, Princeton University, 1988), 21. Of course, there is a difference between trade and investment; AEG and Siemens both wanted to export.
43. Davenport-Hines, *Dudley Docker*, 155–58.
44. Hubert Herring, *A History of Latin America* (New York: Knopf, 1961), 667, and David R. Moore, *A History of Latin America*, rev. ed. (New York: Prentice-Hall, 1942), 489–94, 817–18.
45. Ibid., 817–18.
46. Gall, et al., *Deutsche Bank*, 183; Albert Carreras, Xavier Tafunnell, and Eugenio Torres, "Against Integration: The Rise and Decline of Spanish State-Owned Firms and the Decline and Rise of Multinationals, 1939–1990," in Ulf Olsson, ed., *Business and European Integration Since 1800* (Goteborg, Sweden: Graphic Systems, 1997), 44. Banco Urquijo, incorporated in 1918 (on the basis of an old banking house), was in the 1920s one of Spain's six largest banks; it was involved in "mixed banking, in the style of the German 'universal' banks;" it was a commercial bank, which also undertook promotional and holding activities; it became very much involved in public utilities finance within Spain (and abroad). *Handbook on the History of European Banks*, 868–69.
47. On the Argentinean, Chilean, and Uruguayan properties of DUEG/CATE (at the end of 1917), see Frederic M. Halsey, *Investments in Latin America and the British West Indies* (U.S. Department of Commerce, Bureau of Foreign and Domestic Commerce, Special Agents Series, No. 169, Washington, DC, 1918), 68–69, 364. CHADE would not acquire the largest of the German-owned Chilean properties (see data later in the present chapter; these had not been owned by DUEG before the war). In 1920 in Argentina, the DUEG counterpart name CATE was also dropped. The company was known in Argentina as CHADE or, over time, by its principal subsidiary's name, Compañía Argentina de Electricidad, abbreviated as CAE or, later, CADE. CAE had been formed as an Argentine company in 1909; DUEG had acquired part of the stock, which passed to CHADE in the 1920 transition. CAE initially operated in the Province of Buenos Aires, north of the capital. In the 1920s, CAE/CADE appears to have become the main operating company of CHADE in Argentina. We are indebted to Norma Lanciotti (November 2006) for this information. Maria Ines Barbero, "Grupos Empresarios, Intercambio Comercial e Inversiones Italianas en la Argentina," *Estudios Migratorios Latinoamericanos*, 5:1990), 324, mentions CAE.
48. Gall, et al., *Deutsche Bank*, 183.

49. The difficulties were not confined to the German-Swiss firms. On Elektrobank and Indelec pre-war investments in Germany, see Chapter 3. The holding companies' difficulties were compounded when in 1921 the Italian lire was devalued.
50. Gall, et al., *Deutsche Bank*, 183.
51. Luciano Segreto, "Financing the Electric Industry Worldwide: Strategy and Structure of the Swiss Electric Holding Companies, 1895–1945," *Business and Economic History*, 23 (Fall 1994), 167–68.
52. Serge Paquier, *Histoire de l'Électricité en Suisse* (Geneva: Éditions Passé Présent, 1998), II, 978. More accurately than Paquier, Peter Hertner notes the curtailed influence of AEG and Siemens in Elektrobank and Indelec; their participation in the capital was lowered in each of the two cases to less than 25 percent of the equity. Peter Hertner, "L'Industrie Électrotechnique Allemande entre les Deux Guerres: À la Recherche d'une Position International Perdue," *Relations Internationales*, 43 (Autumn 1985), 299.
53. A Credit Suisse historian writes that in the spring of 1920 Credit Suisse and Elektrobank "participated in the transfer" of DUEG to Sofina and in the creation of CHADE. Joseph Jung, *From Schweizerische Kreditanstalt to Credit Suisse Group: The History of a Bank* (Zurich: NZZ Verlag, 2000), 73.
54. On Motor and Columbus, see Chapter 3; on Motor-Columbus and its predecessors, Paquier, *Histoire de l'Électricité en Suisse*, II, 691–92, 771–72; Segreto, "Du 'Made in Germany,'" 349, and Segreto, "Financing the Electric Industry Worldwide," 167. On Italo-Argentina's investments in Argentina during World War I, see Halsey, *Investments in Latin America*, 68–69. Although Italo-Argentina would expand during the 1920s, it remained small compared with CHADE.
55. Brion, "Le Rôle de la Sofina," 220, for Sofina's working out of its problems with French sequestrations during the war years. Luciano Segreto, "Le Rôle du Capital Étranger dans l'Industrie Électrique," in Maurice Lévy-Leboyer and Henri Morsel, eds., *Histoire Générale de l'Électricité en France*, II (Paris: Fayard, 1994), 982–1014 (on Elektrobank as well as the other Swiss companies).
56. Pierre Lanthier "Les Constructions Électriques en France: Le Case de Six Groupes Industriels Internationaux de 1880 à 1940," Ph.D. diss., 3 vol., Paris: University of Paris X (Nanterre), 1988. Sofina's investments in France were mainly concentrated in SCIE, while becoming a strong partner of Ernest Mercier (a shareholder in SCIE). Among its overseas interests, SCIE was involved in Algeria and French Indo-China. Segreto, "Le Rôle du Capital Étranger dans l'Industrie Électrique," 1006–10.
57. The three properties that were transferred were in Turku, Maarianhamina, and Hämeenlinna. Timo Myllyntaus, *Electrifying Finland: The Transfer of a New Technology into a Late Industrializing Economy* (London: Macmillan, 1991), 56.
58. On Elektrobank's experiences, see Segreto, "Le Rôle du Capital Étranger dans l'Industrie Électrique," 991–92.
59. See notes to Chapter 3 on the investments of Swiss Bankverein (as of 1917 Swiss Bank Corporation) in the Austro-Hungarian Empire and the then existing

corporate structure. In 1923, SBC set up the holding company Elektrowerte AG to consolidate the main assets of its affiliated railroad bank (Schweizerische Eisenbahnbank) that were located in the former Austro-Hungarian Empire; Elektrowerte took over Steiermärkishe Elektrizitäts-Gesellschaft (in English, Steiermark Electric Power Co.), which just before World War I had built the Fala electricity works, in what would become Yugoslavia. SBC's railroad bank was renamed in 1924: Schweizerische Elektrizitäts- und Verkehrsgesellschaft (Suiselectra). See Bauer, *Swiss Bank Corporation*, 162–63, 249, 393.

60. Nikos Pantelakis, *The Electrification of Greece: From Private Initiative to State Monopoly (1889–1956)* (Athens: Cultural Foundation of the National Bank of Greece, 1991), 177–78, 212 (in Greek, with relevant portions translated for us by the author). English summary, *Ten Years of Electricity, 1926–1936 (Athens Piraeus Electricity Company Ltd.)*, in PEA/COWD 3/3, S. Pearson & Son Papers, Science Museum, London; and British Electrical and Allied Manufacturers' Association, *Combines and Trusts in the Electrical Industry. The Position in Europe in 1927* (1927; reprinted, New York: Arno Press, 1977), 180, confirms the continuing French Thomson–Houston connection. This book is henceforth cited as BEAM, *Combines*.

61. In 1923, the Government of South Africa created (under legislation passed in 1922) an Electricity Supply Commission (Escom) to operate and expand electricity supply undertakings. For conditions in South Africa, see Catherine Coquery-Vidrovitch, "La Politique de Réseaux d'Électrification en Afrique: Comparison Afrique de l'Ouest, Afrique du Sud," in Dominique Barjot, Daniel Lefeuvre, Arnaud Berthonnet, and Sophie Coeuré, eds., *L'Électrification Outremer de la Fin du XIXe Siècle aux Première Décolonisations* (Paris: EDF, 2002), 77; and Céline Boileau, "La Production Électrique Destinée à las Minière en Afrique du Sud (1880–1922)," in ibid., 470–71, which explains the complicated relationship between VFTP and Escom. See also Charles H. Feinstein, *An Economic History of South Africa* (Cambridge: Cambridge University Press, 2005), 120, on Escom. *Stock Exchange Year Book 1930*, 1040.

62. See Chapter 3. See also Linda Jones, Charles Jones, and Robert Greenhill, "Public Utility Companies," in D. C. M. Platt, *Business Imperialism 1840–1930: An Inquiry Based on British Experience in Latin America* (Oxford: Oxford University Press, 1977), 80. Pearson's Vera Cruz Light & Power was one of the many foreign companies that suffered financial losses in certain years of the revolution but persisted. Miguel S. Wionczek, "Electric Power," in Raymond Vernon, ed., *Public Policy and Private Enterprise in Mexico* (Cambridge, MA: Harvard University Press, 1964), 35.

63. Jones and Greenhill, "Public Utility Companies, 94–95.

64. David Kynaston, *The City of London* (London: Chatto & Windus, 1995), II, 404; in the notes to Chapter 3, we indicated that Beit died in 1906 and Wernher in 1912. We cannot find any evidence that the British Pearson group had been involved in South Africa before or after World War I. However, there does seem to have been some international business links – if nothing more than on an information basis – between the Victoria Falls developments and those in Chile. Maryna Fraser, "International Archives in South Africa," *Business and*

Economic History, 2nd ser., XVI (1987), 163–73, describes the Corner House group: Werner Beit & Co., London; the Johannesburg House of H. Eckstein & Co. and its subsidiary Rand Mines Ltd.; and the Central Mining and Investment Corporation. Also CMIC had been involved with S. Pearson & Son in 1914, seeking oil concessions in what is now Iraq. See Marian Kent, *Oil and Empire: British Policy and Mesopotamian Oil 1900–1920* (London: Macmillan, 1976), 88, 234n124.

65. Jones and Greenhill, "Public Utility Companies," 95–101.
66. Wilkins, *History ... 1914–1945*, 766n389; on Kindersley, see Kynaston, *City of London*, III, 73, and R. S. Sayers, *The Bank of England, 1891–1944*, 2 vol. (Cambridge: Cambridge University Press, 1976), I, 122n4. Kindersley was a director of the Bank of England (1914–1946).
67. On Brand, see Quigley, *Anglo-American Establishment*, 60, and Sayers, *Bank of England*, I, 153n, 157n, 178n, and II, 363–364n5.
68. Kynaston, *City of London*, III, 38.
69. Ibid., 40. Had British electrification at home (as well as abroad) fallen behind because of the absence of "universal banks"? For some thoughts on the progress of U.K. domestic electrification, see Michael Edelstein, *Overseas Investment in the Age of High Imperialism: The United Kingdom, 1850–1914* (New York: Columbia University Press, 1982), 64–65. Edelstein did not find this absence responsible.
70. J. A. Spender, *Weetman Pearson: First Viscount Cowdray, 1856–1927* (London: Cassell & Co., 1930), 249, 270 (quote).
71. See data in S. Pearson & Son Papers, Science Museum Library, London. At origin, Whitehall Securities owned all the ordinary shares of Whitehall Electric and S. Pearson & Son controlled Whitehall Securities; Jones and Greenhill, "Public Utility Companies," 102 (on the 1922 situation); in 1933, when we have detailed evidence, Whitehall Securities, still controlled by the group, continued to own all the ordinary share capital of Whitehall Electric; see Deloitte's Valuation, S. Pearson & Son Ltd., Whitehall Securities Corporation Ltd. and subsidiaries, Oct. 5, 1933, material submitted with letter dated March 16, 1936, in PEA/COWD 5/11, Pearson papers. See also Jones and Greenhill, "Public Utility Companies," 102–14; J. Fred Rippy, *British Investments in Latin America, 1822–1949* (Minneapolis: University of Minnesota Press, 1959), 245, and Spender, *Weetman Pearson*, 208, 248–49.
72. Kynaston, *City of London*, III, 73.
73. The Belgian branch was in Brussels. According to Bank of Spain records, the Spanish branch was in Madrid. We are indebted to Teresa Tortella, who sent us (September 30, 2005), from the Bank of Spain Archives, a copy of the "settlement deed" for Lazard Brothers' new Spanish firm, set up in 1920; it had a broad mandate: It could engage in "toda clase de asuntos industriales y mercantiles, especialmente comerciales y de Banca, pero sin excluir ninguna clase de negocios, pudiendo adquirir negocios, bienes y derechos de toda clase sin limitacion alguna" (all classes of industrial and mercantile business, especially commercial and of the Bank, but without excluding any class of business, being able to acquire businesses, assets and rights of all types without any limitation).

74. Davenport-Hines, *Dudley Docker*, 206. The links between the Docker and the British Pearson groups were not harbingers for the future. Often, these two British groups proved to be rivals, with the Pearsons associated, for example, with English Electric, while the Docker group sought business for Metropolitan Vickers and related British companies. In 1925, however, Sir Clarendon Hyde (who was a part of the British Pearson business cluster) joined the board of Elrafin after the death of Sir Edward Pearson. Ibid. See notes later in this chapter on Hyde. It was Docker who seems to have had the strongest Sofina connections, although see (in a note below) Lazard Brothers' participation in the "new" Sofina of 1928.
75. This loan appears to have been made in 1922. See Garcke, 1928–1929, 1576–77. A 1922 £2 million first-debenture loan guaranteed by the British government to the Newfoundland Power and Paper Co. was specifically designed to help the British manufacturer Armstrong, Whitworth, which would do the engineering work and supply turbines for the electrical facility. In 1921, Armstrong, Whitworth had a minority interest in the predecessor of Newfoundland Power and Paper, Newfoundland Products Corporation. W. J. Reader, *Bowater: A History* (Cambridge: Cambridge University Press, 1981), 33–34.
76. For a nice summary, see Sir Alec Cairncross, *Control of Long-Term International Capital Movements* (Washington, DC: Brookings Institution, 1973), 56.
77. Ibid.
78. Kynaston, *City of London*, III, 85.
79. Sayers, *Bank of England*, I, 133 ("taking some of the strain off London").
80. Charles H. Feinstein, Peter Temin, and Gianni Toniolo, "International Economic Organization: Banking, Finance, and Trade in Europe Between the Wars," in Charles H. Feinstein, ed., *Banking, Currency, and Finance in Europe Between the Wars* (Oxford: Oxford University Press, 1995), 9.
81. We did not include Puebla Tramway, Light & Power Co. Ltd., which was Canadian-registered, but part of the Cowdray group. For the firms, see Chapter 3 herein. For the 1919 reorganization of Mexican Northern Power Co., see Armstrong and Nelles, *Southern Exposure*, 253.
82. Armstrong and Nelles, *Southern Exposure*, 207–26.
83. Ibid., 171.
84. Ibid., 178–79, 183, 184. The Brazilian milreis fell sharply in value in 1914–1915, strengthened in 1916–1919, and then plunged in 1919–1923. Ibid., 230.
85. There had once been large German interests in the Brazilian electricity supply industry (in Brasilianische Elektrizitäts-Gesellschaft), but these had been sold to a predecessor of Brazilian Traction in 1905. George F. W. Young, "German banks and German direct investment in Latin America, 1880–1920," in Carlos Marichal, ed., *Foreign Investment in Latin America: Impact on Economic Development, 1850–1930* (Milan: Università Bocconi, 1994), 60–61. By the time of World War I, German interests in the Brazilian electricity supply industry were negligible.
86. Armstrong and Nelles, *Southern Exposure*, 229. We have encountered Peacock earlier in this chapter.

87. On Dillon, Read, see Vincent P. Carosso, *Investment Banking in America* (Cambridge, MA: Harvard University Press, 1970), 344, and Robert Sobel, *The Life and Times of Dillon Read* (New York: Truman Talley Books, 1991).
88. Kynaston, *City of London*, III, 72.
89. Robert W. Dunn, *American Foreign Investments* (New York: B.W. Huebsch and Viking , 1926), 57; because Dunn's source is the *Financial Post*, Nov. 16, 1923, these figures are probably in Canadian dollars.
90. Wilkins, *Maturing of Multinational Enterprise*, 43; in 1919, Vickers Ltd. acquired Metropolitan Carriage and changed the name of British Westinghouse Electric to Metropolitan Vickers Electrical Co. Ibid., 43n. On British Westinghouse's problems, see Byatt, *British Electrical Industry, 1875–1914*, 195. Ibid., 194, found that British Thomson-Houston, GE's affiliate in the United Kingdom was before the war an efficiently run enterprise compared with British Westinghouse *and* the British Siemens facilities. On GE's expansion in the immediate postwar years, see Wilkins, *Maturing of Multinational Enterprise*, 65–66.
91. William J. Hausman and John L. Neufeld, "U.S. Foreign Direct Investment in Electrical Utilities in the 1920s," in Mira Wilkins and Harm Schröter, eds., *The Free-Standing Company in the World Economy* (Oxford: Oxford University Press, 1998), 371–73; Gregory P. Marchildon, "The Montreal Engineering Company and International Power: Overcoming the Limitations of the Free-Standing Utility," in ibid., 394–97 (on Cuba); Thomas O'Brien, *The Century of U.S. Capitalism in Latin America* (Albuquerque: University of New Mexico Press, 1999), 42–43 (Guatemala); Halsey, *Investments in Latin America*, 440, writes that Electric Bond and Share made its initial acquisitions in Panama in 1916, rather than 1917; Wilkins, *Maturing of Multinational Enterprise*, 16, says the actual purchase was consummated in 1917; the property acquired was that of the Panama-American Corporation, originally set up in 1904. Halsey, *Investments in Latin America*, 440; Moore, *History of Latin America*, 817–18. We have no evidence of pre–World War I German ownership of the Panamanian properties, but the State Department did not want to take chances. For national security reasons, it wanted a strong American presence near the Panama Canal. On the German activities in Guatemala in electrification, see Regina Wagner, "Actividades Empresariales de los Alemanes en Guatemala, 1850–1920," *Mesoamérica*, 13 (June 1987), 114, 118, 120, which does not get the story exactly right. On the ostensible German interests in Havana Electric, through Speyer & Co., New York, see Sidney Alexander Mitchell, *S. Z. Mitchell and the Electrical Industry* (New York: Farrar, Straus & Cudahy, 1960), 108.
92. This was an area of Brazil where there had been strong German influences.
93. American & Foreign Power Co., "The Foreign Power System," booklet (New York: American & Foreign Power Co., 1953), 8; Wilkins, *Maturing of Multinational Enterprise*, 131.
94. Wilkins, *Maturing of Multinational Enterprise*, 20–22; Marc Linder, *Projecting Capitalism: A History of the Internationalization of the Construction Industry* (Westport, CT: Greenwood Press, 1994), 107–9; and Hausman and Neufeld, "U.S. Foreign Direct Investment," 377 (on Charles Stone and Stone & Webster).

95. *Moody's Manual (Utilities) 1930*, xxi. This figure was up substantially from before World War I, but there was still a long way to go with U.S. as well as global electrification.
96. Based on research by Mira Wilkins for her *Maturing of Multinational Enterprise*. See also, Dominique Barjot, Daniel Lefeuvre, Arnaud Berthonnet, and Sophie Coeuré, eds., *L'Électrification Outre-mer de la Fin du XIXe Siècle aux Première Décolonisations* (Paris: EDF, 2002), passim. There are numerous discussions of company towns in standard business histories. In the 1960s, Mira Wilkins visited about three dozen company towns in Latin America, Africa, and the Middle East that had been established in the 1920s.
97. Thomas Heinrich, "Product Diversification in the U.S. Pulp and Paper Industry: The Case of International Paper, 1898–1941," *Business History Review*, 75 (Autumn 2001), 479–83; Herbert Marshall, Frank A. Southard, and Kenneth W. Taylor, *Canadian-American Industry* (1936; reprinted New York: Russell & Russell, 1970), esp. 38, 40–43; and Hausman and Neufeld, "U.S. Foreign Direct Investment," 369, 381, 390n77. In Newfoundland, which did not join Canada until 1949, the important Corner Brook company (as of 1922, Newfoundland Power and Paper Co., then International Power and Paper Co. of Newfoundland, later (1938) Bowater's Newfoundland Pulp and Paper Mills Ltd.) had plans at the start of the 1920s for a major hydroelectric facility and a large mill at Corner Brook. The origins (the Newfoundland Products Corporation) were with the Reid family of Newfoundland, which did not have the resources for such a large project; a British group (including the manufacturer Armstrong, Whitworth) put together the financial package. Then, in 1927 International Paper acquired Newfoundland Power and Paper Co./International Power and Paper Co. of Newfoundland. For the very complicated story, see Reader, *Bowater*, 33–36, 139 (International Paper's 1927 acquisition). This acquisition by International Paper in Newfoundland was in addition to those in Canada.
98. Hausman and Neufeld, "U.S. Foreign Direct Investment," 383.
99. Later, we will note Alcoa's Arthur Vining Davis as a participant in Italian Power Co. and its successor, International Power Securities Corp., holding companies related to Italian public utilities; Alcoa had no direct investments in power facilities in Italy, but it had purchased in 1923 the power *sites* in Norway and in 1925 in the French Pyrenees. Not long after, it built a small aluminum plant in Italy. It wanted to be sure that it could gain access to adequate power. Cleona Lewis, *America's Stake in International Investments* (Washington, DC: Brookings Institution, 1938), 248 (on Alcoa's European holdings). For background on Alcoa's Canadian investments, Massell, *Amassing Power*, 170–89, with the terms of the 1925 arrangements on pp. 188–189; George David Smith, *From Monopoly to Competition: The Transformations of Alcoa, 1888–1986* (Cambridge: Cambridge University Press, 1988), 143–44. (The Duke-Price Power Co had been formed in 1924, for the so-called upper development. Massell, *Amassing Power*, 174.) For Andrew W. Mellon's role in "actively assisting Alcoa" in its negotiations with Duke, see David Cannadine, *Mellon: An American Life* (New York: Knopf, 2006), 323.

100. Massell, *Amassing Power*, 5, 190–94. Isle Maligne was the so-called upper development.
101. Estimate made by William Hausman based on M. J. Patton, "The Water-Power Resources of Canada," *Economic Geography*, 2 (April 1926), 188, 190, and Hausman and Neufeld, "U.S. Foreign Direct Investment," 390n76.
102. A later Aluminium Ltd. report described the process: The holding company Aluminium Ltd. was formed in Canada in 1928. At its inception, it acquired in exchange for its own shares, equity interests in various companies owned by Alcoa. The shares of Aluminium Ltd. were then immediately distributed as a dividend to the shareholders of Alcoa, which meant that at the time of this spin-off both Alcoa and Aluminium had identical shareholders. Aluminium Ltd., "Prospectus," July 4, 1963.
103. Wilkins, *Maturing of Multinational Enterprise*, 148–49; according to Marshall, Southard, and Taylor, *Canadian-American Industry*, 105, within Canada, in 1928 Alcoa "directly retained only the Alcoa Power Company Ltd., owning the undeveloped site on the lower Saguenay." The best discussion of what was retained and what was not of the Saguenay project is in Brief of the Aluminum Company in U.S. *v*. Aluminum Company of America, Equity No. 85–83 (SDNY, 1940), 139–51, 187–91, 711–24; according to this brief, the reason that the Lower Development (Alcoa Power Co. Ltd.) was not transferred to Aluminium Ltd. in 1928 was that "The value of the property was ... so great that the surplus of Alcoa would not permit its transfer as part of the reorganization and the finances of Limited would not justify that company's acquiring the property." By 1938, there was a new situation, and Aluminium Ltd. paid $35 million for that property. Ibid., 723. The lower site in 1925 was expected to have 780,000 potential horsepower, compared with the upper development with its 400,000 horsepower. Ibid., 331.
104. After World War II, a U.S. antitrust suit would require the common shareholders to choose and to maintain investments in one or the other company; only then did the two companies become fully separate. Wilkins, *Maturing of Multinational Enterprise*, 297.
105. Hausman and Neufeld, "U.S. Foreign Direct Investment," 369.
106. Lewis, *America's Stake*, 670.
107. See notes to Chapter 3 on the prewar situation. See also L. F. Haber, *The Chemical Industry, 1900–1930* (Oxford: Clarendon Press, 1971), 87, 126, 152, 168–69, 276, 286, and Jeffrey Allan Johnson, "The Power of Synthesis (1900–1925)," in Werner Abelshauser, et al., *German Industry and Global Enterprise: BASF: The History of a Company* (Cambridge: Cambridge University Press, 2004), 144–45.
108. From 1925 through the rest of the 1930s, the German share of world exports in electrotechnical products was the highest of any nation globally, even though as a percentage of world exports of electrotechnical products, the share was far lower than in 1913. Hertner, "L'Industrie Électrotechnique Allemande," 304. On the recovery of the German electrotechnical *manufacturers*, see ibid., 289–304, and Feldenkirchen, "Siemens in Eastern Europe," 126. By *1939* (regrettably, Feldenkirchen does not provide this information for 1929), Siemens had once again a worldwide network – outside of Germany within Europe and

overseas – employing 26,000 people. (This 1939 employment figure is to be compared with that of 1914, when Siemens had 24,606 employees in its foreign establishments. Hertner, "L'Industrie Électrotechnique Allemande," 292.) In most countries of the world in 1939, Siemens had branch offices. Its international organization in 1939 consisted of almost 200 companies, of which 109 were in Europe, 33 in Asia, 27 in Central and South America, 13 in Africa, 10 in Australia and New Zealand, and 3 in the United States. Some of these affiliates had manufacturing plants. Most were designed to encourage German exports and to aid in the offering of technical services. Feldenkirchen does not, as noted, provide similar information for 1929, but he does indicate that the process of reestablishing a Siemens presence was well underway by the end of the 1920s, particularly in Bulgaria, Czechoslovakia, Hungary, Poland, Romania, and Yugoslavia, where by the end of the 1920s. Siemens did have local companies and factories that were established (or reestablished) "so that the sale and at least partial production of goods was secured." Feldenkirchen, "Siemens in Eastern Europe," 135–45. Feldenkirchen does *not* provide any information on Siemens's investments in electric utilities. In 1928, Siemens set up a branch in Egypt and began to compete for Egyptian business. Robert Vitalis, *When Capitalists Collide: Business Conflict and the End of Empire in Egypt* (Berkeley: University of California Press, 1995), 236–237n9, 71. There seem to have been plans for some investments in utilities. For the international investments of Siemens-Schuckert and Siemens & Halske in 1927, see BEAM, *Combines*, 118–21. Harm Schröter, "The German Question, the Unification of Europe, and European Market Strategies of Germany's Chemical and Electrical Industries, 1900–1992," in *Business History Review*, 67 (Autumn 1993), 380–86, is basically concerned with sales, technical services, and manufacturing activities, *not* utilities. Schröter offers information on AEG, noting that AEG had 35 sales/technical services offices outside of Germany in 1930. Ibid., 383. He, too, deals with Siemens's expansion, adding material on its restoration of a minority interest in Siemens Brothers, London, and its interest in two production plants in Italy. The reestablishment of the minority interest in Siemens Brothers in the United Kingdom in 1929 was in exchange for the latter's shares in Siemens & Halske, Berlin. (After World War I, as noted in the text, Siemens Brothers, with its Woolwich factory, had kept the Siemens name but become British-owned. The Stafford factory of the Siemens-Schuckert affiliate in the United Kingdom was what went to English Electric.) Siemens, *History of the House of Siemens*, II, 204. For interests on boards of directors, we have relied on *Moody's Manual*, annual reports, and business histories.

109. For AEG's indirect, usually minority, interests in electricity supply companies in the late 1920s, we have relied on BEAM, *Combines*,137, and Frank Southard, *American Industry in Europe* (Boston: Houghton Mifflin, 1931), 207. In Switzerland, AEG interests were in Kraftwerk Laufenburg; in Poland, in Oberschlesische Kraftwerk, Katowice; in Turkey, in Société des Tramways et de l'Électricité de Constantinople; in Portugal in Compagnies Réunies Gaz et Électricité, Lisbon; and in Hungary, in AG für Elektrischen und Verkehrsunternehmungen and Phoebus AG für Elektrische Unternehmungen, which two companies were merged in 1926.

110. Lewis, *America's Stake*, 638–40.
111. On Siemens's borrowings in the United States in 1925, see Dunn, *American Foreign Investments*, 38, and in 1926, Wilkins, *History … 1914–1945*, 259. On AEG borrowings in 1925, U.S. Senate, Committee on Finance, *Sale of Foreign Bonds*, 72nd Cong., 1st sess. (1932), 107. The culmination of Siemens's borrowings came early in 1930, when Siemens & Halske issued a 1,000-year "participating debenture" (maturity date, 2930)! The par value of this U.S. flotation was $23.5 million. This debenture had the same rate of interest as the dividend rate on common shares. GE applied to the banking group that handled the issue (Dillon, Read) for a block of the debentures ($11 million); the request was relayed to Siemens, which gave its consent. Siemens wanted the foreign capital, without foreign influence. GE got no voting rights and did not get a membership on the Siemens board. United States Department of Commerce, Bureau of Foreign and Domestic Commerce, *American Underwriting of Foreign Securities in 1930* (Washington, D.C., 1931), 10, 18, 25, and Southard, *American Industry in Europe*, 26–27. We provide more on the borrowings of Rhine-Westphalia Electric Power Company (RWE) later; the Germans knew this company as Rheinisch-Westfälisches Elektrizitätswerk and prefer the more accurate translation Rhenish-Westphalian Electric Power; we used the translation adopted for American bond issues.
112. BEAM, *Combines*, 98.
113. Segreto, "Du 'Made in Germany,'" 355. See Segreto, "Le Rôle du Capital Étranger dans l'Industrie Électrique," 1002–6, for Indelec's investments in France. The Czechoslovakian investments were new. Alice Teichova reports that Indelec had (as of December 31, 1937, but probably made in the 1920s) a one-third participation in Severočeské Elektrárny (North Bohemian Electric Power Works) in Podmokly. Alice Teichova, *An Economic Background to Munich: International Business and Czechoslovakia 1918–1938* (Cambridge: Cambridge University Press, 1974), 220. BEAM, *Combines*, 160, confirms that the investment was made in the 1920s, but there is no indication of output of electricity as of 1927.
114. See Segreto, "Le Rôle du Capital Étranger dans l'Industrie Électrique," 991–1002, for Elektrobank's "new" French connections and the particular utilities in which it was involved
115. Hughes, *Networks of Power*, 424; as our readers know, but as a reminder, Elektrobank before the war had been AEG's Swiss affiliate; in Germany, the Lahmeyer enterprise was associated with AEG. BEAM, *Combines*, 140.
116. Segreto, "Du 'Made in Germany,'" 357, and Segreto,"Financing the Electric Industry Worldwide," 168–69; *Stock Exchange Year-Book 1930*, 1025. By 1929, Schweizerisch-Amerikanische Elektrizitäts-Gesellschaft (SAEG), with its sister Swiss companies, owned the majority of the shares in Compañía Italo-Argentina de Electricidad (Italo-Argentine Electric Co.), incorporated in Argentina in 1911; Empresas Electricas de Bahia Blanca (Bahia Blanca Electric Co.), incorporated in Argentina in 1927; and Compañía Americana de Luz y Tracción, incorporated in Argentina 1918, which provided all the electric light and power and street railway business in Asunción, Paraguay, and operated electric light and power and water service in the city of 25 de Mayo, Argentina.

Ibid. For the increase in Italo-Argentina's output in the 1920s, see the *Wall Street Journal*, May 5, 1930.

117. Harm Schröter, "Globalization and Reliability: The Fate of Foreign Direct Investment in Electric Power-Supply During the World Economic Crisis, 1929–1939," *Annales Historiques de l'Électricité*, 4 (Nov. 2006), 117. J. G. White & Co., which was in 1928 a subsidiary of a British company and in 1929 once again became American-owned, was also involved in Foreign Light & Power. For more on J. G. White, see later in this chapter.
118. Wavre, "Swiss Investments in Italy," 85–102.
119. Segreto, "Du 'Made in Germany,'" 357, corrected by the author, based on data he collected in the Motor-Columbus archives. He insists that these are rough estimates, for there is great difficulty in assembling these percentages, owing to the holding and sub–holding companies, the networks, and the partial interests.
120. On Franco-Suisse, see BEAM, *Combines*,159–60 (its interests in electricity supply companies in 1927 in Switzerland, France, and Italy), and Segreto, "Le Rôle du Capital Étranger," 982–91. On Italo-Suisse: Wavre, "Swiss Investments," 96; BEAM, *Combines*, 160; and Segreto, "Du 'Made in Germany,'" 350–52. In 1914, Motor had acquired an interest in Italo-Suisse; and after the merger of Motor and Columbus in 1923, Italo-Suisse became closely associated with Motor-Columbus. Franco-Suisse in the mid-1920s took part with the French Petsche and Mercier groups in the formation of the French holding company Union Financière pour l'Industrie Électrique.
121. Rory Miller, "British Free-Standing Companies on the West Coast of South America," in Wilkins and Schröter, eds., *Free-Standing Company in the World Economy*, 234 (on Lima Light). Richard Roberts, *Schroders* (Houndmills, England: Macmillan, 1992), 139, 204–5 (on British registration, the 1910 and the 1923 loans). The 1910 loan came a year before Schröder sponsored a loan for the Peruvian government; the 1923 loan came a year after Schröder did just that. The 1923 loan to Lima Light was at a time when British capital controls were still in place, but that did not stop British government approval of some offerings.
122. Based on data in Miller, "British Free-Standing Companies," 234, 250, and BEAM, *Combines*, 182. According to the *Stock Exchange Yearbook, 1934*, 1856–57, the 1923 debenture issue was brought out simultaneously in London and Switzerland, and of the £1.5 million, £250,000 was assigned to Switzerland. Schröter, "Globalization and Reliability," 118, identified the Italian and Swiss interests as associated with Motor-Columbus.
123. Ranieri, *Dannie Heineman*, 131–80 (Sofina in the 1920s), ibid., 135–36 (the scientific laboratory); ibid., 138 (Giros), 231 (Argentina, 1928); Armstrong and Nelles, *Southern Exposure*, 258–59 (overview of Sofina); Heineman, "Electricity in the Region of London," 1297 (on Argentina); BEAM, *Combines*, 154–56; *Moody's Manual (Utilities) 1930*, 2316–17, Brion, "Le Rôle de la Sofina," 221–25 (on Sofina's activities in France and Société Financière Électrique); ibid., 224–25 (on "Société Financière d'Électricité," which we believe was a shortening of the name Société Financière pour le Développement de l'Électricité; Finelec). On the Société Générale d'Entreprises (SGE) and Loucher

and Giros, see Chapter 3, herein. See also Davenport-Hines, *Dudley Docker*, 204, and Segreto, "Le Rôle du Capital Étranger," 1002–6. The Sofina *Annual Report 1929* listed the following major participations in France: Société Centrale pour l'Industrie Électrique, Paris (SCIE), with its key affiliates; Société Financière Électrique, Paris (Finelec), with its broad activities, including those in French colonies; and the "electrical enterprises": Compagnie Centrale d'Energie Électrique, Paris; Union d'Électricité, Paris; Compagnie Électrique de la Loire et du Centre, Paris; Société des Forces Motrices de La Truyère, Paris. On these last four companies, see Brion, "Le Rôle de la Sofina," 221–23.

124. On the "new" Sofina, see its first *Annual Report 1929*. See also Ranieri, *Dannie Heineman*, 162; *Moody's Manual (Utilities) 1930*, 2317; Brion, "Le Rôle de la Sofina," 227; *New York Times*, Oct. 22, 1928; and Dominque Barjot, Henri Morsel, and Sophie Coeuré, eds., *Stratégies, Gestion, Management: Les Compagnies Électriques et Leurs Patrons, 1895–1945* (Paris: EDF, 2001), 42, 47. In the reorganization, the *New York Times*, Oct. 22, 1928, listed the huge number of subscribers to the equity: American firms included Electric Bond and Share, International GE, Dillon Read, Bankers Trust, Guaranty Co., Kuhn Loeb, Lee Higginson, International Acceptance Bank, and International Acceptance Trust. The broad international involvements were amazing. Participants included Banque de Bruxelles, Brussels, and other Belgian groups. Swiss representation comprised Banque pour Entreprises Électriques (Elektrobank), Zurich, and Credit Suisse, Zurich. From Spain were Compañía Hispano-Americana de Electricidad (CHADE), Madrid, along with several Spanish banks involved in the latter. Gesellschaft für Elektrische Unternehmungen (Gesfürel), Berlin, and a collection of German banks – for example, the large Berlin banks: Deutsche Bank, Dresdner Bank, and others – took part, as did M.M. Warburg & Co., Hamburg. Société Générale d'Entreprises, Paris, Comptoir National d'Escompte de Paris, along with other French firms, had a presence. British participants included Electric and Railway Finance Corporation (Elrafin, an investment trust identified with Dudley Docker), Baring Brothers, Lazard Brothers Ltd., Midland Bank, N. M. Rothschild & Sons, Vickers Ltd., and Edward Peacock. Then there were the Italian Banca Commerciale Italiana (BCI), Milan, and the Dutch Amsterdamsche Bank, Hope & Co., Mendelssohn & Co., and Nederlandsche Handel Maatschappij. A Hungarian bank was involved, as was Petschek & Cie., Prague. There were many others that we have not listed, but as a group they represented a portrait of the financial world involved in electrification in the late 1920s. Vickers Ltd. and International GE were exceptional manufacturers listed among those involved. See Ranieri, *Dannie Heineman*, 35–36, and passim for the close, long-standing relationship between Heineman and Oliven. Oliven (1870–1939) was two years older than Heineman. See also ibid., 162–63, for the greatly expanded group of administrators of the new Sofina. The best description of the broad interests of Sofina is in its fifty-one-page *Annual Report 1929*. The involvements listed in the *Moody's Manual (Utilities) 1930* do not capture, for example, Sofina's participations in Eastern Europe, where through Société Anonyme pour Entreprises d'Électricité et de Communication, Budapest, Sofina had interests in Czechoslovakia, Hungary,

Romania, and Yugoslavia – in electricity, tramways, and local railroads. *Annual Report 1929*, 22.

125. Sayers, *Bank of England*, I, 88n; Steven Tolliday, *Business, Banking, and Politics: The Case of British Steel, 1918–1939* (Cambridge, MA: Harvard University Press, 1987), 199, and Davenport-Hines, *Dudley Docker*, passim (on Reginald McKenna, Midland, Docker, and Sofina). Southard, *American Industry in Europe*, 211 (U.S. interests). *Moody's Manual (Utilities) 1930*, 2137, gives the 1929–1930 Sofina board. The only American listed on the Sofina board was the lawyer Gordon Auchincloss, son-in-law of Col. Edward House. On Heineman's friendship with House, see Ranieri, *Dannie Heineman*, 113, 299–322, 421–25. Auchincloss was at the 1919 Peace Conference in Paris as House's secretary; he had undoubtedly first met Heineman there. On Auchincloss, see *Who's Who in America 1924–1925*, 259, and miscellaneous references in Ranieri, *Dannie Heineman*.
126. *Moody's Manual (Utilities) 1930*, 2316. Mexico was not on the list in *Moody's*, probably because Sofina's control was exercised through Sidro (see below).
127. Information from Luciano Segreto and data in Davenport-Hines, *Dudley Docker*.
128. He was, for example, a long-time friend (from 1907 onward) of Konrad Adenauer. Adenauer was mayor of Cologne, 1917–1933. See Schwarz, *Konrad Adenauer*, I, 119, and passim.
129. BEAM, *Combines*, 61, and "Consejo de Administración de la CHADE, 1926–1930," given in Gabriela Dalla Corte, "Associaciones y Negocias: Las Redes Sociales Vasco-Catalanas en el Cono Sur Latinoamericano (1911–1936)," July 14, 2005, 5 (http://www.euskosare.org/, accessed Sept. 26, 2007). For Oliven on the Sofina board, see Sofina, *Annual Report 1929*, 2, and *Moody's Manual (Utilities) 1930*, 2316.
130. *Moody's Manual (Utilities) 1930*, 2316–17; Brion, "Le Rôle de la Sofina," 230–31, and ibid. 230–231n36, for the various interests involved in Caninlipo. Ranieri, *Dannie Heineman*, 163, notes that the key French holdings were those of the Giros group. (Caninlipo had a short life; it was liquidated in 1935. Ibid., 163n.).
131. BEAM, *Combines*, 61, 155, and Brion, "Le Rôle de la Sofina," passim. In 1928, Gesfürel was raising money in New York. It had a $5 million dollar twenty-five-year 6 percent debenture isssue (due 1953). The price was not discounted. It sold at 100. See *Electrical World*, 92 (Sept. 29, 1928), 662. Heineman, while American-born and retaining his American citizenship and while German-educated, had resided in Brussels since 1905 and by the 1920s had fully identified himself with Sofina and "Belgian" interests.
132. Once more, the reader is warned that F. S. Pearson, who died in the sinking of the *Lusitania* in 1915, was unrelated to the British Pearsons: S. Pearson and Son, Weetman Pearson (Lord Cowdray), and the latter's second son, Clive Pearson, who came to run Whitehall Electric Investments Ltd. Sir Edward Pearson who died in 1925 was Weetman Pearson's brother.
133. *Moody's Manual (Utilities) 1930*, 2204 (date of registration). Armstrong and Nelles, *Southern Exposure*, 258–71, and Ranieri, *Dannie Heineman*, 146–59

(on Sidro), esp. 150–151 (on the leadership at origin). On Maurice Despret (1861–1933), see Herman Van der Wee and Monique Verbreyt, *The Generale Bank 1822–1997* (Tielt, Belgium: Lannoo, 1997), 121–22, and Ginette Kurgan-Van Hentenryk, "Le Patronat de l'Électricité en Belgique, 1895–1945," in Dominque Barjot, Henri Morsel, and Sophie Coeuré, eds., *Stratégies, Gestion, Management: Les Compagnies Électriques et Leurs Patrons, 1895–1945* (Paris: EDF, 2001), 64.

134. Charles F. Mallory, "Financial Problems of the North American Electrical Utilities in Latin America," M.S. thesis, MIT, 1956, 34.

135. Armstrong and Nelles, *Southern Exposure*, 259. For Sofina/Sidro, Mexlight, and the Canadians, 1924–1929, see Reinhard Liehr and Georg Leidenberger, "El Paso de una Free-Standing Company a una Empresa Pública: Mexican Light and Power y Mexico Tramways, 1902–1960," in Sandra Kuntz Ficker and Horst Pietschmann, eds., *México y La Economía Atlántica (Siglos XVIII–XX)* (Mexico City: El Colegio de México, Centro de Estudios Históricos, 2006), 289, 297–98.

136. Sources agree that in 1924 Loewenstein had sold to Sofina a sufficiently large block of Sidro shares so as to put Sofina in control; indeed, looking at the 1923 management, one would believe that Sofina was already the key influence. On the other hand, as Armstrong and Nelles, *Southern Exposure*, 259, and Ranieri, *Dannie Heineman*, 151–52, point out, Loewenstein behaved as though he remained the dominant figure.

137. For the very complicated conflicts between Heineman of Sofina and Loewenstein over Brazilian Traction and Mexlight control, and where the Canadians fit into the disputes, see Ranieri, *Dannie Heineman*, 146–59; Armstrong and Nelles, *Southern Exposure*, 263–71; and McDowall, *Light*, 289–95. McDowall writes that in October 1926 Heineman, "who had no interest in seeing SIDRO become a full-fledged rival of SOFINA, began to voice opposition to any scheme that would affect the influence of SOFINA" on Brazilian Traction. Ibid., 293–94. Loewenstein was furious; the quarrel was prolonged; at a Toronto meeting of Brazilian Traction in May 1928, he denounced Heineman, "using names that were absolutely inexcusable." Ibid., 296. Later in May, Loewenstein attended a board meeting of Mexican Light and Power Co. in Toronto and once more verbally clashed with Heineman. Ibid. On the letter from Heineman to Peacock (Dec. 17, 1926), see Ranieri, *Dannie Heineman*, 153. Ibid., 155, dates the takeover of control by Heineman and his group of Sidro and Brazilian Traction to January 1927. Liehr and Leidenberger, "El Paso de Una Free-Standing Company," 297–98, write that in January 1929 (after Loewenstein was out of the picture) Sofina, through Sidro, consolidated its capacity to control Mexlight, albeit the Sofina/Sidro presence was evident from 1924 onward, and Liehr and Leidenberger suggest that Sofina/Sidro had effective control much earlier than January 1929 (they do not deal with the clash between Loewenstein and Heineman). It does seem, however, that in 1928–1929 Sofina/Sidro increased its role in Barcelona Traction and in the Mexlight companies. Both appear under the rubric Sidro in Sofina, *Annual Report 1929*, 39–40 (Brazilian Traction was not included). During the 1920s, Loewenstein took part in other public utilities holding companies as well as a range of projects in the rayon industry.

John Wasik notes that Cyrus Eaton was in league with Loewenstein in an unsuccessful 1928 speculation related to Insull shares. John F. Wasik, *Merchants of Power: Samuel Insull, Thomas Edison, and the Creation of the Modern Metropolis* (New York: Palgrave Macmillan, 2006), 166. The differences between Loewenstein and Heineman came down to the fact that the former was a market operator, while the latter was an engineer.

138. Lanthier, "Les Constructions Électriques en France" (on the Empain group). Robert Vitalis interprets information from BEAM, *Combines*, as indicating that in 1927 the Empain group had interests in forty-two electric railway and tramway operations in fourteen countries along with twenty-five electricity supply companies in four countries. Vitalis, *When Capitalists Collide*, 67. On Empain in the 1920s, see also Segreto, Milan Paper; Dominique Barjot and Henri Morsel, "Introduction," Barjot, Morsel, and Coeuré, *Stratégies, Gestion, Management*, 15; Dominique Barjot, "Les Entreprises Électriques en Guerre, 1914–1918," in ibid., 180–81; Kurgan-Van Hentenryk, "Le Patronat," 59–60, 67; and Kurgan-Van Hentenryk, "Finance and Financiers in Belgium, 1880–1940," in Youssef Cassis, ed., *Finance and Financiers in European History 1880–1960* (Cambridge: Cambridge University Press, 1992), 318–19, 331. On the Empain group's Egyptian business, Robert L. Tignor, *State, Private Enterprise, and Economic Change in Egypt, 1918–1952* (Princeton: Princeton University Press, 1984), 28, and Vitalis, *When Capitalists Collide*, 36, 67, 69–71. In the Shubra power project, the strong Egyptian-based Misr group were investors, ibid., 71; for the ups and downs of this project, see ibid., 70–71, 75.
139. On the rivalry between the banking interests in this group and in Sofina, see Brion, "Le Rôle de la Sofina," 220; see also Ranieri, *Dannie Heineman*, 164–65.
140. In China, for example, in the French concessions, there were French free standing electrical companies. See BEAM, *Combines*, 182; C. Yun, "A Statistical Investigation of Electric Power Plants in China, 1932," *Transactions of the World Power Conference*, Sectional Meeting, Scandinavia, 1933 (Stockholm: Svenska Nationalkommittén för Världskraftkonferenser, 1934), II, 532; and Barjot, et al., *L'Électrification Outre-mer*, passim.
141. See Garcke, 1928–1929.
142. See comments of Robert M. Kindersley, "British Foreign Investments in 1929," *Economic Journal* 41 (Sept. 1931), 381.
143. Ibid.
144. Ibid., 378.
145. Kynaston, *City of London*, III, 144, dealing with Norman's views in November 1925.
146. See Hannah, *Electricity Before Nationalisation*, Ch. 4, on the 1926 legislation and the plans to reform power generation and distribution.
147. Wilkins, *History ... 1914–1945*, 176–77; Kynaston, *City of London*, III, 73. Higginson & Co. had been established in London in 1906. See notes to Chapter 3.
148. Wilkins, *History ... 1914–1945*, Ch. 3–5, deal with this in detail.
149. Ibid., 206, 732n98.
150. Ibid., 205–6.
151. Garcke, 1928–1929, 1603.

152. On the Sudan Light and Power board, the Calcutta Electric Supply Corporation, and Meston, see Garcke 1928–1929, 1456, 1576; *Dictionary of National Biography, 1941–1950*, 587–88; and Quigley, *Anglo-American Establishment*, 79–80, 113, 183–85. In 1928–1929, Lord Meston not only was on the boards of Sudan Light and Power and Calcutta Electric Supply, but also was a director of English Electric Co. Ltd., Power and Traction Finance Co. Ltd., Greater London and Counties Trust Ltd., and Perak River Hydro-Electric Power Co. Ltd., Garcke, 1928–1929, 1779. Pybus, while he was still on the board of English Electric, joined the board of Phoenix Insurance Company in 1927. He was briefly British Minister of Transport, 1929–1933. He would follow Sir Clarendon Hyde as chairman of Phoenix Insurance, holding that position from 1933 to 1935; he "was created a baronet" in 1934 and became Sir John Pybus. Hyde, his predecessor on the Phoenix board, who had personally chosen Pybus as his successor, had had long experience with S. Pearson & Son and had special interests in the electrical industry. On Pybus's lack of success in English Electric and its sale to Edmundson's, see Hannah, *Electricity Before Nationalisation*, 241. On Pybus and Hyde, see Clive Trebilcock, *Phoenix Assurance and the Development of British Insurance, Volume II: The Era of the Insurance Giants, 1870–1984* (Cambridge: Cambridge University Press, 1998), 518–20, 525–26; *New York Times*, Oct. 24, 1935 (obituary for Pybus); and R.P.T. Davenport-Hines, "Sir Percy John Pybus," in *Dictionary of Business Biography*, IV, 783–85. Davenport-Hines, *Dudley Docker*, 65, describes Hyde as a partner in S. Pearson & Sons in 1909. The connections between Hyde and S. Pearson & Son went back much earlier. See Spender, *Weetman Pearson*, 26, 50, 95, 224.
153. Davenport-Hines, "Sir Percy John Pybus," 784. For the competition between Dudley Docker's Metropolitan Vickers (to be merged into Associated Electrical Industries during 1928–1929), Pybus's English Electric, and the Empain group in Egypt in 1929, see Vitalis, *When Capitalists Collide*, 67–76. Vitalis includes nothing on Sofina's role, but Davenport-Hines, *Dudley Docker*, 208–11, makes it clear that Docker was working closely with Heineman of Sofina. Vitalis notes that the Empain group, which supplied Cairo with much of its electric power, along with the group's local allies, favored the Shubra site in northern Cairo, which was the plan that ultimately triumphed. There was a rival Delta scheme, put forth by English Electric and Siemens. English Electric, readers will recall, had in 1919 acquired a key Siemens plant in England; but our guess is that this related to Siemens's new branch in Egypt and its hope to export from Germany. On Siemens's 1928 branch, see Vitalis, *When Capitalists Collide*, 237–238n9. The third plan was that of Docker and Sofina, and it involved a dam at Aswan. According to Davenport-Hines, and confirmed by Ranieri, Docker "fronted for Sofina" in the Egyptian transactions. Docker's company, Electric and Railway Finance Corporation (Elrafin), in which Sofina had an interest, in the mid-1920s had produced a hydroelectric scheme in relationship to the Aswan Dam. For details and Docker's plans beyond the Aswan Dam, see Davenport-Hines, *Dudley Docker*, 206–11, and Ranieri, *Dannie Heineman*, 171–76.
154. On May, see Wilkins, *History ... 1914–1945*, 39–40, 777n56, and *Dictionary of Business Biography*, III, 203–6. On E.H. Lever, *Directory of Directors*,

1926, 911. Lever was a director of the Power and Traction Finance Co. (Poland) Ltd. and British and Foreign Utilities Development Corp.

155. Makoto Kishida, presentation to the Business History group, Kobe, Japan, Nov. 20, 2005; on this loan, see also *Stock Exchange Year-Book, 1930*, 1030, which says nothing about Prudential's role.

156. Ioanna Pepelasis Minoglou, "Between Informal Networks and Formal Contracts: International Investment in Greece During the 1920s," *Business History*, 44 (April 2002), 52. Minutes of League of Nations, Mandate Commission, June 15, 1928. On Palestine Electric (http://domino.un.org/Unispal.NSF/0/e21107299be780b905256st00065 1656?OpenDocument, accessed Aug. 11, 2005)

157. V. Watlington to W. J. Sainsbury (Whitehall Trust), May 6, 1929, Box B14, S. Pearson & Son Ltd. Papers; we are indebted to Lisa Bud-Frierman (Sept. 23, 2003) for her notes on this letter. Vernon Watlington was at this time "joint-manufacturing director" of English Electric.

158. On Hong Kong Electric, see Garcke, 1928–1929; on Beith and Pearce, see Frank H. H. King, *The History of the Hongkong and Shanghai Banking Corporation* (title varies), 4 vol. (Cambridge: Cambridge University Press, 1991–1997), IV, 30–31, and Austin Coates, *A Mountain of Light* (Hong Kong: Heinemann, 1977), esp. 200–1. From 1900 to 1935, Gibb, Livingston & Co. supplied the chairmen for Hong Kong Electric. Jardine Matheson was key within the company. We debated at great length whether Hong Kong Electric should be considered a "British direct investment abroad." The argument for including it was the domination by trading companies with British headquarters. (Geoffrey Jones insists in his *Merchants to Multinationals: British Trading Companies in the Nineteenth and Twentieth Centuries* [Oxford: Oxford University Press, 2000] that the overall direction of Jardine Matheson in 1929 came from the family in Scotland.) The argument for excluding it is that it appears to have been owned and controlled by interests *resident* in Hong Kong (and we deal with residence not nationality in defining foreign direct investment). We have been greatly assisted in our considerations by Leo Goodstadt and Jones. On Table 1.4, we made the decision that because there was no U.K. head office and the operations were run by British residents in Hong Kong, under our definitions Hong Kong Electric should not be considered a foreign direct investment. R. P. T. Davenport-Hines and Geoffrey Jones, eds., *British Business in Asia Since 1860* (Cambridge: Cambridge University Press, 1989), 10, argued that the separation between the company registered in the United Kingdom and that registered abroad (specifically in Hong Kong) was artificial. They write that locally registered companies, established by locally resident British business interests, were "scarcely to be differentiated" from free standing companies registered in the United Kingdom. In regard to the clusters surrounding some of them, we agree.

159. We have not seen a list of such loans. We have found information on these loans by reading prospectuses, directories, and learning of them from miscellaneous other sources: *New York Times*, March 9, 1925 (Toho Electric); Garcke, 1928–1929, 1456 (Sudan Light); Pepelasis Minoglou, "Between Informal Networks," 52 (General Hellenic); Garcke, 1928–1929, 1602–3 (Perak River Hydro-Electric

Power Co.); Minutes of League of Nations, Mandate Commission, June 15, 1928 (Palestine Electric); and *New York Times*, May 14, 1928 (Hungarian Trans-Danubian). The Hungarian Trans-Danubian firm financed a Hungarian state-owned power plant that provided power to Budapest. Coopersmith, "When Worlds Collide," 29.

160. Barjot and Morsel, "Introduction," 13.
161. The pre-1914 French investments in Spanish electrification appear to have come to an end. See Chapter 3. However, Paribas was involved with the Belgian Sofina in Electrobel (see later in this chapter).
162. Samir Saul, "L'Électrification du Maroc à l'Époque du Protectorat," in Barjot, et al., eds., *L'Électrification Outre-mer*, 491–512.
163. Barjot and Morsel, "Introduction," 13.
164. Saul, "L'Électrification du Maroc," 497–98, and *Handbook on the History of European Banks*, 247–48, 251.
165. As another example, there was the French Durand group in Madagascar. See Catharine Vuillermot, *Pierre-Marie Durand et l'Énergie Industrielle* (Paris: CNRS, 2001), 98, and Catharine Vuillermot, "Le Groupe Durand: Une Multinationale Française de la Distribution de l'Électricité (dans la Premiére Moitié du XXe Siècle)?" in Hubert Bonin, et al., *Transnational Companies (19th –20th Centuries)* (Paris: PLAGE, [2002]), 372.
166. For context, see Kurgan-Van Hentenryk, "Finance and Financiers in Belgium, 1880–1940," 324.
167. Ibid.; Barjot and Morsel, "Introduction," 7. On Electrobel and Banque de Bruxelles, see Van der Wee and Verbreyt, *Generale Bank*, 195. On Electrobel's relationship with Sofina, Ranieri, *Dannie Heineman*, 164–69. Société d'Électricité et Traction, Brussels, according to the Suez Group website became Traction et Électricité in 1929 (known as Tractionel and formally renamed that in 1981). See Suez Group website (http://www.suez.com/, accessed Sept. 26, 2007), for the complicated chronology. According to ibid., Electrobel (Compagnie Générale d'Entreprises Électriques et Industrielles) was formed in 1929 as a merger of three Belgian companies: Société Générale Belge d'Entreprises Électriques (SGB), Compagnie Générale pour l'Éclairage et le Chauffage par le Gaz, and Société Générale des Chemins de Fer Économiques. Electrobel should *not* be confused with Electrabel, which had different Belgian origins and was not organized until 1990, although its predecessor companies went back to 1905. In 1986, Tractabel was formed, a merger between Tractionel and Electrobel.
168. Kurgan-Van Hentenryk, "Finance and Financiers in Belgium," 326; see also Ranieri, *Dannie Heineman*, 164–69.
169. Eric Bussière, "The Interests of the Banque de l'Union Parisienne in Czechoslovakia, Hungary, and the Balkans," in Alice Teichova and P.L. Cottrell, eds., *International Business and Central Europe, 1918–1939* (Leicester, England: Leicester University Press, 1983), 409–10.
170. *Time Magazine*, Feb. 17, 1930, and June 16, 1930, is the first source; the second source is Brion, "Le Rôle de la Sofina," 231; *Moody's Manual (Utilities) 1930*, 2359, gives the Belgian registration of Europel. On Europel, see Luciano Segreto, "Gli Assetti Proprietari," in *Storia dell' Industria Elettrica in Italia*, III

(Rome-Bari: Laterza, 1993), 130, which describes it as formed in Brussels at the initiative of CIBEE (a Volpi company). Segreto notes the involvements of Sofina, Compagnie Financière et Industrielle de Belgique (Finabel), Compagnie Générale d'Entreprises Électriques et Industrielles, Brussels (Electrobel), Credit Suisse, Elektrobank, the Banque Française et Italienne pour l'Amérique du Sud (BFI), and the Paris branch of the House of Morgan. For more on Europel, see *New York Times*, July 18, 1929, which adds that Banca Commerciale Italiana (BCI) was also a participant in this firm's foundation. For the connections between Sofina and Volpi, see Davenport-Hines, *Dudley Docker*, 204–5. The Sofina, *Annual Report 1929*, 22–23, describes Europel as constituted by CIBEE and Elektrobank and acquiring interests in Italy, Spain, and France. Volpi (1877–1974) had long involvements in electrification, going back before World War I (he founded Società Adriatica di Elettricità [SADE] in 1905); on his participation in the 1913 setting up of Società Elettrica Coloniale Italiana, see Luciano Segreto, "Electifier un Rêve," in Dominique Barjot, et al., eds., *L'Électrification Outre-mer de la Fin du XIXe Siècle aux Premières Décolonisations* (Paris: EDF [2002]), 237.

171. Lanthier, "Les Constructions Électriques en France"; Brion, "Le Rôle de la Sofina," 230; and Sofina, *Annual Report 1929*, 19–20.
172. Ulf Olsson, *Furthering a Fortune* (Stockholm: Ekerlids Förlag, 2001), 98–101.
173. Ranald C. Michie, *The London Stock Exchange* (Oxford: Oxford University Press, 1999), 261. For background on PSC and its founders, see Hannah, *Electrification Before Nationalisation*, 81 and Hughes, *Networks of Power*, 402–3.
174. The initial group of founders included Cammell Laird & Co. Ltd., Sir William Arrol & Co. Ltd., English Electric Co., John Brown & Co., and North British Locomotive Co. The last of these companies was no longer included by 1930. See *Stock Exchange Year Book 1925*, 2871, and ibid. 1930, 3168.
175. V. Watlington to W. J. Sainsbury, May 6, 1929, Pearson Papers, Box B14. We thank Lisa Bud-Frierman, e-mail of Sept. 22, 2003, for this reference. See also *Stock Exchange Year Book 1925*, 2871, and ibid., 1930, 3168.
176. Pantelakis, *Electrification of Greece*, 213–30; and Pepelasis Minoglou, "Between Informal Networks," 50–52.
177. Pepelais Minoglou, "Between Informal Networks," 50–52, and data in S. Pearson & Son Papers. Pantelakis, *Electrification of Greece*, 218–30, suggests that in the negotiations the British government hoped Greece would buy British coal and, accordingly, had vetoed a plan for a hydroelectric plant; British manufacturers had no special expertise in equipment for hydroelectric plants.
178. The names are very confusing: Compagnie Hellénique d'Électricité was *not* the same company as Société Générale Hellénique.
179. The "Austrian" group consisted of (1) the Anglo-Austrian Bank Ltd., a British bank, (2) Castiglioni Bank, (3) ELIN Société Anonyme pour l'Industrie Électrique, Vienna, a manufacturer, (4) Établissement Autrichien pour la Circulation par Chemin de Fer Wien, and (5) Wiener Bank-Verein, Vienna. Others in the syndicate included (6) the Nederlandischen Standard Bank, Amsterdam, (7) Société d'Électricité et Traction, Brussels, and (8) several

Greek banks. On the ChdE financing, see Pantelakis, *Electrification of Greece*, 254–55. On the Anglo-Austrian Bank, see Geoffrey Jones, *British Multinational Banking 1830–1990* (Oxford: Oxford University Press, 1993), 228–31, and Herbert Matis, "Disintegration and Multi-national Enterprises in Central Europe," in Alice Teichova and P. L. Cottrell, eds., *International Business and Central Europe, 1918–1939* (New York: St. Martin's Press, 1983), 89; on ELIN, also known as Elin Aktiengesellschaft für Elektrische Industrie, see ibid., 84; on the Belgian, Swiss, and U.S. investments in Wiener Bank-Verein, see P. L. Cottrell, "Aspects of Western Equity Investment in the Banking Systems of East Central Europe," in Teichova and Cottrell, eds, *International Business*, 338; for that bank's outward international involvements, see Teichova and Cottrell, eds., *International Business*, passim. Société d'Électricité et Traction, Brussels, was the predecessor of Tractionel, according to the Suez website, as cited above.

180. Leopold Wellisz, *Foreign Capital in Poland* (London: Allen & Unwin, 1938), 113–16; see also *Stock Exchange Year-Book, 1925*, 3168.
181. Based on data in S. Pearson & Son Papers.
182. Based on Theodore J. Grayson, *Investment Trusts* (New York: John Wiley, 1928), 80. Are these figures to be trusted? Does a look at the investment portfolio exclude foreign direct investment? We do not know. On PTFC, see also R. P. T. Davenport-Hines, "Sir Percy John Pybus," in *Dictionary of Business Biography*, IV, 784.
183. The best study of Whitehall Electric in Chile is Jones and Greenhill, "Public Utility Companies," 94–114.
184. American & Foreign Power Co., *Annual Report 1928*, 4, for a description of the properties. The contract for the purchase was made in October 1928, and the properties passed to the American company on January 1, 1929.
185. Rippy, *British Investments in Latin America*, 103, citing the *Stock Exchange Year Book, 1931*, 1289; see also Jones and Greenhill, "Public Utility Companies," 111, for the same figure, citing *The Economist*, June 15, 1929, 1374, and June 22, 1929, 1416, but indicating that roughly £1.4 million needed to be deducted from that sum, covering obligations of the Pearson group.
186. Jones and Greenhill, "Public Utility Companies," 112.
187. Lord Cowdray died in 1927, but that does not seem to have been the reason for the sale. Spender, whose book was published in 1930, indicates that Clive Pearson, Lord Cowdray's son, was chairman of Whitehall Electric Investments Ltd., which after the sale was "pursuing its electrical enterprises in other regions ...." Spender, *Weetman Pearson*, 208.
188. Rippy, *British Investments in Latin America*, 243. *Stock Exchange Official Intelligence, 1928*, 1133, indicates that Atlas Light and Power was the successor to the Cordoba Light, Power, and Traction Co. Ltd., formed in 1908, and then the Argentine Light and Power Co. Ltd., set up in 1923. This was a typical sequential set of free standing companies, each one raising more money and adding new properties.
189. It was short-lived as Atlas Light, but its predecessor went back to 1908. When Atlas Light sold out, it retained its tramway property in Uruguay, which its

successor did not sell until 1947; its successor was Atlas Electric and General Trust Ltd. (the name change was in November 1929). *Stock Exchange Official Intelligence, 1930*, 1098, and Rippy, *British Investments in Latin America*, 149.

190. *Stock Exchange Year Book, 1930*, 1112.

191. Jones, *British Multinational Banking*, 243 (on the two banks). The first of the banks was founded in 1919, the second in 1920. Prudential Assurance was a subscriber to the stock of the British Overseas Bank at its formation. *Stock Exchange Year Book, 1930*, 1112; *Directory of Directories, 1926*, 545, 911; and *Stock Exchange Yearbook, 1935*, 1988 (for its 1928 Polish investments).

192. We have put "perhaps Atlas Light and Power" because while it was clearly a holding company, it evolved from free standing companies and proved short-lived in its holding company role. Moreover, it could itself be labeled a free standing company. As pointed out in Chapter 2, the line between certain forms could be ambiguous.

193. See 1933 data in the Pearson papers; we have no reason to believe that this description would not hold for 1928–1929.

194. See above and Marchildon, "Montreal Engineering," 397–98.

195. Armstrong and Nelles, *Southern Exposure*, 251–52; Marchildon, "Montreal Engineering," 398–99. In 1926, International Power acquired in Latin America (1) Bolivian Power Co. Ltd. (registered in Nova Scotia in 1925) from Bolivian General Enterprises Ltd., (2) control of the Demerara Electric Co. Ltd. (operating in British Guiana [Guyana] and incorporated there in 1899 under British law), (3) a company in El Salvador that had been organized in 1890, (4) substantial interest in a company in Monterrey, Mexico, registered in Canada in 1905, and (5) Venezuelan Power Co., incorporated in Canada in 1925. Mallory, "Financial Problems," 99–105. Note International Power is not to be confused with International Paper and Power Co. and its subsidiaries, nor is it to be mixed up with International Power Securities, an entirely different company; likewise, International Holding and Investment Co. was a different firm.

196. Roberts, *Schroders*, 210; Garcke, 1928–1929, 1327; Armstrong and Nelles, *Southern Exposure*, 261, 266, 347n50 (on the planned pyramided arrangements with Loewenstein's International Holding and Investment Company); *Economist*, Aug. 10, 1929, 282; Hugh Bullock, *The Story of Investment Companies* (New York: Columbia University Press, 1959), 122–23, 217–18, 221–23 (on International Holding and Investment Company, formed in 1927, and Hydro-Electric Securities), 123 (tax status). Many of the holding companies bore similar titles; thus, in 1929 the Canadian Hydro-Electric Corp. was part of the International Hydro-Electric System, which in turn had at its pinnacle, International Paper and Power Company. Heinrich, "Product Diversification," 491. These were separate from the Loewenstein financial edifices, which included International Holding and Investment Co., as well as Hydro-Electric Securities. When in 1926 Loewenstein's Hydro-Electric Securities was established, Malcolm Hubbard (a London-based director of Brazilian Traction) described it as "water 90 p.c.; electricity 10 p.c.; no security at all." Ranieri, *Dannie Heineman*, 153n2. International Holding and

Investment Co., whose name was changed in 1937 to International Holdings Ltd., came to have the same management as Hydro-Electric Securities. Bullock, *Story of Investment Companies*, 122–23. In 1926, Loewenstein tried in vain to use Hydro-Electric Securities in his attempt to take over Sidro, as well as Brazilian Traction, Barcelona Traction, and the Mexican companies (see the discussion earlier in this chapter). On Loewenstein, Hydro-Electric Securities, International Holding and Investment, and Barings, see Kynaston, *City of London*, III, 145–46.

197. Bullock, *Story of Investment Companies*, 122.
198. Garcke, 1928–1929, 1327; Schröter, "Globalization and Reliability," 116 (White's presidency). Do not confuse this company with International Power Co.; it was separate.
199. Geoffrey Jones, *Merchants to Multinationals: British Trading Companies in the Nineteenth and Twentieth Centuries* (Oxford: Oxford University Press, 2000), 104; the White firm was "British" for the years 1917–1929. When in 1928 White became president of International Light & Power, his firm was still under U.K. shareholders' control, but it was soon to free itself of the Booth connection.
200. Segreto, "Du 'Made in Germany,'" 357.
201. For the Canadian "investment companies," see Bullock, *Story of Investment Companies*, 118–25.
202. Armstrong and Nelles, *Monopoly's Moment*, 300. They suggest that the Power Corporation of Canada bore some resemblance to the "much looser, less structured" Royal Securities and its subsidiary Montreal Engineering. It was actually modeled after the U.S. firm Stone & Webster. Bullock, *Story of Investment Companies*, 119.
203. Bullock, *Story of Investment Companies*, 119, writes that FPSC did not consider itself an "investment trust;" see also Garcke, 1928–1929, 1312–13; Roger Desprès, who was key in the French Durand group, was on the board of FPSC at the end of the 1920s, and this company's holdings overlapped with those of the Durand group. See also Vuillermot, "Groupe Durand," 372. Remember Nesbitt, Thomson was headquartered in French-speaking Montreal, Canada.
204. Wilkins, *History ... 1914–1945*, 84, 206, 210.
205. *Moody's Manual (Utilities) 1930*, xxi. William J. Hausman, "The Historical Antecedents of Restructuring: Mergers and Concentration in the U.S. Electric Utility Industry, 1879–1935," unpublished paper prepared for the American Public Power Association, March 4, 1997, 8, gives urban and nonrural dwellings with electrical service at just over 40 percent in 1920 and almost 80 percent by 1930.
206. The best material on U.S. business abroad in this sector for the 1920s is Hausman and Neufeld, "U.S. Foreign Direct Investment." We have drawn heavily on this article. The importance of U.S. foreign direct investments in public utilities in the 1920s is emphasized by Robert E. Lipsey, "Changing Patterns of International Investment in and by the United States," in Martin Feldstein, ed., *The United States in the World Economy* (Chicago: University of Chicago Press, 1988), 481. The foreign investments in public utilities

included telephones and other utilities, but within this sector the largest involvements were in electric utilities.

207. See Lewis, *America's Stake*, 666, for her frustrations in trying to separate foreign portfolio and foreign direct investments.

208. For GE, see Wilkins, *Maturing of Multinational Enterprise*. To a large extent, the expanded post–World War I network of GE built on its prewar associations. On the latter, see Chapter 3 of the present book and Mira Wilkins, *The Emergence of Multinational Enterprise: American Business Abroad from the Colonial Era to 1914* (Cambridge, MA: Harvard University Press, 1970), 94–95. On the Westinghouse revival, see *New York Times*, June 11, 1930, which indicates that in the years 1929–1930 Westinghouse obtained minority interests in British, French, and Italian manufacturing companies and acquired a major plant in Norway. See also Southard, *American Industry in Europe*, 19–35.

209. There is a large literature on how much "competition" there was among manufacturers in this industry by the late 1920s. One 1927 report concluded that "the free play of competition between firm and firm belongs now to history." BEAM, *Combines*, 280. If the emphasis is on the "free play" or on perfect competition, this is absolutely correct. On the other hand, U.S. participants were highly competitive in their international business. Wilkins, *Maturing of Multinational Enterprise*, 69.

210. See Wilkins, *Maturing of Multinational Enterprise*, 65–69; Mira Wilkins, interviews with W. Rogers Herod, Feb. 24 and March 11, 1964, Wilkins Files, Miami; Southard, *American Industry in Europe*, 17–36.

211. Mira Wilkins, "American-Japanese Direct Foreign Investment Relationships, 1930–1952," *Business History Review*, 56 (Winter 1982), 502. Siemens also made direct investments in Japanese electrical manufacturing. In 1923, Fuji Electric Co. was established as a joint venture of Furukawa Electric Industry and Siemens (which had a 30 percent interest). Masari Udawaga, "Business Management and Foreign-Affiliated Companies in Japan before World War II," in Takeshi Yuzawa and Masaru Udagawa, *Foreign Business in Japan Before World War II* (Tokyo: University of Tokyo Press, 1990), 10, 15–16.

212. Derek F. Channon, *The Strategy and Structure of British Enterprise* (Boston: Graduate School of Business, Harvard University, 1973), 134; Southard, *American Industry in Europe*, 20–23; in 1930, on the expiration of Westinghouse Electric's licensing agreement with Metropolitan Vickers, Westinghouse Electric announced that it had entered into a patent agreement with English Electric and that it would obtain a minority interest in the latter. On English Electric and Utilities Power and Light Corporation, Hannah, *Electrification Before Nationalisation*, 229, 241. As noted earlier, the old Siemens Brothers, which had become British-owned after the war, still existed; in 1929, the German Siemens had reacquired an 18 percent equity interest in this British firm that continued to use the Siemens name. Harm Schröter, "The German Question, the Unification of Europe, and European Market Strategies of Germany's Chemical and Electrical Industries, 1900–1992," in *Business History Review* 67 (Autumn 1993), 385; see also Siemens, *History of the House of Siemens*, II, 204.

213. Southard, *American Industry in Europe*, 28–29.
214. Schuker, *American "Reparations" to Germany, 1919–33*, 47, 49.
215. Wilkins, *Maturing of Multinational Enterprise*, 146–47; in this book, Wilkins did not make the comparisons. Research by the contributors to the present volume and others make this statement incontrovertible. For GE's role in the Swedish ASEA, for example, see [Jan Glete], *Electrifying Experience: A Brief Account of the First Century of the ASEA Group of Sweden, 1883–1983* (Västerås, Sweden: ASEA, 1983), 32–33.
216. The encouragement might be through contracting, as was evident in the case of Siemens, for instance, as well as through foreign investments. The technical services offices of Siemens and AEG provided information on equipment installations that did not involve any foreign investments in the utility.
217. For the spin-off see Hausman and Neufeld, "U.S. Foreign Direct Investment," 372; Wilkins, *Maturing of Multinational Enterprise*, 131.
218. Sometimes, these interests were direct and sometimes were through extended manufacturers' satellites (see Chapter 2).
219. Wilkins, *Maturing of Multinational Enterprise*, 131. In 1928, Intercontinents Power established Compañía Sudamericana de Electricidad (SUDAM), which in connection with Motor-Columbus became active in the Northern Provinces of Argentina. On SUDAM, Annual Memories of the Ministerio de Justicia e Instrucción Pública, Memoria Año 1928 (Buenos Aires, Talleres Gráficos de la Penitenciaria Nacional, 1929), I, 129 (item 66 for the authorization of SUDAM in Argentina; we are indebted to Andrea Lluch for this reference), and Andrea Lluch and Laura Sánchez, *De Movimiento Popular a Empresa El Cooperativisismo Eléctrico en La Pampa* (Santa Rosa, Argentina: Fondo Editorial Pampeano, [2001]), 17–18. There were numerous connections between manufacturers and holding companies and their subsidiaries. Thus, GE was said to be associated with International Power Securities Corporation (and with Union d'Électricité – see later in this chapter), while Westinghouse was linked with the American European Utilities Corporation. BEAM, *Combines*, 57–58 and Frédéric Marty, "Les Grands Projets de la Filière Électrique dans l'Entre-Deux-Guerres," in Barjot, Morsel, and Coeuré, eds., *Stratégies, Gestion, Management*, 109. GE's wholly owned subsidiary for international business, International General Electric Co., had scattered investments in public utilities. Based on data collected by William Hausman, January 2006. Wilkins, *Maturing of Multinational Enterprise*, 65–69 (on IGE).
220. The best source on these banks and their participation in lending is U.S. Congress, Senate, Committee on Banking and Currency, *Stock Exchange Practices, Hearings*, 72nd Cong. 1st sess. (1932–1933), 7 parts in 6 vol; 72nd and 73rd Cong. (1933–1934), 2 parts in 9 vol. (known as Pecora Hearings).
221. Based on data in *Stock Exchange Year-Book 1930* on each Japanese borrower.
222. Ron Chernow, *The House of Morgan* (New York: Atlantic Monthly Press, 1990), 336–37, and Takeo Kikkawa, *Nihon Denryokú no Hatten to Matsunaga Yasuzaemon* [*The Development of Japanese Electric Power Industry and Yasuzaemon Matsunaga*] (Nagoya, Japan: Nagoya University Press, 1995), 146–49.

223. On the Tokio Electric Light bond issue of 1925 that matured in 1928, see Table 4.2. On the new issue, see *New York Times*, June 7, 1928.
224. See *Moody's Manual (Utilities)* and *Stock Exchange Year Book*, various years.
225. U.S. Department of Commerce, Bureau of Foreign and Domestic Commerce, *A New Estimate of American Investments Abroad* (Washington, DC, 1931), 20 (U.S. FDI in Japan), 21.
226. The investments in Manchuria were in connection with the South Manchuria railroad. Korea was of course a colony of Japan in this period.
227. The date for Brown Brothers Harriman & Co. comes from Edwin J. Perkins, *Financing Anglo-American Trade: The House of Brown, 1800–1880* (Cambridge, MA: Harvard University Press, 1975), 82.
228. Based on Lewis, *America's Stake*, 638–40; in first place was Canada: Lewis shows the *face value* of Canadian corporate borrowings (1915–1929) to equal $896.8 million (and for 1919–1929 to come to $842.4 billion). German corporate borrowings, 1925–1929, were $712.8 million, clearly in second place after Canada (there were none listed for 1915–1925). The total for Japan, 1923–1928, was $181.8 million; and in fourth place, 1924–1929, Italy $165.4 million. Other sources (including the one for Japan given earlier in the text), based on different measures (and covering different dates), give different numbers. Segreto, Milan Paper, for example, citing *Electrical World*, Oct. 6, 1928, 710, indicated that "bond loans contracted by [European] electric companies in the United States between 1919 and 1927" totaled $289 million, of which $149 million went to German firms, $78 million to Italian enterprises." The remainder went to Spanish ($25 million), British ($12 million), Austrian ($9 million), Norwegian ($6 million), Polish ($4 million), French ($4 million), and Danish ($2 million) companies. Segreto's list omits Canada and Japan. When we went to the original list in *Electrical World*, Oct. 6, 1928, 710, we found it put Canada ($192 million) in first place. It included Japan ($101 million) in fourth place. In third place, it had Cuba ($110 million). Further research indicates that this third-place Cuban figure covered telephones and docks, as well as electric utilities and is suspect in many ways (the same figure is given by others with different definitions). Moreover, all the investments in Cuban electric utilities were direct investments.
229. See *Moody's Manual (Utilities) 1930*, 1673–75. On the specifics of the bond issues of Società Generale Italiana Edison di Elettricità, see ibid., 1674.
230. Charles R. Geisst, *Entrepot Capitalism* (New York: Praeger, 1992), 134, 140.
231. The figures from *Electrical World*, see several notes above, cannot be legitimately combined with the ones that Cleona Lewis provides.
232. On German issues, see Table 4.2; Lewis, *America's Stake*, 408; C. R. S. Harris, *Germany's Foreign Indebtedness* (London: Oxford University Press, 1935), 116–18; and U.S. Senate, Committee on Finance, *Sale of Foreign Bonds*, 72nd Cong., 1st sess. (1932), esp. 107, 108, 168–73, 179–81. *Moody's Manual (Utilities)* provides data on the borrowings of individual German companies.
233. Harold van B. Cleveland and Thomas F. Huertas, *Citibank 1812–1970* (Cambridge, MA: Harvard University Press, 1985), 150; for state ownership, see BEAM, *Combines*, 60; for the series of RWE bond issues, see U.S. Senate, Committee on Finance, *Sale of Foreign Bonds*, 107 (1925 issue: $10 million),

108 (1927 and 1928 issues: $15 million and $20 million, respectively), 109 (1930 and 1931 issues: $20 million and $7.5 million), 168–73, 179–81. (The 1928 issue prospectus for the $20 million consolidated mortgage gold bonds, 6 percent, due August 1, 1953, indicated that "the various municipalities and provinces served, together with the State of Prussia and the German Empire [*sic*], own a substantial majority of the [Rhine-Westphalia Electric Power] corporation's stock"; associated with the 1928 bond issue there were stock purchase rights for "American shares.") In the 1920s, RWE had the largest installed capacity of any power company in Germany. Hughes, *Networks of Power*, 408–23.

234. Lewis, *America's Stake*, 669–72.
235. For example, Duke Price Power, see Table 4.2.
236. Wilkins, *Maturing of Multinational Enterprise*, 132 (list of nine major U.S. public utilities operating in Canada in 1929 and their operations). With the date of U.S. formation in parentheses, the seven supplying electric power in Canada (two provided only gas) were: Associated Gas and Electric Co. (1906), Central Public Service Co. (1925), Cities Service Co. (1910), International Paper and Power Co. (1928), International Utilities Corporation (1924), Niagara-Hudson Power Corp. (1929), and North American Gas and Electric Co.(1928). By "outside financing," we mean they went to U.S. capital markets, issuing bonds and/or stock for the Canadian operation (or for the general business and thus used pooled funds for their Canadian operations).
237. Grayson, *Investment Trusts*, 294 (for Canadian investments of Metropolitan Life Insurance Co.), 295 (Prudential Insurance Company of America), 297 (Equitable Life).
238. Southard, *American Industry in Europe*, 11–12, 18, 39–41. According to Leopold Wellisz, a comprehensive 1929 plan was presented by Harriman & Co. and turned down by the Polish government "as it was considered that the terms demanded by Messrs. Harriman & Co. were too onerous." Wellisz, *Foreign Capital in Poland*, 245–47 (on Harriman's 1929 plan).
239. As cited in Southard, *American Industry in Europe*, 41.
240. In 1921, Paul Warburg (in New York) in cooperation with his brother at M. M. Warburg & Co., Hamburg, and with the involvement of a large number of American and European banks, formed International Acceptance Bank (IAB) to help in the financing of postwar Germany. In 1924, IAB organized American & Continental Corp. (ACC) to provide assistance to German borrowers. Participating in the later were the Deutsche Bank, M. M. Warburg, Sofina, Skandinaviska Kreditaktiebolaget, Svenska Handelsbanken, and Österreichische Creditanstalt für Handel & Gewerbe, as well as some other European banks. Sofina apparently represented American & Continental Corp. in Europe. Wilkins, *History ... 1914–1945*, 119, 199, 281, and Ranieri, *Dannie Heineman*, 132–33, 141–42, 420 (for ACC and Sofina).
241. Hausman and Neufeld, "U.S. Foreign Direct Investment," 379.
242. The best material on Aldred is in ibid., 368, 378–80. The Aldred "group" also embraced the Aldred Investment Trust (set up in Massachusetts in 1927), which held stock in International Power Securities Corporation, the Italian Edison Company, and Società Generale Elettrica dell' Adamello.

243. Ibid., 377–78, 388–89. For Stone & Webster's domestic activities in the 1920s, see Hughes, *Networks of Power*, 390–92. See Chapter 3 , herein, for its early history.
244. Thus, Robert Fleming and Robert Benson companies as well as other British investment trusts, individual foreign investors, and a range of foreign financial institutions made inward foreign financial investments in these holding companies and their operating companies. Wilkins, *History ... 1914–1945*, 206, for these and other inward investments in U.S. utilities. In certain cases, the inward investments were quite substantial; for example, the Canadian firm Sun Life Assurance Company was a significant investor in Insull properties.
245. Hausman and Neufeld, "U.S. Foreign Direct Investment," 370–71, 382–83; Christopher Kobrak, *Banking on Global Markets: Deutsche Bank and the United States, 1870 to the Present* (Cambridge: Cambridge University Press, forthcoming) on Deutsche Bank's investment. The name Deutsche Bank und Disconto-Gesellschaft was kept from 1929 to 1937, when use of the title Deutsche Bank resumed.
246. For the complex patterns, see Mira Wilkins, "Cosmopolitan Finance in the 1920s: New York's Emergence as an International Financial Centre," in Richard Sylla, Richard Tilly, and Gabriel Tortella, eds., *The State, the Financial System, and Economic Modernization: Comparative Historical Perspectives* (Cambridge: Cambridge University Press, 1999), 271–91, and Wilkins, *History ... 1914–1945*, 189–200.
247. Hausman and Neufeld, "U.S. Foreign Direct Investment," 368–69, for a list; also (not in ibid.), Insull's holding company in 1929 acquired a minority interest in British Power and Light Corp. Hannah, *Electrification Before Nationalisation*, 227–28.
248. In the literature on multinational enterprise, a "greenfield" operation is one started afresh by the foreign direct investor.
249. In the summer of 1919, a preliminary agreement was signed to form a holding company that would buy around one-sixth of the shares of Italian Edison Company. This Italian holding company would have been controlled half by Morgan and other U.S. banks and half by the Edison Company. Banca Italiana di Scoto, involved in the project, collapsed in 1921, which thwarted this endeavor. Leandro Conte, "I Prestiti Esteri," in *Storia dell' Industria Elettrica in Italia*, 2 (Rome-Bari: Laterza, 1993), 630–31; Segreto, *Giacinto Motta*, 172–76.
250. Dunn, *American Foreign Investments*,152–53; *Moody's Manual (Utilities) 1924*, 1511; Conte, "I Prestiti Esteri," 636, 691; and Segreto, *Giacinoto Motta*, 177–84. The directors of Italian Power included John E. Aldred, A.W. Burchard (President of International General Electric Co.), Charles A. Coffin (GE), E.P. Royce (Stone & Webster), and Arthur Vining Davis (Aluminum Company of America). Carlo Orsi of Credito Italiano, Milan, was on the founding board. After the 1921 recession, the American International Corporation (AIC) had greatly curtailed its activities and was recapitalized; Stone & Webster remained affiliated with it, but the other directors resigned. AIC continued as an investment house until 1969, when it was merged into Adams Express Co., a closed-end investment company. Cleveland and

Huertas, *Citibank 1812–1970*, 368n25. See also Bullock, *Story of Investment Companies*, 17, which describes AIC in 1929 as an investment company with assets of over $60 million, for the most part invested in domestic securities; Adams Express had acquired control of AIC in 1945.

251. On International Power Securities, see Hausman and Neufeld, "U.S. Foreign Direct Investment," 379 and Richard F. Kuisel, *Ernest Mercier* (Berkeley: University of California Press, 1967), 8–11 (on Union d'Électricité, which was formed in 1919, a merger of six suburban Paris electricity producers, and expanded greatly during the 1920s; it was controlled by the so-called Messine group. Petsche was president, and Mercier was managing director); BEAM, *Combines*, 57, 64, 129 (on Union d'Électricité and its links with Thomson-Houston, which was, of course, the "GE company" in France). See also Southard, *American Industry in Europe*, 38–39; *Moody's Manual (Utilities) 1928*, 1090–92; ibid., *1929*, 1852–1854; ibid., *1930*, 1668–75 (on IPSC); and *ibid., 1930*, 1075–76 (on the specifics of the financing of Union d'Électricité, particularly the external gold "6½ s" of 1924, authorized and issued $4 million, due 1954, all owned by IPSC); ibid., *1930*, 1673 (Società Generale Italiana Edison di Elettricità); Chernow, *House of Morgan*, 281 (for Volpi's relations with Thomas Lamont and the House of Morgan, vis-à-vis Italian debts); and Segreto, "Gli Assetti Proprietari," 137, 167n73 (IPSC), 137–42 (Italian plans). In 1925, Alberto Beneduce – chairman of the new state-controlled Istituto per le Imprese di Pubblica Utilità, a special financing institute for the Italian electric sector – had explored with Volpi the possibility of establishing a new U.S. holding to issue bonds on the U.S. capital market. For more on the foreign financing of Italian electric utilities in the interwar period see Mirana Storaci and Giuseppe Tattara, "The External Financing of Italian Electric Companies in the Interwar Years," *European Review of Economic History*, 2 (1998), 345–75.

252. *Moody's Manual (Utilities) 1928*, 1090–92; ibid., *1929*, 1852–1854, and sources cited in the previous note on IPSC.

253. The initial capital of Italian Superpower was divided into common and preferred stock without voting rights; a special category of shares with voting rights went 50 percent to BCI and 50 percent to the Americans. It was the American 50 percent that was acquired by American Superpower in 1929. Segreto, "Gli Assetti Proprietari," 136–44; *New York Times*, June 5, 1929; see also *Moody's Manual (Utilities) 1930*, 635, 1870 (Italian Superpower; American Superpower); Southard, *American Industry in Europe*, 38–39 (Italian Superpower); Gianni Toniolo, *One Hundred Years, 1894–1994: A Short History of the Banca Commerciale Italiana* (Milan: Banca Commerciale Italiana, 1994), 51, 131 (Giuseppe Toeplitz); and Wilkins, *History ... 1914–1945*, 196 (Italian Superpower and the complexities of inward/outward U.S. investments in the 1920s; did Italians or Americans "control" this holding company?). On the size of assets, December 1929, Bullock, *Story of Investment Companies*, 217; the assets of American Superpower in December 1929 put it in fourth place in the United States in the SEC category "Management Investment-Holding Companies," after Christiana Securities Co. ($361.5 m), United Corporation ($332.5 m), and Alleghany Corporation (263.7 m). Ibid., 40 ("investment holding"), 217 ("management investment

holding"). Christiana Securities was a holding company for stocks of companies controlled by Du Pont interests, while United Corporation and Alleghany Corporation were both Morgan-created holding companies; the first had investments principally in public utilities on the U.S. eastern seaboard and the second was devoted to U.S. railroad securities. On Christiana, see ibid., 40; Charles R. Geisst, *Wall Street* (Oxford: Oxford University Press, 1997), 184–85 (United Corporation and Alleghany Corporation). Hausman and Neufeld, "U.S. Foreign Direct Investment," 388n38 (American Superpower came to be controlled by United Corporation).

254. Hannah, *Electrification Before Nationalisation*, 228; Hughes, *Networks of Power*, 402.

255. Hannah, *Electrification Before Nationalisation*, 228–31. One of the largest, according to Hannah, 228; the largest, according to Southard, *American Industry in Europe*, 18, 36–38, 213–14. The majority-owned subsidiaries involved in power distribution of the Greater London and Counties Trust as of 1928–1929 are listed in ibid., 213–14. William May of Slaughter and May is not to be confused with George May of Prudential Assurance.

256. The shares of Electric Bond and Share were distributed to GE stockholders, with the shareholder's approval given December 30, 1924. Mitchell, *S. Z. Mitchell and the Electrical Industry*, 132.

257. Hausman and Neufeld, "U.S. Foreign Direct Investment," 374.

258. The statement on GE's having "no stock interest" in American & Foreign Power is based on the GE divestment of its holdings in Electric Bond and Share; it is altogether possible that GE may have had a small stock interest, directly or indirectly, and that "no stock interest" could be an exaggeration.

259. The 1929–1930 board list with the identifications is taken from American & Foreign Power Co., *Annual Reports 1927–1930*. Chernow, *House of Morgan*, 289 (Simpson, Thacher & Bartlett), 308 (United Corporation, Sosthenes Behn). Note that Charles E. Mitchell was not a relative of the father and son team (S. Z. Mitchell and S.A. Mitchell). On American Gas and Electric, see Hausman and Neufeld, "U.S. Foreign Direct Investment," 372; on United Electric Securities, see Chapter 3, herein.

260. In addition to these direct investments, at year's end 1929 American & Foreign Power also had minority holdings in companies with interests in utility properties in Canada, France, Germany, Italy, and Japan. During 1929, it disposed of its minority interests in Spain. American & Foreign Power Co., *Annual Report, 1929*, 5 (the annual report merely notes these holdings, whereas with the foreign direct investments there is a far more extensive treatment).

261. American & Foreign Power, *Annual Report 1929*, 26 (gross earnings 1928 and 1929). For the importance of American & Foreign Power's Cuban business, see its annual reports (which are by far the best source). See also Leland Hamilton Jenks, *Our Cuban Colony* (New York: Vanguard Press, 1928), 269 (on the connections between GE, American & Foreign Power and General Gerardo Machado, who became President of Cuba in 1925), 289–90 (on the "public utility" investments of American & Foreign Power, International Telephone & Telegraph, and the dock companies).

262. American & Foreign Power Co., *Annual Reports 1928–1929*; Robert M. Kindersley, "British Foreign Investments in 1928," *Economic Journal,* 40 (June 1930), 177; Marchildon, "The Montreal Engineering Company," 397; Southard, *American Industry in Europe*, 41n3; Rippy, *British Investments*, 243. On the sale of the S. Pearson & Son interests (Whitehall Electric Investments), see American & Foreign Power Co., *Annual Report 1928*, 4, and Jones and Greenhill, "Public Utility Companies," 111. The Atlas Light and Power Co. group of companies in Argentina supplied electric light and power and street railway service in Córdoba, Tucumán, Santa Fé, and Paraná. American & Foreign Power Co., *Annual Report 1928*, 5. (The 1929 takeover was reported in the 1928 Annual Report.) On Northern Mexican Power & Development, the 1919 successor to Mexican Northern Power Co., see Armstrong and Nelles, *Southern Exposure*, 253. The other half of Tata Hydro-Electric Agencies Ltd. was owned "by prominent citizens of India." This Tata company supervised the operations of a group of hydroelectric companies; the group produced and transmitted power and sold that power to the local electric light and power and street railway company in Bombay, as well as to cotton mills and other large power users. American & Foreign Power Co., *Annual Report 1929*, 5. The process of changing nationalities was not unique. Earlier the British had replaced the Germans in Chile. Whitehall Electric's expansion in Chile, as the reader will recall, was based on what had been before World War I German properties. In the first decade of the twentieth century (see Chapter 3), there had been German interests in Mexico, which Canadian ones had replaced.
263. American & Foreign Power Co., *Annual Report 1928*, 4.
264. In addition, in 1929 it acquired control of North State Power Company Ltd. In Mexico. Ibid., 1928, 5, 9 (number of communities in 1928). Ibid., 1929, 4, 11–12, 15 (number of communities in 1929).
265. American & Foreign Power Co., *Annual Report 1929*, 9–10 (expansion in Brazil), 15 (communities in Brazil).
266. Ibid., 1929, 8. The ANSEC group was so named: A: Cia. de Electricidad de Andes, N: Cia. de Electricidad del Norte Argentino, S: Cia de Electricidad del Sud Argentino, E: Cia. de Electricidad del Este Argentino, and C: Cia. Central Argentina de Electricidad. The 1929 American & Foreign Power annual report gives the five company names, but does not use the term ANSEC, which appears to have been adopted later. See José Gómez-Ibáñez, *Regulating Infrastructure: Monopoly, Contracts, and Discretion* (Cambridge, MA: Harvard University Press, 2003), Table 6.4, note c. Mallory in his excellent 1956 master's thesis includes a summary sheet for American & Foreign Power in Argentina that indicates that in 1929 American & Foreign Power incorporated in Florida a new firm, the Argentine Electric Companies; and by the end of 1930, this holding company had acquired eleven operating subsidiaries in Argentina. Mallory's summary has nothing on "ANSEC." Mallory, "Financial Problems," 85. Andrea Lluch and Laura Sánchez write that those companies under the Florida holding company umbrella *came to be called* ANSEC (they give no date). Lluch and Sánchez, *De Movimiento Popular*, 17.

267. American & Foreign Power Co., *Annual Report 1929*, 4,10–11, and C.F. Remer, *Foreign Investments in China* (New York: Macmillan, 1933), 286–88.
268. See *Stock Exchange Year Book 1930*, 3504; the resolution indicated that all shares by warrants to bearer had to be included in the 20 percent and that stock transfers had to be accompanied by a special declaration as to nationality, foreign shareholdings being entered on a special register.
269. American & Foreign Power Co., *Annual Report 1929*, 7–8. Item 5, "to apply the latest, most modern commercial development to the property, in the process selling new electrical merchandise in well-lighted attractive stores," is particularly to be noted. American & Foreign Power seems to have been far in advance of Sofina, for example, in this attempt to get utilities to promote the uses of electricity. This emerges much later in Sofina's strategies: See Sofina, *Annual Report 1939*, 13.
270. Jones and Greenhill, "Public Utility Companies," 100–14 (the experiences in Chile); ibid., 112 (fear of expropriation). The American & Foreign Power Co., *Annual Report 1929*, 10, indicated: "Negotiations are in progress for rearrangement of the concession contracts covering the Company's business in Chile."
271. American & Foreign Power Co., *Annual Report 1929*, 15; American & Foreign Power also supplied in certain markets gas, water services, transportation services, and telephones, and in addition, operated ice plants. Ibid.
272. Ibid., 13.

5 BASIC INFRASTRUCTURE, 1929–1945

1. For background, see Harold James, *The End of Globalization: Lessons from the Great Depression* (Cambridge, MA: Harvard University Press, 2001). This is not the place to deal with causes and effects of the stock market crash, but rather to consider what followed in subsequent years.
2. Mira Wilkins, *The History of Foreign Investment in the United States, 1914–1945* (Cambridge, MA: Harvard University Press, 2004), 306.
3. Mira Wilkins, "The Role of U.S. Business," in Dorothy Borg and Shumpei Okamoto, eds., *Pearl Harbor as History: Japanese-American Relations 1931–1941* (New York: Columbia University Press, 1973), 353.
4. United States Department of Commerce, Bureau of Foreign and Domestic Commerce, *American Underwriting of Foreign Securities in 1930* (Washington, DC: USGPO, 1931), 17 (henceforth cited as *Underwriting of Foreign Securities*).
5. U.S. Senate, Committee on Finance, *Sale of Foreign Bonds*, 72nd Cong., 1st sess. (1932), 109. For the importance of this German public utility in developing a regional system, see Thomas P. Hughes, *Networks of Power: Electrification in Western Society, 1880–1930* (Baltimore: Johns Hopkins University Press, 1983), 407–28.
6. Christopher Kobrak, *Banking on Global Markets: Deutsche Bank and the United States, 1870 to the Present* (Cambridge: Cambridge University Press, forthcoming); see also *New York Times*, July 20, 1930. On PUHC's new investments, see William J. Hausman and John L. Neufeld, "U.S. Foreign Direct

Investment in Electrical Utilities in the 1920s," in Mira Wilkins and Harm Schröter, eds., *The Free-Standing Company in the World Economy* (Oxford: Oxford University Press, 1998), 383. The Public Utility Holding Corporation should not be confused with Utilities Power and Light Corporation, which made the investments in Great Britain and Canada.

7. *New York Times*, July 20, 1930, and April 6, 1930; in March and April 1930, Deutsche Bank und Disconto-Gesellschaft was arranging to distribute Berlin City Electric Company dollar securities among its clients. Kobrak, *Banking on Global Markets*. The Berlin City Electric Company's $15 million issue was only partly sold in the United States; the "par value of the flotation within the United States" was $12.8 million. *Underwriting of Foreign Securities*, 22.
8. Ibid., 22–27, contains a list of "Foreign Capital Issues Publicly Offered in the United States during the Calendar Year 1930." It has "government and government guaranteed bonds" and corporate issues. The German bond issues for RWE and Berlin City Electric, as well as the smaller issue for Saxon Public Works, were included as government-guaranteed bonds on this list, but on other lists therein as publicly offered "foreign *corporate* securities (including government-guaranteed issues)[our italics]." See ibid., 22, and also 13 and 18, for the latter formulation. In 1930, foreign electric light and power companies (including government-guaranteed issues), according to this report, constituted 42 percent ($191.8 million) of the total foreign corporate securities ($455.2 million) "purchased in the United States." Ibid., 18. The list included companies that in turn made foreign direct investments, such as American & Foreign Power Co.
9. *New York Times*, July 20, 1930; practically all of these names are familiar to the reader of this book. E. Rollins & Sons was a broker, founded in 1876, specializing in the 1920s in municipal, public utility, and corporate bonds; it was involved in South American utilities through Intercontinents Power Company, a firm formed in 1928. G. L. Ohrstrom & Co. was a smaller brokerage house with big 1930 plans for Latin America; it joined with the experienced J. G. White & Co. in those endeavors. Field Glore, about which we will say more, was a Chicago-based brokerage house.
10. Kobrak, *Banking on Global Markets*.
11. Mira Wilkins, *The Maturing of Multinational Enterprise: American Business Abroad from 1914 to 1970* (Cambridge, MA: Harvard University Press, 1974), 168. In 1930, the Utilities Power and Light Corporation purchased the Maritime Coal, Railway and Power Company Ltd.; this was a major investment in a Canadian power company that had significant coal-mining resources as well. Herbert Marshall, Frank A. Southard, and Kenneth W. Taylor, *Canadian-American Industry* (1936; reprinted New York: Russell & Russell, 1970), 112. See ibid., 142–43, 150–51, for Utilities Power and Light Corporation's Canadian investments. On American & Foreign Power Co., see its *Annual Report 1930*.
12. On European Electric Corp., see *Moody's Manual (Utilities) 1930*, 2359–61; *New York Times*, July 20, 1930; Luciano Segreto, "Gli Assetti Proprietari," in *Storia dell' Industria Elettrica in Italia*, III (Rome-Bari: Laterza, 1993), 130–31, 144; and *Underwriting of Foreign Securities*, 18, 25. On SADE and Count Giuseppe Volpi, Giovanni Paoloni, "L'Industrie Électrique Italienne des Réseaux Locaux aux Réseaux Régionaux," in Dominque Barjot, Henri Morsel, and

Sophie Coeuré, eds., *Stratégies, Gestion, Management: Les Compagnies Électriques et Leurs Patrons, 1895–1945* (Paris: EDF, 2001), 90–91, and *Time*, Feb. 17, 1930; on Fummi, see Wilkins, *History ... 1914–1945*, 352; on Banca Commerciale Italiana Trust Co., New York, see ibid., 279–80. On Field, Glore & Co. 's 1929 syndications, see Hugh Bullock, *The Story of Investment Companies* (New York: Columbia University Press, 1959), 38. Field, Glore & Co. was the 1929 successor to the earlier Chicago investment bank/brokerage house Marshall Field, Glore, Ward & Co. The latter had been involved in substantial Italian business – for example, the 1927 $30 million City of Milan loan, which had Dillon, Read & Co., Bankers Trust Co., Guaranty Co. of New York, and Marshall Field, Glore, Ward & Co. as underwriters. See advertisement in *Barron's*, April 18, 1927.

13. *New York Times*, Nov. 23, 1930. Volpi is not listed as a Sofina board member in Sofina, *Annual Report 1929*; he is, however, listed as a board member in *Moody's Manual (Utilities) 1930*, 2317 (and he was listed in subsequent Sofina annual reports).
14. James, *End of Globalization*, 46, 53. Ranald Michie, in "A Financial Phoenix," in Youssef Cassis, and Eric Bussière, eds., *London and Paris as International Financial Centres in the Twentieth Century* (Oxford: Oxford University Press, 2005), 23, writes that "Britain's leaving the gold standard in 1931 provided a more serious financial crisis around the world than the Wall Street Crash of 1929." We believe that prior to September 1931 the crisis had engulfed the European continent. In 1930, however, there was not yet the recognition of how steep would be the downturn.
15. *Ten Years of Electricity, 1926–1936 (Athens Piraeus Electricity Company Ltd.)* (1936; in Greek with English summary), copy in PEA/COWD 3/3 in S. Pearson & Son Papers, Science Museum, London. This history tells of the completion of an Athens power station in 1929, but the need for substantial new funds, which the Pearson group provided, buying out in the process the most important private power stations and merging generation and distribution companies into one; see also Nikos Pantelakis, *The Electrification of Greece: From Private Initiative to State Monopoly (1889–1956)* (Athens: Cultural Foundation of the National Bank of Greece, 1991), 292 (in Greek, with translations provided by the author). "Fuerzas Motrices del Valle de Lecrin," typescript history in Box B11, and Deloitte's Valuation as of 1933, pp. 21, 47, 49–50, PEA/COWD 5/11, both in S. Pearson & Son Papers (on the Spanish direct investment).
16. See data in Box B14, S. Pearson & Son Papers. When negotiations had started, Belgrade was part of the Kingdom of the Serbs, Croats, and Slovenes (name changed to Yugoslavia in October 1929).
17. *Time*, Feb. 17, 1930, and June 16, 1930; on the start of Dawnay, Day & Co. in 1928, David Kynaston, *The City of London: Volume III, Illusions of Gold, 1914–1945* (London: Chatto & Windus, 1999), 327. For Lord Barnby and the Central Electricity Board, Leslie Hannah, *Electricity Before Nationalisation: A Study of the Development of the Electricity Supply Industry in Britain to 1948* (Baltimore: Johns Hopkins University Press, 1979), 103, 360, 374.
18. Hannah, *Electricity Before Nationalisation*, 223. The Italians (specifically Volpi) had been raising a lot of money in the United States; how did they have

resources to invest in the United Kingdom? Would this in time become part of "flight capital"? That is our guess. We do not know whether the purchase was before or after the British devaluation of the pound in September 1931. If after, and Volpi still had dollar resources, then these properties might have seemed a bargain.

19. Catherine Vuillermot, *Pierre-Marie Durand et l'Énergie Industrielle* (Paris: CNRS, 2001), 99.
20. As an example of new activities in the fall of 1930, Continentale Elektrizitätsunion AG (CEAG) was registered in Basel, Switzerland, with the objective of "permanent participation in firms for the generation, distribution, and use of electric power in Switzerland and abroad, the financing of such undertakings in whatever form, and the taking over and execution of financial transactions." The founders included Basler Handelsbank, Union Financière de Genève, AG Leu & Co., the Swiss Bank Corporation, an Anglo-American group of banks, as well as the operating company Preussische Elektrizitäts AG, Berlin. CEAG took over shares in the Berlin company. Hans Bauer, *Swiss Bank Corporation* (Basel: Swiss Bank Corp., 1972), 278. On the new Swedish concessions in Eastern Europe, see Ulf Olsson, *Furthering a Fortune* (Stockholm: Ekerlids Förlag, 2001), 100–1, and [Jan Glete], *Electrifying Experience: A Brief Account of the First Century of the ASEA Group of Sweden, 1883–1983* (Västerås: ASEA, 1983), 41. On the rejection of the Harriman plan, reported in June 1930, see Frank Southard, *American Industry in Europe* (Boston: Houghton Mifflin, 1931), 41, and Leopold Wellisz, *Foreign Capital in Poland* (London: Allen & Unwin, 1938), 247. According to Jerzy Tomaszewski, the Harriman project was not fully rejected by the Polish government until 1936. Jerzy Tomaszewski, "German Capital in Silesian Industry in Poland," in Alice Teichova and P. L. Cottrell, eds., *International Business and Central Europe, 1918–1939* (New York: St. Martin's Press, 1983), 239.
21. Ginette Kurgan-Van Hentenryk, "Finance and Financiers in Belgium, 1880–1940," in Youssef Cassis, ed., *Finance and Financiers in European History 1880–1960* (Cambridge: Cambridge University Press, 1992), 326.
22. Réné Brion, "Le Rôle de la Sofina," in Monique Trédé-Boulmer, ed., *Le Financement de l'Industrie Électrique 1880–1980* (Paris: PUF, 1994), 232.
23. See Robert Vitalis, *When Capitalists Collide: Business Conflict and the End of Empire in Egypt* (Berkeley: University of California Press, 1995), 75; for a while in 1929, it looked like the government would build and own the Shubra power plant. The change in the Egyptian government after the elections revived the viability of the Empain group's project. For where the British government stood and for Dudley Docker's reaction, see ibid., 77. See also R.P.T. Davenport-Hines, *Dudley Docker* (Cambridge: Cambridge University Press, 1984), 210–11. See notes to Chapter 4 for the competition among the various groups in Egypt.
24. On Oliven's plans, see Hughes, *Networks of Power*, 317–18; Brion, "Le Rôle de la Sofina," 228–29 (the Heineman-Oliven project). On the historical relationship between Sofina and Gesfürel and Oliven's June 1930 plan, see Luciano Segreto, "Aspetti e Problemi dell' Industria Elettrica in Europa tra le Due Guerre," in *Storia dell' Industria Elettrica in Italia*, III (Rome-Bari: Laterza, 1993), 367, 395–396n112. Heineman and Oliven were associated in a

number of projects. For example, as noted in Chapter 4, they both served on the board of the Sofina-controlled CHADE. See "Consejo de Administración de la CHADE, 1926–1930," given in Gabriela Dalla Corte, "Associaciones y Negocias: Las Redes Sociales Vasco-Catalanas en el Cono Sur Latinoamericano (1911–1936)," July 14, 2005, p. 5 (http://www.euskosare.org/, accessed Sept. 26, 2007). On the plans, see Ranieri, *Dannie Heineman*, 179–85, and *New York Times*, July 20, 1930, which has the quoted passage and reported on the mid-1930 plans (with Heineman's name misspelled).

25. See Brion, "Le Rôle de la Sofina," 228–29 (Heineman-Oliven); Segreto, "Aspetti e Problemi," 367 (the Oliven project); Dannie N. Heineman, *Outline of a New Europe* (Brussels: Vromant & Co., 1931), published in French as *Esquisse d'une Europe Nouvelle* (Brussels: Vromant & Co., 1931), and in German as *Skizze eines Neuen Europe* (Cologne: Glide-Verlag, 1931). Brion, "Le Rôle de la Sofina," 229n, indicates that there were two other plans for European electrification presented in 1930, but these did not have as much visibility as the Heineman-Oliven scheme. Katowice is sometimes rendered as Kattowitz, the German spelling.
26. An exception was Rostov, Russia: They did not have a tranche in the Russian facility, but they envisaged a network connection. Ranieri, *Dannie Heineman*, 180, suggests that Europel (see Chapter 4) was set up to implement the plans.
27. Heineman, *Outline of a New Europe*, 15 (on technical means), 31 (on banking plans), 36 (on a European customs union), 48 (on the three pillars, italics in the original), 50 (on federation).
28. Robert M. Kindersley, "British Foreign Investments in 1929," *Economic Journal*, 41 (Sept. 1931), 370–84.
29. Robert M. Kindersley, "British Foreign Investments in 1930," *Economic Journal*, 42 (June 1932), 176.
30. Heineman was well aware of the economic crisis in the United States when he gave his talk in November and December 1930. He stated that American prosperity had once seemed "unshakable.... Today they realize that their position is not unassailable." Heineman, *Outline of a New Europe*, 47.
31. Charles H. Feinstein and Katherine Watson, "Private International Capital Flows," in Charles H. Feinstein, ed., *Banking, Currency, and Finance in Europe Between the Wars* (Oxford: Oxford University Press, 1995), 109.
32. Kynaston, *City of London*, III, 227–28, 360; R.S. Sayers, *The Bank of England, 1891–1944*, 2 vol. (Cambridge: Cambridge University Press, 1976), II, 530–32; for July 1931, we used the rate of £1 = \$4.86; for January 1932, the rate was £1 = \$3.38.
33. Ioanna Pepelasis Minoglou, "Between Informal Networks and Formal Contracts: International Investment in Greece During the 1920s," *Business History*, 44 (April 2002), 52.
34. Davenport-Hines, *Dudley Docker*, 211, 272ns. As indicated above, it was the Empain group that prevailed (but its plans were not those for the Aswan Dam and were much less ambitious). In December 1929, the Duke of Atholl, a business partner of Docker, had declared that Docker's group had been intending to spend £26 million in Egypt, with orders to British manufacturers of about £20 million, but Atholl declared "nobody is likely to put a sum of that

sort into Egypt if there is not going to be any protection of foreigners or their trade." Ibid., 210–11. Sofina's plans in Egypt were linked with those of Docker; Volpi was also involved. For Sofina's role in Egypt, 1927–1931, see Liane Ranieri, *Dannie Heineman* (Brussels: Éditions Racine, 2005), 170–79. Ranieri attributes the dream to develop the Aswan Dam to Heineman. See notes to Chapter 4 for the third scheme that did not materialize.

35. The formation of the Canadian holding company European Electric Corp. in 1930 may have been a way of trying to cope with the perceived new difficulties. Gianni Toniolo, *One Hundred Years, 1894–1994: A Short History of the Banca Commerciale Italiana* (Milan: Banca Commerciale Italiana, 1994), 68; Segreto, "Gli Assetti Proprietari," 144–45.
36. On the March 1931 loan of $17,850,000 granted to the city of Berlin by an international consortium, including Harris, Forbes & Co., J. Henry Schroder Banking Corporation, and Chase National Bank (New York), on the May 1931 formation of Berliner Kraft und Licht (Bewag) AG (Berlin Power and Light Corp.), on Oliven as a vice chairman, and on the 38-member board, see *Moody's Manual (Utilities) 1933*, 2572. On Heineman's role, see Ranieri, *Dannie Heineman*, 186. She notes that the international consortium included Sofina, Gesfürel, and Sofina's regular British, Italian, and American partners, as well as a Dutch, Swiss, and Swedish group. Berliner Kraft und Licht was the successor to Berliner Elektricitäts-Werke AG, hence the initials Bewag.
37. U.S. Senate, Committee on Finance, *Sale of Foreign Bonds*, 331. *New York Times*, Dec. 6, 1931. For the holdings of Intercontinents Power in Argentina, Brazil, and Chile, see Hausman and Neufeld, "U.S. Foreign Direct Investment in Electrical Utilities," 368, and Wilkins, *Maturing of Multinational Enterprise*, 131.
38. After the Japanese moved into Manchuria, lenders had Japanese companies revise the collateral on their loans. Makoto Kishida, Presentation to the Business History group, Kobe, Nov. 20, 2005.
39. For the international aspects, see Wilkins, *History ... 1914–1945*, 312. The public perception during 1930 and 1931 did not reflect reality. According to "Relation of Holding Companies to Operating Companies in Power and Gas Affecting Control," Report to the Committee on Interstate and Foreign Commerce, U.S. House of Representatives, 73rd Cong., 2nd sess., House Report No. 827, pt. 5 (Washington, DC: USGPO, 1935), xiii, "The financial structures of Insull Utility Investments, Inc., and Corporation Securities Co. of Chicago were ill-designed to withstand the more or less constant decline occurring in 1930 and 1931 in the values of and income from securities...."
40. The impact of the downturn varied by country. See B. R. Mitchell data, as cited in the notes to Chapter 1.
41. Hausman and Neufeld, "U.S. Foreign Direct Investment in Electrical Utilities,"370 (one-third interest in French utility); Vuillermot, *Pierre-Marie Durand*, 231; see also ibid., 96, 102 (Durand group acquisition). Hausman and Neufeld, "U.S. Foreign Direct Investment in Electrical Utilities," 370, 383, 390n88 (German investment); see also Kobrak, *Banking on Global Markets* (for suggestions that what happened in the French and German cases were

similar). Vereinigte Elektrizitätswerke Westfalen (VEW) was based in Dortmund, not to be confused with RWE, which was based in Essen.
42. See "Odium [*sic*] in Action," *Time*, Aug. 10, 1936, from *Time* Archives (http://www.time.com/time/magazine/article/0,9171,762314,00.html, accessed Sept. 27, 2007); Hannah, *Electricity Before Nationalisation*, 230–31.
43. See Marshall, Southard, and Taylor, *Canadian-American Industry*, 150.
44. American & Foreign Power, *Annual Report 1929*, passim, esp. 6–7.
45. For the Cuban problems that related to the falling sugar prices, see Harold van B. Cleveland and Thomas F. Huertas, *Citibank 1812–1970* (Cambridge, MA: Harvard University Press, 1985), 109–10. Quote is from American & Foreign Power, *Annual Report 1929*, 13.
46. American & Foreign Power, *Annual Report 1930*, 1–5.
47. Ibid., 6.
48. Ibid. On the traditional managing agency system within India, see Geoffrey Jones, *Merchants to Multinationals* (Oxford: Oxford University Press, 2000), 29–30, 164, 181–82.
49. American & Foreign Power, *Annual Report 1930*, 10–11, and *Annual Report 1929*, 8–9.
50. American & Foreign Power, *Annual Report 1930*, 11–18.
51. Ibid., 7.
52. Ibid., 7–8.
53. American & Foreign Power, *Annual Report 1931*, 6–7.
54. Ibid., 4–5; in 1930, it had not paid dividends on common stock, but it had paid on all the other classes of preferred shares.
55. American & Foreign Power, *Annual Report 1932*, 3.
56. Ibid., 4.
57. Ibid., 9.
58. The grandest investigation of utility holding and operating companies was by the U.S. Federal Trade Commission (FTC). It had been authorized in February 1928 and continued on through the depression. Additional congressional inquiries accelerated in 1932, not long after the Insull collapse. After 1933, they mounted. Over one hundred volumes of reports were published in connection with the FTC investigations. For a summary, see U.S. Federal Trade Commission, *Utility Corporations, Summary Report*, Doc. 92, Pt. 72-A, 70th Cong., 1st sess.(1935). On the scrutiny of investment bankers, see Vincent P. Carosso, *Investment Banking in America* (Cambridge, MA: Harvard University Press, 1970), 320–430.
59. Max Winkler, *Foreign Bonds: An Autopsy* (Philadelphia: Roland Swain, 1933), 251.
60. Roosevelt's position was clearly expressed in his 1932 campaign speeches. Moreover, there had been in the United States a decade-long political battle over what to do with the government-sponsored Muscle Shoals, Alabama, project, which had been started up during World War I for the purpose of producing nitrates and included the Wilson Dam on the Tennessee River. TVA was the Roosevelt administration's answer.
61. Cleona Lewis, *America's Stake in International Investments* (Washington, DC: Brookings Institution, 1938), 659.

62. The German government arranged certain buy-back programs, buying German dollar debt that was selling at low prices and thus trying to eliminate or at least reduce German obligations. See Wilkins, *History ... 1914–1945*, 802n115.
63. See ibid., 379–80, for the general situation, not specifically in utilities.
64. Stephen A. Schuker, *American "Reparations" to Germany, 1919–33* (Princeton: Princeton Studies in International Finance No. 61, Department of Economics, Princeton University, 1988), 74.
65. Harm Schröter, "Globalization and Reliability: The Fate of Foreign Direct Investment in Electric Power-Supply during the World Economic Crisis, 1929–1939," *Annales Historiques de l'Électricité*. 4 (November 2006), 121. On Sofina's acquiring majority control of Gesfürel, see Ranieri, *Dannie Heineman*, 226; Sofina, *Annual Report 1939*, 35, has Gesfürel as a company in which Sofina had an important interest.
66. Feldenkirchen seems to suggest that German expansion in eastern Europe in the 1930s was encouraged by the German government as a means of increasing exports. Wilfried Feldenkirchen, "Siemens in Eastern Europe: From the End of World War I to the End of World War II," in Christopher Kobrak and Per H. Hansen, eds., *European Business, Dictatorship, and Political Risk, 1920–1945* (New York: Berghahn Books, 2004), 125.
67. Ranieri, *Dannie Heineman,* 187–88, 195–96, 383. On November 23, 1934, effective as of January 1, 1934, Bewag merged with Berlin City Electric Co. Oliven was no longer listed as vice chairman. *Moody's Manual (Utilities) 1935*, 920. For the incorporation into the Hermann Göring Werke, see Ranieri, *Dannie Heineman*, 188. On the Hermann Göring Werke, see Peter Hayes, *Industry and Ideology* (Cambridge: Cambridge University Press, 1987), 169, 218; R. J. Overy, "Göring's 'Multi-national Empire,'" in Teichova and Cottrell, eds., *International Business*, ch. 11; and Ulrich Wengenroth, "The Rise and Fall of State-Owned Enterprise in Germany," in Pier Angelo Toninelli, ed., *The Rise and Fall of State-Owned Enterprise in the Western World* (Cambridge: Cambridge University Press, 2000), 116–17 (none of these three say anything specifically about electric power companies that were brought into the group). In 1938, no longer protected by his U.S. citizenship, Heineman finally quit as an administrator of *German* companies. Ranieri, *Dannie Heineman,* 195. However, the Sofina, *Annual Report 1939*, 35–36, lists both Gesfürel and Berliner Kraft und Licht (Bewag) AG as among the enterprises in which Sofina maintained an important participation (the size of which was not specified).
68. R. Nötel, "International Credit and Finance," in M. C. Kaser and E. A. Radice, eds., *The Economic History of Eastern Europe, 1919–1975* (Oxford: Oxford University Press, 1985), II, 284. On Elektrowerte AG, see Bauer, *Swiss Bank Corporation,* 162–63, 249, 393. This company was affiliated with the Swiss Bank Corporation. In the fall of 1936, Elektrowerte AG merged with the closely associated Swiss holding company Schweizerische Elektrizitäts- und Verkehrsgesellschaft (Suiselectra). Ibid., 277. Schröter, "Globalization and Reliability," 119 (Bulgaria).
69. The notion of round-tripping involves a company (or individuals resident) in country A having an investment in a company in country B, which in turn

reinvests back in country A. We first encountered the phrase in Andrea Goldstein, "Emerging Multinationals," OECD Development Center, unpublished paper 2005, 22, but see also Giorgio Barba Navaretti and Anthony J. Venables, *Multinational Firms in the World Economy* (Princeton: Princeton University Press, 2004), 9n7 (on "round-trippers"). The reasons for doing this were various. AEG's reasons related to its historical connections, linked with asset protection. According to Schröter, AEG had by the 1930s totally lost its influence in Elektrobank; some observers had their doubts about this. Schröter is our source for Elektrobank's pullout from Germany ("because of exchange difficulties."). Schröter, "Globalization and Reliability," 117.

70. Luciano Segreto, "Du 'Made in Germany' au 'Made In Switzerland,'" in M. Trédé, ed., *Électricité et Électrification dans le Monde 1880–1980* (Paris: PUF, 1992), 360, for the network of its holdings in 1939.
71. Luciano Segreto, "Financing the Electric Industry Worldwide: Strategy and Structure of the Swiss Electric Holding Companies, 1895–1945," *Business and Economic History,* 23 (Fall 1994), 170. This is remarkable when one realized that in the 1920s Elektrobank had no investments whatsoever in the United States.
72. Nötel, "International Credit and Finance," 284.
73. See Wilkins, *History ... 1914–1945*, 373, for Elektrobank's investments in the United States in a general context.
74. Segreto, "Financing the Electric Industry Worldwide," 168 (Basler Handelsbank, Swiss Bank Corporation), 170 (geographical distribution Indelec); on the Luxembourg holdings, see below on SODEC. Nötel, who writes on Eastern European investments, includes nothing on Indelec; on Indelec in the 1930s, see Peter Hertner, "L'Industrie Électrotechnique Allemande entre les Deux Guerres: À la Recherche d'une Position International Perdue," *Relations Internationales*, 43 (Autumn 1985), 289–304; Daniel Imwinkelried, "Die Auswirkungen des Ersten Weltkrieges auf die Beziehungen der Schweizer Banken zur Deutschen Industrie: Die Schweizerische Gesellschaft für Elektrische Industrie (Indelec) und der Siemens-Konzern," in Sébastien Guex, ed., *La Suisse et les Grandes Puissances 1914–1945* (Geneva: Droz, 1999), 324; and Serge Paquier, *Histoire de l'Électricité en Suisse* (Geneva: Éditions Passé Présent, 1998), II, 1029–30.
75. Remarkably, all through the 1930s the Japanese companies kept up payments on their electric utilities' borrowings. Thomas Lamont of J.P. Morgan & Co. had been, as we have seen, very much involved in the financing of Japanese utilities (as well as arranging Japanese government loans). Lamont came to be appalled at the changes taking place in Japan in the 1930s with the rise of militarism. Wilkins, "Role of U.S. Business," 353–58.
76. Franco Amatori, "Beyond State and Market: Italy's Futile Search for a Third Way," in Pier Angelo Toninelli, ed., *The Rise and Fall of State-Owned Enterprise in the Western World* (Cambridge: Cambridge University Press, 2000), 129–31, 143.
77. United States Department of Commerce, Bureau of Foreign and Domestic Commerce, *American Direct Investments in Foreign Countries–1936* (Washington, DC: USGPO, 1938), 11.
78. *Moody's Manual (Utilities)1938*, 961–62.

79. *Moody's Manual (Utilities)1929*, 1852–54; ibid., *1930*, 1668–76; and ibid., *1938*, 643–46.
80. All this is from *Moody's Manual (Utilities) 1938*, 943. The Greek companies were Galileo, Société Anonyme Hellénique; Société Électrique de Volo, and Société Électrique de Mytilene. The Romanian ones were Compania Romana de Electricitate, Brasov, and Uzina Electrica Brasov, SA. Italo-Belge is not included on Table 5.1, for its assets in 1937 were less than those of the companies listed – that is, less than $10 million.
81. Schröter, "Globalization and Reliability," 117, which discusses the reduction of Motor-Columbus's interests in Germany and Italy. See Chapter 4 on Foreign Light and Power, Montreal. For the investment portfolio, see Segreto, "Financing the Electric Industry Worldwide," 170; the Romanian investments are not included in the investment portfolio tabulation, presumably because the group made the investments through the Canadian holding company and Segreto included these as "Canadian" rather than Romanian.
82. Brion, "Le Rôle de la Sofina," 224.
83. Schröter, "Globalization and Reliability," 116–17; Sofina, *Annual Report, 1936*, 32, and ibid., *1938*, 25–26; Teresa Tortella, *A Guide to Sources of Information on Foreign Investment in Spain, 1780–1914* (Amsterdam: International Institute of Social History, 2000) (http://www.ica.org/en/node/30421, item 53, "Barcelona Traction Light & Power Co. Ltd.," accessed Sept. 26, 2007); Ranieri, *Dannie Heineman*, 195.
84. *New York Times*, Sept. 28, 1940. Closer to the events (at an April 15, 1940 shareholders meeting), Heineman in the Sofina, *Annual Report 1939*, 24, wrote of the "substantial damage" in Spain, but that "two damaged hydro-electric stations have since been repaired and put in service. Repair work is proceeding in the steam power-stations, but several generating sets will have to be replaced."
85. On his purchases during the civil war period, see *New York Times*, Sept. 21, 1949; no interest on these bonds was paid during the civil war years.
86. The reasons for the transfer are given in *New York Times*, Nov. 22, 1948, Jan. 31, 1949, and Ranieri, *Dannie Heineman*, 198, which dates the establishment of SODEC as April 1938; according to Sofina, *Annual Report, 1938*, 25, and *Moody's Manual (Utilities) 1939*, 615, SODEC was established December 20, 1938, under Luxembourg law, by CHADE. Details of the transaction are given in ibid., which indicates that the investments obtained from CHADE comprised substantial holdings of European as well as South American corporations. The latter included Compañía Argentina de Electricidad (CADE) and Compañía de Electricidad de la Provincia de Buenos Aires. Companies in Europe in which there were "participations" (a word often used to include affiliates as well as parents, often denoting cross-ownership) included the holding companies Sidro, Gesfürel, Sofina, and the operating companies Bewag, Centrales Électriques de l'Entre-Sambre et Meuse et de la Region de Malmédy (ESMA in Belgium) and Société des Forces Motrices de Truyère (SFMT in France). SODEC was controlled by CHADE, which in turn was controlled by Sofina. On Sofina's important role in ESMA and SFMT, see Ranieri, *Dannie Heineman*, 136, 139, 191–92. José Gómez-Ibáñez, *Regulating Infrastructure: Monopoly, Contracts,*

and Discretion (Cambridge, MA Harvard University Press, 2003), 138, points out that negotiations for the revised 1936 CADE concession had gone from Buenos Aires to Brussels, bypassing Spain entirely. See Sofina, *Annual Report, 1936*, 40, for details.

87. Brion, "Le Rôle de la Sofina," 225. Société Financière Électrique, Paris, is not included in the key firms listed in Sofina, *Annual Report 1939*.
88. On Sofina in the 1930s, see Brion, "Le Rôle de la Sofina"; Schröter, "Globalization and Reliability,"113; Ranieri, *Dannie Heineman*, 190–96; *Moody's Manual (Utilities)*, various years; ibid., 1940, 617 (for the terms of the Turkish sale); Wilkins, *History ... 1914–1945*, 802; and Sofina, *Annual Report 1939*. In Chapter 2, we introduced the iconoclastic notion that a company could make foreign direct investments, but the targeted company was not a "foreign direct investment." Sofina's investments in Middle West Corp. seem to be another case in point. Sofina was expanding strategically into the U.S. public utilities sector; it had a representative on the board of Middle West Corp.; it included in its 1939 annual report the Middle West Corp. as one of its key affiliated companies; and it was making a foreign direct investment. Yet turning the coin over, it would be hard to call its target, Middle West Corp., a foreign direct investment. Ibid., 38 (for the inclusion of Middle West Corp.).
89. The quotations are from Dannie N. Heineman, "International Cooperation in Privately Managed Public Utility Undertakings," address to the annual general meeting of shareholders of Société Financière de Transports et d'Entreprises Industrielles (Sofina), April 28, 1938. For Heineman's overall optimistic outlook, see his address to the annual meeting of Sofina in May *1932:* "Let credit be restored, and with it the capacity to purchase. But how? By enabling lenders again to feel confident their enterprises will be safeguarded and not frustrated by the public authorities and that debtors will be neither prevented nor exempted from faithfully discharging their obligations toward them. And further, by the conviction,... that trade will revive and that a new period of economic prosperity is about to begin." Reported in *New York Times*, May 29, 1932. Although in 1938 Heineman was not predicting a new period of economic prosperity, he was nonetheless still hoping the trends of the 1930s were "transitory."
90. Schröter, "Globalization and Reliability," 113–14. Sofina, *Annual Report 1939*, 34, lists Electrobel as one of its affiliated companies.
91. Schröter, "Globalization and Reliability," 115; Nötel, "International Credit and Finance," 284; *New York Times*, June 18, 1931, described Hydrofina as a "unit" of Sofina, but since Sofina and Electrobel were in the 1930s working in unison, there is probably no inconsistency.
92. For Empain in France in the 1930s, see Pierre Lanthier, "Multinationals and the French Electrical Industry, 1889–1940," in Alice Teichova, Maurice Lévy-Leboyer, and Helga Nussbaum, *Historical Studies in International Corporate Business* (Cambridge: Cambridge University Press, 1989), 147–48, and Luciano Segreto, "Le Rôle du Capital Étranger dans l'Industrie Électrique," in Maurice Lévy-Leboyer and Henri Morsel, eds., *Histoire Générale de l' Électricité en France*, II (Paris: Fayard, 1994), 1010–12.

93. Odlum was on the board prior to his becoming vice chairman and remained on the board of American & Foreign Power all during the 1930s, even though he stepped down as vice chairman. See American & Foreign Power, *Annual Reports*.
94. This company is not to be confused with its British namesake; they were entirely separate. Atlas Corporation was the successor to a small firm that Odlum and George Howard had formed in 1923. On Odlum and Howard's important role in American & Foreign Power in the 1920s (at the same time they had their own predecessor company to Atlas), see Sidney Alexander Mitchell, *S. Z Mitchell and the Electrical Industry* (New York: Farrar, Straus & Cudahy, 1960), 138.
95. See Hannah, *Electricity Before Nationalisation*, 231–32; Hannah, "Commentary," in Teichova and Cottrell, eds., *International Business*, 194, argued that the Americans had been draining GLCT, insisting on extremely high dividends to support UPLC. "The British directors saw that this was against the British national interest and, with the support of the Bank of England and City institutions, they managed to repatriate the capital in order to prevent this exploitation by the capital-exporting country [the United States]." On Atlas, see Bullock, *Story of Investment Companies*, 49–56, 159, and "Odium [*sic*] in Action," *Time*, Aug. 10, 1936 (the amusing misspelling of Odlum's name notwithstanding, this is a very valuable article); this article gives the $25 million figure. Lewis, *America's Stake*, 329, gives a figure of about $32 million.
96. Hannah, *Electricity Before Nationalisation*, 223, 290.
97. *Moody's Manual (Utilities) 1938*, 961; interestingly, at least according to *Moody's*, Italian Superpower did not have any shares in SADE, Volpi's Italian utility. On Italo-Belge, see material earlier in this chapter. As noted, the Volpi group represented a cluster of public utility companies and Volpi himself was a director of Sofina.
98. See *Moody's Manual (Utilities) 1940*, 1347, and display advertisement in *Kentville Advertiser*, May 9, 1940, by the large Montreal brokerage house Johnston & Ward, offering shares in Eastern Utilities Ltd. and describing its properties. It was not clear from *Moody's* manual whether there were Canadian buyers, which seemed likely, but the advertisement confirmed this. The divestments occurred as a major reorganization of UPLC took place in accord with the U.S. Public Utility Holding Company Act.
99. Wilkins, *Maturing of Multinational Enterprise*, 178–79 (the quoted passage is on p. 179).
100. American & Foreign Power, *Annual Report 1937*, 4.
101. Duncan McDowall, *The Light: Brazilian Traction, Light and Power Company Ltd, 1899–1945* (Toronto: University of Toronto Press, 1988), 340–41.
102. Miguel S. Wionczek, "Electric Power," in Raymond Vernon, ed., *Public Policy and Private Enterprise in Mexico* (Cambridge, MA: Harvard University Press, 1964), 60. After the expropriation of oil, the value of the Mexican currency plummeted, which affected the operations of Mexlight. Sofina, *Annual Report, 1938*, 26.
103. Charles Franklin Mallory, "Financial Problems of the North American Owned Electric Utilities in Latin America," M.S. thesis, Massachusetts Institute of

Technology, 1956, 35 (on the overall situation). On International Power Co. Ltd., Montreal, see ibid., 104. On the Chapala company, see Wionczek, "Electric Power," 70, and Hausman and Neufeld, "U.S. Foreign Direct Investment in Electrical Utilities," 382. Morrison-McCall interests acquired the company in 1926. On Standard Gas & Electric, see *Moody's Manual (Utilities) 1930*, 654; ibid., *1939*, 1074; and ibid.,*1940*, 1006; all through the 1930s, there was mention of Standard Gas's Mexican properties, but not in *Moody's Manual (Utilities) 1940*. Wionczek, "Electric Power," 67–68, writes that Mexlight and American & Foreign Power made no new investments in 1936–1938, briefly renewed investments in 1939, and then cut back sharply in 1940, when they recognized the thrust of Mexican government policies.

104. McDowall, *Light*, 280 (on Miller Lash), 303–41 (conditions in Brazil), 326 (on the water code); see also Mallory, "Financial Problems," 86, and Wilkins, *Maturing of Multinational Enterprise*, 202. In the Heineman 1938 speech, cited earlier, when he spoke of the "tendency amongst some governments to view with suspicion or even animosity the participation of foreigners in ... the management of ... public utility undertakings," undoubtedly he had Mexico and Brazil, as well as other countries, in mind. The Sofina/Sidro interests in Mexico and Spain were listed in Sofina, *Annual Report 1929* and ibid., 1939, so the absence of a listing of Brazilian Traction suggests a less important role than in the other ventures taken over from Loewenstein's speculations.

105. American & Foreign Power, *Annual Report 1939*, 26; Mallory, "Financial Problems," 86 (15 companies).

106. See map in American & Foreign Power, *Annual Report 1939* (Map 5.2 herein).

107. See Chapter 4 herein and Peter Hertner, "German Foreign Investment in Electrical Industry and in Electrified Urban Transport in Italy, Spain and Argentina Until the End of the 1920s: Some Preliminary Considerations," unpublished paper, 2005 (CHADE was, of course, the old German DUEG).

108. Ranieri, *Dannie Heineman*, 142 (the quote from a commemorative brochure), 231 (additions to the Puerto Nuevo power station in 1931 and 1934). Ibid., 231, and Gómez-Ibáñez, *Regulating Infrastructure*, 137, for CHADE's conflicts with the Buenos Aires city council, 1932–1936, and the threats of expropriation.

109. Gómez-Ibáñez, *Regulating Infrastructure*, 138. According to Ranieri, *Dannie Heineman*, 194, 214, Heineman was in Argentina for seven weeks in the summer of 1936 and again in February and March 1937.

110. As noted in Chapter 4, in 1929 American & Foreign Power had incorporated in Argentina five regional companies and in Florida the Argentine Electric Companies; by the end of 1930, the latter had brought together eleven operating subsidiaries in Argentina. Mallory, "Financial Problems," 85.

111. American & Foreign Power, *Annual Report 1939*, 26.

112. On Anglo-Argentine Tramways Company Ltd. and its parent Companie Générale de Tramways de Buenos-Ayres, Brussels, see Sofina, *Annual Report 1939*, 28; see also Ranieri, *Dannie Heineman*, 64–65, 229–31, for the very complicated story; this company is mentioned in Chapter 3 herein. On Société d'Électricité de Rosario, Brussels, established in 1910, see Sofina, *Annual Report*

1939, 26; Ranieri, *Dannie Heineman*, 66–67, 229; and Frederic M. Halsey, *Investments in Latin America and the British West Indies*, U.S. Department of Commerce, Bureau of Foreign and Domestic Commerce, Special Agents Series, 169 (Washington, DC: USGPO, 1918), 69–70 (where the name is rendered slightly differently). Gómez-Ibáñez, *Regulating Infrastructure*, 137–38, argues that like CHADE/CADE, Italo-Argentine Electric Co. was targeted by the Buenos Aires city authorities from 1932 to 1936 in a way that seemed to be a harbinger of possible expropriation. Like CHADE/CADE, Italo-Argentine also got an extended concession in the 1936 negotiations. It was the Buenos Aires city government that gave the tramway company difficulties in the 1930s.

113. It also had properties in Brazil and Chile. In South America, it had 74,800 customers in 1938 compared with the 1,304,900 customers of American & Foreign Power. In Argentina, the communities it served were located in the Provinces of Buenos Aires, Chubut, Córdoba, La Pampa, Neuquén, Río Negro, San Luis, Santa Fe, and Santiago del Estero. It was not a profitable enterprise. Stone & Webster ran the operations on behalf of the holding company. *Moody's Manual (Utilities) 1939*, 1662.

114. Andrea Lluch and Laura Sánchez, *De Movimiento Popular a Empresa El Cooperativisismo Eléctrico en La Pampa* (Santa Rosa: Fondo Editorial Pampeano, [2001]), 32ff, and Mallory, "Financial Problems," 85. In 1919, Buenos Aires had a higher per capita consumption of electricity than Berlin (155 kWh versus 135 kWh); in 1938, however – although the per capita consumption in both cities had grown – Buenos Aires recorded 380 kWh, while Berlin had risen to 430 kWh. Sofina, *Annual Report 1939*, 16.

115. See Gómez-Ibáñez, *Regulating Infrastructure*, 134, on some of the reasons why hydroelectric facilities were so limited in Argentina in the 1930s.

116. American & Foreign Power, *Annual Report 1936*; Wilkins, *Maturing of Multinational Enterprise*, 202. CHADE had no Chilean investments (see Chapter 4).

117. We believe that Paul E. Sigmund, *Multinationals in Latin America: The Politics of Nationalization* (Madison: University of Wisconsin Press, 1980), 55, exaggerates when he writes that in 1935 100 percent of the electricity supplied in Mexico was by foreigners, but we have no doubt that throughout Latin America the provision of electric light and power was overwhelmingly by foreign-owned firms.

118. See Victor Bulmer-Thomas, *Economic History of Latin America Since Independence* (Cambridge: Cambridge University Press, 1994), 226–28.

119. Thomas O'Brien, *The Century of U.S. Capitalism in Latin America* (Albuquerque: University of New Mexico Press, 1999), 130. American & Foreign Power, *Annual Report 1940*, 6, contains a table showing the declines of local currencies with the value at the date of major acquisitions, the average value for 1939 and for 1940. The tale would be depressing to any financial analyst.

120. Marshall, Southard, and Taylor, *Canadian-American Industry*, 139–52.

121. Ibid., 141–42.

122. Ibid., 141–43; Gordon Laxer, *Open for Business: The Roots of Foreign Ownership in Canada* (Toronto: Oxford University Press, 1989), 215.

123. Marshall, Southard, and Taylor, *Canadian-American Industry*, 140.
124. Herbert Holt of Montreal, Light, Heat and Power was ubiquitous in the Latin American activities of Canadian companies. His name appears in numerous different contexts. See Christopher Armstrong and H.V. Nelles, *Southern Exposure: Canadian Promoters in Latin America and the Caribbean, 1896–1930* (Toronto: University of Toronto Press, 1988), passim.
125. Marshall, Southard, and Taylor, *Canadian-American Industry*, 139–40, 152, 215.
126. Ibid., 328, on the divestments from Canadian investments of Public Utilities Consolidated Corp., which company, however, retained its properties in Nicaragua (Central American Power) and Honduras (Planta Electrica). Hausman and Neufeld, "U.S. Foreign Direct Investment in Electrical Utilities," 368.
127. Marshall, Southard, and Taylor, *Canadian-American Industry*, 44–45.
128. Ibid., 41, 146–47.
129. See Sections 3(a)(5) and 3(b) of the act.
130. Graham Taylor and Peter A. Baskerville, *A Concise History of Business in Canada* (Toronto: Oxford University Press, 1994), 271.
131. Marshall, Southard, and Taylor, *Canadian-American Industry*, 142, 146–47.
132. Laxer, *Open for Business*, 215.
133. W.J. Reader, *Bowater: A History* (Cambridge: Cambridge University Press, 1981), 139–55.
134. Pierre Lanthier, "Les Constructions Électriques en France: Le Case de Six Groupes Industriels Internationaux de 1880 à 1940," Ph.D. diss., 3 vol., Paris: University of Paris X (Nanterre), 1988, on the takeover of certain French utilities, and Schröter, "Globalization and Reliability," 113, on Sofina.
135. *Moody's Manual (Utilities) 1940*, 617.
136. American & Foreign Power's investment in the Shanghai International Settlement was by far the largest in electrification in China and indeed appears to have been the only one by U.S. direct investors. British resident investors were present in Hong Kong, with the Hongkong Electric Co. There does seem to have been nonresident British direct investment in Tientsin (Tianjin) (the British concession) as well as in smaller installations in Peking (Beijing), Chingkiang (Zhenjiang), Hankow (Hankou), and Kiangsu (Jiangsu) . There were French interests in Compagnie Française de Tramways et d'Éclairage Électrique in the French concession in Shanghai and Belgian interests in the Tientsin Electric Light and Tramway Co. In addition, there were Japanese investments in Manchuria (Manchuoko) and power facilities linked with Japanese cotton mills and mining projects in China. On all of these, see C. Yun, "A Statistical Investigation of Electric Power Plants in China 1932," *Transactions of the World Power Conference*, Sectional Meeting, Stockholm, 1933 (Stockholm: Svenska Nationalkommittén for Varldskraft-konferenser, 1934), II, 532, and C.F. Remer, *Foreign Investments in China* (New York: Macmillan, 1933), 399.
137. American & Foreign Power, *Annual Report 1937*, 3–5. Before the start of hostilities, in Shanghai the peak demand load had been as high as roughly 156,000 kW. After hostilities, it dropped to 22,000 kW.

138. American & Foreign Power, *Annual Report 1939*, 6; this report was dated April 29, 1940.
139. Data from David Merrett.
140. Mallory, "Financial Problems," 98.
141. We infer this from a careful evaluation by the accounting firm Deloitte's of Whitehall Securities and Whitehall Electric, as of October 3, 1933 (material dated March 16, 1936), juxtaposed with a directory type listing in 1950, along with other data. PEA/COWD 5/11 and PEA/COWD 2/2, S. Pearson & Son Papers, Science Museum, London.
142. On these connections, see Chapter 4, Davenport-Hines, *Dudley Docker,* and *Moody's Manual (Utilities) 1938,* 921, which indicates that McKenna, Wyldbore-Smith, and Docker's son, Bernard, served on the Sofina board.
143. Interestingly, among the French directors of Sofina was André Meyer of Lazard Frère et Cie., Paris. But Robert Kindersley of Lazard Brothers, London, was *not* on the Sofina board; indeed, Kindersley's closest associations were with the British Pearson group.
144. *New York Times*, Feb. 2, 1962. In this obituary for Heineman, the *New York Times* gives the employment as that just before the Second World War. Other sources say Sofina employed 40,000 individuals "at the time of Heineman's retirement" (1955). Hans-Peter Schwarz, *Konrad Adenauer,* 1 (Providence, RI: Berghahn Books, 1995). We think the 1939 date is more realistic. American & Foreign Power, *Annual Report 1939*, 4 (employment).
145. American & Foreign Power, *Annual Report 1929*, 13; Wilkins, *Maturing of Multinational Enterprise*, 134.
146. And even this would be inadequate, for it would not cover a number of important foreign direct investments, including those in copper-mining operations in Chile (where there was important electric power supplied) and the investments in Peru by W. R. Grace & Co., International Petroleum Company, and the Cerro de Pasco Mining Co., for example, where company towns had been electrified. So, too, United Fruit's operations throughout the Caribbean had electric power provided. While Motor-Columbus had investments in Lima Light, Power & Tramways Co., there were also important British stakes in this company. In March 1934, Lima Light had sold its tramway concessions to the state-owned company Compañía Nacional de Tranvias SA, and in 1935 its English name was changed from Lima Light, Power & Tramways Co. to Lima Light & Power (in Peru, the company was called Empresas Eléctricas Asociadas). See Rory Miller, "British Free-Standing Companies on the West Coast of South America," in Mira Wilkins and Harm Schröter, eds. *The Free-Standing Company in the World Economy* (Oxford: Oxford University Press, 1998), 222, and *Moody's Manual (Utilities) 1938*, 898. It is doubtful that Brazilian Traction was included in the list of companies in which Sofina had its "principal interests." See discussion above.
147. The tranche in Sofina is based on secondary sources; we can find nothing to verify this in the late 1930s annual reports of American & Foreign Power. A statement – under the heading "plant" – in the 1936 annual report of American & Foreign Power, reads: "In 1936, the Company disposed of for cash its investment in Société Financiere Electrique, an investment trust

controlling utility properties operating in France. The remaining investment of the Company in Europe aggregates $715,878, which is in companies operating in Italy." American & Foreign Power, *Annual Report 1936*, 4. (In 1936, Sofina also sharply reduced its holdings in Société Financière Électrique, Paris (Finelec), as noted earlier in this chapter.) The companies operating in Italy were undoubtedly networked with Volpi's grouping; and Volpi was a director of Sofina. It is possible that American & Foreign Power might have retained some interests in the Edison Company, Milan.

148. The Fair ran from April 30, 1939, to Oct. 26, 1940. The exhibitors of these "marvels" were U.S. manufacturers: TVs, Radio Corporation of America; Dishwashers, Westinghouse; Air conditioners, Carrier Corporation. See also Sofina's *Annual Report 1939*, 18–22, which devoted space to product usage and the applications of electricity over the prior two decades, as well as the prospects for the future.
149. Hughes, *Networks of Power*, 401.
150. Sofina, *Annual Report 1939*, 16 (remarkable growth), 14–22 (documentation); American & Foreign Power, *Annual Report 1929*, 15; American & Foreign Power, *Annual Report 1939*, 27 (communities and customers).
151. American & Foreign Power, *Annual Report 1929*, 17; American & Foreign Power, *Annual Report 1939*, 27. Sofina, *Annual Report 1939*, 22 (increase in electricity output and customers of "companies in which we have our principal interests").
152. Ranieri, *Dannie Heineman*, 207 (Aug. 1939 transfer to Lisbon). The top management (including Heineman) did not flee Belgium until after the Germans moved in. The group assembled in Portugal in June 1940. It included Aloys van de Vyvere (1871–1961), president of Sofina (Van de Vyvere had replaced Maurice Despret as Sofina's president in 1934). Ibid., 208–9, provides a list of the key Belgians who went to Lisbon. On the Sofina move to Lisbon and New York, see also the letter from the German Military Commander in Belgium and Northern France to Karl Rasche (Dresdner Bank), Feb. 3, 1941, Record Group 238, Microfilm T301, Reel 51, NI 6695 (Occupation Records for the Nuremberg Trial–Nazi Industrialists). The *New York Times*, Sept. 28, 1940, had comments from Heineman that after the German invasion of Belgium, Sofina had moved its offices to France and then to Lisbon. See Wilkins, *History ... 1914–1945*, 452–54, 475 (on freezing of Belgian assets in the United States and Sofina). Sofina, *Annual Report 1939*, 38 (on Sofina's interests in Middle West Corporation).
153. Ranieri, *Dannie Heineman*, 207–11; Wilkins, *History ... 1914–1945*, 452–55 (blocked funds and activities of Foreign Funds Control), 461–70 (experiences of German firms in the United States; fears about disguises, cloaking), 473–81 (Belgian, Dutch, French, Swedish, and Swiss firms in the United States). Banque Belge pour l'Étranger (controlled by Société Générale de Belgique, Brussels) had long been established in New York (since 1921, it had had a New York agency, set up through London). On its experiences, see Ibid., 475.
154. *New York Times*, Oct. 31, 1941. Wilmers (who became increasingly important in Sofina) was a young Englishmen, with a Cambridge degree in modern

languages. He would be a significant figure in Sofina in the 1940s and 1950s. On Wilmers, see John Brooks, "Annals of Finance," *New Yorker*, May 21 and May 28, 1979, and Ranieri, *Dannie Heineman*, 212. It seems likely that earlier Sofina may have had a larger interest in Middle West Corp., which it divested (and bought other American securities or put these securities in a "shelter" company) so as to stay under the SEC trigger point. Sofina included Middle West Corp. among its important interests in its annual report of 1939. Sofina, *Annual Report 1939*, 38.

155. *New York Times*, Oct. 31, 1941; the *New York Times* reporter indicated that he did not know whether the October 15 "reported ban" had been lifted by the Treasury Department. See Wilkins, *History ... 1914–1945*, 452–55 (on the freezes and the July 17, 1941, blacklist and its enlargement). Ranieri, *Dannie Heineman*, 212–13, on the national security issues and the outcome of the investigations.
156. Ranieri, *Dannie Heineman*, 213; it also set up Sovalles, Inc., another Panamanian company, to hold stock in CHADE (see below). On the use of Panamanian intermediaries during wartime by European firms, see Wilkins, *The History ... 1914–1945*, 468, 476, 481, 841, 845n216.
157. McDowall, *Light*, 347–48.
158. Wilkins, *History ... 1914–1945*, 425, 430, 475, 477–78, 842n187. The Swiss Bank Corporation's principal ties in the electric power industry were with Motor-Columbus and Indelec. See Segreto, "Financing the Electric Industry Worldwide," 168. Note that foreign banks were not permitted, under New York state law, to have branches in New York prior to 1961; instead, they set up New York "agencies." In addition, as in the Credit Suisse case, they might set up finance subsidiaries.
159. For the freezing of assets, see Wilkins, *History ... 1914–1945*, ch. 8, esp. 453, for the sequencing.
160. One might wonder that Sofina, with its Jewish chief executive, was under scrutiny. But this was not exceptional. The prominent French Jewish Louis-Dreyfus family was also seen as "endeavoring to get credits placed at the disposal of Germany." See material from the British Foreign Office, Oct. 1, 1940, quoted in Wilkins, *History ... 1914–1945*, 844n204.
161. As noted above, McDowall, *Light*, 348, says that the trade through Switzerland and Italy was done with the awareness of prominent individuals in London. Wilkins's research indicates that there were other cases – see the SKF story – where British officials turned a blind eye to trading with the enemy. Wilkins, *History ... 1914–1945*, 530–33. Heineman's political contacts in London would also serve him well.
162. "Fuerzas Motrices del Valle de Lecrin," typescript history in Box B11, S. Pearson & Son Papers. See also Luis Fernández-Revuelta, Donato Gómez, and Keith Robson, "Fuerzas Motrices del Valle de Lecrín, 1936–9," *Accounting, Business and Financial History,* 12:2 (July 2002), 347–66, for the company's experience during the civil war. Neither the typescript history nor the last cited article indicated the buyer of the company and its assets.
163. Gabriel Tortella, *The Development of Modern Spain* (Cambridge, MA: Harvard University Press, 2000), 300, 317–18; Fuerzas would come to be

owned by ENDESA, see Fernández-Revuelta, Gómez, and Robson, "Fuerzas Motrices del Valle de Lecrín, 1936–9," 348.

164. Alan S. Milward, *War, Economy and Society, 1939–1945* (Berkeley: University of California Press, 1979), 166 (Oriental Development and its Korean subsidiary).
165. William W. Lockwood, *The Economic Development of Japan* (Princeton: Princeton University Press, 1954), 126. Lockwood writes that all of Japan's 11,500 towns and villages (except for 199 small hamlets in remote parts of the country) had access to electricity by the end of the 1930s.
166. Vitalis, for example, documents a highly political story of "contesting national [foreign] interests" in the development of energy-intensive fertilizers in Egypt. Vitalis, *When Capitalists Collide*, 112–19.
167. On the switch from Sodec to CHADE (and the dissolution of Sodec), as well as the role of Sovalles, Inc., see Sofina, *Annual Report, 1940–1945*, 23, and *New York Times*, Sept. 16, 1947.
168. Ranieri, *Dannie Heineman*, 214–15 (on Heineman's trip to Argentina in 1942), Simon G. Hanson, *Economic Development in Latin America* (Washington, DC: Inter-American Affairs Press, 1951), 306–7. American & Foreign Power, "The Foreign Power System," booklet (New York: American & Foreign Power Co., 1953), 10; Bulmer-Thomas, *Economic History of Latin America*, 246; O'Brien, *Century of U.S. Capitalism*, 131, writes that in 1943 American & Foreign Power had two of its subsidiaries in Argentina expropriated; then in 1945, the Argentine government expropriated its properties in five provincial cities.
169. *New York Times*, Sept. 16, 1947.
170. Ibid. Heineman traveled to Lisbon in September 1943 to meet with executives of CHADE on the problems in Argentina; in 1944, he was in Spain, discussing the problems. Ranieri, *Dannie Heineman*, 216–17.
171. David F. Cavers and James R. Nelson, *Electric Power Regulation in Latin America* (Baltimore: Johns Hopkins University Press, 1959), 16; this firm had the same name as its Spanish counterpart and was established the same year. The firms were unrelated.
172. American & Foreign Power, "Foreign Power System," 10, 22.
173. For American & Foreign Power during most of the 1930s, it had been the other way around. Remittances from Latin America had been low because of exchange blockages, and for a number of years Shanghai Power's revenues had assisted in compensating for those low returns.
174. American & Foreign Power, "The Foreign Power System," 22, 26.
175. Harold James, *International Monetary Cooperation Since Bretton Woods* (New York: Oxford University Press, 1996), 18. The quoted passage was James's statement; we are attributing it to the 1944 planners.
176. For example, during the war years in Egypt, British policy makers tried to control the involvements of U.S. direct investors in the Egyptian industrial sector, fearing that Egypt might begin direct negotiations with Americans. The British government tried to support British trade over American trade, and this affected policies toward the Aswan Dam. Vitalis, *When Capitalists Collide*, 130, 134.

6 SUMMARY OF THE DOMESTICATION PATTERN TO 1978

1. Articles of Agreement for the International Monetary Fund and the World Bank had been drawn up in July 1944 at Bretton Woods. They became effective in December 1945 when in Washington, DC, twenty-eight governments endorsed the articles. The first explicit loans for electrification by the World Bank were made to the Chilean government-owned utilities Fomento and Endesa in March 1948. See historical chronology on the World Bank website (http://www.worldbank.org/, accessed July 3, 2006).
2. The word comes from Herbert Bratter, "Latin American Utilities' Nationalization Proceeds Inexorably," *Public Utilities Fortnightly*, 66 (July 7, 1960), 1–15. This was true not only in Latin America and not only for American & Foreign Power.
3. In the United States in 1950, investor-owned utilities produced 80 percent of net electricity generation by electric utilities. This percentage had fallen slightly to 77 percent by 1970. United States Bureau of the Census, *Historical Statistics of the United States: Colonial Times to 1970*, 2 vol. (Washington, DC: USGPO, 1975), II, 821.
4. Ulrich Wengenroth, "The Rise and Fall of State-Owned Enterprise in Germany," in Pier Angelo Toninelli, ed., *The Rise and Fall of State-Owned Enterprise in the Western World* (Cambridge: Cambridge University Press, 2000), 121. Bewag, discussed in Chapter 5, did not return to the Sofina fold after the war; its main power stations were in East Berlin, and its activities in a divided Berlin were fraught with difficulties. Liane Ranieri, *Dannie Heineman* (Brussels: Éditions Racine, 2005), 225.
5. Mira Wilkins, *The Maturing of Multinational Enterprise: American Business Abroad from 1914 to 1970* (Cambridge, MA: Harvard University Press, 1974), 302.
6. Duncan McDowall, *The Light: Brazilian Traction, Light and Power Company Ltd, 1899–1945* (Toronto: University of Toronto Press, 1988), 341.
7. Charles F. Mallory, "Financial Problems of the North American Electrical Utilities in Latin America," M.S. thesis, Massachusetts Institute of Technology, 1956, 34. He explains that in 1924 the Société Internationale d'Énergie Hydro-Électrique SA (Sidro) had begun purchasing securities of the Mexican Light and Power Group and soon achieved voting control. Sofina (Société Financière de Transports et d'Entreprises Industrielles) held important interests in Sidro and as of November 15, 1949, the "Sofina group" held 50.7 percent of the voting interest in the Mexican Light and Power Ltd. Ibid., 34n5. A reorganization occurred in 1950, after which "this Belgian group's voting interest dropped to 36.4 percent." His source was a Mexican Light & Power Co. circular from 1949. Mallory, "Financial Problems," 34n5.
8. For Mexlight in these years, see Ranieri, *Dannie Heineman*, 234–38.
9. See European Association for Banking History, *Handbook on the History of European Banks* (Aldershot, England: Edward Elgar, 1994), 1016, 1090. Ibid., 1092, gives its 1989 place in the Credit Suisse group. In the 1990s, Electrowatt (the 1974 successor to Electro-Watt) was described as a holding company in electric power, engineering, and contracting. In 1998, Siemens completed the acquisition from Credit Suisse of the "industrial part of Electrowatt, AG."

See Siemens's webpage (http://w4.siemens.de/archiv/en/index.html, accessed Sept. 26, 2007), and Wilfried Feldenkirchen, *Siemens: From Workshop to Global Player* (Munich: Piper, 2000), 394. For more on the postwar relations between Credit Suisse and Elektro-Watt and its successor Electrowatt, see Joseph Jung, *From Schweizerische Kreditanstalt to Credit Suisse Group* (Zurich: NZZ Verlag, 2000), 61, 94, 105–6. See also A. Steigenmeier, *Power on. Elektrowatt 1895–1995* (Zurich: Elecktrowatt, AG, 1995).

10. During the war years (in 1942), AEG had absorbed Gesellschaft für Elektrische Unternehmungen (Gesfürel), its related holding company in which Sofina had an important stake. After the war, Sofina received certain compensation for its investment in Gesfürel (and possibly for its investment in Bewag as well). Ranieri, *Dannie Heineman*, 226. AEG came out of World War II, revived its manufacturing, and expanded greatly in the 1950s and 1960s within Germany, only to be an ailing company by the end of the 1960s. It would be absorbed into Daimler-Benz in the mid-1980s and subsequently disappear as an independent business enterprise.
11. *Handbook on the History of European Banks*, 1016, and Hans Bauer, *Swiss Bank Corporation* (Basel: Swiss Bank Corporation, 1972), 309–10.
12. In *Moody's Manual (Bank and Finance)1978*, 1707, "Indelec Swiss Co. for Electric Industry, Basel," and "Indelec Finance SA, Basel," are listed as subsidiaries of Swiss Bank Corporation. In the 1930s, SBC had already been involved with Indelec. See Chapter 5, herein. But its post–World War II relationships with Indelec derived from the Basler Handelsbank heritage. Bauer, *Swiss Bank Corporation*, 392–93.
13. Employment figures for Motor-Columbus are in *Moody's Manual (Utilities) 1971*, 2075; these figures do not include the "group" companies in which Motor-Columbus (and Schweizerisch-Americanische Elektrizität-Gesellschaft) and Brown, Boveri had investments. In 1970, Compañía Italo-Argentina de Electricidad had 4,588 employees, while Lima Light & Power had 2,111 employees. *Moody's Manual (Utilities) 1971*, 2075, 2076, 2068. See Chapter 7 on Brown, Boveri's 1988 successor ABB ASEA Brown Boveri and on the subsequent history of Motor-Columbus.
14. On Heineman's role, 1945–1962, see Ranieri, *Dannie Heineman*, 220–95. In 1955, Sofina had 40 percent of its portfolio in U.S. securities. Ibid., 274.
15. Hugh Bullock, *The Story of Investment Companies* (New York: Columbia University Press, 1959), 1.
16. Charles Wilmer, who followed Heineman in the leadership of Sofina, had a modern-language degree; his successor was a banker. On the plans of Société Générale de Belgique, see *Wall Street Journal*, Nov. 27, 1964. The group headed by Société Générale de Belgique in this planned takeover included Medio Banca of Milan; the Luxemburg company Omnilux; the Boel group (an important Belgian family); Lazard Frères & Cie., Paris; and the Pearson group of London. The *Wall Street Journal* article indicated that about 38 percent of Sofina's holdings were in American securities, including large positions in Florida Power & Light, Middle South Utilities, and Oklahoma Gas & Electric Co.; these and others were clearly portfolio investments (note that this was down from the 40 percent in 1955, cited in a note above). By 1972, the value of

Sofina's electrical holdings was only 20 percent of its portfolio. Ranieri, *Dannie Heineman*, 295. The Boel family group was by then playing a key role in Sofina. Ibid.

17. In 1968, there would be a merger between Construction des Batignolles (Schneider) and Empain's principal holding company, Société Parisienne pour l'Industrie Électriques (SPIE), into a new company called Spie Batignolles. In 1981, Empain would split from what had come to be called the Empain-Schneider Group. For the complicated relations, see the websites for Schneider Electric (http://www.creusot.net/creusot/histoire/schneider/schneider.htm) and Areva (Jeumont) (http://www.jeumont-framatome.com/english/html/homepage) (both accessed March 7, 2006).
18. Emmanuel Chadeau, "The Rise and Decline of State-Owned Industry in Twentieth-Century France, in Toninelli, ed., *Rise and Fall of State-Owned Enterprise*, 189.
19. Marc Perrenoud, "La Diplomatie Suisse et les Relations Financières avec la France 1936–1945," in Sébastien Guex, ed., *La Suisse et les Grandes Puissances 1914–1945* (Geneva: Droz, 1999), 409, 409n84.
20. The Belgian firms appear to have had larger investments in France at the beginning of the 1930s than at the end. We noted in Chapter 5, for example, Sofina's reduction of its investments in Société Financière Électrique, Paris (Finelec), which in turn had investments in operating utilities in France. But Sofina retained interests in Société des Forces Motrices de Truyère, Compagnie Centrale d'Énergie Électrique, Compagnie Électrique de la Loire et du Centre, and Énergie Électrique du Nord de la France. For these companies and the postwar indemnification, see Ranieri, *Dannie Heineman*, 227–28. See ibid, 228n6 for the indemnification of Empain and Electrobel.
21. Wilkins, *Maturing of Multinational Enterprise*, 302.
22. Peter Eigner, "The Ownership of Austria's Big Business, 1895–1995," in Margarita Dritsas and Terry Gourvish, eds., *European Enterprise* (Athens: Trochalia Publications, 1997), 57.
23. Based on discussions with Luciano Segreto; see also Franco Amatori, "Beyond State and Market: Italy's Futile Search for a Third Way," in Toninelli, ed., *Rise and Fall of State-Owned Enterprise*, 132, for the 1962 foundation of Ente Nazionale per l'Energia Elettrica (ENEL) or, in English, the National Agency for Electric Power, which was to "monopolize the production and distribution of electric power in Italy."
24. See *New York Times*, Sept. 16, 1947 (on the ownership).
25. Ibid., Sept. 16, 1947, and Jan. 31, 1949.
26. See ibid., Sept. 21, 1949, and March 19, 1962; Albert Carreras, Xavier Tafunnell, and Eugenio Torres, "Against Integration: The Rise and Decline of Spanish State-Owned Firms and the Decline and Rise of Multinationals, 1939–1990," in Ulf Olsson, ed., *Business and European Integration Since 1800* (Gothenburg, Sweden: Graphic Systems, 1997), 46; and Gabriel Tortella, *The Development of Modern Spain* (Cambridge, MA: Harvard University Press, 2000), 352. See also John Brooks, "Annals of Finance," *New Yorker*, May 21, 1979, and May 28, 1979. The bankruptcy was seen by Sofina and others as invalid, for there were abundant assets and the problem was Spanish

government restrictions on remittances, so foreign obligations could not be met.

27. The U.S. view reflected Heineman's opinions. Heineman, a U.S. citizen, after the war decided he wanted to reside in the United States. He had friends in Washington, DC, who pushed Sofina interests (albeit not as strongly as Heineman would have liked). On the so-called Barcelona Traction affair and March, see Ranieri, *Dannie Heineman*, 255–72.
28. *New York Times*, March 19, 1962; Tortella, *Development of Modern Spain*, 352.
29. For the entire extraordinary story, see John Brooks, "Annals of Finance," *New Yorker*, May 21, 1979 and May 28, 1979, and Herbert W. Briggs, "Barcelona Traction: The Jus Standi of Belgium," *American Journal of International Law*, 65:2 (April 1971), 327–45. Brooks describes March as unscrupulous. By contrast, Briggs, who counseled the Spanish government in the preparation of its pleadings in this case over a period of seven years (1963 to 1969), found the judgment of the court "soundly reasoned." By the time of the decision, March was dead of a car accident in 1966 at the age of 81, as was Heineman, who died at age 84 in 1962.
30. *Moody's Manual (Utilities) 1980* (each annual issue of *Moody's Manual (Utilities)* contained unnumbered pages with lists of companies formerly included and the last issue in which they were listed; there followed a brief explanation of the reason for dropping the company).
31. Wilkins, *Maturing of Multinational Enterprise*, 302; American & Foreign Power Co., "The Foreign Power System" booklet (New York: American & Foreign Power Co., 1953), 10.
32. Robert L. Tignor, *Egyptian Textiles and British Capital 1930–1956* (Cairo: American University in Cairo Press, 1989), 100.
33. Céline Boileau, "La Production Électrique Destinée à l'Industrie Minière en Afrique du Sud (1880–1922)," in Dominique Barjot, Daniel Lefeuvre, Arnaud Berthonnet, and Sophie Coeuré, eds., *L'Électrification Outre-mer de la Fin du XIXe Siècle aux Première Décolonisations* (Paris: EDF, 2002), 476. In 1948, when this takeover occurred, South African mining interests had large stakes in Victoria Falls and Transvaal Power Co., as they had for years. It could be argued that "domestication" had occurred earlier, for the mining interests were "South African" and not really "U.K. foreign direct investments." Because these companies in 1948 still had "headquarters" in London, we have counted this as foreign direct investment.
34. http://www.winne.com/algena3/to12frinter.html, accessed Dec.19, 2005. Ranieri writes that two companies in which Sofina had interests were nationalized in 1950 under Algerian law. Ranieri, *Dannie Heineman*, 228. While she does not specify, these were probably Société Algérienne d'Éclairage et de Force, Algiers, and Société des Forces Motrices d'Algérie, Algiers.
35. Based on discussion with and data supplied by David Merrett.
36. Wilkins, *Maturing of Multinational Enterprise*, 302.
37. On the tramway and Rosario companies, see Ranieri, *Dannie Heineman*, 229–30.
38. José Gómez-Ibáñez, *Regulating Infrastructure: Monopoly, Contracts, and Discretion* (Cambridge, MA: Harvard University Press, 2003), 139. On

Heineman's frustrations over what was happening in Argentina, see Ranieri, *Dannie Heineman*, 232–33. Heineman retired in 1955, and after his retirement the new directors of Sofina preferred to disengage from the Argentine business.

39. *New York Times*, Sept. 16, 1947; American & Foreign Power, *Annual Report 1952*, 4, 16.
40. American & Foreign Power, *Annual Report 1954*, 21–22.
41. The quotations are in American & Foreign Power, *Annual Report 1955*, 17–18. On the ANSEC group of companies, see notes to Chapter 4.
42. American & Foreign Power, *Annual Report 1952*, 19.
43. Ibid.
44. Ibid., 5.
45. Ibid.
46. David F. Cavers and James R. Nelson, *Electric Power Regulation in Latin America* (Baltimore: Johns Hopkins University Press, 1959), 16.
47. Ibid., 16–17.
48. Ibid., 16–19.
49. American & Foreign Power Co., "Foreign Power System," 32.
50. Ibid.
51. Ibid., 34.
52. Robert L. Tignor, *Capitalism and Nationalism at the End of Empire: State and Business in Decolonizing Egypt, Nigeria, and Kenya, 1945–1963* (Princeton: Princeton University Press, 1998), 104–10 (on the Aswan Dam affair); on Hoctief history see Marc Linder, *Projecting Capitalism: A History of the Internationalization of the Construction Industry* (Westport, Conn.: Greenwood Press, 1994), 87, 89–90, 137, 140, 201, 204, 211, 220; on the 1920s–1930s unrealized plans for the Aswan dam, the wartime experiences, and the period after 1945, see the well-told narrative in Robert Vitalis, *When Capitalists Collide: Business Conflict and the End of Empire in Egypt* (Berkeley: University of California Press, 1995), 56, 63–103, 105–135, 144–168.
53. Vitalis, *When Capitalists Collide*, 142, 145, 148–150.
54. Tignor, *Capitalism and Nationalism*,108–153 on the events of 1956–1957.
55. The statistics in ibid., 143, suggest some French investments in utilities.
56. Ibid., 154, and e-mail Robert Tignor to Mira Wilkins, March 2, 2006, which indicated that Lebon & Co. involved Belgian capital and was nationalized in this wave of nationalizations. Nasser's expropriations, 1956–1967, involved seven separate acts and seventy firms. See Charles R. Kennedy, Jr., "Relations Between Transnational Corporations and Governments of Host Countries," *Transnational Corporations*, 1:1 (Feb. 1992), 73.
57. Kennedy, "Relations Between Transnational Corporations and Governments of Host Countries," 73, and passim.
58. Mallory, "Financial Problems," 1.
59. See Wilkins, *Maturing of Multinational Enterprise*, on these properties.
60. Ibid., and Mallory, "Financial Problems," 17, which did not include Kennecott or the Oroya refinery.
61. Mallory, "Financial Problems," 14.
62. There were similar problems related to foreign provision of telephone service, which we will not discuss.

63. Mallory, "Financial Problems," 15.
64. Wilkins, *Maturing of Multinational Enterprise*, 361; see also American & Foreign Power, *Annual Report 1960*, 7; see list of major corporate claims against Cuba in Paul E. Sigmund, *Multinationals in Latin America: The Politics of Nationalization* (Madison: University of Wisconsin Press, 1980), 127; the claim is listed under "Cuban Electric Company (Boise-Cascade)," for American & Foreign Power's successor company, Ebasco Industries, was merged into Boise Cascade Corporation in 1969.
65. Mira Wilkins, interviews with key American & Foreign Power executives in 1964. Fidel Castro, as early as July 26, 1953, had spoken of the need to nationalize the electricity "trusts." Sigmund, *Multinationals in Latin America*, 90. No one at American & Foreign Power realized that if he took leadership of the country, he would do just that.
66. Wilkins, *Maturing of Multinational Enterprise*, 362, for the terms; better still, see American & Foreign Power, *Annual Report 1958*, 6, 18–19.
67. Gómez-Ibáñez, *Regulating Infrastructure* 124–25, 139. Heineman retired in 1955; he was extremely unhappy about what was going on in Argentina.
68. *Moody's Manual (Utilities) 1971*, 2075 (on the renewal of its concession). Argentine president Isabel Perón told a Peronist rally in October 1974 that her government was going to "Argentinize" the Italo-Argentine Electric Co. *Wall Street Journal*, Oct. 18, 1974. Gómez-Ibáñez, *Regulating Infrastructure*, 139 (our source for the actual end of the firm's business in Argentina in 1979).
69. American & Foreign Power, *Annual Report 1958*, 47. See Wilkins, *Maturing of Multinational Enterprise*, 362, for the actual payment terms.
70. American & Foreign Power, *Annual Report 1960*, 7; about 12 percent of the securities, $35 million, was owned by the U.S. Export-Import Bank, six major U.S. banks, and other U.S. investors, including large mutual funds, bringing the total U.S. investments to 72 percent; most of the rest appears to have been owned by individuals resident within Cuba. In Cuba, as elsewhere, American & Foreign Power had brought in local investors.
71. There was a loss in Argentina, because the compensation did not fully cover the investment. In Cuba, there was no compensation.
72. See Wilkins, *Maturing of Multinational Enterprise*, 362, and American & Foreign Power, *Annual Report 1960*, 7, for the terms.
73. Gómez-Ibáñez, *Regulating Infrastructure*, 124–25, 129; as noted earlier, in 1950 Sofina's interest had been reduced to a minority holding.
74. Miguel S. Wionczek, "Electric Power," in Raymond Vernon, ed., *Public Policy and Private Enterprise in Mexico* (Cambridge, MA: Harvard University Press, 1964), 75–76; the difference – 27 percent – was made up of small public and private plants, including some remaining foreign investors.
75. *Moody's Manual (Utilities) 1971*, 2007, 2009–10.
76. Wionczek, "Electric Power," Ch. 6, discusses the final steps in 1960–1962 in the Mexican government takeovers.
77. Wilkins, *Maturing of Multinational Enterprise*, 362; American & Foreign Power, *Annual Report 1961*, 17.
78. American & Foreign Power, *Annual Report 1961*, 17; see also American & Foreign Power, *Annual Report 1962*, 10.

79. American & Foreign Power, *Annual Report 1959*, 13.
80. American & Foreign Power, *Annual Report 1961*, 14.
81. American & Foreign Power, *Annual Report 1962*, 9.
82. Wilkins, *Maturing of Multinational Enterprise*, 362.
83. McDowall, *Light*, 393–95.
84. American & Foreign Power, *Annual Report 1963*, 8. The agreement was made on January 17, 1964; the closing took place on February 13, 1964. See also Gómez-Ibáñez, *Regulating Infrastructure*, 146–50, for background.
85. We have put this together from Mallory, "Financial Problems," 105; *Moody's Manual (Utilities) 1971*, 2007–10, on the parent company; and Gómez-Ibáñez, *Regulating Infrastructure*, 125, 150, who suggests that the Barquisimeto subsidiary was nationalized at the same time as the Maracaibo one and gives the 1976 date; we think he is probably wrong.
86. Wilkins, *Maturing of Multinational Enterprise*, 362.
87. Stephen D. Krasner, *Defending the National Interest: Raw Material Investments and U.S. Foreign Policy* (Princeton: Princeton University Press, 1978), 299–302, 312.
88. Gómez-Ibáñez, *Regulating Infrastructure*, 125; Kennedy, "Relations Between Transnational Corporations and Governments of Host Countries," 73.
89. McDowall, *Light*, 395; *Moody's Manual (Utilities) 1971*, 2017.
90. *Moody's Manual (Utilities) 1971*, 2017.
91. See McDowall, *Light*, 395–98.
92. Gómez-Ibáñez, *Regulating Infrastructure*, 116.
93. Kari Levitt, *Silent Surrender: The Multinational Corporation in Canada* (Toronto: Macmillan of Canada, 1970), xix, 121.
94. Dannie N. Heineman, "The Changing International Environment," address to the general meeting of shareholders of Société Financière de Transports et d'Entreprises Industrielles (Sofina), April 22, 1954 (published in booklet form), 19.
95. The present volume has shown a long history of multinational enterprises. On the overall history of U.S. multinational enterprise, readers are once more referred to Mira Wilkins, *The Emergence of Multinational Enterprise: American Business Abroad from the Colonial Era to 1914* (Cambridge, MA: Harvard University Press, 1970), and *Maturing of Multinational Enterprise*. For the history of all multinational enterprise, see Geoffrey Jones, *Multinationals and Global Capitalism from the Nineteenth to the Twenty-First Century* (Oxford: Oxford University Press, 2005); a brief historical summary is in Mira Wilkins, "Multinational Enterprise to 1930: Discontinuities and Continuities," in Alfred Chandler and Bruce Mazlish, eds., *Leviathans: Multinational Corporations and the New Global History* (Cambridge: Cambridge University Press, 2005), 45–79, and Geoffrey Jones, "Multinationals from the 1930s to the 1980s," in ibid., 81–103.
96. There were exceptions. For example, Standard Oil of New Jersey (through Esso Eastern) entered into a 1964 60–40 joint venture with China Light & Power Co. in Hong Kong. See Bennett H. Wall, *Growth in a Changing Environment: A History of Standard Oil Company (New Jersey), 1950–1972 and Exxon Corporation 1972–1975* (New York: McGraw-Hill, 1988), 515–16, 523–25.

97. In 1970, 68.9 percent of the crude oil production outside of the United States and communist countries was produced by the then seven major international oil companies and 8.4 percent by producing countries' state-owned oil companies. In 1979, the figures were 23.9 percent and 68.7 percent. Raymond Vernon, *Two Hungry Giants: The United States and Japan in the Quest for Oil and Ores* (Cambridge, MA: Harvard University Press, 1983), 27. (To get the 100 percent, one needs to add in "other international oil companies," which produced 22.7 percent in 1970 and 7.4 percent in 1979).
98. Ibid., 27 (seven major international oil companies). The estimate of less than 1 percent of world electric power is that of the authors of the present book.
99. In 1979, Brascan was acquired by the Canadians Edward and Peter Bronfman (cousins of Charles and Edgar Bronfman, who inherited control of Seagram's). Edward and Peter Bronfman were buying a collection of companies. Brascan became an investment house. Graham D. Taylor and Peter A. Baskerville, *A Concise History of Business in Canada* (Toronto: Oxford University Press, 1994), 444. By 1986, Edward and Peter Bronfman would control well over 100 companies. *New York Times*, Nov. 9, 1986. For some of the companies in their trust-fund-turned-holding company (as of 1997), see "A Canadian Business Group," in Randall Morck, "How to Eliminate Pyramidal Business Groups – The Double Taxation of Inter-Corporate Dividends and Other Incisive Uses of Tax Policy," NBER Working Paper 10944, Dec. 2004, 39. See also Chapter 7 herein for more on Brascan as of 2004–2006.
100. These generalizations were not true in every country, but overall they seem legitimate.
101. See Raymond Vernon, *Sovereignty at Bay: The Spread of U.S. Multinational Enterprise* (New York: Basic Books, 1971), for the early articulation of the "obsolescing bargain" concept. During the 1970s and 1980s, it was much discussed among students of multinational enterprises. See, for example, Theodore H. Moran, ed., *Multinational Corporations: The Political Economy of Foreign Direct Investment* (Lexington, MA: Lexington Books, 1985), 6, and passim.

7 COMING FULL CIRCLE, 1978–2007, AND A GLOBAL PERSPECTIVE

1. See, for example, R.W. Bacon and J. Desant-Jones, "Global Electric Power Reform, Privatization and Liberalization of the Electric Power Companies in Developing Countries," *Annual Reviews Energy and the Environment*, 26 (2001), 331–59.
2. In the United States, "deregulation" often has been associated with the administration of Ronald Reagan; however, the vast majority of regulatory reform bills actually were enacted during the presidency of Jimmy Carter. No major government-owned electric power operation in the United States (e.g., Tennessee Valley Authority, Bonneville Power Administration, etc.) was ever privatized. Margaret Thatcher, who became prime minister of Great Britain in 1979, is closely associated with the privatization movement, including privatization of the electric utility industry. Richard H.K. Vietor, *Contrived*

Competition: Regulation and Deregulation in America (Cambridge, MA: Harvard University Press, 1994), 15; Richard Green, "Electricity Deregulation in England and Wales," *Topics in Regulatory Economics and Policy*, no. 28 (1998), 179–202.

3. OECD/IEA, *Electricity Supply Industry: Structure, Ownership and Regulation in OECD Countries* (Paris: OECD/IEA, 1994), 23 (http://www.iea.org/textbase/nppdf/free/1990/electricity_supply1994.pdf, accessed June 22, 2006).
4. Martin Chick argues that the breakdown of traditional arrangements in Europe was caused by "the deterioration in public finances during the 1970s, growing exasperation with the agency problems affecting the government-industry relationship, and the recognition that technological progress had made alternatives to the existing vertically integrated monopolies potentially economically and politically attractive." Martin Chick, "The Power of Networks: Defining the Boundaries of the Natural Monopoly Network and the Implications for the Restructuring of the Electricity Supply Industry," *Annales Historiques de l'Électricité* (June 2004), 89–106 at 92. Also see the preface in Pier Angelo Toninelli, *The Rise and Fall of State-Owned Enterprise in the Western World* (Cambridge: Cambridge University Press, 2000), ix, where he notes, "During the 1980s and 1990s, a major wave of disenchantment with state intervention swept through the industrial nations. In those years the fortunes of SOEs [state-owned enterprises] reached their nadir, and countries, such as Italy, that had previously resisted privatization started a massive dismantling of public undertakings."
5. "In the early 1990s, the World Bank decided to finance projects mainly in states that 'demonstrate a commitment to implement a comprehensive reform of the power sector, privatize distribution, and facilitate private participation in generation and environment reforms.' This marks a change from the period before 1993, when the World Bank financed mostly large-scale generation projects. ... The overall strategy of the Asian Development Bank (ADB) for the power sector is to support restructuring, especially the promotion of competition and private-sector participation." OECD/IEA, *Electricity in India* (Washington, DC: OECD/IEA, 2002), 70–71.
6. Witold J. Henisz, Bennet A. Zelner, and Mauro F. Guillén, "International Coercion, Emulation and Policy Diffusion: Market-Oriented Infrastructure Reforms, 1977–1999," Working Paper, June 17, 2004 (http://papers.ssrn.com/sol3/papers.cfm?abstract_id=557140, accessed May 31, 2006).
7. Fernando Manibog, Rafael Dominguez, and Stephan Wegner, *Power for Development: A Review of the World Bank Group's Experience with Private Participation in the Electricity Sector* (Washington, DC: World Bank, 2003), 1. The potential competitiveness of the generation function was enhanced by technological changes in generating equipment. The minimum efficient scale, for example, of combined-cycle gas generators was substantially lower than that of the traditional coal-fired and nuclear base-load generators, leading to a substantial reduction in barriers to entry. U.S. Department of Energy, Energy Information Administration, *The Changing Structure of the Electric Power Industry 2000: An Update*, Oct. 2000 (http://www.eia.doe.gov/cneaf/electricity/chg_stru_update/chapter5.html#tech, accessed June 2, 2006).

8. According to a 1994 OECD report, "The electricity supply industry (ESI) worldwide, and in many OECD countries in particular, has been subject to reform and change for more than a decade. Driven by political and economic considerations, a number of Member countries have introduced significant structural, institutional, and regulatory changes and have drastically transformed their ESI's." OECD/IEA, *Electricity Supply Industry*, 20. Reactions recently have occurred, and the wisdom of unbundling generation from the other functions has been challenged in the United States, even by market advocates. See, for example, the Cato Institute publication by Robert J. Michaels, "Vertical Integration and the Restructuring of the U.S. Electricity Industry," *Policy Analysis* 572 (July 13, 2006).
9. Timothy J. Brennan, et al., *A Shock to the System: Restructuring America's Electricity Industry* (Washington, DC: Resources for the Future, 1996), 10. This legislation was followed by major energy policy acts in 1992 and 2005 that further opened up the electricity system in the United States to competition, thus also opening the door to foreign investment. The 2005 act also repealed the Public Utility Holding Company Act of 1935. At the same time, there were major changes in bank regulation in the United States. The Glass-Steagall Act of 1933 was repealed in 1999, which greatly widened the range of financial services in which banks were allowed to participate. The act opened the way for banks to participate once again in public utilities finance. James R. Barth, R. Dan Brumbaugh, and James A Wilcox, "Policy Watch: The Repeal of Glass-Steagall and the Advent of Broad Banking," *Journal of Economic Perspectives* 14 (Spring 2000), 191–204.
10. Privatization laws were passed in Argentina in 1990, Colombia in 1991, Peru in 1992, Bolivia in 1994, and Brazil in 1995. Victoria Murillo and Cecilia Martínez-Gallardo, "Political Competition and Policy Adoption," Institute for Social and Economic Research Policy, Working Paper 2005–06 (New York: Columbia University, 2005), Table 1. Murillo and Martínez-Gallardo argue (p. 1) that the pressure to adopt market-oriented policies was more intense in capital-scarce developing countries than it was in developed countries. Specifically regarding Latin America, they see such pressures as a legacy of the debt crisis of the early 1980s, with its shortages of domestic capital and heightened fiscal deficits. These factors also played a role in some Asian countries. See James H. Williams and Navroz K. Dubash, "Asian Electricity Reform in Historical Perspective," *Pacific Affairs*, 77 (Fall 2004), 411–36.
11. By 2000, Endesa (Chile) and Enersis had been taken over by Endesa (Spain), which had become a private company in 1998. In 2006, Endesa (Spain) had become the object of a takeover bid by the German utility E.ON (a company that will be discussed below). The remaining domestic Chilean companies continued to expand within Latin America, adding operations in Bolivia, Colombia, and the Dominican Republic. U.S. Department of Energy, Energy Information Administration, *Privatization and the Globalization of Energy Markets* (Washington, DC: EIA, Oct. 1996), Table A3. The online version (http://www.eia.doe.gov/emeu/pgem/contents.html, accessed June 13, 2006) contains cross-national ownership tables updated in June 2000.

12. William W. Hogan, "Electricity Market Restructuring: Reform of Reforms," *Journal of Regulatory Economics*, 21 (2002), 125. For a detailed account of the restructuring in England and Wales, see U.S. Department of Energy, Energy Information Administration, *Electricity Reform Abroad and U.S. Investment* (Washington, DC: EIA, Sept. 1997), Ch. 2 (http://www.eia.doe.gov/emeu/pgem/electric/contents.html, accessed June 14, 2006).
13. OECD/IEA, *Competition in Electricity Markets* (Paris: OECD/IEA, 2001), 29–30. For a more extensive listing of the various forms of market-based reforms in the industry in various countries around the world, see Bacon and Jones, "Global Electric Power," esp. 7–8. While it is still very early to assess the impact of the increased reliance on competition and the electricity market, one recent study of the New York Independent Systems Operator (NYISO) found that extreme volatility in prices existed, much greater than in traditional commodity markets, caused in large part by transmission congestion. As the authors note, "Reducing congestion is a difficult task to implement and is part of the ongoing capital investment problem that continues to plague the electricity industry today." Lester Hadsell and Jany A. Shawky, "Electricity Price Volatility and the Marginal Cost of Congestion: An Empirical Study of Peak Hours on the NYISO Market, 2001–2004," *The Energy Journal*, 27 (2006), 177.
14. Independent power producers generally did not invest in transmission or distribution. Various clusters and consortia often were created to purchase a power generator or build a new one (greenfield investment) in a foreign country. In July 2002, for example, Brazil sold the concession to an existing 1,078 MW plant in Tocantins state to a group led by Tractebel (discussed later in the text of the chapter) that included Alcoa, the British-Australian BHP Billiton, and two Brazilian companies. *New York Times*, July 13, 2002.
15. A study by the U.S. Energy Information Administration contains information on investments made by foreign firms in response to the privatization and liberalization movement, using information from company annual reports in 1998 and 1999. Much of the following discussion is based on U.S. Department of Energy, Energy Information Administration, *Privatization and the Globalization of Energy Markets* (Washington, DC: EIA, 1996), data updated June 2000 (http://www.eia.doe.gov/emeu/pgem/contents.html, accessed June 13, 2006).
16. In 2000 its nuclear power business, head office in the United States, was sold to U.K.-based BNFL, while its power generation business (a 50 percent interest in ABB Alstom Power) was sold to the French firm Alstom. See http://www.abb.com/, accessed Oct. 2, 2007.
17. On the dismemberment of AEG's operations in the 1990s, see *New York Times*, Jan. 26, 1996; on AEG-Telefunken's collapse in the early 1980s, see *New York Times*, Aug. 22, 1982.
18. *New York Times*, Aug. 4, 1998.
19. *New York Times*, May 29, 1999; Oct. 3, 2000; Dec. 23, 2000; May 13, 2001; Sept. 13, 2001; Feb. 20, 2002; Aug. 30, 2002; March 4, 2003; and Aug. 7, 2003. Even with its difficulties, AES continued operating in twenty-four countries and by the end of 2005 was ready to start investing again. It announced a $1.3 billion Bulgarian power project in Dec. 2005. *Wall Street*

Journal, Dec. 7, 2005 (http://www.aes.com/aes/index?page=home, accessed July 3, 2006).

20. ExxonMobil's investments in China (Hong Kong) date from 1964, when Esso and China Light and Power formed Peninsula Electric Power Co. Ltd., 60 percent owned by Esso, to be the main generator of electricity for China Light and Power. Nigel Cameron, *Power: The Story of China Light* (Hong Kong: Oxford University Press, 1982), 200–5.
21. OECD/IEA, *Electricity in India*, 7–73 (http://www.msnbc.com/id/12984163/, accessed May 31, 2006).
22. However, as of mid-2006, Hydro One did not appear to have any foreign assets (http://www.hydroone.com/, accessed July 3, 2006).
23. http://www.fortisinc.com/, accessed July 5, 2006.
24. See http://www.fundinguniverse.com/company-histories/Brascan-Corporation-Company-History.html, accessed Sept. 26, 2007. Several other Canadian firms or funds owned or controlled foreign assets, including EPCOR Power L.P., Algonquin Power Income Fund, Boralex Power Income Fund, and Atlantic Power.
25. "The Odd Couple," *The Economist*, July 29, 2006, 61. EDF is the largest European electric utility in terms of electricity generated. In 2005, EDF received 59 percent of its sales revenue in France, 35 percent in other European countries, and 6 percent in the rest of the world (http://www.edf.fr/html/ra_2005/uk/pdf/ra2005_corporate_01_va.pdf, accessed July 3, 2006).
26. The German utility RWE had acquired a 20 percent stake in Motor-Columbus in 1995, which it held until 2004 when UBS obtained RWE's stake and gained a controlling interest. In December 2005, UBS announced the sale of its shares to a consortium of Atel's Swiss minority shareholders and to EDF. In 2006, Atel generated electricity in four European countries and had operations in sixteen others (http://www.motor-columbus.ch/en/investor/shareholders.html, accessed July 31, 2006; http://www.atel.ch/en/index.jsp, accessed July 31, 2006).
27. International Power in mid-2006 had assets in the United States, six European countries (including the United Kingdom), three Middle Eastern countries, Australia, and four Asian countries (http://www.ipplc.com/ipplc/, accessed June 30, 2006).
28. Some smaller utilities were owned by Canadian companies. See Table 6.1 herein for the foreign interests.
29. Scottish Power did not completely withdraw from the U.S. market, retaining some utility assets in the West (http://www.ppmenergy.com/wwd.html, accessed July 3, 2006). MidAmerican Energy owns distribution assets in the United Kingdom. According to the *New York Times* (Aug. 7, 2003), "One of the few American investors to do well in Britain is Warren E. Buffett, analysts say. Mr. Buffett concentrates on the networks that carry the energy, rather than the power plants themselves."
30. *Wall Street Journal*, Nov. 29, 2006; http://www.scottishpower.com/ accessed Oct. 2, 2007. The newly-formed company announced the purchase of a US generating plant in September 2007.
31. http://www.nationalgrid.com/, accessed July 3, 2006; and http://www.nationalgridus.com/information/, accessed Oct. 2, 2007.

32. *The Economist*, Feb. 25, 2006, 71; *New York Times*, July 29, 2006; Arturo Bris, "Global Growing Pains," *Financial Times* (London), June 2, 2006. As of mid-2006, E.ON operated in twelve Central European countries, three Northern European countries, the United Kingdom, and the United States. EON *Annual Report*, 2005 (http://www.eon.com/en/downloads/EON_GB_E_komplett_geschuetzt_060309.pdf, accessed July 3, 2006).
33. *The Economist*, April 7, 2007, 63.
34. Suez also became in 2003 the majority shareholder of Electrabel (http://www.tractebel.be/index-en.htm, accessed July 3, 2006; http://www.suez.com/groupe/english/histoire/index3.php, accessed July 3, 2006).
35. Stacy Meichtry, "Enel Runs into Dilemma over Where to Spend," *Wall Street Journal*, June 13, 2006, B4; "Patriot Games," *The Economist*, July 1, 2006, 12, "For Europe's Utilities, a Frenzied Power Grab," *Wall Street Journal*, April 11, 2007, A1.
36. http://www.vattenfall.com/www/vf_com/vf_com/365787ourxc/367425histo/index.jsp, accessed July 3, 2006.
37. http://www.acciona-energia.com/, accessed July 6, 2006.
38. http://www.heh.com/hehWeb/Index_en and http://www.ckh.com.hk/eng/index.htm, accessed Aug. 29, 2006.
39. http://www.jpower.co.jp/english/company_info/jpower/aisatu/index.html, accessed Aug. 29, 2006.
40. BTU Power was established in 2001 to invest in energy industries in the Middle East and North Africa, where it owns generating facilities. BTU's shareholders include publicly traded companies as well as individual investors in the Gulf Cooperation Council countries. The company has offices in Massachusetts and Dubai (http://pepei.pennnet.com/Articles/Article_Display.cfm?Section=OnArt&Subsection=Display&ARTICLE_ID=205934&KEYWORD=middle percent20east, accessed Aug. 29, 2006).
41. http://www.meiyapower.com/eng/about/index.htm, accessed Aug. 29, 2006.
42. http://www.singaporepower.com.sg/index.html, accessed Aug. 29, 2006.
43. http://www.ytl.com.my/utilities.asp, accessed Aug. 29, 2006.
44. http://www.sumitomocor co.jp/english/, accessed July 6, 2006.
45. http://www.tepco.co.jp/en/press/corp-com/release/06121101-e.html, accessed Dec. 28, 2006.
46. For a summary, see Steve Thomas, David Hall, and Violeta Corral, "Electricity Privatisation and Restructuring in Asia-Pacific," report commissioned by Public Services International, Dec. 2004 (http://www.psiru.org/reports/2004-12-E-Asia.doc, accessed Aug. 29, 2006).
47. This is the case even though there is a continuing need for investment, especially in developing countries. "In the power sector alone, the IEA (2003) has estimated that to keep pace with growing demand, developing countries will have to invest annually around $120 billion over the period 2001–2010. During the 1990s, private capital flows made a substantial contribution to meeting the needs in some countries. Private flows have fallen considerably in recent years. From a peak of $50 billion in 1997, investment in power projects with private participation in developing countries fell to around $14 billion in 2003." Ian Alexander and Clive Harris, *The Regulation of Investment in*

Utilities, World Bank Working Paper, 52 (Washington, DC: World Bank, 2005), 1.

48. Williams and Dubash, "Asian Electricity Reform," 430. Paul Joskow, an economist who has consistently supported restructuring, cautioned utilities not to blame the reforms for the resulting problems but rather the specific implementation of the reforms in California. He acknowledged, however that the crisis had "attracted attention around the world." Paul L. Joskow, "California's Electricity Crisis," *Oxford Review of Economic Policy*, 17:3 (2001), p 365–88 at 365. Armstrong and Sappington, while warning about some of the pitfalls of restructuring, call the California experience "legendary." Mark Armstrong and David E. Sappington, "Regulation, Competition, and Liberalization," *Journal of Economic Literature*, 44 (June 2006), 329.
49. Carles Boix, "Privatization and Public Discontent in Latin America" (Washington, DC: Inter-American Development Bank, 2005), 1. Also see "Slow! Government Obstacles Ahead," *The Economist*, June 17, 2006, 41, which asserts that "the flow of private money for electricity, water and transport has dried up in many countries, partly because citizens or politicians turned against privatization." Amy L. Chua has argued that there is a natural cycle of privatization and nationalization in less developed countries and that neither condition is likely ever to be permanent. Amy L. Chua, "The Privatization-Nationalization Cycle: The Link Between Markets and Ethnicity in Developing Countries," *Columbia Law Review*, 95 (March 1995), 223–303.
50. William Keegan, "Anxiety of Ownership," *Guardian Unlimited*, June 19, 2006.
51. See Alexander and Harris, *The Regulation of Investment in Utilities*, 2.
52. For insightful comments on some of these risks, see Donald R. Lessard, "Risk and the Dynamics of Globalization," in Julian Birkinshaw, ed., *Future of the Multinational Company* (Chichester, England: John Wiley, 2003), 76–85.
53. This is probably what happened in England and Wales, where several U.S. firms had such trouble recently.
54. See, for example, "The Don't Invest in America Act," *Wall Street Journal*, July 19, 2006. Also see Edward W. Graham and David M. Marchick, *US National Security and Foreign Direct Investment* (Washington, D.C.: Institute for International Economics, 2006).
55. *New York Times*, Jan. 9, 2007.

Select Bibliography

Adams, Edward Dean, *Niagara Power: History of Niagara Falls Power Company*, 2 vol. (Niagara Falls, NY: Niagara Falls Power Co., 1927).

Amatori, Franco, "Beyond State and Market: Italy's Futile Search for a Third Way," in Pier Angelo Toninelli, ed., *The Rise and Fall of State-Owned Enterprise in the Western World* (Cambridge: Cambridge University Press, 2000), 128–56.

American & Foreign Power Co., *Annual Reports, 1927–1963*.

American & Foreign Power Co., "The Foreign Power System" (booklet; New York: American & Foreign Power Co., 1953).

Antolín, Francesca, "Global Strategies and National Performance: Explaining the Singularities of the Spanish Electricity Supply Industry," *Business and Economic History On-Line*, I (2003).

Armstrong, Christopher, and H. V. Nelles, *Monopoly's Moment: The Organization and Regulation of Canadian Utilities, 1830–1930* (Philadelphia: Temple University Press, 1986).

Armstrong, Christopher, and H. V. Nelles, *Southern Exposure: Canadian Promoters in Latin America and the Caribbean, 1896–1930* (Toronto: University of Toronto Press, 1988).

Aubanell-Jubany, Anna M., "Cartel Stability in the Electricity Industry: The Case of Electricity Distribution in Madrid in the Inter-war Period," *Business and Economic History On-Line*, I (2003).

Aubanell-Jubany, Anna M., "La Industria Eléctrica y la Electrificación en Madrid entre 1890 y 1935," Ph.D. thesis, European University Institute, Florence, 2001.

Bacon, R. W., and J. Desant-Jones, "Global Electric Power Reform, Privatization and Liberalization of the Electric Power Companies in Developing Countries," *Annual Reviews Energy and the Environment*, 26 (2001), 331–59.

Baer, Werner, and Curt McDonald, "A Return to the Past? Brazil's Privatization of Public Utilities: The Case of the Electric Power Sector," *Quarterly Review of Economics and Finance*, 38 (Autumn 1998), 503–23.

Bank für Elektrische Unternehmungen, *50. Geschäftsbericht der Bank für Elektrische Unternehmungen, Zurich, 1944–1945*.

Barba Navaretti, Giorgio, and Anthony J. Venables, *Multinational Firms in the World Economy* (Princeton: Princeton University Press, 2004).

Barbero, Maria Ines, "Grupos Empresarios, Intercambio Comercial e Inversiones Italianas en la Argentina," *Estudios Migratorios Latinoamericanos* 5 (1990), 311–41.

Barjot, Dominique, *La Grande Entreprise Française de Travaux Publics (1883–1974)* (Paris: Economica, 2006).

Barjot, Dominique, "Le Rôle des Entrepreneurs de Travaux Publics: L'Exemple du Groupe Giros et Loucheur (1899–1946)," in Monique Trédé-Boulmer, ed., *Le Financement de l'Industrie Électrique 1880–1980* (Paris: PUF, 1994), 69–100.

Barjot, Dominique, Daniel Lefeuvre, Arnaud Berthonnet, and Sophie Coeuré, eds., *L'Électrification Outre-mer de la Fin du XIXe Siècle aux Première Décolonisations* (Paris: EDF, [n.d.; 2002?]).

Barjot, Dominique, Henri Morsel, and Sophie Coeuré, eds., *Stratégies, Gestion, Management: Les Compagnies Électriques et Leurs Patrons, 1895–1945* (Paris: EDF, 2001).

Bauer, Hans, *Swiss Bank Corporation* (Basel: Swiss Bank Corporation, 1972).

Beauchamp, K. G., *Exhibiting Electricity* (Stevenage, Herts., England: Institution of Electrical Engineers, 1997).

Beaud, Claude Ph., "Investments and Profits of the Multinational Schneider Group: 1894–1943," in Alice Teichova, Maurice Lévy-Leboyer, and Helga Nussbaum, *Multinational Enterprise in Historical Perspective* (Cambridge: Cambridge Unversity Press, 1986), 87–102.

Bellevance, Claude, *Shawinigan Water and Power, 1898–1963* (Montreal: Boreal, 1994).

Berend, Ivan T., and Gyorgy Ranki, *Economic Development in East-Central Europe in the 19th and 20th Centuries* (New York: Columbia University Press, 1974).

Berthonnet, d'Arnaud, *Guide du Chercheur en Histoire de L'Électricité* (Paris: Éditions La Mandragore, n.d.).

Boileau, Céline, "La Production Électrique Destinée à l'Industrie Minière en Afrique du Sud (1880–1922)," in Dominique Barjot, Daniel Lefeuvre, Arnaud Berthonnet, and Sophie Coeuré, eds., *L'Électrification Outre-mer de la Fin du XIXe Siècle aux Première Décolonisations* (Paris: EDF, 2002), 459–78.

Bonbright, James C., and Gardiner C. Means, *The Holding Company: Its Public Significance and Its Regulation* (New York: McGraw-Hill, 1932).

Boyce, Gordon H., *Co-operative Structures in Global Business: Communicating, Transferring Knowledge and Learning Across the Corporate Frontier* (London: Routledge, 2001).

Bratter, Herbert, "Latin American Utilities' Nationalization Proceeds Inexorably," *Public Utilities Fortnightly*, 66 (July 7, 1960), 1–15.

Brion, Réné, "Le Rôle de la Sofina," in Monique Trédé-Boulmer, ed., *Le Financement de l'Industrie Électrique 1880–1980* (Paris: PUF, 1994), 217–32.

Brion, Réné, and J. L. Moreau, *Tractebel 1895–1994: Les Métamorphoses d'un Groupe Industriel* (Antwerp: Ford Mercator, 1995).

British Electrical and Allied Manufacturers' Association, *Combines and Trusts in the Electrical Industry: The Position in Europe in 1927* (1927; reprinted New York: Arno Press, 1977).

Broder, Albert, *Alcatel Alsthom: Histoire de la Compagnie Générale d'Électricité* (Paris: Larousse, 1992).
Broder, Albert, "Banking and the Electrotechnical Industry in Western Europe," in Rondo Cameron and V. I. Bovykin, eds., *International Banking* (Oxford: Oxford University Press, 1991), 468–84.
Broder, Albert, "Électricité et Relations Internationales dans l'Entre-Deux-Guerres," *Relations Internationales,* 43 (1985), 269–87.
Broder, Albert, "L'Expansion Internationale de l'Industrie Électrique Allemande ... 1880–1913," *Relations Internationales,* 29 (1982), 65–87.
Broder, Albert, "The Multinationalisation of the French Electrical Industry 1880–1914: Dependence and Its Causes," in Peter Hertner and Geoffrey Jones, eds., *Multinationals: Theory and History* (Aldershot, England: Gower, 1986), 169–91.
Brooks, John, "Annals of Finance," *New Yorker,* May 21, 1979, and May 28, 1979.
Brown, Frederick, ed., *Statistical Year-Book of the World Power Conference,* vol. 1, 1933 and 1934 (London: World Power Conference, 1936), and subsequent volumes.
Bullock, Hugh, *The Story of Investment Companies* (New York: Columbia University Press, 1959).
Buss, Dietrich, *Henry Villard: A Study of Transatlantic Investment and Interests, 1870–1895* (New York: Arno Press, 1978).
Bussière, Eric, "The Interests of the Banque de l'Union Parisienne in Czechoslovakia, Hungary, and the Balkans," in Alice Teichova and P. L. Cottrell, eds., *International Business and Central Europe, 1918–1939* (Leicester, England: Leicester University Press, 1983), 399–410.
Byatt, I. C. R., *The British Electrical Industry, 1875–1914* (Oxford: Clarendon Press, 1979).
Cairncross, Sir Alec, *Control of Long-Term International Capital Movements* (Washington, DC: Brookings Institution, 1973).
Calomiris, Charles W., *U.S. Bank Deregulation in Historical Perspective* (Cambridge: Cambridge University Press, 2000).
Cameron, Nigel, *Power: The Story of China Light* (Hong Kong: Oxford University Press, 1982).
Cameron, Rondo, and V. I. Bovykin, eds., *International Banking* (Oxford: Oxford University Press, 1991).
Cantwell, John, ed., *Foreign Direct Investment and Technological Change,* 2 vol. (Cheltenham, England: Edward Elgar, 1999).
Cardot, Fabienne, ed., *1880–1980, Un Siècle d'Électricité dans le Monde* (Paris: PUF, 1987).
Carlson, W. Bernard, *Innovation as a Social Process: Elihu Thomson and the Rise of General Electric, 1870–1900* (Cambridge: Cambridge University Press, 1991).
Carosso, Vincent P., *Investment Banking in America* (Cambridge, MA: Harvard University Press, 1970).
Carosso, Vincent P., *The Morgans* (Cambridge, MA: Harvard University Press, 1987).
Carreras, Albert, Xavier Tafunnell, and Eugenio Torres, "Against Integration: The Rise and Decline of Spanish State-Owned Firms and the Decline and Rise of

Multinationals, 1939–1990," in Ulf Olsson, ed., *Business and European Integration Since 1800* (Gothenburg, Sweden: Graphic Systems, 1997), 31–49.

Carreras, Albert, Xavier Tafunnell, and Eugenio Torres, "The Rise and Decline of Spanish State-Owned Firms," in Pier Angelo Toninelli, ed., *The Rise and Fall of State-Owned Enterprise in the Western World* (Cambridge: Cambridge University Press, 2000), 208–36.

Cartianu, Paul, and Calin Mihaileanu, "Les Débuts de l'Utilisation de l'Électricité dans le Territoire de la Roumanie," in Fabienne Cardot, ed., *1880–1980: Un Siècle d'Électricité dans le Monde* (Paris: PUF, 1987), 165–73.

Cassis, Youssef, *Big Business: The European Experience in the Twentieth Century* (Oxford: Oxford University Press, 1997).

Cassis, Youssef, ed., *Finance and Financiers in European History, 1880–1960* (Cambridge: Cambridge University Press, 1992).

Cassis, Youssef, and Eric Bussière, eds., *London and Paris as International Financial Centres in the Twentieth Century* (Oxford: Oxford University Press, 2005).

Cavers, David F., and James R. Nelson, *Electric Power Regulation in Latin America* (Baltimore: Johns Hopkins University Press, 1959).

Caves, Richard, *Multinational Enterprise and Economic Analysis,* 3rd ed. (Cambridge: Cambridge University Press, 2007).

Chadeau, Emmanuel, "The Rise and Decline of State-Owned Industry in Twentieth-Century France," in Pier Angelo Toninelli, ed., *The Rise and Fall of State-Owned Enterprise in the Western World* (Cambridge: Cambridge University Press, 2000), 185–207.

Chandler, Alfred D., Jr., "A Framework for Analyzing the Modern Multinational Enterprise and Its Competitive Advantage," *Business and Economic History,* 2nd ser. 16 (1987), 3–17.

Chandler, Alfred D., Jr., *Scale and Scope* (Cambridge, MA: Harvard University Press, 1990).

Chandler, Alfred D., Jr., Franco Amatori, and Takashi Hikino, *Big Business and the Wealth of Nations* (Cambridge: Cambridge University Press, 1997).

Channon, Derek F., *The Strategy and Structure of British Enterprise* (Boston: Harvard Business School, 1973).

Chelpner, B. S., *Le Marche Financier Belge Depuis Cent Ans* (Brussels: Librairie Falk Fils, 1930).

Chernow, Ron, *The House of Morgan* (New York: Atlantic Monthly Press, 1990).

Chick, Martin, "The Power of Networks: Defining the Boundaries of the Natural Monopoly Network and the Implications for the Restructuring of the Electricity Supply Industry," *Annales Historiques de l'Électricité,* No. 2 (June 2004), 89–106.

Chokki, Toshiaki, "'Japanese Business Management' in the Prewar Electrical Machinery Industry: The Emergence of Foreign Tie-up Companies and the Modernization of Indigenous Enterprises," in Takeshi Yuzawa and Masaru Udagawa, eds., *Foreign Business in Japan Before World War II* (Tokyo: University of Tokyo Press, 1990), 197–216.

Chua, Amy L., "The Privatization-Nationalization Cycle: The Link Between Markets and Ethnicity in Developing Countries," *Columbia Law Review,* 95 (March 1995), 223–303.

Cleveland, Harold van B., and Thomas F. Huertas, *Citibank 1812–1970* (Cambridge, MA: Harvard University Press, 1985).
Coates, Austin, *A Mountain of Light* (Hong Kong: Heinemann, 1977).
Collier, Hugh, *Developing Electric Power: Thirty Years of World Bank Experience* (Baltimore: Johns Hopkins University Press, 1984).
Confalonieri, Antonio, *Banca e Industria in Italia 1894–1906*, vol. 3 (Milan: Banca Commerciale Italiana, 1976).
Conte, Leandro, "I Prestiti Esteri," in *Storia dell' Industria Elettrica in Italia*, 2 (Rome-Bari: Laterza, 1993), 625–707.
Coopersmith, Jonathan, *The Electrification of Russia, 1880–1926* (Ithaca: Cornell University Press, 1992).
Coopersmith, Jonathan, "When Worlds Collide: Government and Electrification, 1892–1939," *Business and Economic History On-Line*, I (2003).
Czamanski, Daniel, *Privatization and Restructuring of Electricity Provisions* (Westport, CT: Praeger, 1999).
Davenport-Hines, R. P. T., *Dudley Docker* (Cambridge: Cambridge University Press, 1984).
Davenport-Hines, R. P. T. and Geoffrey Jones, eds., *British Business in Asia Since 1860* (Cambridge: Cambridge University Press, 1989).
Davies, A. Emil, *Investments Abroad* (Chicago: A. W. Shaw, 1927).
Davis, Lance E., and Robert E. Gallman, *Evolving Financial Markets and International Capital Flows: Britain, the Americas, and Australia, 1865–1914* (Cambridge: Cambridge University Press, 2001).
Denison, Merrill, *Canada's First Bank: A History of the Bank of Montreal*, 2 vol. (New York: Dodd, Mead, 1966, 1967).
Deutsche Überseeische Bank, 1886–1936 (Berlin, 1936).
Dickens, Paul D., "The Transition Period in American International Financing, 1897 to 1914," Ph.D. diss., George Washington University, 1933.
Dictionary of Business Biography.
Dictionary of National Biography.
Directory of Directors, various years.
Doria, Marco, and Peter Hertner, "Urban Growth and the Creation of Integrated Electricity Systems: The Cases of Genoa and Barcelona, 1894–1914," in Andrea Giuntini, Peter Hertner, and Gregorio Núñez, eds., *Urban Growth on Two Continents in the 19th and 20th Centuries: Technology, Networks, Finance and Public Regulation* (Granada, Spain: Editorial Comares, 2004), 219–48.
Dritsas, Margarita, and Terry Gourvish, eds., *European Enterprise* (Athens: Trochalia Publications, 1997).
Düblin, Jules, *Die Finanzierungs-und Kapitalanlage-Gesellschaften der Schweizerishchen Grossbanken* (Basel: Philographischer Verlag, 1937).
Dunn, Robert W., *American Foreign Investments* (New York: B. W. Huebsch and Viking, 1926).
Dunning, John, *Multinational Enterprises and the Global Economy* (Wokingham, England: Addison-Wesley, 1993).
Economist, various issues.
Edelstein, Michael, *Overseas Investment in the Age of High Imperialism: The United Kingdom, 1850–1914* (New York: Columbia University Press, 1982).

Eigner, Peter, "The Ownership Structure of Austria's Big Business, 1895–1995," in Margarita Dritsas and Terry Gourvish, eds., *European Enterprise* (Athens: Trochalia Publications, 1997), 49–68.

Electrical World, various issues.

Emden, Paul H., *Money Powers of Europe in the Nineteenth and Twentieth Centuries* (London: Sampson Low, Marston & Co., [1937]).

Etemad, Bouda, and Jean Luciani, *World Energy Production* (Geneva: Librairie Droz, 1991).

European Association for Banking History, *Handbook on the History of European Banks* (Aldershot, England: Edward Elgar, 1994).

Feinstein, Charles H., ed., *Banking, Currency, and Finance in Europe Between the Wars* (Oxford: Oxford University Press, 1995).

Feinstein, Charles H., Peter Temin, and Gianni Toniolo, "International Economic Organization: Banking, Finance, and Trade in Europe Between the Wars," in Charles H. Feinstein, ed., *Banking, Currency, and Finance in Europe Between the Wars* (Oxford: Oxford University Press, 1995), 9–76.

Feis, Herbert, *Europe: The World's Banker 1870–1914* (1930; reprinted New York: Norton, 1965).

Feldenkirchen, Wilfried, *Siemens: From Workshop to Global Player* (Munich: Piper, 2000).

Feldenkirchen, Wilfried, "Siemens in Eastern Europe: From the End of World War I to the End of World War II" in Christopher Kobrak and Per H. Hansen, eds., *European Business, Dictatorship, and Political Risk, 1920–1945* (New York: Berghahn Books, 2004), 122–45.

Feldenkirchen, Wilfried, *Werner von Siemens* (Columbus: Ohio State University Press, 1994).

Fernández-Revuelta, Luis, Donato Gómez and Keith Robson, "Fuerzas Motrices del Valle de Lecrín, 1936–9," *Accounting, Business and Financial History*, 12 (July 2002), 347–66.

Financial Times (London, UK), various issues.

Flowers, Edward B., *U.S. Utility Mergers and the Restructuring of the New Global Power Industry* (Westport, CT: Praeger, 1998).

Fridenson, Patrick, "France: The Relatively Slow Development of Big Business in the Twentieth Century," in Alfred D. Chandler, Jr., Franco Amatori, and Takashi Hikino, *Big Business and the Wealth of Nations* (Cambridge: Cambridge University Press, 1997), 208–45.

Friedel, Robert, and Paul Israel, with Bernard S. Finn, *Edison's Electric Light: Biography of an Invention* (New Brunswick, NJ: Rutgers University Press, 1987).

Gall, Lothar, et al., *The Deutsche Bank, 1870–1995* (London: Weidenfeld & Nicholson, 1995).

Garcke, Emile, comp., *Manual of Electrical Undertakings* (London: Electrical Press, various years).

Geisst, Charles R., *Entrepôt Capitalism* (New York: Praeger, 1992).

Geisst, Charles R., *Wall Street* (Oxford: Oxford University Press, 1997).

Gilbert, Richard J., and Edward P. Kahn, eds., *International Comparisons of Electricity Regulation* (New York: Cambridge University Press, 1996).

Gómez-Ibáñez, José, *Regulating Infrastructure: Monopoly, Contracts, and Discretion* (Cambridge, MA: Harvard University Press, 2003).
Grayson, Theodore J., *Investment Trusts* (New York: John Wiley, 1928).
Greene, S. Dana, "Distribution of the Electrical Energy from Niagara Falls," *Cassier's Magazine*, 8 (1895), 333–62.
Guex, Sébastien, "Introduction," in Sebastien Guex, ed., *La Suisse et les Grandes Puissances 1914–1945* (Geneva: Droz, 1999).
Haber, L. F., *The Chemical Industry, 1900–1930* (Oxford: Clarendon Press, 1971).
Halsey, Frederic M., *Investments in Latin America and the British West Indies* (U.S. Department of Commerce, Bureau of Foreign and Domestic Commerce, Special Agents Series, 169, Washington, DC, 1918).
Hannah, Leslie, *Electricity Before Nationalisation: A Study of the Development of the Electricity Supply Industry in Britain to 1948* (Baltimore: Johns Hopkins University Press, 1979).
Hannah, Leslie, "The Finance of the Electricity Industry in the UK Before 1948," in Monique Trédé-Boulmer, ed., *Le Financement de l'Industrie Électrique 1880–1980* (Paris: PUF, 1994), 271–89.
Hanson, Simon G., *Economic Development in Latin America* (Washington, DC: Inter-American Affairs Press, 1951).
Harris, C. R. S., *Germany's Foreign Indebtedness* (London: Oxford University Press, 1935).
Hausman, William J., "The Historical Antecedents of Restructuring: Mergers and Concentration in the U.S. Electric Utility Industry, 1879–1935," unpublished paper prepared for the American Public Power Association, March 4, 1997.
Hausman, William J., and John L. Neufeld, "The Market for Capital and the Origins of State Regulation of Electrical Utilities in the United States," *Journal of Economic History*, 62 (Dec. 2002), 1050–73.
Hausman, William J., and John L. Neufeld, "Public Versus Private Electric Utilities in the United States: A Century of Debate over Comparative Economic Efficiency," *Annals of Public and Cooperative Economics*, 65 (1994), 599–622.
Hausman, William J., and John L. Neufeld, "The Rise and Fall of the American and Foreign Power Company: A Lesson from the Past?" *Electricity Journal*, 10 (1997), 46–53.
Hausman, William J., and John L. Neufeld, "U.S. Foreign Direct Investment in Electrical Utilities in the 1920s," in Mira Wilkins and Harm Schröter, eds., *The Free-Standing Company in the World Economy* (Oxford: Oxford University Press, 1998), 361–90.
Hedges, Killingworth, *Continental Electric Light Central Stations* (London: E. & F. N. Spon, 1892).
Heerding, A., *The History of N. V. Philips' Gloeilampenfabrieken*, vol. 1 (Cambridge: Cambridge University Press, 1985).
Heineman, Dannie N., "The Changing International Environment," address to the general meeting of shareholders of Société Financière de Transports et d'Entreprises Industrielles (Sofina), April 22, 1954.
Heineman, D[annie N.], "Electricity in the Region of London," in *Transactions of the First World Power Conference*, Vol. 4 (London: Percy Lund, Humphries and Co., 1924), 1285–305.

Heineman, Dannie N., "International Cooperation in Privately Managed Public Utility Undertakings," address to the annual general meeting of shareholders of Société Financière de Transports et d'Entreprises Industrielles (Sofina), April 28, 1938.

Heineman, Dannie N., "Obstacles to Private Foreign Investment," address to the general meeting of shareholders of Société Financière de Transports et d'Entreprises Industrielles (Sofina), April 28, 1949.

Heineman, Dannie N., *Outline of a New Europe* (Brussels: Vromant & Co., 1931), published in French as *Esquisse d'une Europe Nouvelle* (Brussels: Vromant & Co., 1931) and in German as *Skizze eines Neuen Europe* (Cologne: Glide-Verlag, 1931).

Heinrich, Thomas, "Product Diversification in the U.S. Pulp and Paper Industry: The Case of International Paper, 1898–1941," *Business History Review*, 75 (Autumn 2001), 467–505.

Helfferich, Karl, *Georg von Siemens: Ein Lebensbild aus Deutschlands Grosser Zeit*, 2nd ed., vol. 2 (Berlin: Julius Springer, 1923).

Henisz, Witold, Bruce A. Zelner, and Mauro F. Guillén, "International Coercion, Emulation and Policy Diffusion: Market-Oriented Infrastructure Reforms, 1977–1999," unpublished paper, June 17, 2004.

Hennart, Jean-François, "Transaction-Cost Theory and the Free-Standing Firm," in Mira Wilkins and Harm Schröter, eds., *The Free-Standing Company in the World Economy* (Oxford: Oxford University Press, 1998), 65–98.

Hertner, Peter, "Il Capitale Tedesco in Italia dall' Unità alla Prima Guerra Mondiale," in *Blanche Miste e Sviluppo Economico Italiano* (Bologna: Il Mulino, 1984), 209–25.

Hertner, Peter, "Il Capitale Tedesco nell' Industria Elettrica Italiana Fino alla Prima Guerra Mondiale," in Bruno Bezza, ed., *Energia e Sviluppo: L'Industria Elettrica Italiana e la Società Edison* (Torino: Einaudi, 1986), 211–56.

Hertner, Peter, "Espansione Multinazionale e Finanziamento Internationale dell' Industria Elettrotecnica Tedesca Prima del 1914," *Studi Storici* (1987), 819–60.

Hertner, Peter, "Exports or Direct Investment: The German Electro-Technical Industry in Italy, Spain and France from the 1880s Until the First World War," in Hans Pohl, ed., *Transnational Investment from the 19th Century to the Present* (Stuttgart: Franz Steiner, 1994), 103–15.

Hertner, Peter, "Financial Strategies and Adaptation to Foreign Markets: The German Electro-Technical Industry and Its Multinational Activities, 1890s to 1939," in Alice Teichova, Maurice Lévy-Leboyer, and Helga Nussbaum, eds., *Multinational Enterprise in Historical Perspective* (Cambridge: Cambridge University Press, 1986), 145–59.

Hertner, Peter, "German Banks Abroad Before 1914," in Geoffrey Jones, ed., *Banks as Multinationals* (London: Routledge, 1990), 99–119.

Hertner, Peter, "The German Electrotechnical Industry in the Italian Market Before the Second World War," in Geoffrey Jones and Harm Schröter, eds., *The Rise of Multinationals in Continental Europe* (Aldershot, England: Edward Elgar, 1993), 155–72.

Hertner, Peter, "German Foreign Investment in Electrical Industry and in Electrified Urban Transport in Italy, Spain, and Argentina until the end of the 1920s: Some Preliminary Considerations," unpublished paper (n.d. [2005?]).

Hertner, Peter, "German Multinational Enterprise Before 1914," in Peter Hertner and Geoffrey Jones, eds., *Multinationals: Theory and History* (Aldershot, England: Gower, 1986), 113–34.

Hertner, Peter, "Global Enterprise Before the Second World War: The Example of the Electro-Technical Industry," in Tamás Szmrecsányi and Ricardo Maranhão, eds., *História de Empresas e Desenvolvimento Econômico* (São Paulo: Editora Hucitec, 1996), 105–16.

Hertner, Peter, "L'Industrie Électrotechnique Allemande Entre les Deux Guerres: À la Recherche d'une Position Internationale Perdue," *Relations Internationales*, 43 (Autumn 1985), 289–304.

Hertner, Peter, "Les Sociétés Financières Suisses et le Développement de l'Industrie Électrique Jusqu'à la Première Guerre Mondiale," in Fabienne Cardot, ed., *1880–1980: Un Siècle d'Électricité dans le Monde* (Paris: PUF, 1987).

Hertner, Peter, "Technologie et Capitaux Allemands dans l'Industrie Électrotechnique Français Avant la Première Guerre Mondiale: Un Premier Bilan," in Michèle Merger and Dominique Barjot, *Les Entreprises et Leur Réseaux: Hommes, Capitaux, Techniques et Pouvoirs, XIXe–XXe Siècles, Melanges en l'Honneur de François Caron* (Paris: PUP, 1998), 499–521.

Hertner, Peter, and H. V. Nelles, "Contrasting Styles of Foreign Investment: A Comparison of the Entrepreneurship, Technology, and Finance of German and Canadian Enterprises in Barcelona Electrification," *Revue Économique*, 58 (Jan. 2007), 191–214.

Hill, N. K. "The History of the Imperial Continental Gas Association, 1824–1900," unpublished Ph.D. thesis, University of London, 1950.

Himmel, Ernst, *Industrielle Kapitalanlagen der Schweiz im Auslande* (Langensalza, Germany: Druck von Hermann Beyer & Söhne, 1922).

Hines, Mary Alice, *The Development and Finance of Global Private Power* (Westport, CT: Quorum Books, 1997).

Hirsch, Richard F., *Power Loss: The Origins of Deregulation and Restructuring in the American Electric Utility System* (Cambridge, MA: MIT Press, 1999).

Hjerppe, Riitta, "The Significance of Foreign Direct Investment in a Small Industrialising Economy: The Case of Finland in the Interwar Period," *Business and Economic History On-Line*, 1 (2003).

Hoshi, Takeo, and Anil K. Kashyap, *Corporate Financing and Governance in Japan* (Cambridge, MA: MIT Press, 2001).

Huertas, Thomas F., "US Multinational Banking: History and Prospects," in Geoffrey Jones, ed., *Banks as Multinationals* (London: Routledge, 1990), 248–67.

Hughes, Thomas P., *Networks of Power: Electrification in Western Society, 1880–1930* (Baltimore: Johns Hopkins University Press, 1983).

Hull, Richard W., *American Enterprises in South Africa* (New York: New York University Press, 1990).

Imwinkelried, Daniel, "Die Auswirkungen des Ersten Weltkrieges auf die Beziehungen der Schweizer Banken zur Deutschen Industrie: Die Schweizerische Gesellschaft für Elektrische Industrie (Indelec) und der Siemens-Konzern," in Sébastien Guex, ed., *La Suisse et les Grandes Puissances 1914–1945* (Geneva: Droz, 1999), 301–25.

Israel, Paul, *Edison: A Life of Invention* (New York: John Wiley, 1998).

Jacob-Wendler, G., *Deutsche Elektroindustrie in Lateinamerika: Siemens und AEG 1890–1914* (Stuttgart: Klett-Cotta, 1982).

Jöhr, Walter Adolf, *Schweizerische Kreditanstalt 1856–1956* (Zurich: Schweizerische Kreditanstalt, 1956).

Jones, Geoffrey, *British Multinational Banking 1830–1990* (Oxford: Oxford University Press, 1993).

Jones, Geoffrey, *The Evolution of International Business* (London: Routledge, 1996).

Jones, Geoffrey, *Merchants to Multinationals: British Trading Companies in the Nineteenth and Twentieth Centuries* (Oxford: Oxford University Press, 2000).

Jones, Geoffrey, *Multinationals and Global Capitalism from the Nineteenth to the Twenty-First Century* (Oxford: Oxford University Press, 2005).

Jones, Geoffrey, "Multinationals from 1930 to the 1980s," in Alfred Chandler and Bruce Mazlish, eds., *Leviathans: Multinational Corporations and the New Global History* (Cambridge: Cambridge University Press, 2005), 81–103.

Jones, Geoffrey, ed., *Banks as Multinationals* (London: Routledge, 1990).

Jones, Geoffrey, and Tarun Khanna, "Bringing History (Back) into International Business," *Journal of International Business Studies*, 37 (July 2006), 453–68.

Jones, Linda, Charles Jones, and Robert Greenhill, "Public Utility Companies," in D. C. M. Platt, *Business Imperialism 1840–1930: An Inquiry Based on British Experience in Latin America* (Oxford: Oxford University Press, 1977), 77–118.

Josephson, Matthew, *Edison* (New York: McGraw-Hill, 1959).

Jung, Joseph, *From Schweizerische Kreditanstalt to Credit Suisse Group: The History of a Bank* (Zurich: NZZ Verlag, 2000).

Keller, David Neal, *Stone & Webster, 1889–1989* (New York: Stone & Webster, 1989).

Kennedy, Charles R., Jr., "Relations Between Transnational Corporations and Governments of Host Countries: A Look to the Future," *Transnational Corporations*, 1 (Feb. 1992), 67–91.

Kikkawa, Takeo, *Nihon Denryokú no Hatten to Matsunaga Yasuzaemon* [*The Development of Japanese Electric Power Industry and Yasuzemon Matsunaga*] (Nagoya: Nagoya University Press, 1995).

Kikkawa, Takeo, "The Plan for the Establishment of the Japan-Britain Electric Power Joint Enterprise After the Japanese-Russian War," in *Enerugi shi Kenkyu* [*Research for the History of Energy*], 12 (June 1983), 46–60 (in Japanese).

Kindersley, Robert M., "British Foreign Investments in 1929," *Economic Journal*, 41 (Sept. 1931), 370–84.

Kindersley, Robert M., "British Foreign Investments in 1930," *Economic Journal*, 42 (June 1932), 176–95.

King, Frank H. H., *The History of the Hongkong and Shanghai Banking Corporation*, 4 vol. (title varies) (Cambridge: Cambridge University Press, 1987–1991).

Kirchner, Walther, "Siemens and AEG and the Electrification of Russia, 1890–1914," *Jahrbücher für Geschichte Osteuropas*, 30 (1982), 406–9.

Kobrak, Christopher, *Banking on Global Markets: Deutsche Bank and the United States, 1870 to the Present* (Cambridge: Cambridge University Press, forthcoming).

Kuisel, Richard F., *Ernest Mercier* (Berkeley: University of California Press, 1967).

Kurgan-Van Hentenryk, Ginette, "Un Aspect de l'Exportation des Capiteaux en Chine: Les Entreprises Franco-Belges, 1896–1914," in Maurice Lévy-Leboyer, ed., *La Position Internationale de la France* (Paris: Éditions de l'École des Hautes Études en Sciences Sociales, 1977), 203–13.

Kurgan-Van Hentenryk, Ginette, "Finance and Financiers in Belgium, 1880–1940," in Youssef Cassis, ed., *Finance and Financiers in European History 1880–1960* (Cambridge: Cambridge University Press, 1992), 317–36.

Kurgan-Van Hentenryk, Ginette, "Le Patronat de l'Électricité en Belgique, 1895–1945," in Dominque Barjot, Henri Morsel, and Sophie Coeuré, eds., *Stratégies, Gestion, Management: Les Compagnies Électriques et Leurs Patrons, 1895–1945* (Paris: EDF, 2001), 55–68.

Kurgan-Van Hentenryk, Ginette, "Le Régime Économic de l'Industrie Électrique Despuis la Fin du XIXe Siècle," in Fabienne Cardot, ed., *1880–1980, Un Siècle d'Électricité dans le Monde* (Paris: PUF, 1987), 119–33.

Kurgan-Van Hentenryk, Ginette, "Structure and Strategy of Belgian Business Groups (1920–1990)," in Takeo Shiba and Masahiro Shimotani, *Beyond the Firm. Business Groups in International and Historical Perspective* (London: Oxford University Press, 1997), 88–106.

Kynaston, David, *The City of London: Volume II: Golden Years, 1890–1914* (London: Chatto & Windus, 1995).

Kynaston, David, *The City of London: Volume III: Illusions of Gold, 1914–1945* (London: Chatto & Windus, 1999).

Lanthier, Pierre, "Les Constructions Électriques en France: le Case de Six Groupes Industriels Internationaux de 1880 à1940," Ph.D. diss., 3 vol., Paris: University of Paris X (Nanterre), 1988.

Lanthier, Pierre, "L'Électrification de Bombay Avant 1920: Le Projet de Jamsetji N. Tata," in Dominque Barjot, Daniel Lefeuvre, Arnaud Berthonnet, and Sophie Coeuré, eds., *L'Électrification Outre-mer de la Fin du XIXe Siècle aux Premières Décolonisations* (Paris: EDF, 2002), 211–33.

Lanthier, Pierre, "Multinationals and the French Electrical Industry, 1889–1940," in Alice Teichova, Maurice Lévy-Leboyer, and Helga Nussbaum, *Historical Studies in International Corporate Business* (Cambridge: Cambridge University Press, 1989), 143–50.

Laxer, Gordon, *Open for Business: The Roots of Foreign Ownership in Canada* (Toronto: Oxford University Press, 1989).

Lessard, Donald R., "Risk and the Dynamics of Globalization," in Julian M. Birkinshaw, ed., *The Future of the Multinational Company* (London: John Wiley, 2003), 76–85.

Levitt, Kari, *Silent Surrender: The Multinational Corporation in Canada* (Toronto: Macmillan of Canada, 1970).

Lewis, Cleona, *America's Stake in International Investments* (Washington, DC: Brookings Institution, 1938).

Liefmann, Robert, *Beteiligungs- und Finanzierungsgesellschaften: Eine Studie über den Modernen Kapitalismus und das Effektenwesen* (Jena, Germany: G. Fischer, 1913).

Liefmann, Robert, *Cartels, Concerns, and Trusts* (London: Methuen, 1932), originally published in German as *Kartelle, Konzerne und Trusts.*

Liehr, Reinhard, and Georg Leidenberger, "El Paso de una Free-Standing Company a una Empresa Pública: Mexican Light and Power y Mexico Tramways, 1902–1960," in Sandra Kuntz Ficker and Horst Pietschmann, eds., *México y la Economía Atlántica (Siglos XVIII–XX)* (Mexico City: El Colegio de México, Centro de Estudios Históricos, 2006), 269–309.

Liehr, Reinhard, and Georg Leidenberger, "From Free-Standing Company to Public Enterprise: the Mexican Light and Power Company and the Mexican Tramways Company, 1902–1965," typescript prepared for International Economic History Congress, Buenos Aires, July 2002.

Liehr, Reinhard, and Mariano E. Torres Bautista, "British Free-Standing Companies in Mexico, 1884–1911," in Mira Wilkins and Harm Schröter, eds., *The Free-Standing Company in the World Economy* (Oxford: Oxford University Press, 1998), 253–78.

Linder, Marc, *Projecting Capitalism: A History of the Internationalization of the Construction Industry* (Westport, CT: Greenwood Press, 1994).

Lipsey, Robert E., "Changing Patterns of International Investment in and by the United States," in Martin Feldstein, ed., *The United States in the World Economy* (Chicago: University of Chicago Press, 1988), 475–545.

Lluch, Andrea, and Laura Sánchez, *De Movimiento Popular a Empresa el Cooperativisismo Eléctrico en La Pampa* (Santa Rosa: Fondo Editorial Pampeano, [2001]).

Lockwood, William W., *The Economic Development of Japan* (Princeton: Princeton University Press, 1954).

Loscertales, Javier, *Deutsche Investitionen in Spanien 1820–1920* (Stuttgart: Franz Steiner Verlag, 2002).

Mallory, Charles Franklin, "Financial Problems of the North American Owned Electric Utilities in Latin America," M.S. thesis, Massachusetts Institute of Technology, 1956.

Manafa, Marcel N. Azodo, *Electricity Development in Nigeria (1896–1972)* (Yaba, Nigeria: Raheem Publishers, 1979).

Manibog, Fernando, Rafael Dominguez, and Stephan Wegner, *Power for Development: A Review of the World Bank Group's Experience with Private Participation in the Electricity Sector* (Washington, DC: World Bank, 2003).

Marchildon, Gregory P., "The Montreal Engineering Company and International Power: Overcoming the Limitations of the Free-Standing Utility," in Mira Wilkins and Harm Schröter, eds., *The Free-Standing Company in the World Economy* (Oxford: Oxford University Press, 1998), 391–418.

Marchildon, Gregory P., *Profits and Politics: Beaverbrook and the Gilded Age of Canadian Finance* (Toronto: University of Toronto Press, 1996).

Marshall, Herbert, Frank A. Southard, and Kenneth W. Taylor, *Canadian-American Industry* (1936; reprinted New York: Russell & Russell, 1970).

Martinez López, Alberte, "Belgian Investment in Tramways and Light Railways: An International Approach, 1892–1935," *Journal of Transport History*, 3rd ser., 24 (March 2003), 59–77.
Mason, Mark, "Foreign Direct Investment and Japanese Economic Development, 1899–1931," *Business and Economic History*, 2nd ser., 16 (1987), 93–107.
Massell, David, *Amassing Power: J. B. Duke and the Saguenay River, 1897–1927* (Montreal: McGill-Queen's University Press, 2000).
Matis, Herbert, "Disintegration and Multi-national Enterprises in Central Europe," in Alice Teichova and P. L. Cottrell, eds., *International Business and Central Europe, 1918–1939* (New York: St. Martin's Press, 1983), 73–100.
McDowall, Duncan, *The Light: Brazilian Traction, Light and Power Company Ltd., 1899–1945* (Toronto: University of Toronto Press, 1988).
McGraw Central Station Directory (New York: McGraw-Hill Catalog and Directory Co., various years).
McGraw Electrical Directory (New York: McGraw Hill Catalog and Directory Co., various years).
McKay, John, *Tramways and Trolleys: The Rise of Urban Mass Transport in Europe* (Princeton: Princeton University Press, 1976).
Michie, Ranald C., *The London Stock Exchange: A History* (Oxford: Oxford University Press, 1999).
Millard, Andre, *Edison and the Business of Invention* (Baltimore: Johns Hopkins University Press, 1990).
Miller, Rory, "British Free-Standing Companies on the West Coast of South America," in Mira Wilkins and Harm Schröter, eds., *The Free-Standing Company in the World Economy* (Oxford: Oxford University Press, 1998), 218–52.
Millward, Robert, *Private and Public Enterprise in Europe* (Cambridge: Cambridge University Press, 2005).
Milward, Alan S., *War, Economy and Society, 1939–1945* (Berkeley: University of California Press, 1979).
Mitchell, B. R., ed., *International Historical Statistics: Africa, Asia and Oceana, 1750–1993*, 3rd ed. (New York: Stockton Press, 1998).
Mitchell, B. R., ed., *International Historical Statistics: The Americas, 1750–1993*, 4th ed. (New York: Stockton Press, 1998).
Mitchell, B. R., ed., *International Historical Statistics: Europe, 1750–1993*, 4th ed. (New York: Stockton Press, 1998).
Mitchell, Sidney Alexander, *S. Z. Mitchell and the Electrical Industry* (New York: Farrar, Straus & Cudahy, 1960).
Moody's Analysis of Investments (New York: Moody's Investors Services, various titles and years, commonly known as *Moody's Manuals*).
Moore, David R., *A History of Latin America*, rev. ed. (New York: Prentice-Hall, 1942).
Morck, Randall, "How to Eliminate Pyramidal Business Groups: The Double Taxation of Inter-Corporate Dividends and Other Incisive Uses of Tax Policy," NBER Working Paper 10944 (Cambridge, MA: National Bureau of Economic Research, 2004).

Morck, Randall, ed., *A History of Corporate Governance Around the World: Family Business Groups to Professional Managers* (Chicago: University of Chicago Press, 2005).

Morck, Randall, and Lloyd Steier, "The Global History of Corporate Governance: An Introduction," NBER Working Paper 11062 (Cambridge, MA: National Bureau of Economic Research, 2005).

Morck, Randall, Daniel Wolfenzon, and Bernard Yeung, "Corporate Governance, Economic Entrenchment, and Growth," *Journal of Economic Literature,* 43 (Sept. 2005), 657–722.

Myers, Ramon H., and Mark R. Peattie, eds., *The Japanese Colonial Empire, 1895–1945* (Princeton: Princeton University Press, 1984).

Myllyntaus, Timo, "Electrical Imperialism or Multinational Cooperation? The Role of Big Business in Supplying Light and Power to St. Petersburg Before 1917," *Business and Economic History,* 26 (Winter 1997), 540–49.

Myllyntaus, Timo, *Electrifying Finland: The Transfer of a New Technology into a Late Industrializing Economy* (London: Macmillan, 1991).

Myllyntaus, Timo, "The Transfer of Electrical Technology to Finland, 1870–1930," *Technology and Culture,* 32 (April 1991), 283–317.

Nelles, H. V., "Financing the Development of Foreign-Owned Electrical Systems in the Americas, 1890–1929: First Steps in Comparing European and North American Techniques," *Business and Economic History On-Line*, I (2003).

Nelles, H. V., *The Politics of Development* (Toronto: Macmillan, 1974).

Nelles, H. V., and Christopher Armstrong, "Corporate Enterprise in the Public Sector Service: The Performance of Canadian Firms in Mexico and Brazil," in Carlos Marichal, ed., *Foreign Investment in Latin America; Impact on Economic Development, 1850–1930*, B10, Proceedings Eleventh International Economic History Congress, Milan, Sept. 1994 (Milan: Università Bocconi, 1994), 69–82.

New York Times, various issues.

Niosi, Jorge, *Canadian Multinationals* (Toronto: Between the Lines, 1985).

Nötel, R., "International Credit and Finance," in M. C. Kaser and E. A. Radice, eds., *The Economic History of Eastern Europe, 1919–1975,* vol. 2 (Oxford: Oxford University Press,1985), 170–295.

Nye, David E., *Electrifying America: Social Meanings of a New Technology* (Cambridge, MA: MIT Press, 1990).

O'Brien, Thomas, *The Century of U.S. Capitalism in Latin America* (Albuquerque: University of New Mexico Press, 1999).

Ol', P. V., *Foreign Capital in Russia* (New York: Garland Publishing, 1983).

Organization for Economic Cooperation and Development, International Energy Agency, *Electricity in India* (Paris: OECD/IEA, 2002).

Organization for Economic Cooperation and Development, International Energy Agency, *Electricity Supply Industry: Structure, Ownership and Regulation in OECD Countries* (Paris: OECD/IEA, 1994).

Pantelakis, Nikos, *The Electrification of Greece: From Private Initiative to State Monopoly (1889–1956)* (Athens: Cultural Foundation of the National Bank of Greece, 1991; in Greek).

Paquier, Serge, *Histoire de l'Électricité en Suisse,* 2 vol. (Geneva: Éditions Passé Présent, 1998).

Paquier, Serge, "Swiss Holding Companies from the Mid-Nnineteenth Century to the Early 1930s," *Financial History Review*, 8 (Oct. 2001), 163–82.

Parsons, R. H., *The Early Days of the Power Station Industry* (Cambridge: Printed for Babcock and Wilcox Ltd. at Cambridge University Press, 1939).

Passer, Harold C., *The Electrical Manufacturers, 1875–1900* (Cambridge, MA: Harvard University Press, 1953).

Pepelasis Minoglou, Ioanna, "Between Informal Networks and Formal Contracts: International Investment in Greece During the 1920s," *Business History*, 44 (April 2002), 40–64.

Perrenoud, Marc, "La Diplomatie Suisse et les Relations Financières avec la France 1936–1945," in Sébastien Guex, ed., *La Suisse et les Grandes Puissances 1914–1945* (Geneva: Droz, 1999), 385–426.

Perry, Allen M., "Tentative History of the Evolution of the Electrical Industry," 4 vol., typescript (Birmingham, AL: Alabama Power, c. 1936).

Pohl, Manfred, ed., *Arthur von Gwinner: Lebenserinnerungen*, 2nd ed. (Frankfurt am Main: Knapp Verlag, 1992).

Quirico, Roberto di, "Italian International Banking, 1900–1950," Working Paper HEC 98/7 (Florence: European University Institute, 1998).

Quiroz, A. W., *Banqueros en Conflicto: Estructura Financiera y Economía Peruana, 1884–1930* (Lima: Universidad del Pacífico Press, 1990).

Quiroz, A. W., "Financial Leadership and the Formation of Peruvian Elite Groups, 1884–1930," *Journal of Latin American Studies*, 20 (1988), 49–81.

Ranieri, Liane, *Dannie Heineman: Un Destin Singulier, 1872–1962* (Brussels: Éditions Racine, 2005).

Rauber, Urs, *Schweizer Industrie in Russia* (Zurich, 1985).

Recueil Financier, various years.

Remer, C. F., *Foreign Investments in China* (New York: Macmillan, 1933).

Riesser, J., *The German Great Banks and Their Concentration* (1911; reprinted New York: Arno Press, 1977).

Rippy, J. Fred, *British Investments in Latin America, 1822–1949* (Minneapolis: University of Minnesota Press, 1959).

Roberts, Richard, *Schroders* (Houndmills, England: Macmillan, 1992).

Robinson, Henry Leslie, "American & Foreign Power Co. in Latin America: A Case Study," Ph.D. diss., Stanford University, 1967.

Roy, Patricia, "The British Columbia Electric Railway Company, 1897–1928: A British Company in British Columbia," Ph.D. thesis, University of British Columbia, 1970.

Safarian, A. E., *Foreign Ownership of Canadian Industry*, 2nd ed. (Toronto: University of Toronto Press, 1973).

Salings Börsen-Jahrbuch, various years.

Saul, Samir, "Banking Alliances and International Issues on the Paris Capital Market, 1890–1914," in Youssef Cassis and Eric Bussière, eds., *London and Paris as International Financial Centres in the Twentieth Century* (Oxford: Oxford University Press, 2005), 119–50.

Saul, Samir, "L'Électrification du Maroc à l'Époque du Protectorat," in Dominque Barjot, Daniel Lefeuvre, Arnaud Berthonnet, and Sophie Coeuré, eds.,

L'Électrification Outre-mer de la Fin du XIXe Siècle aux Premières Décolonisations (Paris: EDF, 2002), 491–512.

Sayers, R. S., *The Bank of England, 1891–1944*, 2 vol. (Cambridge: Cambridge University Press, 1976).

Schapiro, Raphael, "Why Public Ownership? Urban Utilities in London, 1870–1914," D.Phil. thesis, Nuffield College, Oxford University, 2003.

Schröter, Harm, "Continental European Free-Standing Companies," in Mira Wilkins and Harm Schröter, eds., *The Free-Standing Company in the World Economy* (Oxford: Oxford University Press, 1998), 323–43.

Schröter, Harm, "The German Question, the Unification of Europe, and European Market Strategies of Germany's Chemical and Electrical Industries, 1900–1992," *Business History Review*, 67 (Autumn 1993), 369–405.

Schröter, Harm, "Globalization and Reliability: The Fate of Foreign Direct Investment in Electric Power-Supply During the World Economic Crisis, 1929–1939," *Annales Historiques de l'Électricité*, 4 (Nov. 2006), 101–24.

Schröter, Harm, "Siemens and Central and South-East Europe Between the Two World Wars," in Alice Techova and Philip Cotterell, eds., *International Business and Central Europe 1918–1939* (Leicester, England: Leicester University Press, 1983), 173–92.

Schröter, Harm, "A Typical Factor of German International Market Strategy: Agreements Between the US and the German Electrotechnical Industries up to 1939," in Alice Teichova, Maurice Lévy-Leboyer, and Helga Nussbaum, eds., *Multinational Enterprise in Historical Perspective* (Cambridge: Cambridge University Press, 1986), 160–70.

Schuker, Stephen A., *American "Reparations" to Germany, 1919–33*, Princeton Studies in International Finance, 61 (Princeton: Department of Economics, Princeton University, 1988).

Schwarz, Hans-Peter, *Konrad Adenauer*, 1 (Providence, RI: Berghahn Books, 1995).

Schweizerisches Börsen-Handbuch, various years.

Schweizerisches Finanzjahrbuch, various years.

Scientific American, various issues.

Segreto, Luciano, "Aspetti e Problemi dell' Industria Elettrica in Europa tra le Due Guerre," in *Storia dell' Industria Elettrica in Italia*, 3 (Rome-Bari: Laterza, 1993), 325–98.

Segreto, Luciano, "Capitali, Technologie e Imprenditori Svizzeri nell' Industria Elettrica Italiana: Il Caso della Motor (1895–1923)," in *Energia e Sviluppo: L'Industria Elettrica Italiana e la Società Edison* (Turin: Einaudi, 1986).

Segreto, Luciano, "Ciento Veinte Años de Electricidad: Dos Mundos Diferentes y Parecidos," in Gonzalo Anes, ed., *Un Siglo de Luz: Historia Empresarial de Iberdrola* (Madrid: Iberdrola, 2005), 17–51.

Segreto, Luciano, "Du 'Made in Germany' au 'Made In Switzerland,'" in M. Trédé, ed., *Électricité et Électrification dans le Monde 1880–1980* (Paris: PUF, 1992), 347–67.

Segreto, Luciano, "Electrifier un Rêve: L'Électrique dans les Colonies Italiennes," in Dominique Barjot, et al., *L'Électrification Outre-mer de la Fin du XIXe Siècle aux Premières Décolonisations* (Paris: EDF, 2002), 235–49.

Segreto, Luciano, "Financing the Electric Industry in Europe (1880–1945)," unpublished conference paper, 1993 (cited as "Milan paper").
Segreto, Luciano, "Financing the Electric Industry Worldwide: Strategy and Structure of the Swiss Electric Holding Companies, 1895–1945," *Business and Economic History*, 23 (Fall 1994), 162–75.
Segreto, Luciano, *Giacinto Motta* (Rome-Bari: Laterza, 2005).
Segreto, Luciano, "Gli Assetti Proprietari," in *Storia dell' Industria Elettrica in Italia*, 3 (Rome-Bari: Laterza, 1993), 89–173.
Segreto, Luciano, "Imprenditori e Finanzieri," in *Storia dell' Industria Elettrica in Italia*, 1 (Rome-Bari: Laterza, 1992), 249–333.
Segreto, Luciano, "Le Rôle des Investissements Suisses dans l'Industrie Électrique Française Jusqu'à la Deuxième Guerre Mondiale," in Monique Trédé-Boulmer, ed., *Le Financement de l'Industrie Électrique 1880–1980* (Paris: PUF, 1994), 199–216.
Segreto, Luciano, "Le Rôle du Capital Étranger dans l'Industrie Électrique," in Maurice Lévy-Leboyer and Henri Morsel, eds., *Histoire Générale de l'Électricité en France*, 2 (Paris: Fayard, 1994), 982–1014.
Siemens, Georg, *History of the House of Siemens*, 2 vol. (Freiburg/Munich: Karl Alber, 1957).
Sigmund, Paul E., *Multinationals in Latin America: The Politics of Nationalization* (Madison: University of Wisconsin Press, 1980).
Smil, Vaclav, *Creating the Twentieth Century: Technical Innovations of 1867–1914 and Their Lasting Impact* (Oxford: Oxford University Press, 2005).
Smith, George David, *From Monopoly to Competition: The Transformations of Alcoa, 1888–1986* (Cambridge: Cambridge University Press, 1988).
Sofina, *Rapport du Conseil d'Administration à l'Assemblée Générale Ordinaire des Actionnaires*, 1929–1948, cited as *Annual Report*, with date.
Southard, Frank, *American Industry in Europe* (Boston: Houghton Mifflin, 1931).
Spender, J.A. *Weetman Pearson: First Viscount Cowdray, 1856–1927* (London: Cassell & Co., 1930).
Steigenmeier, A., *Power on. Elektrowatt 1895–1995* (Zurich: Elecktrowatt AG, 1995).
Stock Exchange Official Intelligence, London, various years.
Stock Exchange Year-Book, London, various titles and years.
Stone, Irving, *The Composition and Distribution of British Investment in Latin America, 1865 to 1913* (1962 diss.; reprinted New York: Garland Publishing, 1987).
Stone, Irving. *The Global Export of Capital from Great Britain, 1865–1914* (Houndmills, England: Macmillan Press, 1999).
Storaci, Marina, and Giuseppe Tattara, "The External Financing of Italian Electric Companies in the Interwar Years," *European Review of Economic History*, 2 (1998), 345–75.
Storia dell' Industria Elettrica in Italia, 5 vol. (Rome-Bari: Laterza, 1992–1994).
Strobel, Albrecht, "Die Gründung der Zürcher Elektrobank," in Erich Hassinger, ed., *Geschichte, Wirtschaft, Gesellschaft: Festschrift für Clemens Bauer* (Berlin: Duncker and Humblot, 1974).
Strouse, Jean, *Morgan* (New York: Random House, 1999).

Survey of Current Business, various issues.

Szmrecsányi, Tamás, "Infrastructural Services and Foreign Capital in the Brazilian Economy (1850–1930)," in Bart De Prins, Eddy Stols, and Johan Verberckmoes, eds., *Brasil* (Leuven: Acco, 2001), 197–201.

Tate, Muzaffar, *Power Builds the Nation: The National Electricity Board of the States of Malaya and Its Predecessors*, 2 vol. (Kuala Lumpur: National Electricity Board, 1989, 1991).

Taylor, Graham D., and Peter A. Baskerville. *A Concise History of Business in Canada* (Toronto: Oxford University Press, 1994).

Teichova, Alice, *An Economic Background to Munich: International Business and Czechoslovakia 1918–1938* (Cambridge: Cambridge University Press, 1974).

Teichova, Alice, Maurice Lévy-Leboyer, and Helga Nussbaum, eds., *Multinational Enterprise in Historical Perspective* (Cambridge: Cambridge University Press, 1986).

Teichova, Alice, and P. L. Cottrell, eds., *International Business and Central Europe, 1918–1939* (New York: St. Martin's Press, 1983).

Thobie, Jacques, "European Banks in the Middle East," in Rondo Cameron and V. I. Bovykin, eds., *International Banking* (Oxford: Oxford University Press, 1991), 406–40.

Tignor, Robert L., *Capitalism and Nationalism at the End of Empire: State and Business in Decolonizing Egypt, Nigeria, and Kenya, 1945–1963* (Princeton: Princeton University Press, 1998).

Tignor, Robert L., *Egyptian Textiles and British Capital 1930–1956* (Cairo: American University in Cairo Press, 1989).

Tignor, Robert L., *State, Private Enterprise, and Economic Change in Egypt, 1918–1952* (Princeton: Princeton University Press, 1984).

Tolliday, Steven, *Business, Banking, and Politics: The Case of British Steel, 1918–1939* (Cambridge, MA: Harvard University Press, 1987).

Tomaszewski, Jerzy, "German Capital in Silesian Industry in Poland," in Alice Teichova and P. L. Cottrell, eds., *International Business and Central Europe, 1918–1939* (New York: St. Martin's Press, 1983), 227–47.

Toninelli, Pier Angelo, ed., *The Rise and Fall of State-Owned Enterprise in the Western World* (Cambridge: Cambridge University Press, 2000).

Toniolo, Gianni, *One Hundred Years, 1894–1994: A Short History of the Banca Commerciale Italiana* (Milan: Banca Commerciale Italiana, 1994).

Tortella, Gabriel, *The Development of Modern Spain* (Cambridge, MA: Harvard University Press, 2000).

Tortella, Teresa, *A Guide to Sources of Information on Foreign Investment in Spain, 1780–1914* (Amsterdam: International Institute of Social History, 2000).

Trebilcock, Clive, *Phoenix Assurance and the Development of British Insurance, Vol. II: The Era of the Insurance Giants, 1870–1984* (Cambridge: Cambridge University Press, 1998).

Trédé, Monique, ed., *Électricité et Électrification dans le Monde 1880–1980* (Paris: PUF, 1992).

Trédé-Boulmer, Monique, ed., *Le Financement de l'Industrie Électrique 1880–1980* (Paris: PUF, 1994).

Twomey, Michael J., "Patterns of Foreign Investment in Latin America in the Twentieth Century," in John H. Coatsworth and Alan M. Taylor, eds., *Latin America and the World Economy Since 1800* (Cambridge, MA: Harvard University Press, 1998), 171–201.

Uchida, Hoshimi, "The Transfer of Electrical Technologies from the United States and Europe to Japan, 1869–1914," in David J. Jeremy, ed., *International Technology Transfer: Europe, Japan and the USA, 1700–1914* (Aldershot, England: Edward Elgar, 1991), 219–41.

Udagawa, Masari, "Business Management and Foreign-Affiliated Companies in Japan Before World War II" in Takeshi Yuzawa and Masaru Udagawa eds., *Foreign Business in Japan Before World War II* (Tokyo: University of Tokyo Press, 1990), 1–30.

United Nations Department of Economic and Social Affairs, Statistics Division, *Energy Balances and Electricity Profiles (2000)* (New York: United Nations, 2004).

United Nations Department of Economic and Social Affairs, Statistics Division, *Energy Statistics Yearbook (2001)* (New York: United Nations, 2004).

United States Congress, Senate, Committee on Banking and Currency, *Stock Exchange Practices, Hearings*, 72nd Cong. 1st sess. (1932–1933), 7 parts in 6 vol.; 72nd and 73rd Cong. (1933–1934), 2 parts in 9 vol. (after January 1933 known as Pecora Hearings).

United States Congress, Senate, Committee on Finance, *Sale of Foreign Bonds, Hearings*, 72nd Cong., 1st sess. (1932).

United States Congress, Senate, *Report on Electric Power Industry: Control of Power Companies,* Sen. Doc. 213, 69th Cong., 2nd sess. (1927).

United States Department of Commerce, Bureau of Foreign and Domestic Commerce, *American Direct Investments in Foreign Countries–1936* (Washington, DC: USGPO, 1938).

United States Department of Commerce, Bureau of Foreign and Domestic Commerce, *American Underwriting of Foreign Securities in 1930* (Washington, DC: USGPO, 1931).

United States Department of Commerce, Bureau of Foreign and Domestic Commerce, *Central Light and Power Plants in the Western Hemisphere, with Notes on the Market for Electrical Goods*, Trade Information Bulletin 469, (Washington D.C.: USGPO, April 1927).

United States Department of Commerce, Bureau of Foreign and Domestic Commerce, *A New Estimate of American Investments Abroad* (Washington, DC: USGPO, 1931).

United States Department of Commerce, Bureau of the Census, *Historical Statistics of the United States, Colonial Times to 1957* (Washington, DC: USGPO, 1960).

United States Department of Commerce, Bureau of the Census, *Historical Statistics of the United States: Colonial Times to 1970,* 2 vol. (Washington, DC: USGPO, 1975).

United States Department of Energy, Energy Information Administration, *Privatization and the Globalization of Energy Markets* (Washington, DC: Energy Information Administration, 1996).

United States Federal Trade Commission, *Report on Cooperation in American Export Trade*, 2 vol. (Washington, DC: USGPO, 1916).

United States Securities and Exchange Commission, *Investment Trusts and Investment Companies*, House Doc. 707, 75th Cong., 3rd sess. (1939); House Doc. 279, 76th Cong., 1st sess. (1940); House Doc. 246, 77th Cong., 1st sess. (1942).

Van der Wee, Herman, and Martine Goossens, "Belgium," in Rondo Cameron and V.I. Bovykin, eds., *International Banking 1870–1914* (Oxford: Oxford University Press, 1991), 113–29.

Van der Wee, Herman, and Monique Verbreyt, *The Generale Bank 1822–1997* (Tielt, Belgium: Lannoo, 1997).

Varaschin, Denis, "EDF in the Global Market Since the Beginning of the Nineties," in Hubert Bonin, et al., *Transnational Companies (19th–20th Centuries)* (Paris: Éditions P.L.A.G.E., [2002]), 377–87.

Vernon, Raymond, *Sovereignty at Bay: The Spread of U.S. Multinational Enterprise* (New York: Basic Books, 1971).

Vernon, Raymond, *Two Hungry Giants: The United States and Japan in the Quest for Oil and Ores* (Cambridge, MA: Harvard University Press, 1983).

Vernon, Raymond, ed., *Public Policy and Private Enterprise in Mexico* (Cambridge, MA: Harvard University Press, 1964).

Vitalis, Robert, *When Capitalists Collide: Business Conflict and the End of Empire in Egypt* (Berkeley: University of California Press, 1995).

Vuillermot, Catherine, "Le Groupe Durand: Une Multinationale Française de la Distribution de l'Électricité (dans la Premiére Moitié du XXe Siècle)?" in Hubert Bonin, et al., *Transnational Companies (19th–20th Centuries)* (Paris: Éditions P.L.A.G.E., [2002]), 367–75.

Vuillermot, Catherine, *Pierre-Marie Durand et l'Énergie Industrielle* (Paris: CNRS, 2001).

Wagner, Regina, "Actividades Empresariales de los Alemanes en Guatemala, 1850–1920," *Mesoamérica,* 13 (June 1987), 87–123.

Wake, Jehanne, *Kleinwort Benson* (Oxford: Oxford University Press, 1997).

Wall Street Journal, various issues.

Wallich, Hermann, and Paul Wallich, *Zwei Generationen im Deutschen Bankwesen 1833–1914* (Frankfurt am Main: Fritz Knapp Verlag, 1978).

Wavre, Pierre-Alain, "Swiss Investments in Italy from the XVIIIth to the XXth Century," *Journal of European Economic History,* 17 (Spring 1988), 85–102.

Weiher, Sigfrid von, *Die Englischen Siemen-Werke und das Siemens-Überseegeschäft in der Zweiten Hälfte des 19. Jahrhunderts* (Berlin: Duncker & Humblot, 1990).

Weiher, Sigfrid von, and Herbert Goetzeler, *The Siemens Company: Its Historical Role in the Progress of Electrical Engineering, 1847–1980* (Berlin and Munich: Siemens AG, 1977).

Wellisz, Leopold, *Foreign Capital in Poland* (London: Allen & Unwin, 1938).

Wengenroth, Ulrich, "The Rise and Fall of State-Owned Enterprise in Germany," in Pier Angelo Toninelli, ed., *The Rise and Fall of State-Owned Enterprise in the Western World* (Cambridge: Cambridge University Press, 2000), 103–27.

Wilkins, Mira, "Conduits for Long-Term Foreign Investment in the Gold Standard Era," in Marc Flandreau, Carl-Ludwig Holtfrerich, and Harold James, eds.,

International Financial History in the Twentieth Century (Cambridge: Cambridge University Press, 2003), 51–76.

Wilkins, Mira, "Cosmopolitan Finance in the 1920s: New York's Emergence as an International Financial Centre," in Richard Sylla, Richard Tilly, and Gabriel Tortella, eds., *The State, the Financial System, and Economic Modernization: Comparative Historical Perspectives* (Cambridge: Cambridge University Press, 1999), 271–91.

Wilkins, Mira, *The Emergence of Multinational Enterprise: American Business Abroad from the Colonial Era to 1914* (Cambridge, MA: Harvard University Press, 1970).

Wilkins, Mira, "The Free-Standing Company Revisited," in Mira Wilkins and Harm Schröter, eds., *The Free-Standing Company in the World Economy* (Oxford: Oxford University Press, 1998), 3–64.

Wilkins, Mira, *The History of Foreign Investment in the United States to 1914* (Cambridge, MA: Harvard University Press, 1989).

Wilkins, Mira, *The History of Foreign Investment in the United States, 1914–1945* (Cambridge, MA: Harvard University Press, 2004).

Wilkins, Mira, "Hosts to Transnational Investments-A Comparative Analysis," in Hans Pohl, ed., *Transnational Investment from the 19th Century to the Present* (Stuttgart: Franz Steiner, 1994), 25–69.

Wilkins, Mira, *The Maturing of Multinational Enterprise: American Business Abroad from 1914 to 1970* (Cambridge, MA: Harvard University Press, 1974).

Wilkins, Mira, "Multinational Enterprise to 1930: Discontinuities and Continuities," in Alfred Chandler and Bruce Mazlish, eds., *Leviathans: Multinational Corporations and the New Global History* (Cambridge: Cambridge University Press, 2005), 45–79.

Wilkins, Mira, "The Role of Private Business in the International Diffusion of Technology," *Journal of Economic History*, 34 (March 1974), 166–88.

Wilkins, Mira, "The Role of U.S. Business," in Dorothy Borg and Shumpei Okamoto, eds., *Pearl Harbor as History: Japanese-American Relations 1931–1941* (New York: Columbia University Press, 1973), 341–76.

Wilkins, Mira, "Swiss Investments in the United States 1914–1945," in Sébastien Guex, ed., *La Suisse et les Grandes Puissances 1914–1945* (Geneva: Droz, 1999), 91–139.

Wilkins, Mira, "Two Literatures, Two Story-Lines: Is a General Paradigm of Foreign Portfolio and Foreign Direct Investment Feasible?" *Transnational Corporations*, 8 (April 1999), 53–116.

Wilkins, Mira, ed., *British Overseas Investments, 1907–1948* (New York: Arno Press, 1977).

Wilkins, Mira, and Harm Schröter, eds., *The Free-Standing Company in the World Economy* (Oxford: Oxford University Press, 1998).

Williams, James H., and Navroz K. Dubash, "Asian Electricity Reform in Historical Perspective, *Pacific Affairs*, 77 (Fall 2004), 411–36.

Wilson, J. F., *Ferranti and the British Electrical Industry, 1864–1930* (Manchester, England: Manchester University Press, 1988).

Winkler, Max, *Foreign Bonds: An Autopsy* (Philadelphia: Roland Swain, 1933).

Wionczek, Miguel S., "Electric Power," in Raymond Vernon, ed., *Public Policy and Private Enterprise in Mexico* (Cambridge, MA: Harvard University Press, 1964), 19–110.

World Development Report 1994 (Oxford: Oxford University Press for the World Bank, 1994).

World Investment Reports, various years.

World Power Conference, *Transactions* (1st, London, 1924; 2nd, Berlin, 1930; 3rd, Washington, DC, 1936; 4th, London, 1950; 5th, Vienna, 1956; 6th, Melbourne, 1962; 7th, Moscow, 1968; 8th, Bucharest, 1971), title varies.

Yamasaki, Kakujiro, and Gotaro Ogawa, *The Effect of the World War upon the Commerce and Industry of Japan* (New Haven: Yale University Press, 1929).

Young, George F. W., "German Banks and German Direct Investment in Latin America, 1880–1920," in Carlos Marichal, ed. *Foreign Investment in Latin America: Impact on Economic Development, 1850–1930* (Milan: Università Bocconi, 1994), 57–65.

Yun, C. "A Statistical Investigation of Electric Power Plants in China 1932," *Transactions of the World Power Conference*, Sectional Meeting, Scandinavia, 1933, vol. 2 (Stockholm: Svenska Nationalkommittén for Varldskraftkonferenser, 1934), 530–38.

Index